ELEMENTS OF SOCIAL SCIE

SEXUAL, AND NATURAL RELIGION.
True Cause and Only Cure of the Three
POVERTY, PROSTITUTION, and CELIBACY. By a Doctor of Medicine. London : E. TRUELOVE, 256, High Holborn. Fourteenth
Edition. Twenty-third Thousand.

Translations of this Work have been published in the following
languages, and may be had of E. TRUELOVE :—

IN FRENCH.—*Eléments de Science Sociale.* Paris: GERMER BAILLIÈRE,
rue de l'Ecole de Médecine, 17. Second Edition, 1873.

IN GERMAN. —*Die Grundzüge der Gesellschaftswissenschaft.* Berlin:
ELWIN STAUDE. Second Edition, 1875.

IN DUTCH.—*De Elementen der Sociale Wetenschap.* Rotterdam: NIJGH
& VAN DITMAR. In two Parts, 1873 and 1875.

IN ITALIAN.—*Elementi di Scienza Sociale.* Milan: GAETANO BRIGOLA.
Second Edition, 1875.

IN PORTUGUESE. — *Elementos de Sciencia Social.* Lisbon: SILVA
JUNIOR. 1876.

OPINIONS OF THE PRESS.

"This is the only book, so far as we know, in which at a cheap price and with
honest and pure intent and purpose, all the questions affecting the sexes, and the
influence of their relations on society, are plainly dealt with. It has now been
issued in French as well as in English, and we bring the French edition to the
notice of our friends of the International Working Men's Association, and of our
subscribers in France and Belgium, as essentially a poor man's book."—*National
Reformer*, edited by Mr. Charles Bradlaugh.

"The *Elements of Social Science* is a most remarkable work, written by a man
evidently with great knowledge of pathology and political economy. It will be
greatly liked or disliked, according to the 'school' of the reader; but no one can
fail to consider it as one of the most remarkable works of the day, on the subjects
of which it treats. We are told that it has been largely read in London by medical
men."—*Medical Press and Circular*, February 23rd, 1870.

"A very valuable, though rather heterogeneous book. . . . This is, we believe,
the only book that has fully, honestly, and in a scientific spirit recognised all the
elements in the problem—How are mankind to triumph over poverty, with its
train of attendant evils?—and fearlessly endeavoured to find a practical
solution."—*The Examiner*, January 4th, 1873.

"In some respects all books of this class are evils: but it would be weakness
and criminal prudery—a prudery as criminal as vice itself—not to say that such a

book as the one in question is not only a far lesser evil than the one that it combats, but in one sense a book which it is a mercy to issue and courage to publish."—*Reasoner*, edited by Mr. G. J. Holyoake.

"We have never risen from the perusal of any work with a greater satisfaction than this."—*Investigator*.

"That book must be read, that subject must be understood, before the population can be raised from its present degraded, diseased, unnatural, and immoral state. We really know not how to speak sufficiently highly of this extraordinary work; we can only say, conscientiously and emphatically, *it is a blessing to the human race.*"—*People's Paper*. By Ernest Jones.

"Though quite out of the province of our journal, we cannot refrain from stating that this work is unquestionably the most remarkable one, in many respects, we have ever met with. Though we differ *toto cœlo* from the author in his views of religion and morality, and hold some of his remedies to tend rather to a dissolution than a reconstruction of society, yet we are bound to admit the benevolence and philanthropy of his motives. The scope of the work is nothing less than the whole field of political economy."—*The British Journal of Homœopathy*, January, 1860.

"It is because, after an impartial consideration of this book, we feel satisfied that the author has no meretricious professional object to subserve, that we are induced to use its publication as a text for the discussion of a vital and pressing subject; and because it bears evidences of research, thorough although misapplied, professional education, some pretensions to philosophy, and a certain earnestness of misguided conviction of the truth of peculiar prevalent economical theories, which seems to have led him off his feet, and to have induced him to venture upon any extravagance in their support. It is in vain to attempt to hide these subjects out of sight. This one book of 600 closely printed pages is in its third large edition. It is of no use to ignore the topic as either delicate or disgusting. It is of universal interest. It concerns intimately every human being."—*From an adverse review, occupying six columns in* THE WEEKLY DISPATCH, *January and February, 1860.*

Extract from an Article by Professor MANTEGAZZA, *of Florence, in the Journal* MEDICO DI CASA, *of 16th January,* 1874.

"This work has had eleven English editions, two French, a German and a Dutch one; and is about to be published in Italian and in Portuguese; and we who have read and meditated on it, rejoice with the author at this success, auguring for it new and increasing good fortune.

"He is convinced that in this lower world too many people are born, and hence very many of them are condemned either to a premature death, or, what is worse, to a wretched life, oppressed by hunger and suffering. He comes forward therefore to propose what we ourselves have modestly urged in our 'Elements of Hygiene' since 1864, when we said 'Love, but do not have offspring.' A disciple of Malthus and of Stuart Mill, he is well versed in modern philosophy and in political economy, and studies the abstruse problem in all its aspects, setting out from the most elementary domestic hygiene to raise himself gradually to the lofty regions of human dignity and civil progress. A foe to all hypocrisy and prejudice, the author of the 'Elements of Social Science' calls things by their real names, and shrinks only from the excessive sufferings and privations to which the poor children of Adam are condemned. He is firmly convinced that to measure human fecundity in accordance with the economical production of families and of nations is the most certain means of destroying pauperism and all the forms of want; and in this perhaps he is in error, for the evils of modern society have many sources, and with the drying up of one (perhaps even the most fruitful), another and another would present themselves, which only the combined and constant labours of future generations will perhaps be able to overcome. However this may be, the courage with which the author faces one of the most formidable problems of human society is most praiseworthy.

"Human morality is gradually changing its centre of gravity to rest upon a more solid and durable basis. In this new morality the doctrines of Malthus and those of the author of the 'Elements of Social Science' must also have a large share.

In the place of alms-giving which humiliates, in the place of charity which caresses an evil that it does not know how to cure, there will be substituted preventive philanthropy, which by studying want and suffering in their most hidden and deep-seated springs, will be able radically to remove them. Jurisprudence, medicine, and morality follow the same movement, are aiming at the same end—to prevent rather than to cure."

" The motto of the work : 'The diseases of society can, no more than corporeal maladies, be prevented or cured, without being spoken about in plain language" (John Stuart Mill), and its dedication to the poor and suffering, are sufficient to show the tendency of the author. He uses, indeed, a directness of expression, an outspokenness, which is seldom met with in our times, and will probably in most circles of so-called refined society be styled *very shocking* if not *cynical*, though in reality it is not so. The author only calls by their names things which we medical men also have to discuss openly among ourselves and with patients, but which are treated by polite society according to the Parisian proverb, 'cela se fait, mais cela ne se dit pas.' The author, as appears from the title and from his professional knowledge, is a medical practitioner. He merits, therefore, the attention of his colleagues, the more so because, in the first place, they would scarcely guess from the title that this is a book for medical men—and secondly, because his medical colleagues alone possess the education which permits them to estimate without prejudice the aims and efforts of the author, to try the truth of the facts which he lays down as premises, and, after due consideration, either to accept or reject, or to limit and amend, his conclusions and proposals. . . . The author's remarks on the social questions in general are among the best and most deeply-felt we have ever read."—*Schmidt's Jahrbücher der gesammten Medizin*. Band 152, Heft 1.

"This is one of those books of which little is spoken, but which nevertheless are wont to produce a quiet lasting effect, while finding their readers at length in this way that under the influence of peculiar circumstances one person confidentially tells another that in such and such a work there is something to be found . . . The author is, as a natural inquirer, what one must perhaps still call a materialist and a Darwinian ; as a political economist—and he is by no means an insignificant political economist—he belongs to the left wing of the free trade school, to which, in spite of some differences of opinion, he lends on the whole a great impulse, anticipating with confidence its ultimate and complete victory throughout the whole cultured world."— *Vierteljahrsschrift fur Volkswirthschaft und Culturgeschichte,* edited by J. Faucher. XII. Jahrg.

" One must first accustom himself to the openness with which the author treats his themes ; but the work is unquestionably most instructive and interesting, and is written with great knowledge of the subject."--*Hessische Morgenzeitung*, Dec. 24th, 1871.

"No one, who has turned his thoughts to the solution of the most burning of all questions of the day, the *social* question, and who wishes to devote to it his mental and practical energies, will be able to leave unread this book, whose anonymous author, basing himself on the Malthusian essay ' On the Principle of Population,' deduces from it with keen logic a peculiar and most striking theory on the cure of the three primary social evils—poverty, prostitution, and celibacy . . . Whatever may be said against this fearless laying bare of the most intimate relations of social life and against his whole theory, purely and undisguisedly materalistic as it is—even the opponent of the daring socialist will be unable to deny him the merit of scientific closeness of reasoning, and what is quite as important, of warm and zealous philanthropy ; he will rather honour the moral courage and mental energy which the author must have had to work his way out of the bewildering maze of hitherto unsolved problems and conflicts, to a conviction so logically consistent, so luminous, and yet so opposed to established institutions and to the moral sentiments in which men have been brought up."— *Königsberger Hartungsche Zeitung*. December 4th, 1871.

" The author treats, in an open and unreserved manner, the diseases of the human frame, as well as those of society, because he is convinced, with Stuart Mill, that they can only in this way be prevented and cured. In truth we have learned from many years' experience that such is the case. We bring therefore to the notice of our readers, and recommend them to procure, this excellent book." *Sonntags-Blatt, Organ für die Freidenker Deutschlands,* edited by Dr. Aug. Specht. January 26th, 1873.

"Many of the author's views are diametrically opposed to our own, but we cannot refrain from describing the book as in very truth an epoch-making one, whose perusal must interest in the highest degree, both the professional man and the educated general reader. Nothing is gained by a prudish avoidance of the subjects treated in the work; they *must* be discussed, and mankind might congratulate themselves if this were always done in so candid and disinterested a manner as by the author of 'The Elements of Social Science.'" — *Hanoversche Anzeigen und Morgenzeitung.* November 14th, 1871.

"A very remarkable book. . . . A regard to the nature of the subjects treated of forbids us to enter further into its contents—an exposition of the inner conditions of social life which, for obvious reasons, lie outside the sphere of the daily press. Suffice it to say that we have here to do with a work which differs widely from the common-place productions of the book market, and which will very probably go through no fewer editions in philosophic Germany than in England." — *Reform,* Hamburg, 28th October ,1875.

ELEMENTS OF

SOCIAL SCIENCE.

THE ELEMENTS

OF

SOCIAL SCIENCE;

OR,

PHYSICAL, SEXUAL AND NATURAL, RELIGION.

An Exposition of the true Cause and only Cure of
The Three Primary Social Evils:

POVERTY, PROSTITUTION, AND CELIBACY.

BY

A DOCTOR OF MEDICINE.

"The Diseases of Society can, no more than corporeal maladies, be prevented
or cured, without being spoken about in plain language."—John Stuart Mill.

FOURTEENTH EDITION, ENLARGED.
(TWENTY-FIRST THOUSAND.)

London:

E. TRUELOVE, 256, HIGH HOLBORN,

REMOVED FROM TEMPLE BAR.

——

1876.

DEDICATED

TO

THE POOR AND THE SUFFERING.

PREFACE.

Had it not been from the fear of causing pain to a relation, I should have felt it my duty to put my name to this work ; in order that any censure passed upon it, should fall upon myself alone.

I feel deeply indebted to Mr. TRUELOVE for the service he has done me in its publication; and the more so that he has been actuated, by no means by a full acquiescence in its opinions, but by a generous desire to promote the free discussion, and earnest investigation, of the most important, though unfortunately most neglected, subjects. In particular, he is desirous to afford expression to whatever may throw light upon the great social difficulties, and the condition and prospects of the poor and oppressed classes. He wishes to give to the author the opportunity of advocating his views, and to the reader that of examining them, and forming his own conclusions.

I earnestly hope that the time is not far distant, when each individual shall be enabled freely to bring forward his conscientious beliefs, without incurring the intolerance of others; and when the subjects of the following pages shall be generally understood, and openly discussed.

December, 1854.

PREFACE TO THE THIRD EDITION.

In the present edition of this work, a fourth part, on Social Science, has been added, in which I have endeavoured to present in a somewhat more systematic form the views advocated in the earlier parts, and have also given a short outline of the chief laws of political economy. Most of the additional matter has already appeared in a small periodical, the Political Economist and Journal of Social Science, which was discontinued some time ago.

In giving to the work the title of the Elements of Social Science, instead of its original one of Physical, Sexual, and Natural Religion, it need scarcely be said that I do not make the slightest pretension to have offered any comprehensive or adequate exposition of this great science. My chief reason for changing the title was, that the Malthusian Principle and the laws of nature involved in it, are in my opinion incomparably *the most important* elements of social science; so much so, that, while they enable us readily to comprehend the chief social phenomena, the theory of society without them is in reality a mere chaos. I was very desirous also, as far as lay in my power, to direct attention to that science, whose name has of late years been gradually becoming more familiar to the public, and whose character and method have been so admirably described by Mr. Mill in his Logic, and by M. Auguste Comte in his Positive Philosophy. Although differing entirely from the latter writer on many of the most vital points of moral and social doctrine, (and especially in regard to the principle of population, the truth and importance of the sciences of political economy, logic, psychology, and metaphysics, properly so called, the sphere of woman, the marriage question, &c.,) I cannot here refrain from expressing the profoundest admiration of the manner in which he has carried out the leading idea of his great and noble work. No single work has ever done so much to emancipate the human mind from the fatal errors of supernaturalism in any form, or to prepare the way for the great intellectual regeneration, when mankind shall be united in a purely natural faith, and when human life shall again be governed by sincere and openly expressed convictions.

The characteristic principles of positive philosophy, as shown by M. Comte, are in the first place, to regard all phenomena as determined by invariable natural laws; and secondly, in the inquiry into the laws of phenomena, rigorously to exclude, as unreal and unfit for consideration, all causes which are not themselves susceptible, either of demonstration by means of evidence, or of direct perception by our consciousness. Positive philosophy therefore excludes all supernatural or theological causes, whether first or final, together with those fictitious, or, to use M. Comte's expression, metaphysical entities, such as gravity, attraction, vital essence, &c., which have been so often supposed to account for phenomena, especially in the earlier periods of philosophy. M. Comte classifies the abstract sciences in six great departments, gradually ascending in their order of complexity and dependence, namely, mathematics, astronomy, physics, chemistry, biology, and social science. He shows that each of these sciences has, in the course of its development, passed through the theological and metaphysical stages; and that all of them have been gradually emancipated from these erroneous methods of philosophizing, and have attained more or less completely the positive stage, with the exception of social science, the last and the most important of all. " This branch of science," he says, "has not hitherto entered into the domain of positive philosophy. Theological and metaphysical methods, exploded in other departments, are as yet exclusively applied, both in the way of inquiry and discussion, in all treatment of social subjects, though the best minds are heartily weary of eternal disputes about divine right and the sovereignty of the people. This is the great, while it is evidently the only gap which has to be filled, to constitute, solid and entire, the Positive Philosophy. Now that the human mind has grasped celestial and terrestrial physics—mechanical and chemical; organic physics, both vegetable and animal, —there remains one science, to fill up the series of sciences of observation—Social physics. This is what men have now most need of; and this it is the principal aim of the present work to establish."

I believe that a very large proportion of thinkers in this and other countries, thoroughly agree with the following opinion expressed by Miss Martineau in the preface to her admirable translation of M. Comte's work:—"The only field of progress is now that of Positive Philosophy, under whatever name it may be known to the real students of every sect."

November. 1859.

CONTENTS.

PART III.

NATURAL RELIGION.

PART IV.

SOCIAL SCIENCE.

PART I.

PHYSICAL RELIGION.

PHYSICAL RELIGION.

THERE is nothing from which mankind in the present day suffers more, than from the want of reverence for the human body. The mass of men, even the most cultivated, are content to pass their lives in the deepest ignorance of its structure, and of its most simple laws. All active sympathy with its fate, or interest in the infinitely varied details of its health and disease, is handed over to the medical profession, into whose modes of thought, aims, and principles of action, the public care not to enter. In the education of childhood and youth, no knowledge of the body is imparted, no instruction given for the conduct of the future physical life. No reverence is inculcated for physical laws, no aspirations cherished after physical excellence. Beauty of form, that imperishable source of joy and stamp of nobility, to be perpetuated through successive generations, so far from being held out as an object for our reverence and constant endeavour after, is rather regarded as a dangerous snare, and vanity, which may mislead men from the path of virtue. Physical strength is held in slight estimation by those who cultivate the intellect, and they who take delight in the sports and exercises which call it forth, are rather looked down upon as men of low tastes. Bodily health, the proof of a virtuous physical life, is not proposed as a chief end of our endeavours, nor regarded as an honour to its possessor. It is rather thought of as a blessing bestowed by providence, or inherited from our parents, with the attainment of which the individual's self has comparatively little to do. The laws of health are as little reverenced as understood. While the infringement of a moral law involves the deepest guilt, and is considered worthy of infinite punishment, to break a physical one, and thereby incur disease, is not deemed an offence at all, but only a misfortune. The animal or sensual passions as they are called, are viewed in a most degrading light, and the youth is warned to beware of indulgence in them, and rather to train himself in the vastly nobler enjoyments of the moral and reasoning faculties. These are thoughts

to be of a much higher and loftier nature than the others, which it is
their duty to control and direct.   Men set no high value in their
theories on life itself, which some even view in the light of a penance,
while they regard death as the greatest blessing.   Length of life, and
its proper and only beautiful termination in extreme age, after the
gradual extinction of the vital powers, is by no means considered a
noble goal for man's aim.   The ill-regulated mind rather shrinks from
the idea of natural decay, and admires much more the lamentable fate
of martyrdom, or the premature death of interesting youth, just nature's
punishment for broken laws.   The whole material universe shares in
this neglect with the body, its representative in man.   The physical
sciences with their infinite treasury of novelties and wonders are followed only by a few devoted adherents, while to society in general they
are an unknown region. Besides this, all the so-called manual pursuits,
are held as vastly inferior in dignity to the mental ones, which, under
the name of the learned professions, claim for themselves the highest
place in man's respect.   The fine arts, sculpture and painting, and the
mechanical arts, all of which are concerned with material objects,
although their dignity and powerful influence are daily more and more
felt, are yet very far from occupying their due position.

In short, in whatever direction we look, we find that the body and
matter in general, hold a very secondary place in man's reverence.   We
see that almost the whole of mankind, with the exception of the few
who expressly follow material pursuits—grow, live, and die, with their
thoughts and interests turned in quite a different direction.   It is mind,
and not body, moral and intellectual, not physical themes, which possess
their heart.

"Spirit," they say, "is infinitely higher and nobler than matter: the
soul is the truly glorious part of our humanity.   Does it not constitute
the attribute of man, by which he is raised above the rest of nature to
the likeness and comprehension of the Deity himself?   How poor in comparison is the body, its humble companion, whose tardy movements and
coarse sensibilities but clog its etherial essence!   The latter shall soon
perish, and with it all its excellences; but the other, glad to be released
from its prison-house, shall soar away into everlasting bliss.   Why then
waste our time in laying up treasures that corrupt?   Let us, first of all
things, attend to our spiritual part; and then, even though our body
perish, we have still saved that which is alone all-sufficient."   Thus do
men reason, and thus are all their sympathies and aspirations bound up
in their spiritual welfare.   As they judge of themselves, so do they of
others.   A well-spent moral life, and endeavours to elevate the spiritual
condition of others, command their warmest admiration; but of a
virtuous physical life they have no conception; and for the struggles and
aspirations of those, who have sought to ennoble men physically, little
sympathy. While the names of poets, moralists, and mental philosophers,
are in every mouth, and their lines and precepts in every heart; few are
acquainted even with the names, far less with the deeds of those who
have striven in the cause of the human body.   It is well for them, physicians and physiologists, if they escape the charge of materialism, or the

disgust attaching to the charnel-house or vivisections. Sad is it indeed to look back on the fate of the apostles of the body! For if any ideal object of pursuit be looked down upon, or not sufficiently reverenced, those who follow it will necessarily share in that irreverence. Therefore, has the clergyman, who has the care of souls, been for ages held in much higher esteem and love than the physician, who has the cure of bodies.

And not only have these professions been ranked on such principles, but every other profession and calling has had its place assigned by the same standard. The spiritualist has ever been esteemed above the materialist; the thinker above the doer; the musical composer above the finished musician; the dramatic writer above the actor; the mental above the manual pursuits. A few mental directions of man's energy are elevated above the others, and chiefly honoured, so that the young man of liberal education, is impelled by all his accustomed sympathies and feelings to adopt one of them, whether or not it be fitted for his nature. According to this gauge, the nearer a man's pursuit approaches to pure spirit, the more is he esteemed—the nearer to matter, the less.

Whence, then, has arisen this extraordinary and arbitrary mode of judging of the elements of nature? Who has presumed to settle the claims of precedence between the twin elemental principles of the universe; and thereby cause so powerful an influence on man's existence? If we look for the main source of this universal preference for spirit, and things connected with it, we shall find it in the Christian religion. This religion, springing as it did out of the ancient Hebrew worship, which delighted in representing the infinite material universe, as dependent on the nod of a supreme spiritual Self-existent being, is essentially a spiritual faith. According to its doctrines, the Deity himself, from whom all things originated, and to whom all are subject, is a spirit, infinite, eternal, and unchangeable. He first called matter into existence, and imposed on it laws after his own will, reserving to himself the power of changing or annihilating them, whenever he thought it necessary. Man, the wondrous compound of mind and body, also owed his origin to this spirit; who gave him life by a pure act of his will. Believing then in the infinite supremacy of the spiritual element, and worshipping it exclusively, he naturally bestowed his chief reverence on the representative of the Deity in himself. Hence his soul was the grand object of all his thoughts, while the body was little regarded, or at most borrowed a reflected light from its more favoured companion. The soul, it was believed, was joined in some mysterious way to the body at birth, and condemned for a brief period to travel through this life in its company, clogged and confined by its ignoble associate. At death, however, it resumed its own privileges as spirit, infinite, eternal, and unchangeable, and soared away into an immortality of weal or woe, while its despised companion was consigned to the darkness of a grave, and to disgusting decay, from which the ignorant mind shrank with abhorrence.

Who could entertain such views of the nature and ultimate destinies of the twin parts of man, without becoming almost entirely absorbed in the fate of the one, and as wholly neglecting that of the other? Such is the Christian doctrine of life, and such the effect it has had on man.

Wherever it has made its way, supported by the beautiful character of its originator, it has given an intensely spiritual direction to men's minds; and their tastes, judgments, social scale, and various pursuits, have been modified by it in the way mentioned above.

But physical religion is diametrically opposed to the Christian and spiritual beliefs. It can allow none of them, seeing that they give to mind a superiority over matter, and so deprive the latter of its rightful place in the affection and reverence of man. Its fundamental propositions are—matter is as noble as spirit, the body as the soul. To separate the one from the other is to destroy the truth of nature; to place the one above the other is a monstrous presumption, destroying the harmony of the universe, where all things are equally important, and where the laws of one substance never yield to those of another.

The belief that the Deity is a spirit is completely untenable. The natural theologians, who have attempted to prove it, and who, doubtless, have followed the same line of reason as the ancients, who proposed the doctrine, argue thus:—"In the universe around us, we everywhere see marks of design; from this we must infer a designing mind, reasoning by analogy from what we find in ourselves."

But they forget, that the mind which designs in man, is inseparably connected with a vitally organized brain; therefore, to conclude that the designer of the universe is pure spirit, is to reason against all analogy. According to our experience, mind is invariably found in connection with brain, and never creates matter.

Not only does physical religion deny the possibility of spirit having originated matter, or of the laws of matter being ever in one iota subject to those of spirit, it cannot allow a prerogative to the one, in any particular, over the other. Thus it entirely denies the possibility of the immortality of the one without the other. Such a belief tends inevitably to destroy the equal place both should hold in our reverence, thus entailing the most ruinous consequences. The narrow conception of salvation for the one, without, or even at the expense of the other, is utterly condemned by physical religion, according to whose views no scheme of salvation can be received, which omits any part of humanity. Our bodily and mental interests are inseparably bound together, and no part of us can rise or fall, without the rest taking a share. Thus physical evil always infers moral evil, and the reverse. Our body cannot be diseased without our mind becoming so likewise.

It is the duty of all men to study the laws of their body, no less than those of their mind. If they do not, if they have not sufficient reverence for the body to take due care for its healthy development either in themselves or in others, when they break any of its laws, which they are certain to do, it will be little excuse to plead ignorance. All moral sin may exactly in the same way be resolved into ignorance, but nature accepts no such excuse. The conduct of our physical life is just as difficult as that of our moral one. To live a virtuous physical life deserves, therefore, as great admiration and praise as the other. The ennoblement of the body in ourselves and in others is just as high an aim for man as that of the spirit. Can you have a healthy mind without a healthy brain? Certainly, this is impossible, whatever mistaken moral views have led some to suppose. Therefore provision for the one is as lofty, and moreover, just as difficult an endeavour as for the other; and indeed the only true method of attaining the highest development of man, is by equal regard and attention to the interests of both.

The man who is only conversant with spiritual reasoning and mental phenomena, who has confined his attention to the region of mind, and is ignorant of the body with its infinitely complex states of health and disease, is incapable of a true and comprehensive view of man—in the same way is he, who knows only the physical side, equally imperfect. In every act, every thought, every relation of man, there are a double train of forces at work, and he who attends only to the one is not fitted to reason on the whole result. In every act presented to the eye of the moralist, there is a physical line of causation, equally important, equally difficult to unravel, which must be taken into account, before he can be said to reason on man, as a whole being, at all. Therefore, since the moralist and the physicist have hitherto been separated in the world's history, we possess no comprehensive or true views of man, and our reasonings both in morals and in medicine will all need complete revision by minds equally conversant with body and mind, and their several phenomena of health and disease; and ready to assign to each their due importance, unbiased by partiality for either.

There has not yet lived a man, who has done this for the world; who has brought to bear on the problem of life a brain equally trained in spiritual and bodily experience, educated equally in the phenomena of the mental and material universe. Unstirred by the unhappy party distinctions of spiritualism and materialism, seeking instruction on all parts and sides of nature, omitting equal reverence to none, would not he show more fully than our fathers have done, his duty and devotion to man and to nature?

But physical religion does not leave it to us as a matter of choice, whether we will study the laws of our body or not; it enjoins their study on all men as a duty, second in importance to none.

If you do not wish to live a physically virtuous, that is, a healthy life, you are an immoral being; if you do, there is but one way to it; study the laws of health and obey them. Physical virtue is as lofty an aim for man as moral virtue, and no man can be called good, who does not combine and aspire equally after both. To break a physical law is just as culpable as to break a moral one, and therefore all physical diseases must be regarded as a sign of sin, and as little in the one case as in the other, can ignorance be received as an excuse. No man whose body is diseased whether hereditarily or individually, can be called a virtuous being.

All moral and all physical excellencies may be mutually resolved into each other, for a noble mind or a good or true spirit may be just as fairly regarded as a noble and true brain, and all physical good may equally be traced to a moral one. Thus, by following the trains of thought of spiritualist and materialist, we will be able, equally legitimately, at one time to resolve all things into spirit, at another all into matter.

Beauty of form, and physical strength and activity, as well as health, should be sought after, and valued no less than beauty and power of mind. Is the development of the brain to be the supreme object of man's aspirations? A fuller wisdom will show us, that we must value equally all our parts, since no one can thrive alone. Ugliness and bodily imperfection or deformity are always marks of sin, and show us that some error has been committed, or that we have not duly sought after bodily excellence. Physical beauty, whose expression forms the glorious ideal of the painter and sculptor, is as high an aim as any other that could be proposed. For it is inseparably associated in nature's plan with all other beauties and powers, and we can attain to truth just as surely by following beauty, as by any other path. In fact all the ideals of man which are founded on a reality in nature, are equally infinite, and therefore equally capable of forming a religion. For there is not one religion, but as many religions as there are parts of nature to absorb us in their pursuit. The real religion of each man is that pursuit and that idea, which most holds his heart, and which awakens in him a lofty enthusiasm. It is the perception and feeling of the infinite, and our duty to aspire to it, to which the name of religion has ever been given. Unfortunate the pursuit and those who follow it, which has not its own equally recognised and equally reverenced religion.

Spiritualism is at present the great obstacle to this recognition; to the extension of the idea of Catholic humanity, which is now pervading the civilised world; the equal reverence for all men and for all parts of nature. It is the prevailing error of past and present times, and is not confined to our own country merely, but extends perhaps over all the globe. It is the true aristocratic element in our society, which interposes its chilling barriers between men's hearts, for where there is not equal mutual reverence, there cannot long be true love. Itself at first an advancing revolution, it has now become a stationary despotism. It has shown no quarter to its opponent materialism, which at present as a theory can scarcely be said to exist in the world, and is not therefore much to be dreaded as an evil.

It is spiritualism, that men of our age have to fear, and do what they may, they will find it almost impossible to extricate themselves from its prejudicing influence, so subtly is it interwoven in all our thoughts and feelings. For the man who has not paid equal attention to physical pursuits, and to the study of the human body in its varied phases of health and disease, must be a spiritualist; and his unequal knowledge of the different parts of our nature, while it shows his preference for the one, will bias and falsify all his views on man as a whole.

As all parts of our nature are of equal perfection, and therefore all equally claim our reverence, it cannot be for a moment allowed, that the so-called animal passions are of an inferior kind to the spiritual. They exercise an influence on man just as divine as any other, and shape and mould the human character as powerfully and as nobly. It is not the place of man to say:—"This part of my nature is more beautiful or more noble than another, let me therefore cultivate it chiefly." His duty is to study to perceive an equal beauty in all, and to endeavour that all shall be duly and equally developed.

If a healthy life be the crown of the physical virtues, death in all its forms, except the natural spontaneous one of gradual decay in old age, is the greatest of all physical sins. The gravity of a physical sin is to be measured by the severity of the disease, nature's punishment; and when death follows, the physical sin must have been the greatest. All premature deaths, therefore, are sinful, and abhorrent to physical religion, showing that the evil powers have been at work. It matters not what other noble qualities, moral or physical, the individual may have had; if he die before his time, his life is an imperfect one, and so far must be condemned.

The death of martyrdom, which has been so dangerous an example to the world, is but a confession of the imperfect state of existing things. "All men around me are sinning," says the martyr, "therefore must I also sin, and submit to a mutilated career in order to save them." Beautiful, truly; but the highest ideal allows of no sacrifice of any real good.

It is by no means martyrdom, or premature death in any conceivable form, that men are to aim at; but rather a physiologically perfect life, perfect in every stage, perfect in its natural termination. It is from the want of a reverence for our physical life, from an inadequate appreciation of its infinite value and majesty, and the duty that we lie under, to guard it as a most sacred possession, that the recklessness of life, both in themselves and in others, in great part arose, which has been, and still is, so dark a stain on mankind.

The grand aim of the natural and only beautiful death should be kept steadily before the eyes of all throughout life. To live and die naturally, and to help others to do the same! Have we ever thought how much of virtue, of duty, of religion, lies in this aim, apparently so simple, yet in its attainment so infinitely difficult?

As physical religion teaches us to reverence the body as highly as the spirit, so does it also teach us to view with equal reverence all the different parts and organs of the body itself. There are few things from which humanity has suffered more than from the degrading and irreverent feelings of mystery and shame that have been attached to the genital and excretory organs. The former have been regarded, like their corresponding mental passions, as something of a lower and baser nature, tending to degrade and carnalise man by their physical appetites. But we cannot take a debasing view of any part of our humanity, without becoming degraded in our whole being. It would be hard to enumerate all the evils which have flowed from this unhappy view of the genital organs; whose functions and influence are second in importance and in transcendant perfection to none. Their health and disease have been neglected, their misfortunes have called forth rather the sneer and the reproach than the divine pity and assistance which should wait upon all error, physical and moral.

I have endeavoured elsewhere, in the treatise on the sexual organs, to give a short sketch of their laws, which should be studied and obeyed by all men and women as reverentially as those of any other organs, else will their consequent ruin involve the ruin of the whole being. Before the calm eye of nature, all flimsy veils of morbid modesty, shame, an indolence, vanish like a dream; and when she demands penalty for broken laws, such excuses die away on the lips of the offender.

In the same way that physical religion enjoins reverence for the genital organs, so does it prohibit all low and degraded ideas connected with the organs of excretion. All such are an abomination unto it, and it will not hold him guiltless who stoops to entertain them. Every one should endeavour absolutely to free his mind from these unhappy views of our ancestors, and learn to regard all parts of his body with the same reverential eye, undisturbed by feelings of mystery, shame, or disgust. Too long alas! too long have these indignities defiled our humanity, and baffled the efforts of the physician! What sufferer from the diseases of these organs has not had his woes aggravated ten-fold by these unhappy feelings! The universal study of anatomy, enjoined on all men by physical religion, will alone succeed in dissipating these morbid and irreverent ideas.

But in what direction can we turn our eyes, and not find man degraded by the want of physical reverence? Have not all the various classes, who follow material pursuits, become themselves degraded, from the want of a religious enthusiasm for them? Have not the physician, the artist, the actor, the labourer, and artizan, become degraded thereby? If a man have not a sufficient reverence for his pursuit, it will hang a dead weight round his neck, and sink him to the level of a mercenary drudge. It is deplorable to see the way in which some of these glorious branches of human endeavour are looked down upon, not only by society at large, but by their own followers. The noble profession of the actor or actress is viewed in so degrading a light by society that it is almost ignored. Is the perfection of art in that vocation, which forms as integral an ingredient of our social life as any others, less difficult in its attainment or less unbounded in its influence than they? In a more perfect state of society it will not be viewed so.

The interests of all concerned in physical studies or pursuits, are, no less than the physician's, bound up in the spread of physical religion. Without it, medicine is, as it has been up to this time, comparatively paralysed, and can have but a minor influence on the physical regeneration and progress of man. How can the voice of the physician be heard, if he can urge only the feeble motives of expediency, while the moralist and clergyman have at their command the armoury of duty and religion, with the array of eternal rewards and punishments, to enforce reverence for their precepts? To all of these assumptions of spiritual superiority, as it has been seen, physical religion inexorably returns a denial, while it claims, and will have from all human beings, exactly an equal share of their reverence. The individual and the age which resist those claims shall not escape punishment, but shall surely suffer; not that it loves spirit less, but that it loves the whole man more. The true interests of the spiritualist are no less involved in this, for, where injustice is done, all must suffer.

MAN, THE PHYSICIAN.

The noble science of medicine has never yet received due reverence from mankind. This arises chiefly from the cause that has been mentioned above, namely, the want of reverence for the body, the special object of its attention. In the neglect shown to their subject, medical men have shared, and thus has the profession become a little world in itself, separated from the interests and real sympathies which only mutual understanding can give, of the main world around them. The physician, to the eyes of other men, appears as one apart, who is initiated into mysteries which their imagination dreads, yet dwells upon; who is devoted to studies, the materialising and debasing influences of which are still, in the light of the nineteenth century, vaguely whispered of, though society is now-a-days too polite to utter openly the coarse and irreverent accusations of our forefathers.

It is not, however, with the degradations of the physicians of the past that I have to do; those who will may find the records of them in history, and having studied them, will be prepared by their light to read the condition of the physician of the present. For the seeds sown by our ancestors still flourish among us, and long will be the struggle before the prejudices against medicine and its followers, and the materialising tendencies of the science, be totally uprooted. It is rarely that we see in the writings, even of the most cultivated men of past times, the medical profession alluded to, except with a sneer at their low-mindedness, or expressed contempt at their want of skill. It would have been better for these writers and for society, had they rather tried themselves to solve those problems of health and disease, which medical men knew so little about.

But what was there to induce these men of lofty ambition and great powers, to devote themselves to a subject which shut them out of the sympathies of the world; which offered to them few of the prizes of fame, influence, or even that, which, with the true philanthropist, outweighs all other rewards—the wide love and sympathy of their fellow beings! Truly there was little in the body, neither religion, poetical ideal, nor wide-spread human interest to invite their regards. Hence there have been comparatively few of the most powerful and genial minds in the medical profession · as these, with their insatiable demand for human sympathy,

chose the more certain paths to it. Poets have shunned it, and therefore
has the poetry of the body, as lofty and as beautiful as any, never yet
been adequately conceived ; religious and moral philosophers have shunned
it, and therefore, have its religion and morality remained unrecognised.
How much has been lost by this, the body will yet make us feel.

Neither in former times nor at present has the youth even a fair choice
given him, at his entrance upon life, of adopting the medical profession.
His whole previous education, none of which has been concerned with
physical studies, and more especially with the study of the human body,
gives him a bias to mental ones, the more powerful in proportion to the
abilities he has shown. Hence in the present day, if a boy distinguish
himself at school, or a youth at college, medicine is the last profession
either he or others think of his entering. It is completely out of the
sphere of his own sympathies and associations, which are bound up in the
great world of poetry, literature, religion, and morality, to which medicine
is almost unknown. Do not these facts show the little reverence in which
the medical profession is held? While these things are so, men may
render it lip-service, saying, "Oh, medicine is a noble calling, what
could be more honourable than to heal the sick and comfort the afflicted!"
But with such vain words no true physician will be satisfied, knowing that
the hearts of the faint praisers are in reality far from us. I have heard
it said by a medical man, "No one who has any money, chooses medicine as a profession," and as a general rule this is true. Few who have
free choice enter it ; no man of independent means takes it as the delight
and recreation of his leisure hours, for the sake of study and science, and not
of art and practice. Medicine is generally looked upon as a calling of a
prosaic, plodding, and uninteresting, if not of a materialising and disgusting
nature, which repels the man of ardent mind. Hence it is comparatively
seldom entered from disinterested love or aims of a lofty character. It
is too often viewed by those who adopt it, as a mere art, whereby to
make their bread ; and in general it is chosen by men not of the highest
mental culture, or of even moderate fortune.

Of course, there are many brilliant exceptions to this, but I speak
merely of the general rule. It is true that the further they proceed in
their pursuits, the more devoted becomes their love for them, for who can
know any part of nature without loving it? So that there is no class of
men perhaps who ultimately become more enthusiastic in their profession
than medical men. From the time they enter the dissecting room,
and having got over the unpleasant feelings caused by their previous
prejudices, learn at every step more and more to love and admire the
wondrous new world they have been admitted to, until they quit the scene
of their labours, the ruling passion of love for the human body in all its
ages and stages, joys and sorrows, the stronger that to them alone have its
secrets and its beauties been unfolded, waxes more and more powerful in
the true medical breast. But their love, intense as it often is, is by no
means generally of a pure nature. So far from wishing to extend to men in
general the knowledge which has been to them the source of so much
enjoyment and advantage, they have done all they could to prevent others
having an access to these secrets.

They have constantly discouraged all unprofessional attempts to reason en medical subjects, by hints of the dangers of little knowledge, and by keeping up as much as possible the mysteries and technicalities of their science. - Even any attempt by a medical man to enlighten society on his subject has ever been discountenanced by his brethren, and sneered at under the name of popular medicine.

A true physical religion will introduce very different views on these subjects. Jealousy, always the mark of some error, has long been an acknowleged fault of medical men. This feeling, called forth by their wish to reserve for themselves the monopoly of their subject, has pervaded their minds, as is ever the case, in other directions also, and the mutual jealousy of reputation among the members of the profession has become proverbial. How could it be otherwise, seeing that they have to do with a public which has no true standard, by which to judge their merits? which cannot distinguish between the pretender and the real man of science? with whom all the unreal accessories of affected manners, boasting phrases, and the assumed mystery of wisdom, have more weight than the dignity of knowledge and the simplicity of love? What medical man has not felt the unpleasantness of having to deal with those who have no true standard of judgment? How many have been seduced by this into the endeavour, rather to cheat the uninitiated, and to hide their own ignorance, than to attain to true knowledge? The faults of medical men lie in a great measure at the door of society, and a physically ignorant and incompetent society—such as now exists—must have comparatively ignorant, incompetent, and slovenly physicians.

According to the amount of physical knowledge and discrimination possessed by men in general, will be that attained to by physicians themselves. Until all men become more or less physicists, as all have become more or less moralists, the profession itself will remain in comparatively a degraded state.

The want of a sufficiently high and comprehensive aim has also had a very prejudicial effect on the medical character. Too few have pursued it from disinterested motives, or from a pure wish to benefit mankind in the highest degree possible by its practice. Such an aim, recognised in other branches of human endeavour, has comparatively seldom been deeply felt by medical men, however ardent may have been their devotion to science. We hear the love and advancement of science much talked of among them, but the love of humanity comparatively little. Not that love should be more highly esteemed than knowledge—that common error, which has done, and still does, so much harm—but the claims of both should be equally felt and equally dwelt upon. In this respect, viz., the prominence of the feeling of devoted and disinterested love for man in the medical character, there are, I know, many exceptions to what I have stated, but they who well know the medical profession, will recognise, that in this matter their aspirations stand far below a desirable level. How could it be otherwise? Have they not been left to themselves, withdrawn from the eye and criticism of the world, and when did secrecy and irresponsibility not lead to carelessness and indifference?

Another great cause of the lowering of the tone of the profession, has been the fact that the first men in it are so overwhelmed with practice

that they have little time for attending to the moral dignity of them
selves or their brethren, for purifying and analysing their aims and
position, and elevating their ideal—a work which demands much reflec ·
tion, and solitude, without which reflection is impossible. They become
too completely absorbed in the practical business of their lives, and have
scarcely even time to keep up with science on their own subjects,
much less to take a comprehensive view of all, or to enter on the nicer
moral questions which surround the medical position.

There are certainly great advantages to be gained from this thoroughly and constantly practical life, and many are the valuable works
which distinguished physicians have given to the world ; but there are
other advantages which cannot be obtained in this way. Every science
and mode of life require to be viewed from various points ; and there
are aspects given to the pure scientific inquirer, who works out his
problems, in solitude or society, according as he sees the necessary
paths to knowledge ; collecting, comparing, and reflecting on ever
increasing stores of experiences from all quarters ; which aspects cannot be revealed to him who is overwhelmed by practice. Now, there
are very few who have pursued medicine in this scientific spirit, resolutely refusing to allow themselves to be engulphed by practice,
and thus lose the power of always advancing in knowledge. Practice
is necessary to make a great physician, but too much practice is destructive.

Another, and perhaps, next to the want of religious reverence for
their subject—the greatest cause of the impairment of the dignity of the
profession, is the narrow view that has been taken of its sphere. Medicine, according to the common acceptation of the term, is merely the
management of the body in disease—not the healthy, it is thought, but
only the sick need the physician. Thus, while the moralist has a
relation to all men in every state and stage of life, the physicist has
merely a little corner assigned him, and the most of men pass through
the greater part, or perhaps, if they are particularly fortunate, the whole
of their lives, thanking their stars that they never had anything to do
with doctors ! Thus did the name become almost a bugbear, which an
ardent nature shrinks from assuming, always bringing with it sad and
unpleasant associations, so that it is used even to frighten children!
But how different is the true sphere of the physician! His subject is
by no means limited to the diseased body, but embraces the whole life
of man in health and disease, for health has its laws and its treatment,
no less difficult, no less necessary, than disease. It was from this immense omission, that so little attention has been paid till within very
recent times, to hygiene, and the prevention of disease—these mighty
subjects which are now proceeding to change the face of the world—
subjects, which have scarcely yet been adopted into medicine proper,
and are not taught in the schools. As soon as these vast ideals began
to be conceived, it was immediately seen that medicine bore the closest
relation to every human being, in health as well as in sickness ; that
physical knowledge was needed by man at every step through life,
exactly as much . as moral knowledge—that without the former all

mental acquirements and cultivation, were the sport of chance, and proved too often in vain; that not only was it needed to prevent disease, but to fortify and elevate health itself, which, without a hygienic life, was not health ; that to it alone could men trust to attain to a healthy old age, and transmit an untainted constitution to their posterity.

But there are many other paths of medicine, which are yet unexplored, and which must be laid bare to the world, before the medical sphere receive its due completeness, and the profession be fully knit to the sympathy of men. He who would be enabled to take a true and comprehensive view of the subject, should study no less the spiritual than the bodily part of man, in health and disease, for they are indissolubly united; and the one cannot be understood without the other. He must show how and in what manner, the physical enters equally with the moral element into every human question. Insanity, and the various diseases of the mind—of which there is a peculiar one to correspond with every diseased bodily state—all should come under his patient investigation. To understand the diseases of the body and to prevent them, he should have an extensive acquaintance with the physical habits of all the different classes of society; and, as a knowledge of their mind is as important as of their body, with their mental habits also. The various arts and sciences, moreover, he should aspire to become acquainted with ;. for, if he be not conversant with the musical, mathematical, or mechanical world of ideas, and sympathies, how shall he know the different causes of health and disease, physical or mental, that operate in each of these ; and how shall he be able to prevent or cure disease in them, or to elevate their physical state ? He should seek to enter into the thoughts of poets, of religious and moral thinkers ; for all of them are in their own sphere physicians, and their every thought has a physical and medical import. This is not to be done by one man, but by the persevering and combined efforts of many ; and not until the intimate connection of medicine with all the other sciences has thus been shown, and generally recognised ; and until the public are as well informed on physical as on moral subjects, and as fully convinced of their paramount importance, will the medical profession hold its due place in their esteem, and exercise its natural influence on human affairs.

WOMAN, THE PHYSICIAN.

Mankind can never have a comprehensive view of any subject, until the mind of woman has been brought to bear upon it, equally with that of man. The two sexes have separate points of view; different thoughts, feelings, and modes of judgment; and no theory of life, nor of any part of it, can be complete, till the distinct views of each have been formed on it, and mutually compared. The religion, the morality, the duties of woman, differ no less from those of man, than their bodily organisation, and the states of health and disease, to which it is subject. No religion, no moral or physical code, proposed by one sex for the other, can be really suitable; each must work out its laws for itself in every department of life. Therefore have women, properly speaking, at present no religion, physical or moral, no morality, and no medicine. They trust to man for these, unaware that themselves alone can solve their life's problem in its minutest particular. I am aware of the great progress, in various directions, which many of the sex have lately made, but there still remains an immensity to be done, as none feel more than they do. Women have hitherto been content to regard the universe and themselves through men's eyes; and their self-consciousness is thus very imperfectly developed. The attainment of self-consciousness is to be gained in the same way as that of man, only by discovering their moral, intellectual and physical relations to all parts of nature. Hence there is no subject, which man has conceived or shall conceive and pursue; which woman should not also conceive and pursue according to her peculiar powers. Until she shall do this, neither she nor man will have a full or natural conception of the whole, as one of the grand sexual paths towards it will be unexplored.

There is no department of knowledge, from which woman has been more debarred than from medicine. If it was often thought unadvisable for man to penetrate the mysteries of the body, for woman it was held almost a sacrilege. The narrow ideal which our imperfect conceptions have shaped for woman—of purity, modesty, love, and grace, which are supposed to constitute her peculiar and sufficient sphere—revolts from the very thought of her engaging in pursuits of presumedly so opposite a character. In all ages all nations has the development of woman been crippled and impeded by man's interference. Like the Chinese bandaging, and the Turkish prison-house, does their conventional character at the present day among ourselves confine their natural energies and prevent their expansion. Innocence, purity, chastity, delicacy—let us rather read ignorance, morbidity, disease, and misery: how long shall this semblance of a moral character hang about the neck of woman? Does nature move thus with downcast eye, and sidelong regard, fearing everywhere to encounter objects it is ashamed to meet? No; the front of nature is calm, open, and fearless: her steady gaze penetrates everywhere beneath the sun, and if man or woman would be in harmony with her, they must emulate her fearless deportment. Hence should neither woman nor man shrink from the view of decay and death; they should meet them boldly and by wrestling with them, learn to embrace them too in their sympathies, to know that they are as sublime and beautiful parts of our being as any other. Who can value an existence spent in hiding from the presence of the inevitable, which will meet us in every step through life? By our knowledge of the destructive side of nature, and our acknowledgment of its equal justice and beauty, we are brought into harmony with the whole; while without this knowledge our characters remain most imperfect. This side has ever been assiduously hidden from woman in other things as well as in medicine, and thus has her character suffered infinitely.

No pursuit would have a better effect in restoring the balance of the female character than medicine, in which the destructive processes meet us on the very threshold, and command our most devoted attention. Nothing could be better adapted for unspiritualising woman, as well as man, and for restoring her to the realities of life and of the material universe. Here is the scene of our human joys and sorrows; our real trials and triumphs. Ah! not for woman only, but for all of us, is mother earth our paradise, our everlasting abode, our heavens, and our infinity! It is not by leaving it, and our real humanity behind us, and sighing to be anything but what we are, that man will become ennobled or immortal. Is this our gratitude for all that has been done for us, for the grandeur and sublimity by which our life is surrounded?

But medicine does not rest its claims on woman's reverential study, any more than on man's, merely on the feeble grounds of expediency. It is not the "rights" of woman that are concerned, but her duties. On her as well as on man, the study of her physical part and its laws, is enjoined by nature, as a religion and a duty, second to none in its claims. All those who do not study them, as is the case with all women, and nearly all men in the present day, live a life of sin, and are under the ban of nature. Ignorance of the physical laws is in woman no less culpable than in man; and nature has no excuse for the softer sex for any breach of them. Gallantry and cumbrous chivalry enter not into her code towards them; she does not load them with lip service, and yet deny them access to her heart's recesses. She lies there, open and inviting to the gaze, with one calm and impartial front turned towards both sexes alike.

The consequences of the want of physical reverence and knowledge in woman, have been as disastrous, perhaps more so, than in man. The ignorance and carelessness of women, in all things appertaining to their bodily welfare, is proverbial, and the despair of the physician. Men may perhaps, as has been said, be brought to attend to their stomach when death is staring them in the face; but to make woman attend to her bodily state, and reverence the laws of health in her own person, is too often a hopeless endeavour. But in all things, in all matters in life, this want of the feeling of duty to themselves, which is so often erroneously praised under the name of unselfishness, characterises women. They have never deeply thought or felt what it is right for themselves to do: what are the laws of their being, moral or physical, which they must obey. They have taken the will of man for their law, instead of that of nature; and yielded to him with little thought of their own duties. They have sanctioned by their apathy towards all other objects, the fallacious words of the poet, that "man is made for God only, woman for God in him." Does this deserve man's gratitude or approbation? would he then wish to absorb in himself woman's thoughts, and allegiance, jealous of the claims of all the rest of nature which demands no less her love, jealous of her attention and reverence for the laws of her own being? Alas! such has been and is too much the case: but this jealousy is a most narrow and mistaken feeling. We cannot be happy, unless woman be happy; and it is impossible she can be so, if she do not study and reverence her relations to the rest of nature as well as to us. Nature will not be neglected for man; and it demands her love. Can we love nature for woman? can we live her life, bear her penalties for error, die her death for her? If a woman do not herself possess moral and physical knowledge, which are inseparable from a genuine love of nature; if she do not possess them of herself and for herself, will all the knowledge on these subjects that was ever possessed by man, bear her safely through her life? Nothing can ever come to us from another, everything we have we must owe to ourselves; our own spirit must vitalise it, our own heart must feel it: for we are not passive machines—women, any more than men who can be lectured, and guided, and moulded this way and that; but living beings, with will, choice, and comprehension, to be exercised for ourselves at every step in life.

All the sciences, all the arts, wait at present for woman's hand and thought, to give them new life and impulses; and none solicit her attention more imperatively than medicine. The physical organisation of woman is, in many respects, different from that of man; their physical lives are different, their healthy and diseased sensations different. If the merely objective consideration gives one man so imperfect an idea of another, how much more imperfect must be his idea of woman, based on similar grounds? We cannot explain woman; her diseases, many of which are quite peculiar to her sex, are a mystery to us, which no objective reasoning will ever resolve. Woman alone, by her trained self-consciousness, can represent to us her peculiar sensations, and when these are disordered, it is she alone who possesses in her own sex the healthy standard, wherewith to compare them. When she relies on man to explain or to cure her, she leans on a broken reed. Nay, more than this, it is a sad error for either man or woman to believe, that it is the part solely of the physician to cure them. Men and women must equally co-operate in their cure; there is no royal road to health, nor is it often to be obtained by the mechanical pouring of medicine down the throat. Here, as in all other parts of life, it is to be regarded as the reward of individual exertion; our own body must labour for it, and our own reason and good endeavours must co-operate to the best of our powers. To throw the whole responsibility on the medical shoulders, is an evil which leads to the most ruinous results.

Each sex has a relation of objective reasoning to fulfil towards the other. Each has to reason for the other on all subjects; criticise, and endeavour to mould the other, according to its conceptions of what is just and good; and in every way strive to present to the other as complete as possible a picture of the aspect it bears towards itself. But, hitherto, man only has thus reasoned on woman. Man has been for ages shaping his model of the female physically and morally; dwelling upon, and endeavouring to elevate, and perfect her ideal, as it appeared to him. In medicine too, man alone has reasoned on woman; she has never ventured to think for him, and to render him his portrait in return. How much men lose by this, has been deeply felt in the moral world, where there are constant complaints, that woman, with regard to man, knows not her own mind, and therefore, that all men come in a manner alike to her. She will not criticise, or at least not reflectively, and, therefore, little dependence can be placed in her judgment of men, which is guided in great measure by caprice or conventionalities. In medicine this is even more the case than in morals; and not till woman shows her care for us by the keen investigation of our physical part with all its healthy and diseased states, shall we have a satisfactory picture of our wondrous two-sexed humanity. Does woman's heart never prompt her to this? is she never urged by the sight of the sufferings or death of those near and dear to her, to make herself something more than a cup-bearer in the sick room? Does intense love never suggest to her that there may be secrets in nature, kept for her solution alone, which tardy science would without her slowly or never reach? Do these things never awake in her an earnest determination, that will make its way through all obstacles, to work for those she loves, and for mankind, regardless of the wonder or stare of those, whose laugh would soon be hushed to a prayer for her. For a fountain of admiration for virtue and noble endeavour springs perennial in the human breast, and never yet did man trust to it and was deceived.

But rarely, alas! too rarely, does woman succeed in choosing for herself an independent path. She is yet too weak from the swaddling clothes, and can scarcely be expected to surmount the great obstacles which obstruct her freedom in almost every direction. When the first glow of self-reliance and independence, kindled by her intense feelings, has passed, doubts and irresolution succeed; the old woman, trained in long passive habits, and dependence on the opinion of others, re-asserts its sway; and after a sad and agonising struggle, she falls back into the accustomed beaten tracks, and her noble aspirations for the unknown and untried are dissolved like the melting vapour. "How should she presume to think for herself; how did she ever imagine she had the power to open up, or the privilege to enter upon a new world; why was she disturbed by elevating thoughts, she whose soul was so conscious of its own weakness and utter nothingness? The very wish to serve mankind, and develope herself in unaccustomed ways, was a deadly sin, showing the secret presumption of the heart, and the pride of the intellect. Oh, no! humility and gentle submission were her element; and love and contrition, not bold aspirings, her duty;" and thus is she in all probability, sooner or later absorbed into the Christian ideal, which by the mesmerism of the supernatural fascinates all those who lose their self reliance. For the power exercised by any dogmatic belief, whose essential characteristic ever is, that it reposes on faith, not on reason, is in exact proportion to the want of self-reliance of an individual in his own reason. Those who propose such doctrines, and those who receive them, alike forget, that the propositions they subscribe to are absolutely impossible; that there is no such thing as faith, not grounded on reason. Individual reason, good or bad, right or wrong, is at the bottom of every one's nature, and a man or woman's religion, right or wrong, must always be their own, whether they will or not, and cannot be that of any other.

Instead of urging woman onwards on the untrodden paths of new virtue and enterprise, Christianity tends greatly to keep her back, in the same way that it prevents men in general from reverencing duly the body. If the salvation of her soul by entertaining certain beliefs, and educating her mind and her life on certain all-absorbing feelings of love, purity, and devotion—if this be the one grand necessity for her, the all-sufficient crown of her existence, why imperil it by seeking to develope herself, or benefit mankind by such dangerous paths, as medicine; or, to give another example of a so-called unfeminine pursuit, the stage? Are not both professions more or less degraded in the eyes of men, and shall she not share in their degradation? are they not, especially for woman, scandalous, if not unheard of? what shall she gain by exposing herself to all the trials, temptations, seductions, and materialising influences which surround them, compared to the one thing needful, she endangers by the attempt? But more than this, does not the study of medicine, besides the mysteries of the body, with its sexualities, its putrescences, all of these subjects from which her uncultivated imagination has hitherto shrunk in alarm or disgust, does it not necessitate an acquaintance with the various habits and diseases, brought on by every vice, every sin of man and woman? Must not the venereal and genital diseases of both sexes be revealed to her eye, and studied with unaverted gaze? Must not she mix and converse with every class of human beings, with the debauchee of the one sex, and the prostitute of her own?

Yes, all this must she do, and far, far more besides. She must learn to shrink from nothing, and from no human being. She must learn to regard all with an equal love and reverence, totally irrespective of their actions; for in this consists the true character of the physician of the soul or the body—not to hate and reproach any, but to love and succour all. Does the true physician refuse to devote equal care to the worst case of sin or disease, as to the least? Nay, he loves and tends it, even the more, the more it requires his love. The true friend of man turns the same face of benevolence towards all; towards all, his endeavours are the same; namely, to benefit them to the utmost of his power.

SUBJECTIVE MEDICINE.

Every human life has a two-fold aspect, a subjective and an objective one. The first is the view it presents to an individual's self; the other, to those around him. In order that we may have a comprehensive knowledge of any individual, we must enter into both these views. Medicine, which embraces the whole physical life of man in health and disease, is also naturally divided into these two parts, both of which are equally necessary to render the science complete. One part of the knowledge of an individual's physical state, is to be got by the observation of the physician; the other can come only from the revelation of the individual himself.

Now in the latter part, namely, in subjective medicine, the science is as barren and incomplete, as was that of religion or morality, before men began to think for themselves on these matters. Neither in medical works, nor elsewhere, have we anything at all approaching to satisfactory subjective descriptions of disease. Very few medical men have ever thought of allowing their patients to speak for themselves in their reports of cases. Intent chiefly on arriving at physical facts and physical conclusions, they have paid comparatively slight attention to the mental state of the patient, which forms no less integral a part of the disease. Thus, in questioning a patient, they strove as much as possible to bring him to the physical point, checking his digressions, and the outpourings of his suffering heart. It is this want of sympathy and value for the mental part of the disease, and the mere attention to the physical, that has proved one of the chief barriers between medical men and the public. But it is no less the physician's duty to embrace in his reverence and scientific attention the mental element, than it is that of the moralist to embrace the physical. Both have suffered equally from the omission, and such a division of labour in so indissoluble a compound as man, cannot but lead to the most imperfect results.

Every one must have felt, in reading medical works, the dull and mechanical tone, which the want of the subjective element imparts. Instead of the intense glow of life and individuality, with which each stamps his own soul's or body's tragedy, in a personal narrative, we have all pruned down to a sober routine list of facts and symptoms, evidently not designed to interest men generally, but merely the scientific few. How many are cheated by such a method! The patient is deprived of the appeasing of that yearning demand for sympathy, which dwells in every human bosom, and which, though it has not yet been fully awakened for physical, as it has been for moral woes, surges in the breast of every sufferer with an agony that increases by resistance, and will yet overwhelm the world. Who can bear to have merely a calm and dispassionately scientific view taken of his fate or of his woes, which to him are in themselves an infinite world? But society, too, lose as greatly as the patient. Not only do they forfeit the valuable lesson of experience, and the deep impression for good, which no dull routine description that does not reach the heart, can excite, but they lose the power of giving sympathy and consolation, as blessed as the receiving, for we cannot sympathise with that which we do not intimately understand. And the physician himself, and science, lose in as great a degree, not only by the blunting of the feelings caused by mechanical views of living and thinking beings, but also in their insight into the *psychology of health and disease*, which is as valuable a part of medical knowledge, as any other, and as important for the prevention and treatment of disease, and the advancement of health. Every physical state has its peculiar mental one, and to discover what this is, and what influence on the mind all bodily states from so-called perfect health, to hypochondria, insanity, delirium, or death, is a most essential branch of medical science. This psychology of health and disease is to be obtained only by the study of every individual's mind compared with his bodily condition, and a full knowledge of this is to be arrived at only by his own revelations. We want a whole man to know and sympathise with, not merely a body or a soul.

How few subjective records of physical life are to be found in history. Among the numerous autobiographies that have been written by so many noble human beings, who has given to us any but the most meagre details of his physical life, even though its history may have been the most extraordinary, the most sadly eventful of the twin parts of his nature? Hence do all these men present to us most imperfect pictures. Through all the tissue of their lives we know not what physical threads have been interwoven, and therefore we can pass no satisfactory judgment on themselves or their actions. But how immensely does the world lose by not having the fruits of their physical as well as their moral experiences! Had their penetrating minds been as keenly directed to the physical goods and evils they encountered, as to the mental ones; had they used, each in his own case, the subtle insight which personal experience alone gives, would the world have been in so wretched a physical state as it still is, with so low a physical standard, that health is not health, and that there is a skeleton in every house, and a disease, secret or open, gnawing at the vitals of almost every one of us! Would we be still stumbling on from age to age in the same erroneous tracks, and falling one after the other like sheep, into the same physical pit-falls?

If it be impossible to build a moral world out of objective reasoning alone, it is no less vain to seek to build a physical one with these poor materials.

If we seek for a physical criticism on men of past ages, we must say, "We have not the elements for it; we know them not, they knew not themselves, and their physical motive influences escaped their consciousness." Shall we be content to remain in the same undeveloped unconscious state; shall we continue still to view ourselves and our neighbours with a spiritual eye only, and thus for ever remain hidden from ourselves and from them? If we will not remain thus ignorant, we must imbue our minds equally with physical knowledge; we must study the language of the body, a language not confined to an age or a nation, but wide and universal as humanity, in order that we may attain to a higher self-consciousness, and be able to interpret ourselves and comprehend others

LIFE AND DEATH.

THESE form the two great divisions of human existence. They are the sums of the various forces which are at work within us. The one is the result of all the constructive, the other of the destructive processes. In man's body the two several processes of reparation and destruction, of life and death, go on together throughout the whole of his existence. If it can be said of him that he is living at any moment, it may be no less truly said of him that he is dying; for it is only through constant death that we live; through constant waste of tissues that our forces are supplied. Thus we see that even of life, death forms an integral part; that the processes of destruction are equally necessary and equally valuable to man, with those of construction. If the destructive processes be impeded at any moment, disease is just as certainly produced as if the others be impeded.

But there is always an exact analogy between the body and the mind. There is no bodily truth, which is not represented by a spiritual one; no physical law, which is not reflected in a moral law: as there is no change in the mind without an exactly corresponding change in the brain. Therefore in the moral world also, we find the same powers of construction and destruction balancing each other. These are known under the names of belief and scepticism. Like the parallel powers in the body, these different kinds of moral processes are equally necessary, equally valuable. If the powers of scepticism have not their full and natural scope, if their healthy destructive processes be arrested, man must suffer just as certainly as if the powers of belief were impeded. Death and scepticism are just as essential and as much to be reverenced, as life and belief.

In the body, every particle dies in the very act of living; and so does a truth, as soon as it is conceived, become a falsehood. It has been acutely, said that nothing but what is new is true; and every new truth must to the old be false and destructive.

Nothing can be erected by one process in the body, which will not be destroyed by another; and so nothing can be erected by one part of man's mind which another will not overthrow. Nothing can be affirmed which cannot be denied; nothing believed which cannot be disbelieved. There is a destructive and sceptical tendency in man's mind, just as infinite, just as insatiable, as a constructive and believing one.

As death springs from life, so does life ever arise from death. As denial is evolved from affirmation, so does new belief ever arise from scepticism. Had there been the possibility of arriving at settled truths, by which men could abide, the infinity of nature would not have been recognised; but scepticism for ever prevents the possibility of limiting her domains. Scepticism or destructiveness is therefore the grand power, which nature has given to enable us ever to preserve the sense of infinity. While life gathers together, defines, and bends to its will the elements of our being, death constantly strives to disperse and restore them to their former freedom. It is good for a man that life shall at one time prevail; it is no less good for him that death shall at another time prevail.

One part of man strives powerfully and victoriously for life and belief; another as powerfully and as victoriously for death and denial. But as they not only alternate with each other, but go on simultaneously during the whole course of existence; therefore in our moral nature are truth and falsehood, belief and scepticism, necessarily going on together, whether we recognise this or not. To constitute a well-balanced mind, the destructive and sceptical workings must keep pace with the constructive ones. If the former processes are interfered with, or not sufficiently called into play, the mind will become diseased. Again, if the believing and constructive part of the mind have not equal scope, disease will likewise be produced. The equal claims and necessities for both should be recognised by us.

But hitherto this has been little the case. Instead of feeling the equal value of these two sides of our nature; instead of paying equal reverence to the destructive side, we have striven as much as possible to hide it from our thoughts and sympathies. We have averted our faces from death and scepticism, forgetting that these are as inevitable, and, therefore, as beautiful parts of our being as life and belief. Until ignorance, error, and finiteness, are banished from the world; until life stands by itself and is not irseparably linked with death, throughout our whole existence; until, in short, man have a totally different nature from what he has, so long will every thought, every feeling, every moral and physical act have its necessary amount of sin, destruction, or imperfection. Since this is so, if we avert our faces from sin, destruction, and death, we can know but little of man; we can see but the one half of his being, and our knowledge of that will be radically defective. Man's wishes and thoughts must be in harmony with his nature or he will surely suffer. If we wish to exclude death from our thoughts; if we wish to have absolute life, absolute virtue, or absolute belief, at every point nature will rise in arms against us. Death will overwhelm us with anguish and disappointment; sin, the inevitable, will bind us, clinging to our heartstrings, and clogging our every thought: scepticism, the infinite, the inexorable, will crush to pieces our flimsy beliefs, and fill our bosoms with terror and dismay. If we refuse to recognise them; if we hate the idea of death or scepticism, and do not acknowledge their equal powers; if we impede their healthy destructive actions, disease and misery will most certainly result. But if on the contrary we acknowledge their natural beauty; if we study them and learn to take delight in their

contemplation, we shall soon perceive, that the powers we shunned are
in reality our glorious privileges, and that without them our life were
shorn of its sublimity.   It is only by embracing them, that we shall be
in harmony with nature, and attain to a fuller knowledge of our mysterious being.   The weapons of destruction, will be to those who reverence, and learn to use them, most powerful for the service of mankind.
Scepticism and all the destructive forces are not toys for the young mind
to play with, till it obtains a settled faith—but glorious privileges to
be carried with us, and constantly exercised for knowledge and for improvement throughout life ;   acting in continual harmony with the
constructive powers.   The individual or the society who fear scepticism
or natural death, must live in constant discord and antagonism with
nature ;   and will not be at peace till they have embraced them in
their sympathies.   There are few things, from which we have suffered, and still suffer more, than from this grand error ;   even at the
present day, scepticism and death, along with all the destructive
forces, are subjects from which the mass of men shrink.   Scepticism,
that transcendent power, has become a sort of watchword to their ears,
the very sound of which torments, if it does not horrify them ;   and indeed it, like death, will remain a horror, till it be recognised as a blessing and delight.

With regard to death, as well as its ministers, man is in the most unhappy antagonism with nature.   He shrinks from the idea of death on
every side.   Although he cannot but admit physical death, when it is
brought before his eyes with the certainty of physical demonstration, yet
he claims for his soul or spiritual part complete immunity from the
common lot, and by so doing utterly subverts the harmony of nature.   He
will not bear to have it said, that the soul and the body are inseparably
linked in their destinies, and yet this is a fact so certain, that nature
challenges it as an axiom in all our reasonings.

It is true that matter never dies, nor loses any of its properties, but
it changes its combinations, which do not retain their identity.   By
gaining more and more insight into the wondrous processes of material and
spiritual development and change, never for a moment attempting to
separate where nature has joined—by following the universal laws of
induction in this matter, as well as in all others, we may hope to
discover our true relation to the infinite on the destructive side of life
as on others, but by no other method is it possible.   Too long
have these subjects been withdrawn from science and the common
sense of man, and given over to the mere assertions of authority
and self-styled instinct ;   and the consequence is, that they have
remained a dead unproductive theme amid the living and expanding
sciences around.   The voices of men are silent on these great subjects of
the futurity of the individual and the race ;   no one likes to speak of them,
except those whose opinions on the infinite are so well known, and so
little grounded on reason, or any satisfactory principles, that their words
fall dull and powerless on our ears.   Meanwhile, Life and Death—the two
indefinable mysteries, the beautiful twin brothers of eternity— move on
through the universe, in perfect and loving harmony and mutual under-

standing, heedless of our theories, and inscrutable to the prejudiced eye. All gaze on the one, all knees bend before him, but the other is despised and reviled; we loathe him, we shrink from him, as from pollution. We do not seek to know his laws, we do not wish even to look upon his face. But by this we lose immensely in knowledge, power, and happiness.

There is no greater loss to mankind at present, no greater waste of treasures unpurchaseable by gold, than the way in which our bodies are disposed of after death. Instead of every one of us having the utmost reverence paid us, having every part of us analysed and attended to in death as in life, with as persevering care and devotion; being neglected in no scrutiny which science can devise, as a means of approaching nearer to the mystery of our peculiar being, and of general humanity; instead of all this, we are shunned as a pestilence, our dearest friends fear to look on us, and shrink from mentioning even our names; and our invaluable remains, instead of still in death blessing their companions, who remain behind, in a manner, in which they could not, while living, are huddled out of sight, and consigned to the thankless worms. Death was intended by nature as the grand key to the meaning of life, by which alone man could arrive at her secrets; but this priceless boon we wantonly cast away. Nay, so far are we from eagerly seeking to avail ourselves of this privilege, that we shrink from the very idea of using it. Some few years ago, there was so great a prejudice against the dissection of human bodies, that it was regarded as one of the greatest punishments for the criminal, that his should be so treated. And even yet the prejudice against the examination of the dead pervades all ranks of society. The dissecting room is viewed with a kind of horror and disgust; it is thought about the last degradation for a human being to be brought there. None are dissected except the friendless ones, who die in the hospitals and poorhouses, and whose latter hours are often embittered by the knowlege of the fate which awaits them. Their relations, if they know of their death, are too poor to bury them, and can but lament over the miserable alternative. But even to obtain an examination of the body after death, to discover the nature of the fatal disease, is no easy or pleasant task for the physician; often it is absolutely impossible. The mistaken friends will not hear of such a thing, and view with a kind of horror the physician who makes the proposal. Matters are not quite so bad among the richer classes; but among the less educated they are most painful to all parties. How well do I remember the sickening feelings of degradation I had when living in hospital, where our examinations of the dead bodies, far from being sympathised in by the heartfelt interest of the patients and their friends, were viewed with loathing and horror; ourselves regarded at times as butchers, and every attempt made to baffle our laudable endeavours. The patients were afraid of dying in hospital, and would sometimes cause themselves to be carried off, when nearly at the last gasp, to escape those whom they regarded as the sworn foes to the decency of death. No provision had been made to allow of the examination of the dead, and therefore it was done clandestinely by the physicians and students; and at every death there was a series of stratagems between the doctors on the one hand, and the friends of the deceased on the other, to effect or prevent the examination. At these most indecent and degrading scenes the deep glow of sorrow and indignation entered my heart. What then, are we to be considered butchers for doing what love and duty enjoin upon us? Shall the sympathies of men shrink from us because we take the necessary mode to serve them? Shall the cause of mankind suffer, and all of us be alike degraded by these most sinful impediments, thrown in the way of our religion and our science? Who will submit to wrongful degradation?

But if we find these unhappy prejudices so dominant among the poorer classes, it is because the rich and better educated entertain them also. In these classes also, how often do the thoughts of friends shrink from the examination, which in every case should be made. Are the ways of death so easy, that in any case we can afford to pass them by without the profoundest consideration? But it is not merely to discover the nature of the fatal disease, that our bodies claim the attention of man after death.

No human being, man, woman, nor child, should die, without being dissected in their every nerve and fibre, as carefully, as minutely, as reverentially, as love and science can suggest. To squander such glorious subjects for our contemplation, the most perfect types of material organization, on the grave, is the greatest and most wanton waste that is now committed by man. At present the supply of human remains, is in this country too scanty, even for the instruction of the medical profession; when every educated human being, man and woman alike, shall study anatomy, as one of their chief duties and privileges, we shall learn better the uses of universal death. Human anatomy and physiology are the key-stones of the physical sciences, and without them all attempts to interest man or woman in the latter—to make them comprehend them, or their own relation to the material universe, are utterly vain and impracticable. He that does not know anatomy, can have but a skin-deep knowledge of man. Therefore, as it is impossible for any of us to live a good or true life without self-knowledge, every one should study anatomy. He or she who does not, sins; and any one who throws impediments in the way of our obtaining this indispensable knowledge, also sins. Instead of shrinking from this necessary path of duty, we should account it a great privilege. Has any one so little love for man, so little reverence for truth, that he would not consent, or rather earnestly desire, that men should not neglect him after death; that he should be able even in death to serve them, after death's own incomparable manner; that in death as in life he should be judged of, and thus a wider and deeper revelation of his being, obtained! He who is not dissected after death, has an imperfect fate, and must so far remain unknown to us. Not only this, but he in this particular, does less good to his kind, and therefore less deserves their gratitude than he who is. Until the educated classes feel deeply these things, and bring themselves and the medical profession into harmony, by being every one in his heart and sympathies, no less than in his knowledge, a physicist, how can we expect that our poorer neighbours will view these matters aright? How many sore feelings, how much anguish to patients, friends, and physician; how much degradation to all will be spared, when we attain to truer ideas of life and death!

HEALTH OF TOWNS.

LARGE towns are the grand arena of disease of all descriptions. It is in them that the various causes of bodily suffering, both physical and moral, operate most powerfully, and produce their most fearful results. It is to them, therefore, that the physical reformer must chiefly direct his attention; it is their evils that most urgently claim the sympathy and pity of every feeling heart. What a difference is there between the physical state of town and country! In the vigourous rustic, where the rural population are not sunk in poverty, we see health glowing in every feature; we can note the action of pure air and bracing exercise in his ruddy cheek and stalwart frame, and delight in the joyous hilarity of his ready laugh, the sign of an exuberance of health. But how sad a contrast does the townsman present? Even in the appearance of the richer classes, when we enter a town, we may observe a wide difference from their country neighbours of the same rank. The pale cheeks of the young ladies tell of late hours, lives spent within doors in reading, working, or exchanging visits, or of exercise limited to a saunter along a fashionable street. In the young men too, how constantly do we observe the signs of the evil effects of the town's influence. Here we pass the student, whose sallow complexion, quickened pace, and absorbed expression, show how much his body and external senses are neglected for his more cherished pursuits; there the pleasure-hunter, whose jaded looks let us guess the nature of his nocturnal dissipation. Scarcely even the healthiest among them, but presents some indication to the instructed eye, of the infinity of noxious and weakening influences of the city.

But let us quit the better streets, and wander through the quarters occupied by the poor. Let us penetrate to the core of the crowded city and view the corruption which harbors there. In this part, the most sadly interesting of all to the sympathising eye, where my feet have often lingered and my heart saddened and burned within me, the rich man is rarely to be seen; it is separated from the haunts of the more fortunate by a broader line of demarcation than that which severs land from land, or sea from sea.

What a scene of woes too deep for tears, does the poor's quarter present! Little children with pale sickly faces, blear-eyed, covered with eruptions, with rickety limbs, and scrofula written in every feature, playing about among the gutters, if such beings can be said to play at all! Men and women, still pale, and all prematurely old and haggard, with the furrows of care ploughed deep in their brows, and a common expression of despondence and anxiety. Here we see the deep yellow hue of incurable liver disease, brought on probably by intemperate habits; there the puffy watery face that tells of the kidneys degenerated from similar causes; next the hollow ghastly visage of the consumptive, the labouring chest of the asthmatic, or the defaced features of the unhappy victim of syphilis. Wherever we go, care, squalidness, and disease, meet our eyes.

From such a scene, let us go with what appetites we may, to admire the beauties of the city, the works of art, magnificent buildings, gardens, and institutions, of which the wealthier citizen is so proud. Alas! how little compensation can these offer for the human ruins we have been contemplating! The splendid edifices and luxuriant gardens, where the happier children of the rich are fenced from all harm, and allowed to grow up in the sunshine, like the young flowers, contrast too painfully with the narrow filthy streets, dilapidated houses, and scrofulous features of the unfortunate little ones, whose playground is the kennel and crowded thoroughfare, fraught with so many dangers.

Can we be contented with bestowing our thoughts and our expenditure in beautifying the more fortunate parts of our cities, in erecting monuments to the dead, and grand buildings for the wonder and admiration of the stranger, while we thus neglect our poorer living brethren? Shall we take pride and glory in our towns, in whose secret recesses, which the stranger cares not to see, and which the citizen avoids as an eye-sore and focus of infection, corruption riots at its pleasure? One town vies with another in its beauties, natural and artificial, but does any fully feel the noble aspiration to excel, not in architectural beauties alone, but in the dutiful and loving provision made for the physical well-being of all its citizens? Should we not earnestly feel the desire to be able to pass ourselves and to conduct the stranger, not through magnificent squares or splendid streets alone, but through every part, every lane and alley, and to feel that there is none we are ashamed to meet, none which our brotherly sympathies have not entered, and invested with a peculiar and equal beauty?

How very far are we at present from so blessed a condition! There is not a large town in the country which is not a disgrace to our nation; not one which does not cry out to heaven against us. There is not one which is even moderately healthy; not one which is not hideously diseased. If men had given to their own bodies, or to the bodies of their fellow beings, the thousandth part of the devoted attention and enthusiasm they have given to their souls, should we have come to this!

Our ancestors knew little about the laws of health. They built their streets narrow, their chambers small; they huddled their buildings as closely together as possible, leaving few if any open spaces, either as squares or gardens, which are the lungs of a large town ...without which it must languish and suffocate.

Our better informed generation builds in a more healthy manner, although among us too, there is often little or no provision made for free air, but our improvements are almost entirely confined to the quarters of the rich. The poor succeed to the houses we have long abandoned, which are now, besides their radical defects, rendered ten times as unhealthy by their old age, the surrounding extension of the city, and their over-crowded population. Hence these quarters are the focus of disease; no one abides in them for any time without being destroyed physically and morally; the unhappy children, if not cut off, as the great majority of them are, during the first few years of life, grow up pale, weak, vicious, criminal; the healthiest stock becomes in a few generations extinct, and the vacuum thus created is filled by new healthy victims, who are soon brought through the tedious chronic processes of destruction to a similar end; syphilis and typhus have it here all to themselves, and spread from hence over the whole city.

What avail all the exhortations of the preacher, or of the moralist; what our penal codes and our hospitals, while these things remain so? If the town be itself diseased, nothing which lives in it will be healthy. Will all the prayers ever poured out under the skies widen these streets one inch? will all the penal codes, all the medicines that are, or shall be known to man, make up for the want of the air of heaven? It is good to bind up the bleeding heart, to console the sufferer; it is good to cure disease, when a cure is possible, but it is better that the suffering or disease should never have existed.

What then can we do to remedy this hideous blot on our civilisation, to restore to health our great towns, and thus be able to enjoy the freedom of our cities, and inspire the fresh air ourselves without the remorseful consciousness, that our neighbours are gasping, languishing, and dying, for the want of it? For it is pure air which our large cities especially require; it is the want of that, which most of all destroys them; and the admission of it to every part is the grand problem of the physical reformer. No other immediate cause of disease, among the innumerable host which operate in large cities, is at the present day nearly so impor-tant. Others may more attract our attention and are better recognised, because they are more palpable; but this invisible agent, with its insi-dious chemistry, saps the foundations of our being, while it eludes our observation. In its subtle menstruum how many poisons enter into our frames? Every infection, noxious exhalation, and destroying product of destruction, by its agency penetrates to our inmost bosoms, and taints us at the core.

No living thing, plant, animal, or human being, can live in a tainted atmosphere, or can have health or enjoyment, unless pure air and sun-shine have free admission to it. Hence the stunted diseased state of the scattered trees in the midst of a crowded city. Do we think that a man can flourish, where a plant languishes? But even these plants have many advantages over the poor man. They live at least in the open air so as to obtain the greatest benefit possible from the atmosphere, impure as it is; while he is confined to the house, nearly the whole of his existence, toiling in musty, airless rooms, where the sunshine, almost as necessary as pure air for the health, never penetrates.

To remedy these immense evils a radical change will be needed in the construction of our large towns, and in the habits of the citizens. Every care that enlightenment and philanthrophy can suggest, should be expended in the remodeling of our old towns and poors' quarters. No new street should be allowed to be built in a large city, of less than a certain width, in proportion to the supply of fresh air; and in those which have been bequeathed us by our ancestors, we should never rest till we have succeeded in altering them to a healthy standard. But there is nothing perhaps of so much importance, or which is so totally neglected in the poorer districts, as that open spaces should be left at intervals, in the midst of the most crowded parts, to serve as reservoirs of fresh air. These small parks should be simply covered with grass, with a few trees here and there, whose healthy effect in decarbonising the atmosphere is shown by science; and whose flourishing condition would be a test of the salubrity of the air around. Unfenced by envious railings, they should be freely open to all. Although all the community, young and old, would benefit by such spaces, yet to none would they be so great a boon, nay, so absolutely necessary, as to the children. These have as yet no business to occupy their day, and it must be spent in play somewhere, whether in the filthy musty rooms, or in the dangerous thoroughfares.

One's heart sickens over the thought of a childhood spent in such places. No wonder that thus they become spectres instead of children; that about two-thirds of them die of scrofulous diseases, and that the rest grow up withered and stunted, with watery blood and cold dull hearts. Shall we love and care for our children (for all children are ours as belonging to our common humanity) less than for the animals and plants? In truth it seems so, when we observe, as we often do, in large towns, public gardens, or meadows, from which the children of the poor at least, are totally excluded, whether for the sake of a few wretched plants, or from mere caprice.

To the feeling heart there is no spectacle more delightful, than that of healthy and happy children sporting on the grass, and at every breath and every frolic, laying in stores of health, which in after years shall bless themselves and the city which gave them birth. There is no spectacle so miserable, as that of the pale, dirty, spectres of the streets, building mud-pies, peevish and quarrelsome, the future tenants of the hospitals and gaols. As long as the children have the streets alone to play in, there is no hope for them. The high streets are ever dangerous, and on this account they are often kept at home by their parents.

Nor is it of much use that there should be parks and gardens, outside the city, even though it be of moderate size. Little children can go but a short distance to seek their play-ground, and if it be not close at hand, they will confine themselves to the puddles before the door. One grass park in the middle of their homes, is to the children of more value than all the churches, monuments, or institutions of the city.

Besides the making of these lungs to the town, the widening of the strictured streets, and the improvement of the houses everything should be done to bring the inhabitants as much as possible into the open air All of us live far too much in the house; but the poor artizan, at his constant sedentary employment, is almost entombed in it. That man is a chief benefactor to his species, who by shortening the working hours, by the discovery of means of amusement, social pleasures, or any other inducements, prevails on his fellow citizens, to spend as much of their time as possible in the open air. Any human being who spends his or her life without passing a considerable portion of each day in the open air, lives a life of sin. The open heavens are nature's temple, and those who do not reverence her, she will not reverence. We should endeavour as much as possible to carry our enjoyments and our pursuits, nay, as far as may be, our meals and our studies into the open air.

The close domestic life for which our country is so proverbial, is much less healthy in this respect than that of the continent, where the inhabitants of town and country often almost live in the open air, taking for months together, many of their meals, and most of their social pleasures in it. It is not the difference of climate nearly so much as the difference of manners, which prevents us from adopting such admirable customs.

In the present sickly state of society, especially among the poorer classes, the poor townsman works during the whole day, at a sedentary trade, which confines him to the house; and then instead of being able to pass the evening in the open air, which might make amends for the unhealthy day, he spends it either at home, in the tavern, or in some place of public amusement, as the theatre, whose pestilential atmosphere is well known.

Evening lectures and mechanics' institutes, good though they be, will not atone for the want of the open air. Amusements are as necessary for man as instruction, and form no less important a part of his real duty; for without joy and hilarity, the man and the child will alike become diseased. It is a mistake too to suppose, that a taste for amusements exists naturally, while one for information requires to be cultivated. The taste for amusement and the pleasure derived from it, need constant cultivation through life, both by the individual and the society, and those who neglect this will surely suffer.

Nothing is more hurtful to man's health, physical and moral, than an austere, serious state of mind, which cannot be amused, and is constantly prone to gloomy views. This serious cast of mind is one of the great evils in our national character, especially in the Scotch; our theory of life, favoured by the Christian religion, is a serious one; we cannot understand the equal beauty and truth of the laughing philosophy, and this has the most unhealthy effect on both mind and body.

There is nothing in which this serious view of life operates more banefully, than in the influence it has on the mode of keeping the Sunday. This day is our workman's only holiday; the day in which his weary labours have a pause, and he has time to enjoy the fruits of his toils. On this day he should lay in a stock of health, happiness, and content, to carry him through the week, to delight him in his retrospect and prospect. Released from the necessities of his sedentary life, he should spend his Sunday entirely in the open air—in the country, if possible, bracing his lungs and limbs by the unwonted exercise. Having one day's respite from the serious monotonous life of work, his Sunday should be devoted to amusement, gaiety, and hilarity, as boisterous, as free and unrestrained, as possible. With every hearty laugh the burden of his cares will be lightened, and his heart will open to the love of his fellow creatures. Instead of this, the admirable and religious manner in which the Sunday is spent, for the most part, on the continent, how sad and melancholy is our Sunday to him who has an insight into the laws of health, physical and moral, and an interest in the welfare of his fellow beings.

Instead of the working classes being exhorted, and induced by every temptation of cheap and numerous railway trains, public gardens, and promenades, with musical bands and various social amusements, (for it requires no slight inducements to prevail on a pale and sickly frame to make any effort for its own regeneration) to spend their whole day in the open country air; they are pressed by every means into the church service, amusements are forbidden, and even to go out to breathe the fresh air, is in many parts, especially in Scotland, scarcely thought proper. In the latter country, especially, all thoughts of the mind, all acts of the body lie under a restraint more galling to many, than even the week-day confinement.. The thoughts, it is said, should then be serious, the bodily deportment sober and sedate. No amusements are permitted, even to sing or whistle is looked upon as a sacrilege. Even the little children are prevented from playing, and their toys lie idle. Many of those whose bodies have been pining in narrow rooms the whole week, and who would now, if left to nature, burst into the free air with the exuberant delight of school-boys, spend their day at church, still sedentary, still serious.

But far more of the poor inhabitants of our large towns, do not go to church, as they must have excitement; and where do the unfortunates, ashamed to be seen abroad, resort to? To the tavern, where they consume nearly as much whiskey on the Sunday, as on all the rest of the week together. I have no hesitation in saying, that our Sunday is one of the chief causes of the drunkenness in our large towns, for which the Scotch are proverbial, and which is one of the greatest national causes of disease and misery. In the country, and to the hardy rustic, the evil effect of this day is not so manifest, but to the blighted artizan of the city, it is destructive. Alas! how does the heart which has rejoiced over the happy continental Sunday, sadden at the contrast!

But we should not only grieve at such things, but seek to enforce the reverence for the natural laws, which have been neglected. We should earnestly endeavour to make it clearly understood, that the moral and physical laws, are exactly of equal sacredness, and that to be ignorant of, or to break either of them, is equally culpable. Thus we must recognise that it is a great sin for any man, whose body from confinement during the week, requires fresh air and exercise, to go to church on a Sunday; it is no less a sin in those who endeavour to induce him to do so, or throw obstacles in the path of his physical duties, in defiance of the interests of his being. I say these things, in the deep conviction that unless all of us learn to reverence the physical, as much as the moral interests, of ourselves and our neighbours, there is no safety for man.

D

Is the question of the air we breathe a slight matter, or one easily solved? Is the construction and health of our large towns, and their teeming populations, each individual with a claim on our sympathy, which cannot be over-estimated, a trivial thing, which is to be left to the doctors, the sanitarians, and those who busy their heads with these simple physical questions? A simple question truly, the false solution of which has entailed on us such an infinity of evils, such a labyrinth and abyss of miseries, that it will require the most strenuous untiring efforts of mankind for generations, with all the genius and self-devotion of the wisest and most persevering men, to enable us in part to escape. It will not be in a day, scarcely in a century, that men will recover from the contempt and neglect that have been shown to the body and all its requirements.

Besides the above mentioned means for ensuring a supply of fresh air in a town, every precaution should be taken to prevent its contamination by noxious elements. The most baneful and important of these in our large towns is the smoke, whether from private houses or from public works. This pollutes the air by poisonous gases, and still more by the small particles of coal and soot, so that the carbon enters into the very core of the citizens. No smoking factory should be tolerated in a large town; every one should be forced to consume its own smoke. Until this is done, there is no safety for any of the inhabitants, but more especially for the poorer classes, who dwell in the neighbourhood of these sooty giants, more pestilential than the dragons of old. Society should by common consent, enforce the consumption of the smoke, which could be easily accomplished, and should not rest till this be obtained. If they cannot afford to change these things, can they better afford to forfeit their own or their neighbours' lives by them? There is never a gain by that carelessness and want of attention, which neglects the laws of health in their full perfection. Whenever any individual's health or forces suffer, there is a dead loss in every way to society, as well as to himself, and the sin as well as the penalty must be shared by all.

None of the exhalations in a town, whether from graveyards or sewers, are, I believe, nearly so fatal to health as smoke; although the former also, are often very injurious, and should be carefully guarded against. But the smoke in some towns, especially in London, is ruinous to the health and strength of almost every one who dwells amid it. In this town, there are but few public factories, and the chief part of the smoke comes from private houses. Until this be got rid of, every human being who lives in London, will suffer more or less in health, and the whole race of its inhabitants must be deteriorated. It has been shown, I believe, to be perfectly practicable, by conducting the smoke from the different houses in each row into a common vent, and there consuming it, to prevent any of these deleterious sooty particles from escaping into the air. Scarcely anything would be of equal value to the town as such a measure, if universally adopted.

Much has been done of late years to improve the ventilation of the houses of the rich, and of those parts of public institutions, which are set apart for them. But how little in either respect has been done for the poor! How pestilential are the upper galleries of our theatres! How many a fever and consumption might be traced to them! How wretched and unwholesome are the rooms of their own houses! How little has been done to make themselves feel the sovereign importance of fresh air, the religion and duty which they owe to their bodies! It is seldom that the women among the poorer classes in the large towns ever leave their houses, except on necessary errands, and when they thus become diseased, a constitutional walk is beyond the power of their medical adviser to obtain.

But religion and duty form but one part of our lives, not one whit superior in importance to others. A life guided by principle alone or chiefly, is an imperfect one, and by no means the ideal of humanity, which with its innate demand for freedom, cannot bear to feel itself the slave of laws, and is spoiled in its completeness and beauty by such a feeling.

Thus there should be inducements of pleasure, happiness, and spontaneous choice, to lead us along the paths of duty; and in the matter of air and exercise, it is not to be expected or desired, that man or woman should take them merely on principle or as a duty. They are too often prescribed as medicines, like the moral virtues, without means being taken to combine their benefits with the happy freedom of spontaneous choice, without which all medicines or duties are imperfect.

Therefore, constant habit from early infancy, teaching us to regard fresh air as a necessary of life; all manner of inducements and social pleasures linked with the idea of the open air, should combine with the recognition of our religious and dutiful relation to it, to make men eagerly seek after it, in every condition and circumstance of life.

There is another great reason of the awful degradation of our poor townsmen. It is the separation between them and the richer classes. Had there been any bond of union, any connection of intimacy, of friendship, of social enjoyment; any heart sympathy or understanding between them, could the unfortunate poor have got into such a wretched state? Had the foot of the wealthy often sought the streets, had it ever passed the threshold of the poor, and beheld the stifling squalor behind it, had his sympathies been mixed with those of his fellow-being in but an infinitesimal proportion of that amount which our common humanity demands, could these evils have remained so? No; it is in great part because the poor have been excluded from our friendship and sympathies, because we are class conventionalists, and not real men, because we have no communion with them at home or abroad, that there have arisen such miserable evils in their state. Neither physically nor morally, can the poor be sufficiently elevated, save by the habitual mingling among them, for mutual instruction and sympathy, of those who have more time and opportunity to cultivate their various faculties.

MENTAL DISEASE.

IT is not yet sufficiently recognised, that the mind has its health and disease, exactly like the body, dependent on fixed natural laws. The term, mental disease, is restricted to insanity; but it must be viewed in a much wider sense, comprehending every case in which a mind suffers by erring against any natural law. If our thoughts and our feelings are in harmony with truth and nature, our minds will be healthy and happy; if not, they will be unhappy and diseased. Sorrow in the mind corresponds to pain in the body; wherever it is found it is a mark of sin and disease.

Whenever we observe, either in ourselves or in others, any grief, we may be certain that some evil is the cause of it. Happiness is the sign of moral health; it is one grand gaol for human aspiration, just as physical happiness or health is in the material world. Joy and sorrow are our guides to truth, showing us where we are right, and where wrong, in the exploration of our being. Wherever we find joy, we should seek the cause and follow it; wherever sorrow, the reverse is our duty.

But sorrow, in another light, may be regarded as a kind of good; thus having an exact analogy with bodily disease. It is now well known, that the body never works for its own destruction, but constantly for its preservation; and thus, that all disease is an effort of nature to regain health. Thus if a man receive a bodily injury—for instance, a blow, inflammation or pain will follow. These consequences constitute a disease; but still they are necessary for the restoration of the part to health; therefore they may be called a healthy disease.

In like manner let us analyse all the destructive processes of the most complicated forms of disease—of cancer, consumption, &c.; we will invariably find that all of them, though they are rapidly destroying life, are yet used and intended by nature to save it—one of the most wondrous and instructive paradoxes in our being. In exactly the same way, sorrow, fear, and all the evil or diseased states of the mind, are nature's remedies for an injury received by it; and in their most unlimited and destructive developement we shall still invariably recognise the natural and necessary struggles for good, to which man's nature, physical and moral, is essentially bent, like the plant to the light. Thus we feel sorrow naturally, for any calamity which befalls us, or those we love: this sorrow is always a disease in us; while it remains, we are in a state of imperfection, or sin, if you will. Still, without it, as in the case of the bodily inflammation, we could not be restored to our healthy equilibrium, and thus it may be called a healthy disease, or a good evil. The inflammation was a thing heartily to be deprecated and prevented; so was the sorrow.

But the inflammation, or other bodily disease, may far overstep the limits necessary for the restoration of health; the injury received may have been too severe, or the constitution too feeble to resist it. The consequences may become themselves causes of new evils, and endanger the safety of the whole economy. In the same way the sorrow may pass all healthy bounds, and become itself the main cause of disease. The physician is always on the watch to see that the inflammation do neither more nor less than is necessary to restore health, and so must we watch over sorrow. If it become chronic and linger in the mind, we must use all means to eradicate it.

All the depressing and sorrow-causing passions and feelings are also diseases of the mind. Fear, jealousy, anxiety, or ennui, are all signs to us that there is evil somewhere, of which we must seek out the cause, however obscure, and remove it, before the suffering mind regain its health. Nay, more, every error in judgment, every untruth of thought is, like every untruth of bodily conduct, a cause of disease.

The mind and the body are inseparably linked together, so that the health and happiness of the one involves that of the other. Thus if the mind be diseased by any of the evil moral states, the body will also become diseased; while all bodily disease equally necessitates a want of sanity of mind. Every imperfect moral state, at once reacts on the body, and if it be very intense, or long continued, the body will be deeply injured. Thus does our mental element play as important a part as any other, in the causation of physical disease, and to cure the latter it is just as often requisite to apply remedies to the mental, as the bodily state. To do this, we must first be able to recognise what is mental disease, and then to treat it according to the principles of mental health.

But men, in general, do not recognise moral disease, they do not allow sorrow, fear, &c., to be diseases; and instead of wishing, or feeling it their duty, to escape from them, often hug them to their bosoms and glory in them. There is as yet, scarcely any defined or tangible moral science; we think and feel according to the caprice of the hour, and when long-continued misery, arising from our ignorance of the laws of our mind, has involved us, body and soul, in ruin, we pride ourselves on our woes, and glory in our contempt of them! Truly this is carrying paradox rather too far. We say sorrow is good, for it chastens and elevates the mind, teaches it new lessons and sympathies, and gives it a loftiness and intensity of aspiration, which we should not have had without it. This may be true in some cases, but

SPIRITUALISM

ALTHOUGH 1 have already spoken on this subject in the first of these essays, yet it appears to me to be of such vital importance, that I would wish to add a few farther remarks.

By spiritualism is to be understood the modes of thought and feeling, which seek to elevate mind above matter, and take a greater pleasure in mental than in physical pursuits, and in the cultivation of the moral than of the physical virtues.

Spiritualism is one of the most widely diffused of all diseased modes of feeling in the present day. It pervades the minds of almost all the educated classes in this country. If each of us, whether Christian or not, analyse our own thoughts and feelings, we shall find that we are deeply imbued with spiritualism; ingrained into us by our earliest education, and by the prevailing moral atmosphere around us. All the educated classes instinctively prefer moral to physical excellencies, and aspire rather to the former than the latter.

To be a distinguished poet or thinker, to acquire renown by literary merits; to have a cultivated intellect, a warm heart, and deep sympathies—all of us aim at these, and regard with comparative indifference, if not contempt, the physical virtues of a powerful, athletic, and healthy frame, and the excellence in feats of bodily prowess. Little reverence is paid to these virtues, if possessed by any one, but all bow down in admiration before a man of superior mental powers. The tastes moreover of the great mass of the educated classes are thoroughly spiritual. Literary pursuits, intellectual enjoyments, poetry, morality, and spiritual religion, engross their attention; but the physical sciences, and bodily sports and exercises, have but little comparative interest for them, and the equal claims of the physical laws of life, to their study and religious obedience, are unfelt. The educated classes seem to think, that athletic frames and a keen relish for bodily exercises and sports, are characteristics of the poorer classes, and that their own peculiar province is the cultivation of the mind and not of the body.

But there could not be a mistake more fatal to happiness or to the real culture of mankind. The consequence of this has been, that the two sets of virtues are rarely seen united in the same individual; but, as a general rule, the physical virtues are found, if found at all, in the poor; and the mental ones, in the rich and educated classes. A strong, robust frame, is seldom seen among the men of letters, or the members of the learned professions. They are for the most part, a puny, degenerate race, whose bodies are too weak for their over-worked minds. But they care little for this, unless it tells palpably upon their sensations in the form of indigestion, nervousness, or some other of the Protean evils of spiritualism. What is it to them though their body is weak, provided their mind is strong? They console themselves with boasting of the triumph of mind over matter, the vainest boast ever uttered by man; and feel, it may be, even proud of their physical insignificance.

But this is a most dangerous error. No one of our powers, either mental or physical, can ever be neglected with impunity. If the man of letters does not suffer sensibly, from his one-sided culture, and from the weakness of his physical frame, his unfortunate children shall assuredly do so. They will be born exactly so far degenerate, puny, and exposed to disease, as he has failed in his attention to his bodily powers. Unhappy are the children of the feeble spiritualist, what-ever renown he may have won for himself from short-sighted mortals, by his literary achievements. But he who neglects his bodily powers, need not hope to be truly a healthy writer or thinker. If the body is feeble, puny, and prone to disordered sensations, and if there be not a keen relish for the pleasures of the senses, such as proceeds from healthy and well-exercised bodily organs, the mind will to a certainty, be wanting in some of the elements which aid in forming true literary excellence. There will be a want of healthfulness, of serenity, of sus-tained vigour, of natural tastes and enjoyment of life, which are the characteristics of a healthy and equally-balanced mind.

Spiritualism has weakened immensely, not only the body, but the mind of man, for the one cannot be enfeebled without, to an absolute certainty, dragging with it the other. There is a conspicuous want of *manliness*, not only in the bodily, but the mental character of our age. This has been fostered of late years by the long continuance of peace; whose numerous advantages have been, in some measure, counter-balanced by this great evil.

In former times, physical courage and manly vigour were considered excellences inferior to none; but war having, until recently, been almost unknown among us, there was little scope or estimation for these virtues. Hence the world has been gradually sinking more and more into spiritualism, under the enervating influences of a spiritual religion. We have been losing our healthy relish for bodily exercises and enjoyments; setting up intellectual, at the expence of corporeal pleasures; and despising and neglecting our bodily powers, until our manliness and vigour have been tainted at the core. Let any one com-pare the educated classes among us at present, with what they were in the times of the ancient Greeks and Romans, or with some of the hardy peasantry in the present day, and he will see the immense difference in physical virtue. Let us walk through the crowded streets of our large towns, and observe the pale faces, spare and puny frames of those we meet, and we shall form some estimate of the awful state of physical degeneracy in which we live. Scarcely shall we see a single one, man or woman, whose physical state is not a disgrace, and a profound grief, to our humanity.

But it is not in the outward appearance alone, and in the want of manly strength, and nervous energy, that we see this degeneracy, it is in the wide-spread prevalence of the deseases of debility. Chief among these stands consumption; the terrible destroyer of our race, by whose hand one sixth of our population perishes, and from whose baneful influence but few families among us wholly escape. Consumption is the sure and unerring sign of physical degeneracy, and the enfeeblement of the physical powers, and this age is pre-eminently to be called "the consumptive age" of the world. The disease never was so prevalent as it is at present, and one of its most certain and prolific causes is spiritualism. Do we think that any one of us, whatever be his mental merits, can allow his physical strength to decline, can leave his bodily powers uncultivated, without becoming degraded and imperfect, and without paying the sure penalty? Will nature spare either him or his children for neglecting the one part of his being, whatever he may accomplish by the culture of the other? No; she demands that an equal and impartial attention be paid to all the faculties, and that an equal interest be taken in physical as in spiritual culture. There is scarcely one of us of the educated classes, whose physical state is not a disgrace to him. Poor, weak, diminutive, thin, pale, puny, dyspeptic beings we are, unworthy of the name of a *man*, whatever learning or mental attainments we may possess. We may dazzle our fellow-men by these one-sided accomplishments, we may win their short-sighted praise; but we shall not cheat nature, nor reap ought but her punishment for us and our children.

When our day of physical affliction comes, as come it certainly will, to every one who neglects his body, when the retributive hand is laid heavily on ourselves or our children, then shall we feel the vanity and delusiveness of our preference for one set of our faculties above the other.

It is true that the average length of life, is gradually increasing, but I feel convinced that this is accompanied by a compensatory diminution of health and strength in the human frame. The longer average of life is produced, I believe, chiefly by our increased knowledge of the nurture of children, and the substitution of long wasting chronic diseases, for the short and fatal epidemic of small pox, fever and ague, dysentery &c., as well as the ravages of wars, which were formerly so prevalent. It is also favoured by the increase of the preventive, compared with the positive, check to population (as advocated by Mr. Malthus, whose views will be considered subsequently,) by which means an individual may refrain from reproducing his species, and thus help to raise the average of life, at the expense of losing his share of offspring, together with other evils hereafter to be mentioned. In less civilised countries a large proportion of children die, from the general ignorance of the mode of rearing these tender beings; while in our times, when the importance of fresh air, avoidance of undue exposure, &c., are better recognised, the rate of infant

mortality has greatly decreased, and delicate children are kept alive till
the time of puberty or thereabouts, then to perish by consumption. This
difference in the mortality of delicate children, tells greatly on the average of human life, but comparatively little on human happiness. So
does the substitution of slow chronic miserable diseases for short and de-
cisive ones.

The diseases of debility are the prevalent and characteristic ones of the
present age. Consumption, dyspepsia, and nervous weakness are universally diffused through our country; but were comparatively little
known, more especially the two last, among our ancestors. They were
decimated at intervals by terrible acute epidemics, such as small pox,
ague, scurvy, &c., which have now become almost extinct, owing to the
splendid discoveries of medical science.

We surpass them also greatly, in prolonging the lives of invalids, and
in our general medical treatment. In less civilised communities, as
among the lower animals, any one who falls into bad health has comparatively little chance of recovery, as he is either neglected or badly
treated. But can it be said, that we have really gained by the substitution of these miserable diseases of debility, some of which may indeed
permit a man to drag on a life in death, till a great age, but poison all
his enjoyment?

It is a common, and I believe a very true remark, that our constitutions are not nearly so strong as those of our forefathers; and while that
is the case, let us not boast of the longer average of life. A long life, if
sad, is hardly preferable to a short and vigorous one. The longer average
of life, like other marks of apparent progress, is a vanity and a delusion
and helps to blind us to our actual state of physical degradation.

The mind as well as the body has degenerated in manly vigour under
the influence of spiritualism. A morbid effeminacy pervades all our
moral atmosphere. There is a want of healthy enjoyment of life, as
must always be the case when the natural pleasures of the senses
are disparaged, a want of self-reliance, of manly vigour, and courage, in
the mental character of all of us. Thousands among us are so much
oppressed with shyness and the want of self-confidence, that it looks as
if we felt almost ashamed of living at all.

There is a pervading timidity in declaring our real convictions on the
most important matters, especially on religion and on sexual love, which
are, as far as open and candid discussion is concerned, almost interdicted
subjects among us. A sort of doleful spiritual whine meets our ear on
every side, as if man, the mightiest and most glorious of all the manifestations of nature, existed only on sufferance, and were too vile to
deserve anything but sorrow and humiliation. The fear of the opinions
of others is one of the most prevalent of all feelings in our society; a
feeling which is more destructive than almost any other, to sincerity and
manliness of character. We are afraid of departing one step from the
beaten track of conventionalism, for fear of incurring the odium of our
neighbours. How unlike is this to the manliness and self-reliance of
those, who have dared death and torture rather than disguise their
principles!

How different is the morbid state of sorrow, self-abasement, irr lution, despondency, or despair, which we observe so prominently in our modern poets and writers, from the manly vigour, healthfulness, and enjoyment of life, which is so delightful in the authors of the Elizabethan age. There are certainly many other causes than spiritualism, which have helped to work this change; the great social difficulties, which are only of late years coming to be adequately recognised, are enough to load the hearts of each of us with sorrow, if not despair; but besides these, a great part of the mental morbidity is caused by spiritualism, which blights all healthy enjoyment of life, and weakens the mind with the body.

The spiritual religion which is dominant among us, by its threats of endless punishment, and its constant inculcation of the weak and effeminating qualities of humility and resignation, has broken in a great degree the spirit of man. No man can seriously entertain the belief in endless punishment, without his whole nature being demoralised, and without being cowed into a state of fear as to his own and his neighbour's actions, incompatible with manly dignity and freedom. Humility and resignation are, it is true, often desirable virtues, but neither they nor any other conceivable modes of feeling, can be always termed good, and to inculcate them in a wholesale way is to do infinite mischief. To be constantly urging them upon those who are already broken in spirit from shyness, want of self-reliance, energy, and the power of actively enjoying life, (which are just the prevailing defects in our characters at present), is exactly like the old system of repeated bleeding and purgation, now happily abandoned by medicine, by which the whole energy of the constitution was gradually exhausted. What is wanted in mind as well as in body at present, is not piety nor tenderness, nor humility, nor spiritual fervour; but self-reliance, manly energy, and an active enjoyment of life; in a word, *health*.

Health of body and mind, should be the chief aim of mankind, not pietism or spiritualism, or any other one-sided ideal, which our imperfect religions have set up; all blessings are comprehended in health, for it is not obtainable except by a well-regulated conduct of all our faculties of body and mind alike. Where there is not an active and keen enjoyment of life in all its different parts, where there is not happiness, there cannot be health; and where there is not health there cannot be virtue. It is absolutely impossible for either body or mind to be truly healthy and well-balanced, when the chief attention is paid to one set of faculties, and the others are comparatively neglected. This great truth has been completely disregarded in our theories of life, and the consequences have been most disastrous to all of us.

However powerfully spiritualism has operated in degrading man, it has far more degraded woman. The physical virtues are scarcely thought to belong to her province at all: strength, vigour, courage, and activity, are not considered feminine virtues, but, if possible, rather detract from woman's peculiar charms in the eye of spiritualism. Hence the physical character of women, is, as a general rule, degraded to the last degree; poor, weak, nervous, delicate beings, who can scarcely walk half-a-mile, whose muscles are unstrung, and whose nerves are full of weakness and irritability.

Compare the ladies in our ball-rooms· or the women in our streets, with the strong healthy country girl, or with the women of Ruben's pictures, and their awful inferiority in physical virtue will be seen. Not only to her own health and happiness is the physical degeneracy of woman destructive, but to our whole race. The strength and bodily power of woman, are just as indispensable to the health and strength of mankind, as that of man, for the vigour of the child depends as much on the mother as on the father. It is a folly to desire to see powerful and athletic men, without desiring to see the same virtues in woman; such a division of the virtues is absolutely impossible.

The mind of woman is as much enfeebled as her body, by spiritualism. A vigorous relish for sensual pleasures, an energetic study of the sciences, and especially of the physical ones, is thought unwomanly, and the sex is limited to a narrow range of thought and feeling, which cripples all the mental power.

It is in vain to hope that a mind will be powerful, if certain subjects are forbidden to it ; if death and the evil side of nature are hidden, as they are at present from woman. Such interdictions prevent any true power or freedom of thought and feeling; for who cares to study nature, if they are only allowed to advance a short distance, and if all the subjects necessary to give completeness to their views, are shut from them as from children? In the emotions, as well as in intellect, woman is bound in the effeminating bonds of spiritualism. Love, tenderness, and humility, are thought to be the special female virtues ; and the qualities of self-reliance, energy, and mental intrepidity, are rather discouraged than otherwise, by those who wish to keep up the unfortunate state of dependence, in which woman exists at present. Hence the character of woman is full of weakness and irresolution, fear of the opinion of others, and hysterical emotions, which are diametrically opposed to health and strength of mind. Woman is, as a general rule, dwarfed in body and mind, by her one-sided and narrow spiritual culture.

Spiritualism has not only prevented us from taking an equal interest in the physical sciences, and attending equally to our physical culture; it has also blighted the progress of *moral* science. This is shown not only by the narrow and erroneous views of mental health and disease, and their treatment, of which mention has already been made; but also by the existing state of mental and psychological science.

The spiritual moralists have ever maintained, that there is a complete and fundamental difference between the mind of man and those of the inferior animals ; so that no true comparison could be instituted between them. But this is an enormous error, and has stood in the way of all philosophical acquaintance with the human mind. The truth is, that there is not, and cannot be, by one single iota, a greater difference between the mind of man and the minds of the lower animals, than there is between his body and theirs. Every conceivable shade of mental difference must be accompanied by an exactly equal difference in the shape and substance of the brain; and the brain of man must differ exactly in the same degree, not one atom more or less, from the inferior brains, as his mind from the inferior minds. Now until the body of man was compared, minutely and perseveringly, with that of the lower animals, down to the very humblest, it is well recognised that we did not understand it at all, that we had no true and philosophical knowledge of it. Professor Owen refuses to give the name of "Anatomy" at all to the mere dissection of the *human* body; that, he says, is merely "anthropotomy," while "anatomy" is a term merited only by the whole comparative science.

But exactly on the same principles, we must recognise, that there is at present no true science of "Mind," at all; we have no real "Psychology;" we have merely an anthropo-psychology. There has never yet lived a man, who deserved the name of a moralist; there have merely been humanity-moralists.

A true knowledge of man's spiritual and moral nature is to be obtained only in the same way as that of his body, namely, by the comparative examination of the minds of all living beings, and by tracing our faculties upwards from their simplest expression in the humblest animals, to their most complex state in man. Until this be done in mind, as it has been done in the body, there can be no real "mental science," and we must continue, as we are at present, in the dark, as to the meaning and origin of our faculties. The science of Comparative Psychology, though it has yet scarcely an existence, opposed as it has been by our narrow conceptions of the human mind, will ultimately be recognised as equally indespensable with comparative anatomy, in order to attain to a true knowledge of man.

The morbid ideas of spiritualism are well seen in the little reverence that is paid to the bodily appetites. It is by no means thought a great merit to have a good appetite for food: nay, many people, especially effeminate ladies, are rather ashamed of it, and abstemiousness is often practiced as an evidence of refinement and spirituality. A keen relish for the pleasures of eating, is thought coarse and unbecoming, especially in women; the attention, it is thought, should rather be directed to intellectual enjoyments, and the mind, as little as possible, occupied with the pleasures of the senses. But these are most dangerous and destructive errors. The truth is, that a good appetite is one of the greatest virtues either man or woman can possess, and is one of the things of which, far from being ashamed, they have most reason to be proud. It is one of the best of all signs and tests of health, and of a well-spent physical life,

No one who has not a keen appetite is deserving of the name of a good man or woman; and the individual who allows his appetite to languish or to be habitually feeble, is equally reprehensible with him, who permits his feelings of love or truth to become blunted.

The vigour of our bodily appetites is the test and the invaluable safeguard of our virtue, if we attend to it; by the keenness of our appetites we shall know whether our physical life is a true and healthy one; but if we neglect them, disease and destruction are certain sooner or later to make us repent it. A good appetite for food is just as great a virtue, and just as much to be admired wherever it is seen, as an ardent love and just appreciation of truth and beauty. The same principle applies to all the other physical appetites. By these tests, it can be seen how exceedingly unhealthy, or in other words, sinful, are the lives of the great majority of those of us who live in towns, and work constantly at sedentary occupations. Our appetite languishes, and is rarely strong; and this should be taken as the unerring sign that the powers of life and virtue are growing feebler, and those of death and evil gaining the ascendancy.

When the appetite is habitually feeble, consumption, or the other diseases of debility, will to an absolute certainty, be induced, either in the individual's self or in his posterity, if the same want of physical virtue continue in them.

The great physical problem is to endeavour to secure to all human beings, the essentials of life in abundance; and in the purest form. Air, water, food, healthy exercise for all the organs &c., to procure for every human being the power of enjoying these in their greatest purity should be our steadfast and religious aim—an aim as lofty and as difficult as any ever proposed by man, and to be zealously aspired after, not only by the physician and the sanitary reformer, but by every man and woman among us, as comprehending the most important essentials of virtue. If we cannot habitually breathe pure air, eat abundantly of wholesome food, and obtain healthy and sufficient exercise for our various organs and faculties, let us not deceive ourselves; it is absolutely impossible that we can live virtuous lives. Pure air and wholesome food are just as indispensable necessaries of virtue, happiness, or true religion, as any conceivable moral qualities. This has never yet been sufficiently attended to; for mankind have not become generally aware of the exactly equal duty they owe to their body and mind.

All our tastes and modes of judgment are more or less perverted and effeminated by spiritualism. As an instance of this, the prevailing opinions with regard to beauty may be taken. To have delicately cut features, a prettily turned figure, neat little feet and hands, and a sweet and amiable expression, are considered the chief beauties in a woman. But health and strength are in general scarcely at all considered. Now the truth is, that without these fundamental qualities, there cannot be real beauty. Health is the very first essential of beauty; and permanent health, continuing for many generations, cannot possibly exist without great physical strength, for the active exercise and natural life which ensure the one, ensure the other also. Elegance in shape and form are something, and are sufficient in a lifeless object to constitute beauty, but in a living being health is a far more fundamentally important quality. Strength, power, and activity, are also among the most essential of all parts of beauty, in woman as well as in man. Without strength, which is to be obtained only by the active and regular exercise of the body in out-of-door pursuits, health cannot long continue, and will soon decay, if not in one generation, then in the next; and without health the beauty even of form and expression will soon disappear.

We hear little tiny delicate girls, who have perhaps a prettily chiselled face, and an interesting pallor of complexion, called beautiful; but the truly instructed eye can see in them but mournful proofs of the physical degeneracy of our age. Height of stature, and weight of body, not produced by fat, but by healthy and powerful muscular developement, are in woman as well as man, a great part of true beauty.

In large towns, the stature always becomes diminutive under the influence of a smoky and confined atmosphere, and the want of exercise; and hence the stunted, pale, and puny appearance of the inhabitants of London, and others of our large towns. Let us never be deceived into confounding the symptoms of delicacy and imperfect nutrition, which we see among them, with true beauty. Let us not regard the tiny waist, the little impotent feet and hands, the delicate complexion, even though they belong to our own selves, or to those we love most dearly, as really beautiful; such a judgment confounds all principles of good and evil. True beauty cannot possibly exist among those who have lived constantly amid the smoke of a large town. The golden rule in the cultivation of beauty should be, seek first *health and strength*, a powerful frame, and a healthily cultivated mind, and all the rest shall be added unto you.

In man, physical beauty is looked down upon, and intellect is thought his peculiar province. This is an admirable instance of the false and short-sighted judgments of spiritualism. A man who cultivates his personal appearance, and takes a pride in his athletic and handsome figure is called a coxcomb; while the puny delicate man of letters, who exults in his mental superiority, and the feeble care-worn clergyman, who boasts of the triumph of mind over matter, are thought to have a noble and excusable pride. In truth, physical beauty is exactly as important and desirable in man as in woman, and is just as much to be cultivated and admired in the one sex as in the other. The attention and reverence for physical beauty, is one of the best safeguards of health and manly vigour. Beauty of face and figure is only to be maintained, and perpetuated to coming generations, by exercise of our bodily powers, and is one of the best signs of a well-spent physical life. A powerful and a handsome frame is just as valuable as a powerful and beautiful mind. From the want of attention to their personal beauty and to the culture of their bodies, we see men becoming slovenly and ungraceful, thin pale and sallow from wasting their looks and their health over the midnight lamp; we see their hair dropping out prematurely, their faces getting ploughed by the wrinkles of thought and care before their time, their teeth decaying and dropping out under the influence of a failing digestion, their noses filthy with snuff; their figures, which might have been manly, powerful, and agile, becoming weak, stooping, and exhausted, as if a breath could blow them over. Where is a woman to find in these learned scare-crows the glowing realisation of her youthful dreams of love? A lady said to me a short time ago, "What can be the reason that men are so dreadfully ugly? I was looking round the lecture-room the other night, and positively I scarcely saw a single handsome face. The most of them were very plain and vulgar, and very many, especially the elderly men, had such distorted and misshapen faces, that it was painful to look at them. We don't see this in the lower animals. we don't see in them that perversion of features, those bloated, wizened, and unhealthy countenances, with all the features out of proportion, which we see in men. What can it be that makes men often so very ugly?" In truth the great want of physical beauty and manly strength and elegance of frame, which is so wide-spread among us, and which is so blighting to the romance of love, is as distressing and as deeply to be deplored as the prevalence of moral evil, of which in fact it is the outward and visible type. No qualities of mind can make up for this sinful and miserable neglect of the body.

The unnatural practice of shaving, has tended most powerfully to increase this disregard of physical beauty in man. It has done so, by in reality destroying man's beauty. The peculiar beauty of the male countenance consists very much in its contrast with the female one, by the possession of those hairy appendages which impart to it a dignity and manliness. The beard is peculiarly a *sexual* distinction, it only appears at puberty, and is intimately connected with—in fact, is the outward expression of sexual maturity, of that which distinguishes the man from the woman and the boy. To cut it off is to effeminate the male face, and has a greater effect than is generally supposed in weakening the sexual feelings between man and woman, which are powerfully awakened by contrast. It is thus a part of those effeminating and debilitating influences on the sexual feelings, which have so much degraded the vigor and manliness of all of us, as I shall endeavour to show hereafter. It spoils the natural ideal of manly beauty, and that admirable contrast between the two sexes, by which each acts as a foil to the other, and the peculiar sexual characteristics of each, are duly symbolised and called forth.

It is not by spiritual, but by physical reformation, that mankind can at present be chiefly benefited. Even were the views of our moral teachers with regard to the moral virtues correct; even though mental health were substituted as the object of men's aims, instead of the diseased spiritualism, which is now inculcated, comparatively little could be done at present by any moral training. It is physical and not spiritual religion, of which we are at present most urgently in need. More could be done in a few years by due attention to the physical virtues, than in a century by moral exhortations, however pure and exalted; for the physical virtues are those which have been far the most neglected, and stand far the most in need of attention. The moral virtues themselves are to be promoted at present chiefly through the physical ones, for in the present awful state of physical degradation in which we live, it is a vanity to imagine that high moral excellence can prevail. Therefore, the social sanitary movements, together with the earnest culture of the bodily powers by every one of us, are at present the most important means to elevate mankind.

We should not be contented with a low standard of physical elevation. We should make it our religious aim, that every one of us, man, woman, and child, should possess a large, powerful, vigorous frame, whose blooming health shall set consumption and the other diseases of debility at defiance. Each man and woman should take exactly as much pride in the cultivation of the bodily, as of the mental virtues, feeling deeply the grand truth, that the interests of our race are just as much bound up in the promotion of the one as of the other.

D

We should not be content till the thews and sinews, the powerful bodies and manly minds of our ancestors, are again become prevalent among us, and are blended with the advantages of our increased civilisation, with our greater enlightenment and refinement, and a longer average of life. We should cultivate all those sports and manly exercises, which promote bodily health and vigour, just as sedulously as we cultivate the moral virtues, and should have an equal honour for physical, as for mental excellence, wherever we see it. We should learn to take an equal pleasure and to have an equal reverence for the sensual as the intellectual enjoyments, for the physical as the mental sciences, and in every thing to attain to an impartial and well-balanced sense of the equal grandeur of the material and the moral universe, of a true Physical and Spiritual Religion.

END OF PART I.

PART II.
SEXUAL RELIGION.

PART II.

SEXUAL RELIGION.

REPRODUCTION AND DEVELOPEMENT.

THE subject of the following essays—namely, the nature and laws of the sexual organs, with their diseases, and the allied evils of poverty and hard work, is, it appears to me, by far the most important of all subjects for our consideration in the present day. There is nothing unfortunately, which has been so much neglected, and on which such wide-spread ignorance prevails ; and yet I feel convinced, that there is no subject so deeply affecting the interests of man. From the mystery and secrecy in which sexual matters have been involved, and from the consequent want of due attention to them, the whole of our moral and social philosophy has been rendered unsound at the core, and the progress of our race has been blighted.

Before entering upon the diseases of the sexual organs, which arise as all diseases do, from our disobedience to the natural laws, and upon the associated evils of poverty, I shall give a short sketch of these organs and of the function of reproduction.

I entreat the reader's attention to this, not only from the surpassing interest of the subject, but because some knowledge of the nature of the sexual organs is necessary to follow the subsequent descriptions of their diseases. There is no part of physiology which is less understood by the generality of mankind, and yet there is not one of deeper interest, and which more urgently demands the attention of us all.

Reproduction has been, and still is, viewed as a mysterious and incomprehensible subject, with which none but scientific men should have to do; and feelings of sexual bashfulness and disgust have restrained the generality of mankind from acquiring a knowledge of these organs and their laws.   But such feelings are unworthy alike of the dignity of man, and the infinite perfection of nature

Nature demands our calm and reverential study of all her works and laws alike; she has given us no organs which she intended to be shrouded in mystery and concealment; but on the contrary she lays her mighty commands upon us to seek to become acquainted with every one of her all-perfect productions.   It is not for us to pick and choose among her works, which we please to attend to, and which we please to avoid; but to pay a like reverential study to all.   If the sexual organs be omitted, the knowledge of all the rest of the human frame will avail us little; and we should seek to acquire just as true and as thorough an insight into their laws, as into the processes of respiration or digestion.   I have already dwelt upon the sacred duty that rests upon all of us, both men and women, to study a subject which concerns us so nearly as the human frame; and of all the bodily organs there is none which should have more special attention than the reproductive ones, which have been so much neglected by our ancestors.   No others are so deeply implicated in the most urgent problems of the present age.   All of us should therefore strive to divest ourselves of the childish and degrading feelings of morbid delicacy, which foster the ignorance on these subjects, and have been the causes of greater miseries to our race than almost any others, as I shall endeavour hereafter to show.

Dr. Carpenter in his most admirable work on *General and Comparative Physiology*, says of the function of reproduction, "a very unnecessary degree of mystery has been spread around the exercise of this function, not only by general enquirers, but by scientific physiologists. It has been regarded as a process never to be comprehended by man, of which the nature and the laws are alike inscrutable.   A fair comparison, however, with other functions, will show that it is not in reality less comprehensible or more recondite than any one of them; that our acquaintance with each depends upon the facility with which it may be submitted to investigation; and that if properly inquired into by an extensive survey of the animated world, the real character of the process, its conditions, and its mode of operation, may be understood as completely as those of any other vital phenomenon."

All living beings, both plants and animals, have a limited existence, and the race is kept up by a constant succession of new individuals. It is a law which we never see departed from at present, that every living organism has sprung from a pre-existing organism.   The doctrine of spontaneous generation, which held that in some cases living beings might originate out of lifeless matter, and which was formerly very prevalent, has gradually lost almost all its supporters, and "has not now any claim," says Dr. Carpenter, "to be received even as a possible hypothesis."

Another law which seems at present to be universal, is that every living thing springs from a parent like itself, so that the different species do not pass into each other, although great modifications may arise from the influence of external circumstances, especially in the lower organisms.

All living beings are endowed at birth with a certain degree of vital power, by which they are enabled to develope themselves into their perfect form, and to maintain themselves in it for a season. This power is called the *germinal capacity*, and it varies in degree in different beings. In all, however, it sooner or later becomes exhausted, and the race would perish, were it not that the germinal capacity is renewed by an act of generation, by which a new individual is produced, and endowed with a new measure of vital power. Thus then, life and generation are antagonistic; the former exhausts, while the latter renews the germinal capacity. In their essence also, the two processes are quite opposite. All the actions in which the germinal capacity manifests itself, are accompanied by the *subdivision* and *continuous growth* of the minute cells, of which our frame is built up, whereas generation consists in the very reverse of this—namely *the reunion of the contents of two cells*. By this reunion a new impulse is given, and the fading powers of the parent are produced afresh in the offspring.

It seems almost certain from the most recent discoveries in physiology, that such an act of *true generation* occurs in every living being, whether plant or animal, and is absolutely necessary in all to prevent the vital powers from dying out. But it is only lately, that this has been recognised. Formerly, it was believed, that many of the lowest classes of plants and animals never truly generated, but that their race was kept up entirely by *gemmation*; or, in other words, by buds or offshoots, and not by seeds. It was supposed that no true generation took place in the large class of plants, called the Cryptogamia, or flowerless plants, which include the sea weeds, mosses, lichens, ferns, &c., but that these propagated only by little buds or spores. But it has lately been discovered, that both in the lowest species of these plants, namely, the inferior sea-weeds, and in the highest, namely, the ferns—a true act of generation by the reunion of the contents of two cells does take place, and, therefore, we may conclude that it occurs in the other tribes also; although it has not yet been seen in them. In the same way, true generation has been detected in some of the very lowest animals, and may be presumed to exist in all.

In very many of the lower plants and animals, the ordinary mode of reproduction, is by gemmation, or budding. Gemmation consists in the sprouting of a new individual from some part of the body of an old one. Gemmation is essentially the same process as *fission*, by which many of the lower tribes of plants and animals propagate. In fission, the parent splits into two nearly equal parts; each of which is developed into a complete individual.

A familiar instance of propagation by gemmation is seen in the potato and in fruit trees. These plants are commonly propagated by buds, which are either inserted in the ground, or engrafted on another tree, instead of being sown by seed. This method of reproduction can be continued for a long time, but not indefinitely; for, after a certain time, the germinal capacity dies out, and has to be renewed by an act of true generation, which

gives birth to a seed. Thus, however long gemmation may be continued, it must at last, in all living beings, give place to generation.

Among animals, a very interesting instance of gemmation, is seen in
the Hydra, or Polyp. This little animal, which lives in the water, attaching itself by a sucking disc to some solid substance, and fishing for
its food with its long tentacles, propagates ordinarily by gemmation.
Little polyps spring like buds from its surface, and when fully developed,
are cast off and become independent individuals. But in the polyp, like
the potato, a true generation also takes place, by means of the reunion of
contents of two cells, and thus eggs are formed from which young are
natched. Gemmation continues, like the crops of buds and leaves on a
tree, till the cold weather comes on, and threatens the animal with
death. Then it gives place to the true generative act, by which eggs that
can stand the winter's cold, and are hatched in spring, are produced.

Another very remarkable instance of gemmation occurs in the insect
called Aphis. This is the only insect in which gemmation occurs, for insects are too high in the scale of being for such a mode of reproduction.
The parent Aphis gives birth in the autumn to true eggs, which are
hatched by the warmth of spring; but the young so produced, remain imperfectly developed, unprovided with sexual organs, and give birth to a
new family, without any sexual intercourse. Their offspring, which are
born alive, beget others in the same way, and so on, during the whole
summer, and it is only when the cold of autumn checks this process, that
the young are developed into perfect insects, provided with complete sexual organs; and that a true act of generation takes place by which fertile eggs are produced. In this case, by one act of generation, so much
germinal power is imparted, that no more is needed till after many repetitions of gemmation. Here the process may be called *internal* gemmation, for the young are born alive from the female passages; but it is
essentially the same with external gemmation, which takes place from
the surface of the polyp; both of them consisting in the production of
new individuals without previous sexual intercourse. By this means an
incredible number of offspring may be produced by the Aphis. It has
been calculated, that if all lived, about six thousand millions would result from five repetitions of the process of gemmation; and this process
is repeated twenty times in the year, so that the numbers following a
single generative act, pass the power of our imagination to conceive.

None of the higher animals ever propagate by gemmation, but invariably by true generation. In them the germinal capacity is so much
expended in producing all their complex organs, and in maintaining their
integrity, that it has not the super-abundant developemental power
which enables it to give rise to new individuals. The only modes in
which the persistence of this developemental power is shown, is in the
regeneration of parts which are accidentally lost. Thus the lobsters and
spiders can reproduce whole limbs, when the old ones are torn off or injured. In man this cannot be done, although there are one or two extraordinary instances on record, of fingers &c., being completely reproduced;
but in general the only parts of our frame which can be regenerated, are
those which are of the simplest nature, and thus most like the lower or-

ganisms. Such are the bones, which are of a simple chemical composition. A whole bone with its muscular and ligamentous attachments can be regenerated, and this is truly a more complicated process than the restoration of entire limbs in lower animals. Those parts also, which arise by a simple process of nutritive repetition, as the small blood-cells &c., can be regenerated, and also connecting parts, such as nerves and blood-vessels, which lie amid the other tissues. With these exceptions, no part of the human frame can be restored if injured, but only *repaired* by a lower form of tissue. The power of regenerating parts is, as might be expected, greatest in those humble beings which usually propagate by gemmation. Thus the hydra may be divided into fifty pieces, and each piece will reproduce the whole animal. Many animals which do not propagate spontaneously by gemmation, will reproduce their entire structure if artificially divided; as, for instance, some worms and star-fishes. When this artificial fission succeeds, it shows that there is a natural tendency to spontaneous gemmation.

A very curious phenomenon, which occurs in the reproduction of some plants and animals, has been termed *alternate generation.* In this the parent gives rise to an offspring unlike itself, which lives independently, and in its turn gives birth to a progeny, which is like the original stock. Thus the Hydroid Polyps develope buds, which have the form of Medusae (jelly-fishes,) and these after living independently for some time, give birth to the original Polyp. In the same way, the Fern developes small buds, called spores, which when cast off, grow into a little plant to which the name of pro-embryo has been given. This in its turn gives birth to a Fern. Here the grand-child, and not the immediate offspring, is like the parent. But in all these cases of so-called alternate generation, it is to be carefully remarked, that one of the generations is produced by *gemmation* and the other by true *generation.* Thus the medusae come from buds, while the polyps they give rise to come from eggs. In like manner, the spores are buds, while the pro-embryo which springs from them, contains true generative organs, and gives birth to a seed, from which springs the young Fern. In all cases the immediate product of the true generative act is the same. Thus the expression "alternate generations" is incorrect, and it may be seen, that this is only in appearance an exception to the law, that every being resembles its parent.

The occurrence of gemmation has led to much interesting discussion on the question, "What is an individual?" If every part of an organism which can exist independently and re-produce the rest, is to be considered an individual, it would do violence to many of our usual ideas on the subject. For instance, in many trees, the buds will grow if detached and planted—nay, some trees spontaneously detach buds, or bulbels, which grow into new plants. But not only will buds do so, but even single leaves in some plants, as the Bryophyllum; and not only leaves, but even fragments of leaves. The very lowest forms of plants, (such as the red snow,) and animals, (as the gregarinae) consist of a single microscopic cell. This cell is a complete individual. It breathes, feeds, digests, reproduces, lives, for and by itself. It is certainly a separate individual, and so do we name the seed of a plant, or egg of an animal, because they

are capable of living independently and reproducing the whole. The
individual life of the human egg in the womb, is considered as sacred as
that of the adult; and to cause its abortion, when it is no bigger than
a nut-shell, is deemed murder. Now, why should not the same name of
"individual" be given to every fragment of a leaf, which is capable of
living alone? And why should not a tree be called a huge collection of
individuals, instead of a single individual? Professor Owen and many of
the first scientific men do so regard it. But it must always be remembered
that there is a great difference between an individual produced by gemmation and one produced by true generation.

The individuals produced by gemmation, such as the Polyps, or the
buds or bulbels of a plant, are not really homologous (or essentially corresponding) with an individual such as man, who is produced by an act
of generation, but are rather comparable to the different parts of his
body, which are produced by a process truly resembling that of gemma_
tion, namely, the subdivision and continuous growth of cells. Gemmation
is only a form of nutrition, (the processes by which the body is nourished and maintained), and like it, exhausts instead of renewing the
germinal capacity. Each little cell in our body, may be called an individual, and we may be termed a congeries of individuals, nearly in the
same way as each bud and leaf of a tree may be so styled; each little cell
in us lives a life of its own, and the chief difference between it and the
leaf-bud is, that it cannot exist if separated from the rest of the frame,
nor re-produce the whole. Dr. Carpenter proposes to call all individuals produced by gemmation, *Zooids* (or apparent beings), and to
restrict the term *Zoon* (or true being) to the collective product of one
generative act. Thus it would need both the Medusa and the Polyp to
form one true being, analogous to a perfect plant or animal; and the potato
with all its buds and all their descendants till the germinal capacity is
exhausted, should be regarded as forming only one complete individual.
It is generally in the presence and absence of the sexual organs, that the
two zooids, proceeding from the same stock, principally differ. One of the
chief purposes of the alternation of forms seems to be the dispersion of
the species of plant or animal; and thus the zooid which contains the
sexual organs, and produces eggs, consists frequently of little more than
these organs, furnished with locomotive appendages.

In investigating any organ or function, the usual, and the best way to
proceed, is to follow it upwards through the scale of being; for the simplest and most comprehensible form is found in the humblest organism,
and after becoming acquainted with that, it is comparatively less difficult
to unravel the mysteries of complex scructures. Indeed it is utterly
hopeless and impossible to comprehend a being like man, either physically
or mentally, without comparing him with all other living beings, and
without tracing upwards his organs and his faculties, from their simplest
condition, as it appears in the lowest plants and animals. When we do
so compare him, we are struck by the fact, that the *essentials* of life, and
the essential nature of all the organs and functions, are the same throughout
all the chain of being, and that it is only in the *accessories* that the infinite variety which we observe, exists.

This is well seen in the function of generation. The generative act is essentially the same in the very humblest plant as in man. It consists in the reunion of the contents of two cells. A cell is a very minute body, invisible to the naked eye, with a thin transparent wall, containing various substances. It generally contains a *nucleus*, a small dot formed by a collection of granules, and in this the chief powers of the cell generally seem to be centred. It seems to be the point of attraction to the matters which the cell absorbs, and to be prominently engaged in the production of new cells and other vital operations. Cells propagate in several ways, sometimes by subdividing into two, each of which again subdivides into two more, and so on till a large mass is produced, just like fission in the lowest plants and animals, sometimes by giving birth to new cells in their interior, which are liberated by the bursting of the parent &c. The cell feeds by absorbing nourishment through its walls; and it is from the transformation of cells that almost all the living tissues—the muscles, nerves, blood-vessels &c., are built up.

Now, the very simplest being consists of a single cell, which is not usually found alone, but in masses produced by these processes of multiplication; each single cell however, being capable of living independently. Each cell performs all the essential vital functions for itself. It feeds and it reproduces by itself. In them, the simplest form of generation, or as it is here called *conjugation*, is seen. In this process one of these cells approaches close to another, and then they burst, and their contents are mingled together, and from the mass so formed, new cells arise, which give birth to an immense progeny by the ordinary processes of cell-growth. In this process there is no apparent distinction of sexes, both cells seeming to take a similar part in the generative act. Conjugation has been best studied in the *zygnema*, one of the Algae. This little plant consists simply of a filament of cells, united end to end in a single row. Two of these filaments approach each other and stick together, and then the intervening walls burst, and the whole of the contents of one filament are emptied into the other. This shows that here there is some sexual distinction between the two sets of cells.

Now this intermingling of the contents of two microscopic cells is the real essence of the generative act throughout the whole chain of being, and is exactly the same in man as in the humblest plant. The difference is only in the accessories. In the more complex organisms the function of generation is not exercised by every cell, but is confined to a certain set of cells, specially set apart for the purpose, and elaborated by special organs. There are also complex organs developed in both sexes for effecting the union of these cells; and in proportion as mind becomes developed in ascending the scale of being, more and more complicated emotions and ideas are interwoven with the generative act. But all these are accessories, and the most impassioned enthusiasm and exaltation of love has for its essential object to effect the union of two microscopic cells, and thus continue the race. In this we see an example of the invariable law of development, namely, *the progress from the general to the special*. The simplest forms of generation are the most general, they are common to all living beings, and as it were include the subsequent accessory developments, as the little egg potentially includes the future adult.

In the Mosses and Ferns these accessories of generation are considerably more complex. In these plants we find two sets of organs, essentially corresponding to the male and female sexual organs of animals. These organs in ferns are found on the pro-embryo, which is *monoecious*, that is to say, possesses both the male and the female sexual organs in the same plant. The male organs are called *antheridia*, and correspond to the anther of a flowering plant and to the testicle of an animal. They consist of large parent cells, each of which gives birth to a number of smaller cells inside it, and in every one of these secondary cells there is a small spiral filament, furnished with long *cilia* or hair-like bodies, by whose constant vibrations it is moved rapidly about. These spiral filaments are called *phytozoaires*, and are analogous to the spermatozooids, which exist in the semen of animals, and which they greatly resemble in appearance. The female organs are called *pistillidia*, and correspond to the pistil in flowering plants and to the ovary in animals. In them lie the germ-cells, corresponding to the ovules of flowering plants and the eggs of animals. The phytozoaires, which are let loose by the bursting of the cells which enclose them, penetrate to the germ-cell and conjugate with it just as the cells of the zygnema do with each other. By the intermixture of the contents of these two cells, which takes place by transudation through their walls while they are conjugating, a fertile germ is produced, which grows up into the fern.

In *Phanerogamous*, or flowering plants, the sexual organs are found in the flower. They consist of the *anthers*, containing the *pollen*, and the *ovary* containing the *ovules*. In the anthers the pollen grains, or sperm cells, are produced. These are elaborated by a complex process, as is always the case with important secretions. Two or three generations of cells, produced one within the other, are needed to elaborate sufficiently the little pollen grain, which corresponds to the phytozoaire of the ferns and to the spermatozooid of animals, being the male conjugating cell. It has two coats like other cells, the outer of which is hard, and has several little pores in it, while the inner one is very delicate. The ovule, or germ cell, on the other hand, is produced in the ovary. It corresponds with the egg or female conjugating cell of animals. Conjugation takes place between the sperm and germ cell as follows. The pollen, set free by the bursting of the anther, falls upon the stigma, or end of the pistil, which is covered by a viscid secretion. By this the pollen swells, and then its inner coat is protruded through the small pores in the outer one, and insinuates itself downwards in the shape of a long tube, among the loose tissue of the style, till it reaches the ovary. There it impinges upon the germ cell, and thus conjugation is effected, and their contents mingled, just as was done by the self-moving filaments of the Fern. By the mixture of the contents of the pollen cell, and the germ cell, a fertile seed is produced, from which springs the plant.

In animals, while the essential nature of the generative act remains just the same as in plants, the accessories gradually rise in complexity. Except in the very lowest animals, there are special organs set apart for reproduction, and these produce the sperm and germ cells, the *sperm-*

zoosoids and the *eggs*. The sperm cells are elaborated in organs, called *testicles;* which are generally composed of long and delicate tubes. In these tubes, the parent cells of the sperm are envolved, which contain self-moving microscopic bodies called *spermatozooids.* These are quite analogous to the phytozoaires, and are found throughout the whole animal kingdom, with the exception of the very lowest species. They have the form of a lengthened filament with a little oval head and a long and very delicate tail. By this tail, which is in constant motion, they are propelled amid the viscid fluid, in which they float, and which is called the *liquor seminis,* or seminal liquid. They were long thought to be animals from their peculiar movements, but are now recognised to have no claim to that title. The movements, like those of the phytozoaires, are owing to mechanical causes, and help to bring the spermatoozoids into proximity with the egg. These little bodies are the active agents in impregnation, the immediate fathers of us all ; they find their way to the neighbourhood of the egg, and conjugate with it, thus producing a fertile germ. They are discharged from their parent cells by the bursting of the latter, and are then conveyed by the duct leading from the testicle into the urethral canal, whence they are poured into the female organs, in the act of copulation. They retain their fertilising power for but a short time after their discharge in warm-blooded animals, namely, birds and mammals. In birds, their movements cease in a quarter of an hour after their discharge. In the cold-blooded vertebrate animals,—namely, reptiles and fishes, and in the invertebrata, they can live much longer, and remain active for days and even months in the female organs, fertilising several crops of eggs in succession.

The germ cells or eggs are produced in organs called *ovaries.* These in many animals are exceedingly like the testicles, being tubular and vesicular glands. So they are in the human embryo, for our organs, in their gradual developement in the womb, pass through stages similar to those which remain permanent in the lower animals. Among all adult vertebrated animals, including woman, the ovaries are solid bodies, composed of dense fibrous tissue, in which the germ cells or eggs lie imbedded. Each egg is enclosed in a parent cell or *ovisac,* called the graafian vesicle, and consists of a *yolk sac,* with a little cell called the *germinal vesicle,* amid the yolk. The egg of some animals, as, for instance, of the fowl, is very large, but the egg of woman, and of all the mammalia, is so small as not to be visible to the naked eye. The size varies according to the degree of developement the embryo is to reach at the expense of the egg alone ; for it is on the yolk of the egg that all embryoes are first nourished. The egg on quitting the ovary, before fecundation, consists only of the yolk sac with its contents ; in its passage down the oviduct it often receives, as in the fowl, a covering of *albumen* or white, and a shell.

The means which nature adopts to effect the union of these sperm and germ cells, are very various throughout the animal kingdom. In the lowest animals consciousness and volition are scarcely at all awakened, and their actions seem merely of an automatic kind. In them there is probably no more sexual feeling, nor sexual effort, than in plants. Many

of them are, like plants, hermaphrodite, each individual having both sets
of sexual organs, and preparing both sperm and germ cells, which fer-
tilise each other automatically. But as we ascend the scale of being, and
mind becomes gradually developed, the sexes are no longer united in one
individual, but are divided ; one individual producing the sperm, and another the germ cells, one possessing the male and the other the female generative organs.

All the higher invertebrate and all the vertebrate animals are mono-
sexual. In them, accordingly, the union of the two sets of cells is effected
by sexual intercourse, for which nature furnishes a special set of accessory organs, and to which each animal is impelled by desires, strong and
complex in proportion to the power and elevation of its being. Some
animals, such as the snail, are hermaphrodite, but not self-fertilising ;
each individual has both male and female genital organs, but the congress of two is necessary for fecundation, each impregnating the eggs of
the other. Others, such as fishes, have but an imperfect provision
for bringing together the sperm and germ cells. The female sheds her
roe in the sand, and then the male pours over it his seminal fluid. But
in this way, very many eggs are wasted, and hence the enormous number of eggs which many fishes produce. In the higher animals, there is
a much more perfect sexual union. The male is furnished with an intro-
mittent organ, called a *penis*, which penetrates into the *vagina* of the female, and sheds the semen there, so that it is brought into close proximity with the egg. Hence, in the higher animals, the eggs do not need
to be so numerous, as their fecundation is much more certain.

The sexual system of the higher animals may be divided into three
parts; namely, the germ *preparing* organs, comprehending the testicle
in the male, and the ovary in the female ; the germ *transporting* organs,
which convey outwards the semen and the eggs, and which consist of
the vas deferens in the male, and the oviduct in the female ; and the
emitting organs, the penis and the vagina, which serve also for sexual
intercourse. Of these the first are the essentials, the others the accessories. These organs are gradually developed, becoming more and more
complex and specialised as we ascend the animal series, or follow the
processes of developement in the human embryo, or other embryo of the
higher class of animals. I shall give a short description of them as they
exist in man, entreating the reader's attention, in order that the subsequent account of their diseases may be better understood.

In man there are two *testes* or testicles, suspended in a bag, called the
scrotum, by the *spermatic chord*. They consist of a mass of thin and delicate tubes, which if unravelled would form a continuous tube of about
one thousand feet long. In these tubes are produced the parent cells of
the seminal fluid. These cells elaborate the spermatozooids, which in
man are very small, requiring a high magnifying power to be visible.
They resemble those found in other animals, having a broadened oval
head and a long tail, by which they are rapidly moved about in the seminal liquid. The length of time they may continue to exist when
poured into the female organs, is not exactly known, but probably it is
but short. Pure water soon puts an end to their motions, but in a denser

fluid, such as mucus or urine, they can live for some time. When the semen is matured, the parent cells burst, and discharge it into the tubes by which it is conveyed into the *vas deferens*, a single larger duct which leads from each testicle, and conveys the semen into the penis. The vas deferens is tortuous, and forms a thick convoluted mass called the *epididymis*, just on leaving the testicle. It conducts the semen upwards through the spermatic chord, then winds round the bladder, and meets a duct coming from one of the two *seminal vesicles*, which are narrow pouches, about an inch and a half long, in which the semen is stored up so as to form a sufficiently copious discharge. After the confluence of the ducts from the testis and seminal vesicle, the common duct receives the name of *Ejaculatory canal*, of which there is one on each side. They open into the *urethra* or urinary canal, at the base of the *prostate gland*. The prostate is in shape something like a chestnut, and surrounds the urethra just after it leaves the bladder. It is nearly an ounce in weight, and is one of the firmest glands in the body. It secretes a thin fluid, like a very thin mixture of milk and water. This fluid is increased in quantity like the seminal fluid under venereal excitement, and it mixes with the latter as it is being ejaculated through the penis. It probably serves to dilute the semen, and to lubricate the canal. It is not however to be regarded as essential to fecundation, for the power of procreation often remains when the prostate is greatly diseased.

The body of the *penis*, or emitting organ, is composed of the two *corpora cavernosa*, and the *urethra*. The former are on the upper surface of the penis, and constitute its main bulk. They are composed of what is called erectile tissue, (like the nipples in the breast, and the wattles on the head of a cock), the erection of which is caused by a suddenly increased flow of blood being sent to it by the arteries, under the stimulus of a sexual desire, and its exit being checked by muscles which compress the veins. Erection is not producible by will, but by sexual emotions.

The *urethra*, or urinary canal, commences at the neck of the bladder, and terminates in its external orifice, in the glans penis. It is divided by anatomists into three portions, namely, the prostatic, which is surrounded by the prostate gland; the membranous, where the canal is somewhat contracted in its passage under the arch of the bony *pelvis*, and where stricture is most apt to occur; and the spongy portion.

The head of the penis is called the *glans* or nut. It is covered by a prolonged piece of skin, called the *prepuce* or foreskin. which can be drawn back in most individuals, and helps to preserve the sensitiveness of the glans. At the base of the glans are a number of little follicles, which secrete a whitish sebaceous matter.

Of these organs the testes are the essentials, the others the accessories. The testis prepares the seminal fluid; the vas deferens conveys it outwards to the seminal vesicles, where it is stored up till required; and the penis ejaculates it into the female organs, where it meets with the germ cell or egg.

In woman the sexual organs may be divided in like manner into three sets, the germ preparing, transporting, and emitting organs; the *ovaries*, oviduct, and vagina. The external slit or opening of the female organs is called the *vulva*, and it is bounded by the two *labia* or lips. In the anterior part of the vulva is a small erectile organ, analogous in form and structure to a diminutive penis, differing however in not being perforated by a canal. It is called the *clitoris*, and is highly sensitive like the glans penis. It is probably the chief organ of sexual enjoyment.

At the posterior part of the vulva is the opening into the *vagina*, the passage which leads up to the mouth of the womb, and into which the penis is introduced in coition. The vagina is about four inches long, and is very distensible, so as to admit the passage through it of so large a body as the child. It is membranous, and surrounded by bands of muscular fibres, which form a *sphincter* or closing muscle, which constricts the orifice of the vagina, where it joins the external genital fissure. In the virgin, before connection has taken place, there is generally a fold of membrane which stretches across the mouth of the vagina, leaving however space for the passage of the menstrual discharge. This is called the *hymen* or maidenhead, and was formerly sought for as a test of virginity, as it is generally ruptured in the first sexual connection, but it is now no longer depended upon. The pain felt in the first intercourse is caused by the rupture of this membrane, and the forcible dilatation of the vagina.

The vagina leads up to the *uterus* or womb, which opens into it at its upper and anterior side, about three inches from the orifice of the vagina. The womb, that most important and wonderful organ, the first cradle of the human race,is, when unimpregnated, a small flattened pear-shaped body, about 3½ or 4 inches long, and 2½ broad, whose broad end is uppermost, while its lower end rests on the vagina. It is a hollow muscle like the heart, and like it, is composed of involuntary muscular fibre, whose actions are not dependent on the will.

The upper and broadened part of the womb is called the *body*, and the lower, which is narrower, is the *cervix* or neck.

The cervix is the part which rests on the vagina, and in the middle of it is a small opening, leading into the womb, called the *os uteri* or mouth of the womb. It is so narrow as only to admit a small sound. The womb contains two little cavities, one of them in the body, the other in the neck. They can hold about equal quantities of fluid, namely, about nine or ten drops. Between them there is a narrow passage called the *os internum* or internal mouth.

There are considerable anatomical differences between the body and the neck of the womb. The body is of a low vitality, consisting of muscular tissue, closely welted together, and with very few blood-vessels; its cavity also has a very imperfect and rudimentary mucous membrane. The neck, on the other hand, has a higher vitality, it is much better supplied with blood-vessels, and its cavity, which is called the *cervical canal*, is lined by a thick mucous membrane, studded with numerou-secreting follicles. Hence the neck is much more liable to inflammatory disease than the body, and hence also, it is rare that inflammation spreads either to the substance, or to the mucous membrane of the latter, though when it does so, it is exceedingly chronic and obstinate, like all in flammations in tissues of low vitality

The *ovaries*, which, like the testes in the male, are the most essential of all the generative organs, as they prepare the germs, which the others only serve to bring together and foster in their growth, are two small bodies, in size and shape like an almond, which are attached by membranous folds, called the *uterine ligaments*, to either side of the womb. Towards each of them a very minute tube, called the *fallopian tube* or oviduct, proceeds from the cavity of the uterus.

The fallopian tubes are not united to the ovaries, but are provided with a bell-shaped mouth, which erects itself and clasps the ovary, when an egg is about to be discharged.

The inside of the vulva and vagina is lined by a mucous membrane, which secretes, like similar membranes in other parts, a colourless fluid, serving to lubricate the passage.

The female sexual organs lie between the bladder in front, and the *rectum* or lower portion of the intestines behind. The *urethra* or urinary canal, is very short and wide in the female, not being more than two inches in length. It opens into the vulva, immediately in front of the orifice of the vagina. Behind the vulva, and separated from it by a space about an inch and a half in length, which receives the name of the *perineum*, is the *anus* or opening of the intestine, which runs up behind the wall of the vagina. The uterus and ovaries lie between the bladder and the rectum in the middle of the pelvis, (which is the lower part of the skeleton of the trunk, and is formed by the union of the haunch-bones and others). The knowledge of these relations between so important organs, and the intimate nervous connection which exists between them, explain why in pregnancy, or in diseases when the womb alters in size &c., the contiguous organs may be disturbed in their functions.

The generative organs in both sexes are the last in the body to arrive at maturity. They are quite immature at birth, and it is not till the epoch of puberty, that they become fully developed. Puberty consists essentially, in the ripening of the sperm and germ cells. It takes place in the male at about the fifteenth or sixteenth year, and it is only then that the seminal fluid begins to be elaborated by the testicles, and that the young man becomes capable of reproducing his species. Other changes accompany this maturation of the sperm cells. A larger supply of blood and nervous influence is sent to the sexual organs, and they grow rapidly, and hair appears about them. The larynx also becomes wider, and the voice deeper and rougher, and fresh vigour and energy pervade the frame. The sexual desires are also awakened, and become very powerful; while involuntary emissions of the seminal fluid with erections of the penis occur at times during sleep, showing the maturity of the sexual system.

In woman, puberty occurs in our country, generally between fourteen and sixteen years of age. In hot climates it is one or two years earlier, and in cold ones later. It consists in the maturation of the reproductive organs. An increased supply of blood and nervous influence is sent to these organs, so that they rapidly acquire their full developement, and begin to exercise, as in the male, a most powerful influence over the rest of the constitution, physical and moral. All

F

the sexual organs, together with the breasts, increase in size, and hair grows upon them. , When the organs are fully developed and the eggs are ripe, there commences that wondrous chain of periodical actions, known under the name of *menstruation* or *ovulation* (the monthly lay-ing of eggs). At intervals, generally of four weeks, sometimes of a few days more or less, one egg, or in some instances more than one, is ripened and discharged from the ovary. This is accompanied by a periodical flow of blood to all the sexual organs, so that the ovaries become red and turgid, and the vagina and vulva have a dark red hue, instead of their usual pink one. At the same time blood is discharged from the cavity of the womb, and escapes from the external genital fissure in drops. This is called the menstrual discharge, or the *cata-menia* (in ordinary parlance, " the courses " or "monthly illness ") and lasts for from three to five days, amounting to about as many ounces.

Menstruation in woman corresponds exactly with the period of heat in female animals, and differs only in the unessential particular, that in woman there is an external sanguineous discharge. In all, the essence of the process is the periodical flow of blood to the sexual organs, and the maturation and spontaneous discharge of eggs from the ovaries.

This theory of menstruation—namely, that it is connected with the *spontaneous discharge of eggs*, is one of the most recent and most impor-tant discoveries in physiology. Formerly, it was believed, that eggs were discharged from the ovaries only in consequence of sexual inter-course, and subsequent to fecundation, but now it is well ascertained that such is not the case. It was M. Raciborski who first discovered the fact of the spontaneous discharge of eggs, quite independently of any intercourse with the male, and who showed clearly that impreg-nation does not take place before but *after* the egg quits the ovary, and while it is in the oviduct. His theory has been corroborated by many subsequent observers, and is now received by the great majority of scientific men.

· The egg escapes from the ovary by the bursting of its ovisac or pa-rent cell, and falls into the bell-shaped mouth of the fallopian tube, which, during the menstrual period, applies itself to the ovary and embraces it tightly. It is in this tube that fecundation takes place, if there have been previous sexual intercourse. If not, the egg passes slowly down through the fallopian tube into the cavity of the womb, where it continues to live, and to be capable of impregnation for a few days, then dies, and is discharged from the external passages. If fruitful intercourse have taken place, the seminal fluid, shed in the vagina, enters the mouth of the womb, and penetrates into its cavity, aided partly by the movements of the spermatozooids, partly by the action of little hair-like cilia, with which the mucous lining of the cer-vical canal is covered. It then mounts into the fallopian tubes, and there meets with the egg on its descent. The spermatozooid conjugates with the egg, just as the two reproductive cells do in the humblest plant, and by this union a new human being is produced. It is worthy of remark, that the essential part of the generative act, namely, the meeting of the sperm and germ cells, is as totally unaccompanied by consciousness or volition on our part, as it is in the lowest links of the chain of being. In us also, generation is truly an automatic process.

The fecundated egg now enters the cavity of the womb, and proceeds to develope itself into the future human being. The mouth of the womb becomes sealed up by a tenacious mucus, secreted by neighbouring glands, and the womb gradually enlarges, as the *fœtus* or embryo becomes developed within it. For its developement the powers of the mother's economy conspire; a connection is effected between the blood-vessels of the fœtus and of the parent, a plentiful supply of blood is sent to the womb, and the monthly discharge is suppressed. Thus from the blood of the mother the embryo is nourished and grows apace, and the womb also grows to an enormous size, so that at the end of pregnancy the little pear-shaped body has, without any thinning of its walls, become a huge globular mass, upwards of a foot long, and eight or nine inches broad, within which lies the infant, floating in a liquid, whose soft and yielding volume protects its tender limbs, as well as its mother, from injury. After nine calendar months have expired, the womb, which is a large hollow muscle, begins sponta neously to contract, and expel its contents, the vagina and vulva becoming at the same time relaxed and loose, so as to permit the pas sage of the child through them. The womb's contractions, which take place at regular intervals of from five to twenty minutes, or there abouts, (gradually increasing in power and frequency,) and occasion, together with the dilatation of the passages, the pains of labour, proverbially so excruciating, first dilate the mouth of the womb, and then gradually force down the child, head-foremost, through the vagina and vulva into the world, which extraordinary distension is performed without any harm to the child or rupture of the maternal tissues. Having expelled the child, and shortly afterwards the *placenta*, or after-birth, (the mass of blood-vessels by which the embryo drew its nourishment from the blood of the mother), the womb contracts into a hard ball, and in a few days has returned almost completely to its original size. These extraordinary developements and actions are peculiar to the womb alone among muscles, and are without a parallel in the human frame.

The physiological explanation of the venereal act is the following. At the stimulus of a sexual desire, the only true and healthy stimulus, the blood rushes into the erectile tissue of which the penis is composed, and thus it becomes capable of penetrating into the vagina. Its erection is aided by the contraction of muscles at its base. The sensitive nerves on the surface of the glans, gradually roused by friction to a state of intense excitement, transmit this to the brain and spinal chord, which by a reflex action cause spasmodic and rhythmical contractions of muscles, which compress the seminal vesicles, and expel the seminal fluid with considerable force through the ejaculatory ducts and the urethra into the vagina of the female. Let it be carefully observed with regard to the perfection of this act that no stimulus but the normal one—namely, a venereal desire, should be needed to call up a full erection of the penis; that the excitement and sensation of delight experienced, should continue constantly increasing till it reaches its acme, which should be neither too soon nor too lingering in its arrival; that the pleasure experienced depends in great measure on the manly vigour of the organs, which have not been exhausted by any of the causes hereafter to be mentioned; that all dalliance or protraction of the act is enfeebling to the organs and effeminating to the whole constitution, physical and moral; that after coition a feeling of drowsiness is often experienced, none of which considerations are rashly to be neglected. All our bodily functions and actions have their ideal perfection, just like the moral types, upon which it is most important that the attention of man be fixed, for it is only by his knowledge of, and regard for, these, that he will understand how to conduct his physical life.

In the inferior animals, the seminal fluid is secreted only at intervals. This frequently occurs in the spring, and at that time the testicles increase greatly in size and furnish the sperm in abundance. During the rest of the year they shrink and remain inactive. The females also will admit the male only during the period of heat, namely, while the eggs are being ripened and discharged, at which time alone they are capable of impregnation. In woman also, the sexual desires are strongest just after the menstrual discharge. Sexual intercourse however, and sexual enjoyment are, in her case, by no means confined to this period; a privilege which is consistent with the higher endowments of intellect and self-restraint possessed by the human race.

The reproductive powers cease far sooner in woman than in man. In her they terminate with the cessation of ovulation, which generally takes place from the 45th to the 50th year. The sexual desires and enjoyment do not, however, cease then. In man, the power of procreation remains much longer; it may last, if the constitution be vigorous, till extreme old age. Old Parr showed himself capable of reproduction in his 142nd year; and it is to be observed, that the continuance of strong sexual desires, instead of being regarded as a reproach to old age, as is often done, should be held one of the best of all signs of a healthy and well-spent physical life. It is the premature exhaustion of his powers and desires that disgraces a man; their long retention ennobles him.

After the egg is fecundated, the processes of *developement* immediately commence in it. By developement is meant the series of changes which the egg passes through, until it reaches the form of its parent. The phenomena of developement are of surpassing interest and importance. They are the best guides that we have to the systematic classification of plants and animals, and by studying them we obtain the greatest insight into the origin and the meaning of life.

The womb is the workshop of organisation; in it take place those mysterious and occult transformations, by which the microscopic cell is changed into the perfect being. Hence, very great pains have been taken by scientific observers in watching the developemental processes in the embryoes of a vast variety of plants and animals, and in endeavouring to gain a knowledge of the wondrous plan on which nature builds up the fabrics of the animated world. An immense number of the most interesting facts have thus been ascertained, and several most important laws deduced from them; but the subject is wide and deep as nature, and much remains to be done before the relations between the various phenomena are clearly perceived, and the plan of organic structure satisfactorily made out.

Probably the most important law of developement yet discovered is that which was first clearly enunciated by Von Baer, "that developement always proceeds from the general to the special." By this, is meant that the earlier stages of any embryo are always the more general, that is, common to a greater number of living beings, and that by each successive stage of developement, it becomes more specialized, and gradually proceeds through less and less general types of structure, till, at last, it ends in the individual. This will be better understood by an illustration. The human embryo is at first exactly like all other embryoes, and like the simplest form of a living being; namely, it is a simple microscopic cell. All living beings commence with this, and there is no distinguishable difference between the germ of the humblest plant and of man. This, then, is the most general form of life. As yet, it is impossible to say whether the embryo is an animal or a vegetable. Soon, however, the *special* marks of animality appear, but it is impossible to say, to which great class of animals the embryo belongs, as it contains characters, which are *general* in all. Gradually, however, and by successive stages, it becomes apparent that the animal is vertebrated, next that it is a mammal, and afterwards that it is of the human species. Lastly, the sex becomes apparent along with the peculiar and special characters which distinguish one individual from all others. In this, we see an exemplification of the great law of progress from the general to the special, which law comprehends every fact yet known. The scientific classification of plants and animals proceeds in the same way from the general to the special. One great type of structure for instance, is found to be general throughout a large division of the animal kingdom: the modifications of that type are formed according to less general types; and thus we proceed through a series of less and less general, or more and more special types, till we get to the species and individual. Thus are formed the kingdoms, sub-kingdoms, orders, families, genera, and species of the botanist and zoologist; nay more, it is exceedingly probable, as Dr. Carpenter says, that the whole scale of being from the simple cellular plant, up to man, has been developed in the course of myriads of ages, according to the very same law, as that which presides over the developement of any single being. The organisms which first originated on the surface of the earth were probably those of the most general form; and every plant and animal has successively arisen in strict accordance with this great principle of gradual progress from the more general to the more special.

From this account it will be seen that the embryoes of all beings invariably resemble each other during some part of their developement, however unlike the adults may be; and that a man is not more dissimilar to the humblest plant, than he is to his own self when commencing life. Those animals are most nearly related to each other, whose developement proceeds furthest in the same direction, and those are most widely separated, which soonest diverge from each other in their developement. The fact that the powers of nature are sufficient to produce a human being from a single cell, make it more comprehensible to us, how they may of themselves have sufficed in the lapse of ages to develope the great chain of animated existence. In truth, the developement of man in the womb, is just an epitome of the developement of the whole living world; beginning in a single cell, and ending in the wondrous perfection of humanity. It is the key, could we but rightly understand it, to the whole natural history of the origin and succession of life upon our planet. Nature here as it were repeats in miniature, and in the space of a few months, those grand evolutions and developements, which it cost her millions of ages to accomplish.

Another great law of organic structure is the *unity of type*. By this is meant that a number of beings are formed upon the same fundamental plan, and have the same essential organs differing only in their relative developement. In the animal kingdom there are four great plans of structure, on each of which a large class of animals is built. These are the Radiate, the Molluscous, the Articulate, and the Vertebrate plans. All the animals constructed on any one of these, and more especially on the highest or vertebrate plan, are strictly comparable with each other. Thus all vertebrated animals are formed according to the same archetype or ideal plan, and all of them have essentially the same organs, although an organ which is largely developed in one animal may be merely rudimentary in another. A vertebrated animal however is not in the same way comparable with a radiate or articulate one, for their plans of structure are widely different. Still, a very close and remarkable connection exists between the very lowest members of the vertebrate class, and the other classes, namely the molluscous and articulate ones. This is shown in the extraordinary little fish called the Amphioxus, whose peculiar organisation was only lately pointed out. It is the lowest of all known vertebrate animals, and approaches in many respects very nearly to the lowest forms of the other classes. This is one instance of the general and instructive fact, that it is the *lowest* members of the various groups of living beings, which resemble each other, and not the highest of an inferior class and the lowest of the one above it, as is sometimes supposed.

Moreover, all animals and all plants are comparable together in their earliest embryonic stages, and therefore there is doubtless some much more general plan of structure, which includes all living beings, could we but understand it. Newton, when reflecting on the wonders of animated nature, said, "I cannot doubt that the structure of animals is governed by principles of similar uniformity with that of the rest of the universe."

The vertebrate type to which man belongs is common to four classes of

animals, namely fishes, reptiles, birds, and mammals. These are all
formed on the same plan, and possess essentially the same organs, and
the great difference we see in their shapes, arises from the wonderful way
in which the same parts are modified in different animals to suit special
purposes. Thus the wing of a bat is essentially the same as the hand of
a man ; the only difference being that the bones are developed in an extraordinary degree, and connected together by a membrane adapted for
flying. The vertabrate type exists in its lowest and most general form
in fishes, and gradually reaches its highest and most specialised one in
man. The human embryo in the womb passes through an analogous
series of stages. It presents the characters successively of the embryonic
fish, reptile, and bird, and all its organs successively pass through transitory stages, which remain permanent in these inferior animals, and
thus gradually reach their final highly specialised and complex form.
In this adherence to a fixed type, and to immutable laws, we see the
signs of the workings of nature, which are so different from those of
man. All the works of man, or of any voluntary being, are directed to
the accomplishment of some design, and we are constantly imputing the
same designs to the works of nature. But this is a great error. The
works of nature are produced by unconscious agencies, which do not
operate from design, but from necessary adherence to fixed laws. Rudi-
ments of organs appear sometimes in the embryo and then fade away
again ; and parts often remain through life in a rudimentary state, and
without subserving any purpose in the economy, but merely showing the
fixity of the laws of developement, and the necessary adherence to one
type. Thus it is not from design that we are endowed with any of our
organs, but from necessity ; the eye was not given to us in order that we
might see with it, but we see with our eye, because it has been developed
in us, in obedience to the resistless laws of progressive evolution.
The first processes of the developement of the human being, are as
follows. The microscopic egg, it has been said, contains a minute yolk,
and a little cell in its centre called the germinal vesicle. When ripe, this
germinal vesicle becomes filled with young cells in its interior, then
bursts, prior to fecundation ; and if the egg be then impregnated, developement begins in one of these liberated young cells. It multiplies itself
by splitting into two, and these two into four, and so on, just as the
simplest plant or animal does. Each of the cells so produced draws
round it a part of the yolk, which becomes invested with another cell-
wall, and thus a *mulberry mass* of cells is formed, each having a share of
the germinal capacity. The spermatic power, derived from the union of
the contents of the spermatozooid and the egg, is shared among all the
cells which spring from the one first fecundated, and by this power the
cells are enabled to transform themselves into the various organs of the
body and to develope the faculties of the mind. It is a great law of
developement, discovered by Professor Schwann, that all the tissues
and organs in the body commence in *cells*, just in the same way as the
entire organism. Nature never forms any tissue, whether a muscle, a
vessel, or a nerve, *directly* by the aggregation of molecules, but she first
makes a cell, and this cell is transformed into the tissue. All our organs

originate in masses of cells, which are the most *general* form of living tissue, and their gradual developement takes place by the *special* transformation of these cells. When once a cell has been transformed into a tissue, it loses its power of undergoing further developement, and hence the phenomena of gemmation in the lower organisms arise from the fact, that a number of the original germinal cells which are endowed with the spermatic influence, remain untransformed within them. Thus the buds of a plant are produced from the central pith, which consists of untransformed cells, and the Polyp buds spring from germinal cells, which remain untransformed within the body of the parent. The more cellular a plant or an animal is, the greater in general is its power of propagating by gemmation, for the germinal capacity of the cells is not exhausted by their transformation.

The generative organs are in all animals the last to attain their full developement. In man they, like the other parts of the body, pass through states resembling the permanent forms of the genital organs in the lower vertebrate animals, and gradually rise through the fish, the reptile, and the bird, to the mammal, and ultimately to the human type. For a long time the external organs of generation in the embryo are so alike in both sexes, that they are undistinguishable ; their form is *general* to both male and female, but gradually the *special* characters of the sexes are produced. It is from the persistence of this embryonic similarity that the malformation called *hermaphroditism*, is sometimes occasioned. Developement is arrested at a certain stage, by some cause or other, and the external genitals continue to present the characters of both sexes. Several very curious cases of such hermaphroditism have taken place, in which the individuals have passed their lives, married, and been received in society, as belonging to a different sex from their true one ; and the mistake has in some cases been discovered only on minute investigation after death. Other cases have occurred, where even the most scientific men were totally unable to come to a conclusion as to the sex of the individual, from the appearance of the external genital organs during life. These cases, in which there is merely an arrest of developement in the external organs, are called *spurious hermaphroditism ;* but it is doubted whether there ever was a case of *true* hermaphroditism, namely, where the essential generative organs, the testicles and ovaries, were fully developed in the same individual, and both sperm and germ cells produced, as is the case in hermaphrodite animals, as the oyster or snail, or in monoecious plants.

But a theory has lately been proposed, and received by many of the profoundest anatomists, that in truth all living beings, including man, are hermaphrodite. This deeply interesting view is supported by many facts in the animated world, and seems consistent with the fundamental unity of type. We have seen that in the lowest plants there seems to be no distinction of sex between the conjugating cells. Both of them seem to have the same reproductive properties, and to combine in themselves the sperm and germ power. On ascending the scale we find very many plants and animals possessing both sets of sexual organs, some of them self-fertilising and others not. In the snail, both sets of organs are fully developed, but a double sexual congress is necessary to impregnate the eggs. Now in the higher animals, including man, there is great evidence to show that each individual is really hermaphrodite, and possesses both sets of organs, and the only difference in this respect between them and the snail is, that one set of organs remains rudimentary and undeveloped in each sex. Man has the male organs fully developed and the female ones in a rudimentary state, and *vice versa.* Thus, the clitoris in the female is in reality the male penis. In the embryo the two organs are so alike, as not to be distinguishable; but the developement of the clitoris is arrested at an early stage, so that it remains small and imperforate, while the penis increases in size, and is closed beneath so as to form the urinary canal. In like manner the womb is represented in man by a minute cavity called the *sinus pocularis* in the prostate gland, &c. Thus, according to this view, the difference of sex is rather apparent than essential, and all of us are truly hermaphrodite beings.

Before taking leave of the interesting subjects of generation and developement, some singular reflections arise on considering these wondrous phenomena.

We call each human being a distinct individual, because he has been produced by an act of generation, and lives independently. But in truth we are not distinct individuals. Each of us is formed of a part of his two parents, a part which is indeed separated from them, but which once was included in their individuality. Hence we are merely a part of our parents, largely developed, and existing independently; and therefore, a man who has given birth to children, does not wholly die at death, but a part of him survives in his offspring. In this way, man is in a manner immortal on this earth. Children of the same families are in reality parts of the same parental organisms; allied to each other something like the different buds on a tree, or different polyps on a compound polyp stock, except that they spring from two instead of one parental organism, and the connection between them has been cut at an early stage.

But the whole human family, whether they are descended from a single pair of first parents, or from many, are so connected together by intermarriage, that in reality they form one great consanguineous whole. The progenitors of all of us have at some time or other formed parts of the same body. Thus, mankind may be termed one great composite individual, instead of a collection of individuals, nearly in the same way as the compound polyp. We form an organism, whose earlier parts are dead, and whose life is ever renewed afresh to the latest posterity by the reunion of certain of its component parts.

Following the same train of thought further, it may be said that we are in the same way, though more remotely, connected with all other living beings, and form with them one great individual; if it be true, as everything leads us to believe, that we have been developed in continuation with them. This great *unity of life* should serve to bind us more closely to our fellow men and to all living things, and to increase the heartfelt sympathy between the different races and individuals of mankind. However widely separated by time and circumstances, we are in reality all parts of the same being, and our interests are indissolubly woven together. It is as impossible for one class of human beings to be wretched without ultimately affecting the happiness of all the rest, as for one organ of the body to be long diseased without involving the others.

Another interesting reflection connected with the subject of generation is, that every child must include in itself the mingled qualities of its two parents. Neither parent furnishes alone, the embryo, as was at one time believed, but both together, by the union of the sperm and germ cells. Therefore the child is just midway between the parents, and can possess no quality which did not exist in them. The qualities of the parent, both mental and bodily, are blended together in the child so as to form a third being. The parental characters may indeed be disguised, as the properties of oxygen and hydrogen are, when they combine to form water; but still they must be there, and it is most interesting to trace them.

By an analytic comparison of the child with its two parents, we may gain an insight into the laws, just as definite and fixed as those of chemistry, or any other part of nature, according to which two sets of qualities of mind and body are blended together, so as to form a third. If we possess any prominent gift of mind or body, the seeds of it must have existed in our parents; and whether we inherit a good or a bad constitution, and a healthy or a delicate mind, depends entirely on them, subject of course to the modifying influence of circumstances. It is commonly and vaguely said, that such a child is like its parents and such another unlike; but the truth is, that every child is the mingled essence of its two parents, and must, if we look deep enough, be a thorough representation of them. The laws of hereditary transmission, and of the commixture of parental properties in the child, are as yet little understood, but are a most important province for investigation.

Neither is it yet known what decides the sex; what are the causes which produce at one time a male, and at another a female. Some interesting experiments on this subject have been made on plants, (and here, as elsewhere, it is only by studying the problem in the lowest organisms, and so reducing it to its simplest expression, that we can hope to solve it) and it has been shown that in some monoecious flowers, male organs alone are produced, if they be subjected to an excessive heat with little light; and female ones alone, if these conditions be reversed. But with regard to the decision of the sex in the human being, nothing certain has been discovered.

Having thus given a short sketch of the phemonena of generation and developement, I proceed to that which I believe to be by far the most important of all subjects, in the present state of the world, namely, the diseases of the generative organs, viewed in connection with the evils of poverty and hard work. I shall give a short description of these diseases, and endeavour to trace them along with poverty to their great primary source.

It is in vain to treat of disease as a separate subject in the manner generally pursued: almost all prevalent diseases depend primarily on some great cause opèrating widely throughout our society, and unless they are traced to this, and means be taken to remove it, they cannot possibly be remedied or prevented. There is not a better instance of this than the sexual diseases. These are inseparably bound up, as will appear hereafter, with other great social miseries ; and thus the researches of medicine are so thoroughly interwoven with those of political economy, that neither science can lead to any good result without the other.

It is from the want of perception of the dependence of these, and many other diseases, on deeply rooted social difficulties and errors, that so little has yet been done to prevent them. It is from studying disease as a separate entity, and not tracing its causes far enough back, by which its dependence on the great social embarrassments, and its inseparable connection with other fields of inquiry would be seen, that the efforts of medicine are so frequently frustrated. It is not by endeavouring to cure individuals merely that human health can be advanced; if the mainspring of the disease remain hidden and unattended to, individuals may indeed be cured, but an endless succession of new diseases will constantly arise so that the health of the race on the whole will make no advance.

DISEASES

OF THE

MALE GENERATIVE ORGANS.

IT is deeply to be regretted, that mankind are in general so little acquainted with the laws of bodily health, and the penalties or rewards consequent on their observance. In the young world, it was long the custom to leave the care of men's spiritual welfare in the hands of a certain class, and it is only after progressive reformations, that we can clearly see how vain it is for us to trust to another, in matters where our own knowledge and judgment are required.

The case is the same now-a-days with man's bodily welfare; he is too pre-occupied by other pursuits, to pay attention to this, and delivers himself over in health and sickness to the guidance of chance or the physician, a passive unreasoning instrument.

And yet but little reflection is needed to show us, that in this, as well as in spiritual and moral matters, our own knowledge and independent judgment are required at every step in life; that if we have not as full a knowledge of the body and of the paths to physical health and disease, as of the mind and the phenomena of its virtues and vices, our life is the sport of chance, and our brightest hopes are all liable to end in disappointment and misery; that no mental culture or moral excellence will avail us, if we are borne to the ground by bodily disease. The laws of our body will not be neglected; they demand our attention, and woe to him who offends against them.

Shall we then, like our ancestors, be content to remain as children, on matters of such infinite importance? It is said, that a little knowledge is a dangerous thing, but truly none at all is still more dangerous, and far more unpardonable. Deeply convinced as I am, that there is no safety for man, till the laws that regulate our bodily health and disease be as well known to all, as any of the other most widely-spread branches of knowledge, I shall endeavour in this essay to give a short sketch of a class of diseases, perhaps more fatal at present to the health and happiness of our race than any other, and also from their peculiar nature, if possible, less understood by the world at large.

It is of the diseases of the genital organs that I shall speak, to which man and woman are most liable in the years that follow puberty. This is probably at the present day the most dangerous period of life, with the exception of the first year or two of existence; not so much because more die in it, but because the foundation of many chronic lingering diseases is then laid, which may embitter all the rest of life's cup.

The great danger of the period arises from the fact of the genital organs, these mighty powers for the happiness or misery of each individual, then coming first into play; and from the lamentable ignorance in which youth, and indeed the whole of society, is plunged, as to the laws of these organs. There is no subject at present on which such a dense cloud of ignorance, prejudice, and every imperfect and degrading feeling lies brooding, as upon the genital organs, and their whole nature and duties. To raise this veil of obscurity and shame, which degrades the sexual part of man, and to strive to show, by the lights which modern research has thrown upon it, the simple and beautiful natural laws to which it is subjected, like other parts of the economy, shall be my endeavour in this essay. It is not sufficient that all men should become acquainted with the laws of health, as has been so admirably dwelt upon in some late popular works on physiology; it is necessary also that we should be acquainted with the history of *disease;* for it is as important that we should be aware of the penalty for breaking a law, as of the reward for obeying it.

The great causes of the deplorable ignorance and prejudice which prevail on sexual subjects are, first, the erroneous moral views which are entertained regarding them; and, secondly, the ideas of mystery and shame which are attached to them, and which must be completely overcome throughout society, before we be rescued from the innumerable evils that overwhelm mankind at present from their diseases. Mystery always causes ignorance, which is of itself sin, and the parent of sin; and therefore every one of us should seek entirely to rid ourselves of such feelings on sexual subjects, and to view that part of nature, like all others, with the calm and reverential spirit that the pursuit of truth demands.

PUBERTY IN THE MALE.

This period, which generally occurs about the age of fifteen or sixteen, is accompanied by important changes in the economy, connected with the developement of the genital or reproductive organs. Were anatomy and physiology as well known as the comparatively unimportant dead languages, it would be unnecessary to explain to any one, with a liberal education, the nature of these changes. They consist mainly, as has been already mentioned, in the production of a new secretion, called the seminal fluid, by the testicles, and the simultaneous growth of the generative organs, and increase of strength and manliness in the whole frame. With this new bodily developement, come the fresh and powerful feelings of sexual love, and the young man is impelled to new energy of thought and action.

It is at this time that the senses, and that part of our nature, which we have been unhappily in the habit of regarding as a sort of slave or rebel against the other mental faculties, demand their free scope; and if these animal passions be unheeded, or unreasonably repressed, the whole organism is liable to become diseased. This is the season for youthful gaiety, and the amusements in which the two sexes join in friendly intercourse; for passionate love with all its hopes and fears, delights and griefs; in short for that part of our experience, which we are meant to draw more from the exercise of the passions, than from reflection. "The man who reflects is a depraved animal," said Rousseau; and the paradox, however exaggerated, is too often applicable to the youth of our time, prematurely enfeebled by care and thought. For our country is sadly deficient in those amusements so necessary for the health and happiness of youth; too frequently the free and joyous communion which should prevail between the two sexes, is overawed by the asceticism of our morality, and shrinks into morbid shyness and bashfulness, rendering distasteful the most agreeable society. How constantly do we see young people, poring over books till they become mere thinking machines; or so intensely spiritual, that it would seem they had escaped from their bodies; or with natural tastes so perverted, that they become at last almost incapable of vigorous manly love! These evils arise from mistaken ideas of their duties to themselves and to their neighbours, from ignorance of the great sexual laws, which I shall now endeavour to the best of my knowledge to explain.

LAWS OF THE SEXUAL ORGANS.

One physiological law of supreme importance and universal application in our constitution is, that every several member must, in order to be vigorous and healthy, have a due amount of exercise, and that of the normal kind. Thus the eye must have light, the limbs motion, the intellect reflection, and our appetites and passions their normal gratification, else will they infallibly become enfeebled and diseased. Either excessive or deficient exercise is injurious; and in order to have a well-balanced bodily constitution, (just as much our honor and our duty, as a well-balanced mind), we must obey this law. The generative organs are subject to 't as well as every other, and hence we shall see the duty and necessity of their having due exercise from the time of their maturity, which takes place at puberty, till that of their decline. If this be neglected, they will be enfeebled, and although in some cases, when other parts of the system take on a vicarious action for the unexercised genital organs, according to another admirable physiological law; in other words, though, by directing the mind to other thoughts and pursuits, and strengthening the frame by exercise, (according to the advice so often given by physicians to the youth of both sexes, whose health is suffering from their ungratified sexual appetites), though thus in some cases health and vigour may apparently be retained, yet it is comparatively rarely, and only in very favourable circumstances, that this will be the case ; and even in these, I do not consider the health perfect, where one organ or passion acts vicariously for another, and has thereby double work to do. I feel convinced, that when we have a far higher standard of health than passes current in the present sickly state of our society, such deviations from it will not be permitted.

If on the other hand, the genital organs be excessively exercised, they will in like manner become enfeebled ; just as the excessive indulgence and dwelling on the feeling of love, detracts from the beauty of the moral character ; as is exemplified in some amatory poets, and in the dissipated pleasure hunters, who sacrifice all the rest of their nature to this one passion.

Further, if the mode of their exercise be not the normal one, the consequences will be still worse, for nature allows no departure from her plan with impunity. By the most beautiful and delicate adjustment, she has so united our health and happiness to the natural and normal mode of sexual gratification, that we cannot depart in the least from it without being injured. This, every one will understand to be the case in the injurious habits of self-pollution ; but it is not so generally understood, that even in sexual intercourse, the more intense and genuine is the passion felt, the more will its gratification stimulate and elevate mind and body. Love should be real and intense, free from all fear and suspicion, in order to produce its best effects on man. When mercenary or clandestine, in which case the mind is suspicious, solicitous, or, especially on the female side, apathetic, it cannot be said to be normally indulged.

I now proceed to speak of the diseases of the genital organs arising from the ignorance and neglect of these laws of healthy exercise. These constitute a most important class of diseases, which may be named the *genital* diseases, in contradistinction to the venereal ones, from which they are totally different. The former arise from neglect of the laws of healthy exercise, &c., and are not infectious ; whereas the latter are propagated by contagion, and are of a completely different nature.

EVILS OF ABSTINENCE.

It is most unwise to suppose that our chief duty with regard to our appetites and passions is to exercise self-denial. This quality is far from being at all times a virtue; it is quite as often a vice; and it should by no means be unconditionally praised. Every natural passion, like every organ of the body, was intended to have normal exercise and gratification; and this it is to which every individual and society at large should aspire. It is always a sign of imperfection in an individual, or in society, if the normal requirements of all their members be not duly provided for. At present, in this country, abstinence or self-denial in the matter of sexual love is much more frequently a natural vice than a virtue; and instead of deserving praise, merits condemnation, as we may learn from the mode in which all-just nature punishes it. Wherever we see disease following any line of conduct, we may be certain it has been erroneous and sinful, for nature is unerring. Sexual abstinence is frequently attended by consequences not one whit less serious than sexual excess, and far more insidious and dangerous, as they are not so generally recognised. While every moralist can paint in all its horrors the evils of excess, how few are aware that the reverse of the picture is just as deplorable to the impartial and instructed eye!

The young man enters on the period of puberty with an imagination glowing with the ideas of love and romance he has read of, or conceived in his own visions of happiness, and all these receive ten-fold intensity from the stimulus of the new bodily developement. If this have no natural outlet, the consequences may be most fearful and deplorable. Thrown upon himself by the asceticism of our morality, he is very liable to contract the habit of solitary indulgence, the baneful effects of which I shall describe under the head of the *abuse* of the sexual organs. If he do not: if, persuaded by the theoretically received, but by no means generally practised, views on moral subjects which surround him, he abstain from all sexual gratifications, he is exposed to the following evils, of which, if we look around us, we may see too many examples. Haunted by amatory ideas, and tormented by frequent erections of the sexual organs, the spirited youth wars manfully for the citadel of his chastity; he takes refuge in study, in severe bodily exercise, in platonics, the unhappy one ! and reasons on love instead of feeling it; and perhaps at last is so unfortunately successful, that the strong sexual passions and erections vanish together.   But not with impunity, do we triumph over any part of our nature.   He now becomes restless and dissatisfied, he loses his serenity and active vigour of mind, he is distracted by nervous irritability and probably dyspepsia, that frequent attendant on mental anxiety ; weak and exhausted, he cannot fix his attention on the objects he would wish to study ; his intellect, formerly vivid and elastic, has become turbid and sluggish, and instead of the objective and impetuous passions of youth, he becomes morbidly shy and bashful, wrapping himself in subjective speculations, so that the very thought of woman's society is often distasteful to him.   Poor fellow! is this the result of his imagined good conduct ? Nay, but the penalty for a youth unphysiologically spent.   If we examine into the cause of this train of evils, we shall find it to be the enfeeblement of the genital organs from *disuse*, besides the exceedingly pernicious effect, that a powerful natural passion has when repressed upon all the rest of the mind.   Subject to the frequent excitement of erotic ideas, the genital organs have been denied all normal exercise, and the effects of this are now manifest. The penis may be shrunk and flabby, the testicles soft, and even, in extreme cases, greatly atrophied ; the erections which, when vigorous, are a sign of power in the organ, have in great part disappeared, and perhaps involuntary discharges of the seminal fluid have been established.   These discharges, when they occur unfrequently and in a healthy person, have often but little bad effect on the health, although perhaps they should always, when proceeding from abstinence, be considered as a warning that sexual exercise is required; they occur generally at the time of puberty, as a sign of the maturity of the organs ; but when they are frequent, proceeding from irritability and enfeeblement, and acquire a morbid habit of recurrence, they form one of the most miserable diseases to which man is liable, and which I shall describe more fully under the head of spermatorrhœa.

If this disease be established, the young man sinks gradually into a gloomy hypochondria, an invariable attendant in a greater or less degree, on any seminal weakness ; he begins perhaps a system of mental analysis, which may lead, according to his disposition, to a hopeless scepticism, or to a religious melancholy ; society is a burden to him, and the love of his friends an annoyance. His health becomes much impaired, all the symptoms marking nervous weakness, for such is always the effect of loss of the seminal fluid.   Night brings no consolation after the gloomy day, for he lives in constant dread of nocturnal discharges of semen, which weaken him so much, that in the morning he feels as if bound down by a weight to his couch.   He goes from one physican to another, but is probably rather injured than benefited, for all but the natural remedy, namely, sexual connexion, can do little good, and may do much evil.   And how few English physicians are there, who have the courage, even if they have the knowledge, to prescribe, nay even to tell the patient, of this one and only physiological remedy ! No ; overawed by the general erroneous moral views on these subjects, they shrink from their duty of asserting the sacredness of the bodily laws in opposition to all preconceptions. At most, perhaps, some more scientific physician will tell the unhappy sufferer from abstinence, that marriage is the only thing for him; but this is like the prospect of the distant shore to the drowning man. It would be the most rash and immoral act, for a man hypochondriacal and impotent, to stake another's fortunes, as well as his own, on so uncertain a chance; were it even possible that he should change his robes of grief for a marriage garment, in so sudden a manner. The true and only remedy for the evils arising from abstinence, is a moderate indulgence in sexual intercourse, together with the freedom from study, exercise and amusements in the open air, and other means of satisfying the wants of our animal nature. By these means, if the disease have not progressed too far, and if the constitution have not been tampered with by unnatural remedies, health and happiness will in general be soon and readily restored. Vigour of body will return along with a generous self confidence and manly bearing, without which youth is not itself.

It may be objected to these facts, that there are others, who remain strong and healthy, though they be rigorously abstinent. This may be true in some cases, where the constitution is strong, the temperament not very erotic, and the pursuits not of too sedentary, indolent, or studious a nature. But there is nothing that leads to more unphilosophical views, than this idea, that what one man may do with comparative impunity is equally safe for another. Complete sexual abstinence is in every case an evil, and more especially so in the years immediately after puberty, as then the imagination on sexual subjects is most vivid and powerful from their novelty, and also from the instinctively sensuous direction of that part of life; in after years, when the body has gained greater firmness of fibre, and the mind more sedateness and reflection, especially if the sexual passions have been duly and naturally gratified in their fitting season, the injurious effect of abstinence is not so great. We may observe on looking around us, every different degree of its evil effects; in some young men it may proceed to the extreme results I have mentioned above, the establishment of great seminal weakness, and total loss of energy of mind and body; while in the majority of cases but minor degrees of lassitude of body, and irritability, depression, and sluggishness of mind will be produced, a benumbed and confused state of the mind being a very frequent and characteristic symptom; but in no case will the physical and moral nature of a man who is rigorously abstinent, be so high as it should be, had it the due and necessary stimulus of moderate sexual gratifications.

What prevents this certain truth from being acknowledged, is the fact, that all but married love, which it is impossible for the young man to obtain, is so degraded by the commonly received moral views on sexual subjects, that the youth who indulges in it, is necessarily to a certain extent degraded, besides running great risks from the venereal diseases, which have been so shamefully neglected and looked down upon. Hence the young man is placed in this most unhappy dilemma; either he must be abstinent, and in so doing not only make himself wretched, dissatisfied, or diseased, by the repressing of the most powerful passion, on the due regulation of which the whole of his youth's and manhood's developement depends, more than on perhaps, any thing else at the time, but also be false to his duty, and the principles of physical religion, which enjoin the due exercise of all parts of his body; or, if he follow the dictates of his nature, he has to indulge in an intercourse generally, nay invariably, of a most degraded kind, where true love, honour, openness, and sense of right, are replaced by mercenary, suspicious, and heartless feelings, and the obscure sense of sin and degradation; besides this he runs the risk of catching venereal complaints, which may destroy his whole life, and which from their nature, mode of origin, and the degrading light in which society regards them, are the most painful and bitter of all diseases.

To remedy these great evils, it is the part of every well-wisher of his kind, and more especially of all the youth, to endeavour to attain a truer knowledge of this most important subject in its physical and moral aspects, and to remove the mass of ignorance and secrecy which surrounds it, and to which so many have been sacrificed. The principle which should be kept steadily in view is—that a due and natural amount of exercise for the organs, and gratification of the passions connected with them, should be aimed at for every individual in society; and that if a society be so constituted, that this cannot be obtained, there must be something radically defective in its constitution, which we should seek with all patience and diligence to rectify; that abstinence and excess are alike pernicious, and that an individual is equally culpable, if he allow mind or body to be weakened or thrown off its balance, by either too much repressing or too much indulging these natural feelings; and that the ideal of a good character is as little possible, with the exclusion or imperfect exercise of the sexual passions, as of any other natural or virtuous quality.

Hence, we must acknowledge, that every man, who has not a due amount of sexual exercise, lives a life of natural imperfection and sin; and he can never be certain how far nature's punishment for this will proceed in his case. I am well aware how intricate and difficult are many of the social questions, which are involved in these relations of the sexes; but such questions are incapable of solution without reference to the physical laws of the generative organs; and nothing but confusion and misery can arise from the mysterious way in which these subjects are at present viewed. The youth of both sexes are at present almost uniformly suffering to a greater or less degree from the evils caused by this ignorance; the female sex especially, as is seen in the matter of prostitution, are placed in the most appalling and heart-rending position of degradation and misery, in which any class of human beings, not even excepting the slaves, have been placed in the world's history; and such evils are more than sufficient to show the inadequacy of our present moral views, and to make us strive in every possible manner to gain more insight into so important a subject.

EVILS OF EXCESS.

The evil effects of excessive venereal indulgence are not so often met with among us as those of abstinence or abuse. The reason is, that there are many natural checks on excessive sexual intercourse, which do not exist in solitary indulgence. Besides this, any abnormal gratification of the sexual passions is much more dangerous both physically and morally, than the natural one.

Venereal excesses arise in many cases more from ignorance and imprudence, than from confirmed sensuality. There is nothing perhaps, in which constitutions differ more, than in the amount of sexual exercise they can severally bear. Among men we shall find every degree of difference in this respect, from those of exceedingly erotic temperament and powerful frame, like the extreme case of a Greek mentioned in M. Lallemand's work on spermatorrhœa, who for years indulged in sexual connection on an average fourteen times a day, to those who are injured by indulging oftener than once, or at most twice, a week. The cause of this difference lies, first, in the nervous temperament; those who are of an erotic disposition being *caeteris paribus*, more capable of, and less injured by immoderate venereal indulgences than the more lymphatic; also in the strength or weakness of the muscular developement; and also to a great degree on men's habits of life. Those who take plenty of exercise in the country air and live well, are less subject to injury from frequent venereal indulgence, than the studious or indolent. Nothing seems to have greater influence in weakening sexual power than overwork of the brain. The student is therefore liable to suffer from slight excesses, which would be unfelt by one of more healthy pursuits. In this matter, as in all other physical gratifications, we must sedulously bear in mind, that a greater indulgence demands from us greater exertions to maintain the balance of the constitution. Thus if a man drink, smoke, or exercise his brain, or his sexual organs, to a great extent, he will infallibly become exhausted and diseased, unless he at the same time take plenty of exercise in the open air, and live otherwise a healthy life.

Although it is difficult to give any general rule in a matter, in which different constitutions vary so much, yet it may perhaps be said, that about twice a week is the average amount of sexual intercourse of which the majority of those who live in towns are permanently capable, without injury; while for the delicate, once a week, or even less, may often be sufficient. But each individual should be guided by his own sensations; and whenever he feels at all exhausted or enervated by sexual indulgences, he should recognise that he has exceeded his natural powers, and practise greater moderation. Excesses are often committed from ignorance of the amount of sexual intercourse which the constitution can bear; as well as from the desire to please, and not to appear deficient in what is justly regarded as a proof of manly vigour; but no man should allow himself to be tempted to exceed his true powers by such feelings, nor should any woman permit so dangerous an error. A great deal of mischief is done by two persons of unequal constitutions being matched together, as is so frequently seen in married life. Here the wife either exhausts the husband, or the husband the wife, the weaker party being constantly tempted to exceed their strength. This shows us, that in all sexual relations, as in the other relations of life, we should have a careful consideration for the health and happiness of others, as well as of ourselves, and never allow our partner to overtask his or her energies for our own gratification. It is not so much from selfishness that such a mistake is made, as from ignorance, and still more from the lamentable morbid delicacy, which prevails o sexual matters, and which prevents all open and rational conversation on them, even between those who have the most intimate knowledge of each other.

Those who are most frequently found to suffer from venereal excesses are young married couples, especially if they be of weak constitutions, and excitable temperament; young men of very dissipated habits; and those who are at the same time, hard students. The effects are very similar to those of abstinence—namely, increasing weakness, nervous irritability, loss of appetite, impaired digestion, hypochondria and disgust with life, and distaste for female society; mental irresolution and enfeeblement, and all the symptoms of nervous exhaustion, which may well be expected to follow the lavish expenditure of a fluid so vitally important as the semen. A weakness of the genital organs is here also produced, and involuntary seminal discharges may be established, which will reduce the patient to the last degree of wretchedness. Besides this, the moral character, in the very sensual and dissipated, becomes selfish, and in many other respects most imperfect and lamentable; results which we should endeavour to remedy by training the mind to self-denial, exercise in other directions, and the noble aspiration for the happiness of others equally with their own; just as in the opposite case of abstinence, we had to urge attention to the gratification of the sensual passions, as constituting no less important a duty.

As for the treatment of disease from excesses, if the case be a slight one, and the result of ignorance, the individual should be warned to be more moderate, to take exercise in the open air, the shower bath, and other means of strengthening the constitution; and at the same time not to give himself up so much to the relaxing and effeminating feelings of love and sexual pleasures, which never fail, when too much indulged in, to detract from the beauty and health of the whole character. It is from being too exclusively devoted to these feelings, that southern and oriental nations, amatory poets, and also many of our youth of both sexes with keen and ungratified passions, lose the beauty and force of their character; that luxury and effeminacy have crept in and spoiled the civilization of so many lofty empires.   The true principle is, that all parts of our being should be alike duly exercised; that none should be either too much repressed, or too prominently indulged; and this balance of character is what we should aspire to attain.

We shall not in general have nearly so much difficulty in checking excess in this case, as in that of solitary indulgence; for, as Rousseau says in his Emille, "Shouldest thou fall into the unhappy habit of self-pollution, my poor Emille, I would pity thee; but I would not hesitate a moment; I would bring thee at once to know woman's society, well aware that it is far easier to detach thee from her, than from thyself." This, as will be seen hereafter, is the height of science on the subject.

But if the case have proceeded far, we may have to deal with the most aggravated form of seminal weakness.   The patient may have involuntary nocturnal, or, still worse, diurnal discharges.   In this case it will be requisite to resort to powerful remedies.   Cauterization of the prostatic portion of the urethra, over the mouths of the ejaculatory ducts, has been found by M. Lallemand very serviceable in such cases, but it should not be done till other hygienic means have failed; and, as M. Lallemand expressly cautions us, it should not be applied more than twice in the same case, as this will shew the benefit it is capable of doing.   But it is an infinite pity, that the disease should be allowed in any case to proceed so far unchecked; for, if they only knew their duty, few would be so foolish or unrestrained as to risk all their hopes in life in the headlong pursuit of one sensual enjoyment.

EVILS OF ABUSE.

I COME now to consider one of the most serious and frequent causes of disease in youth; one which ruins more constitutions than enters into the conception of the uninstructed. Any one who reads M. Lallemand's work will see, that by far the majority of the worst cases of seminal weakness are owing to this cause. Its evil effects are confined to no one class, but are found in all ranks of society; and there are few rocks, on which the health of more individuals is wrecked. The unfortunate habit of solitary indulgence or masturbation, is frequently contracted at schools or elsewhere, and often adopted more out of sport or ignorance of the consequences it may lead to, than from any more serious purpose. However, the habit grows on the young man, and if he be not diverted from it, may gradually master his powers of mind and become almost irresistible. Some of the cases given by M. Lallemand show the surprising extent to which this practice may be carried; some of his patients owned, that they had been in the habit of exciting seminal emissions from ten to twenty times daily, and this during a long period of time. In others, a far more moderate indulgence soon brought on the worst results; for in this, as in the case of venereal excesses, different constitutions will be very differently effected. Hence, of those who acquire the habit, some may escape with little injury, while others may bring on the most intractable seminal disease, which will prostrate their powers. Those who are most likely to suffer, are young men of a shy and retiring disposition, whose bashfulness prevents them from stepping across the gulph, which in this country separates the sexes. Others of a more forward character, though they may for a while indulge in the practice (which, were the truth known, probably few men have not done more or less) yet soon relinquish it, for the more natural and infinitely more desirable sexual intercourse, and thus any injury they may have done themselves is soon corrected.

But in the case of the shy or studious youth, or the sensualist, who is too absorbed in the pursuit of his new pleasure to think of any other consideration, the habit, once formed, has a great tendency to increase. The more it is indulged, the weaker does the will become, and the more perverted the imagination; the shyness increases to a morbid degree, and indeed this great irresolution and timidity is one of the most marked signs of the existence of the practice. After it has been continued for a length of time, proportioned to the frequency of its repetition, and the strength of the individual, the powers of the constitution begin gradually, or sometimes suddenly, to break down. All the symptoms of exhaustion and debility, which have already been described, as consequent on seminal weakness, appear. Nocturnal, and in the further progress of the complaint, diurnal involuntary seminal losses take place. The countenance often becomes pale and wan, the sight weak, the frame emaciated, and the whole nervous system much enfeebled. Incapacity for study or any mental exertion, gradually comes on, and may proceed in extreme cases to such an extent as to border on idiocy. M. Lallemand gives several cases, where idiocy or insanity was produced by the long continued practice of this habit. The moral effects are as striking as the physical. Morbid shyness and timidity, especially in female society, is one of the most frequent effects, and is much more marked in these cases than in weakness resulting from abstinence or excess. The patient looks like one conscious of some secret shame. Poor fellow! this very dread, so uncalled for, of the judgment of the rest of us fallible mortals, is one of the chief obstacles to his emerging from the slough of despond. There are of course many also of bolder disposition, in whom this shyness is not so marked.

All these symptoms are connected with, and dependent on, the enfeeblement of the genital organs from *abuse*, and the consequent involuntary discharges of the seminal fluid. This is probably the first thing to excite the youth's attention and alarm, at the consequences of his acts. Awakened from his sickly joys by the frequent occurrence of nightly pollutions, (which I shall describe more fully under the head of spermatorrhœa), he is horror-struck at finding himself entangled in the net of disease. His imagination heightens tenfold his real danger; and when he finds that his strength daily decreases under this fatal drain, and that nothing he can do will arrest it, he at length resorts to medical advice, overcome by shame at his confession, which he thinks will sound dreadful to the medical ear. Did he but know how little the physician, who has seen the worst that disease and rashness can do, thinks of judging either his boyish folly or his complaint too seriously. Lucky is he if his tale come to the kindly ear of a benevolent and skilful man, whose object will be to bind up the wounds of his bleeding conscience, and cure his malady, and not to the advertising and generally ignorant empiric, who builds his fortunes on the sufferings of his fellow-beings.

It is a disgrace to medicine and mankind, that so important a class of diseases, as those of the genital organs, have become the trade and speculation of unscientific men, because forsooth they are looked upon unfavourably by society, and even by some of our own profession. Until this class of diseases receive due respect from all, and till no greater blame attach to them, than to any other violation of natural laws and consequent disease, so long shall we be disgusted by the degrading advertisements of "silent friends," "cures for certain diseases," &c., in reading which one's breast glows with indignation and sorrow, or, if he be a sufferer from these miserable diseases, sinks to the dust in humiliation. The very existence of these degrading advertisements shows the erroneous mode in which the sexual organs and their diseases are regarded; and it is not the empiric on whom the real blame for them should rest, but the spurious delicacy which makes a mystery of all these subjects, and thus inevitably consigns them to the destructive and mercenary treatment of this body of men. Is not the misery entailed by these complaints desolating enough, without the consciousness of the reproaches or contempt of our fellows, instead of their heart-felt pity? What generous mind does not feel the beauty of M. Lallemand's remark, "Instead of blaming these unfortunates, ought we not rather to pity. and still more to relieve them?" Let us go yet a step further in the path of the true physician, acknowledging it as our principle, ever to reverence and love every human being, totally irrespective of his actions; and in all cases not to seek to hate or reproach, far less to despise any, but rather to love and benefit them to the utmost of our power. There is no subject in which these beautiful principles of the true physician are so lost sight of by the world, as in all sexual matters; whoever offends against any law of the prevailing moral code, however little grounded on truth, or however much his errors may have been owing, as in this matter of self-pollution, to the unnatural strictness of the code itself, is visited by a shower of contempt, hatred, and all evil passions: whenever any one ventures to dispute the moral code, society treats him worse than a dog; in short there is perhaps no subject at present, the very mention of which rouses such a host of prejudices, and so completely deprives a man of his usual moderation and common sense, as the sexual one.

But such a state of things has lasted too long and cannot continue; too many of us have deeply suffered, and keenly feel the degradation caused to mankind by so scandalous a treatment of a subject so near to its deepest interests; and it would be desirable that those who entertain truer and more rational views on sexual matters, should energetically strive to introduce a better and happier state of things than now exists. Times have changed since the so-called animal passions endangered by their excesses the other parts of·man's nature, when the sympathies and exertions of the physicians of mankind were enlisted on the side of the latter; at the present day, it is our sensual part which is unduly repressed, and thus must philanthrophy change its aspect. It is amazing, how little general philanthropy has yet done for these sexual diseases, or indeed for any disease; and yet what spectacle is more deplorable, than the noble spirit of man wallowing in the gulph of misery, into which these and the numberless other fleshly ills plunge him! He who has known the depths of physical impotence or agony, feels how slight in comparison seems to him all purely mental suffering. I would not enlarge so much on these things, were it not in this essay, my earnest purpose as much to prevent disease, as to describe its nature and cure. And how shall disease be ·prevented, unless all of us become keenly alive to its infinite evil and misery, and learn to sympathise as profoundly in physical as in moral suffering?

Nothing has done more harm to medicine and to humanity, than the low and grovelling ideas attached most irreverently to some parts of the hu-

man body, and especially to the organs of which I am treating, and the
excretory organs. Unhappy mortals, it pleases us to make a jest or a
mystery of these parts of our frame and their necessities. We would be
purely spiritual and soar above these bodily indecencies, and strive if we
can to forget them. But they will not be forgotten, and all our folly returns on our own heads. If we do not reverence and study them, and
their laws, exactly as much as any other parts, our sufferings will surely
teach us our neglect. The one great remedy for this, is to make anatomy
and physiology as well known to all men and women, as any other
branch of necessary knowledge. Then will the mystery, shame, and disgust, disappear before the most perfect, and in all its parts equally beautiful,
type of material organisation; and the mind, ever degraded by mystery
and ignorance, lose its morbid feelings in the clear light of truth. Without the hope that these changes will ere long be effected, how could we
behold, without a feeling of despair, victim after victim perishing of the
same disease, through ignorance of its nature and cause?

The disease before us—namely, self-pollution, is one of the most fatal
examples of this ignorance. Who is there to warn the youth against this
habit, and to instruct him in the laws of his sexual nature? Society
stands aloof with the air of offended purity; the subject is an interdicted
one, even to family confidence; the youth is thus left to his own devices
in utter ignorance of the way to guide this new power, which, at that
time of life, sways, and was meant to sway the whole being, more absolutely
than almost any other feeling; and thus are thousands ruined without a hand being stretched out to save them.

The true and only preventive means for this most ruinous habit, is to
instruct youth in the laws of the genital organs, and to alter the strictness of the moral code; of which subject I shall speak more fully hereafter.
As long as the present rigorous sexual code continues, so long will the
whole of our youth of both sexes be liable to this disease, along with the
other genital and venereal complaints. Masturbation is practised only
because the natural sexual intercourse cannot be attained, or because
its attainment is difficult and dangerous. Were it readily attainable
without the danger of disease and the degradation of illicit intercourse,
masturbation would rarely if ever be resorted to, and one of the most
fearful and prevalent causes of disease, moral and physical, eradicated.

I now come to speak of the treatment of the evils arising from masturbation. It is in vain to seek to cure such a patient, when once seminal weakness has been established, without natural sexual exercise. In
this disease it is doubly requisite, not only to give a healthy exercise to
the enfeebled parts, but to prevent a morbid one; and we may be assured
that even in the most favourable cases, where the patient's will is still
powerful, and the beauty of his character but little obscured, he will not
long be able to resist entirely, but unless a natural outlet be given for his
passions, he will sooner or later recur in some degree to his former habits.
It is not enough that he be informed of the true physiological remedy
but the necessity and natural duty of it should be impressed upon him
as he will otherwise most frequently be deterred from using it, either

by bashfulness, irresolution, or fear of contracting disease. There are some physicians, who, convinced by M. Lallemand's eloquent demonstration of the necessity of this remedy in such a complaint, mention it indeed to the patient, but in so careless and unimpressive a way (as if they were ashamed of their advice, or made a jest of the matter,) that the patient never adopts it; and indeed it is evident, that in the existing sexual circumstances of our society, there must always exist considerable obstacles to its adoption.

If there be much seminal weakness present, sexual intercourse should at first be moderate, according to the universal law for the exercise of weakened organs; but afterwards, with progressing health, its frequency may be increased. In this way, attending meanwhile to the general health, by exercise, bathing &c., the symptoms of debility will gradually disappear. The gloomy hypochondria and mental confusion will rise, like mist, from the brain; the sexual appetites and erections will become more powerful; the involuntary seminal discharges cease; the patient will regain his health, spirits, and self-confidence; his perverted imagination will be corrected, and he will again begin to take pleasure in the beautiful world, and in the society of mankind. There is no more interesting mental phenomenon, than this gradual and steady progress from the depth of gloom, to the healthy light of day, under means so simple and natural. The cure, if the disease have gone far, may be slow, and almost imperceptible in its gradations, and from two or three months, to a year, may be required. It is not to be expected in some cases, when the constitution has suffered severely, that a restoration to health, as perfect as before, will be obtained; but whatever dregs of nervous weakness may remain, the patient will still be inexpressibly thankful for the blessed change.

There are many adjuncts to the treatment of this complaint; such as in some very bad cases, cauterization of the urethra, the occasional passage of a bougie to strengthen the canal, and other matters connected with diet and regimen; but these I shall describe more fully under the head of spermatorrhœa, and they are all subsidiary to the main part of the treatment, sexual intercourse, to which they should be merely preparations or accessories. I shall end the description of this disease with a case which occurred under my own observation, and which is full of instruction on many points.

A young man about fifteen years of age, of active, studious, and erotic disposition, but of almost feminine bashfulness, as is so often the case in this country, discovered by chance the practice of self-indulgence. Delighted with this easy mode of satisfying his passions, which had for a long time been the source of unrest and torment to his vivid imagination, he indulged in it, being in the habit of exciting two or three discharges daily, for the space of about a year. During this time he was studying at college, and with distinguished success. At the end of the year he began to feel his health declining; he grew rather weak, his bowels became constipated, and involuntary discharges of semen began to appear in the night, during sleep. His excited imagination and ignorance of bodily disease at once filled him with terror at these symptoms. He read an article on Onanism in the Encyclopædia, written by some anti-quated horror-monger, and of course applied all the extreme effects of this disease to his own case. He, the favourite of fortune, loved and admired by all, the centre of so much hope and promise, to be threatened with an abyss of wretchedness and degradation, where it seemed as if all the world had a right to revile and despise him! Poor fellow, that glance let him far down into the depths of human woe!

He was not so careless or ignorant, notwithstanding all his shame, as to let himself waste away, under this seminal drain, which none of his own endeavours had the least effect in checking, without seeking advice; so he consulted, with tears of fear and shame, a medical friend, who quieted him by telling him his complaint was a common one, trifling, and easily curable; and in fact by applying some counter-irritant oint-ment, and a course of tonic medicines, he did succeed in stopping the discharges.

How different would his future fate have been, had the true physio-logical remedy of sexual intercourse been at that time applied! Then would the matter have indeed been a trifle and rapidly cured. But the physician merely prescribed for the effect, without seeking to remove the cause; for in such a case to abstain from self-indulgence, even if this can be effected, is not to remove the cause; but the organs weakened by abstinence from normal sexual intercourse, injured by abuse, and still more exhausted by the involuntary discharges, require to be gradu-ally restored to vigour by regulated sexual exercise.

In this case, the patient was so much terrified by his first warning, and had besides so much firmness of moral character, that he at once gave up the practice of self-pollution. For about a year and a half, he re-mained in pretty good health, except that he was often troubled by con-stipation, a very frequent symptom in seminal disease. At the end of this period, while still at college, he began to perceive his health again declining, but this time the symptoms were different. He became sen-sible of a growing confusion of mind and inability to fix his attention on his studies. Having completely abandoned the practice of masturbation, and there being no appearance of seminal discharges, (which had probab-ly however been going on in the insidious form of diurnal ones, which will be described hereafter) he could not discover the reason of this; but his medical friend, a man of first rate eminence, told him it was a determi-nation of blood to the head, that he should cut his hair close, sponge, exercise &c. However the cause of his symptoms was soon indicated. Involuntary seminal discharges soon began to appear in the night, and inspired the unfortunate youth with all his former horror. Though it was close upon the end of the session, and high honours awaited him, he threw up all without the least hesitation, and devoted his whole energies to the cure of his complaint. He applied to the same physician, who had by this time heard of Lallemand's great work, and, without reading it, which would have shown him, how erroneous was the practice he adopted, at once applied cauterization to the internal surface of the urethra. This is a measure, which is advisable only in cases of extreme weakness, where there is no prospect of checking the destructive discharges by milder means. But in this case, the weakness was not excessive, the discharges were seldom more than four or five in the week, (although they were probably accompanied by diurnal unconscious ones, which neither patient nor physician were aware of,) and the result of abstinence from sexual intercourse, doubly injurious to the previously weakened organs. A due sexual intercourse would here, beyond all doubt, have soon given new strength to the organs, and health to the patient; and restored to the light of day, and to his sorrowing friends, a valuable life. But it was not yet to be so, and a deeper lesson of sorrow was to be engraven on the inmost heart of the youth.

The cauterization caused some pain and a retention of urine, for which, after trying baths &c., it was necessary to pass a catheter. The operation was repeated after a short interval, and this had the effect of stopping the nocturnal discharges, and relieving the patient for a while. Then he tried a long pedestrian tour, during the whole of which his health was pretty good. But as soon as he came home, his remorseless persecutor reappeared. The nocturnal discharges began, again and with them his former grievances. The constipation became obstinate, and, as he had the kind of superstitious fear, so common in this country, of having his bowels unopened, even for a single day, he used a warm-water clyster daily, for nearly a year. He applied again to the doctor, who, with persistent ignorance, continued to apply from time to time the severe and totally unphilosophical remedy of cauterization, which always produced a temporary, but never a permanent relief. Within the space of a year he cauterized the urethra seven or eight times, a practice highly and expressly reprobated by M. Lallemand.

The poor young man was, during all this time, in the depths of wretchedness and degradation. He tried every kind of exercise, on horse and foot, in athletic sports and games, but nothing could give him any essential relief. At last the nocturnal emissions became rare, and gradually ceased entirely; but instead of improving, he grew worse. This delusive occurrence is generally found in such cases, and is especially noticed by M. Lallemand.

He says that his patients often told him, that they had been worse, since the cessation of the nocturnal discharges. In such cases they cease from the increased weakness of the organs, which now pour out the seminal fluid by day, when the patient goes to stool or makes water, without any pleasurable sensation, or at most a slight titillation. When diurnal pollutions are fairly established, the disease has proceeded far.

All his studies were now neglected, and his energetic spirit consumed itself in the gloomiest hypochondria. He resolved again to try travel, and he found that by this means, and perfect abstinence from study, he could keep his disease in check, though his confusion of head remained the same. By these hygienic means, invaluable in the treatment especially of chronic disease, his muscular developement remained good, and in outward appearance he seemed in vigorous health; a fact often observed by M. Lallemand, in patients, whose nervous system was shattered by the disease in the worst manner, and who might even be reduced to the verge of idiocy.

He now settled for a couple of years on the continent, and from the change of scene and of associations, his spirits began to rise a little, and the unhappy one ventured to fall in timid love. But his day dream was soon ended. Unable long to abstain from study, he began to learn a foreign language, and after applying to it cautiously for less than two months, his health, unable to bear this slight burden, broke down worse than ever. His sleep became dreadfully disturbed, so that he feared to go to bed. After sleeping for a couple of hours, he would wake from some frightful dream, with a crushing oppression in his head and stomach, so that he could scarcely turn on the pillow. After lying in a heavy lethargy for a short time, as if his whole body and especially his brain, were turned into lead, he would again sink to sleep, to awake again after a short interval with the same exhausted feelings aggravated; and thus would the weary night go by, leaving him in the morning so prostrated that he could hardly rise. A few nocturnal discharges appeared at this time, but soon ceased. He became perfectly incapable of reading, which had never before been the case. On attempting to read even one page of a light book, he felt a crushing sensation in his head, and his stomach began to work and ferment as he called it, and if he persisted, this soon grew so oppressive, as to force him to stop.

He sank at once into the greatest despair and disgust at life, and also at the object of his love. He girt up his loins for travel, which he found to be the only thing that kept his foe at bay, and walked in solitary moodiness for a couple of months, over a distance of about eight-hundred miles. This gave him a little relief, and on his return home, his nights were not quite so bad; but still he lived in a sort of lethargy, unable to open a book, and spent most of his day lying on a bench in the open air, weighed down by a stupor which he dare not indulge by going to sleep; else, as he expressed it, he thought he could have slept on for months, as he always felt more exhausted and lethargic on wakening, than on going to sleep. If he had an emission in the night, the next day would be one of double gloom.

In this manner, with a life in the open air, and total abstinence from books, he gradually slept away some of the worst symptoms. His nights became pretty good, and his spirits and intellect began to recover a little, though the total inability to read still continued. Like the flower that ever anew opens itself to the sun, as soon as the bitterness of the wind has abated, his mind at every intermission from its sufferings, struggled to unfold itself to the warmth of love and hope.

The fermentation of self-conciousness now began in his mind, as it does whenever we have time and peace to reflect, and analyze ourselves and our position. His views began to widen, and his hopes to revive partly under the influence of a new attachment he had formed; and, as he became enthusiastic under the conciousness of increasing knowledge of life and the dear-bought lessons of experience, his ardent mind turned him towards the busy world in the hope of being able to do some good to others even with his impotent brain. But as soon as he began to direct his mind to any pursuit, he perceived the helplessness of his state. He could not dream of entering into any profession which required study, and for any other he had at the time no inclination. Thus after several struggling months, he sunk into a still deeper gloom, than any he had yet experienced; he blamed himself for not having the courage to finish his miserable life by suicide; his mind became half-addled by its physical weakness, and by the wear and tear of his passions, so that he seemed to himself ever on the verge of madness, and probably, had his constitution not been naturally a very tough and strong one, he might have become so; unable to rest anywhere, he tried several physicians, and systems of cure. Homoeopathy, to which he gave a short trial, had no effect, and the water cure, with all its immense curative powers in chronic disease, afforded but little benefit. He stayed at a hydropathic establishment for two months, and gained considerably in muscular strength and weight, but the cerebral impotence continued as before.

He now got hold of Lallemand's work, which he contrived with difficulty to peruse, and gained from it the knowledge of the true sexual remedy for his case. However, this only added to his wretchedness, for there ensued a struggle between his knowledge of the means of cure, and his morbid bashfulness, in which the latter ever prevailed.

He went over to Paris for the purpose of consulting M. Lallemand, who told him that by employing the physiological means, namely, sexual intercourse, he would certainly recover. However his insuperable bashfulness, and powerless will, made it impossible for him to follow this advice, though convinced of its necessity. He returned to this country, and another year passed by in the same impotent and hypochondriacal state; his mind tortured by a divided and paralysed will, and restlessness and irritability making him a burden to himself, and a sorrow and mystery to his friends. He was then advised to try change of climate by some of the English physicians, (not one of whom, though acquainted with his past history, knew, or would recommend, what was necessary in his case,) and he set off for a long tour in the south of Europe. On his way however, he passed through Paris, and again consulted M. Lallemand, who was surprised that his previous advice had not been followed.

M. Lallemand, as he always does, demanded a written account of his case, and having read it, said, that all that he should advise, was, duly regulated sexual intercourse, and washing the genital organs every morning with cold water. By such means, health would gradually be restored, though it would probably require about six months to complete the cure. This time, these necessary means were at length adopted. Coition was at first permitted only once a week, and nothing that could have an exciting effect on the organs, such as being in female society, which called forth the venereal desires, taking spiced dishes &c., was allowed in the interim. A bougie was also introduced to strengthen and tonify the organ, when it was found, that there was a stricture of the urethra, produced by the previous cauterization. Dilatation of this, became of course a prominent part of the treatment; for stricture is itself one of the most dangerous causes of seminal losses, and had doubtless in this case greatly aggravated the disease; and in two months the patient began to feel a slight improvement in his symptoms, and to entertain new hopes. However, he now contracted a gonorrhœa to his excessive chagrin. In the course of it he had bubo, and swelled testicle, the pain and tedium of which, besides the complete arrest of his treatment, brought him of course back to his former despair; for in a long chronic disease, after years of hopelessness and constant relapses and disappointments, far slighter evils are sufficient to prostrate the patient's fortitude.

The gonorrhœa lasted for six miserable months, in spite of all sorts of treatment, but was at last cured. After its stoppage, the treatment of the stricture, and the regular sexual intercourse, both of which had been of course entirely arrested, were renewed; and the stricture being by a treatment of two months, sufficiently dilated, health began gradually to return. He began almost imperceptibly, to recover the power of reading, and his nervous tone, physical and moral. Gradually, the gloom, which had so long brooded over his mind, was dispelled, and after about seven years of as great misery and impotence, as often falls to the lot of youth to endure, he began again to waken to life. Since then, his convalesence has progressed steadily, under the constant use of the natural means of health, and he has been able to enter on a profession, and to study with energy and vigour, though his mind has by no means its first elasticity, which could not be expected, after such long illness.

However, though his health will probably ever remain somewhat delicate, compared with those whose constitutions have not received such rude shocks, and though a strictly hygienic life is more evidently necessary for him, than for the more robust, yet has he cause for inexpressible thankfulness for the blessed change in his state, and to the hand that saved him.

In reading the above history, which gives so imperfect a sketch of the years of real suffering, that clouded the brightest days of a young and ardent spirit of no ordinary energies, let us regard it, not as a mere individual case, but as a type of a whole class, and involving most of the moral questions on sexual subjects, whose true solution is of such immense importance. Who was the true and good physician, the saviour of this youth? It was he, who, undisturbed in his clear perception of natural truth and duty by world-wide prejudices, could give him the invaluable results of his years of patient enquiry on the subject, and thus with the certainty of demonstration enable him to escape from his abyss of misery to the world of hope and joy. The ignorant physicians on the contrary, were they, who, influenced by the common moral prejudices on these matters, left the door to his recovery for ever barred against him; and, had there not been truer views, and a braver and more scientific man to apply them, would have permitted the unhappy sufferer to drag on his miserable life, and probably in a few years to have sunk into idiocy or hopeless hypochondria, a horror to himself and a cause of the deepest affliction to his friends and relatives. These things are true, and no fiction, and the world must before long admit them. The subject of love cannot, more than others, bear the supernatural mode of reasoning. In it, as in all others the world is escaping at the present day, from the

assumptions and dogmas of the supernatural, to the clear and demonstrable region of nature ; and it is only by examining every individual
case, as it occurs in nature, that we shall attain to true views on the
subject.

Would that all mankind could learn to consider of infinite importance
the fate of every single individual ! We do not live, joy, and suffer, for
ourselves alone, but every one of us is a type of the whole of humanity,
and if we could understand all the wants and requirements of his being,
we would understand those of all mankind. We are too ready to sacrifice the interests of the individual, for what is falsely called the general
good. No good can be general, which does not include the good of every
being in the universe. The real interests of each individual will invariably be found, if we search deeply and patiently enough, to be inseparably bound up with those of all mankind.

The true physician cannot bear the very name of sacrifice. If we begin
by sacrificing the interests of any individual, which of us is safe? Are
we not all individuals, and essentially implicated in every question
which involves the rights or duties of any human being? Every single
case of disease is of infinite importance to one individual, namely, to the
sufferer, but of no less real importance to us, as also individuals, liable
ourselves, or our children, and friends, to the same evils ; and world-wide
theories must fall, if they unrighteously stand in the way of his cure.

SPERMATORRHŒA

OR,

INVOLUNTARY SEMINAL DISCHARGES.

HAVING now treated of some of the chief causes of this disease, I shall proceed to give a fuller description of its nature and symptoms. Until the researches of M. Lallemand, although recognised, it was very little understood, having been involved previously in the mystery and ignorance which brooded over all sexual subjects, and which even to a greater degree obscured the diseases of the female genital organs, as we shall see hereafter. It was whilst observing diseases of the brain, that M. Lallemand was first led to suspect, and examine into, the effects of seminal disease on the male system. Having once got hold of the clue, he followed it with the most admirable steadiness and sagacity, and after twenty years labour, he laid bare to the world, in his work on "involuntary seminal discharges," published only some few years ago, a host of the most important and original facts, exemplified by the histories of cases written by the patients themselves; which throws over the whole work the sad and living interest that subjective descriptions alone can give. His discoveries are in their originality and importance comparable with those of any other medical benefactor of his race, but are yet comparatively little known, or at least openly admitted and approved by our profession in this country; for this chief reason, that, shaking as they do the very foundations of the theoretical morality between the sexes, they are opposed by a host of prejudices.

Unhappy is it at all times when we have to do with supernatural prejudices, the most difficult of all to overcome; trebly unhappy is it, when they stand between a miserable sufferer and his rescue from what is almost worse than death. Had they, who would rigorously enforce abstinence or chastity, on him who is wasting from the surface of the earth from its effects, but a glimpse into his real hell of misery, they would pause, and at any rate wipe their hands of so dangerous and responsible a matter, as interfering with those who can and will rescue him. Men will not now-a-days submit to be made *auto-da-fes* of, for the edification of their zealous neighbours.

The venereal and genital complaints would be the most painful of all, were it only for the painful feelings which they almost invariably rouse 'n the breasts of those, who have suffered much from them. While in other complaints, the public sympathy is at least with the sufferers, and all efforts that love and skill can devise, are made for their relief, in these diseases, and these only, quite the reverse is the case. So far from pitying and relieving, the public do all they can, however little they know what they are doing, and how sinful their feelings are, further to degrade and desolate the unfortunate sufferer, and throw every obstacle in the way of his recovery. Therefore, there is no class of diseases, which is characterised by such irritability and bitterness of feeling in the abused victims, none which so spoils the moral character, however noble it may be. Oh! that we may yet live to see these most ruinous and unhappy feelings disappear from the human breast; that the sexual diseases, perhaps the most important and widely spread of all at present, may be, like the rest, included in the true brotherly love and sympathy of all of us; and that every thing may be done to promote their cure, and to banish them, as far as possible from the world, which they have too long desolated!

By spermatorrhœa, or involuntary seminal discharges, is meant the loss of seminal fluid without the will of the patient, which, when it occurs frequently, constitutes, as we have seen, a most dreadful disease. These discharges may be divided into the nocturnal and the diurnal. In the *nocturnal* ones, the patient has generally a dream on some venereal subject, an erection of the penis, and a discharge of semen, and wakes just as the discharge is taking place. This form of the nocturnal emissions, which may occur in the strongest men, and is generally attendant on the period of puberty, is the least injurious, as it contains all the elements of the venereal orgasm except that, Ixion-like, the dreamer embraces a cloud.

Many persons, who live a life of abstinence, have such emissions, at shorter or longer intervals, for years, and yet remain tolerably strong and vigorous. However, they are always suspicious, and prove, even when they do not reduce the strength, that the genital organs are ready for, and in want of due exercise, just like the feeling of muscular irritability which we have when we take no exercise. All such warnings, if long disregarded, are apt to be followed by enfeeblement and disease. When this does take place, the emissions increase in frequency, and the patient begins to feel his health declining. The emissions may now take place nightly, or even three or four times in the night in bad cases, and this soon brings on a state of great exhaustion. The proportion in which nocturnal emissions weaken the strength in any one, must determine how far they constitute a disease. Sometimes, when few, they are of little consequence; at other times, if frequent, they bring on the greatest prostration and melancholy.

As the disease progresses, discharges take place without a venereal dream or erection. The patient wakes suddenly from a stupor, just as the discharge is pouring out, which he will try in vain to check; or, perhaps, he does not wake till after it is over, and then, as a lethargic consciousness, which of itself tells him what has taken place, slowly awakens, he puts down his hand and sickens with despair, as he perceives the fatal drain, and thinks on the gloomy morrow, which will follow

As the disease advances still further, the organs lose their natural powers of pouring forth a large quantity involuntarily at one time. The

semen becomes thinner, and deteriorated in quality; and as fast as it
forms, it drains off, whenever any exertion is made; as at stool, in going
into a cold bath, in making water, or even in thinking on a venereal subject. These constitute the *diurnal* involuntary discharges, which are
always a sign of a worse form of the disease, and greater weakness.

When the patient goes to stool, he will observe, that after he has expelled the contents of his bladder, a few drops of a thick viscid whitish-
looking fluid, like the mucus from the nose, follows, and if he has to use
much exertion, as for instance, to overcome constipation, more of this
will appear, with a sensation of slight venereal titillation; and, at last,
though rarely, even an erection and a full discharge may be produced;
the semen may also, though more rarely, appear before the stream of
urine. If this fluid be examined, under a microscope, it will be found to
be semen from the presence of the spermotazooids. In the urine, if semen be discharged also in making water, it floats about like a cloud, and
can be recognised by the same test. This mode of recognising the disease
by the microscope is a very valuable one, and reveals frequently the cause
of the most obscure symptoms. It is to be observed, that a cloud is very
often present in urine, which contains no semen.

When spermatorrhœa has existed long, the semen sometimes becomes
much deteriorated in quality, so as to be incapable of serving for impregnation. The spermatozooids in these cases are sometimes scarcely
to be recognised, and do not appear to have their normal developement.

As soon as the nocturnal emissions have become so numerous, that
the patient's constitution cannot support the drain, the powers begin to
break down. The one prevailing feature in all the symptoms caused by
seminal losses, is *weakening of the nervous system.* There is perhaps, no
chronic disease, not having its seat in the brain itself, in which this part
becomes so enfeebled. The signs of nervous exhaustion are at first slight
a feeling of weakness on rising in the morning, especially after a nocturnal emission, and still more after two or three in the same night; a
sort of mistiness or haze in the thoughts, and dimness in the sight, while
the eye loses its lustre; enfeeblement of muscular power, with irritability
of its fibre, often shown by palpitation of the heart, (so constant an attendant on nervous exhaustion,) which has caused in many cases,
groundless fear of organic heart disease; indigestion and constipation,
from insufficient nervous tone; and wasting of the frame more or less.
In different patients, different parts are chiefly affected. Thus one (who
has probably not studied hard, and in whom the brain is not the vul-
nerable part,) will not complain so much of his head, but rather of indigestion, emaciation, and muscular debility; whilst others retain the
appearance of blooming health, whose mind may be greatly enfeebled.

However on the whole, there is a great and striking similarity in the
symptoms of all affected with the disease; which will enable him who has
well studied, readily to recognise it, and will afford to every intelligent
patient, in the interesting histories contained in M. Lallemand's work,
a transcript of his own sensations.

As the disease advances, all the symptoms become aggravated. The patient gradually and slowly sinks into the greatest emaciation and weakness, if unrelieved ; he becomes impotent, *i. e.* cannot have sexual connection, for the weakened brain can no longer call up an erection in the no less weakened genital organs ; or if sexual connection be effected, the emission comes almost immediately, and with little enjoyment. Along with this, there is often at one time a disgust at, and at another a morbid bashfulness in the presence of women. The mind may be variously affected, according to his disposition ; he may become savage and repulsive, so as to avoid the society of his friends, and feel hatred and disgust at mankind or gloomily despairing, hypochondriacal, and timid ; the intellect gradually loses its clearness and elasticity, and ceases to obey the powerless will, which may seek in vain to bend it to attentive thought, and this may proceed even to insanity or idiocy, in the worst cases ; but though these extreme results have taken place, let us hope that, as the disease and its cure become better known, it will rarely again be allowed to proceed so far. For it is one which advances slowly, so that many years would be required in general to bring a man to this state ; and its treatment, if judicious, is in most cases very effective ; unlike many other, far more intractable, though not so miserable, diseases.

It is one of the most grievous diseases of humanity, but one in which an immensity might be done, *which is not done,* for its prevention and cure. Would we could say as much for all diseases ! When we think of cancer, organic heart disease, &c., of the first of which the causes are almost unknown, while we often see the second produced in a day under our eye in rheumatic fever, to cause years of insupportable anguish—states hard of prevention and incapable of cure—how does the thought of all the miseries that poor humanity is exposed to, awake our pity ! Give us but a glimpse into the nature and cause of a disease, and shall we not move heaven and earth to prevent it !

Spermatorrhœa is not likely to cause structural disease in the chief vital organs, contrary to what has been thought. Many a patient and physician have been deceived in believing that the functional diseases of the head, heart, stomach, &c., produced by seminal weakness, proceeded from an organic affection of these parts themselves. Many have consulted M. Lallemand, believing themselves to be labouring under such diseases, or consumptive, in whom the emaciation and weakness proceeded from the far more manageable spermatorrhœa. In particular, very many of that class, to whom the name of hypochondriacs has been given, as an excuse for our ignorance of their malady, and its cure, have been discovered to be affected with this disease, in which hypochondria, or a gloomy state of mind, is perhaps the most constant symptom.

In male animals, such as the bull, dog, &c., in whom this disease has been observed, the very same effects, moral and physical, have been found, as in man. The animal became solitary, gloomy, and unwilling to be disturbed ; retired from his fellows, and gradually grew weak, emaciated, and at last sank exhausted.

As for the termination of the disease ; if left to itself, it has a constant tendency to increase. The patient may after years of suffering, sink into the lowest stage of weakness, and die. M. Lallemand describes some cases, in which death was caused by a kind of apoplexy, characteristic of this disease, and induced by the exhausted state of the brain. The disease has in many cases preceeded to insanity, and idiocy; in one case, which was cured by treatment, the patient had lost the knowledge of his friends, and the power of speech. From this extreme, there are of course infinite gradations, up to perfect soundness of intellect. M. Lallemand makes many observations, full of interest, on some of the distinguished men of past times, whom he suspects to have been affected by this disease; and as far as we can judge of them by their own description of their symptoms, his suspicions seem well founded. From the description of his ill-health which Rousseau gives in his confessions, and of the sufferings, which brought on his death, having previously reduced him to a state almost of madness, Lallemand judges him to have laboured under spermatorrhœa, which produced many of the extraordinary moral and intellectual effects, depicted by that unfortunate man with such matchless vividness. To the eye of Lord Brougham, Rousseau is a man of rare, but narrow genius, full of vice and crime; while, to the penetrating gaze of the truer philosopher, he is a sad, and infinitely instructive instance of a most noble mind, struggling under the inevitable ruin of a secret bodily disease. I do trust, that this will be the last century, when any one will believe himself qualified to judge of man, a physico-psychical being, while in utter ignorance of his material part, and its workings. Are the laws and diseases of the body a less important part in man's history, than every sophistical idea, proceeding from the countless theory-spinning brains, that have left their webs in the lumber-room of moral and metaphysical speculations?

Pascal, he also suspects to have had the disease, and probably so had Sir Isaac Newton, who is said to have lived a life of strict sexual abstinence, which produced before death a total atrophy of the testicles, showing the natural sin which had been committed. It is certain that his matchless intellect declined after middle age, and it is even said, I know not with what truth, that he almost lost his mind late in life. It is a disease, whose progress is greatly favoured by study; and as no human brain can withstand it, we may well believe that very many cases of premature mental decay have been owing to it. No man is safe from a greater or less degree of seminal weakness, who does not exercise his genital organs, or reproductive part, as duly as the brain, stomach, or any other organ.

The appearances found after death, in patients labouring under this disease, complete the chain of inductive reasoning. M. Lallemand found in many cases, the ejaculatory canals widened, and their orifices inflamed; the testicles generally much softer than natural, and some other signs showing the diseased state of the genital organs.

I have already described several of the principal causes of the disease, in speaking of the *disuse*, *overuse*, and *abuse* of the genital organs.

M. Lallemand met with several instances of the disease, among Roman Catholic priests, who rigidly adhered to their vows of celibacy, (ore of the most flagrant instances of the ignorance of, and disregard for, bodily laws); many among young men, who had brought it on by masturbation at school, and elsewhere; many among old debauchees, exhausted by excesses and venereal complaints. Other causes of it are found in anything which weakens or irritates the genital organs. Thus a very common and most important cause is a gonorrhœa, especially if it have lasted for a long time.

In this case, the inflammation gradually extends down the canal, till it reaches that portion where the ejaculatory ducts empty themselves, and thus often gives rise to most obstinate spermatorrhœa. A stricture in the urethra is also a very common cause. The urine arrested behind the obstruction, distends the canal, and enters into the ejaculatory ducts, which become widened, and thus may great seminal weakness be brought on. The debility and hypochondria, which often forms so marked a characteristic of strictured patients, is in most cases attributable to the loss of semen. Another cause—(which operated in one of the most interesting of M. Lallemand's cases, written by the patient himself, and giving the most graphic and affecting picture of his unaided fruitless struggles with his terrible foe,) is the existence of ascarides, a species of small worm, in the adjacent intestine. The constant irritation caused by their neighbourhood occasioned the discharges.

The immoderate use of tobacco, and of malt or spirituous liquors, has also a very weakening effect on the genitals, and predisposes to disease. They also aggravate the nervous symptoms in those affected with the disease, and should be entirely abstained from. When the nervous system loses its tone, from any debilitating cause, such as seminal weakness, it cannot bear the least irregularity. It is a distressing feature in the complaint, that the patient cannot indulge in any such sensual gratification, without injuring himself; slight irregularities, which would not be felt by one in health, cause dreadful jarring in his shattered nerves.

Other predisposing causes, which render a man more liable to the disease, and the disease itself, if once established, more difficult to cure, are, naturally weak and imperfect genital organs, which in some rare cases do not develope themselves at puberty, but continue through life in the rudimentary state; a long foreskin, or a congenital phymosis, (which consists in the inability to draw back the foreskin over the glans,) in which case, unless great attention be paid to cleanliness, the sebaceous matter collects round the base of the glans, becomes acrid, and causes irritation. In many of M. Lallemand's cases there was a long foreskin, large urethral orifice, flabby and soft testicles and scrotum, with a feeble growth of hair. Where the length of the prepuce favours irritation, he practises circumcision.

He gives also one or two cases, in which seminal discharges habitually took place backwards into the bladder, instead of forwards, and in which the patients sank gradually into the impotent and exhausted state. This was caused, by their having been in the practice of checking the discharge when about to come, by compressing the urethra, in order to prevent impregnation; a most dangerous habit. Anything at all abnormal in the venereal act, such as dallying with it too long, or any other effeminating practice is very weakening to the organs and the nervous system.

Let us not imagine that this disease is of rare occurrence ; the extreme effects are indeed not so common, perhaps, as those of some other diseases ; but from its peculiar nature, the ignorance of the laws of the genital organs among men and women, and the great difficulties which oppose the natural healthy exercise of the sexual organs, there are probably few men, who have not suffered more or less in their health, moral and physical, from sexual derangement.

Never do we see that ignorance and mystery do not lead to disease and misery ; and can we suppose, that so vitally important a subject as the human body generally, and the sexual organs, of which we are more particularly speaking, can remain unknown, and their laws unstudied, without the most grievous consequences ? One great reason, why men do not take a more vivid interest in, and do not more reverently study bodily laws, is that their rewards and punishments are hid from them : all insight into disease is confined to the physicians, and thus the valuable lesson is lost to the public. For we learn reverence and respect for laws, just in proportion as we are brought into close relation with them, and have the opportunity of seeing how their observance and neglect affect us, or our neighbours. Thus, until all men are called upon to witness, make themselves acquainted with, and pass judgment upon the various states of physical health and disease, no less than on the moral ones, they will never take a due interest in the study and observance of the physical laws.

With regard to the cure of spermatorrhœa, from what has already been said, it will be seen, that the great object is to bring the genital organs into such a state, that they shall be able to enjoy and profit by sufficient and normal exercise. To arrest the spermatorrhœa, and then leave the organs to be again enfeebled from disuse, is as profitless, as to cure a broken leg, and allow the patient to remain ever after on the sofa. The indications for treatment in every case of seminal weakness, are, as in all other diseases, first to remove the cause of the complaint, secondly, to remedy the effects, and thirdly, to restore the constitution as far as possible to its original strength, by enforcing attention to physiological laws, whose infringement has caused the disease. Thus, if on examination we find a stricture, it must be, it possible, dilated ; if ascarides, they must be dislodged. If the patient trace his ill health to a former gonorrhœa, the urethra should be explored by a bougie, and if the irritability be apparently caused by chronic imflammation of the mucous membrane over the ejaculatory ducts, M. Lallemand recommends the application of the armed bougie. This instrument, intended to cauterize the internal surface of the urethra, consists of a metallic bougie, through which a stilet is passed, containing at its end the caustic nitrate of silver, with which he slightly touches the tender part of the urethra, on which the irritability seems to depend. To this application, M. Lallemand, who was the first to introduce it, ascribes very great virtues in many intractable cases ; and it certainly possesses wonderful powers in checking spermatorrhœa. However it should be used only in bad cases, or in those arising from gonorrhœal imflammation, when sexual connection, and hygienic means are incompetent to check the discharges ; it should be applied very slightly, and in no case more than twice. We have seen above its rash application produce stricture, (not an uncommon occurrence), a disease often more difficult to cure than the spermatorrhœa itself. Dr. Dawson, a pupil of M. Lallemand, has introduced another application, which ne believes from long experience to possess many advantages over the nitrate of silver. He uses an ointment, composed of iodine and the chloride of zinc, which he applies directly to the surface of the prostate gland, by means of a bougie passed along the urethra. The advantages of this preparation are, that the application does not give the ·least pain, (while cauterization by the nitrate of silver is somewhat painful), and does not hinder the patient from going about as usual. It also produces a more satisfactory and lasting cure, by removing inflammation, and any swelling of the prostate gland, which may exist; and this swelling of the gland is, according to Dr. Dawson, very frequently present in bad spermatorrhœa.

With regard to the natural remedy of sexual intercourse, it is of great consequence that it be duly followed. We must remember that the organs are in a very feeble state, and hence that an immoderate exercise at first, might have an effect directly contrary to our desires. Hence coition should at first be very moderate; once a week, or so; and should be gradually increased with the waxing powers. The signs of its favorable action are, an increase of tone both of mind and body, improved appetite, spirits, and self-confidence. The patient should not be much in the company of women at other times, if they excite venereal desires, which are not to be gratified. He should live in the open air, take enough of exercise, but not too much, which might weaken him and cause a seminal discharge.

Medicines will be found generally not only of little use, but of positive injury. Here, as in so many other complaints, they are often used as an excuse for doing nothing, and tend to take off the attention of the patient and physician from the one grand and really efficient remedy. Purgative medicines are almost always ill-borne in this disease, but a clyster of warm or cold water should be used frequently, if there be constipation, which has a very bad effect in promoting the diurnal discharges, by the exertions it causes at stool.

Wine, beer, vinegar, &c., are also bad, and should be avoided, especially if there be a stricture, when they should never be indulged in. Very great care must be taken that the patient in the progress of the treatment do not contract a venereal disease. In him it is ten-fold to be dreaded, for it arrests his cure, greatly complicates his case, and is dreadfully disheartening to one who has suffered so long. This risk is often made an objection to the sexual mode of treatment, but it is one which does not call in question its scientific truth, but merely its practical advisability. Of course the patient should be most earnestly cautioned against this danger; and unless a reliable connection can be obtained by him, which is unfortunately too rarely the case, he should sedulously use the preventive means I shall speak of under the head of venereal diseases. Still, even though such a disease be contracted, it will not often stand much in the way of a scientific treatment, which will ultimately conduct the patient to health.

The introduction of an elastic bougie, once every week or fortnight, to give tone to the canal, is highly recommended by M. Lallemand ; and even when this is not employed, the passage should always in this disease be explored by a bougie, which gives hardly any pain, to ascertain whether there be stricture, or unusual tenderness at any part.

He also recommends mineral baths in many cases, and I should advise much more strenuously the water cure, (though of course only as an accessory to the sexual treatment,) as by far the most concentrated and systematic hygienic treatment hitherto introduced.   Were I to express, how much I admire and what results I hope for, from this immense addition to therapeutics, the praise might seem extravagant ; though not to those, who know the paramount importance of the physiological or natural conditions of health, so ably explained in the works of Dr. Andrew Combe, Liebig, and many others.

It may seem strange, that men well conversant with the natural laws of health, should not admit, how admirably in most respects the hydropathic system, when skilfully applied, carries out these principles ; being, as it were, the concentrated essence of the ordinary and natural means of health, upon which it is of such infinite importance that the minds of all of us, both in health and disease, should be fixed. How can those, who should know better, talk of this system, one of the greatest marks of the age's advancement, as in the same category with homoeopathy ; from which it differs utterly, except in the single respect that its claims have been too arrogantly and exclusively asserted, as is always the case with new doctrines, which have to establish a position for themselves in our esteem?   As for homoeopathy, it is quite different from our natural experiences of the influences, which produce health and disease ; and as such,—(although it should not, now-a-days that it has so large a body of followers, be treated with neglect, but rather patiently investigated, and disproved, if found false,) it lies far from the beliefs and conceptions of the most of us.   But the water cure is systematised common sense ; exercise for weak and lazy muscles, pure country air for pining lungs ; powerful, regular, and invigorating baths for skins, all their lives suffering from hydrophobia ; cold water and plain food, for blood pampered by wine, and spiced dishes ; may not these, which go to the very root of so many of the diseases of man, be expected to do more good in general, than courses of double-edged medicines, so often prescribed for effects, while the causes remain unremoved?   If any one read the works of some of our best physicians, as Holland, Forbes, Andrew Combe, and many others, he will see how much an essentially hydropathic treatment enters into the most scientific medicine of the day, and be prepared for the desirable adoption of some of the most valuable hydropathic remedies, such as the wet sheet, (a cold water bandage, extended to the whole body), the douche, and vapour bath ; and ultimately, (and at a period, it is to be hoped, not far distant,)—for the union and incorporation in one, of the two systems, without which hydropathy can exercise comparatively a slight influence on the health of society.   At present however, it is rather homoeopathy and hydropathy, from their both being classed and run down together, that seem inclined to make common cause.

To prevent this disease, like every other—a subject, whose vast importance is as yet only dimly conceived—we must seek to remove all the causes of it. Some of these consist in other diseases, as for instance, gonorrhœa, a most important cause, which by producing stricture or chronic inflammation of the mucous membrane, is the ultimate origin of the spermatorrhœa.

The modes of preventing disuse, overuse, and abuse, of the genital organs, have been shortly considered above; and consist chiefly, as does the prevention of all diseases, in universally diffusing among all human beings, men and women, a knowledge of the laws and structure of the body, and of all its organs, and in affording them the power of obeying these laws. There is no other possible prevention of disease, than knowledge of the laws of health and the history of disease, and reverence for them, as universally spread as any branch of human knowledge may be.

In taking leave of this part of my subject, I must beg the reader, if he wish to obtain a further knowledge of it, and an insight into a field of moral and physical experiences, teeming with novelty and importance, that he read M. Lallemand's great work on involuntary seminal discharges, of which so imperfect an idea has been given in this essay.

VENEREAL DISEASES.

I now come to a class of diseases, much better known and almost more widely spread, than the true genital diseases, which I have been describing; nay, it may be said, than any other disease. For there is scarcely a corner of the globe in which they are not to be found, and they knot and gender most of all in the very heart of our civilization. Like the poison in the cup, they embitter all youthful love, and breed suspicion, hatred, and despair, among young and trusting minds. Like the dragon of the gardens of old, they bar the gate often of very salvation upon youth. Not only are the poor, wretched, friendless daughters of pleasure their victims, but the respected wife and hapless child are thus often rotted from the surface of the earth. They fall alike on the inexperienced and the most dissipated; and, like the old laws, have as severe a punishment for a first transgression, as for the old offender.

And who dares, in the present day of morbid morality, to take up the cause of these neglected, nay, often despised and abhorred victims, and contend with adequate energy against the ravager, that spreads corruption from the lowest to the highest ranks of society, so that there is scarcely a family, scarcely a constitution, untainted by it! No one among the fair-weather moralists will approach the subject, or if they do, it is only to make corruption and degradation ten-fold more overwhelming to the unfortunate sufferers. Nothing is done by society at large, nothing by any philanthropic individual heart, to try in the least to prevent this hideous evil; and thus is an incalculable amount of misery permitted to continue among us. Even for the very reason that others neglect, laugh at, or reproach the victims of these sexual diseases, especially when they are poor and friendless, and the voice of their bitter woe is dumb, should they claim double reverence and sympathy from every generous breast. Oh, ye poor ones! shall I not respect your desolation and shame, when the Levite passes by on the other side?

An immensity could be done to check these diseases, and great and laudable have been the efforts made in France to this end; although never, in any part of the world, have adequate means been taken to prevent any disease, nor will there be, till all men become deeply impressed with the importance and sacred duty of this endeavour. There is scarcely any disease which does the same degree of mischief, physically and morally, to mankind. Can any of us still believe that physical evil can exist without necessarily causing moral degradation?

By putting a check upon these diseases, the axe would be laid to the very root of a great many of the most fearful evils that infest mankind, and of which they are the fountain-head. Scrofula, consumption, insanity, mercurial poisoning, stricture, and an innumerable host of other ills, may often be traced to this source. Does it not then become our sacred duty to arrest and nip in the bud these miseries? Let none of us, whether men or women, say, "It belongs not to me to attempt to remedy these evils, nor to meddle with such a subject." The commandments to love and to know, to benefit not ourselves only but all others, lie equally on all; and the generous heart is urged to advance the good, and repress the evil, on all subjects alike, which come within its comprehension.

The venereal diseases are divided into two great classes; the virulent, and the non-virulent. The first class consists of *syphilis*, the second of *gonorrhœa* and its modifications.

The *non-virulent* diseases, which I shall first describe, are those which are merely local, and do not in their progress contaminate the general system. Their effects are, therefore, for the most part, not so lamentable, as those of the virulent affections. The non-virulent diseases consist in an inflammation of the mucous membrane, which lines the glans and the urinary canal of the penis, excited by the contact of irritating matter deposited during sexual intercourse. This irritating matter is, in the immense majority of cases, the product of a venereal disease in the female, although in some few instances, it may arise from a leucorrhœa, or white discharge, to which women are very subject (a simple inflammation of the vagina, not arising from any infectious source). Therefore, it must not be concluded, that a woman from whom a gonorrhœa is contracted, is necessarily labouring under a venereal disease; though this is the case in the vast majority of instances.

According to the different part of the mucous membrane of the penis, which is affected, the disease has received different names. Thus when the smooth surface of the glans, with the opposite surface of the foreskin, is inflamed, the complaint is called *balanitis*, (the termination, *itis*, always means inflammation of, and is applied to every organ in the body) or *external* gonorrhœa. When the interior of the urethra is affected, it is called simply *gonorrhœa* (commonly styled *clap* which is much the more common disease.

BALANITIS.

THE most frequent cause of this disease is the contact of gonorrhœal matter in sexual intercourse. It may also, though very rarely, be caused by the monthly discharge in the female, or by the whites; and it is frequently found in boys, who allow the secretion of the sebaceous glands to accumulate under the foreskin, and become acrid. It is a disease, which depends on the presence of the foreskin, and is never found in those who have been circumcised; and therefore it might in every case be prevented, by washing the glans well, after any sexual connection, where there is a possibility of contagion; a precaution which should never be neglected.

Balanitis, or inflammation of the glans, begins with slight itching, which is soon followed by heat and swelling of the part, and by a more or less purulent discharge from beneath the foreskin; which swells also, some times to a great degree, so that it cannot be drawn back over the glans. This disease is generally readily curable, especially if taken in time, and it seldom becomes chronic; but in some cases, where circumstances, such as a dissipated mode of life, and allowing the inflammation to run on from neglect, combine to exasperate it, the consequences may be very serious. Mortification of the prepuce may result from the intensity of the inflammation, and the strangulation of its blood-vessels by the swelling; and proceed, if not checked, to the destruction of the whole penis.

Balanitis is a complaint easily recognised, but it is often difficult to tell whether it be complicated by the virulent affection of chancre or syphilis. A chancre may exist under the foreskin at the same time as the running from the glans; and it cannot, in some cases, be detected, from the inability to draw back the foreskin, owing to the swelling and inflammation. Its existence is then only to be discovered by the test of inoculation, which I shall describe hereafter in speaking of syphilis. However, its existence does not alter the treatment, which is as follows.

The treatment of Balanitis, in its mild and common form, is very simple. It consists in washing the parts well, and keeping the foreskin and the glans separated by a piece of dry lint, to be changed several times a-day. This will generally suffice to effect a cure. No method is more efficacious in arresting discharges from mucous surfaces which

lie against each other, than keeping them separate by some dry substance; as the two hot and inflamed surfaces act like mutual poultices,
and keep up the discharge. First wash and dry the part, then introduce a piece of dry lint at the base of the glans, and draw the foreskin
over it. If the parts be much inflamed, nothing has so great an effect
in reducing the inflammation, as passing a stick of nitrate of silver
lightly over them, so as simply to whiten the surface, which should be
previously dried by lint; and on the subsequent days, the part should be
washed with Goulard's lotion and dry lint kept constantly applied.

GONORRHŒA.

This disease is a greatly more important one than the preceding, not only from its much greater frequency, but also from its severity, and from the grievous effects it in too many cases leaves behind. Yet there is no disease, which the young and thoughtless are more in the habit of making a jest of; and while the inexperienced regard all venereal diseases with the anxious fear that ignorance inspires, the initiated often take a pride in telling of the dangers they have passed, and in drawing a ludicrous picture of the sufferings the novice has before him. It is often held rather a proof of manliness and experience among the youth, to have had a few claps, like the scars of the German duellist; and as they do not, like syphilis, leave a Damocles' sword, in the shape of secondary poisoning, suspended over the head, the sufferings they may have caused are soon forgotten, or but used for banter, by the many, whose vigorous health has brought them through in triumph. But far different is the tale told by the unfortunate, already struggling under the burden of a weak—it may be, scrofulous constitution; by him, whose shyness makes such a complaint anything but a subject for public glorification; by the exhausted sufferer from spermatorrhœa or other causes, whose reviving health has received a rude arrest from this new enemy; by him, in whom gonorrhœa proves the cause of stricture, seminal weakness, diseased prostate, and other miserable complaints, which bring the proudest head to the dust; by the unhappy infant, who at life's portal, is deprived of sight by the mother's disease; in short, by the countless host of victims to those diseases of which this unreverenced gonorrhœa is the origin.

What have the genital organs done, to deserve that their diseases, so serious, so universally spread, should be treated so differently from any others? "Offended against the moral laws," says the moralist; and the youth, whose instincts whisper to him a truer morality, would disarm the censure by submitting to the penalty with a laugh—a laugh but the rattle of his chains; as if death, or any of his artillery, were to be merely a subject for jesting! Thus, favoured by the neglect of the mistaken moralist, by the irreverence of the youth, and the ignorance and heedlessness of the poor girls, whose degradation in the eyes of the

world cannot be increased by their spreading the poison, which they
themselves have received, this yellow stream of misery is permitted to
flow ever onwards, while scarcely any efforts are used for its prevention.

To prevent these diseases, it is first of all requsite that they, (like the
subject of digestion and the laws of the rest of the human body, which
have been dwelt upon with such admirable and religious enthusiasm by
Dr. Combe, and others,) be rescued from their secrecy, and become
universally known to mankind, and not alone to our profession; and
that they be no longer made a subject for jesting and reproach, but
viewed exactly in the same light as all other diseases—namely, as offences
against natural laws, but equally claiming our pity, our reverence, and
our every effort to cure them.

Gonorrhœa, commonly called clap, consists of an inflammation of
the interior of the urinary canal. It is caused by the contact, during
sexual intercourse, of matter secreted by the female organs, affected
with a similar disease. Its symptoms are as follows. Within a few
days after an impure connection, some itching and heat are felt at the
orifice of the canal, and soon a discharge appears, at first thin, but
in a short time becoming thick, yellow, and purulent. Then scalding
begins to be felt in making water, as it flows through the inflamed
canal; and the inflammation, which began at the orifice, travels
gradually downwards, the symptoms meanwhile increasing in severity.
When the disease is at its height, great pain is felt in making water;
and sometimes the swelling of the walls of the canal is so great, that the
urine can scarcely, if at all, be passed.

Chordee also is often present in severe cases, which consists in the acute
inflammation causing the effusion of lymph (the plastic substance of
which the solid tissues of the body are built up) around the walls of the
urethra; and this lymph, which has always, when poured out from the
blood-vessels, a tendency to coagulate and harden, makes the penis so stiff,
that when an erection takes place, the under part cannot go along with
the rest, and a curve or chordee is produced, causing great pain. These
erections take place chiefly at night, excited by the warmth of the bed,
and cause the patient frequently to waken with a start by the violence of
the pain. Often have I laughed, though against my soberer judgment,
at the ludicrous descriptions of his sufferings by a fellow-student; with
what lightning speed he would wake, bound out of bed, and seek the
comfort of the cold hearth-stone, or the still greater luxury of a cold wet
sponge placed on his loins, allowing the water to trickle down; and then
how relentlessly his enemy pursued him all night through, with its elec-
trical arousings, just when his wearied senses were dropping to rest.

If the gonorrhœa travel very far down the canal, or the inflammation be
very high, the prostate gland, the neck of the bladder, or even the bladder
itself, may become inflamed, but these very serious and lamentable
occurrences are fortunately not very common. A more frequent occurrence is inflammation of the *epididymis* or upper part of the testicle,
which must always be regarded as a serious and important complication.
Buboes, or swellings of the glands in the groin, are sometimes caused

I

by simple gonohrrœa, but rarely, not more than once in a hundred cases.

The gonorrhœal discharge may vary in colour and smell, being generally of a greenish yellow, sometimes tinged with blood, but this is of little importance. Like other inflammatory diseases, gonorrhœa generally tends, in process of time, to a spontaneous cure. Thus in a fortnight it will probably have reached its greatest severity, and after remaining stationary for a week or so, it will gradually decline: and in some cases, where the constitution is vigorous, cease without treatment. But this is not to be expected, and the disease has a great tendency to become indefinitely chronic, unless actively treated: and I shall now describe the treatment of the different stages.

This is divided by M. Ricord (the admirable surgeon, who has the charge of the great Venereal Hospital in Paris, with' greater opportunities of observing the venereal diseases than any man in Europe, and who has done perhaps more than any other to throw light on their nature and treatment,) into the abortive treatment, and the treatment of the acute and chronic stages; all of which are distinct from each other.

By the *abortive* treatment, (which it is peculiarly important for the public in general to be acquainted with, as their prompt adoption of it on the very first signs of the disease can alone make it available,) is meant the endeavour to arrest the disease at its very outset; an object much more desirable than to permit it to run on to the acute stage, in which it is so severe, and sometimes so intractable. The abortive treatment consists in using injections of a solution of nitrate of silver, which has an unequalled power in altering the character, and arresting the inflammations, of mucous membranes. The solution should be very weak, in the proportion of one-fourth of a grain of the nitrate, to the ounce of distilled water, and should be used as follows:

A glass (not a pewter) syringe should be half-filled with it, and the fluid injected into the urethra, and allowed to remain for a minute or two. These injections should be repeated once every four hours, for forty-eight hours. They will cause some little pain, and a slightly rosy, purulent discharge, which is to be looked on as a good sign, showing that the disease will soon yield. No spirituous liquor or heating food should be taken. Neither warm baths nor any other relaxing measures should be used during the abortive treatment, which if duly and early enough employed, will effect a cure at once in a half of the cases, according to Ricord's experience.

I need not dwell on the immense importance of this method, and of its being generally made known to the public; so that those who have been exposed to infection, may seize the very first signs of disease, and so save themselves all the pains and dangers attendant on gonorrhœa. This treatment is of great value to the public, but little to the surgeon, as in general, especially among the poorer classes, (who never attend to a disease, till it has caused them some great inconvenience,) he sees the case too late for its adoption. It can be used only in the first day, or perhaps

two days, of the discharge, on the very first appearance of the yellow matter, and before much redness and inflammation have been set up, as then it would only aggravate the disease. After the twelve injections have been used, cubebs or copaiba should be taken for a few days, in the doses hereafter to be mentioned, all sexual intercourse and spirituous liquors avoided, and in a fortnight the patient may resume his usual habits. It is no easy matter to nip in the bud an incipient gonorrhœa, and unless all these directions be carried out, the complaint will probably return in a day or two (for it has as many heads as the hydra), and may then last for months. This treatment is without any risk of causing stricture or other evils; which, by cutting short the disease, it rather tends powerfully to prevent.

Instead of using injections, copaiba or cubebs alone will very often succeed in checking the disease at its outset. They should be given the moment the first drop of yellow matter is perceived, and should be used in rather larger doses than those adapted for the later stages, as the object is to cut the disease short at once by vigorous means. Thus two or three drachms of cubebs should be taken thrice a day. M. Ricord says, that this abortive treatment is more likely to succeed, where there is little or no pain or scalding, in the commencement of the disease; and also that even although it fail in wholly arresting the discharge, it never fails to modify and mitigate the symptoms, so that by persisting in remedial measures, the disease is generally brought to a close in from fifteen to twenty days. He says, moreover, that much harm is often done by a popular prejudice against trying speedily to arrest the discharge; whereas his object always is, to cure the disease as quickly as is consistent with caution in the use of the remedies; for, he says, the danger of a gonorrhœa depends upon two things; first, the severity to which the inflammation is suffered to attain, and secondly, its duration.

But if the golden moment have been allowed to pass, or if the abortive treatment have failed; if the symptoms have gradually increased in severity, and there be present much scalding in making water, with heat, redness, and swelling at the orifice of the urethra, the abortive treatment can no longer be applied, as it would exasperate the inflammation. Antiphlogistic (or anti-inflammatory) treatment should now be used. The patient should take plenty of mucilaginous drinks, as barley-water, syrup and water, or plain cold water, to render the urine as little irritating as possible. He should rest on a sofa, and have low diet. A general warm bath every night for from a half to one hour is an excellent means of quieting the inflammation. Local warm baths are not so good, as they tend to congest the part. Leeches may be applied to the perineum (the space between the *scrotum* or pouch of the testicles and the *anus* or opening of the intestine,) but not to the loose skin of the penis itself, as in that situation their bites may be followed by erysipelas. Some authors recommend cubebs and copaiba in this acute stage, but Ricord does not approve of them; for he says, they often do more harm than good, when the inflammation runs high, and, besides, lose the virtues they would have had, in a later stage. The bowels should be freed by purgatives, which cool the system, and so subdue the inflammation; and, if it run high, tartar emetic should be given.

This medicine is the most powerful means of subduing active inflammation in almost all parts of the body; except where, from the nature of the organs inflamed, it cannot be given, as in inflammation of the stomach or bowels. If given in sufficient doses, it brings on a state of extreme sickness, which, as can readily be understood, is the most powerful opponent of inflammation. This invaluable medicine, whose general adoption now-a-days in inflammatory diseases has superseded in very many cases the use of the lancet (which, by its expenditure of the vital fluid, is a remedy never to be resorted to, if safer means can be found), may be given in doses of from one-fourth to one-half a grain, in an ounce or two of water, every two hours, according to the quantity found requisite in each case to cause the state of nausea.

The chordee, which will be more severe in proportion to the violence of the inflammation, and also to the depth it has reached in the canal, should be treated by avoiding everything that could excite erections. These are generally caused by the warmth of bed; therefore a hard mattrass and light bed-clothes should be used. M. Ricord praises camphor very highly as a sedative in chordee, and gives it either in pills with opium—namely, six grains of camphor, and one grain of opium, made into two pills, to be taken at bed-time; or ten grains of camphor, one of opium, the yolk of an egg, and four ounces of water, given in an ejection, an hour before going to bed.

By these antiphlogistic means, the intensity of the gonorrhœal inflammation, will probably be subdued, and the scalding, heat, and other signs of acute inflammation diminished, although the yellow purulent discharge still continues copious. The patient should now begin to take some of those remedies which have a specific action, and most powerful control over gonorrhœa—namely, cubebs or copaiba. These are both remedies of very great value, and in the great majority of cases succeed in curing the complaint, if skilfully used. Sometimes the very first doses will reduce the discharge to a single drop in the morning. Copaiba is a kind of resinous balsam, with a taste which to many is exceedingly nauseous; and so it has been ingeniously enclosed in little gelatinous capsules (the capsules de Mothes) that are equally efficacious with the plain balsam; which may itself be taken in water, or suspended in a mucilaginous liquid. Cubebs —a hot pepper-like powder, containing as its active ingredient a volatile oil, very similar to that which is the active principle of copaiba (both of which volatile oils may be taken pure, and are thus equally efficacious, and not so apt to disagree)—may be used in the following formula, which is exceedingly effective, and in some constitutions succeeds much better than copaiba. Take two or three ounces of cubebs, and make them into a paste with honey. Begin with three tea-spoonsful the first day, and increase the dose taken on the following days to five or six tea-spoonsful, drinking at the same time plentifully of barley-water, milk of almonds, or other mucilaginous drink, so as to prevent the cubebs from irritating the stomach or kidneys. The medicine acts equally well if taken merely in water, in similar doses.

These medicines should not be given up as soon as the gonorrhœa has ceased, for, if so, it would most probably re-appear; but they should be continued for a few days longer, in gradually diminishing doses. Some constitutions are most benefited by one, others by the other; so that if the one do not succeed, we may have recourse to its fellow.

But we cannot expect to find such a thing as an unalloyed blessing, and thus there are evils, which in some cases arise from the use of these medicines. Among them is a rash, which they sometimes bring out over the body, attended with smart fever, and arrest of the gonorrhœa; which however returns when the rash disappears. It seems to be owing to a disordered stomach, and to exposure to cold and damp, which should be carefully avoided, while taking the medicines. Copaiba also sometimes causes nausea, diarrhœa, and griping, which, when slight, need not be attended to, except by avoiding cold, damp feet, &c. Cubebs has in some few cases, when given in too large doses, caused symptoms of inflammation of the stomach, which occurrence must be guarded against by ceasing at once the medicine, if any incipient signs be perceived.

Cubebs are also often adulterated, and may thus prove injurious, and should, as well as many other medicines, be got at the best druggists. All medicines are to be viewed as double-edged weapons, in themselves most important causes of disease, and being so, we should desire to use them as rarely as possible.

At the same time that these internal remedies are used, Ricord employs, whenever the inflammation has been sufficiently subdued, a local treatment also, as the conjunction of both is much more certain. Injections of nitrate of silver, of the strength before recommended—namely one fourth of a grain to the ounce of distilled water, should be employed as before directed, viz, twelve in the forty-eight hours, when they may be stopped, and the internal remedies continued. In some old standing cases, when the mucous membrane has become relaxed and thickened, this injection may not be sufficiently strong to produce the reddish discharge and other signs of salutary action; and, if so, it may be increased to from one to two grains, to the ounce of water.

There are different forms of the chronic stage of gonorrhœa, whose treatment I have been describing. In some cases the yellow discharge continues as thick and copious as in the acute stage, although the scalding in making water is in great part, or altogether, absent. In others the discharge is reduced to what is called a *gleet*, in which it has lost its yellow colour, and has become nearly colourless, like gum, or small shreds of vermicelli; in other cases no discharge is visible during the day, and only a drop or two, gluing together the orifice in the mornings, remains.

These gleets, though some persons care little for them, are to others a source of great annoyance, in proportion to the susceptibility of their nature, moral and physical; and they often, by their long continuance, and by inducing stricture, or, as we have seen above, spermatorrhœa, bring the patient into a state of the most miserable hypochondria.

Some cases of chronic gonorrhœa, or gleet, are exceedingly obstinate, and resist all sorts of treatment, causing endless annoyance and impatience in those affected with them. Thus they often last for months, and not unfrequently from one to two or three years; and Ricord mentions one which lasted thirty years; so that it is of immense importance that, by a vigorous and well directed treatment at first, the risk of such consequences should be prevented. A gonorrhœa is not a complaint to be trifled with; in some constitutions it is exceedingly difficult to subdue, whether from their weakness, incapability of bearing the remedies, unhealthy relaxing life of confinement, neglect, want of self-restraint in applying for, a sufficient time the remedies, or abstaining from drinking, and other sensual enjoyments; and perhaps above all, from the unfortunate and pernicious social feelings on the subject of this disease, which cause it to be concealed, prevent the sufferer from applying for assistance in time, hamper and obstruct all the remedies employed, and too often reduce the patient and the humane physician to despair of the cure.

There is no matter perhaps in which concealment does more harm to mankind, than in this of genital and venereal diseases. The grand point ever to be kept in view, in remedying diseases, is, that they be treated as early as possible. Not a moment should be lost, on the first appearance of any disease, in taking measures to arrest it; for the first few golden moments are often the most important of all. Now, the miserable shame and fear attending on venereal and genital complaints, in almost all cases, prevent the inexperienced youth, and still more the woman, from applying for relief, till the irrevocable time is past; till the mischief is fully developed, and the disease riots and revels in its strength, exulting at our impotence to arrest it, and proceeding to bring on consequences which no man can answer for, and which may be most disastrous. Must we not then consider the odium attaching to venereal diseases, as being most sinful in every individual who entertains it, since it is the cause of so many miseries to man and woman?

If a gleet have lasted a long time, we should try to make out, in each separate case, the cause of this chronicity. And first, the canal should be explored with a bougie, to see whether there be not a stricture, which is a frequent cause of lingering gleet. Sometimes, when the inflammation lingers deep in the canal, at the orifices of the ejaculatory ducts, there are frequent seminal emissions in the night, which aggravate in their turn the gleet, and frequently are the cause of bringing back a gonorrhœa, which was on the wane. From this exhausting complication, all the horrors of spermatorrhœa may in time be established. In such cases slight cauterization of the walls of the urethra, over the mouths of the ducts, with M. Lallemand's porte-caustique, has sometimes an excellent effect.

Impotence may be caused in this as in other cases by spermatorrhœa; and here I may say a few words on this subject, which to many is one of great importance. Impotence may be the result of anything which tends to weaken, either mentally the venereal appetites, or physically the genital organs. Mentally, the most frequent causes of impotence are—hard study, which consumes the nervous power in a different direction; and still oftener, all the depressing emotions, such as fear, shyness, apathy,

&c., which by their admixture, destroy the force of the venereal appetites. Physically, a want of tone in the genital organs, which are
scarcely capable of full erection, at least solely at the stimulus of venereal
desires ; want of exercise of the organs, which, like all others, are greatly
strengthened by habitual exercise ; spermatorrhœa, or the general
exhaustion of the frame from long disease of any kind. If the disease be
of mental origin, John Hunter's advice was, that a man should sleep
with the woman, with whom he was impotent, resolving to have no connection with her. A man may be impotent with one woman, into his
affections towards whom any of the paralysing feelings enter, and may
not be so with another. As a preventive or cure of impotence, the
regular exercise of the genital organs, and a healthy life in the open air,
without the exhaustion of protracted study, are the best of all means.
Besides this, it must be remembered, that there are great natural constitutional differences in these powers in different individuals, and each
one must be contented with those which have been given him ; and not
waste his thoughts and strength, as is so often done, in vain regrets that
they are not greater than is natural to him.

Sometimes a gleet will persist in spite of all the above-mentioned
remedies, which may not have the power of wholly stopping the discharge,
but perhaps of reducing it to a single yellow or gummy drop in the
morning, which will not be driven away, and, the moment the remedies
are discontinued, increases rapidly till the running be as bad as ever.
Sometimes too, the remains of a chordee may continue after the gonorrhœa is cured. In cases of obstinate gleet, various means should be
tried.

It must always be borne in mind, that diseases do not become chronic
and lingering without a cause. Chronic disease is always a sign, that
either the part effected, or the constitution generally, is too weak to
throw off its enemy. In a healthy man living in the country, and still
more in the vigorous savage in the woods, disease rarely becomes chronic ;
but wounds and inflammations heal with surprising quickness, aided or
unaided, so great are the natural powers. But in the poor unhealthy
townsman, the case is very different ; every indefinite disease, like inflammation, &c., tends to become chronic, from the weak powers and unhealthy life. This constitutional weakness is in many cases the chief
cause of the continuance of a gleet, and must be remedied, before the
latter can be got rid of. Thus the man who has an old gleet, should
adopt the most bracing life possible ; should be in the country, and
always in the open air ; should live regularly, rising early and going
early to bed ; should take cold baths, twice or even oftener, daily,
remaining in the water only a short time, and always taking a smart
walk afterwards, to restore the circulation ; and probably a good remedy
also, is the cold sitz-bath, taken several times a-day, with a walk after
it. These directions which will apply to many other chronic diseases,
should at once be adopted, if the powers of the constitution seem inadequate to cure the disease ; for delay is, in this complaint, like all others,
only wasted time, besides favouring the evil consequences, which may
arise from old gleet. Along with these general means, a local treatment

by injections should be used, employing the milder astringent, the sulphate of zinc, (which is often more successful than the nitrate of silver,) in the proportion of one or two grains, to the ounce of water: this to be used twice or thrice-a-day, and continued for eight or ten days. Other astringent injections may be employed, as the decoction of oak bark, &c. By these means, the bracing change of air, and *al fresco* life, along with the local astringents, the complaint may almost always be subdued, if they have a due trial ; but without the general means, all local ones will often prove unavailing.

Before proceeding to the complications of gonorrhœa, I may mention, that the disease is sometimes, and not very infrequently, produced by other causes than infection. A yellow discharge may be excited by hard drinking, or by undue exercise of the sexual organs, especially in those in whom there are some lingering remains of inflammation from a former gonorrhœa, or who suffer from an irritable prostate gland. To these cases the name of *spurious* gonorrhœa has been applied. They may often be distinguished by commencing suddenly with little or no previous itching; and by the discharge appearing to come at once from the inner part of the canal, and not beginning at the orifice and gradually passing inwards, as in the true disease. They are in general mild, and readily curable by a few injections of the solution of nitrate of silver, or sulphate of zinc.

I shall now speak of some of the complications which may arise in the course of a gonorrhœa. *Buboes*, or inflammatory swellings of one or more of the glands in the groin, sometimes, though rarely, occur ; but are in general readily subdued by applying a few leeches and poultices, and using the tartar emetic. In a gonorrhœa, buboes depend merely on the neighbouring irritation, in the same way that a swelling of contiguous glands may be caused by a blister. They generally arise in the first week in simple gonorrhœa, when the inflammation is at its height.

Another much more serious complication of gonorrhœa is *Epididymitis* (commonly called swelled testicle,) or inflammation of the epididymis, the upper part of the testicle. It was long thought, that in this affection the testicle itself was inflamed, but this is fortunately only rarely the case. Inflammation of the epididymis is occasioned by the gonorrhœal inflammation, when it has reached the orifices of the ejaculatory ducts far down in the canal, causing sympathetic inflammation of the epididymis at the other end of the seminal duct ; according to the law, that the two extremities of a canal may be sympathetically excited, without intervening inflammation. As the gonorrhœa must have penetrated far down in the canal, before it reaches the ejaculatory ducts, we do not find inflammation of the epididymis come on early in its course. It seldom occurs before the third week of gonorrhœa, and from that till the end of the fifth week, it is most common. This is an important fact, as it enables us to be on our guard against it, and take precautions against its occurrence.

The chief means of prevention are, to cure, if possible, the gonorrhœa before the third week, and to wear a suspensory bandage for the testicles; to avoid anything which would increase the inflammation of the urethra;

and above all, to be on the watch for the first symptoms of the affection of the testicle, and nip it in the bud, which, in general, might readily be done.

These first symptoms are as follows. About the fourth or fifth week of a gonorrhœa, the patient may feel a slight aching pain in the groin, which gradually extends down the spermatic chord, and fixes in a small spot at the upper and back part of the testicle (generally the left one, which, from want of the support given by the trousers to its fellow, is much the most frequently attacked). On feeling this spot it will be found that the epididymis is here enlarged, hard, and tender to the touch. The gonorrhœal discharge is probably at the same time a little diminished, and seminal emissions are liable to take place at night, and are followed by increased pain in the testicle, lasting for some hours ; but as yet there is no blood mixed with the seminal fluid. If the patient now at the golden moment take the warning, and attend to these first symptoms ; if he give the organ the most perfect rest, by remaining constantly in the recumbent posture for a couple of days, foment the parts with warm cloths, and take a dose of opening medicine to cool the system, the affection will subside entirely, and none of the following serious symptoms will arise. But if he neglect them, as so many do, chiefly from ignorance of their nature, heedlessness, or a foolish reluctance to be laid up for a couple of days, when by so doing, they would avoid weeks of suffering, which will most certainly follow; or finally, from that most deplorable dread of their disease becoming known, which so constantly operates in this case, where confinement to the sofa is absolutely requisite; if he walk about or take other exercise, even the slightest, the disease will advance very rapidly. The affected testicle now becomes greatly swelled, and exquisitely tender and painful. The constitution sympathises with it, and a good deal of fever arises. The gonorrhœa often stops entirely, from what is called revulsion, but begins again when the other affection has subsided. When the swelling of the testicle has been very rapid, the pain is most excruciating.

The course of this affection, severe though the symptoms be, is in general favourable, where the constitution is good. Under the use of appropriate antiphlogistic treatment, the inflammation and swelling subside, but some enlargement and hardness of the epididymis almost always remain for some time, and pain and consequent relapses are liable to occur from sexual intercourse for months after ; evils which are to be guarded against by the continued use of the suspensory bandage, and abstinence from, or but rare indulgence in, sexual intercourse, if it cause pain. The testicle in general regains all its reproductive powers : which consolation we are enabled to give the patient, from the knowledge that in the great majority of cases, it entirely escapes the disease, and the epididymis alone is affected.

But in many cases unfortunately, the result of epididymitis is not so favourable—is most disastrous. This is especially the case in scrofulous constitutions. In these, the inflammation of the epididymis has a great tendency to become chronic, and gradually to engage in its progress the whole testicle, causing slow suppuration in it, or the deposition of tubercle, (that degenerated product, which is the sign of scrofulous disease, and may be deposited in any part of the body, causing consumption in the lungs, mesenteric disease in the abdominal glands, &c.,) in its substance, which in time softens, and causes complete disorganisation of the whole testicle. Meanwhile the feeble constitution, from the long confinement and weakening treatment of such an affection, may gradually fall a victim to consumption. How frequently do we we see in hospitals such lamentable results of the despised gonorrhœa! In the same way that scrofulous disease may be thus roused by epididymitis, so may in those predisposed to it, the still more formidable disease of cancer. The indurated and enlarged state of the epididymis which is left behind, sometimes at a future period, excites cancerous degeneration in the part; from the law that previous inflammation in an organ makes it particularly liable to cancer, in those who seem to have a natural predisposition to this disease. When we contemplate even the possibility of two such fearful diseases resulting, how great should be our endeavours to prevent the epididymitis, which may give rise to them, and still more the gonorrhœa, which is the source of them all!

In the treatment of epididymitis which has passed the incipient stage, we must use energetic means to arrest the inflammation. In the first place, it is absolutely necessary that the patient remain in the recumbent position; the testicle should be supported, so as to take the strain off the inflamed chord, and leeches should be applied to the groin, or perineum, but not to the loose skin of the scrotum, where they might cause erysipelas. Besides this, the patient should take pretty large doses of tartar emetic with epsom salts, a mixture whose effects in reducing the inflammation are sometimes wonderful. It may be used as follows:—Dissolve two grains of tartar emetic, and two ounces of epsom salts in a pint of water, and take four ounces every third hour, till great nausea and purging be produced. (Of course the medical attendant will prescribe such or other fit remedies, but it is very desirable that the public should be acquainted with the general actions of the most valuable medicines in the various diseases.) This most powerful of antiphlogistic medicines will sometimes effect a cure in twenty-four hours. Poultices should be applied locally.

When by these means the inflammation has been checked, and the pain is lessened, but the swelling remains, compression should be applied, a powerful mode of speedily restoring the testicle to its original size. This is to be effected by straps of adhesive plaister, passed round the testicle, some horizontally, and others vertically, so as to cause a moderate and equal compression. Pressure is one of the most effectual means of causing the absorption of any effusion, after the inflammation, which caused it, has abated. The great swelling of the testicle, in this disease, arises from the effusion of *serum*, (the watery part of the blood) into the tunic or case which encloses the testicle. The application of compression will occasion, for a short time, some increase of pain, but this will soon subside; and, if the method is to succeed, in a few hours the strapping will become quite loose. As soon as this takes place, the straps should be removed and others applied, so that no reaction shall follow; which would probably be the case, were the compression not carried forward uninterruptedly. But if at the end of an hour, after applying the first strapping, the pain do not subside, we may infer, that here compression will not succeed; remove the straps, and continue antiphlogistics. By compression, Mr. Acton, (the pupil and friend of M. Ricord, whose valuable work on venereal diseases embodies the experience of his master,) has seen many testicles reduced to their normal size in twelve hours; and in two hundred well chosen cases, which he saw, no bad results followed its use.

The next disease arising from gonorrhœa, of which I have to speak, is one of very great importance, from its frequency, and its disastrous consequences in many cases.

Stricture of the urethra, consists of a narrowing of the calibre of that canal, which may be caused in several ways. Thus it may arise from a fall or a blow on the perineum, which ruptures the urethra, and may cause, when the wound heals, a great narrowing, perhaps even obliteration, of the canal by the contraction of the cicatrix. This is the most dangerous and difficult to cure of all forms of stricture, for the cicatrix of a wound is so hard, that it cannot be distended or absorbed, as takes place in the cure of other strictures. Chancre, or syphilitic sore in the urethra; vegetations which grow from the walls of the passage, irritated by some long discharge; and some other causes, may also produce stricture. But by far the most frequent cause is gonorrhœa, and especially when that disease has continued long in the chronic stage, or when the patient has had several attacks of it.

Stricture from gonorrhœa may consist either in a relaxed and swelled state of the mucous membrane, which proves an obstruction to the urine; or, which is much the commonest form, in the deposition of lymph at some point beneath the membrane, which in time by its coagulation, hardening and contracting according to its natural tendency, as before explained, becomes callous, and narrows the canal gradually more and more. This, the usual form of stricture, is generally limited to a narrow band, not more than one or two lines in length, as if a ligature surrounded the canal at the point; but sometimes it is much longer. In most cases, there is but one stricture; but sometimes two, and in a few rare cases, several, in the course of the canal. The situation of a stricture is generally far down in the canal, at the membraneous part.

These permanent strictures form a most important class of diseases. It may well be understood how dangerous to the system is any obstruction to the passage of a fluid of such vital importance, and so constantly formed, as the urine. I will describe some of the disastrous results which may, and often do, follow stricture, if it be not early detected and removed. It will be seen that these effects are all felt in the parts *behind* the stricture.

When a stricture exists in the urethra, the urine, which is arrested behind it, and can escape only with difficulty, gradually dilates the portion of the canal behind the stricture, and may enter into the mouths of the ejaculatory ducts, and so give rise to the most inveterate spermatorrhœa. Many of Lallemand's cases were owing to this cause, and he says that the marked hypochondria into which strictured patients so often fall, even when they do not know that they have any disease, is

generally owing to the seminal losses, whose characteristic effect in
producing hypochondria we have seen above. Proceeding further backwards from the stricture, we come to the bladder, which, in cases of long
standing stricture, is very liable to become diseased, and in the following
way. It becomes gradually hypertrophied, i. e. it increases in the thick-
ness of its muscular coats, from the greater force needed to expel the
urine, and its capacity is increased. This is in accordance with a general
law of the economy, whereby organs can, within certain limits, adopt
themselves to new exigencies. In the same way the heart becomes enlarged and thickened, when there is a similar obstruction in its valves.
The urine, prevented from freely escaping, and retained in the bladder,
putrefies there, as it would do out of the body, (for the vital preservative
power of the bladder to prevent putrefaction lasts only a short time),
and the putrid urine irritates the bladder, and causes disease of its internal or mucous coat, which discharges large quantities of mucus.
The bladder becomes so irritable, that the patient is constantly tormented by vain strainings to pass water, though there may be only a
few drops in the bladder, and their passage causes intolerable pain ; and
thus the unhappy sufferer can get rest neither by night nor day. This
disease of irritable bladder, is described by Sir Astley Cooper, as the
most painful one he had to witness.

If we go back a step further, we come to the kidneys, those most
vital organs, and they too, are liable to become diseased in the
course of the evils. The urine, retained in the bladder, is prevented
from escaping freely from the kidneys also, which secrete it. Besides, the irritation is propagated to the kidneys from the bladder, by
the law of sympathy, and from these causes the kidneys may become
organically diseased ; a necessarily fatal affection, whose palliation is
unfortunately all that is left for the physician.

Another terrible accident, which not unfrequently happens in old,
neglected, and very narrow strictures, (and how common is such neglect
in the poor, who have never been taught the duty they owe to their
bodies!) is the bursting of the urethra behind the stricture, and the in-
filtration of urine into the surrounding tissues. It is in strictures that
have become almost impervious, the urine escaping perhaps only drop by
drop, that, in one of the violent efforts of straining, which this state of
things calls forth, the urethra, weakened by long disease, gives way, with
a feeling of present relief. But soon the dreadful effects follow. The
urine by its irritating qualities, acts like a strong poison on the parts
unaccustomed to it, and very speedily causes their death, and with
that, if the surgeon do not act with great promptitude and skill, the
death of the patient too.

On reviewing this sad list of diseases, it will be seen, how they all depend by a backward chain of influence, on the stricture ; and thus that
the first step either for their prevention or cure, is the cure of the
stricture.

Sir Benjamin Brodie has well said, that there is no class of diseases
so important and so dangerous, for which so much can often be done, as
for the urinary diseases. But in order to do this, they must be treated

in time ; and it is to be borne in mind as a general law in strictures
that the earlier they are treated, the more easily they are cured.   It is,
then, of immense importance that the public, who alone can observe and
discover for themselves their early symptoms, should be well acquainted
with these.

In few diseases is minute attention on the part of the patients more
necessary, than in stricture ; as it is a disease, which almost always
remains undetected, till it has gone a considerable length.   Many—nay,
we may say, the great majority of patients, live for years without knowing, that they have a stricture; and during that time they may suffer
from . hypochondria or increasing debility, of which neither they, nor
their physicians know the cause.   For, from the pernicious feelings of
delicacy prevailing on sexual subjects, physicians generally neglect to
inquire into the history, past and present, of the genital organs in each
patient, who presents himself with chronic or obscure disease ; and thus
do sexual diseases constantly escape detection, though they may be at
the root of all the symptoms.   It is a general rule now in scientific medicine, introduced especially by the admirable French physicians, M. M.
Louis, Andral, and others, in questioning patients, to inquire minutely
into the past and present state of *all* the important organs in the body,
of which the genital ones, both in man and woman, are among
the most vitally influential ; and this rule should always be followed,
especially when a case is in the least obscure or complicated, as most
chronic diseases are.   Among young people in particular, in whom the
genital organs, and the passions connected with them, may be said to
be the keystones of the being, an inquiry into the sexual history of all,
men and women alike, should never be omitted.   From this morbid
delicacy, which cannot but be veiwed as culpable, both in patient and
physician, thousands of diseases pass undetected and uncured.

The hidden existence of a stricture may at length be discovered,
whether from the gradually increasing difficulty of making water, according to the natural tendency of strictures to become narrower ; from
the vigilance of the patient or physician, or other cause.   Thus the early
symptoms of this disease, as well as of all others, should especially be
studied by the public, as it is themselves, and not the physicians, who
generally have opportunities of knowing these.

And first, in whom may stricture be expected to exist ?   He who has
had frequent gonorrhœas, or in whom that disease, the great cause of
stricture, has lasted for a long time, should be particularly on his guard
against stricture.   If the gleet still continue, and have lasted long, a
bougie should be passed, to see whether a stricture be not keeping it up.
If the gleet have ceased, the individual should be ready to notice any
diminution in the size of the stream of urine, which is the chief sign of
stricture.   Other signs are, if, after making water, the last drops cannot
be discharged, but are retained behind the stricture, and dribble away
afterwards: also in seminal discharges, the feeling that the semen is not
freely ejaculated from the orifice, but slowly wells out after the orgasm
is over, having been retained behind the stricture ; also the slow escape of
the urine, which cannot be propelled far but drops to the ground near
the orifice of the penis

If from these symptoms, one, who has had gonorrhœa, be led to suspect he has stricture, the sooner he has it investigated and treated, the better; for a stricture cannot exist long without causing evil effects in the exceedingly important parts behind it.

I do not wish to make men imaginative or over-anxious, in their solicitude about their health, by dwelling on these matters; the fallacious objection which has been always made to the public's learning anything of that which may preserve their health and their life, and which it is not only expedient for them, but their solemn duty, to become acquainted with;—an objection which could be made exactly with the same force to our learning any new truths, and escaping from any old ignorance whatever; but I wish, as far as I may, and as the generous co-operation of my readers can effect, to prevent these most miserable disasters, which the apathy and ignorance of us all have hitherto allowed to be so very common. What generous heart does not exclaim, on witnessing the quivering lip, the anguished brow, and the feelings full of bitterness, degradation, and despair, of the unfortunate victims of these and other diseases, "On me, on me be the guilt; it was my heartless prejudices, my ignorance, my apathy, which stood in the way of the prevention of all this woe! What have I done, what can I do, to atone for this neglect, and to prevent in future, as far as lies in my power, the occurrence of like calamities?"

I now come to the treatment of permanent stricture. This consists, in the great majority of cases, in the dilatation of the stricture, by means of *bougies* or narrow rods, made of various materials—as metal, wax, or elastic substances, and of a series of sizes; and in most cases this treatment is successful. Strictures caused by gonorrhœa, depend for the most part on lymph being effused by the violent inflammation, beneath the mucous membrane, and not being afterwards absorbed. This lymph has a tendency constantly to increase in hardness, and at the same time to contract; which explains the gradual narrowing that takes place in most cases of stricture. This shows us the great importance of having stricture dilated early, before the lymph has become too hard.

The mode in which dilatation is effected, is the following. A bougie of moderate size is first introduced, and if this cannot pass into the bladder, a smaller one is tried, and so on till one be found which can enter the stricture; and this at times, in very narrow strictures, can be effected only by a piece of catgut, and with the greatest difficulty. When this has entered the stricture, which grasps it tightly, it is left there, according to Ricord's practice, until it can be moved easily through the stricture; which, in most curable cases, soon takes place. It is then removed, and any irritability of the canal, which may have been excited by the presence of the instrument, is allowed to subside; and on the following day the same instrument is introduced, and if it enter readily, it is withdrawn, and another of a little larger size substituted. This is allowed to remain, like the former, till it move readily; and thus the treatment advances daily till the widest dilatation is obtained, which is possible or necessary. In this manner a cure may be effected in most cases, in a space of time varying from three to six weeks or so, according to the size and hardness of the stricture.

Strictures have a great tendency to return after being cured, and to prevent this, the patient should, after his cure, pass an instrument of requisite size every fourth day for the first fortnight, and once a week for some time after. As this tendency to return often continues indefinitely, he will probably be obliged to pass one once a month, or at other intervals according as he finds it necessary, during the rest of his life; and to this end he should learn to pass them himself, which, with a little care, is a very simple operation in an open canal. In the course of the treatment, the urethra, which may at first have been very irritable, becomes generally quite habituated to the instruments, so that they cause little uneasiness.

The mode in which dilatation acts, is not by mechanically widening the stricture, so much as by causing the absorption of the effused lymph under the pressure; according to the same law, by which we have seen above, that compression rapidly reduces the size of the enlarged testicle.

Besides the above method of slow dilatation, there is another, praised very highly by M. Lallemand, namely, rapid dilatation; which, however, M. Ricord and most surgeons disapprove of, as relapses are so common after it. It consists in introducing first the largest bougie the stricture will admit, leaving this until it becomes readily moveable, then withdrawing it, and replacing it at once by another of a larger size, and so on in succession, till the largest sized bougie can be introduced. By this treatment, a cure can often be effected in less than forty-eight hours. Probably in many cases, where there is not too much irritability of the canal, to bear the protracted presence of the instruments, and also where the intelligent co-operation of the patient aids in preventing the closure of the stricture again, the rapid method would be a great advantage, but of this I cannot speak from personal experience.

Dilatation is by no means applicable or successful in all strictures, and therefore in each the nature of the constriction must first be determined. Stricture depending on indurated chancre in the urethra (which will be described hereafter), is generally not far from the orifice, may be felt hard and gristly exteriorly, and is in general accompanied by symptoms of secondary syphilis in other parts of the body. This stricture would only be exasperated by dilatation, but will usually yield with readiness to the general constitutional remedies for secondary syphilis. Stricture, resulting from the cicatrix of a wound, as from a fall or blow on the perineum, where the urethra has been ruptured, will not yield to dilatation, however long continued; as the cicatrix, being organized, is not absorbed under pressure, and constantly returns to the same state, nay,—contracts still closer. The only thing to be done in these most intractable and melancholy cases, is incision, which is accomplished by introducing a knife, concealed in a hollow catheter (a bent tube, like the bougie, only with an opening at its end), down to the stricture, and then pushing it out, and so dividing the obstruction. After that, a large catheter is introduced, and left for some days in the bladder, to prevent the cicatrix uniting again. In this way many such cases are cured; but others, of a worse nature, give rise to some of the most difficult and fatal operations in surgery. It is chiefly in strictures produced by gonorrhœa, that dilatation is successful, in which the obstruction consists of effused, and as yet

unorganized lymph. These are generally far down in the canal, and
tightly grasp the instrument. If they have been too long neglected,
their lymph becomes organized, and so hard that they may be almost
as intractable as a cicatrix; and the surgeon must often be content, if
he can introduce through them a bougie of two or three lines in dia-
meter.

Stricture is also sometimes caused by vegetations, which are generally situated near the orifice, and bleed very easily, when a bougie
is passed. These are not easy to remove, and are very apt to grow
again. A softened puffy state of the mucous membrane, after a long
gonorrhœa, may also cause stricture, and this is perhaps the most
easily curable form; to wit, by injections, or slight cauterization with
the nitrate of silver. In speaking of injections, it may be remarked,
that it is a common belief, that they are a great cause of stricture, but
the best authorities on the subject, as Ricord and Sir B. Brodie, deny
that they are so, if used judiciously, i. e. not during the acute stage of
gonorrhœa, nor of improper strength.

With regard to the prevention of stricture, and with it the host of
serious evils it gives rise to, we must in the first place use every means,
social and individual, to prevent its great cause, gonorrhœa. If this
disease, however, should be incurred, we must bear in mind, that the
sooner it is cured, the less risk will there be of stricture. Thus, if
the gonorrhœa be stopped at its outset by the abortive treatment,
neither stricture nor any other evil will ever occur. If the gonorrhœa
have, by neglect or misfortune, degenerated into a lingering gleet, and
so stricture been produced, its early detection, and prompt treatment,
will in general readily remove it.

Besides these permanent forms of stricture, where there is a lasting
change of structure in the canal, there are two other varieties of a less
serious nature—viz. the inflammatory, and the spasmodic. *Inflammatory* stricture is a temporary obstruction of the canal, with frequently complete retention of urine, from the swelling caused by
inflammation. This form may occur in the acute stage of gonorrhœa,
or after cauterization of a part of the canal. For this affection, which
is generally easily remediable, soothing measures should be used first,
viz., a Dover's powder, and thirty or forty drops of laudanum in a
clyster; and if these measures are not sufficient, a small elastic catheter
should be passed, to draw off the urine, and then the soothing measures
continued.

By the *spasmodic* stricture is meant one which depends merely on
temporary spasm of the muscles, surrounding the urethra; which in
irritable constitutions, if stimulated by an acrid state of the urine,
sometimes contract spasmodically and so prevent the emptying of the
bladder. The sign that a stricture is spasmodic, is its occurring suddenly in a person, who has till then been able freely to pass water.
These spasms are generally brought on by drinking freely of spirits,
or wine, which make the urine very pungent and irritating; so that
when it attempts to flow along the canal, the muscles contract spasmodically on it, and obstruct its passage. Thus a person during, or

after a debauch, may suddenly find himself quite unable to urinate, and after trying several times, if he be not relieved, his vain efforts to strain out a few drops will become most agonising; his face flushed, and covered by sweat, and his whole frame quivering with the fruitless efforts. But the case should never be allowed to proceed so far, for here, as well as in other diseases, the sooner relief is obtained, the less injury is done to the parts. Luckily, relief for the time is generally easily rendered. The patient should be put to bed, warmth applied, a Dover's powder given to favour sweating and relaxation of the fibres; and this after a few hours should be followed by a dose of opening medicine, when he will generally be able to pass water in a full stream. Opium, whether given by the mouth or in injection, is the most powerful of all means of relaxing spasm (except the very recently introduced chloroform), and in this case of spasmodic stricture, thirty or forty drops of laudanum, used in injection, is a most excellent remedy, superior in efficacy to the warm bath, which is also a valuable anti-spasmodic. In cases which have been allowed to run on, till the patients' straining and sufferings are very urgent, or where the above means do not overcome the spasm, the smallest sized elastic catheter should be passed.

But though relief may generally be given in spasmodic stricture, it has a great tendency to return according to the universal law of habit, especially in irritable constitutions, and where drinking is persisted in; and thus in different cases, it occurs from once in the fortnight, to perhaps once in the year. Now it is a known natural law, that functional diseases—of which this is one, have in process of time, a great tendency to become organic and permanent, and thus may a spasmodic stricture at last become a permanent one. Therefore he, who is subject to it, should be doubly careful to avoid all its causes. These include every thing which weakens, and so renders irritable the nervous system, such as late hours, too hard study, &c.; and above all, what in all cases of stricture becomes of the very highest importance, he should forswear the use of fermented liquors. There is perhaps no disease, in which spirituous liquors are so uniformly injurious, as in strictures of every kind. He should also exercise the genital organs in duly regulated sexual intercourse, for nothing gives tone and strength to muscles, and deprives them of morbid irritability, more than a proper amount of exercise. Also sponging the genitals with cold water, morning and evening, is one of the best tonics for this, as well as every other case, where they are effected by irritability or weakness.

Spasmodic strictures are very important, not only in themselves, but because they constantly complicate and aggravate permanent stricture. When a man has a permanent stricture, he may get on well enough, as long as he avoids drinking or other causes of spasm, but as soon as he indulges, he is liable to have the stricture completely closed by spasm, which requires the use of a catheter for its relief; and this may sometimes be a very difficult matter, if the permanent stricture be narrow. How constantly are these, and all other evils,

K

seen in our hospital and dispensary practice, among the ignorant, negligent, and neglected poor?

It is not science that at the present day is most required in medicine; there is scientific knowledge enough, accumulated by the efforts of ages, to build a new world for man, such as has scarcely yet been conceived, were it only vitalised by the earnest love and reverence of us all. It is not the head so much as the heart, which is most needed; and were there more physicians, who partook of the noble enthusiasm for the prevention of disease, and universal diffusion of natural knowledge, which animated Dr. Andrew Combe and others, our country and mankind in general would not long continue in their present state of physical misery and degradation, which in so many respects every one must see and lament. With our national strict allegiance to law and duty, and power of self-denial, did we but know our true laws and duties, there is no people which might be expected more earnestly to study and reverence them. But enthusiasm, or any ardent appeal to the feelings of society upon medical subjects, has generally been coldly regarded, if not sneered at, by the profession, in the few instances in which it has been attempted. Medical men seem generally to suppose, that their peculiar province lies merely in the plain, matter-of-fact, physical treatment of disease; and leave the sympathetic appeals and wordy lamentations over human ills to poets, clergymen, and others, whose ignorance of real disease betrays them into the most false and exaggerated views; and who must keenly feel how utterly vain and useless is all their sympathy to alleviate or to cure a bodily disease. But though enthusiasm and sympathy are often of little comparative importance in the management of disease, yet, without them, no great impression can ever be made on mankind; and in respect of the *prevention* of disease more especially, the arm of the physician is paralysed without them.

Obstruction to the passage of urine may be caused by another most serious disease, besides stricture, viz., by chronic enlargement of the prostate gland; which, as was previously mentioned, surrounds the urethra at its deepest part, where it leaves the bladder. This is a disease of elderly life, very rarely occurring during youth, or middle age, at which time on the contrary, stricture is most common. The most common cause of it, as of most diseases of the urinary passages in man, is gonorrhœa; which when it makes its way far down in the canal, is sometimes very difficult to eradicate, and gives rise to irritation and unhealthy states in the prostate gland, which later in life favour the developement of the disease in question. Other causes often assist, or of themselves occasion it, such as excessive venereal indulgences, hard drinking, which is so especially hurtful in all urinary diseases, from the kidneys and their appendages being the vehicles by which the stimulating liquids are carried out of the system; also a sedentary life, which favors the morbid growth of different parts, by preventing the balanced circulation of the blood attendant upon exercise.

Enlargement of the prostate, so as often to cause some slight inconvenience, takes place naturally in almost every man, along with other changes, which mark the approach of old age, such as the hair becoming grey, earthy deposits in the coats of the arteries, &c.; so that, when it does not exceed this limited degree, it may be called natural and healthy. But in many cases the enlargement proceeds beyond these bounds, and the prostate may attain a size twice or thrice—nay, even ten, or fifteen times its natural one; an enlargement which finds a parallel only in the goitres, caused by the monstrous growth of the thyroid gland, surrounding the throat.

From the enlargement of the prostate, the bladder becomes somewhat irritable, and the urine flows slowly; but these first symptoms generally attract little attention, till from some accidental cause, as wet feet, hard drinking, or venereal indulgences, the swelling suddenly increases, and causes complete retention of urine. But the disease frequently, from not being understood or attended to by the patient, proceeds much more insidiously, just like stricture. The urine is gradually expelled more and more frequently and slowly, the patient not having the power entirely to empty his bladder at once. The consequence is, that some of the urine, being constantly left in the bladder, undergoes the same putrefying changes, that were mentioned in speaking of stricture. This causes disease of the coats of the bladder, and perhaps the formation of stone; diseases, especially under such circumstances, of a most lamentable and often hopeless nature. Ultimately the kidneys also may become diseased, and lead to a necessarily fatal termination. It will be seen from this description how very serious are the effects of this disease in many cases, and it generally shatters and prostrates the moral character of a patient as much as the physical.

With regard to the treatment, its early application is of paramount importance. If the enlargement be not detected, till disease of the coats of the bladder have been produced, the treatment will be rendered much more difficult. The great object to be kept in view in treatment, is not to try to diminish the size of the prostate, which is for the most part, beyond the power of medicine; but to prevent the evil effects, which must result from an obstuction to the free passage of urine. Therefore the treatment here, as in so many diseases, is not curative, but palliative, or preventive. However, if treatment be adopted early, and strenuously persevered in, the patient may live to an old age with scarcely any inconvenience from the enlargement.

The grand essential in the treatment, as was pointed out by Sir Everard Home, is the constant use of the catheter. By this instrument, supplying the want of the natural powers, the bladder should be completely emptied of urine twice a day, as soon as it is discovered that the patient has not the power of voluntarily emptying it completely. By this simple means, if unremittingly persevered in, all the ill effects which would inevitably follow from the retention of the urine, are in many cases entirely obviated; and the man, who, if untreated, would have sunk to the grave, amid the most wretched sufferings, may carry his grey hairs thither in peace after many years of a grateful life.

But besides this chronic enlargement, the prostate is subject by no means infrequently to acute affections, which are generally caused by gonorrhœa; and it is these, which lay the foundation of its more serious diseases in elderly life. The prostate or the mucous membrane covering it, becomes sometimes inflamed, either from the gradual extension of the gonorrhœal inflammation down to that part of the canal, or, still more frequently, from the use of violent remedies to arrest the discharge. It is dangerous to use too powerful means to stop the discharge while at its height; for such are very liable to throw the inflammation *backwards* upon the more important organs, such as the prostate, testicle, bladder, &c. The symptoms of inflammation of the mucous membrane, covering the surface of the prostate, are, an uneasiness at the end of the glans, and an urgent desire to pass water. The urine gives little pain in passing along the canal, but great pain is felt in forcing out the last drops, along with the sensation, as if a foreign body were being expelled from the bladder. There is a very frequent desire to make water, and the moment the mind thinks of doing so, the impulse becomes irresistible. These symptoms depend on inflammation of the mucous membrane of the neck of the bladder and prostate, and are soon relieved by restoring the gonorrhœal discharge, whose injudicious arrest is generally the cause of them.

But the *substance* of the prostate is not unfrequently inflamed, and this is more serious. The great irritability and incontinence of urine, which are symptomatic of inflammation of the mucous membrane, may have greatly subsided, but the urine is now expelled with some difficulty and without force. There is also deep-seated throbbing pain in the perineum, increased on pressure. The orifice of the urethra is red, and the end of the glans has a dark reddish blush. On examining the prostate by the finger, passed into the bowel, it is found a little swollen, and there is pain on firm pressure. The discharge becomes thin and gleety, and not so purulent as before, and there are sometimes a few drops of blood in straining at stool. These are the symptoms of subacute inflammation of the prostate in gonorrhœa, as it generally occurs.

In the more acute and violent inflammation of the prostate these symptoms are all aggravated. There is often complete retention of urine from the swelling of the gland. The pain in the perineum is increased, and shoots round to the loins, thighs, &c. The discharge quite stops, and the redness of the orifice increases. Examined through the bowel, the gland is hot and very painful to the touch; and the patient has constantly the feeling, as if there were a foreign heavy body in the bowel. Acute prostatitis often ends in abscess. As long as a gleet continues, inflammation of the prostate is liable to be brought on by cold or damp, or excesses in drinking.

Inflammation of the prostate often becomes chronic, the symptoms growing less intense, and assuming a slow wearing character, most prostrating to the bodily and mental powers. In chronic inflammation the pain in the urethra and the weight in the bowel continue though duller and more obscure. There is great irritation of the anus, accompanied often by piles. The discharge is slight, sometimes a mere colourless gleet, but now and then purulent. This often leads to permanent enlargement, and is the most frequent cause of this dangerous malady under the age of forty.

These affections of the prostate are a serious class of diseases. The prostate is a very important gland, not so much perhaps on account of its own functions, as from its position. It surrounds the neck of the bladder, and therefore its diseases often most dangerously interfere with the discharge of the urine. Through it also the seminal ducts pass, and therefore its inflammation is very apt to cause seminal disease. Moreover the affections of the prostate have a dreadfully depressing effect on the spirits, and on the bodily sensations. This is probably owing to the intimate connection of the prostate with the seminal ducts, and with the sexual powers; otherwise it is not easy to account for the overwhelming feelings of obscure and undefinable misery, which oppress the sufferer from these diseases. He feels as if bent down by a weight of lead; and there are perhaps no diseases, which more thoroughly unman a patient, than these. They moreover frequently lay the foundation of incurable enlargement of the prostate later in life; which, especially if it be neglected, is one of the most miserable of all diseases, and utterly breaks down a man, physically and morally. The only way adequately to prevent this miserable class of diseases is to prevent gonorrhœa.

There is another, and a common affection of the prostate, not of so serious a nature, but which causes a great deal of misery. It is called *irritable* prostate. In this there are obscure sensations about the region of the gland, viz., uneasiness in the perineum, weight in the bowel, rather frequent desire to pass water, and a slight gleet, just enough to moisten the linen. The orifice of the canal has a peculiar appearance; it is rather more patent and redder than natural. If the patient drink, or indulge much in sexual intercourse, the discharge may become purulent, and is often mistaken for a fresh gonorrhœa. On going to stool there are often a few drops of a fluid, like a thin mixture of milk and water, pressed out of the urinary canal, by the passage of the fæces, before the stream of urine comes. This is the prostatic fluid. The urine moreover, in this and other prostatic affections, is often turbid with a white cloud, caused by the secretion of alkaline phosphatic salts. These symptoms depend on irritation of the prostatic portion of the urethra, and of the ducts and follicles of the prostate. It is often, like the other prostatic affections, very obstinate, and depresses the mind of the patient greatly. It is frequently accompanied by spermatorrhœa with all its prostrating effects.

Mr. Adams in his excellent treatise on the prostate, gives directions for the treatment of these various diseases. He has found the Chia turpentine, given in five grain doses thrice a-day, a very valuable means of checking the gleety discharge, which proceeds from the surface and follicles of the prostate.

There is yet another and most lamentable consequence, which is liable to follow gonorrhœa. This is an inflammation of the eyes, or ophthalmia, caused by the accidental contact of any of the gonorrhœal discharge with the eyeball. If the slightest particle of this matter be conveyed by the fingers or other substances soiled by it, to the eye, the most frightful form of inflammation of that organ will speedily be set up. Gonorrhœal ophthalmia is perhaps the most violent of all, and the usual methods applied in other diseases of the eye, generally prove here of little avail. The inflammation may run so high, that the eye bursts and sight is irrecoverably lost in twenty-four hours. Generally one eye only is affected; but great care must be taken, especially in the night, that none of the yellow matter from it enters the other, or both may be lost. It is an affection much more common in men than women, chiefly because the male organ, being necessarily so much more handled by the patient, makes contagion more apt to take place.

In the treatment of this disease, almost everything depends on its adoption as early as possible, for if the inflammation be once fully developed in all its fury, medical aid can do little to save the eye. Therefore all who suffer from gonorrhœa, should be especially careful that none of the discharge come in contact inadvertently with their eye, taking care to dip their fingers in water if they touch the matter, and if any symptoms of redness, itching, or a feeling as if of sand rolling under the lids (the usual symptoms of commencing ophthalmia) be perceived, they should at once apply for assistance, as it is only the abortive treatment, or the attempt to nip the disease in the bud, that can here be expected to save vision. The abortive treatment consists in using a strong solution of nitrate of silver, of four or five grains to the ounce, so as to change, if possible, the character of the inflammation. This should be repeated at intervals, if the disease be checked by it; but if it have proceeded to the acute stage, other powerful remedies will be necessary, to give the patient a chance. Thus, bleeding from the arm, leeches round the eye, as well as the caustic solution, should be used; and in some few instances, if these means be energetically employed, sight may be saved.

But it is not only in the adults affected with gonorrhœa, that it may by contagion destroy vision: infants at birth not unfrequently lose both eyes, if their mother happen at the time to have a gonorrhœa. The discharge enters into the child's eyes, as its head is passing through the vagina, and in two or three days after birth, inflammation, with the discharge of pus, heat, and swelling set in; and in many cases both eyes are lost in spite of all the efforts of the physician. Many of the unfortunate tenants of the blind asylums, who awaken our pity in the streets, have lost their sight at birth in this way.

Having now given an outline of most of the important diseases, which may and very often do, arise from gonorrhœa, I come next to the most interesting question; how is this disease, the fountain of so much misery, to be prevented? Prevented it will never be, till mankind in general be roused from their apathy about all physical evils, and most of all about the venereal complaints, and set themselves earnestly to work, to prevent, and, as far as possible, eradicate them. This is one of the diseases, whose prevention is comparatively easy, as we know well its cause, which is single and definite. To effect its prevention therefore, what we want is earnest endeavour and co-operation. In our own persons we should carefully avoid spreading the disease, and in others we should do all we can to prevent their catching it, and to cure it if caught. We should seek, above all, completely to do away with prostitution, which is the grand cause of the venereal diseases. I shall speak hereafter of the mode in which this great object is to be effected.

Besides these social and moral means for the prevention of gonorrhœa, there are means which each individual should use, who wishes in the present dangerous state of the sexual world, and as long as prostitution exists among us, neither to receive nor to give infection. No one should ever neglect, after a suspicious sexual connection, (and all mercenary love is to be viewed as such,) to make water immediately, and also to wash well the genital organs, whether with pure water, or with a chlorine or alkaline wash, which is more effectual, but not so easily to be had. The external washing will prevent any chance of balanitis, and will render the occurrence of chancre much less probable. The urine will cleanse the canal internally, and probably prevent a gonorrhœa, even though the female should be highly diseased.

Even though one has great confidence in a woman's assertion that she is not diseased, yet if she have been exposed to infection, these precautions should never be neglected; as she may communicate a disease from infectious matter having been retained in her organs, though without causing disease in her. In fact, it should be recognised as a settled rule in all mercenary intercourse, as long as it lasts in the world, that both parties should wash carefully immediately after connection; which simple precaution, so easy of application, would of itself prevent the great majority of diseases. It is now very generally adopted, both by men and women, among those who have experience, self-regard, and prudence in these matters; but it is too often neglected, whether from carelessness or inexperience, or still more from ignorance and intoxication, especially among the poorer classes. Women of the better description, both expect and are glad to see precautions used, which are a guarantee of their own safety, and themselves habitually employ them. Besides these means, the venereal act should not be prolonged, and ejaculation should take place, as the semen helps to cleanse the canal.

But by far the most certain preventive of gonorrhœa, and of all other venereal diseases, is the *condom*, an artificial sheath for the penis, made of very delicate membrane; which, if well made, so as not to be torn, renders gonorrhœa impossible. It is so thin as not very greatly to interfere with the venereal enjoyment; and yet from many causes it is comparatively seldom used in this country. In the first place, the shyness between the sexes, which is much greater here than abroad, prevents the man from using, what he may think would show him to be suspicious, or might be disliked, or thought unnatural, by the woman; who probably for the most part is perfectly apathetic about the matter, or would rather be glad to see means used, which would save herself also from any risk. Moreover, the sheath has been proscribed by moralists, as an unnatural, and therefore immoral interference with the normal act, and final cause, of sexual intercourse; and therefore it is sometimes difficult to procure it in this country, as it is sold only in a few shops, which have a low moral character, and in an under-hand way. Nay, on its first invention and introduction into France, as a means of preventing venereal diseases, we learn from M. Parent Duchatelet, that a body of medical men, who met to deliberate on the subject, published to their own shame, their strong disapprobation of the invention and its author, not on account of the facility it might give to the secret indulgence of sexual desires, unburdened by the fear of offspring, but because they held it a sin to attempt to prevent these diseases! It gives one pain to think that the good Duchatelet, whose life-time was devoted, like that of Dr. Andrew Combe, to the prevention of disease, and whose great work on prostitution I shall afterwards treat of, should have also adopted this perverted, and in him too strangely illogical, opinion.

It is a very great pity that ideas, many of them so sinful, for by no other name can one term those prejudices, which stand in the way of the sacred cause of the prevention of disease, should prove a barrier to the introduction, and free liberty of using, according to the necessities of each case, a means which in the present condition of society is of so very great value. Indeed its discovery, if rightly viewed, may be, and I trust one day, shall be considered, as a very great benefit to society. As a preventive of venereal disease, the sheath is most invaluable; with its aid, one may pass scatheless through the very midst of infection; and for any one in whom disease is particularly to be dreaded, as in a weakly constitution, or a patient with spermatorrhœa or other evils, its protection is often the greatest blessing.

But it has fared with this instrument, just as with all other efforts to prevent venereal diseases; all have been alike discountenanced, or at best, viewed with apathy, by the mistaken moralist; to whom these hideous and desolating diseases appear more as a salutary warning to men, the existence of which he would rather coldly ascribe to providence, than to his own and other's lukewarmness. Would that the reader may feel, as strongly as I do, the injustice, immorality, and want of human sympathy, contained in such opinions!

When society has become fully alive to the desire to prevent venereal diseases, as well as all others, then and not till then, will the great value of the sheath be perceived, as a most powerful means of such prevention. Meanwhile it were very desirable that it should come into more general use, and that there should be a greater facility of obtaining it; so that each individual who wishes to avail himself of it, may readily do so. All attempts to interfere with its sale, or with the perfect freedom of procuring it, must be looked on as injurious to the interests of society, and liable to occasion the most deplorable diseases.

Care should be taken that the sheath, if used, should be made of good materials, not pervious, and that the same one should not be used frequently, as thus it becomes less trustworthy. Along with its use, the other precautions of making water and washing should not be neglected; and were these precautions generally made known and adopted we should have in a short time the number of venereal diseases wonderfully reduced, and endless human misery, hate, crime, and bitterness spared.

Besides these precautions during and after coition, there are some other prophylactics, which are very useful for those who expose themselves much to infection, especially if they do not use the sheath. They are more efficacious as preventives of balanitis and chancre, than of gonorrhœa; consisting as they do, in means for hardening the external mucous membrane. Those who have been circumcised, as I stated before, never have balanitis, and they are also much less subject to chancre; because the mucous membrane of the glans becomes hardened by constant exposure, and excoriations rarely take place in coition, into which the chancrous matter may find a way. Those who have much promiscuous sexual intercourse might imitate this, by drawing back the prepuce, and so keeping the glans habitually exposed, a state of things which in many persons is natural. This is a powerful preventive of balanitis and syphilis, and is especially necessary for those, in whom the mucous membrane is apt to excoriate and tear in coition, which renders them very liable to chancre. Under exposure the mucous membrane will become tough and insusceptible of infection. Sponging with cold water, or what is more powerful, washing frequently with some astringent, as the decoction of oak bark, acts also as a preventive by hardening the parts.

However unfortunate a man may be in getting a gonorrhœa, no one who has a true heart, with love for his kind, will ever give one to another. Neither in carelessness nor sport, for as we have seen, it may be a death-sport; nor from a wish to be revenged on the sex in the person of a helpless girl, innocent at least towards him, and who has so few friends, or kind treatment, an action unmanly and unfeeling; nor from ignorance whether his gleet be infectious—knowing that while a sign of yellow matter remains, it is probably still infectious, and in such a case, if he will not abstain, he must wear the sheath; nor from heedlessness, irreverence for the girl, want of heart, nor bluntness of conscience, from which feelings may the reader ever be free. A man in the present state of society has far less excuse for giving the disease to another, than a woman, as the latter, from the peculiar form of the female genital organs, may possibly not know that she is diseased; and besides she has often the powerful excuses of destitution, the necessity of gaining a livelihood, friendlessness, and, last not least, her shameful degradation in the eyes of society to plead for her, while we have none of these. But I trust that the reader, very far from doing anything to spread these or other diseases, will rather, to the best of his powers, co-operate in the endeavour to prevent them.

SYPHILIS.

If the disease, which I have just been describing, viz., gonorrhœa, be frequently viewed in a light and jesting manner, by those who are unacquainted with the lamentable consequences it so often occasions, and by the young and thoughtless,—such is not the case with the much more formidable and dreaded disease, which comes now before us. While the former is merely a simple inflammation, rendered frequently serious only by the vitally important nature of the organs, where it occurs, syphilis consists in a peculiar and specific poison; which, if it be once fairly introduced into the system, contaminates the whole frame, and produces the most deplorable effects.

Of all the plagues and scourges of mankind in the present day, this disease may certainly be said to be the most fearful. It does not overwhelm us with sudden panic and destruction, like cholera, or other epidemic evils, which come but rarely, and therefore, however fearful their visitations, have not a permanent influence on our fate; but it is always with us, preying on our vitals, and slowly sapping the constitution, moral and physical, of thousands; and these the young, hopeful, and vigorous, the pride and the promise of our race. Mankind will yet, and let us hope ere long, become universally alive to the fearful prejudice and inhumanity, which have suffered this disease to run on so long without any means being taken for its prevention and eradication.

Syphilis, commonly called pox, is the disease produced by a poisonous matter, introduced into the frame during sexual intercourse. It first appears locally on the genital organs of either sex, in the form of a small ulcer; the poison of which is in many cases absorbed into the general system, giving rise to the most dreadful consequences. The symptoms of the disease are therefore divided into three classes, according as they mark different stages of the poisoning, local or general. These classes are the primary, the secondary, and the tertiary.

Primary syphilis consists in a small ulcer, secreting a poisonous and contagious matter, and seated on the part which has been exposed to contagion. It is produced by the contact of the secretion of a similar ulcer, with an unprotected surface. When any of the matter of a syphilitic ulcer, in an individual affected with the disease, finds its way beneath the skin or mucous membrane of a healthy person, the following results take place. During the first twenty four-hours, the point of the skin where the virus is, becomes red; in the second and third day, a little pimple rises on it; in the third and fourth, the pimple becomes a vesicle, filled with clear fluid; on the fourth and fifth, this fluid becomes thick and yellow, and the vesicle thus becomes a pustule with a slightly depressed centre, exactly like one of the small-pox pustules. In the sixth and seventh days, the matter dries up, and forms a crust, which in a few more days falls off, disclosing a small ulcer, about the size of a split pea. Its base is rather hard from the effusion of some lymph around; its sides are abrupt and a little everted, so that it looks as if cleanly cut out with a punch; its surface covered with a whitish tenacious film, and secreting a thin acrid pus, which possesses the contagious properties.

Such is, in many cases, the apparently slight and simple origin of this terrible disease. A *chancre*, for so the small ulcer is named, is, in the male, generally seated on some part of the glans of the penis, or on the internal or external surface of the prepuce; sometimes, though rarely, inside the urethra, like gonorrhœa. A chancre is not, like gonorrhœa, confined to mucous membranes; it may arise on all parts of the body alike, provided the contagious matter be introduced beneath the skin. Hence, accoucheurs sometimes contract the disease, in examining pregnant women affected with it, if they happen to have a scratch on the finger.

To give rise to chancre, a closer contact of its peculiar poisonous matter is necessary, than in gonorrhœa, which is caused merely by the pus coming in contact with a mucous membrane. The matter of chancre however must be introduced below the surface, whether of the skin or of a mucous membrane, so as to come in contact with the blood, else it will not act. Hence infection is produced either by its meeting some abrasion of the surface, or by its getting into a little follicle or pouch, where it lies dormant for a short time, till it has eaten its way into the quick, and then it is developed into the ulcer. It may also perhaps, if allowed to remain long enough, eat its way through a mucous surface by its acrid properties. If it meet an abrasion, the ulcer begins immediately to be developed, and frequently without going through the previous stages of pimple, vesicle, and pustule; if it has to eat its way through the tissues, some days may pass before the disease shows itself.

But the primary ulcer is in many cases by no means of so mild and simple a nature, but may be a most serious disease. There are several different forms of chancre, occasioned, according to some authors, by specific differences in the nature of the poisonous matter, but according to others, (among whom is M. Ricord, and who believe that there is but one syphilitic poison), by the differences of constitution in the patients. One of these is the *gangrenous* or phagedænic (or eating) ulcer—a most terrible disease. In it the inflammation caused by the poisonous matter, runs so high, that mortification is produced, which has a tendency to spread on every side, destroying the tissues, so that a part and sometimes even the whole of the penis is lost, and even death may result. This is by no means an uncommon form of the disease, and in the hospitals in our large towns, most deplorable instances of it are constantly to be seen. Those who admit but one kind of syphilitic poison, assert that this fearful kind of sore is owing to the badness of the patient's constitution. It is chiefly found in young plethoric persons of dissipated habits, who are weakened by intemperance or other noxious influences Others say that the character of the sore depends on the kind of matter which produced it, and thus that a gangrenous ulcer is generated by one of a similar nature. Probably both of these causes influence its development.

Another important variety of chancre is the *indurated* one, in which a large quantity of lymph is thrown out into the surrounding tissue, giving it a hard cartilaginous base, which remains after the ulcer is healed.

These are the most important forms of the primary ulcer, as well from their local peculiarities, as from their comparative likelihood to give rise to secondary symptoms. General poisoning of the system may follow all of them, but it is much less likely to occur after the simple and the phagedænic, than after the indurated chancre. While the former varieties are followed by secondary symptoms in comparatively a small proportion of cases, indurated chancre gives rise to them almost invariably, becoming thus the most formidable of all the varieties of chancre. M. Ricord, to whom, more than perhaps to any other, mankind are indebted for the most valuable statistical and explanatory facts connected with venereal diseases, says that general poisoning succeeds to indurated chancre in eighty-eight cases in a hundred.

The poison is absorbed into the system from a chancre by the veins and absorbent vessels, through whose thin coats it penetrates and mingles with the vital current; and after a short time, generally in from six to eight weeks, it shows itself by the following symptoms, which have received the name of *secondary* syphilis. Different forms of eruption, frequently accompanied by ulceration of the mucous membrane of the throat, break out over the body. In this secondary stage nature tries to throw off the poisonous matter by the skin and mucous surface. But if the disease remain still uneradicated, which will probably be the case, unless proper treatment be adopted, symptoms of a still graver nature will arise, constituting the third stage, or *tertiary* syphilis. In this stage, it is the bones and deeper tissues, which are chiefly attacked. The bones of the palate, the nose, the skull, the shin, and in general, all the bones which lie nearest the surface of the body, may become inflamed and mortify, thus giving rise to deep abscesses and most melancholy deformities. Thus may the disease, when once it has fairly gained admittance into the system, continue in it for years, causing one after the other, symptoms ever more and more calamitous; and it is sometimes very difficult wholly to dislodge it, or to know when the patient is safe from its recurring persecutions. But I will speak more fully of these later symptoms hereafter, and meanwhile revert to the primary stage and its treatment.

If a man be so unfortunate as to contract a chancre, it is of the utmost importance, that it be destroyed as soon as possible. The shorter the time it is allowed to exist, the less risk will there be of the occurrence of secondary poisoning. Thus any one, who has exposed himself to the shance of contagion, should watch carefully for the first signs of the disease, and if he observe any traces of the different stages, the pimple, the vesicle, the pustule, or the ulcer, he should at once resort to treatment. This should consist in destroying the poison by cauterizing the sore; if there be a vesicle or a pustule, it should be broken, and a fine point of the nitrate of silver introduced, and the part thoroughly cauterized. If an ulcer be already formed, cauterization is still the best of all methods of healing it speedily, and preventing secondaries. It should be cauterized at intervals, until the surface presents a healthy appearance, secreting a simple yellow pus, instead of the thin poisonous matter. It should be also frequently washed with some stimulating astringent, which will wipe away the acrid secretion, and harden the surrounding parts, so as to prevent, if possible, the absorption of the virus. A piece of lint soaked in this lotion, should also be kept constantly applied. Ricord uses for this purpose the aromatic wine, a French preparation; and if it cannot be had, Mr. Acton recommends a lotion composed of eight ounces of the decoction of oak bark, and half an ounce of the tincture of catechu, which will answer equally well. Under this simple treatment, the mild form of chancre generally heals readily in eight to ten days; and even if left to itself, it may heal in three or four weeks; and in the majority of cases secondary poisoning will not follow.

In the gangrenous form of chancre, Ricord's treatment is to soothe the inflammatory sore, by the constant application of lint dipped in a strong solution of opium; and, by regulating the diet and other hygienic means, to brace the depraved constitution of the patient, which he believes to be the chief cause of this formidable variety of the disease. By these means, he says, the disease is soon arrested, only destroying the part first engaged, and being succeeded by a healthy ulcer that soon heals. Other surgeons prefer to treat it by the most powerful caustics, such as the nitric acid, which burns out the poisoned part, and leaves a healthy surface underneath. Either mode is sometimes powerless in checking the ravages of the disease, which, as has been mentioned, may in severe cases destroy the whole penis. If a cure take place, as generally happens, the reparative processes of nature often leave much less deformity than might have been expected, even though a considerable part of the penis may have been destroyed. This form of chancre is followed by secondary poisoning only in a minor proportion of cases; although when they do occur, they are usually of a peculiarly severe nature.

If a chancre become indurated either before or during treatment, cauterization and the astringent applications should not be resorted to; as the disease is no longer a simple one, and these means will scarcely succeed in curing it. The ulcer may indeed heal under their use, but the induration remains, and is very liable to break out again into ulceration. Therefore in cases of indurated chancre, Ricord gives mercury, a medicine which seems to have a specific power over syphilis; and under its action the induration generally soon disappears. The indurated sore is the only variety of primary syphilis in which he gives mercury; and his reasons for doing so are, first, that without it the induration is very difficult to remove, and secondly, that secondary symptoms almost invariably follow this variety of chancre, and the mercurial treatment often prevents their occurrence.

There is scarcely any question on which surgeons are more divided, than on the propriety of giving mercury in syphilis. In former times it was thought to be impossible to cure the disease without it; and the unfortunate patients were one and all subjected to the most severe salivation, a remedy which was often worse than the disease. But it was afterwards discovered, that many cases were perfectly curable without mercury at all; and hence the non-mercurialists, proceeding to the opposite extreme, refused to give that medicine, whose baneful affect on the human frame is well known, in any case. Between these opposite opinions arose the eclectic school, of which Ricord is one, and from his immense experience in the Parisian hospitals, there is no one whose views deserve more deference. He made extensive experiments in both modes of treatment, with, and without mercury, in all the various stages, and it is from his results that the treatment here recommended is chiefly taken. He does not give mercury in any form of primary chancre, except it be attended with a certain degree of induration. In simple cases, where most probably no general poisoning will occur, it would be very injudicious to give so dangerous a remedy as mercury; which is only to be used when a greater evil is by its means alone to be overcome. Ricord gives mercury at all times very cautiously and in small doses, rarely, if ever, producing salivation, (which is an inflammation and swelling of the gums and sides of the mouth, with a profuse discharge of saliva, caused by the powerful action of mercury on the system), which he sedulously avoids as an evil. He gives generally, one grain of the protoioduret of mercury with one grain of henbane in pill every night to begin with, and increases gradually the dose by a grain at a time, every five or six days, if the disease remain stationary; but if healing commences, he continues at the same dose, and does not leave it off at once, but gradually diminishes it, after a cure has taken place.

Before Ricord's investigations on syphilis, it was often impossible to be certain, whether an ulcer on the genital organs was syphilitic or not, for ulcers may arise from other causes. The appearance of the ulcer was the chief criterion by which surgeons were guided; the syphilitic ulcer having often a peculiar form, which the practised eye readily recognises. But in many cases the ulcer did not present this characteristic form, and as the statements of the patients, especially females, as to previous exposure to infection, were unfortunately not to be relied on, it was often impossible to say whether an ulcer was syphilitic or not; a question of course of the utmost importance. Ricord however, discovered a certain and simple test for this, namely, by inoculation. If some of the matter secreted by a chancre be introduced on the point of a lancet below the skin on another part of the body, it will give rise to a similar sore, which will go through all the stages of pimple, vesicle, pustule, and ulcer described above. By this inoculation, (exactly similar to that used in small-pox, and vaccination,) the mysteries of syphilis were cleared up, and a means was given for drawing a definite line between different forms of disease, till then too often confounded. It had often been thought before, that chancre and gonorrhœa were produced by the same poison, and could mutually cause each other, but Ricord's test shows them to be totally distinct. The matter of gonorrhœa when inoculated will not produce a chancre; it is merely the product of an inflamed mucous membrane, somewhat similar to the thick matter that runs from the nose, or is expectorated from the chest in a bronchitic attack, (although there must be something peculiarly acrid and irritating in its nature,) and hence, no poisoning of the system can result from it. All venereal diseases are thus divided into the virulent and the non-virulent, distinguishable by this test of inoculation; the one capable of causing secondary poisoning, the other not. Inoculation is performed by introducing some matter from the sore under the skin on the thigh of the patient; if an ulcer forms, it is at once destroyed by cauterization. The sore formed on the thigh is similar in character to the one on the penis; therefore a gangrenous sore should not be inoculated. Ricord never permitted himself to inoculate one individual with matter from another; and therefore it is not known whether, in such a case, a similar variety of sore would be produced.

Animals cannot be inoculated with chancre,—a very singular fact—whilst it has been recently discovered that the cow-pock, or pustule formed on the udder of the cow, from which we derive the inestimable boon of vaccination, may be caused by the introduction of the matter of a small pox-pustule under the skin of that animal. Therefore we owe our protection from that fearful disease to the modification it undergoes in passing through the system of an animal; one of the most striking and wonderful facts, presented to us by science, showing how subtly linked together are all parts of the animal world.

A chancre may, though rarely, be developed inside the urethra, and it was owing to its secretion being mistaken for gonorrhœa, that the latter disease was supposed in some instances to cause general poisoning. The symptoms of urethral chancre are; generally in not less than a fortnight after the infection, (during part of which time the virus has doubtless lain dormant in one of the follicles in the canal), a thin yellowish secretion, sometimes streaked with blood, begins to flow from the orifice of the urethra. Pain is felt in making water at one point of the canal, and here pressure also is painful, and perhaps some hardness may be felt. On opening the orifice of the canal, the chancre may often be seen. By these marks, and by the fact that the secretion does not begin to flow till about a fortnight after infection, the ulcer taking some days to pass through its previous stages, this disease may be distinguished from gonorrhœa. Inoculation will, if need be, help to decide the question.

The treatment here is the same as for external chancre, according to the different varieties. If a simple chancre, cauterization and injections of aromatic wine; if it become indurated, causing stricture, then mercury; if it be gangrenous, it is a fearful disease, and may extend to the bladder and cause death, though happily such a termination is rare.

Any of these varieties of chancre may be accompanied or followed by a *Bubo*; which is included among the primary symptoms, as it is a local complaint, and does not show that the system has become infected.

Secondary symptoms are not more frequent, where there has been a bubo, than where there has not. A bubo, as has been already described, is the inflammation of one of the glands of the groin. In gonorrhœa it occurs sometimes, but then it is a simple non-virulent affection, caused merely by the irritation of the neighbouring disease. But the bubo which accompanies chancre, is often caused by the presence of syphilitic matter in the gland, to which it has been conveyed by the absorbent vessels from the chancre. In such a case the inflammation of the gland proceeds rapidly; it swells, reddens, and suppurates, disclosing an ulcerated surface, which is in fact a large chancre, and secretes the same virulent inoculable matter as the primary sore. But all buboes occurring during chancre, are not virulent; they may be caused just as in gonorrhœa, by the simple irritation produced by the neighbourhood of the chancre. These buboes are not virulent, and if they suppurate, the matter they secrete is not inoculable. Now, when a bubo occurs during a chancre, how can we distinguish whether it be virulent or not; whether it be caused by the absorption of poisonous matter, or merely by irritation? Before suppuration has occurred and inoculation is possible, it is often beyond our power to determine whether a bubo be, or be not virulent; and we can only presume it to be so by the greater rapidity and intractability of its progress. But this does not make any difference in the treatment, which should always aim at preventing, if possible, suppuration.

Buboes generally occur during the second or third week of chancre, rarely earlier; and it is remarked by Ricord, that they occur chiefly when a chancre is situated at or near the *frœnum* or little band of mucous membrane, which joins the glans and prepuce. The first symptoms of bubo are, a pain in a gland in the groin, which gradually swells, inflames and becomes very tender and painful, so as to prevent all motion. The swelling increases, if the disease be not arrested, and suppuration takes place attended by shivering. The matter either makes its own way to the surface, or is let out by the lancet, and an ulcerated surface is left, secreting a virulent or non-virulent pus, as the case may be. This sore sometimes heals readily, but in other cases, where the constitution is bad, or the disease very virulent and extensive, it may be tedious and intractable.

In the treatment of bubo, it is of great importance that suppuration, with all its tedious and uncertain course, should be if possible prevented; and therefore every means should be taken to cut short the disease. The most important of all these means is, that the disease be taken in time. Whenever the least pain or swelling is felt in any gland of the groin, by a patient affected with chancre, he should at once lay himself up, as every step of exercise he takes will aggravate the complaint, which advances very rapidly, and soon proceeds beyond our power to check it. Cold water or ice should then be diligently applied, and this often at once arrests the disease. However if the cold do not succeed, or if it seem rather to increase than to arrest the swelling, compression should be next tried. This is effected by a spiral bandage, wrapped round the loins and over a pad placed on the swollen gland in the groin. This means, if employed early, often succeeds in suppressing the disease. But if the inflammation gain ground, and be too powerful for these measures, they must be left off, and antiphlogistics resorted to, viz: the application of leeches and poultices to the gland, and tartar emetic given internally to produce nausea, just as in the case of inflammation of the testicle. By these means also, success is frequently obtained, and suppuration prevented. But often, and especially when the bubo is a virulent one, caused by the absorption of syphilitic matter, this desirable end cannot be obtained, and pus begins to be formed in the gland. As soon as suppuration takes place, (which is attended here, as in other parts of the body, usually by shivering and feverish creeping of the skin), and the surgeon learns that pus is present by the feeling of fluctuation imparted to the fingers, the sooner it is let out the better. It is much better to let it out by the lancet, than to wait till nature makes an opening, because the latter process is slow, and accompanied by a greater spread of the ulceration. When the suppurating surface of a virulent bubo is laid open, it is to be treated just as a simple chancre, which in fact it is, by cauterization and aromatic wine; or, if it be gangrenous or indurated, the same treatment should be used as for the corresponding primary ulcers. When the constitution is scrofulous, a bubo is often a most intractable and tedious disease, and may bring on the worst consequences, by the long confinement and other weakening influences it necessitates.

I now come to speak of secondary symptoms. These are caused by the absorption into the blood of the poisonous matter from the primary sore, and make their appearance generally in from six to eight weeks after its commencement. They rarely appear earlier than this, but are often postponed till later, from various causes. Thus a course of mercury taken for the primary sore, seems sometimes wholly to prevent, and at other times to delay, their appearance, so that they do not break out till considerably later than usual. Ricord does not believe that they can occur after an interval of years, as some authors assert. The dread of this secondary poisoning is one of the great terrors of the disease, for after the occurrence of a primary sore, the patient is kept for a long time in anxiety and suspense, whether the whole system have been contaminated or not.

Secondary symptoms are not capable of being transmitted by contagion from one individual to another, and they are not inoculable; but they are so far hereditary, that the child in the womb may be infected by the disease of the mother. They consist of various eruptions on the skin, often attended with ulcerated sore throat, and rheumatic pains in different parts of the body. There are several kinds of these eruptions, of various appearance and severity. Some consist of rosy spots very like measles, others of pimples scattered over the body, both of which gradually assume a peculiar copper-coloured appearance, which is very characteristic of the syphilitic disease. These are the most common and the most readily curable. Others, which are of a much graver nature, and are generally found in broken-down constitutions, consist of a number of small corroding ulcers, scattered over the skin, and covered by hard dark scabs. This eruption is generally accompanied by great exhaustion of the powers, and the patient may even sink under it. Another form is that called *lepra* or *psoriasis*, in which the body is covered by patches of eruption, on which scales of dry cuticle constantly form and fall off. This scaly disease is exceedingly obstinate and intractable. Another consists of what are called *condylomata* or mucous tubercles, which are smooth fleshy elevations, rising on soft parts of the skin, especially on the scrotum and groin, and round the anus. They may extend and cover the whole of these parts, and thus form a most loathsome mass of disease. Their surface ulcerates and secretes an offensive fluid, which however, like all other products of secondary symptoms, is incapable of transmitting the disease.

These constitute the most important forms of the syphilitic eruptions; they are generally preceded or accompanied by feverishness, loss of strength and appetite, a pale leaden complexion, and sometimes by a pustular eruption on the scalp, causing the hair to fall out, so that baldness is produced.

They are often accompanied moreover, by the important and serious complication of ulcerated sore-throat, which begins by redness and swelling of the mucous membrane at the back part of the mouth, causing hoarseness, and pain in swallowing. This affection is generally a chronic one, and may continue for months in this first stage without ulceration, if care be taken; but at other times, and especially under exposure to wet, or intemperate habits of the patient, it may become deeply ulcerated, and be very intractable.

Another organ which is often attacked in the course of the secondary poisoning, is the eye, the *iris* of which may become inflamed; and if prompt treatment be not adopted, vision may be lost. This affection is generally found in very bad constitutions,—in the miserable, half-starved, and intemperate poor of both sexes.

These then, the various eruptions, the sore-throat, the iritis, and the rheumatic pains in the limbs, constitute the symptoms of secondary poisoning; various degrees and combinations of which occur in different cases. It has been said, that it is chiefly after indurated chancre that they occur; the other varieties, viz., the simple and phagedænic, comparatively rarely giving rise to them. After the poison has been taken into the system, it lies dormant for awhile, and it is generally after exposure of some kind, whether to wet, cold, or other depressing influence, that these secondary symptoms appear. The moment that any of them are observed, treatment should be resorted to; and where this is done, and circumstances are otherwise favourable, a cure will generally soon be obtained. The favourable circumstances are, that the constitution of the patient be good, that he should take every pains to co-operate in his cure by avoiding exposure to cold or excesses of any kind; and that his system be not weakened by previous injudicious courses of mercury, so as to be intolerant of this medicine, which is Ricord's grand remedy for secondary poisoning. In his experience he has found, that though secondaries may get well without mercury, merely by care, warm baths, low diet, and other simple means, yet they prove often very obstinate under such treatment, and are very apt to return in a severer form, which mercury may no longer have the same power to control. He therefore, gives mercury in the moderate doses mentioned before, so as never, if possible, to produce salivation, in nearly all cases of secondary symptoms. Besides this, the peculiar treatment of each of the various symptoms is as follows.—For the different kinds of eruption, warm baths are exceedingly useful, as they soothe the skin, and excite it to a healthy action. In most cases they may be taken twice a week, the patient remaining in them for from half an hour to two hours. If there be mucous tubercles, they should be kept very clean, as inattention to cleanliness is a great cause of them. They should be washed at intervals with a solution of chloride of soda, then dusted over with calomel, and dry lint placed between their surfaces; a method which we have seen in balanitis to have so good an effect in checking mucous secretions. The sore throat should be lightly cauterized every three or four days with the nitrate of silver, and gargled with some astringent gargle, as the following: four ounces of the decoction of oak, or cinchona bark, and one drachm of dilute muriatic acid. Great attention should be paid to diet, and manner of life, which should be strictly hygienic, avoiding late hours, excitement, or any other debilitating influence. A light, plain, and nutritious diet should be taken during the treatment; and great care must be observed in avoiding all exposure to damp or cold, while under the mercurial course.

By these means a cure is generally effected, although some cases are very tedious and intractable. It is especially in scrofulous and lymphatic constitutions that syphilis, like all other diseases, is most to be dreaded, and when once it has taken root, is most difficult to dislodge.

If, from any cause, whether from the neglect of treatment, or the employment of injudicious or inefficient means, or, it may be, from the weakness of the constitution, or the deep root which the poison has taken in it, the disease be not eradicated in this secondary stage, other symptoms succeed, of a still more formidable nature. The secondary symptoms either gradually merge into them, after having lasted for months, with constant relapses; or an interval of two or three years may take place between the cessation of the secondary symptoms, and the outbreak of their still more formidable successors. In the latter, it is now no longer the skin which is the seat of the affection, but the deeper tissues, viz: the bones, and the periosteum or membrane which covers them, and also the submucous or subcutaneous tissues. This stage of syphilis is styled by Ricord, the tertiary, as it generally occurs later than the secondary one; which usually, though not in all cases, precedes it, and often by degrees merges into it.

In the secondary symptoms, says Ricord, the specific nature of the syphilitic poison still remains, although greatly modified by its transfusion through the economy; therefore these may be inherited by the child in the womb, though they are not inoculable; and they require a specific treatment by mercury. But in the tertiary stage, the poison is quite transformed by its long sojourn in the system; therefore are tertiary symptoms not hereditary, and should be treated by general and not specific means.

The tertiary symptoms are as follows: A large abscess may form at the back of the throat, burst, and disclose a deep, tawney, and sloughing ulcer, at the bottom of which the dead bone may be felt with a probe. The root of the nose may be attacked in the same manner, and large portions of the bones of the nose and the palate die and come away. Here it is the bones of the nose, palate, etc., which are first attacked by inflammation, either in their substance, or in their lining membrane; and as the vitality of bones is of a low character, they soon die when their nutrition is interfered with by disease, and are then cast off. Along with these lamentable occurrences, a pustular or scabby eruption often appears on the extremities; the unfortunate patient, whose constitution has been reduced to the lowest state by the long continuance of the disease, emaciates rapidly, and, if not relieved by proper treatment, may die from the hectic induced by the diarrhœa, and profuse suppuration, the want of sleep from pains in the bones, loss of appetite, and all the other powers of nutrition; although death is a result which very seldom proceeds from syphililis, when alone and uncomplicated with other diseases.

In other cases, different bones throughout the body are attacked in a similar way by inflammation, followed by abscess, suppuration, and discharge of the dead parts of bone. It is chiefly the bones nearest the surface that are attacked, for instance, the shin-bone, the skull, and breast-bone. When disease occurs in these, there are first general rheumatic pains felt, which soon become fixed in certain spots of particular bones, and are very much aggravated during the night, so as to prevent sleep. In these spots the bones or their lining membranes inflame, and if the inflammation be not subdued, they may go on to suppuration and caries, or mortify, and pieces of them come away. It is generally the bones themselves which are inflamed, more rarely their investing membrane. When this membrane, the periosteum, is inflamed, *nodes* or painful swellings are formed, by the effusion of lymph or other product of inflammation. These nodes are generally situated on the subcutaneous bones, as the shin, collar-bone, etc. They are very painful, chiefly at night; sometimes chronic, sometimes acute, proceeding to suppuration, and disclosing, when they burst, dead bone underneath. For the periosteum not only invests the bone, but supplies it with nourishment from the numerous blood-vessels, which it contains; and when it becomes inflamed and separated from the bone, the latter perishes from want of nutriment.

Another symptom of tertiary syphilis, is the occurrence of *subcutaneous tumors*, (tumors beneath the skin). These occur, like the other tertiary symptoms, in cases where the poison has been long rooted in the system, and generally long after the first appearance of secondary symptoms. They are small tumors about the size of a hazel nut, either solitary or in several parts of the body, situated beneath the skin or mucous membrane. They remain perhaps for months indolent, without causing any inconvenience, but when they have attained the size of a small nut, they burst and discharge a thin ichorous matter. An irritable little cavity, prone to inflammation and difficult to heal, is left behind; and no sooner is it healed, than other tumors spring up in its place, and go through the same course. These tumors may form in the substance of the tongue and back part of the mouth, bursting and forming splits and fissures which pour out a fetid discharge, forming a most loathsome disease, and impeding the movements of the tongue. This affection has often been mistaken for cancer of the tongue, to which it bears a great resemblance in many respects, but it is curable, while cancer unfortunately is not. These tumors are generally accompanied by other tertiary symptoms, as pains and inflammation of the bones, &c.,

Both in the secondary, and in the tertiary symptoms, the co-existence of various affections gives mutual proof of their syphilitic nature. Thus we can judge whether an attack of sore throat be syphilitic, by observing whether there be any other secondary symptoms present, as for instance a syphilitic eruption. Sometimes it is very difficult to determine whether an affection be of syphilitic origin or not, as there are scarcely any of the syphilitic symptoms secondary and tertiary, which are not to a great degree similar in outward appearance to other non-venereal affections. Thus there are common sore throat; rheumatic pains and inflammations of the bones; rosy, pimply, and pustular eruptions, which have a close resemblance to the syphilitic ones, although of totally different origin. There are however differences in the peculiar appearance of the diseases, which generally enable the practised eye to recognise those arising from the syphilitic poison.

Now it is of immense importance to be able to distinguish between a venereal and a non-venereal disease, as the treatment in the two cases is very different. The patients themselves, whose chief interest it is, that a correct judgment should be formed and proper treatment adopted, too often, instead of giving every assistance to the physician in arriving at the nature of the disease, do all they can to mislead him, by denying exposure to infection. This arises from the deplorable social ignorance of the seriousness and true meaning of diseases, and the necessity of our having every possible guide to the treatment of them; and still more from that most pernicious and sinful mode of looking with abhorrence on venereal diseases, which makes people ashamed to confess them, and which we have already seen in so many cases to do such incalculable mischief.

It is especially women, who in these matters destroy themselves, by their endeavours to deceive the surgeon : they scarcely ever admit, until closely pressed, their exposure to infection, but seem to expect, that it is enough for the physician to see their complaint and undertake its treatment, in the dark as to its real nature. There is no end to the mischief done by these foolish courses, and by their reluctance to apply for aid till they are forced to do so by the severity of their symptoms; evils, which lie at the door of those who take such harsh and degrading views of the genital organs and their diseases.

The treatment of tertiary symptoms is very different from that of secondaries. Here mercury, instead of doing good, would rather exasperate the disease, and still more enfeeble the patient; for the specific syphilitic nature of the poison is now so much changed, that mercury has no longer power over it. Ricord's grand remedy for tertiaries is the hydriodate of potash. Iodine, which is the chief ingredient in this compound, has a very powerful influence in removing, and checking chronic inflammation and its effects in the tertiary symptoms are often marvellous. It is given in the tertiary inflammation of the bones and periosteum of the palate, nose, shin, skull, &c., of which I have spoken, in doses beginning with ten or twelve grains taken during the day, and mounting up to even one hundred and twenty grains in the twenty-four hours, if the disease do not yield. At the same time, the constitution of the patient, which is generally much shattered, must be supported by plain and nourishing diet, and braced by fresh air, and other necessary hygienic means. Under the influence of the hydriodate of potash, the putrid ulceration of the throat generally soon puts on a healthy character, and heals up; though the bones and other tissues which have been lost, can never be restored.

For the indolent and painful nodes on the shins and elsewhere, Ricord uses the following treatment. A blister should be applied over them, and allowed to rise well. When this has been taken off, poultices, or lint steeped in a strong solution of opium, and covered with oiled silk to prevent evaporation, should be applied. This treatment often acts like a charm with indolent nodes, though it is of course not applicable to the acute ones; the severe pain being allayed and the wearied sufferer dropping to sleep, even while the blister is rising.

The water cure is said to be exceedingly powerful in tertiary syphilis, especially in cases where the constitution is greatly broken down by the combined effects of the disease and the mercury used in its treatment; and where the hydriodate of potash fails or cannot be borne. There are few diseases in which this treatment is said to have produced more striking results.

Tertiary symptoms, it has been said, are not hereditary, and cannot be communicated by the mother to the child in the womb. But secondaries may be so transmitted, and are a very frequent cause of abortion and still-born children, as well as of disease in those which are born alive. Sometimes the syphilitic spots are already apparent on the child at birth, but in general they do not appear till some weeks after, when an eruption of rosy patches or pimples comes out, chiefly in a neighbourhood of the genital organs and the anus, but also scattered over the body. They gradually assume that deep copper-colour which is so characteristic of syphilis. The unfortunate infant becomes peevish and fretful, declines in health, and often dies.*

---

* Two very important doctrines with regard to syphilis have lately been brought forward, which invalidate several of the statements made above. One of them, which was arrived at from the researches of MM. Ricord, Bassereau, Clerc, and others, is that the different varieties of primary chancre—the hard, the soft, the phagedænic, and the gangrenous—do not arise from one and the same disease, but from *two distinct diseases*, which have hitherto been confounded together. According to this doctrine (which seems to me to have much the greater weight of evidence in its favour) there are two affections—the *hard*, or indurated, and the *soft* chancre—which differ from one another in their nature, symptoms, and origin, and of which the former alone is really syphilis. The radical difference between them may be seen from the following description. In true syphilis, the ulcer is hard; it has an incubation of three or four weeks, that is to say, it only appears three or four weeks after infection; it cannot be made to abort by cauterisation, for when once it appears, it shows that the constitution is already infected; it cannot be re-inoculated on the patient himself, or contracted again at a future period, for syphilis, like small-pox, or measles, is a disease which occurs only once in a life-

The above is a short and imperfect sketch of this terrible disease, at whose very name humanity shudders. This is the pest, which, on its first appearance in Europe some four or five centuries ago, having been introduced it is supposed from the new world, and before its nature or treatment were known as they now are, is said by many authors to have almost decimated our race; spreading its ravages on every side, among the highest and the lowest ranks of society. Monarchs have died of it; and its unhappy victims among the poorer classes, were not even permitted to rot in peace from the surface of the earth, but treated as the worst of criminals, and shunned as walking leprosies by their uncultivated and pitiless fellow-beings. Are these barbarities at an end in our more advanced age? Have we reversed the merciless verdict of our ancestors, and striven to atone by every kindness and assistance in our power to those, on whose fellow-sufferers of a former age, was piled a load of contumely and shame, which blackens the sky, a lasting memorial of the inhumanity and moral obliquity of men? Do we pour balm, instead of poison, into the wounds of the desolate and miserable ones, who become the prey of this ravager? whose genital organs are destroyed, whose constitutions are ruined, whose bones and hearts are full of aches and miseries innumerable, and from whose glazed eyes the light, life, and joy of the world have faded before their prime?

Alas! would that such were the case. Many a sufferer would almost be content to die, did he know that he had what every human heart yearns for, the infinite sympathy and reverence of his fellow mortals; many a dull heart, sunk in apathy, or hardening into the sullenness of hatred, would waken again to hope and love, if those of others were not coldly, and oh! how sinfully, shut against him. For the heart of the world is shut against all venereal disease. To the common ear, and even more, shall it be said? to those who seek to be called pure and morally elevated, they are a subject unknown and nearly unheard of; at least unheard of for any purposes of active sympathy, aid, or prevention—the only purposes for which the true physician's heart loves to speak or to think of disease or evil, whether moral or physical. They are regarded as a mystery, and as a degrading subject, into which the moralist, and still more the female mind, dreads to enter.

___

time; it is always accompanied by hardness and swelling of several neighbouring glands, which, however, do not suppurate; and it is always followed by secondary symptoms, showing the general poisoning of the system. In the other affection, the ulcer is soft; it has no period of incubation, but begins to develop itself immediately after infection; it can be repeatedly re-inoculated on the patient himself, and contracted again at a future time; it aborts whenever it is completely cauterised; it is sometimes, but not always, accompanied by the swelling of a neighbouring gland, which suppurates like the ulcer itself; and it is merely a local affection, which never gives rise to secondary symptoms. The other doctrine which has lately been established with regard to syphilis, and which is of extreme practical importance, is that secondary symptoms are infectious. This was long denied by Ricord and others; but several experiments made on healthy persons, in one of which M. Ricord himself took part, along with some other medical men in Paris, have proved conclusively that if the matter from a secondary ulcer, or even the blood of a syphilitic patient, be inoculated on a healthy individual, it may communicate the disease. 1872.

Alas for mankind, when any such thing is held a mystery! Are the real joys and sorrows of humanity to be sacrificed to childish and morbid mysteries? Mystery and secrecy, born of ignorance and heartlessness, are certain to corrupt any part of our nature, where they are allowed to abide. What can we do in any matter of which we are ignorant? We are helpless, aidless, powerless to serve, powerless to comfort or advise. Ignorance and mystery can never possibly be right; they are invariably in themselves most destructive sins. How many thousands, how many millions of human beings have fallen and are now falling victims to the general mystery and ignorance surrounding the body, and above all the genital organs! Does nature, like spiritualism, make a mystery of these things? Is she too delicate and morally pure, to meddle with them, to visit these organs with her rewards and punishments any more than other parts? Does a sense of shame prevent a man or a woman from agonising and dying of their diseases; or will it comfort them, through long years of misery, which they are ashamed to speak of to their fellows, or in their premature, and, it may be, unpitied death, that a tinsel of mock delicacy adorns their shroud?

There are but two ways; either all men and women must learn to study the body and all its laws, with the reverence and calm worship due to all nature's elements; or they must break these laws on every side, from ignorance and unrighteous contempt of them, and anguish and die in consequence. He who studies and obeys them is a moral being; he who does not, as neither men nor women do, except the professional few, in the present day, is an immoral being. Forsooth *we* will not speak of these diseases; but nature will, and in the groans from smitten thousands around us, in every country, we may hear her voice.

There is probably no disease, which has so much corrupted and deteriorated the human race as syphilis. Among the poor population, especially of the towns, it may almost be said, that there is not a single constitution untainted by it. If the individual himself has not incurred it, some of his ancestors have, and thereby transmitted to him a constitution more or less deteriorated. Among the richer classes almost the same might be said. It is not only the disease itself, but the fearful mercurial poisoning induced in its cure, which gives it so pernicious an influence on mankind. Nothing deteriorates the human constitution more certainly than mercury; it is one of the great causes of disease in our present society. There is not one of us perhaps, whose constitution is not impaired more or less by the mercurial poisoning of ourselves or our forefathers. How great then should be our care to prevent a disease, which, like syphilis, is rendered twice as dangerous to the race by the remedies which are needed to counteract it! There is perhaps not one who reads this, whose constitution might not have been purer, and therefore whose whole nature of mind and body might not have been higher and nobler, had there been no syphilitic or mercurial poison in the veins of man. For, inseparably linked together as are all mankind, the diseases of the parents descend through generations to the children, modified and transformed by time and circumstance.

Syphilis, which corrupts and lays low the strongest constitutions, when it gains root in them, is one of the greatest sources, along with the mercury used for its cure, of scrofula, insanity, and all other diseases and debilities in their descendants. It is one of the grand fountain-heads of diseases, miseries, evil moral and physical natures, and their resulting vices and crimes, by which our society suffers so much. Is this a subject for secrecy and mystery; one upon which we can be content to remain in wilful ignorance—nay even to make a virtue of it; one which our love for our kind, and interest in its welfare and progress, allow us to pass unregarded? Shall we continue to permit this dreadful pestilence to spread its desolation, and poison our cup of life, without taking any measures for its prevention? or, if our hearts are not yet alive to the feeling of the necessarily inseparable connection of all mankind in good and evil, joy and sorrow, how do we know, who shall be the next to suffer? that the next victim may not be a son, or a brother, or beloved friend? Alas! how often are the hopes and the support of a family blighted, by the ruin of those nearest and dearest, by this remorseless disease!

No class of human sufferers have been so sinned against, as the victims of venereal disease. Less sympathy and interest in their fate has been felt by mankind in general, than in that of the greatest criminals, for the cure and prevention of whose moral diseases many truly noble endeavours have been lately made, while the venereal diseases remain neglected and unregarded; and yet wherein have their victims offended? As I shall more fully endeavour to show hereafter, the commonly received code of sexual morality is most erroneous, and erected in ignorance of, and opposition to, natural truth; the real natural duties of every human being (however social difficulties may interfere with the discharge of them) towards his reproductive organs, and the passions connected with them, consisting in their due and normal exercise, for which the social provision of marriage is quite inadequate. Nature lays one command on us, "Exercise all thy functions, else art thou an imperfect and sinful being." Society lays another, "Obey my institutions and my fashions of thought, however little thou or any of us may understand their natural truth or rectitude, or it will be the worse for thee." Let men reflect, and decide whose commandments are to be obeyed.

When another and truer moral code, founded on the recogniton of our natural duties towards all parts of our being, has become established among mankind, all will feel the enormous injustice that has been shown to those who have suffered from venereal diseases, and to the unhappy girls—the outcasts of society, who may be viewed as the unconscious martyrs to the sexual difficulties, and whose cause and sufferings must lie so near to every generous heart. Long, long will it be, oh ye poor inarticulate ones! ere the dumb voice of your sorrows reach the cold ear of man, and still longer of your own sister, woman—whose estrangement from your side, and the common duties of love and sympathy, is one of the foulest blots on our humanity; many a one of you shall yet perish, rot away in anguish with no friend near, with hardened hearts and lips defiant of the pitiless world; many a one of us, too, shall go down with you in degradation and misery to the grave, before society receive you into her bosom, and shed the tear of sorrow and repentance over her unhappy daughters. And you too, my fellow-men, whose life is matured, and whose infinite nature is agonised and distorted by this hateful disease, will you only bow your heads to the smiter, and suffer in silence? Is such your duty either to yourselves or to others? Is this all the lesson of love or of knowledge, that experience has brought? Will you not rather use your utmost endeavours to eradicate this evil; and thus to feel, and to show others, that you have not suffered in vain?

We have now come to the infinitely important subject of the prevention of this disease, a matter of as deep an interest for the human family, as almost anything which could be named. It is a new subject, like the prevention of almost all diseases. Man has scarcely yet attempted or conceived even the possibility of regenerating the world by this means. But daily are we becoming more alive to its paramount importance; daily is the truth dawning upon us, that the body of man is not one whit inferior in majesty or in influence on his destiny to his spirit. If he would be virtuous or happy, or deserve the name of a cultivated being, he must attend to the one as much as to the other; he must equally seek its ideal developement, and prevent its diseases.

How then is disease to be prevented? As soon as the question was asked, and it is only a few years ago that it first was seriously asked, it was seen that there was but one answer, viz., " By mankind in general becoming acquainted with its nature and its causes, and so avoiding it." A simple answer, and one which indeed seems self-evident, but involving what a mighty change in man's education and habits of thought!

While we are unacquainted with the nature or source of anything, we have no power over it; but when its cause is known to us we have it under our control. Now there is no disease of which the cause is more palpable than syphilis; we see the fountain-head, whence all this torrent of poison has overflowed the world, and by seeing this we have the disease in our own power. There is probably no disease, not even infectious fevers, of which the cause is so definite and so completely distinct. It has but one specific source, and cannot by any possibility, that we are aware of, arise but by direct contagion. Other diseases have innumerable roots; if you destroy one, another springs up in its place; but here we have the single solitary Upas tree, and if it were fairly uprooted, the world would remain ever after, as far, as we can see, free from its influence. Have we thought what a difference the freedom from any disease, however insignificant, would make in the destiny of our race? and if so how enormous a change would be effected by the extirpation of its deadliest foe; of that which M. Ricord calls " the most terrible contagion that ever threatened mankind?" Four centuries ago, some say, syphilis was unknown in Europe. Shall we never more see these fortunate times? is this accursed pest for ever to prey on the vitals of us and our remotest posterity? to poison for ever the loves of the race, and wound us in the most tender part—sexual confidence and endearments, turning our love and trust into suspicion and hatred?

Until mankind make common cause against it, there is no hope of its radical extirpation; none even of its powerful repression. Until it has become a well-known subject to every mind, (and what youth's path of life is not darkened by its shadow?) and has a deep interest in the heart of every man and woman, we are powerless against it; it will triumph. But when our human family on such points is not divided against itself; when the genital organs, their laws and their diseases are recognised with reverence by us all; when more universal sympathies, unshaken by class or creed prejudices, have bound men closer together in mutual confidence; and above all, when love is no longer mercenary, that chronic disease under which it labours among us—then may we hope that the total extirpation of our foe is not far distant.

I will speak hereafter of the social means which have been taken in France to repress syphilis, and which contrast with the melancholy neglect which in this country has so favoured its progress; and meanwhile I shall mention the measures which each individual who exposes himself to it should adopt, for its prevention, as long as this disease and prostitution exist in our society. These are very similar to those already recommended for the prevention of gonorrhœa. Washing the parts frequently with cold water or some astringent, as the decoction of oak, or cinchona bark, is a powerful preventive. It is still more useful to keep the prepuce habitually drawn back, and the glans left uncovered, which makes the mucous membrane tough and not easily abraded. It must be remembered, that abrasions are one of the chief causes which favor chancre, as it can eat its way but slowly, and often not at all, through a mucous membrane or follicle. Abrasions should therefore be carefully avoided, and if any be present before a suspicious connection, it should not take place. A narrow vagina favours abrasions both of the male and female organs. Besides these general prophylactics, the individual should carefully wash the parts immediately after coition, either with water, or with alkaline or chlorine washes, which have the property of destroying the poison. He should also make water, to prevent the occurrence of chancre in the urethra, as well as gonorrhœa. Above all, he should be on the watch, after any suspicious intercourse, and destroy the disease by cauterization; which means, M. Ricord says, he has invariably found successful during the first four or five days, if efficiently applied. It should be mentioned that the nitrate of silver, unless used very early, is often not strong enough to destroy the poison, and only irritates the part. Therefore, in many cases, M. Ricord prefers the acid nitrate of mercury, which more powerful caustic seldom fails completly to burn out the poisoned part, and to leave a smple sore underneath.

But there is one safeguard more powerful than all of these, and that is the sheath. Even where it is used, the parts should still be well washed after coition, as it may nave been torn; and besides it does not protect the scrotum, the groin, and other parts, on which the virus may be deposited, and chancre arise if there be any abrasion. With this invaluable instrument and these additional precautions, contagion, whether of syphilis or gonorrhœa, is rendered almost impossible; and well would it be for our race if its use were more universally spread in this age, when the genital organs are in so miserably corrupted a state. Nay, it is not impossible that to this instrument humanity may in part be indebted for the total eradication of the syphilitic disease. Were we for instance to suppose it possible, that all those who expose themselves to the slight-est risk of infection, should for three or at most six months (during which even in untreated cases the contagious properties would probably die out) to unite in the use of this instrument ; and if the most jealous watch were put upon all the cases which might remain, and these be carefully prevented from spreading the disease, and cured as speedily as possible; in short, were mankind earnestly and unitedly to enter into a war of extermination against syphilis, as has been done in the case of wild animals, or other noxious plagues, this terrible disease could be in a short time eradicated from the world, and become a thing of the past. The generations of man to the latest posterity would bless the age in which such a boon had been conferred on humanity!

But we are indeed far removed at present from the hope of such an achievement. The world treats with a sinful neglect all diseases, and most of all syphilis. There are few united efforts, few noble aspira-tions, to shake off any of the physical evils, which desolate our society ; and until a common cause be made against them, as against others, there is no hope of their eradication. Can physicians prevent disease ? Can they keep men in health, or ennoble each individual's physical, and through it, his moral nature ? No : in this matter, as in others, every in-dividual must be self-governed, must depend chiefly on himself for his direction in life, for his elevation, or for his ruin. We have our united political endeavours, our united educational, peace, and other movements, but where are our united efforts for physical regeneration ?—a matter perhaps more important than any other at present, as none has been so much neglected. There are few or no such efforts, because man as yet knows, and cares little for his body, because mind and spirit rule his thoughts, and form his religion ; but when we shall have a far wider and truer religion, and an equal reverence for all parts of our nature, then will these questions of the eradication of syphilis and other diseases, claim our most devoted attention.

[Since the first edition of this work appeared, an interesting and valuable trea-tise on syphilis and its treatment has been published by Dr. Charles Drysdale. In this work—entitled "The Treatment of Syphilis and other Diseases without Mercury ; being a collection of evidence to prove that Mercury is a Cause of Disease, not a Remedy"—the author has brought together a mass of evidence to show, firstly, that mercury ought not to be given in syphilis ; that instead of being of use, it acts as an additional poison to the system, and does a great deal of mischief; and secondly, that syphilis, when not interfered with by mercury, but treated by rest, diet, local applications, baths, iodide of potassium and other simple means, though in many cases a most serious and obstinate disease, in general gets well, and is less frequently attended with grave symptoms than when mercury is employed. In proof of this the author gives the history of the non-mercurial treatment of syphilis within the present century, and quotes largely from the works of Fergusson, Rose, Guthrie, John Thompson, Desruelles, Fricke, Syme, Hughes Bennett, Weeden Cooke and others, who have adopted this plan of treatment. He shows that the most extensive comparative experiments—amounting, according to M. Desruelles, to upwards of three hundred thousand published cases—have been made in civil and military hospitals between the simple and mercurial treatment, all of which, he holds, have demonstrated the superiority of the former. Dr. Drysdale, however, has lately stated, in a paper read in 1875, that he has changed his opinion, and that he now thinks mercury useful, especially for the prevention of tertiary symptoms. Recent researches have shown that the tertiary syphilitic products, the so-called gummy tumours,

DISEASES

OF THE

FEMALE GENERATIVE ORGANS.

I now proceed to speak of the sexual diseases of women, and of the peculiar morbid states to which the female constitution is liable. Until a few years ago, the subject of female disease was in many parts shrouded in the profoundest darkness. It is only since the invention of the speculum by Professor Recamier of Paris, who is, I believe, still alive, and the gradually spreading use of the digital and ocular means of examining the female sexual organs, that these affections have become tolerably understood, and another ample page in the history of human suffering been opened to us. Thousands and millions of women have spent years of misery, have languished and died, for the want of the aid, which knowledge of these affections could have afforded them.

What is the reason, that so very extensive and important a class of diseases remained so long hidden from mankind? The one great reason is—the mysterious and unnatural manner in which the female sexual organs have been regarded. The knowledge of the male sexual diseases has been, and still is, most unhappily impeded by the same cause; but in the case of woman it has acted with tenfold force. If we attend to the history of the science of female disease, we will easily understand its very slow progress. The Greek and Latin physicians, who had not these morbid feelings of sexual delicacy, had considerable knowledge of female disease. They used an instrument, which some say was similar to the speculum, and have left us descriptions of ulceration of the womb, &c. But after them, medical science fell into the hands, first of the Arabs, and next of the Roman Catholic priesthood, who were for centuries the sole physicians. Both these classes of men were restrained by their religious and moral opinions from investigating female disease; and thus the knowledge possessed by the Greeks fell completely into abeyance. "It does however seem most marvellous," says Dr. Bennett, in his admirable work on Inflammation of the Womb, "that the influence of these former social conditions should still be felt in the medical profession, should still exercise an evident control over medical science in England. And yet, unless we admit that such is the case, how can we account for the existing state of uterine pathology, or explain the opprobrium, thrown till

---

are sometimes formed in internal organs, such as the brain, lungs, or liver, and that several lamentable and fatal cases of epilepsy, paralysis, consumption, &c., are due to this cause It is in order to prevent these and other tertiary accidents, which constitute the great danger of syphilis, that Dr. Drysdale now thinks mercury of service. Still, the facts given in his work and the opinions of so many distinguished men show how much may be said in favour of the non-mercurial treatment. 1875.]

within the last few years, by the governing bodies of our leading medical corporations, on those who devote their attention to mid-wifery, and the diseases of females?" In the standard work on female disease, by Sir Charles Clarke, published in 1831, ulceration of the mouth of the womb, one of the commonest female diseases, is not even alluded to ; which shows how very great was the ignorance of these diseases before the introduction of the speculum.

This invaluable instrument constitutes an era in medical science, and in the history of our race. It has been as great a boon to man-kind as the stethoscope. It has cleared up innumerable obscurities, and been the means of giving health and happiness to thousands. Happy would it be for medicine and for mankind, if we could say that its benefits have been fully reaped ; and that the false sexual delicacy, which has for ages shut the door of medical aid against suffering woman, is a thing of the past.

But such is very far from being the truth. Although the world in other matters has made such advances in enlightenment, still in the depths of the dark ages in all things pertaining to sexual feelings. The sexual organs, especially of woman, are still regarded with the old Hebrew feelings of mystery and shame, as if they differed from the rest of our humanity ; and as if it were either our duty or our safety to permit their nature and their laws, their health and their disease, to remain hidden from us. I do not know any class of ideas, which produce more unhappiness or more disease at the present day, than these. Instead of the sexual organs and sexual appetites being studied and reasoned upon, in a natural and open manner, exactly as any other organs and functions of our frame, the subject is regarded as one which must be avoided and kept secret. The consequence is, that the grossest ignorance prevails upon it ; that the physical and moral ideas entertained with regard to it are a tissue of errors ; that sexual diseases and morbid sexual feelings are excessively prevalent ; and that the knowledge and eradication of these diseases is very greatly impeded.

There is no physician, who is conversant with female diseases, who does not deplore the false delicacy so constantly found in woman when suffering from any sexual disease. Dr. Ashwell and Dr. Ben-nett frequently complain of this, saying that the repugnance of women to have recourse to the necessary examinations, or to communicate any information with regard to their symptoms spontaneously, is a constant cause of delayed and erroneous treatment. It may be said, that nothing more retards the knowledge, the prevention, and the cure, of female diseases, than this false delicacy. When a woman becomes affected with a genital complaint, especially if she be a virgin, or un-married, she shrinks from informing a medical man ; and thus the irrevocable infancy of the disease, when it is always so much more tractable, passes away. When she does at last call in assistance, in-stead of openly informing the physician of her symptoms, as she would do in any other affection, she tells nothing spontaneously, but leaves it to him to elicit the necessary information piecemeal ; which of course is very frequently the source of the most lamentable errors. Again, in vast multitudes of cases, where the disorder is considered not to be of a serious nature, medical aid is not sought at all, but the woman continues to bear her ills in silence, as long as they are at all endurable. In this way leucorrhœa, menorrhagia, dysmenorrhœa, &c. are often borne for years, and cause an immensity of suffering, often breaking down the health irretrievably. This false delicacy is not confined to the diseases of the sexual organs; piles, constipation, diarrhœa, &c., and morbid states of the urinary organs are also disclosed by the patient with great reluctance, and often neglected for years, from motives of false delicacy.

Disease, with our present scanty knowledge of therapeutics, is alas! difficult enough to treat, when every advantage is given to the medical man; but when no alacrity is shown in anticipating it, when the patient by reluctance and reticence rather perplexes than aids the diagnosis, and when the means of investigation and treatment are received with repugnance, rather than with the anxious co-operation we should expect from her, whose interests are chiefly at stake, the task becomes arduous and unsatisfactory indeed. There is no safety for woman, till these morbid feelings of sexual delicacy have been thoroughly eradicated, and till the sexual organs and their diseases are regarded in exactly the same rational light, as any other part of our frame; till a knowledge and reverence for these organs have been substituted for the present ignorance, mystery, and childish and degrading feelings of shame; till their states of health and disease be so generally understood throughout society, that on the one hand, disease will be prevented, and on the other, when it does it occur, that it will be met, as promptly, as openly, and as earnestly, as disease of any other bodily organ.

The main cause of all diseases is the general ignorance regarding them, which prevails throughout all but the medical part of society; and the first necessary step to their prevention, is to remove that ignorance and to bring the subject into the clear light of day. There is no part of our nature, which has been so peculiarly enveloped in mystery as the sexual part; there is none about which there is such general ignorance, and in consequence so much disease and misery; and there is none in which more requires to be done, to remove these obstacles to human welfare. The mystery attaching to the sexual organs, has, as it were, overshadowed the whole body. This lies at the root of the neglect of the study of anatomy, and consequently of the other physical sciences; which, without human anatomy and physiology, their *keystone*, will never be really interesting to man. There are few questions more nearly affecting our happiness, than to investigate the causes of the exceptional manner, in which the sexual organs are viewed, and the origin of the peculiar feelings of mystery and shame attaching to them, particularly in woman; for these are the chief causes of the pervading ignorance on the subject, and the vast accumulation of sexual disease and misery.

The Greeks and Romans knew little of these feelings, and it may be said that they have been introduced and fostered amongst us, chiefly in connection with the spiritual views of the Christian and ancient Hebrew faith. There is nothing which more particularly character- ised the ancient Hebrews, than this sexual mystery and shame, and also the excessive harshness with which a breach of their moral code was punished.

Of the intensity of these morbid feelings the following instances may be given as illustrations. It is recorded that Noah cursed Ham and Canaan for having seen him naked. A woman after her confinement was to be considered unclean for a week, if the child was a boy ; if a girl, for two weeks ; then she was to continue in the blood of her puri- fying thirty-three days for a boy, sixty-six for a girl, (as if there were some peculiar pollution in the female sex), being forbidden during that time to touch any hallowed thing, or come into the sanctuary ; and then she should make a sacrifice, to be offered by the priests for her as an atonement, and then she should be cleansed. If any man's seed of copulation should go out of him, he should bathe and be unclean till evening. Every garment and skin, whereon this seed was, should be washed and be unclean till evening. Also the woman with whom a man had lain, should bathe, and be unclean till evening. A men- struating woman was put apart for seven days, during which she and everything she touched were considered unclean, and then she had to make a sacrifice of atonement.

As instances of the extreme harshness of their judgments in sexual matters, the following may be given. The sons of Jacob treacherously slew Shechem, and all the males in his city, which they sacked, be- cause he had lain with their sister, Dinah. The Lord is said to have slain Onan, for spilling the seed, before going in to his brother's wife, not wishing to have a child by her. Tamar, the daughter-in-law of Judah, disguised herself as a harlot, and was lain with by Judah ; who afterwards in his character of judge, ordered her to be burnt for thus playing the whore. According to the laws of Moses, the daughter of a priest was to be burnt alive, if guilty of prostitution. Both parties in adultery were to be put to death. If a man lay with a menstrua- ting woman, and uncovered her nakedness, both were to be put to death. If a man took a wife and found that she was not a virgin, she was to be stoned to death for playing the whore. The unnatural practice of circumcision, wantonly inflicted on helpless infants, still exists among the Jews, as a symbol of their sexual code and the feel- ings which gave rise to it.

These awful cruelties, the very thought of which fills us with horror, are, as far as I am aware, the most remarkable proofs of sexual bar- barism recorded in history. They illustrate the manners of a people, great indeed, but semi-savage, which, so far from being to us a model for imitation, should be a solemn warning for avoidance. And yet they are the real source of our present views on sexual subjects ; and thus have caused an incalculable deal of misery to our race, and espe- cially to the female sex. Probably of all the dangerous modes of feeling and action, which have been perpetuated by the Bible, none has had so blighting an influence on the happiness of mankind. Many of these harsh views have been partly mitigated by time ; and it is chiefly in the case of self-abuse or Onanism, (which superstitious term, intended to inspire a mysterious horror, should be totally discarded), and also in the breach of the moral code by woman, that their spirit, at least, has been kept up.

If we analyse these views both in the Hebrews and in ourselves, we will find that their merciless character depends essentially on the mystery and shame attaching to the genital organs; which feelings are so opposed to a true physical religion. *Sexual disgust*, the product of these morbid feeling, enters as a peculiar element into all our judgments on sexual matters, blinding us as it were, and depriving us of the charity and moderation we may possess on other subjects. It thus doubles the misery of all sexual sufferers, who have to endure, not only the natural burden of their diseases, but also the unnatural disgust attaching to them. But let us not suppose that it is these unfortunates alone, who suffer from this morbid feeling ; it is constantly mingling itself in all the relations between the sexes, causing impotence, perverted sentiments, and diminished enjoyment both in married and unmarried life. It infuses a peculiar bitterness into the jealousy of the pleasures of others, which is no where so keen as in sexual matters ; and there is probably no feeling, not even religious intolerance, which has made men take such contemptuous and abhorrent views of their fellow-creatures. Verily the generative organs have been amply avenged for the neglect and irreverence with which they have been treated !

Almost all those, who have been imbued with the Christian beliefs, have given a great superiority to what they have termed the spiritual part of our being, over the animal ; meaning thereby chiefly the sexual appetites, and enjoyments. The latter they have studiously endeavoured to degrade and disparage, and they have always striven to exalt what they call the moral and intellectual over the sexual enjoyments of man. They have ever endeavoured to check in themselves the sexual appetites, and to find their happiness in so-called higher aims. It was these feelings which gave rise to the celibacy of the Roman Catholic clergy, (who, as we have seen, were unfortunately for woman, so long the guardians of the healing art,) and to the system of monks and nuns, who made it their grand merit to mortify the flesh by denying their sexual appetites.

The monasteries and nunneries have indeed passed away in some countries ; but the ideas which gave birth to them have by no means passed away. They flourish nearly as much as ever amongst us, though we have not the flagrant solecism of such public institutions. The pernicious idea of the mortification of the flesh still rules among us in fact, if not in express word. One of the main christian beliefs is, that it is a great merit to crucify the bodily lusts, and to exercise great self-denial in the gratification of the natural sexual impulses. The moral and intellectual parts of sexual love are elevated at the expense of the physical, which is viewed in a degrading light · and this has

M

given an unreal and unnatural character to our society, for the passion, if deprived of its natural physical basis, (which is as beautiful and as much worthy of admiration as the moral part) is totally incomplete, and works rather for evil than for good.

Chastity is considered one of the greatest of all virtues in woman, and in man too, though in his case it is practically less regarded. We have no longer voluntary nuns, but of involuntary ones there are myriads; far more in reality than ever existed in any Roman Catholic country. Millions of women pass a great part of their sexual lives, and immense numbers pass the whole, in total sexual abstinence, without any of the enjoyments of sexual pleasures, or the happiness of a mother's affections. For all this incredible self-denial, which causes more anguish and disease than any mind can conceive, they have for their reward the barren praise of chastity. But if we examine earnestly and without prejudice the real nature of this quality, which is so highly prized, we shall discover in it a totally different meaning.

Chastity, or complete sexual abstinence, so far from being a virtue, is invariably a great natural sin. We are short-sighted beings, full of errors and false theories, but nature is absolutely unerring, and it is only by consulting her, that we can gain a true knowledge of our virtues and vices. If we attend to nature, we shall find that all our organs are subject to the same law of health; the great law of normal and sufficient exercise. There is no organ in our body, nor any faculty in our mind, which to be healthy, (or in other words, virtuous,) does not require its due share of appropriate exercise. The sexual organs are subject to this law exactly as all others; and, whatever theories we form about them, nature invariably rewards or punishes them, according as the conditions of their health are observed. She cares not for our moral code; marriage has nothing sacred in her eyes; with or without marriage, she gives her seal of approbation to the sexually virtuous man or woman in a healthy and vigorous state of the sexual organs and appetites, while she punishes the erring by physical and moral sufferings.

It is strange to observe, and can only be accounted for by the intense nature of the sexual prejudices, that the law of healthy exercise, which every physiologist knows to apply equally to every organ, and which has been sedulously applied to every other organ, has never been insisted on in the case of the genital organs. Hydropathy, whose fundamental principle is the scientific application of appropriate exercise and stimulus to the various bodily organs, and which has, by these great natural means, had such wonderfully beneficial results, dares not apply this great principle to the sexual organs; and is, consequently, of little power in true sexual diseases. The only man, who has had the courage and the wisdom to insist on the application of the law of exercise to genital disease, is M. Lallemand in the case of spermatorrhœa. Although his conclusive reasoning and experience on this subject were met with a torrent of obloquy in this country, and still are neglected by the majority of physicians, yet they are irresistibly gaining ground; and it is now comparatively common among our most skilful medical men to recommend sexual intercourse to young men suffering from genital debility.

But for suffering woman no one has yet raised his voice, no one has applied to her case the only true and scientific remedy ; that remedy which is the keystone of female therapeutics, and without which all treatment or prevention of female disease is a vanity and a delusion. The great mass of female sexual diseases, even more than those of men, arise from sexual enfeeblement, consequent on the want of a healthy and sufficient exercise for this important part of the system. From the want of this, the green sickness, menstrual irregularities, hysterical affections without number, proceed ; and it is utter vanity to expect to cure, and still more to prevent these miserable diseases, without going to the root of the matter. It is a certain and indubitable fact, that unless we can supply to the female organs their proper natural stimulus, and a healthy and natural amount of exercise, female disease will spring up on every side around us, and all other medical appliances will be powerless against the hydra.

I would entreat the reader not to prejudge this most important question, nor to allow his mind to be diverted from a calm and earnest investigation of the real facts of the matter, by the vehemence of sexual prejudices, which all of us know are so very violent in this country. Let him survey the state of the sexual world; let him think of the fearful amount of prostitution, of venereal and genital disease; of the impenetrable ignorance brooding over the subject, and the tide of headlong and irrational feelings, which are connected with sexual topics ; and he will acknowledge that surely there must be some grand error somewhere, to account for so much misery. Love indeed, instead of being one of the sweetest blessings of life, seems rather to be a curse, to such innumerable evils and miseries does it give rise. Let him now review our code of sexual morality, and try it by the grand touchstone of nature ; he will find it a chaos of theories, on which no two nations are agreed. and in which nature has been almost wholly left out of sight, and authority and blind prejudices allowed to take her place. Physical as well as mental health has been disregarded in framing these codes, and if he open his eyes to their working, he will see the ground strewn with sexual victims. It is absolutely certain, that nature meant the sexual organs in either sex to have a due amount of exercise, from the time of their maturity till their decline ; and no one who knows anything of the bodily laws, can doubt, that every departure from the course she points out, is a natural sin; and she shows this herself by the punishments she inflicts. She forms no organ, that she does not intend to be exercised ; rouses no desires merely to torment by their self-denial. It is not by shutting our eyes to these facts, that we can hope to progress either in knowledge or in virtue.

I know the great natural difficulties, which lie in the way of the sufficient exercise of the sexual organs in each individual, and shall speak of these hereafter, and examine how far they are insurmountable. But whether or not it is possible to attain this desirable result,

we must recognise, that the diseases, which arise from sexual abstinence, are always a proof of a sin against nature, even though from
social considerations it be impossible to avoid them.   The principle of
population, as Mr. Malthus has so admirably pointed out, is the true
difficulty, which stands in the way of the sufficient exercise of the sexual organs in each individual; and it is upon this natural foundation
that all the false reasoning on chastity, self-denial, and self-mortifica-
tion is really supported.   I shall speak hereafter of the best way of
meeting this difficulty ; and meanwhile proceed to give a description
of the chief forms of female sexual disease.

CHLOROSIS.

THIS disease is a very common one, and therefore of great importance. It is generally found in young girls about, and shortly after puberty, but it may occur at any age during the continuance of menstruation, and is not unfrequently found in married women who have been exhausted by various causes, such as miscarriages, over-lactation &c. It very rarely, if ever, occurs before puberty, or after menstrual decline. It seems therefore, evidently to be connected with the sexual system; and it is a disease peculiar to women, for although pallor and debility occur in man, yet genuine chlorosis does not.

The symptoms of the disease are as follows. A young girl, who has perhaps been always rather delicate, approaches the period of puberty. At this time, instead of an increase in the strength and vigor of the frame, coincident with the natural developement of the sexual organs, her health gets worse, she becomes more delicate, and does not pass on to womanhood. The sexual system does not develope itself, or but imperfectly; and menstruation, which must be preceded by this sexual developement, is either absent, or scanty and pale. The disease also very frequently arises after puberty and menstruation have been established, from causes which weaken the general health, and especially from such, as interfere with the sexual functions, or disappoint the sexual desires. The patient becomes very pale and sickly, and from this deadly paleness the disease may generally be at once recognised. She loses her appetite, her strength declines, and slight exercise produces fatigue, palpitation of the heart, and breathlessness; her stomach becomes disordered, her digestion difficult, and her bowels are generally constipated. Her spirits flag, she becomes listless, and prone to melancholy and solitude. If the disease be allowed to advance, the symptoms all become aggravated. The stomach is greatly disordered, there is flatulence and heartburn; frequently a total want of appetite, and at other times a craving for unwholesome food, such as green fruit, or sometimes even chalk or slate-pencils. The tongue is pasty and white, and the breath foul. The pallor becomes deeper, the face is deadly white, with often a kind of dirty greenish-yellow hue, (whence the name of the disease). The lips and gums are pale and bloodless. Headaches of fearful intensity are very frequent, with the pain, or a feeling of weight and pressure, often confined to the top of the head. There is impairment of all the senses ; sight and hearing are weakened. The mental powers are greatly impaired ; memory and concentrativeness fade, while an impotent listlessness and apathy overpower the mind, or the patient resigns herself to despair. Hysterical symptoms also generally occur.

In short, there is not a function or faculty of the body or mind, which is not more or less interfered with ; all of them become enfeebled. The reason of this is, that the blood itself, which nourishes all these organs, is impoverished. Chlorosis essentially consists in a watery state of the blood. That fluid is found in this disease to have lost a great part of its solid constituents ; the clot is very small and dark-coloured, when it separates, on standing, from the serous or watery part. It is this watery state of the blood, which causes the deadly pallor, the great debility, the arrest of the catamenial and fæcal secretions, and the failure of the bodily and mental powers. If we listen with the stethoscope over the heart or one of the large veins, a morbid rushing noise is heard, made by the watery blood in passing along the vessels. The serous part of the blood, when the disease is far advanced, often exudes through the vessels, and causes dropsy of the legs, eyelids, or other parts.

In different cases different organs are most interfered with. Thus in one case the prominent symptoms may be connected with the head and nervous system, such as intense headaches, and neuralgic or paralytic affections of various parts of the body. In another, the digestion may be chiefly disordered ; while in another, the chest may be the principal part to suffer. It is in this last case, that there is the greatest danger ; for a fatal issue does not frequently attend on chlorosis, unless from consumption. Unless there be a scrofulous taint in the constitution, whether hereditary or not, chlorosis does not generally tend towards consumption, nor indeed to the establishment of any organic disease, although the derangements of the nervous, digestive, circulatory, and other systems are often so very violent. But when a girl of a consumptive family becomes chlorotic, symptoms of consumption are very apt to attend, and unless prompt and efficient remedies be used, fatal organic disease will very probably be established. In such a case the pulse is generally rapid, there is a short hacking cough, with pain in the chest, and there may be night-sweats, with the other symptoms of incipient consumption.

Let us now examine, what are the *causes* of chlorosis. They consist in all those general influences which weaken the young girl ; and more especially in those which weaken or prevent the developement of the sexual system.

The education of young girls is exceedingly erroneous. In our boarding schools, and other places of female instruction, very little attention is paid to the developement of the bodily powers. Stiff and false ideas of what is proper for young ladies prevail, vigorous and exhilarating sports and games are discountenanced, and exercise is limited to a formal walk. There is a much greater want of physical religion in the training of young women, than even of men. Bodily strength, physical courage, and activity, are not regarded at all as female excellences, indeed they are rather looked upon as unfeminine; and gentleness, quietness, and an amiable amount of timidity are rather cherished—qualities which flatter the pride of man, in his mistaken character of protector of the weaker sex.

But there is no such natural distinction between man and woman. In woman, exactly as in man, superior bodily strength, physical daring, and nervous power, are indispensably requisite to form a fine character; and these are only to be obtained by strengthening the frame, and by training the nervous system to a healthy and elevated vigour. It is not true, that the masculine and feminine virtues are frequently in contrast with each other. The two natures are built on the same original model, and in the main, they are alike in their laws. The great law of exercise of every part applies equally to both sexes; and in woman, as in man, physical strength is more virtuous than weakness; courage than timidity; nervous power, than nervous debility; and it is a sign of an effeminate and unnatural theory of life that these truths are not deeply felt by all of us. In all the physical virtues, which are just as important as the moral ones, woman is dreadfully deficient. Her education, and the erroneous views prevailing as to what is admirable or beautiful in the female character, bring her up weak in body and mind: her strength is not developed by sports and proper exercises, and she is feeble and delicate; her courage is not brought out by cultivation, but on the contrary repressed, from the mischievous idea, that timidity is rather amiable in a woman, and therefore she becomes nervous and hysterical. Her mind also is left feeble by the exclusion of the solid parts of knowledge from her studies, as being unfitted for her narrow sphere in life. Again, the crippling idea of chastity and female decorum binds her like an invisible chain, wherever she moves, and prevents her from daring to think, feel, or act, freely and impulsively. She must not do this, she must not study that; she has nothing to do with a knowledge of her own frame or its laws; she may not read the works, nor acquire the knowledge that is open to men; she must not sport nor play boisterously, nor go out unattended, nor in the evening walk alone in the streets, nor travel alone, nor make use of the thousand and one privileges, which are open to the more fortunate sex.

If we examine into the origin and meaning of these singular ideas with regard to woman, we shall find that they are based upon no natural distinction between the two sexes, but upon the erroneous views of man, and especially upon the mistaken ideas as to the virtue of female *chastity*. It is to guard this supposed virtue, that all the restrictions on female liberty and female developement in body and mind have arisen. In all ages and in all countries the treatment of woman has been very irrational. We know how very oppressive it is at the present day in China and Turkey; but even among ourselves, the liberty and privileges of women are very far behind what is just and natural.

Their erroneous education leads to infinite forms of misery, debility, and disease. " Were our present system of female education altered," says Dr. Ashwell, in his admirable and standard work on Female Diseases, " chlorosis and the allied affections would be rare, instead of as at preser exceedingly common diseases." By the cramping and enfeebling training, the girl receives in early youth, she grows up so delicate, that her constitution is quite unable to rouse to life, and to give adequate vital energy to the new set of organs at the age of puberty. The girl is not strong enough to afford to lose three or four ounces of blood every month, nor has she, therefore, such superabundant vital powers as to be able to reproduce her species; for which privilege, nature demands a certain amount of vigour. This delay in the evolution of the sexual organs at puberty reacts upon the blood; which, from the want of the new nervous influences the frame should receive at that time of life, becomes impoverished, and so the series of miserable chlorotic symptoms is set up.

But chlorosis may be caused by more peculiarly sexual influences. Masturbation is said to be a very frequent cause of it, and although this is a subject, which has not been at all sufficiently investigated, in consequence of the difficulties thrown in the way by the sexual delicacy, both of medical men and their patients, there is little doubt that these unfortunate practises are just as common among young women, as young men. It is no wonder that patients are unwilling to speak of these errors; the world, in the spirit of ancient Judaism, looks with such harshness on any sexual fault, that the poor young sufferer would rather bear anything than disclose it. But in reality, society is itself to blame for all such errors as unnatural sexual indulgences, in either sex. Until we can supply to the violent sexual passions of youth a proper and natural gratification, we may be absolutely certain, that an unnatural one will be very frequently resorted to. Instead of the healthy and happy state of sexual feeling, which a proper amount of the natural sexual intercourse can alone produce, the two sexes in youth are kept at arm's length; no intimacies are allowed between them, nor any healthy outlet for the violent and novel sexual impulses. Sexual shame and embarrasment therefore come in to cloud and agitate the mind; and morbid tastes take the place of the healthy ones, and lead to unnatural indulgences.

Chlorosis is often brought on after the establishment of puberty, by ungratified sexual longings, independently of masturbation. These longings are generally connected with some love affair, in which there has been disappointment or delay. The poor young girl's whole being is absorbed in the one passion, and she pines away, refusing consolation from her well-meaning, but ignorant friends. It is in vain, that they seek to divert her by tenderness or varied amusements; it is love, not friendship, that the mind seeks at that age, and without which it knows neither rest nor peace. There is no class of human griefs, which has been to me a greater cause of sadness, than those endured by the young unmarried females amongst us. People in general have no idea of the immense numbers of women who pass a single life in this country. According to the classified returns of the population, made lately, although the number of young men and young women, between the years of fifteen and thirty-five, is in the country nearly equal, in the towns of England, there are 230,912 more women than men. In London alone, there are 72,312 more women. In Scotland the case is the same. In Edinburgh there are 15,556 more women than men; a larger proportion, than in any other town in the kingdom. When we think of this, and consider moreover the great number of men who do not marry, but either live in sexual abstinence, or content themselves with the society of girls of the town; and the very large proportion of either sex, who are unable to marry till late in life, from inability to support a family; we will be able to form some slight conception of the misery endured by the female sex, from ungratified sexual desires, want of love, and all the joys of a family. How often alas! do we see young blooming girls, full of life and hope, entering on their womanhood, and year after year passing over them without any outlet for the strongest passions and affections of their nature ! Their beautiful natural gaiety and enjoyment of life soon droop, they become uneasy, discontented, unnatural; the bloom fades from their cheeks, and the laugh from their lips; fretfulness and capriciousness succeed to the buoyant sunny disposition; and hysteria, and the gloomy train of sexual diseases, chlorosis, amenorrhœa, or dysmenorrhœa, claim them as their prey.

Why do we shut our eyes to these things, or steel our hearts to such realities ? Is there one among us, who does not know from experience the universal strength of the sexual passions, and the tortures attendant on their constant and systematic denial? Who can bear to see their life passing away, uncheered by the sweetest of human pleasures; to see their fellows around them enjoying advantages and blessings, of which they are deprived, without a feeling of deep-seated discontent, envy, jealousy, and despair, rankling in their breast? On woman too it is especially hard, for she is, from our unfortunate social arrangements, far more wholly dependent on love than man. There are many other pleasures open to man, from which woman, and especially unmarried woman, who has so little liberty, is debarred. Truly of all the slow and wasting tortures, that ever were endured by humanity, there is scarcely any more painful to contemplate, than those endured by myriads of women, who pass their lives amongst us. The halo passes from their lives, the short-lived dream of romance and poetic love fades into the dull reality of a monotonous and unfulfilled existence, and the iron eats into their soul.

Chlorosis occurs sometimes also in married women, who have been exhausted by too frequent child-bearing or by long-continued white or sanguineous discharges. In short, any wasting or exhausting cause, especially those which affect the sexual system, physically or morally, tends to produce it. Amenorrhœa, when protracted, very frequently induces chlorosis.

I shall now proceed to the treatment of this affection. The great principle on which this must be based, is to brace and elevate the constitution, and to render the blood richer. If we can effect this, the whole train of disordered symptoms will disappear, the skin will regain its hue, the mind its tone and buoyancy, and puberty and menstruation will be thoroughly established. The girl should be sent into the country, should be out constantly in the open air, and should take as much exercise as can be borne without fatigue. She should also take one or two cold or slightly tepid baths daily in the hydropathic manner, applying the cold water for a very short time, and afterwards strong friction, and taking a walk before and after the bath, to ensure sufficient reaction. She should keep regular hours, and live upon a nutritious and wholesome diet, avoiding slops.

The medicine which is chiefly relied upon in this disease is iron, the effect of which in enriching the blood, and invigorating the frame, is often so marked, that some have considered it a specific in chlorosis. It is often beneficial when given along with the natural means, as pure air, exercise, &c.; but it frequently fails, and often cannot be borne by the constitution, causing flushing and headache. Iron may be used either by repairing to a chalybeate spring, which is the best mode, or by giving it in medicinal doses. One or even two grains of the sulphate of iron may be given thrice a day. But the iron will probably do harm rather than good, if the digestive functions be not first improved, and the system prepared for it. In order to do this, a course of mild purgatives, such as rhubarb or aloes, is greatly recommended by Dr. Ashwell. But it would be better if the bowels could be regulated, and the digestion reinvigorated by more natural means, such as country air, exercise, bathing, and the other admirable hygienic means so beneficially applied by the hydropathic treatment. A course of aperient medicine certainly does great good in some cases, but it is always an uncertain remedy, of a lowering nature, and is very liable to be abused. In fact, there is an immense deal of harm done in chlorotic affections by these means, for there is a popular prejudice in favour of "a good active purgation." When the digestion has become better, the appetite improved, and the tongue cleaner, then the iron should be given.

But a remedy far more essentially important in the great majority of chlorotic cases, than any medicinal means, is one that obtains at most but a slight and passing allusion in medical works. It is sexual intercourse, the direct and healthy exercise of that part of the system whose enfeeblement or disorder is so frequently at the root of the general disease. Andral, the great French physician, says, "all lowering remedies do harm in chlorosis; but it frequently happens that by stimulating the nervous system by the physical and moral emotions of matrimony, the anaemia (or bloodlessness) is removed, and the whole train of diseased actions vanishes." Dr. Ashwell says, "Marriage is frequently curative of chlorosis; but as its prospect is in general far distant, and besides as it is scarcely a proper subject for the medical man's discussion, it calls only for a passing allusion."

But it is assuredly the part of the true physician to seek in every case the safest and most energetic means for the recovery of his patient, and to make that known, whatever social obstacles may stand in the way of its adoption. Had M. Lallemand thus refrained from pointing out the true and natural remedy for spermatorrhœa, and from recommending it to his unhappy patients, many a one who owes to him his restoration to health and happiness, would now be the tenant of a mad-house, or wallowing in the depths of seminal wretchedness, a torment to himself and to all around him. Chlorosis and hysteria in the female are diseases quite analogous to spermatorrhœa in the male. Both are a general enfeeblement and prostration of the system, connected with genital enfeeblement. Now in man we have already seen, that the only real natural cure for spermatorrhœa, (without which in almost all cases the disease lasts indefinitely, causing its own insufferable miseries,) is a proper healthy exercise for the sexual organs, and a healthy outlet for the sexual emotions and passions. Spermatorrhœa may be perhaps checked in some cases by instrumental means, such as nitrate of silver &c., but this is not sufficient to give permanent vigour to the organs, nor to correct thoroughly the diseased and morbid state of the mind; which can be done alone by the grand natural means of appropriate exercise. In woman the case is just the same; her nature languishes for the want of the natural stimulus to be imparted only through these organs: her mind and her feelings become morbid from the same cause, and the only true and permanent remedy is a proper amount of sexual exercise. This would give an appropriate stimulus to her system, satisfy the natural passions which consume her strength, and give to her mind the natural healthy sexual feelings, instead of the morbid sickly sense of shame and sexual timidity, which overwhelm her. Sexual intercourse is particularly necessary, when chlorosis has been caused by masturbation; for here there is not only a natural habit to be established, but an unnatural one to be eradicated, and this in both sexes is sometimes a difficult matter. Indeed, there is no means, which can be relied upon in either sex for checking the habit of masturbation, except the supply of the normal gratification. Were such gratifications attainable, masturbation would rarely, if ever, be resorted to; and one of the most prevalent causes of bodily and mental disease would be extirpated.

I know the host of prejudices that will oppose the recognition of sexual intercourse, as the great remedy in sexual enfeeblement in woman, but I am absolutely certain too that it will be recognised. It is in vain that we strive against the decrees of nature; we may exhaust ourselves in forming unnatural theories, and in forbidding any attempt to compare them with the natural laws; we may be content that the subject should continue shrouded in mystery, and that our young women should be racked and tortured by innumerable diseases, rather than allow the least departure from our prejudiced schemes; we may persecute and anathematise all those poets, philosophers and physicians, who, horror-struck at the amount of sexual misery, endeavour to find a new path out of the labyrinth; but not one jot, not one iota, does nature move for all our vehemence, and she will force us at last, exhausted by our sufferings, to confess our errors and recognise her infallibility. I do not see how any man of common sense, far less a scientific physician, can fail to see, that nature intended that the sexual organs should be used, as soon as they are fully developed. The sexual passions are strongest at that time, and we might foresee with certainty, that if the natural intentions be defeated, disease and misery must result. It is clear too, that for diseases arising from such a cause, the natural and obvious remedy is to supply the normal exercise, the want of which occasions the disorder. In the case of genital enfeeblement in man, M. Lallemand has shown clearly by the results of his treatment, as well as by his general reasoning, that sexual exercise is the true natural and efficient remedy; and his views have been adopted by a great many of the most enlightened medical men in this country, and must eventually be accepted by all, however much they are opposed by Christian prejudices.

Now, I ask, how is it possible that a similar reasoning should not apply to woman? In her, too, the sexual organs are early developed, and powerful sexual appetites roused; she is liable to analogous states of sexual enfeeblement and derangement, consequent on the non-exercise of her sexual organs; and can any philosophical mind infer otherwise, than that a proper exercise is the treatment required for her cure? Nay, we find that in the chance cases in which marriage has come to the succour of these unfortunates, it has generally proved curative; and we may be satisfied that if the sexual means were duly used, (which is frequently by no means the case in marriage, over-indulgence producing exhaustion and satiety instead of reinvigoration), along with other means of bracing the health, very few cases of chlorosis, or the allied affections, could resist it. But the fact is, that there are few men, who, on calmly considering the subject, would fail to see that a due amount of sexual intercourse is one great thing needed to preserve and restore the health in the youth of both sexes; and it is a common remark among men on seeing a girl languid and sickly, that what she needs is venereal gratification. It is impossible to avoid the conclusion that the natural exercise is the great means, without which it is absolutely impossible to prevent or cure an immense amount of disease and misery. When once we have clearly recognised this grand truth, —certainly one of the most important which the physician, or the moral philosopher, can apprehend at the present day—we will be in a fitter position for reasoning upon the possibility of procuring for every human being this great essential of health, happiness, or virtue: but upon this question I shall speak hereafter.

There is a great deal of erroneous feeling attaching to the subject of the sexual desires in woman. To have strong sexual passions is held to be rather a disgrace for a woman, and they are looked down upon as animal, sensual, coarse, and deserving of reprobation. The moral emotions of love are indeed thought beautiful in her; but the physical ones are rather held unwomanly and debasing. This is a great error. In woman, exactly as in man, strong sexual appetites are a very great virtue; as they are the signs of a vigorous frame, healthy sexual organs, and a naturally-developed sexual disposition. The more intense the venereal appetites, and the keener the sense of the normal sexual gratifications, provided it do not hold a diseased proportion to the other parts of the constitution, the higher is the sexual virtue of the individual. It is exactly the same with the venereal appetite as with the appetite for food. If a woman be healthy, and have a frame braced by exercise and a natural life, she will have a strong appetite and a keen relish for food, and it is exactly the same with the sexual desires. The strongest appetites, and the greatest enjoyment in their gratification, have been fixed by nature as the reward of obedience to her laws, and the preservation of health by a due exercise of all the functions, neither excessive nor deficient. The man or woman who is borne down by a weakened and diseased digestion, will recognise strength of stomach and vigour of appetite to be the greatest of all desirable virtues for them, that which lies at the root of every other advantage; and in the same way he who is wallowing in spermatorrhœa, impotence, and sexual disgust, or the morbid and chlorotic girl, may recognise sexual power and strong sexual appetites, as the highest and most important of all virtues for them in their position. Other virtues are in such cases a dream and a delusion to the sufferers—unattainable, or even if apparently attainable, of little real and permanent advantage. Instead of a girl being looked down upon for having strong sexual passions, it is one of her highest virtues; while feeble or morbid desires are the sign of a diseased or deteriorated frame. Those who have the most healthy desires are the chosen children of nature, whom she thus deems worthiest to continue our race. In sexual diseases, the venereal desires are generally deadened or rendered morbid; and one of the best signs of restoration to health is the return of powerful sexual feelings.

Before leaving the subject of the treatment of these affections, I would entreat especial attention to the subject of their prompt and early treatment. Dr. Ashwell says, "These diseases are very frequently neglected at their commencement. Menstrual irregularities and general delicacy, are matters of every-day occurrence, and the disease is often suffered to attain a great height before advice is sought. I have often been consulted in such cases, where, from what the relations had told me, I should have thought the case a slight one, and yet I have found it almost hopeless." It is, alas! too true that delicacy in young women and menstrual derangements are at present—at least, in towns—rather the general rule than the exception; and when we consider the female training and the state of the sexual world, we cannot be surprised at this. The standard of female health and strength is miserably low. If we go through one of our large towns—London, for instance—we will observe how pale, thin, and feeble the young girls are, as a class. Contrast one of them with a blooming and powerful girl from the country, and we will see the immense difference in physical virtue. Such low states of the vital powers border closely upon disease, and favour the occurrence of innumerable diseases. Pallor, feebleness of frame, want of appetite, and any menstrual irregularities, should never be neglected; nor should a girl be permitted to grow up in a delicate state, if the means of invigorating her be at all attainable.

For the *prevention* of this important disease every means must be taken to elevate the physical powers in woman, from her childhood upwards. Female education, and the cramping views as to female decorum, should be greatly altered. Their bodies should be strengthened, just as those of boys and young men, by active sports and exercises—such as all young people delight in. They should be taught that physical strength, courage, and blooming health are as excellent and desirable in woman as in man, and they should learn to take as much pride in the physical as in the mental virtues. It is not for themselves alone, that they elevate their bodily powers, but for their future offspring also; pale and sickly mothers beget pale and sickly children. Solid and real knowledge should be given them, as well as the graceful arts; and above all, that which is far the most urgently required in the education both of man and woman—a knowledge of the human body and the human mind, with their nature and their laws. Without the study of human anatomy and physiology, and of moral and mental science, in short without the study of human nature, no education is worthy of the name. The ignorance and spurious delicacy of woman necessitate the same deplorable qualities in man; for no sexual subject can be freely discussed, or written about, among us, unless woman also be able to reason upon it.

The nature of the various organs of the body and mind, their purposes, their states of health and disease, the great law of healthy exercise as applicable to our whole frame—all these should be pointed out, and thus would the young woman be prepared to encounter the difficulties of life. The study of anatomy would do away with the childish and irreverent ideas connected with the sexual and excretory organs, along with the mystery and shame, which have done such incalculable mischief. At present a morbid curiosity is excited by the general ignorance on these subjects; to gratify which, purient and stupid books are written, which are read by immense numbers of all classes and sexes. Fanny Hills, Aristotles, &c., are eagerly sought for and read in secret, to the degradation of all parties concerned. Who would care to read such sickly and ignorant productions if they had an honourable knowledge of the real nature of our being, and the lofty and dignified sense of our wondrous humanity, which such knowledge must always impart? The mystery on sexual subjects keeps men and women constantly in a state of childhood. Childish curiosity and ignorant imaginations, with a degraded feeling of mystery, shame, or disgust, varied by a vulgar pretence of knowingness, pervade our society on all sexual matters.

The natural sexual feelings, which awaken at puberty, should not be discountenanced or unduly suppressed in the girl. To do so is infallibly to render her morbid and unnatural. In Scotland, where there is a stricter sexual code than in perhaps any other country, and where the lusts of the flesh, as they are called, are stigmatised and controlled as much as possible, sexual shyness and timidity constitute a great *national disease*, and cause more unhappiness among young people, than can well be conceived. The youth of both sexes are so often warned of the sin of indulging even in the very feeling of sexual passion, that their whole nature becomes distorted, and they become shy and awkward to a most painful degree. It is indeed bewildering to the young mind, when nature and human ideas are so completely at variance. Scotland is the shyest country in the world; and this is among the surest signs of its sexual code being one of the most unnatural.

When the girl has been trained to the possession of a powerful and healthy frame, and a healthy mind, invigorated by sound knowledge for her guidance in life, puberty will be readily and easily established, menstruation will follow, and she will enter upon womanhood with the fairest prospect of happiness. But at this period it is absolutely requisite, in order to maintain and elevate the health, and prevent the occurrence of sexual disease, that she should have before long, a healthy exercise for the new organs, and the normal gratification of the new desires. If this be not attainable, all our former efforts will prove in vain, and we shall have elevated her powers only to their own destruction; for her mind and body will indubitably be thrown into disorder by the workings of the new physical and moral influences. She may indeed retain her health for a time, but gradually menstruation will become irregular or painful, she will become hysterical and nervous, and discontent and unhappiness will take the place of her former amiability. We may do what we please in the way of other healthy influences; we may bestow every other care on the nurture and education of our beloved ones; but it is absolutely impossible to make woman healthy or happy without a due amount of sexual enjoyment. Irrespective of the question of its attainability, we may recognise the indisputable fact, that without it, it is equally impossible to prevent or to cure the greatest part of their sexual diseases and unhappiness; and female therapeutics are an impossible science. If the sexual organs are to remain, as at present, totally unexercised throughout a great part, and, in numberless cases, throughout the whole of life, and if chastity must continue to be regarded as the highest female virtue, it is impossible to give woman any real liberty; it is impossible to give her a true and genuine education, and to cultivate her bodily powers and animal passions, as they should be cultivated; and it is out of human power to make the lot of woman other than an unhappy, a diseased, and a degraded one, as it is at present, when vast quantities of the sex pass their lives as involuntary nuns, or as prostitutes.

HYSTERIA.

THIS extraordinary disease is a still more important one than chlorosis, from its very great frequency, and the amount of unhappiness it causes, both to the patients, and their friends. Dr. Ashwell calls it "The incubus of the female habit," and Sydenham says "Hysterical affections constitute one-half of all chronic diseases." From this it may be judged how very prevalent is this affection in its various forms. It is peculiar to woman, for although morbid nervous states, weakness, and excitability, are common to both sexes, when in weak health, the regular hysterical fits, and hysterical counterfeits, are never seen in man. It is evidently connected with the female sexual system, for it is not found before puberty, and it is very frequently dependent upon a disordered state of the sexual organs or feelings.

A regular hysterical fit presents the following symptoms. Painful sensations are felt about the navel; these gradually, with a rumbling noise following the windings of the intestines, mount upwards till they reach the throat, where they assume the character of a ball, rising in the gullet, and producing a sense of suffocation. There is here evidently spasm of the passage, just as the abdominal pains are probably owing to spasm of the bowels gradually mounting upwards. The fit is now at its height, and a burst of hysterical laughter or crying occurs, followed by a copious flow of limpid urine, and the patient gradually returns to her usual state. In many cases these fits occur very frequently, and are brought on by very slight causes. Any thing that agitates or vexes the mind, or that exhausts the body, is likely to bring them on.

Besides these regular fits, there are various nervous symptoms that characterise the hysterical disposition. The patient is weak, excitable, nervous, and irresolute; very changeable in her likes and dislikes, and with a general instability of character, showing the delicacy of the nervous system. There is a want of concentrativeness, and of the power of continued effort in any direction. But besides these, there is in almost all cases some deep-rooted *sexual* morbidity, which, if we analyse the case well, we shall find to be the very essence of the disordered mental state. If the patient be a single woman (and in the vast majority of cases it is in the single, and in women who are not happily married, or who are without children, that the aggravated form of the disease is seen) she is generally full of sexual shyness and timidity, with a conscious and stealthy look, as if she were accustomed to indulge in feelings, whose expression is forbidden.   There is a considerable similarity between the timidity and self-consciousness of this disease, and that of spermatorrhœa in man. Doubtless in many hysterical cases masturbation is practised, and serves to increase the nervous weakness, and the morbid state of the sexual feelings.   The hysterical fits and allied symptoms of nervous weakness and excitability are very common, and as they are often to a certain extent under the control of the will, and may continue for years in some cases, without materially affecting the health, they are frequently treated only by laughter and sarcasm.   But there are many other forms of this protean malady, which present far more serious appearances.   The common fits, if the patient encounter serious trials and disappointments, may become so aggravated in character, as to assume the severity of epileptic paroxysms.   In this form of the disease, the patient falls down as in epilepsy, becomes totally unconscious, struggles and gasps for breath, foams at the mouth, and is convulsed on one or both sides of the body. The face becomes blue and livid, and she seems on the verge of suffocation, so that the fit presents a very alarming appearance, and causes great terror to those around.   It is often very difficult, even for a practised eye, to distinguish at first this attack from true epilepsy, but there is one great criterion to guide us, namely: that in the hysterical convulsion, the larynx, or head of the wind pipe, is not quite closed, as it is in epilepsy, and the patient can breathe a little, though with great difficulty.   In epilepsy there is complete closure of the larynx, and a total inability to respire, which makes that fearful malady so much more fatal in its effects. Besides this, a knowledge of previous hysterical seizures will aid us in the diagnosis.   The insensibility in the hysterical fit is sometimes apparent only, and the patient is not without knowledge of external things.

But hysteria does not consist only in fits of greater or less severity, and in the various symptoms of nervous excitability.   Another peculiarity of this disease is that it *counterfeits*, or assumes the form of, a vast number of different diseases.   Thus there are hysterical diseases of the spine, hysterical asthma, palsy, affection of the joints, retention of urine &c., in all of which hysteria takes the form, and gives rise to the symptoms of the different affections ; and often so closely, that it it is almost impossible to distinguish between the real and the spurious disease.   This most extraordinary feature in hysteria is one of the great difficulties in medical practice, and has been the cause of errors without number.   Many a patient has been long treated for spinal disease, many have had their limbs amputated, or their constitution seriously injured by energetic treatment, when there was no real structural disease, but merely a series of disordered nervous actions simulating one.   Hysterical epilepsy is, as we have seen, one instance of an affection, very difficult to distinguish from the true one.   Hysterical cough and loss of voice are frequently met with.   The cough has a peculiar croupy, spasmodic character, and together with the nervous loss of voice may be brought on by very slight causes, often by mental agitation. Painful and hurried breathing, simulating asthma, is also frequent. Irritable and painful states of the breasts, in which these glands are enlarged and indurated, are common, and are generally found along with amenorrhœa. The most violent colics, lasting sometimes for days, are met with, and enormous quantities of wind are frequently generated in the intestines, giving rise to pain, excitement, flushing, and frequently hysterical fits. Violent and circumscribed pulsations of the blood-vessels often excite suspicion of organic disease in them. Pain and tenderness in the spine is common, and still more so is a most trying and wearing pain in the left side of the abdomen, which often continues for years, and is exceedingly intractable. This pain is probably in most cases, sympathetic of an irritable or inflamed state of the ovaries or womb ; just as a pain in the right shoulder is sympathetic, in many cases, of disease of the liver. The most intense and continued headaches are of very frequent occurrence. They are often so severe as to drive the patient nearly to distraction. Apparent obstructions in the natural apertures of the body frequently occur, such as difficulty of swallowing, retention of urine, &c. Stiff and rigid states of various parts of the body, such as the neck, the arms, &c. and also paralysis and spurious affections of the joints are frequent. Affections of the rectum and of the urinary organs are often simulated. In short there is scarcely an organ which may not be interfered with, scarcely a disease which may not be counterfeited by hysteria.

It is often a very difficult task for the medical man, and one requiring great tact, to distinguish between the true and the hysterical diseases. A great guide in this matter is a knowledge of the previous history of the patient, and also a something unreal, transient, and exaggerated, in the character of the disease before him. The pains in these affections have not the fixed and permanent character that they bear in the true diseases, and they shew more the marks of a nervous, than a structural origin. There are generally too the signs of excitement and nervousness in the bearing of the patient, and it seems as if she herself does not believe in the real nature of the disease, but is rather anxious to deceive herself and her attendants into this belief, and to excite a romantic pity ; or in other cases her fears and her vivid imagination seem to call forth the symptoms. However it is always a nice, and also a most important matter, to distinguish between the true and the hysterical affections, for a mistake either way may have very injurious results.

The hysteria of some approaches very near to insanity. The mind becomes so perverted, so wild, excitable, and violent, that their friends become alarmed, and sometimes wish to subject them to confinement. But this should never be permitted, as to put such a patient among lunatics would be the very way to complete the ruin of her mind.

If we review the endless array of symptoms found in this disease, and analyse them, we will find that they all arise from a weakened and excitable state of the nervous system, depending upon or connected with a similar state of. the numerous and important nerves of the sexual organs. As chlorosis is mainly a disease of the blood, so is hysteria of the nerves, though symptoms of both are often found together. The sexual system is connected by the sympathetic chain of nerves with all the important viscera in the body, such as the heart, stomach, and spinal cord, and irritability and enfeeblement arising in it, is propagated to all these organs, and gives rise to the endless variety of sympathetic affections mentioned above. *A morbid sexual state*, both physical and mental, lies at the root of hysteria. Girls menstruating healthily, and women happily married, are seldom afflicted with this disease; it is the single, or widows, or barren women, or such as are indifferent to, or dislike their husbands, (which last class, in this country of indissoluble marriage, is unhappily so large a one) in all of whom some sexual derangement of mind or body may be suspected to exist, who are its victims.

Hysteria is as much a mental, as a bodily disease, and consists as much in morbid and disordered emotions, as in disordered bodily functions. The parts of the body which are liable to be affected, are those which are most under the influence of the emotions, acting through the medium of the spinal or reflex nervous system. Thus we all know how much the heart, the stomach and bowels, the breathing, and the natural orifices of the body, such as the throat, the anus, and the neck of the bladder, are under the influence of the emotions. Fear and rage make the heart beat violently, make one gasp for breath, produce a choking sensation in the throat, and take away the voice. Bashfulness sends the blood rushing to the face, and often, like other kinds of fear, produces a looseness in the bowels, or violent desire to make water. It also disorders the sexual feelings, making a man impotent, and a woman hysterical. The emotions have moreover a great power over the will; and this explains the palsy and rigid states of various parts of the body in hysteria, where it is the will, which is powerless, not the muscles. The emotions exercise also a great control over the organs of secretion; hence the flow of limpid urine which follows the hysterical fit, and the immense secretion of air in the bowels. The convulsive affections, so often found, whether of a graver or milder character, depend on the irritability of the spinal cord, excited by the irritability of the emotions, or the organic nerves, especially those of the sexual system. According to the principle that all disease is a restorative effort of nature, the fits seem intended to restore the balance of the nervous system, and patients often say that they feel better and calmer after them.

A singular feature in hysteria is its *imitative* character, seen, not only in its simulating so many diseases, but also in its great infectiousness. It has been often observed by hospital physicians, that when a hysterical girl is admitted into a ward, the disease frequently spreads throughout the whole band, and all the patients begin to present hysterical symptoms. This arises from the great impressibility of the female character. Woman is constantly in the habit of acting from example, and is very much under the control of sympathy. Her will is not nearly so strong nor so firm as that of man in general, and the emotions and feelings have a greater sway over her mind than his. Probably this arises partly from the natural difference between them, but it certainly in great part depends on her imperfect education, (in which those subjects which develope the reasoning powers, and those actions and endeavours which fortify the will, are so much neglected,) and on the dependent state in which she lives; wh'ch causes weaken her will and self-control, surrender her to uncontrollable emotions, and make her so subject to external influences. We have a curious parallel to these hysterical sympathies, in the effects of electro-biology, as it is called. Women are much more generally mesmerisable than men; and the rigid state of the muscles, the impotence of will, &c., produced in these experiments by strong external impressions, are closely analogous to the hysterical phenomena; and it is probable that mesmerism might have beneficial results, as a remedy in these affections.

The *causes* which pave the way for the developement of hysteria, are in many respects similar to those of chlorosis, except that they are more especially those which act upon the mind and the nervous system, instead of such as interfere chiefly with nutrition and the elaboration of the blood. Such are faulty physical and moral education, which leave the nerves and the mind weak and prone to disorder. But the peculiar causes which give rise to the disease, are those which excite without gratifying the sexual feelings, thus rendering these feelings and the sexual nerves morbid and irritable. This, in by far the most cases, is the cause of hysteria. A young Indian officer once told me, that hysteria is almost unknown among the Hindoo women; and we know that it is a matter of religious feeling among that people, to procure a husband for a girl, as soon as menstruation first begins. They think it a sin that a single potential child should be lost. In this country on the other hand, there is probably no disease so widely, so universally spread. It is most common among the upper classes, among whom the sexual feelings are much more prominently developed, from the want of a necessary employment to occupy the mind, as well as from the various causes—such as novel reading, poetry, romance, dancing, theatricals, and so many other excitements, which elevate to the highest pitch the sexual desires, and paint the delights of love in the most glowing colors. But it is found in all classes, from the palace to the hovel; and in all classes we know, that the great majority of women pass a large part, and immense numbers the whole of their lives, without any gratification of the sexual feelings, or satisfaction of that yearning wish to love and to be beloved, which is the divinest and strongest instinct in the breast of young people.

Let the reader consider these facts; let him think of who are the victims of the disease—the single, widows, or women unhappily married; let him analyse the peculiar mental and physical phenomena of hysteria, and let him consider the powerful disturbing influence, which the systematic denial and disappointment of the strongest of our natural desires must have upon a delicate and susceptible girl; and it is impossible to avoid the conclusion, that this is the main cause of the disease. The natural emotions are checked and thrown back upon themselves, and it is inevitable that they should become disordered; and their disorder gradually implicates the whole nervous system. The stream of feeling, instead of being allowed to flow onwards in its natural channel in the eve of day, gladdening and fertilising all around, is pent up in the gloomy secret caverns of the mind, to cause there a deluge and a desolation.

That which should have been the young girl's pride and delight, becomes her shame and her torture; she must conceal, the unhappy one! and studiously repress her eager and beautiful emotions, and can we wonder that bewilderment, timidity, and impotence result? Nature cannot bear this constant state of slavery; and ever and anon she shows in the hysterical convulsions, in the wild tumultuous hysterical emotions, or in the delirious excitement of nymphomania (love-madness,) that she will not be repressed. The passions of youth are a volcanic fire, which in the end will burst through all obstacles.

Is it the part of a wise and feeling man to refuse to see these facts? Whatever we may be able to do, to cure or to prevent these enormous evils, their main cause is undeniable. Men refuse to look at the melancholy results of sexual abstinence, and rather blame the patient for indulging in sexual feelings which cannot be gratified. It may not be that their peculiar idolised virtue should be attended by so much misery: the fault cannot surely be in it, but must be in our own original sin and perverse nature. Thus, according to the inveterate error of the christian moralist, they lay the blame on nature, the all-perfect; and hopelessly mourn over the evil nature of man, instead of trying to remedy their own erroneous system.

Hysteria is very frequently associated with diseases of menstruation, such as amenorrhœa, dysmenorrhœa, menorrhagia, or chlorosis. It is rather with these, than with the marked inflammatory affections, such as ulcers of the womb, inflammation of the ovaries, &c., that convulsive hysteria is found; although the peculiar sexual bashfulness and nervous irritability are common to all sexual diseases; arising, as has been already explained, from the morbid delicacy on these subjects. However it would seem, that where there is a real serious structural disease, the hysterical emotions are, as it were, calmed by it, and the imagination bound down by the real physical suffering. Many young women thus say, that they would rather have some real physical ailment, than the exceedingly unpleasant, vague feelings of nervous weakness, uselessness, and discontent, which make them miserable without an assignable cause; but which in reality arise from the want of definite occupation and of sexual love, the two great wants in woman's life. Relations say of a young girl, who shows signs of discontent and unhappiness, "why is she unhappy? surely she has everything to make her satisfied, all her wishes and wants are supplied;" but they do not see. that by far the most essential of all wants at that age is not supplied, without which every luxury, every tenderness of friends or relatives, are to the ardent young girl quite insufficient for her happiness; namely sexual love, and also the power of working for herself at something, which her mind tells her is worthy of her energies.

The *treatment* of hysteria is, as may be expected, often very difficult. The means usually applied are—as is readily understood, when we reflect on the general cause of the disease, and its nature, which is often more mental than bodily—totally irrational, and unsuited to produce a radical cure. Dr. Ashwell acknowledges this; he says that " few physicians desire the treatment of hysteria; for the symptoms are so variable, one springing up after another, that different remedies are successively tried and abandoned, till both the doctor and patient are worn out, and the disease is suffered to take its course." In reality, Love is the only physician, who can cure his peculiar diseases ; and it is vain for a medical man to expect to supply his place. The passions, which have been repressed and thrown into disorder, must be gratified, and the proper healthy stimulus given to the sexual organs, so as to restore their nervous balance, before we can have any rational expectation of a cure. The mind will thus become contented and happy, the tumultuous emotions be calmed and restored to health, and the sexual organs will regain their normal state. Dr. Ashwell says, that marriage frequently cures hysteria, but hysterical women often make bad nurses, having scanty and innutritious milk. A happy sexual intimacy is the grand remedy in hysteria ; but besides this, various accessory means would often be necessary.

In a hysterical fit, the usual treatment is, to lay the patient down, loosen the dress, and dash cold water over the head and neck. The various affections of the head and chest, stomach, bowels, &c., should be met as they occur by appropriate means, chiefly by remedies of a soothing and anti-spasmodic nature. In all cases of hysteria we should discover whether there be any co-existing genital disease, and endeavour to remove it : for hysteria, if depending on such an affection, is never cured without its prior removal.

But the main object of treatment in all hysterical cases, should be to go to the root of the disease, and remove the morbid state of the sexual system and feelings, which causes the general nervous irritability. It is in vain that we treat symptom after symptom, headache, colic, fits ; or mental irritability, vehemence, or caprice. We may overcome one enemy after another, we may load the patient whether with blame or compassion, but we cannot cheat nature ; and until the required remedy is applied, the radical sexual disorder in mind and body will continue, and only become aggravated by continuance.

It is a miserable thing to see the usual treatment of a hysterical girl. Friends and relations either laugh at, or dislike her ; for irritability, peevishness, and often violent temper are a part of the disease ; and that effeminate amiability which is so highly lauded in the female character, at the expense of the far higher virtues of force and independent energy, is sadly defaced by stern nature, whose destructive tendencies will not be silenced in either sex. Such unkind and mistaken treatment often aggravates the disease, and pushes it to the verge of insanity, or frequently into complete insanity : for hysteria often ends in this, where the mind is naturally weak. The medical man must generally content himself with treating symptoms, and directs his attention chiefly to bracing the general health, and at most palliating the affection.

Few medical men pay much attention to the mind, but consider chiefly the bodily state ; and in a disease like hysteria they are quite at fault, and find their agents powerless. For it is necessary, in order to remove disease, that we should make an individual *happy* or contented (in other words, healthy) in mind as well as healthy in body ; and unless we attend to this in hysteria, which is as much a mental as a bodily disease, we cannot expect success. To produce a happy and contented mind, we must give the patient that which her nature demands.

Lecturing and contempt will not bully the disease, kindness and pity will not persuade it; youth turns a deaf ear to all but its own beautiful instincts, which for ever point out to it the path of truth; and none of these means will produce a quiet and a happy mind, which is essential to the patient's recovery. The only one who can cure a hysterical young woman, is a young man whom she loves, and with whom she may gratify her natural feelings, and have a free and happy outlet for the emotions which have been so long disordering her.

Along with this essential for the cure, other means of bracing the general health and restoring the mental balance should be taken. Change of scene is especially advisable, and removal from home influences, which are so often prejudicial in such cases. Travelling is an excellent auxiliary, especially a pedestrian tour, which women so seldom have the power of indulging in; not because they could not undertake it, but because it is thought indecorous in women. There are few things more salutary or delightful than a walking tour, whether in pleasant society or alone. It is much more strengthening than a driving one, and a most powerful means of invigorating the frame. I have frequently heard ladies express a great desire that they had the freedom that men have, in travelling about, and especially in making walking tours, which are becoming so common among our sex. But a girl is never allowed to go about alone, like a young man; she is subjected to a constant espionage, from which not one of her actions or motions can escape; and so she is frequently forced to do things, excellent in themselves, in an underhand manner, to the destruction of her sense of dignity and rectitude. It is to guard the great female virtue of chastity, as has been mentioned above, that all these intolerable restrictions and espionage, are placed upon the movements of woman; and as long as the present ideas regarding this so-called virtue remain, it is impossible for woman to obtain greater freedom. The difference in the privileges of man and woman, depends essentially on the difference of their *sexual* privileges; and until this question is attended to, the various efforts which are being made at present to give greater freedom and a wider sphere to woman, can have but a very limited success.

Every young mind, whether in man or woman, burns for romance, love, and adventure; these are the great natural stimuli to the health and virtue of youth, the pole-stars which cheer us on, and shed a glory on our every-day working-life. At home among her relations the young hysterical girl has in many cases a constant feeling of degradation; the emotions which she instinctively feels are the most ennobling and exalting for her, are coldly looked upon or laughed at; her romantic longings are sneered down, and the main springs of her virtue trodden in the dust. Familiarity, in the home circle, far too often breeds contempt; and it is very frequently a love affair, that first shows a girl what she can be, and elevates her into another sphere of self-respect. In countries such as Scotland, where spiritual puritanism reigns triumphant, romance and love have no quarter shown to them, and all the ardent sexual aspirations meet with double discouragement. Kindness and reverence should be used towards the hysterical, instead of the contemptous way in which they are usually treated, so as to increase their self-respect and self-control. A great part of the disease consists in a sense of weakness, and want of self-confidence. How can a girl have confidence in herself, if all around laugh at her, and treat her feelings as unreal? It must never be thought, that hysteria is an unreal disease. It is a weakened state of the nervous system, physical and mental, and the physical weakness and irritability are just as marked as the mental. It is easy to laugh, but it is rather the part of the wise and feeling heart to reverence and to cure.

One great reason of the simulation of various diseases, and also of the vague and unreal nature of many of the sufferings of which the hysterical complain, is that they are forbidden to disclose the real cause of their sufferings, or of their unhappiness. In every sexual disease both in man and woman, and especially in the latter, the miserable necessity for concealment makes the patient invent other subjects of complaint; and thus sexual patients are almost always accused of hypochondria, and falsification or exaggeration of symptoms. When a man or a woman suffers, whether in mind or body, they must give some reason for it, and if they are forbidden by our unnatural ideas of propriety to speak freely of the real cause, they are forced into deceit; and this is one cause which greatly heightens the miseries of all these diseases, and is the source of great degradation to the sufferer. No diseases cause such a feeling of insufferable degradation as the sexual ones; and in a minor degree those of the excretory organs. Not to believe in an individual is one of the greatest injuries we can do him, and is as philosophically false as it is unfeeling. It has been truly and beautifully said "Love thy neighbour as thyself;" but the precept "Believe in thy neighbour as thyself" is not less true, and still more needed among us. Every man believes in himself, and knows that his nature is true at bottom; that his joys and his sorrows are real, although his external character may be at variance with the inner man. But it is the part of the moralist and the physician to endeavour to see into this inner man, which is always real, and seek to make the exterior correspond with it. It is only when the inner man is in harmony with the outer, and when a person thus lives a true life, that there can be satisfactory happiness. Nature always strives to be true, and to have a true expression; although in our complex and imperfect society her purpose is so often defeated.

If a genital disease co-exist with hysteria, it will be necessary to cure it, but in many of the functional genital diseases by far the most effectual cure is sexual intercourse; and medicinal remedies will be needed chiefly in the inflammatory diseases, and in cases where sexual intercourse and child-bearing prove insufficient. It is important to remark, that sexual intercourse may frequently fail thoroughly to cure a sexual disease in woman, while child-bearing, lactation, and the thoroughly new world of physical and moral emotions which is thus opened up to her, and which is necessary in that sex to complete the chain of the sexual functions, may succeed. The immense impulse that is often given to the health of woman by child-bearing; the change which it produces, dispelling morbid states of body and mind, and giving a renewed freshness and vigour to both, in those cases where it proceeds naturally and happily, is well known. If it be not possible to procure for hysterical women these great remedies, let us not flatter ourselves that the disease will yield throughout our society to any other means. If we must still adhere to the old routine, to valerian and musk, assafœtida and opium : to lecturing, persuading or upbraiding ; the cure of hysterical disease is a physical and moral impossibility.

As to the still more important question of the *prevention* of this widespread malady, the same remedy which will cure, will also prevent, like all the natural remedies. The only possible mode of preventing hysteria, is by fortifying the general system by the appropiate exercise of all the bodily and mental powers from childhood upwards ; and more especially by providing for the healthy exercise of the sexual organs and emotions, as soon as nature requires this. If we could possibly attain this so desirable aim throughout society, hysteria would almost disappear, instead of being as at present, probably the most widely spread af all diseases, and therefore creating an enormous mass of misery. It is the most widely spread of all diseases, simply because, of all the human organs, the female genital organs and sexual feelings are placed at present in the most unhealthy circumstances.

Woman's peculiar torments begin at puberty, and from that time, in innumerable cases, till her marriage, she is the constant prey of anxiety. Ungratified desires distract her, endless temptations and excitements surround her, marriage is for her so critical a step, and yet she has not the power of selection. The fatal question, shall she be married at all? gradually dawns upon her, and the clouds and whirlwinds of anxious and conflicting passions darken her sky. If these be not natural and real sufferings, and if we are not to recognise and do all we can to remedy this fearful state of matters, let us close at once the book of human knowledge, and give up the farce of philosophy and philanthrophy. It is our part to investigate diligently and recognise all truths ; nor to bend what we see to a preconceived theory, but rather to form if possible, a theory based upon all the natural truths. If we do thus in the case before us, we will see, that unless we can remove the main cause of hysteria, namely, insufficient sexual gratifications, it is totally impossible to prevent that disease. Let us look this truth steadily in the face, whatever difficulties it occasions us.

I have now spoken of two of the most important female diseases, which are dependent, in the vast majority of cases, mainly on sexual abstinence. Before proceeding to the diseases of menstruation, many of which have the same cause, I shall say a few words on the subject of sexual excess.

SEXUAL EXCESS

A VERY meagre account is given in medical works of the frequency or the effects of venereal excesses in the female. Venereal excesses are not, in this country, nearly so [prevalent a cause of disease in woman as venereal abstinence ; and in this we see the great error of those, who are constantly declaiming on the evils of the former, while they never allude to the latter. In the pulpit, and among Christian moralists generally, we have fearful pictures given of the evils of sexual excess ; but in reality they are very rarely seen, compared with those of abstinence. Men war with shadows, and neglect the dreadful realities under their eyes. Chastity or sexual abstinence causes more real disease and misery in one year, I believe, in this country, than sexual excesses in a century. We must not include venereal disease among the evils of excess, as it has nothing to do with it ; it depends always on infection, not on over-use of the sexual organs.

However there is no doubt that sexual excess is capable of producing, and that in many cases it does produce, serious evils. Over stimulus of the sexual system will cause disease and exhaustion ; and this not unfrequently results in newly-married women. Hysterical and chlorotic symptoms may be induced in this way by debility, and various organs may suffer in their functions. This is especially seen, when a weak and delicate girl marries a powerful man. Menorrhagia is apt to be induced from over stimulation of the ovaries, together with exhaustion and sexual apathy. In such cases the constitution should be allowed to regain its strength by separation of the parties for a time, and greater moderation must be used afterwards. I have seen several cases, both in men and women, where sexual excesses after marriage were the cause of great enfeeblement ; and there is in these cases far too much delicacy in the medical man about telling the parties of their error. Why should such scruples be allowed to interfere with the most important of all considerations—the health and happiness of the individuals ?

But there is another aspect in which we should view the question of sexual excess. A moderate amount of sexual indulgence braces and ennobles body and mind, and heightens the virtue of each · but to be always thinking on amatory subjects, or constantly indulging in vene-real pleasures, has a very bad effect on both man and woman, even though it do not produce tangible bodily disease. The mind becomes effeminate, and the nerves lose their tone ; the power of thought be-comes impaired, cloyed as it were by sweetness. Nature never meant that we should be absorbed in one set of feelings, nor steeped in sex-ual indulgences, as some of the southern nations are. The great object of our aims should be to cultivate all the different faculties we possess, and so to vary and perpetuate our enjoyments. Self-denial, although so much abused in this country, especially in sexual mat-ters, is often a most valuable quality. But the very way to ensure the rank and morbid growth of the sexual passions, is to deny them any gratification. By so doing, let us not suppose that we become their masters; rather we become their slaves, and they tyrannise over our thoughts, and absorb us completely. There are no people who think so habitually on sexual matters, as those in whom love has been most repressed; the youth suffering from seminal weakness, the hysterical girl, the single woman, or the priest. Married people soon become accustomed to the pleasures of love, and learn to divide their thoughts and affections among the many objects around them ; but to the young single woman love is all in all. This is in one way a true sexual excess, and shows the folly of imagining that we can defeat the purposes of nature. Among many of our poets and young female authoresses we can see the effects of this effeminating one-sidedness ; they can write and talk of nothing but love, and if we analyse their works, we will find how much this absorption in one set of feelings interferes with their general developement and happiness. They can-not escape from the passion, because they have either been sexually unfortunate themselves, or because their sympathising eyes see so much sexual misery around them, that they can think of little else.

DISEASES OF MENSTRUATION.

THIS function which has been aptly called " the sign and the guardian of the female health," is so very frequently disordered to a greater or less degree, that its perfect health is the exception, instead of the rule, in our society. Dr. Tilt informs us, that in a large number of apparently healthy women taken indiscriminately, it was found on enquiry, that only in one-fourth of them, was menstruation perfectly free from morbid symptoms. In the others it was preceded or accompanied by more or less disturbance, pain, or uneasiness. Dr. Ashwell moreover, says of the ovaries, the organs which preside over the menstrual function, " No organs of the body seem to be so prone to disease as the ovaries, for I can truly say that I have seldom found them after death perfectly healthy." A fellow student once told me, that he was informed by a female friend, that among the young ladies of her acquaintance, there was scarcely one in whom menstruation continued healthy for many years, if they remained single. It was often healthy at first, but about the twentieth year or so, it gradually became painful, and more or less disordered.

These facts are exceedingly significant, and prove to demonstration, how very unhealthy must be the hygienic conditions, that surround the female sexual organs. Disordered menstruation, attended by more or less pain, is so common, that women look upon it as a natural and inevitable evil, and unless it be severe, pay little heed to it. But this is a very false and a very dangerous opinion. That menstruation was 'ntended by nature to be quite free from pain and uneasiness is proved as well by our experience of the painless elimination of all the other secretions, when perfectly healthy, as by the complete absence of pain in many women, and in those who are otherwise in the most robust health. Why too are the ovaries so very frequently found diseased ? Even though the pain might possibly be deemed natural, this cannot be. It must be concluded, that menstruation cannot be called typically healthy, where there is any pain or uneasiness attending it, although, in the present low standard of female health, very considerable disorder may pass current; and it is certain that serious menstrual disease is often induced, by disregarding the common and slighter symptoms at its commencement. The perfect condition of menstruation, which should be to woman so very valuable a criterion of health, is at present of little comparative use, if its warnings are so little heeded.

Child-birth, moreover, (which consists like menstruation in the discharge of an egg, and differs only in the fact that this egg has been fecundated, and has arrived at maturity) is a much more painful process in civilized woman than in the savage, and in some women than in others. This, which is also a sign of degeneration from the natural standard of health, is probably owing partly to the feeble developement of woman, and partly to the disproportionate size of the brain in civilized man.

I now proceed to the disorders of menstruation, which are so important as to become serious diseases.

ABSENT MENSTRUATION.

THIS signifies an absence of menstruation. and is a very common disease. It is classified under two kinds, the amenorrhœa of suppression, and of retention. By retention is meant that the catamenia have never appeared; by suppression that they have been stopped, after continuing for a time.

Retention of the menses may arise either from a congenital defect of the sexual organs, or from a want of power in the constitution to establish puberty, or to set agoing the menstrual functions. Congenital deficiency is very rare, although of all the organs in the body none are so frequently subject to malformations as the sexual organs, both in man and woman; nature seeming to find the perfect developement of these organs her most difficult task. There are some women in whom the ovaries, others in whom the womb, are naturally wanting or imperfectly developed, and in such cases of course no menstruation can take place. In these cases the sexual desires are absent, and the appearance, tone of voice, &c., may have somewhat of a masculine character. However, according to Dr. Ashwell, who has seen a few such cases, the health is generally delicate, and the mind irritable. Of course there is no remedy in these cases, and all that can be done by those who have the misfortune to be born sexually imperfect, just as others are born deaf, dumb. or blind. is to console themselves with the reflection that there are many other blessings in the world besides those of sex; which indeed prove at present too often a curse instead of a blessing. There is one mode too, in which any natural defect like this, might be put to advantage, and used for the service of mankind. Every one who is born defective, stands in an exceptional position, the sexually neuter among the rest; and has experiences and perhaps opportunities of insight into nature, that others cannot have. All evil in one aspect may be viewed as good; and it is well known in pathology, that disease reveals to us important truths with regard to the nature of health, which we could not have learned in any other way and in like manner all monstrosities and congenital deficiencies are now recognised by physiologists, as among the most valuable of all revelations of the operations of nature. Some of us in this life inherit health and happiness, others disease and misery; but all are, in one point of view, equally valuable and important in the scheme of nature.

Retention of the menses is, in the great majority of cases, owing to delicacy of frame or other causes, which retard the developement of puberty or the sexual functions; and we should be very slow to suspect any congenital deficiency, unless it be quite apparent, even in cases where the menses are delayed for years beyond their usual time of appearance. We have seen that retention often occurs in chlorosis, and that the frame is here unable to develope perfectly the sexual organs or to set up menstruation. The feebleness of the system causes the sexual arrest; and this reacts on the general health, and produces the peculiar chlorotic cachexy. This kind of retention is found chiefly among delicate girls in towns, engaged in sedentary occupations, or confined in unhealthy rooms or factories. But there is another class of cases, where the menses are kept back; namely, in full plethoric girls, in whom congestion and torpor of the system, and especially of the sexual organs, prevent the elimination of the secretion. In these cases there are the symptoms of fulness of blood, viz. flushing of the face, giddiness, and oppression of head, specks floating before the eyes, a full and usually a slow pulse, and alternate heats and chills of the extremities, showing a disordered circulation. These cases are sometimes found in robust and plethoric country girls, and in those in towns, who have had a luxurious or indolent life, favouring fulness of habit.

I have already described the treatment of the chlorotic cases, which should consist in a bracing and invigorating plan to establish puberty, and then the proper sexual stimulus to excite the menstrual discharge. In the congestive form, means should be taken to remove the plethoric state. Plenty of walking exercise should be taken, with a cold bath once or twice daily, and a plain and somewhat sparing diet; in fact the patient should go for a while into *training*. These means will tend to remove the fulness of blood, and will equalise the circulation and the nervous influence, for which purpose nothing is so effectual as plenty of active walking exercise. The great natural remedy, the sexual stimulus, should now be used; and there are very few cases of such disease, I am persuaded, that would resist these means.

The direct stimuli used at present to excite menstruation are a class of remedies called *emmenagogues*, whose intention is to stimulate the sexual organs, and urge them to the performance of their functions. The ones chiefly used are the mustard hip-bath at 96 or 98 degrees, taken every night for from half an hour to one, or even two hours. This is one of the best, and frequently induces menstruation. Various medicines are also given with the same view. Iron, by enriching the blood, often causes menstruation, especially in chlorotic cases. Aloes is very frequently given, and is the best purgative for producing menstruation. It acts chiefly on the rectum, and by irritating it, produces the menstrual discharge from the neighbouring sexual organs. It is well to give it in combination with iron, which prevents it from irritating the rectum too much. Electricity applied to the sexual organs is in some cases very effective, a single spark sometimes producing the discharge. Stimulating injections into the vagina, especially one made of one drachm of the pure liquor ammoniae to a pint of milk, are often very good.

These are the chief means at present used to produce the menstrual discharge directly; and they are commonly employed, in cases where, after the general health has been braced, congestion removed, and puberty established, menstruation still continues absent; where in short the way has been paved for the flow, and yet it does not appear. These various means prove successful in many cases, but they are all very uncertain in their action, and, like all other unnatural medicinal means, do an immense amount of harm to counterbalance the good. Electricity, if much used, may over stimulate and destroy the natural nervous susceptibility. Aloes often cause piles, and always derange the stomach and bowels. Iron is apt to cause fulness, headache, and giddiness. Besides this, there is not one of them for a moment to be compared in efficiency, any more than in safety, to the natural sexual stimulus. It is by this alone that nature intended that the ovaries should be urged to action, that the proper nervous equilibrium of the system should be maintained, and the monthly flow regulated; and it is an utter delusion to hope to supplant the natural stimulus by iron, electricity, hip-baths, aloes, or other means foreign and poisonous to the frame. Dr. Ashwell says that marriage often, though not always, cures amenorrhœa; and I am convinced that if sexual intercourse were used early enough in these diseases, before the susceptibility of the organs is worn out by long disease or by unnatural stimulants; if other means of invigorating the system were used at the same time, and, if need be, mustard hip-baths, aloes, &c., sometimes resorted to as auxiliaries, where the sexual stimulus alone proved insufficient; very few cases of absent menstruation would resist. We should not then see, as is now frequently seen, the retention of the menses persisting for years, sometimes for the whole of life, in spite of all our unnatural remedies; causing endless anxiety and debility, and frequently leading to fatal structural disease, which, like the vulture, ever hovers round the weakened prey. There will yet come a time, when it will be clearly seen, that it is as wrong to stimulate the female sexual organs with these unnatural means, unless in exceptional cases, as to stimulate a jaded frame and toil-worn mind with whiskey or opium.

"When menstruation is absent, a woman is never quite well," says Dr. Ashwell; the powers of the constitution gradually become disordered, chlorosis and white discharges are very frequently induced, and the greatest prostration comes slowly on. Even where menstruation is retained for many years, we must be slow to suspect congenital defect, for that is of very rare occurrence, and menstruation in the great majority of cases comes on at last, even under the present inadequate treatment.

The amenorrhœa of *suppression* is a far more common disease than that of retention; and therefore of much greater importance to society. It is divided by medical writers into two kinds, acute and chronic suppression. By *acute* suppression is meant the sudden checking of the discharge, when actually present. The two great causes of this are, cold, and violent mental emotion. When menstruating women are exposed to cold, damp feet, &c., or receive a sudden mental shock, as of terror or grief, the discharge is often suddenly arrested, and acute symptoms of either inflammation or great irritation in the ovaries and womb follow. I shall speak afterwards of the acute inflammation of the womb or ovaries, which is sometimes the result of arrested menstruation. But more frequently irritation and congestion of the organs alone result, especially in delicate and irritable women, in whom such an accident is most likely to occur. Here there is acute pain felt in the lower part of the abdomen, and a feeling of weight and uneasiness in the pelvis. The pulse is quick, and the patient is anxious and excited. Nausea is also a frequent symptom. It is often difficult in such a case to distinguish whether there be not acute inflammation, but the character of the pain, which occurs in severe paroxysms with intervals of ease, and flies rapidly from one part to another; also the occurrence of hysterical fits or fainting, and other marks which denote irritation rather than inflammation, will enable the physician to decide. Here a soothing and relaxing treatment should be used. A general warm bath at 96 degrees should be given (that is, warm, not hot), and also some purgative medicine, and Ipecacuanha in small doses, so as to produce nausea, and thus deaden pain and calm down fever and spasm. The injection of assafœtida and opium into the rectum often produces an almost magical relief. The injection should be kept in for awhile with a piece of sponge. By these means the pain and congestion will be relieved, and the discharge will perhaps return at the time, though this cannot always be expected. Whether it do or not, no subsequent treatment should be used, till just before the next menstrual period. Then every precaution should be taken to favour the return of the flow. Fatigue or cold should be sedulously avoided, the bowels kept free, and hot mustard hip and foot-baths taken on alternate nights for a few nights previously. If menstruation occur, all is well; but if it do not, and if white discharges be set up instead, then the case becomes one of chronic suppression, and must be treated accordingly.

Chronic suppression is of very frequent occurrence. Its constitutional effects are somewhat similar to those produced by other suppressed secretions, such as the bile, the fæces, &c., and indicate, in the first place, a fulness of blood, and disorder of the nervous system, and afterwards a gradually increasing debility, and impoverishment of the whole frame. There are diffused and obstinate headaches, occasional giddiness, with specks floating before the eyes and dilated pupils. The surface is irregularly hot and cold, and easily chilled; the bowels are constipated; there is disordered respiration, palpitation of the heart, pains in the chest, &c. The health often seriously fails, all the different organs being liable to be implicated; and organic disease may be established in some part. Chlorosis is frequently caused by chronic menstrual suppression; and hysteria is very generally found along with it.

Chronic suppression may be brought on in many ways. An attack of acute suppression may gradually pass into it. After such an attack, the function may not return or only imperfectly; a painful effort being made at each menstrual period, and a small quantity of blood secreted, but this gradually dying away. It may also be caused by gradual impairment of the health, from the want of the proper sexual stimulus. This is a very frequent cause; indeed it is rare for a single woman, especially in towns, to continue long to menstruate healthily. Irregularities occur, monthly periods are frequently missed, and menstruation becomes painful or often ceases.

It must always be kept in mind that the ovaries receive their natural stimulus from sexual intercourse. The flow of all the secretions depends on the application of their appropriate stimulus. Thus the flow of saliva is promoted by the stimulus of food in the mouth; that of bile by the substances passing through the alimentary canal; that of gastric juice by the presence of food in the stomach. There is no secreting organ which can possibly remain long active and healthy, unless it receive a due proportion of its appropriate stimulus; and the only appropriate stimulus to the ovaries is sexual intercourse and child-bearing.

Chronic suppression frequently depends also on ulceration of the mouth of the womb; and also, as Dr. Tilt has shewn, on inflammatory states of the ovaries. Every case therefore should be carefully analysed, and its peculiar cause and complications ascertained, before a proper treatment can be adopted. Independently of inflammatory disease, there is frequently especially in recent cases, a congested state of the ovaries and uterus. White discharges are generally found where menstruation is absent, and show the congested state of the sexual organs, which it is their object to relieve. Chronic suppression is also sometimes, though comparatively rarely, the result of slow organic disease in the ovaries, such as ovarian dropsy, and in this case is incurable.

In *treating* this very common disease, it is first necessary that we should learn the true cause of each case. To do so, it is very frequently necessary, and in probably all cases it is advisable, that an examination should be made by the finger or the speculum, to see if there be any ulcer of the womb, ovarian inflammation, &c. The general neglect of such an examination at the present day, is the cause of an immense number of errors in this, as well as almost all other genital diseases. The symptoms of ulcerative or ovarian disease are often so obscure, that without a physical examination it is impossible even for the most experienced man to come to a conclusion, whether or not such disease exist. If it do, and be not discovered, we cannot expect to be successful in the treatment. No conscientious man thinks of treating any other part of the body, which is accessible to our view or our touch, without using every possible means to aid his diagnosis.

There is nothing so satisfactory as ocular inspection, and there is scarcely any mere description of symptoms, that can be depended on. Whenever there is disorder in an organ, it is next to impossible to say in any case that there is no structural disease, and that it is merely functional, without looking at the organ, if that be at all possible. And surely it is a very wrong, as well as a very slovenly, neglect of the power which nature has given us of seeing and touching the womb and other sexual organs, to allow a false delicacy to interfere with this inspection, in any case where these organs are implicated. We cannot tell from the mere detail of symptoms exactly what is the matter even in the very simplest case ; and it seems to me to be a grave dereliction of duty, in both physician and patient, even to hazard in the slightest, so valuable a thing as human life and health. If it be the case, as I do not believe, that it is not advisable that man should frequently inspect the female sexual organs, and if these morbid feelings of mystery and shame between the sexes are to be kept up at any price, let women be trained (as they certainly should be in any case) to aid in the examination and treatment of these organs ; but do not let it be said of human beings, arrived at the age of reflection, that they allow such feelings to stand in the way of their obvious and paramount duty—the conscientious investigation of every disease by all the means in their power. Until scruples of sexual delicacy throw as few obstacles in the way of the investigation and treatment of sexual diseases, as they do in diseases of the throat, eyes, or ears, it cannot be said that the genital diseases have any fair chance given them ; and such scruples must be recognised as among the most important causes of the ignorance and neglect of these diseases, and therefore of a vast amount of misery.

Human life and health are dirt-cheap at the present day, when the world is so full of poverty, misery, and disease ; but I earnestly hope, that in time, when a higher standard of health prevails, such carelessness and imperfections in the modes of investigating disease will not be generally seen. In our dispensaries—nay, even in our hospitals, all must deplore the summary and inefficient manner in which diseases are so often diagnosed and treated. The doctor's hands are far too full, and he can pay no adequate attention to the immense numbers, and consequently the treatment is often a mere farce. These hasty and imperfect habits of diagnosis are carried into the treatment of all diseases in all classes : and in fact the amount of disease prevents proper attention to almost any single case.

If, after a proper examination, the chronic suppression be found to depend on ulceration of the womb, or on subacute inflammation of the ovaries, these diseases must be first cured ; and then if menstruation do not return spontaneously, the sexual stimulus and a bracing treatment will probably induce it. If there be congestion of the sexual system, and a plethoric habit, leeches applied to the mouth of the womb are very beneficial, together with plenty of walking, exercise, bathing, &c., all of which means tend to equalise the circulation, and remove local congestions They thus prepare the way for the bene-

ficial action of the sexual stimulus, which in all these cases is the one
that is ultimately to be relied on.   When the system is chlorotic and
enfeebled, a bracing treatment is necessary along with sexual intercourse ; which should be used (here as in other cases where the sexual
organs are in a weak state), in moderation, so as not to over stimulate
the weakened ovaries.   This is evidently too the treatment requisite
for the very frequent cases of irregularity or complete suppression of
the menses, brought on by sexual abstinence.   Mustard hip-baths or
other auxiliaries may be needed in many cases, and would probably be
frequently beneficial.   Epilepsy, St. Vitus' dance, and other nervous
diseases, are sometimes dependent on chronic menstrual suppression,
and are cured by the return of the discharge.

In order to *prevent* amenorrhœa, care should be taken by women
not to expose themselves to cold or wet while menstruating.   Habit
however accustoms the body to this, and bathing women go into the
sea, whilst menstruating, without injury.   Other causes, which are
said sometimes suddenly to arrest menstruation are, sexual intercourse or violent emetics or purgatives during menstruation, and these
causes should be carefully avoided.   Dr. Tilt says, that if women were
generally in the habit of wearing drawers, the number and severity of
sexual diseases would be greatly diminished.   These articles of dress
are gradually coming into use, but are still not nearly so much worn
as they should be.   Cotton stockings too, and thin shoes, expose the
feet to cold and wet, and are said by one of the French physicians to
be among the chief causes of the universal prevalence of white discharges among the Parisian women.   To prevent chrónic suppression,
the great means is a due amount of the proper stimulus for the ovaries, and a healthy life in other respects.

VICARIOUS MENSTRUATION.

THIS is a curious affection that sometimes occurs in the absence of natural menstruation, and has been termed "a freak of nature. A quantity of blood is discharged from some other organ, generally the stomach or the lungs, and sometimes this discharge takes place periodically at the menstrual epochs. It causes much alarm to the patient, but is not dangerous, and ceases after a time. It is sometimes difficult to distinguish it from true primary hermorrhage; but the guiding facts are, the presence of amenorrhœa; the occasional periodicity, and the absence of the signs of disorder and disease, which accompany primary hemorrhage. White discharges sometimes take the place of absent menstruation, occurring at the usual periods, lasting the usual time, and attended by the usual catamenial effort. This is most common in delicate girls at the beginning of menstruation.

The treatment of these vicarious affections is, to restore natural menstruation.

DYSMENORRHŒA

OR

PAINFUL MENSTRUATION.

THIS is, as Dr. Ashwell says, a very common disease, and causes intense suffering. In fact the disease, in its aggravated form, is something like the pains of child-birth occurring every month. It not only causes intolerable suffering, but very frequently sterility likewise; so that a celebrated physician said of it, "one half of the life of such a patient is devoted to suffering, and the other blighted by sterility." "Single women are particularly prone to it," says Dr. Ashwell, "and it often seems to be associated with a tendency to strong mental emotion."

The symptoms of painful menstruation are as follows. Menstruation becomes irregular, and is sometimes excessive, but generally scanty. The discharge is emitted with indescribable pain, and is shreddy or clotted; lancinating and shooting pains are felt in the womb and vagina. Severe pain is also felt in the loins, shooting towards the groin and down the inside of the thighs; expulsatory throes, like those of labour, occur, and the patient bears down, and sometimes, after expelling a clot, experiences a temporary relief. In some cases where there is considerable congestion of the womb, what are called "spurious abortions" occur. These are membranes containing a clot of blood, which are expelled from the womb with agonising throes. Acute pain in the breasts sometimes precedes menstruation for some days; and in other cases headaches, flushing of the face, weight in the pelvis, full and quick pulse precede the attack, showing that there is inflammatory action going on, and foretelling the coming storm. Sometimes the menstrual pains, after lasting a day or so, go off, and the remainder of the period is easy; but frequently they last throughout.

In the intervals there is often no suffering, and at first but slight constitutional disturbance. But gradually the health becomes impaired; the bowels become now constipated, now loose; there is loss of appetite, emaciation, and pallor. Profuse white discharges occur during the menstrual intervals, and sometimes amenorrhœa ensues. The breasts now become flaccid, and almost quite disappear.

The *causes* of this excruciating malady are various. It is sometimes co-existent with menstruation from puberty upwards; but often arises at a subsequent period. It lasts in many cases throughout the whole sexual life of the woman, and only ceases at last by the cessation of menstruation. Hysterical and irritable single women are especially its victims. It very frequently comes on gradually from impairment of the general health, as amenorrhœa does; and in the most of these cases in single women, doubtless depends mainly on the want of healthy exercise of the organs. It sometimes, but very rarely, arises from a congenital narrowed state of the os uteri, and cervical canal. In this case it begins with the commencement of menstruation. It is also frequently dependent on ulceration of the mouth of the womb, or ovarian disease.

In the *treatment* of dysmenorrhœa, great care must be taken to arrive at the cause of the particular case before us, and an examination with the finger and speculum is almost always necessary, else the treatment may very probably be erroneous. By the use of these means of investigation it will be seen, whether there be ulceration or ovarian disease. If found, these must be treated, and their cure, which can generally be effected, if they are recognised, will probably remove the dysmenorrhœa. If there be congenital narrowing of the canal, it must be dilated by sponge tents, and this has in several instances produced a cure. If no inflammatory disease be found, sexual intercourse, along with a general bracing hygienic treatment should be used, and is by far the best remedy. Healthy exercise is always the best treatment for organs which are in an irritable nervous state, calming and soothing the nervous excitement, and gradually training the disordered parts to a regulated and healthy discharge of their functions. "Idleness is the root of all evil," in the various organs, as well as in the whole being; for when these are not healthily employed, each in their own special manner, pain and disorder are certain sooner or later to mark their dissatisfaction. Dr. Ashwell says that "dysmenorrhœa is often cured by marriage and child-bearing; but not always, and aggravated cases occur in married women." Of course sexual intercourse cannot be expected to produce a cure, if there be ulceration or subacute ovarian inflammation; in these cases it will rather do harm. Impregnation frequently takes place in this disease, and is even more powerful than sexual intercourse in producing a cure; for during the period of pregnancy and lactation, menstruation is stopped, and the sexual organs have time to escape from the habit of morbid action; and they receive fresh impulses and a more healthy tone from the new train of actions during pregnancy. Frequently however, the patients are barren, and this great natural curative process unavailable.

But it is of great importance also to give relief in the menstrual attack. At the first onset of pain, the patient should take a hip-bath at 96 degrees, for from half an hour to one hour, and repeat this thrice a day, going into bed after it, till warmth is restored. Small nauseating doses of Ipecacuanha, such as half a grain every hour, should also be given, which greatly ease menstruation. The injection into the rectum of 15 or 20 drops of laudanum in a little warm water, is also very good.

To *prevent* this disease, we must endeavor to eradicate throughout society, the causes which lead to it. Of these by far the most important is sexual abstinence. It is chiefly in single women that it occurs, and whether it be merely a functional disease or depend on ovarian inflam mation, it is sexual abstinence, ungratified sexual desires, and doubtless in many cases masturbation arising from these ungratified desires, which chiefly cause it. It is also very important, that the slighter pain and uneasiness in menstruation, so universally neglected, should be met at the beginning, and should not be allowed to assume an aggravated form. This is especially requisite, if these pains be not co-existent with menstruation, but come on later; if menstruation becomes gradually more painful than it has been, it is a certain sign that there is growing disorder, and the causes which lead to this should be investigated and removed. In many women menstruation is habitually attended with more or less pain and disturbance throughout the whole of sexual life, and in these cases the morbidity may be so much a part of the original constitution, as to be irremediable. Dr. Bennett says " It is only with the patient herself in health, that you can compare her in disease;" and thus when menstruation, having been previously easy, becomes difficult, we may be certain that some morbid cause is at work, which should at once be attended to, and removed.

Dr. Ashwell says " Every case of painful menstruation is not to be called dysmenorrhœa; if the pain and tightness in the head and loins, which have preceded menstruation, pass away as the secretion increases, it is not dysmenorrhœa." Although in some women menstruation takes place without the least pain, yet it is generally accompanied and preceded by symptoms. These are, fulness in the pelvis, pains in the loins and ovarian regions, and sometimes bearing down pains of an expulsive character. These are very general, and constitute what is called the " usual catamenial effort." But these symptoms are not to be looked on as natural, because they are general. They are a sign of the common deterioration of the female constitution in our society, and as such are a sign of error. In the same way child-birth is known to be very much more painful among civilized nations than among savages. Savage women bear children with little pain, and I presume that menstruation, which is a kind of parturition, is in them usually attended with no pain, as it is with the most healthy women among ourselves. It should be our endeavour, therefore, to elevate this function in woman to the natural and typical standard of health, just as in the case of all the other organs and faculties of our being. The causes of the general sexual deterioration are the peculiarly unhealthy sexual life of our society, and especially of its female part; and also the generally imperfect state of all the physical virtues, in which respect civilized man stands in such marked inferiority to his savage brother. It is not our part to pique ourselves on possessing a different and a higher class of virtues, but to aim at the equal developement of all, knowing that all are equally necessary to our health and happiness; nor to neglect the valuable knowledge we may get, by comparing ourselves with a ruder part of our race. The female reproudctive organs, moreover, are the work-shop of life; all of us are in fact secretions from these organs, and from the testes of the male; and if the secreting actions of these most important organs be allowed to be habitually in a disordered and vitiated state, the effect on the health of all of us must be most injurious.

MENORRHAGIA.

OR

PROFUSE MENSTRUATON.

By this is meant menstruation, characterized by excess in quantity or in frequency. There are two kinds ; one, in which there is merely the natural secretion in excess, and the other in which pure blood is discharged by the uterine vessels. The latter variety is recognized by the presence of clots of blood in the discharge, or by its stiffening the linen, which appearances are not seen in the normal menstrual fluid. In the majority of severe cases, there is this direct uterine bleeding.

The symptoms of the disease are the following. The flow of blood at the menstrual periods becomes much more profuse than natural, continuing for several days longer than it should do. The menstrual periods are also frequently approximated, so that menstruation occurs every three weeks, or every fortnight. Thus in many cases the woman is almost always menstruating ; one lengthened period being scarcely over, when another begins. In the menstrual intervals there is usually profuse leucorrhœa. In some cases, especially in women who have had children, the discharge comes on suddenly in gushes, unlike the slow dropping exudation, that characterizes the natural secretion. The constitutional effects are those which are produced by a drain on the system, or by loss of blood from any other part. At first languor and weakness in the loins ; then severe aching in the loins and back, coming round to the thighs and groins ; acute headaches, often confined to one spot, as if a nail were driven into the head; ringing in the ears, dimness of sight, giddiness, and sometimes the sensation as if a clock were ticking in the head ; increasing pallor and debility, derangement of the stomach and bowels, palpitation of the heart ; melancholy and nervousness, at times almost to insanity ; dropsy of the eyelids and feet, from the increasing thinness of the blood ; also sometimes prolapse of the uterus and vagina from relaxation.

If the disease occur in a plethoric married woman who lives freely, it is often of an *active* and more violent character, while in the delicate (among whom it is much more frequent,) it is rather of a passive kind. In the former case it is often caused by the application of cold during menstruation, which, if it do not arrest the discharge suddenly, as we have seen it often does, may on the contrary, produce a profuse flow, attended by feverish symptoms : and the habit of profuse menstruation continues at subsequent periods. In these cases menstruation is preceded by a feeling of tension and fulness in the pelvis, with weight and throbbing in the womb. The discharge is often emitted with pain and expulsatory throes, the flow lessening during a pain, and increasing on its subsidence.

The *passive* form of the disease is of frequent occurrence, and is generally found among delicate and nervous women. In it there is frequently little or no local pain during the flow, but extreme debility and exhaustion is often produced. Although a fatal result is very rare, yet life is often reduced to the lowest ebb by the great losses of blood. The disease also frequently occurs about the period of menstrual decline. This takes place in many women about the age of 44, but in the greater number from 47 to 50. This period is in many cases attended with great losses of blood from the womb. These continue long, often for several years, and are sometimes very excessive. The bleeding sometimes continues for weeks, or even months, without complete cessation, and the prostration of health may be extreme. Fear of organic disease, such as cancer, is often excited by these protracted bleedings, and life is sometimes lost from mere exhaustion. These hemorrhages may continue for from one to four years, and yet terminate in health, and the decline of the function.

As the forms of menorrhagia are various, so are its *causes*. The essence of the disease consists in an over-excited state of the ovaries, which discharge too rapidly immature eggs; and in a congested and irritable state of these organs, as well as of the womb, which gives rise to the profuse attendant menstrual discharges. When once morbid and excessive action has been excited in these parts, it is kept up by habit; and the discharge of eggs and of blood at last assume a passive and habitual character. As chlorosis and amenorrhoea are frequently the effect of insufficient stimulus to the ovaries, so menorrhagia often proceeds from their over stimulus. Excessive venery is very apt to produce it, especially where the sexual organs have been unaccustomed to the venereal stimulus. Thus in women who have married late, even a moderate amount of venereal excitement might induce it. The same may be said of delicate and susceptible girls, who take little exercise, and therefore all whose organs are in a habitually weak and excitable state. But the over stimulation of the organs by too frequent child-bearing is also a most important cause of the disease. This, together with over lactation, often causes menorrhagia. Abortion frequently causes, or is caused by, previous menorrhagia; for this is really an ovarian abortion. The eggs are cast off by the ovaries every fortnight or three weeks, prematurely, just as the child is cast off by the womb before the proper time. An inflammatory state of the ovaries, and ulcers of the womb are frequent causes of menorrhagia, as of the other diseases of menstruation. Cold, especially during menstruation, is another frequent cause, producing congestion and disorder of the secreting organs. Dr. Ashwell says moverover, that the form of the disease, which occurs at menstrual decline, is caused more frequently than is supposed, by the avoidance of complete sexual intercourse, and the consequent derangement and congestion of the ovaries and womb. This abstinence is, he fears, not seldom practised, to avoid the risk of adding to an already numerous family. Masturbation is also without doubt a frequent cause in the single; the excessive abuse of the organs being more apt to cause this disease, than an excess in the normal stimulus. Menorrhagia is in some respects analogous to profuse spermatorrhœa in the male; the sperm cells and the germ cells being too rapidly discharged, and in a crude and immature form in the worst cases.

In *treating* a case of menorrhagia, we must first ascertain its peculiar cause. An examination by the finger and speculum should be made to see whether there be any ulceration of the mouth of the womb or ovarian disease. Dr. Ashwell says that a digital examination frequently reveals nothing, but a flabby state of the neck of the womb and vagina, and an os rather more patulous than natural, together with profuse white discharges. If the disease be the result of excessive venereal indulgence, of frequent abortions, or over-lactation: separation from the husband should be enjoined for a time, or the child weaned. During the menstrual intervals, in the passive forms of the disease, every means should be tried to brace the general health. A life in the open air, with cold shower baths to the loins and lower part of the abdomen, and also astringent vaginal injections, should be employed, to cure the leucorrhœa and give tone to the parts. All causes of excitement of mind or body should also be avoided, and sexual intercourse either quite discontinued, or used in great moderation. In the cases of active menorrhagia in the plethoric, purgatives are useful; or, still better, exercise and spare diet, with the avoidance of unhealthy excitement.

But besides the constitutional means to be used in the menstrual intervals, especial attention must be paid to restrain the actual flow. For a few days previous to menstruation great care should be taken to avoid excitement or fatigue, and the patient should lie in the recumbent posture a good deal, so as to prevent the congestion of the pelvic organs. "Without the use of the recumbent position," says Dr. Ashwell, "all means will prove unavailing." When the flow begins, this posture should be strictly maintained, and continued till the period is over, as very slight exertion increases or renews the discharge. The patient should be kept cool; and if the loss of blood be great, cold clothes should be applied to the vulva, and over the hips, and astringent injections used. The cold is not to be applied at the beginning of the period, or it is apt to produce spasm of the womb, but rather when the natural secretion seems nearly over, and clots are passed. In some cases, where there is extreme exhaustion, every possible means must be taken to arrest the bleeding, for fear of an immediately fatal issue. Here the best of all means is to plug the vagina with dry tow. This directly presses on the bleeding vessels and stops the discharge. The best internal medicine in passive menorrhagia is the ergot of rye, which has a specific action on the womb, causing contraction of its muscular fibres. Five grains of the powder or thirty drops of the tincture should be given every six or eight hours.

In the plethoric variety, if there be quick pulse, with spasmodic pain in the womb, attending the discharge, nausea should be induced by one grain of ipecacuanha given every hour. This is a most admirable remedy, and relieves the pain, while it lessens the flow. An injection of assafœtida and opium into the rectum, is also excellent in quieting the uterine irritation.

To *prevent* this disease, its various causes must be extirpated. It occurs much more frequently in delicate and irritable women ; and these, as Dr. Ashwell says, "are a much more numerous class than the robust." Until therefore, the general strength of the sex is greatly elevated, we cannot hope satisfactorily to prevent this disease. The prevailing habits of sexual abstinence, which render the sexual system weak and irritable, and prone to over-excitement, must also be changed before adequate prevention is possible. Venereal excesses and masturbation should be carefully avoided, and only a moderate amount of the natural sexual stimulus used. Frequent pregnancy can be borne with impunity only by very robust women ; and is full of danger to the delicate, and to those whose life is not a very healthy one. Over-lactation is very weakening to the general health, and especially to the sexual organs, between which and the breasts there is so intimate a sympathy. Sudden arrest of the secretion of milk is often the cause of inflammation of the ovaries ; and an unnatural prolongation of suckling may readily make the ovaries irritable and enfeebled. Ulceration of the womb and ovarian disease must also be prevented. The avoidance of complete sexual intercourse, mentioned by Dr. Ashwell, as a frequent cause of the menorrhagia of advanced life, is a very important subject, of which I shall speak afterwards.

Menorrhagia is also greatly favoured by a prevalent idea among women, that copious menstruation is a healthy sign ; just as it is a common idea among the poorer classes, that it is healthy to pass much urine, a belief which favours the progress of diabetes. This belief often induces women to neglect the disease in its commencement. The amount of the natural discharge varies in different women, in some being more abundant than in others ; but each woman should judge by what is natural to herself in health, and if menstruation become more abundant, than it has been, should not neglect this indication

LEUCORRHŒA.

By this is meant the various non-venereal and non-infectious discharges of mucus, pus, &c., that proceed from the vagina, and are popularly called "the whites." Of all female diseases, none is so common as this. "Few married women, especially mothers, escape it," says Dr. Ashwell. The delicate and middle-aged are more prone to it, than the young and robust, and it is commoner in the married than the single, like all other inflammatory diseases; thus contrasting with the nervous functional diseases, which are far more common in the single. The disease is found in all varieties of severity, from the very mild, to the most aggravated form.

The discharge is caused by an inflamed or congested state of the mucous membrane of the vagina, vulva, or womb. The symptoms of an acute attack are, a feeling of heat and tenderness in the parts, followed by a mucous or muco-purulent discharge. There is also some scalding in making water, and more or less febrile reaction. If the disease be not cured, it may gradually become chronic; the pain, heat, and scalding disappear, but a copious discharge continues; and in this chronic state, the disease has a tendency to prove very obstinate, and to exhaust greatly the strength. The pain, heat, and scalding, often last also indefinitely in a subdued form, and are very easily re-excited.

The great cause which renders this disease, as well as other inflammations of the female sexual organs, so very chronic and obstinate, is the periodical return of *menstruation*. This congests these organs, and thus at every monthly period, fans anew the flame of their inflammatory diseases. Thus these white discharges, when once well established, often last for a great part of life, and gradually produce the most serious impairment of health. The constant drain breaks down the system, producing pallor, debility, pain in the back, palpitations, dyspepsia, &c. and all the train of symptoms more quickly induced by menorrhagia. In the young, chlorosis, amenorrhœa, and consumption, are apt to be induced by it. Prolapse of the womb and vagina, and also sterility, are not infrequently caused by it.

In most cases however, the disease is of a milder nature, and produces only a certain amount of weakness and pallor. Many women, except when in unusually good health, are never free from leucorrhœa ; and there is probably no disease so much neglected. It is only when the symptoms are aggravated, that aid is anxiously sought.

The discharge is sometimes very copious, wetting several napkins in the day, and we cannot wonder that this should soon exhaust the strength.　Sometimes it is not abundant, but very acrid, causing excoriation of the lips of the vulva and the inside of the thighs.　The discharge varies in colour and nature ; sometimes it is colourless, and then it is pure mucus ; at other times it is yellow, and then it is pus ; and frequently it is muco-purulent, which is a mixture of the two characters. Pus is alway a sign of inflammation, being the matter secreted by an inflamed surface ; and the muco-purulent secretion shows a minor state of inflammation, such as is found in the chronic stage of leucorrhœa. Pure pus is very seldom discharged in abundance from the female genital organs, except in infectious gonorrhœa, when large quantities of it are formed.　The colourless mucus often comes from congestion alone, without any inflammatory action.　A white curdy matter that is sometimes seen is of little consequence, as it comes from the mucous follicles on the neck of the uterus when simply congested ; whereas a peculiar glairy transparent mucus, like unboiled white of egg, comes from the follicles, inside the cervical canal, and is a sign of its inflammation, which is an important affection.

The natural mucous which moistens the passages, is, when perfectly healthy, never enough to constitute a discharge ; but in a great part of women who live in towns, its secretion is considerably increased for a day or two before and after menstruation, so as to form a discharge. This over-secretion, although it is so frequent, and produces so little bad effect on the health, that it is not regarded, is a sign of a somewhat congested state of the parts ; and the congestion may readily be increased by various causes, and give rise to a permanent discharge, or be aggravated into inflammation.　Although in many cases of leucorrhœa, when the discharge is of a colourless nature, there is merely congestion ; yet whenever the discharge is yellow, and in almost all cases, in which it has seriously weakened the system, the disease is of an *inflammatory* nature.

It is generally impossible to tell certainly, by the discharge, the difference between leucorrhœa, and gonorrhœa.　The only apparent differences are, that pure pus is seldom seen in abundance except in gonorrhœa, in which disease moreover the symptoms are generally more violent, and the urethra is more apt to be inflamed.　And yet there must be a great difference in the nature of the diseases, for gonorrhœa is very infectious, whereas leucorrhœa is very rarely so ; still there are cases, in which the husband may be infected by a peculiarly acrid leucorrhœa.　However in the vast majority of cases where a man gets a gonorrhœa, he may conclude that the female, from whom he has contracted it, has a regular venereal disease.

Leucorrhœa is severe and obstinate in proportion to the amount of the mucous surface affected.　In many cases the disease is confined to the vulva, for it may be cured by applying astringents to that part alone, by separating the labia.　But in the severe chronic cases the whole of the vagina is generally involved, and these cases are very frequently complicated by ulcers of the mouth of the womb, and inflammation of the cervical canal.

The *causes* of this most important disease are very various. It is most common in married women, and in those who have borne children ; because after child-birth the womb does not return quite to its virgin size, but remains somewhat larger and more vitalised, and the vagina is always more relaxed, and more prone to congestion and inflammation, than in the virgin. Besides this, abortion and child-birth are in many cases followed by inflammatory disease of the mouth of the womb, which gives rise to leucorrhœa. The sanguineous congestion, moreover, of the womb and external passages during pregnancy and child-birth, throughout the whole of which period the vagina and vulva are of a deep red colour, may remain in a minor degree afterwards, predisposing the parts to inflammatory action. It must be remembered, that the more the vitality of any part is elevated, the more prone does it become to inflammation. Sexual intercourse also, if excessive, may produce leucorrhœa. The various diseases of menstruation are in general accompanied by leucorrhœa, which helps to relieve the congestion, or inflammation, of the other sexual organs. Cold, and the wearing of insufficient clothing, especially thin shoes and cotton stockings, are also frequent causes.

All these causes are greatly promoted, and the disease, when once established, is made so very difficult thoroughly to cure, from two principal reasons ; namely, first, the periodical congestion of the sexual organs every month, and secondly, the very unnatural and sedentary life that most women lead. They take little exercise, but remain always within doors, which weakens the general health ; and very many of them are engaged in sedentary occupations, which keep all the pelvic organs constantly in a heated and congested state, and render it almost impossible thoroughly to cure severe cases of leucorrhœa. From the same reasons the rectum becomes inactive, and piles and constipation are exceedingly frequent in women, and when present, keep up the leucorrhœa.

The custom of two persons sleeping together, which is so general in this country, is not, I believe, so healthy as the continental one of using separate couches. It increases the warmth, just as too large a quantity of clothes would do; and thus is often relaxing, and tends to favour the origin and continuance of diseases of debility, especially in townspeople, who require all the cool air, and other bracing influences they can get. Moreover the involuntary movements during sleep are a frequent cause of disturbance ; and the rest (that invaluable restorative) is seldom so good as when each individual sleeps alone.

In the *treatment* of this disease it is of great importance, that means should be early adopted. There is no disease which women neglect so often as it is so common ; and thus the acute and first attacks of it are disregarded, and the disease allowed to take firm root in the system. In fact women, especially in the lower classes, seldom or never apply for aid, unless either the acute symptoms are very severe, or the disease has existed for a long time, and has begun seriously to impair the health. Women will go about for years suffering from this weakening malady, if it be at all endurable, and submitting to a languid and imperfect existence, rather than bring themselves to consult a medical man. It is not delicacy alone that restrains them, but neglect also, which is unfortunately very common in women, at least in their own illnesses. This want of attention to self, is a part of the general self-sacrificing character of that sex ; but there is no doubt that, whenever this leads to the promotion of disease, it is a great evil. No woman should allow any symptoms of ill-health to exist, either from delicacy or neglect, without taking proper means to remove them.

In acute leucorrhœa, where there is heat, tenderness, and active inflammation, the *treatment* should be mild and soothing ; rest, a dose of opening medicine, washing with tepid water, together with the avoidance of late hours, sexual intercourse, and other excitements. By these means the attack will in general speedily subside. But if it do not, and if the discharge becomes chronic, then the best treatment is by *astringent injections* into the vagina ; which, if well managed, and assisted by a regular life, will generally effect a cure. The best astringents are alum, sulphate of zinc, acetate of lead, oak bark, or nitrate of silver ; the first three used in the proportion of one drachm to the pint of water. The alum injection is the best for general use, and if used properly, rarely fails to effect a cure in two or three weeks. But injections constantly fail because they are not properly used. The vagina is a long canal, and unless the injection reach the whole surface affected, a radical cure cannot be looked for.

The way to give injections is, to support the hips by a hard cushion, and place beneath the patient a flat bed-pan or other dish ; then inject the lotion, using the pump-handled syringe, and an elastic tube six inches long, so that the injection will be carried to the end of the vagina. Inject about a pint at a time, and retain it for five or ten minutes by a napkin. This requires the help of another person, but is far more effectual than injecting one's-self. The injection should be used at first twice a day, and after a fortnight once a day will be enough. If one kind of injection fail, another may be tried, and it is sometimes good to vary them at intervals. When a cure has been effected, cold water should be injected once or twice a day for some time, to restore tone to the parts. No tonic is equal to this. Dr. Ashwell says, that there is an unfounded dread of ablution of the external genitals with cold, or even with tepid water, but this can do no harm, and is often very beneficial. Its injection is equally harmless, and frequently of service. The injection of a few ounces of cold water into the rectum daily, is greatly recommended by Dr. Ashwell, in cases of inveterate leucorrhœa, where the discharge is limited to a few drops, but still has produced serious impairment of health. He has seen the discharge rendered very obstinate by the habitual use of thick napkins to the parts, which have a relaxing effect. An excellent remedy in obstinate cases, is to plug the vagina with dry tow. This dries up the moisture as it flows, and keeps the mucous surfaces asunder, which is one of the best of all modes of stopping their discharges. The surfaces act just like poultices to each other, causing relaxation and indefinite continuance of the discharge. This remedy is not employed so often as it deserves.

English physicians do not generally make an examination in leucorrhœa, but this is a great error, and the source of mistakes without number. In very many cases leucorrhœa is caused or kept up by ulcers of the womb, and if they are not discovered and treated, injections can do litte good. It should be made a rule, that in all cases of leucorrhœa of any severity or obstinacy, a digital examination at least should be made; and in general the speculum should also be used, for few physicians have so educated a sense of touch, as to be able to rely upon it alone. Besides, by the speculum it can be seen how high the disease reaches in the vagina, &c., When leucorrhœa is connected with diseases of menstruation, these must be cured first, before it can be expected to yield.

The *general* treatment in addition to the local means is of very great importance. Sedentary habits, heated rooms, and all stimulants should be avoided; the patient should live as much as possible in the open air, and should use cold baths. the coldshower over the loins, the cold sitz-bath, and strengthen the frame by moderate exercise. Without these constitutional means, the local ones will frequently fail in old standing cases. Moreover it is very important to persevere for some time in the remedies; the disease is very obstinate and slow to yield; and unless it be thoroughly cured, a relapse will probably take place. In this and the foregoing diseases, and indeed in the treatment of chronic disease in general, the best by far of all constitutional mode of treatment is, it seems to me, what is called the Water Cure; although this name or that of Hydropathy, does not rightly designate the system, which consists in the scientific application of the various natural means of strengthening the frame, namely bathing, air, exercise, regular diet and hours, together with society and healthful amusements, in an establishment where every thing is systematically regulated for the restoration of health, and a patient is not subject to the innumerable temptations and irregularities, which make it so very difficult to treat chronic disease at home. The water cure is a very valuable auxiliary in the treatment of sexual diseases, although alone it generally fails to produce a cure, as it does not include the great natural remedy for such diseases; still it is said to have a marked effect in regulating and favouring menstruation in many cases.

To *prevent* this wide spread disease its various causes must be eradicated. Frequent child-birth, and protracted suckling, to which the lives of so many women are devoted, and which are almost sure to bring on leucorrhœa, should be avoided, unless the circumstances of the woman are very healthy, so as to enable her to bear it. A constitution of iron could not, if subjected to the sedentary lives and hard in-door work which many town mothers have. These sedentary lives also, which the great majority of the sex live, must be materially altered, before this weakening malady can be effectually prevented. There are few modes of life so unhealthy, as those of the poor sempstresses and milliners in our large towns; and their confinement and want of exercise make them very liable to all the diseases of debility. Women moreover should never neglect the com-

P

mencement of this disease, nor should the habitual mucous over-secretion before and after menstruation, so constantly seen in townspeople, and denoting a weak and congested state of the sexual system, be allowed to continue.

DISORDERS AT MENSTRUAL DECLINE.

I SHALL now say a few words on the disorders sometimes attending the cessation of menstruation. It is a very general opinion, that this period must be attended with illness, but this is a great mistake, for healthy women frequently pass over it without the least inconvenience. Women themselves regard it as a very critical and perilous time; and this is a most unfortunate idea, for it causes much needless anxiety, and indeed often gives rise itself to symptoms of ill-health. There is no more danger naturally connected with the decline or menstruation, than with its commencement; and a woman, who is healthy, and who lives temperately need not look upon the " turn of life," with any apprehension.

The most frequent symptoms of disturbance, observed at this period are mental. A hysterical nervous state is so common, as to excite little attention. The woman has a tendency to solitude, disordered sleep, impaired appetite, &c., with frequently a dread of organic disease. In some cases there is great agitation of mind and nervousness, amounting nearly to insanity; but soothing quieting means, not restraint, should be used.

Now all these symptoms are so prevalent, most probably, just because women have an unfounded dread of this period. Their mind is unnecessarily anxious about it, and this gives rise in very many cases to the nervous symptoms. Another reason probably is, that in this country, where there are so many involuntary nuns, it must be a most painful thought to many, that the season of their youth, the last rose of their summer, is fading; that their sexual life has been totally unfulfilled, and that there is no more hope for them of a child to gladden their old age. Alas that such lives and such sad thoughts are so common among us! I believe that if these causes did not operate, and if the general health of women were stronger than it is, these mental disturbances would rarely appear; although they are probably in part owing to the alteration in the nervous currents at the decline of the uterine functions.

In other cases, in corpulent, indolent women, there is apt to be an increased tendency to congestions and inflammations in other organs, such as apoplexy, and pulmonary congestion. The reason of this is, that a periodical safety valve is now shut, and if plethora exist, there is no natural mode of relief for the fulness. In these cases stimulants should b-forbidden, and plenty of exercise taken, along with a somewhat spare diet. But it is a very common and very pernicious error among women, to use purgatives frequently at this time, and to reduce themselves by spare diet to avert fancied dangers. A great deal of mischief is done by this mistaken opinion, which is akin to the old prejudice among the poor, in favour of a precautionary bleeding in the spring, which has now happily almost died out. There is no time of life, and no natural changes in the system, which call for these artificial precautions. If a woman have been living healthily and temperately, she may trust with perfect confidence, that nature will do her own work, without any disturbance; and if she have been living too luxuriously, and requires to reduce herself, the proper means is always to increase the exercise, give up inordinate indulgences, and brace the system by natural and not by artificial means. For reducing plethora and averting a threatened apoplexy, there is, I believe, no constitutional means so powerful as a course of hydropathic treatment. Dr. Gully, in his excellent work on the "Water Cure in chronic disease," states, that were he to choose the case in which the benefits of the water cure are most certainly and strikingly evinced, it would be one of apoplectic fulness.

There is a very general idea, that incurable organic affections, such as cancer, are liable to come on at menstrual decline, but the cessation of the natural function can evidently have no tendency to cause them. These diseases generally occur in both sexes in advanced life, and if there have been a latent pre-disposition, it may be favoured by the congestion of the sexual organs, which is apt to accompany menstrual decline, but no malignant disease can be directly caused by it.

The mode in which the cessation occurs, varies in different women. Sometimes, but rarely, it is sudden; something having occurred to arrest a menstrual period, nature takes the opportunity of putting an end to the function at once. More generally the decline is gradual; there may be a long interval, and then an excessive return; then another long interval and a scanty return, and so on till the function entirely disappears. From months to years may be required to accomplish this change.

INFLAMMATION OF THE SEXUAL ORGANS.

THE next class of diseases which I shall speak of are the *inflammations* of the various sexual organs; an exceedingly important and common class. The diseases which have been already treated of, are often termed in medical works the *Functional* ones, as they are frequently seen without any structural alteration, to be recognised either during life or after death. Still, all of them are frequently connected with, and dependent upon, inflammatory disease, and there has been a growing tendency of late years, since the more accurate investigation of the sexual organs by the speculum, to consider them more and more of an inflammatory nature. Leucorrhea used to be constantly regarded, as well by the medical profession as by women in general, as a disease of debility, and " the whites" are still prevalently thought to be only "a weakness." But Dr. Bennett has shown that in the great majority of cases of any severity, these discharges are of an *inflammatory* nature, connected very frequently with ulceration of the mouth of the womb; and that, instead of being the *effect* of the dyspepsia and general debility usually found along with them, they are the *cause*. He has shown likewise, that all the disorders of menstruation are frequently owing to such ulceration. Dr. Tilt has in like manner traced many of these diseases to an inflamed state of the ovaries, showing that amenorrhœa, dysmenorrhœa, menorrhagia, &c., are frequently dependent on this cause. Hence arises the extreme importance, in all cases of these so-called functional diseases, of making a careful examination, whether they be not connected with an inflammatory affection.

I shall begin with the ovaries, which are the most important parts of the female organs. There are very few organs in the body, which are so little understood, and have been so little attended to, as these most important ones. In reality they preside over the female sexual system, just as the testicles do over the male; and the peculiar sexual sympathies and feelings, both moral and physical, depend on them, and not on the womb. From their small size, their hidden position, and still more from the ignorance of their physiology, (for the new views of ovulation and menstruation are among the most recent discoveries in physiology,) they have been neglected; and the womb has received the main share of the attention of physicians, and to it were ascribed the various sexual sympathies. Hence the pathology, (or knowledge of the diseases) of the ovaries, is still quite in its infancy, and medical works are very meagre on this sub-

ject. It is indeed known that the ovaries are exceedingly prone to
disease, for in no organs are morbid appearances more common after
death. But the causes of these appearances, and the symptoms of disease, which they produce in life, are still wrapped in great obscurity;
although the new light thrown on the functions of the ovaries by the
theory of ovulation, and the labours of physicians who are now
earnestly investigating these organs, will, it is to be hoped, soon illustrate the subject. Nothing more retards our knowledge than the false
sexual delicacy, which prevents women from speaking of the minor
derangements of menstruation, or of applying for aid in the incipient
stages. Science and the female health alike suffer by this most unfortunate feeling. Moreover the repugnance to the necessary modes
of examination is a great obstacle. Dr. Tilt remarks, that it is only
when the patient's sufferings are habitually intense, or when the
prospect of marriage has overcome her reluctance, that an examination is permitted; from this insufficient examination also the disease
is frequently only partially cured, and relapses take place.

The necessary modes of examining the ovaries are through the walls
of the abdomen, vagina, and rectum. All of these must be carefully
used, where there is a suspicion that the ovaries are in a diseased
state; and it is fortunate for woman that it is possible by these
means to arrive at a true knowledge of the nature of some of her most
miserable diseases, and to be able therefore to relieve them. But
there are very few physicians, who have the tact and experience necessary to make such an examination with profit. To make a physical
examination, to use the speculum or the finger with advantage,
requires a long and careful training, of the difficulties of which the
public seem to have no idea, but to suppose that all medical men
have such knowledge by a kind of intuition, or as a matter of course.
Now the fact is, that with regard to the examination of the female
organs, and especially the ovaries, very few physicians have had a
proper training, and most of them have had absolutely no training at
all. The reason of this enormous medical deficiency is, that such
training does not form a part, unless as a rare exception, of the ordinary medical education, on account of the unfortunate scruples of
sexual delicacy; and thus the great mass of physicians, though frequently called upon to treat female disease, are really quite incompetent to do so. Thus unfortunate woman, even when she does reluc-
tantly make up her mind, after long concealed suffering, to apply for
aid, very probably consults a man, who is not much more capable of
forming a true opinion in her case than she is herself.

It is not correct to say, that this class of diseases is specially cultivated by certain physicians, and that it is sufficient for these to be
conversant with female complaints; a large proportion of sexual diseases are *masked* diseases, whose real sexual nature is not recognisable
without a careful analysis and examination of the organs, by a man
who is competent to form a fair opinion on the matter. Although it
is a great advantage, that some men should devote a special attention to certain organs and diseases, yet every medical man should be

able to examine all the different organs in the body, and have a tolerable degree of skill in the management of each. This is especially requisite for the great proportion of medical men, who live in the country, and in small towns, where there is no distinction of medicine into special branches, and each man has to treat every disease that may present itself.

In the abdominal mode of examining the ovaries, the patient lies on the back with the legs flexed, so as to relax the abdominal muscles. Unless however, the ovarian swelling be large, it will not be felt thus. In examining through the vagina, the patient lies in what is called the obstetric position, namely, on the side, with the legs drawn up. The fore-finger of one hand is introduced into the vagina, while with the other hand the examiner presses on the lower part of the abdomen, so as to bring the ovaries within reach of the finger. In examining by the rectum, the obstetric position should be used. The ovaries can be felt in this way, even in their healthy state, although with difficulty; but when enlarged by inflammation they are readily reached. The finger passed into the rectum can feel half of the posterior surface of the womb, bulging through its wall, and on each side the ovaries like two knuckles. When these bodies are healthy, pressure on them gives no pain, but it does, if they be inflamed. Increase of volume can also be recognised in this way. Another method of examining is by what is called the double touch, the fore-finger being in the rectum and the thumb in the vagina. This is very useful in recognising tumours between these two passages.

ACUTE OVARITIS.

On acute inflammation of the ovary--(itis being the termination used to signify inflammation in any organ.) It used to be thought by physicians, that this affection was almost confined to the puerperal period, namely, that period which immediately succeeds child-birth, and during which inflammatory diseases in the sexual organs are most apt to occur, and to be of unusual violence. But ovaritis occurs not unfrequently at other times, as Dr. Bennett has shown, but is constantly overlooked by the medical attendant, who confounds it with inflammation of the womb, or with iliac abscess, or "inflammation of the bowels," a general loose expression for obscure and undetermined inflammation in some pelvic organ, of whose nature the practitioner, from his inexperience in the examination of these organs, is uncertain.

Ovaritis may be spoken of along with the inflammation of that loose areolar tissue, which, as well as the ovaries, is contained between the fold of the peritoneum, called the broad ligament; for it is not possible to tell what exact part of these contained substances is affected. The general cause of this disease is the acute suppression of menstruation, whether by cold, or violent mental emotions. The symptoms are very like those of acute metritis (inflammation of the womb,) namely, severe deep-seated pain in the lower part of the abdomen, with a feeling of weight and uneasiness in the pelvis; also pain in the loins, and tenderness on pressure in the abdomen. There is fever, with a hot skin and quick pulse. A digital examination through the vagina, is absolutely necessary here to learn what part is affected. It is very frequently neglected, and this neglect is the source of great evils. By the vaginal examination it will be found, that the painful tumour is not in the median line, but applied to the side of the womb. It is so closely applied, that it needs some tact to distinguish them. But it is very important to distinguish between the two, for metritis generally ends by resolution (or complete subsidence of the inflammation,) whereas ovaritis generally proceeds to suppuration, unless very active treatment be used. In this case matter forms, and escapes in time, either through the vagina or the rectum. Through the vagina is the most favourable method, for in this canal the pus causes but little irritation. If the abscess open into the rectum, much greater irritation with griping and dysentery, frequently lasting for days, is produced. The bursting of the abscess, and discharge of pus, is rarely noticed by the patient, unless she be warned to expect it; or if noticed is not mentioned, from the reluctance to communicate information spontaneously in sexual diseases.

After the discharge of the pus, there is a decided improvement in the symptoms, and the patient is thought convalescent. But the disease is by no means radically cured; a chronic state of inflammation still continues, and this is aroused anew by each return of menstrual congestion. Fresh matter then gathers, and the former symptoms in a subdued shape are repeated. In this manner may this lingering affection last for one or more years; the patient suffering all the time from the symptoms of chronic inflammation in the sexual organs, namely, pain and weight in the pelvis, tenderness in the ovarian region, pain in the back, inability to walk much, and disorders of menstruation. The reason of her state is a mystery to herself, as well as to her medical attendant, if the real nature of the disease have not been recognised at first.

From this description it will be seen, what great evils may arise from not distinguishing this affection from inflammation of the womb, or of the bowels; which so constantly happens at present, from delicacy and medical inexperience in these diseases, preventing the necessary examinations. If this affection were recognised at first, suppuration might in some cases be prevented by active treatment, and if it did occur, well-directed means might subdue the lingering remains of the inflammation.

The general *cause* of this disease in the unimpregnated womb is sudden arrest of menstruation. It is very rare that acute ovaritis, or acute metritis, arises during the menstrual interval. After confinement however, acute inflammation of these organs is apt to arise from various causes, especially from too early exposure to cold, arrest of the secretion of milk &c.; and in this case the peritoneum is very apt to be involved, constituting a most dangerous and general fatal disease. But in the unimpregnated condition, the peritoneum is very seldom implicated, and a fatal result rarely, if ever, occurs.

SUBACUTE OVARITIS.

THIS is a much more common disease than the preceding. Dr. Tilt, who has lately directed the attention of the profession to the subject, says, he believes no disease is more common than, though so little understood as this. In subacute ovaritis, in general, the whole ovary is not affected, but the inflammation is limited to certain parts, as the Graafian follicles, &c. The symptoms of this important affection are, a dull pain in the ovarian region, increased by walking, riding, or pressure on the part, and also by straightening the leg. The pains radiate from the ovary to the loins, thighs, and anus, and are of a dull, dragging, and sometimes overwhelming character. But they are seldom so acute as to make advice be early sought, and are thus often endured for years. Sexual intercourse increases the pain. This wearing affection, like other inflammatory states of the ovaries and womb, deadens the sexual feelings. It very frequently gives rise to hysteria. It also frequently causes the various disorders of menstruation, which it produces either directly, or by occasioning a secondary congestion or inflammation of the womb, whose health depends greatly on that of the ovaries. It also gives rise to sterility, which Dr. Tilt believes to be much oftener connected with disease of the ovaries, than of the womb, although the contrary is the general opinion.

The morbid appearances so commonly found in the ovaries after death, and which have been caused by subacute ovaritis, are a red and inflamed state of the Graafian vesicles, which are sometimes full of pus. They are also frequently swollen to the size of a pea, denoting a state of chronic inflammation. The fallopian tubes are frequently found bound down by adhesions, so that they could not be applied to the ovaries. This appearance is very frequent in prostitutes, and is one cause of their general sterility.

The chief *causes* of subacute ovaritis, according to Dr. Tilt, are, "excessive venereal indulgence, which sometimes produces it in newly married women, but particularly in prostitutes, whose ovaries after death almost always present some morbid lesion ; privation of the sexual stimulus, whether its absolute privation, as in single women, or sudden withdrawal as in widows, both of which leave the ovaries in a congested state;

late marriages, in which the venereal stimulus is liable to prove too powerful for the ovaries, unused to it ; the decline of menstruation, both in the case of the involuntary nuns of a society over-stocked with women, and in those who have indulged in venereal excesses ; moral emotions and ungratified desires, which are known in the male sex to have the effect of increasing the seminal secretion, and naturally have an analogous action on woman ; arrest of menstruation, which is apt to be followed by this disease, along with dysmenorrhœa and hysterical symptoms ; gonorrhœa, leucorrhœa &c." Dr. Tilt remarks, that the want of the appropriate stimulus to the ovaries, which should promote their healthy action, is often the cause of their becoming the seat of morbid affections.

Subacute ovaritis is thus a most important affection, from its great frequency, and from its obscure nature. There are doubtless very many such cases existing unknown at present, the hidden root of various miserable diseases, which cannot be cured without the prior removal of the ovaritis. Thus very many cases of amenorrhœa, menorrhagia, dysmenorrhœa, sterility, and hysteria, are owing to this disease, and in all these affections a careful examination should be made, if there be any symptoms of ovaritis.

The *treatment* recommended by Dr. Tilt is, leeches applied over the ovarian regions, succeeded by successive blisters to that part, so as to break the morbid chain of nervous action, and lastly to rub in an ointment composed of mercury and belladonna. The bowels should be kept open by aperients ; and emollient injections into the rectum, with the chill taken off, should be used thrice a-day. Three or four ounces should be injected at a time, (the pelvis being elevated,) and retained as long as possible. They bathe and soothe the parts affected. By these means, which can be used only in the menstrual intervals, a radical cure may generally be effected ; and after it, cold water injections, morning and evening, should be used. Sexual abstinence and a regular healthy life should be enjoined during the treatment ; and for some time after the cure, sexual intercourse should be taken in moderation. Sterility and the various menstrual and hysterical affections, connected with subacute ovaritis, frequently cease after its cure.

INFLAMMATION OF THE WOMB.

I now proceed to the inflammations of the womb, of which much more is known than of the ovarian inflammations, in great part through the admirable work of Dr. Henry Bennett. In examining the diseases of the womb, we have fortunately a much more certain guide than the finger, namely, the eye. There are two kinds of specula used, the round and the bi-valve one, the latter of which consists of two separable blades, and is the best, for by means of it the mouth of the womb can be opened, and the cervical canal seen, which is very important, as disease often lurks in this part. But it is more difficult to manage than the round one, which answers excellently for many purposes. The patient should lie on the back, opposite a window, in specular examinations, so that the light should fall on the parts examined. Candlelight will do in the absence of daylight, though not so good. The womb is also examined by means of the touch, through the abdomen, vagina, and rectum. It is only when enlarged that it can be felt through the abdominal walls. Through the rectum, one half of the posterior surface of the womb can be felt, as the prostate gland in the male; and unless the examiner be experienced, he may think the healthy womb morbidly swollen. But the general mode of examining the womb is through the vagina. The fore-finger here readily reaches the mouth of the womb, and can in this way obtain most valuable information.

But the finger, to be a reliable guide, requires a great deal of education. Women seem to suppose that all they have to do is to consent to a digital examination, and all will be ascertained. But the fact is, that there are very few medical men, except those who give special attention to midwifery and female diseases, who can diagnose by the finger many kinds of uterine disease. It is a very difficult thing to tell by the finger, that the mouth of the womb is ulcerated; and the proof of this is, that this very common disease remained almost entirely unknown, till the free use of the speculum. It is necessary to educate the finger by the eye, with the greatest care, before it can be trusted to. Thus, unless a man's finger be a very sure guide, he should always use the speculum also. A woman should consider, that instead of ending, the real difficulties in the recognition and treatment of her case are only beginning, when she consults a medical man; but her mind, if she have had little sexual experience, is generally so much occupied with the unpleasantness of revealing her disease and consenting to an examination, that she loses sight of the only really important matters to her, namely, the competence of the man she consults, and the judiciousness of his treatment. No patients submit to so much erroneous treatment, are so much quacked, and have so little to say in their own case, as sexual patients, especially women; for the unfortunate sexual bashfulness paralyses their common sense, and prevents them from reasoning vigorously as becomes grown up human beings, on a matter of such vital importance to them as their own health.

A very common and most unfortunate defect in medical men, is a dislike to confess their ignorance, and very great evils arise from this. Each one vies with his neighbour in vaunting his own knowledge and his own success. The great reason is, that the public are so utterly ignorant of medicine, that anything passes current with them; and thus is a man tempted to impose upon them, and to pretend to more knowledge than he really possesses. Public ignorance is certain to lead to pretence and to deception, and while that continues to exist, it is in vain to hope that these will not flourish.

There is no possible remedy for these evils, but an increased knowledge of health and disease throughout society generally, so that they shall be able to distinguish between true and pretended science, and to judge for themselves on so infinitely important a matter as their own health. There is no class of diseases in which there is so much assumption of knowledge, with so much real ignorance, as the sexual ones, just because they have been wrapped in such special obscurity. Every one connected with medicine, even to the midwives and nurses in our hospitals, affects to talk knowingly upon sexual matters, as if the most obscure and ill-understood part of our nature were patent to them. This assumption is favoured by the profound ignorance and secret curiosity of the public on sexual matters, and the pride of appearing to be one of the initiated. In fact, turn where we may, there are few things connected with the present sexual state of mankind, which are not the source of sorrow and humiliation to an ingenuous mind.

ACUTE METRITIS.

Or · acute inflammation of the womb, (from the Greek word signifying the womb,) generally arises from the sudden arrest of menstruation, when it occurs in the non-impregnated state. The symptoms are similar to those of acute ovaritis; severe pain in the hypogastrium, pelvic weight, fever and constant nausea. A digital examination by the vagina should always be used to ascertain this affection. The vagina will be found hot and dry; the cervix swollen, and often sensitive; while the body of the womb is exquisitely painful, any touch causing nausea. *Nausea* is a very frequent symptom in affections of the womb, and arises from the intimate sympathy between that organ and the stomach. In incipient pregnancy, nausea generally occurs, and shows the sympathy of the stomach with the changes going on in the womb. In acute metritis the passage of the faeces is exquisitely painful, for the womb lies just upon the rectum, and, in passing, they lift it up.

Acute metritis generally ends by resolution, that is, complete subsidence of the inflammation, in from five to ten days. It rarely ends fatally, but in some cases, it degenerates into chronic metritis, which is an exceedingly wearing and painful affection. This is particularly likely to happen, if the acute disease be not recognised, (as is frequently the case in the absence of the necessary digital examination,) and styled loosely "inflammation of the bowels." If. not recognised, it is not treated promptly enough; and there are few diseases which cause so much suffering, as the chronic metritis, which may follow.

The *treatment* should consist in the application of a large number of leeches, from ten to twenty, to the hypogastrium. This should be followed by large thin poultices to that part, or by warm fomentations, if the abdomen be too tender. Internally, tartar emetic should be given in small doses, which is a most valuable remedy in the majority of acute inflammations, producing sickness, relaxation, and perspiration, quieting the pulse, and reducing fever. Gentle saline aperients should also be given, to soften the faeces, and prevent them from irritating the womb, and to cool the system.

In acute ovaritis the same treatment should be used, and more actively to prevent suppuration if possible.

CHRONIC METRITIS.

This disease is generally partial, being confined to the posterior wall of the uterus. This arises from the fact, that the muscular fibres of that wall are continuous with those in the neck of the womb, and chronic metritis is generally caused by the extension of inflammation from the neck to the body of the organ. The symptoms of the disease are, a dull aching deep-seated pain in the hypogastric region, just above the pubis ; also still more constantly, a pain in the loins and sacral region, extending down the inside of the thighs. These pains are increased by walking, and are accompanied by an oppressive feeling of pelvic weight. On examining by the finger in the vagina, an extremely sensitive protuberance is felt on the posterior surface of the body of the womb, sometimes smooth, sometimes irregular and knotty. Pressure here causes exquisite pain and nausea. The womb being an organ very delicately poised in the pelvis, any increase of weight in one part makes it incline in that direction ; and therefore it is in this disease *retroverted*, and lies upon the rectum, causing obstinate constipation, and the passage of the faeces gives great pain. There is generally some leucorrhoeal discharge.

The constitutional symptoms are the usual ones expressive of impaired health, namely, headache, want of sleep and bad dreams, foul tongue, want of appetite, and dyspepsia. No organ sympathises so much with the womb as the stomach, and there is very generally nausea, along with much dyspepsia, present in this disease. A peculiar appearance of pallor and languor, which is very characteristic of inflammatory diseases of the sexual organs, and hence called the *facies uterina* (uterine face) is in no affection more strongly marked than in this. The patient looks worn out by habitual suffering. Although this affection is a most wearing and distressing one, yet it is not incompatible with what a superficial observer might think tolerable health, especially in the menstrual intervals. But during menstruation all the pains are greatly increased, and are often agonising. The disease is of an exceedingly chronic and obstinate nature, like all inflammations in tissues of low vitality, for instance bones, ligaments, &c.; and also because it is kept up by the periodical congestion of menstruation. Indeed Dr. Bennett, who was the first accurately to describe this, and several other uterine inflammations, says, he never saw a case get well spontaneously, as long as menstruation lasted. He says, that in most of the cases he had seen, the disease had continued for years unknown, the patient having been supposed to suffer from irritable or displaced uterus, or from functional dysmenorrhœa. We see in this, what miserable and protracted sufferings may arise from erroneous diagnosis.

The *cause* of this painful disease is in some cases an attack of acute metritis, which is not perfectly subdued. But in general it results from the extension of inflammation from an ulcerated cervix, and when so, it is peculiarly intractable.

The *treatment* is, first to cure the ulceration of the cervix, if such exist. This often removes the chronic metritis, but not always, and in these cases the tenacity of the disease is extreme, and from months to years may be necessary for its treatment. The means to be used are, rest in the recumbent position, with emollient or astringent vaginal injections, and the occasional applications of leeches to the os, before, during, or after menstruation. At the menstrual exacerbations, opiate injections into the rectum should be used, or the inhalation of chloroform, if the pain be agonizing. The constipation, which is almost always obstinate, is very difficult to treat. Injections cannot be used, for they cause great pain. It is a good sign, when the patient becomes able to bear them. Mild aperients should therefore be used. By these means, long and perseveringly applied, together with lying out in the open air, whenever the weather is favourable, tepid sponging, and other modes of bracing the general health, the disease can almost always be at last cured; but this depends greatly upon the patience and perseverance of the sufferer, and whether she have the power of using the various requisite means for so long a time.

To *prevent* this disease, its chief cause, ulceration of the cervix, should be prevented, or if it do occur should be met by prompt treatment, so as to prevent its giving rise to this much more tedious and painful affection.

ULCERATION

OF THE

NECK OF THE WOMB.

THIS is an exceedingly important disease, and the greater part of Dr. Bennett's inimitable work on the uterine inflammations is devoted to it. He says it is of infinitely more frequent occurrence than any other inflammation of the womb, and is the principal cause of leucorrhœa, prolapsus, painful, scanty, and hemorrhagic menstruation, sterility, abortion &c. The great frequency and importance of this disease was quite unknown in this country, till Dr. Bennett wrote upon the subject, and doubtless in many cases it still remains undetected.

The disease consists in an inflamed and ulcerated state of the mouth of the womb and the surface of the cervix.

The size of the cervix varies naturally in different women, but whatever be its size, shape, or direction, it may be considered healthy, if it be not inflamed, nor indurated, and if the os be normally closed. When healthy it has a soft, elastic, and unctuous feel, is of a pale rosy hue, and not the least painful on pressure.

Before puberty the womb is dormant, and very little subject to inflammation; but afterwards, the menstrual secretion is liable to be prevented, diminished, increased, or arrested, by a variety of social, moral and other causes. Hence ulceration is not very unfrequently found in virgins, while in married women, in whom it is much more common, sexual intercourse is another cause; and in some very susceptible women ulceration follows intercourse almost immediately, without immoderate indulgence. Hence many young females are attacked by this disease soon after marriage and remain sterile; or if they conceive, are very subject to abortion. Child-birth often causes ulceration, for the mucous membrane, lining the os and cervical cavity, is apt to be contused and lacerated; and though such contusions rapidly heal, when all goes on favourably, yet if there be any cause to prevent this, such as the retention of pieces of the after-birth, &c. ulceration may follow. Women who have borne children, are much more subject to this disease, for the womb remains always somewhat more vascular. Ulceration also frequently arises from gonorrhœa or leucorrhœa.

The symptoms of inflammation of the cervix, which generally precedes its ulceration, are as follows. The cervix becomes swollen and enlarged,

Q

and gradually falls in the vagina from its increased weight. When examined by the speculum it is of a vivid red hue, and covered by muco-pus, which must be wiped off in order to see it. This muco-pus must not be confounded with the white creamy secretion often found in this region, which is the product merely of congestion, and is seen in many healthy women before and after menstruation.

When the cervical cavity is inflamed, the os is always *opened*. This is a most valuable sign, for in health the os is invariably contracted : and whenever the finger in examining meets with a well-marked depression, instead of a scarcely perceptible orifice, there is certainly inflammation, and the speculum is indispensable.

The mucous membrane, lining the cavity of the cervix, when inflamed is of a dark livid red hue, and secretes adhesive muco-pus, and a glairy transparent mucous, like raw white of egg. The presence of this glairy discharge in large quantities, and an open os, are certain signs of inflammation of the cavity of the cervix.

Ulceration generally soon follows. It may present different characters; the granulations sometimes being very small and red, (as they generally are in the cavity of the cervix,) or large and livid, showing torpor and congestion of the part. This is generally their form in pregnancy. The ulcers are never excavated, nor have abrupt margins ; therefore they are very difficult to recognise, unless by a thoroughly educated finger, and are constantly overlooked, when a digital examination alone is made. They present to the touch a soft, velvety, mossy feeling. In almost all cases the ulcer penetrates into the cavity of the cervix, but never passes the os internum. An ulcer always secretes pus, whether scanty or abundant; but when scanty, it is often absorbed in passing through the vagina, and thus a patient may have no external discharge. But in other cases there is abundant purulent discharge, mixed with mucus from the congested vagina, creamy milky fluid from the congested follicles of the cervix, and the glairy transparent secretion from the cavity of the cervix, constituting copious leucorrhœa. The discharge is sometimes tinged with blood from the ulcer, especially after intercourse.

The cervix may remain a long time in an inflamed and ulcerated state, without its volume being materially increased ; but very frequently, especially in women who have had children, it becomes more or less enlarged and hypertrophied. It sometimes increases surprisingly, reaching even the size of a man's fist. The inflammation and swelling sometimes, though rarely, extend to the body of the womb, constituting the painful and obstinate affection, chronic metritis. There is generally induration, as well as hypertrophy; a stony hardness of the tumor, which has been frequently mistaken for cancer, giving rise to the greatest misery and anxiety. But this mistake need not again occur after Dr. Bennett's masterly analysis of the different appearances of the two diseases: and it is a great consolation to those afflicted with these inflammatory diseases of the cervix, to know that they have little, if any, tendency to degenerate into cancer. Dr. Bennett says, he has never seen a case so degenerate, even after many years' continuance.

Inflammatory hypertrophy causes prolapse of the womb, and the neck is often carried backwards as well as downwards, so as to press on the vagina or rectum. This gives rise to a disagreeable feeling of weight and dragging, as if a body were about to escape from the vagina. When the patient is sitting, there is the feeling of a tumor pressed up by the seat. When the cervix is ulcerated, the inflammation generally extends to the vagina. Sometimes the vulva is inflamed, although the vagina is not; and this is often attended with a most distressing itching, which is the source of great torment, sometimes banishing the sufferer from society, and nearly driving her distracted. This itching, when very great, is usually dependent on internal inflammation, and is to be removed only by the prior cure of the latter.

The two other pelvic organs, the *rectum* and the *bladder*, are generally affected, when the uterine disease is severe and chronic. The rectum almost always suffers by being pressed upon, which causes constipation. The bowel is also often congested and irritable, and much mucus is expelled with the fæces. Piles and prolapsus ani also frequently occur from the obstruction to the circulation in the blood-vessels of the part. These diseases are aggravated during menstruation, and add greatly to the patient's discomfort. The bladder also becomes irritable, and there is frequent desire to pass water, with scalding. The irritability of the bladder is often caused by the morbid state of the urine, which in this disease is frequently loaded with deposits. The morbid urine causes a dull aching pain at the neck of the bladder, and irritability of that organ.

One chief reason that ulcers of the womb are so often undetected is, that pain is frequently absent, or at least often felt in other parts. It is not in the cervix itself that the pain is felt, but in the loins, in the ovarian, and sometimes in the hypogastric regions. The permanence of these pains is an important character. Better or worse, they are never absent; while back-ache from mere weakness is essentially intermitting. The pains are in general of that dull aching character, which characterises pain when seated in the sympathetic nerves. But the back-ache is sometimes agonising, as if the back was broken.

Menstruation generally soon becomes disordered. It becomes irregular, and either too scanty or too abundant. During menstruation all the above-mentioned pains are greatly aggravated, and the sufferings of the patient are often very great. Many cases of the most severe dysmenorrhœa are owing to ulceration of the womb.

Ulceration very frequently causes sterility: and when a patient does conceive, pregnancy is painful and laborious, and abortions frequently occur. The cure of the ulcer often removes sterility.

It also greatly deadens the sexual feelings, like almost all inflammatory affections of the womb, or the ovaries, and like the analogous inflammations of the prostate gland and testicles in man. This is frequently carried even to the extent of disgust, although no pain may attend intercourse, and often gives rise to great misery in married life; the husband attributing his wife's altered feelings to personal dislike and other moral causes.

This, it may be remarked in passing, is cre of the innumerable instan-

ees of the daily mistakes made in estimating character by all, who are
not acquanted with physical influences, and bodily disease.   In fact it is
not possible for any one, man or woman, however great may be their
knowledge of mental and moral subjects, to form correct judgments of
their fellow beings, unless they are as conversant with our physical as our
moral nature.   From the want of this physical and medical knowledge,
all the current opinions upon mankind, religious and moral, social and
individual, are radically vitiated.

The return of sexual desire is to be regarded in this, as in other sexual
disorders, as one of the best of all signs of a radical cure ; just as the
return of a healthy appetite in affections of the stomach, or the general
system.   In ulceration there is frequently pain in congress, but it is frequently absent.

The most marked and prominent constitutional symptom is indigestion ;
for no organ sympathises so much with the womb as the stomach.   In
general the dyspepsia becomes gradually severe, and leads both patient
and physician erroneously to believe, that it is the real disease.   In
all chronic diseases there is no greater source of error than this, to mistake a secondary disease for the primary one.   In chronic diseases, one
organ after another becomes gradually implicated, and without great care
and skill, the secondary diseases are constantly mistaken for the primary
ones.   In this way we have seen that in spermatorrhœa, the source of
the symptoms was always thought, before M. Lallemand's work, to be in
the brain, stomach, or other organ.   In like manner Dr. Edward Johnson
has ably pointed out the fact, that the exceedingly prevalent disease of indigestion is in a great majority of the cases in this country, rather a disease
of the brain than of the stomach ; arising from the over-work, anxiety,
&c., to which the mind is constantly subject in our society.   Thus in the
case before us, although the stomach becomes greatly disorderd, and the
impaired appetite, the pain, flatulence, &c., absorb the patient's attention,
in reality these are not the primary disease at all, but merely symptoms
of the ulcerated state of the womb.   Dr. Bennett says, that whenever he
sees severe dyspepsia in a young female, he suspects disease of the womb.
For the same reason, whenever we see severe dyspepsia or great nervous
prostration in a young man, we may suspect genital enfeeblement, and why ?
because in youth the sexual system is the prominent one, and is the grand
key to the diseases of that time of life.   There are comparatively few diseases in youth, in which the sexual system does not play a prominent
part, either in causing or in complicating them.   For this reason, whenever
we see a case of chronic disease in the young of either sex, particular care
should be given to examine the state of the sexual organs.

It is indeed essential in cases of chronic disease at every age, to examine into the state of all the different organs in the body, and it is
becoming a rule with scientific physicians to do so ; but there are no
organs, which are so constantly omitted in this general scrutiny as the
sexual ones, in consequence of the lamentable feelings of delicacy so often
alluded to.   Hence the treatment of the diseases of youth is, as a general
rule, exceedingly unsatisfactory and unscientific, and there is no age

which is so constantly mistaken and ill-treated. The sexual organs preside over youth both in health and disease; and to overlook this most important fact is to ignore nature.

The other viscera also, the lungs, liver, and heart are liable to disordered action, such as palpitations, severe pain under the breast-bone, bilious attacks, &c; and consumption is one of the dangers to which this, as well as all other debilitating diseases, indirectly exposes the patient. The weakness, pallor, and uterine face are often extreme; but there is seldom feverishness, and the patient does not look like one labouring under an inflammatory disease. She is nervous and hysterical, with bad sleep and frightful dreams, especially when the dull aching pains are present. There are sometimes mental delusions and dread of insanity, as in other chronic diseases, which gradually weaken and disturb the nervous system.

In some cases the local symptoms may predominate; in others, the constitutional, while the local ones are almost absent; and it is in these cases that the disease is so apt to be overlooked. Hence the medical man can frequently only suspect the possible existence of the disease, and his task, Dr. Bennett observes, is a very delicate one, for women have such a reluctance to a digital examination.

The disease tends to last indefinitely, and rarely subsides spontaneously, before the decline of menstruation. It may exist from ten to twenty years without endangering life. No disease has been more frequently overlooked, the back-ache, leucorrhœa &c., being thought to arise from a "weakness." This is an inveterate popular error. "The opinion has hitherto prevailed," says Dr. Bennett, "that extreme general debility may exist spontaneously in the female, but it does not do so in her, any more than in the male, without some tangible reason; either there must be some organic disease present, or she must be exposed to very bad hygienic conditions."

Ulceration of the cervix not unfrequently occurs in virgins, as Dr. Bennett was the first to point out. He says that to it may be referred most of the cases of severe and obstinate dysmenorrhœa, and inveterate leucorrhœa, occurring in them. "These cases" he says, "are very delicate, but the scruples of delicacy must be overcome; no such feelings prevent surgical relief being offered to girls with disease of the rectum, anus, &c., though here it is equally repugnant." "In most of the cases I have seen," he says, moreover, "the disease had existed for years unrecognised, and it is certain that some of them must have perished. I have restored to perfect health many young females, who were mere wrecks, and had lost all hope of recovery. It would be an opprobrium to medical science, if this disease, when discovered in the virgin, should remain untreated."

So strong is the language, which Dr. Bennett finds it necessary to use in speaking of the feelings of false delicacy, even among medical men; for it must not be thought that these scruples are confined to women alone. In fact in this respect unfortunate woman is as much sinned against as sinning, and the scruples of medical men, and of surrounding friends, have frequently as much to say in the neglect of their diseases, as their own morbid delicacy. There is one simple axiom of morality in all these matters, that whatever feeling stands in the way of the most satisfactory examination and treatment of disease, whether in the virgin or married woman; and whether such feeling exists in the patient herself, in her friends or medical attendant, it is to be considered a serious moral error. Human health and disease, happiness or misery, are far too sacred to be sacrificed to such morbid ideas. Woman has already suffered too deeply from this deplorable false delicacy; and every one who feels for his fellow creatures, and for the dignity of mankind, should endeavour, that such feelings should be rooted out from among us.

Ulceration is not unfrequent in pregnant women, and is said by Dr. Bennett to be the key to most of the accidents of pregnancy, such as obstinate sickness, hemorrage, and abortions. There is here generally copious leucorrhœa, and frequently pain in congress, and slight hemorrage after it. The patient is racked by pains, thin and debilitated, and waits for delivery as the only term to her sufferings, which she believes to be dependent merely on the pregnancy. Ulceration was not known to be frequently present in pregnancy, till Dr. Bennett wrote, chiefly in consequence of a groundless fear of using the speculum in pregnant women. The disease when detected, is generally easily curable, and should be treated as early as possible to prevent abortions.

Abortions, and laborious child-birth, frequently cause ulceration, and here the prominent symptom is the continuance of hemorrhage for many weeks. When such hemorrhages do occur after delivery, and are succeeded by leucorrhœa, they generally depend on ulceration, and it is in these cases that chronic metritis is most apt to be induced.

Ulceration is sometimes found after the cessation of the menses, and is generally the remains of former disease; for menstrual decline does not always cure inflammatory uterine diseases, though it very frequently does so. The ulcerations in advanced life sometimes arise from gonorrhœa. They are much more difficult to cure than in young women.

It will be seen from this description, that ulceration of the neck of the womb is a most important disease. It is very common, and causes most severe and prolonged sufferings. When we reflect on this, and also on the many ages that have elapsed before this disease was revealed to us through the speculum, we may form some slight idea of the immense amount of female misery it has caused. Myriads of women have dragged through a life of wretchedness, or have at last sunk beneath the slow undermining ravages of this relentless foe. And it is certain that even at the present day, there are many who are suffering from this disease unrecognised; although from the masterly analysis of Dr. Bennett, which is a model of medical description, it has been clearly exposed, and would very rarely escape detection, if the speculum were used as often as it should be, or if the finger of medical men were duly trained to the investigation of female disease. Although the use of these necessary means are obstructed among all classes of women, it is especially in virgins, that mistaken scruples are allowed to interfere; and there is no doubt that very many cases of this and other sexual inflammations exist at present among them unrecognised, and cause an immensity of suffering. Amenorrhœa and dysmenorrhœa are of frequent occurrence in the virgin; and these diseases are frequently owing to ulceration, or subacute ovaritis.

The *treatment* of this disease is one of the most satisfactory of all. Ulceration, if left to itself, tends to last indefinitely, and rarely subsides spontaneously while menstruation lasts; but there is scarcely a case which will not yield to good medical treatment. However great the debility, or protracted the sufferings, the disease may in most cases be cured, and the patient restored to health and strength.

The principles of treatment in ulceration of the cervix are, first, to subdue inflammation by emollient and astringent vaginal injections, and by leeches; and secondly, to modify by cauterization the ulcerated surface, so as to substitute healthy reparative inflammation for morbid ulcerative inflammation.

The application of leeches to the os relieves congestion and favours the cure; but they are not indispensable, and it is wrong to apply them frequently. When they are applied, a small plug of cotton tied by a thread, should be fixed in the mouth of the womb, to prevent them biting in the cervical canal, where they cause agonising pain; while on the cervix, they cause no pain. The emollient injections consist of linseed tea, or milk and water, either tepid or cold. They should be retained in the vagina for some minutes, and are very soothing; and chiefly useful, where there is much irritability, increased by astringents. The astringent injections are of very great value in ulceration, as well as in leucorrhœa, and may succeed alone in curing slight ulceration. But this is not to be expected, and the grand treatment for the ulcers is *cauterization*. The ulcers generally pass into the cavity of the cervix, and thus are out of reach of injections. Much time is often lost in using injections, and it is much better to use the speculum and cauterization at once. The caustic generally used, and frequently sufficing for the cure, is the nitrate of silver. The application of this invaluable salt, generally at once arrests the ulcer, which becomes smaller and healthier, and secretes healthy pus. It should be applied every fifth or sixth day, till the ulcer is completely healed; for if it be left to itself, no matter how far the healing process have advanced, it will fall back again. The last part of the ulcer to heal, is that which dips into the cervical cavity; and to treat this, it is necessary to have a bi-valve speculum, by which the os can be opened, and the ulcer within cauterized. If this is done, there will never be a relapse, but if any of the ulcer be left, relapse is almost sure to occur. Astringent injections should be used, as well as the cauterization.

By these means a cure is generally effected in a few weeks, if the ulcer is small and recent. Even in livid and fungous ulcers, the nitrate of silver produces a clean and healthy state; but here it is seldom strong enough to cause complete cicatrisation. It is best applied in the solid form, except in the cervical canal, where a strong solution may be used on a hair pencil, lest the solid stick break. If it does run down on the neighbouring tissues, it does rather good than harm, for its action is not at all violent. Its application to the cervix causes little pain, but more to the cervical cavity. After the pain has abated, there is generally a lull in the symptoms; but if the ulcer be then left to itself, it soon again becomes irritable, and the patient often begs for the re-application of the caustic.

When the ulcer is large and unhealthy, the nitrate is not strong enough to produce a cure, and in this case the acid nitrate of mercury should be used. This is the best of the more powerful caustics. From ten to fourteen days should intervene between its applications. In these cases from six weeks to three months may be needed for the cure. But sometimes all these means fail, and the ulcer, partly healed, becomes stationary, generally in the cervical cavity. Then the most powerful of all caustics, the potassa fusa, should be used. The pain is little more severe, than in ordinary cauterization with the nitrate of silver, sometimes even less. Dr. Bennett says, he has scarcely ever seen bad effects follow even severe cauterization, and he infers that this treatment does not involve more risk to the patient, than the minor surgical operations, such as toothdrawing, opening abscesses &c. Still, he says, all surgical operations have some risk, and he has twice seen acute metritis brought on by weak astringent vaginal injections.

The cure of ulceration by these means removes slight hypertrophy of the cervix; but in many instances after the ulcer is cured, hypertrophy remains, sufficient to drag down the womb; and this will probably cause return of the ulcer, as the cervix remains red and congested. This hypertrophy, Dr. Bennett says, never resists the melting influence of the potassa fusa, which is by far the best, and indeed the only necessary kind of treatment for it. The purpose of the application of this powerful caustic is not to burn away the swelled part, but only to excite a certain amount of inflammation. This extends to the swelled and indurated tissues, and they melt, and are absorbed. The artificial ulcers, produced by the potassa, always heal readily in from four to six weeks; and this shows the rationale of the treatment of diseased ulceration by cauterization.

After the cure of ulceration and hypertrophy, the cervix rises in the pelvis; and although it may not regain completely its position, yet if all inflammation be subdued, it seldom causes any uneasiness, and vaginal injections of cold water are all that is needed. There is considerable difference of opinion among those conversant with female disease, as to the effect of displacement of the womb. Many physicians think that the displacement of the womb backwards or forwards, or its prolapse, is frequently owing to mere relaxation of the ligaments and vagina, by which it is kept in its place. Dr. Bennett however, and many others, are strongly opposed to this idea, and assert that the womb is very rarely displaced, except as the result of inflammation of some part of its substance, which increases its weight, and makes it incline in one direction. They say that unless there be inflammation present, it is very rare that displacement causes any uneasiness whatever; and that the artificial and mechanical means of support, such as pessaries, which are in very common use, are almost always productive of evil, rather than good, as they only increase the inflammation, which causes the displacement. Dr. Bennett says that in forty-nine cases out of fifty, where pessaries are now used, the patient is injured rather than benefited. Cure the inflammatory disease, which is almost always the cause of the displacement, and the womb will regain its position ; and even if it do not entirely regain it, will cause no uneasiness. Dr. Bennett says that almost the only cases requiring pessaries, are those where there is complete procidentia, (by which is meant, that the womb has fallen completely out of the vagina,) which does not yield to the removal of the inflammation.

In ulceration the patient should remain as much as possible in the recumbent position, especially after cauterization. Carriage exercise, and even a gentle walk, more for air than exercise, are good, if they can be borne. Sexual abstinence is always necessary. The torpid and irritable state of the rectum, should be treated by the daily injection of about half a pint of cold water after breakfast. This is a most valuable remedy. After the cure of the ulcer, the secondary diseases will gradually disappear.

"The system," says Dr. Bennett, "seems almost always to have the power of rallying even when depressed by a long life of disease. One of the most striking results of a cure is the removal of the fretful, irritable, and hysterical state of mind, which so often accompanies this disease, and which deserves pity rather than blame, for the irritability is all but uncontrollable. The treatment of the disease is very satisfactory. Women who have been for years in misery, stranded as it were on the shores of life, have a resurrection, and are restored to happiness and usefulness."

VENEREAL DISEASES IN THE FEMALE

THESE diseases in the female are of the same nature as in the male, namely gonorrhœa and syphilis—the non-virulent, and the virulent affections ; but the different form of the sexual organs causes some important differences in their progress and treatment.

Gonorrhœa in the female is characterised by swelling of the lips of the vulva, redness and inflammation of the mucous surfaces, and a copious discharge of pus. The irritation, pain, and itching, are often intolerable. The entrance to the vagina may be much swelled, and excessively tender. The urethra is also frequently inflamed, which is seldom the case in common leucorrhœa ; but the scalding in passing water, is not nearly so great as in the male. The disease generally extends, unless early checked, to the whole internal surface of the vagina, and neck of the uterus, and often to the cervical canal.

During the acute stage, the tenderness of the parts forbids the use of the speculum ; but after it has subsided, that instrument should be used, and the walls of the vagina are then seen to be either simply red and turgid, or covered with isolated patches of redness, vesicles, pimples, or superficial ulcers, the products of the inflammation, and not of a syphilitic nature. After the disease has lasted some time, the mouth of the womb is always more or less affected : it is swelled and red, and generally covered with small ulcers or granulations.

The *treatment* is divided into three parts, as in the male ; namely, the abortive, and the treatment of the acute and chronic stages.

With regard to the first of these, M. Ricord says, " Women rarely consult a medical man soon enough to allow of the gonorrhœa being cut short in its developement ; either because they do not acknowledge the disease till it is too late, or because they do not at once perceive it. However, if applied soon enough, that is to say, within the first two or three days, astringent injections and applications would be generally crowned with success, in cases where the vulva, vagina, or uterus is affected."

Were the immense importance of arresting this disease at the outset generally known by women, and did not a morbid delicacy, or culpable neglect so often interfere, (and even among prostitutes, the first of these feelings operates as powerfully as perhaps in any other class of women,) the most protracted sufferings might be spared. But the disease, in almost every case, is allowed to run on to the acute stage; whose violent symptoms and tedious course show the folly of procrastination. The most absolute rest is now of very great importance, along with sparing diet, and general baths. But the local treatment is the most essential. The diseased parts should be separated from each other, and emollient fomentations with solutions of some narcotic substance, as opium or poppy-heads, applied to allay the irritation. A piece of lint, dipped in this solution, should be placed between the inflamed lips. Injections into the vagina cannot be used at first, from the swelling and tenderness; but should be employed as soon as possible, and repeated several times a day; and, if not too painful, a roll of lint dipped in the same liquid, should be introduced into the vagina, and wetted thrice a day. Sometimes the acute stage resists these soothing means, and, if so, they should not be long continued. In these cases the nitrate of silver applied in the solid form, as in balanitis, often produces a wonderful effect. After its use, a roll of dry lint should be introduced to keep the mucous surfaces apart.

When the acute stage has subsided, the main treatment consists in *injections*, as in the case of other vaginal discharges. Emollient injections should be used, in general, tepid; astringent ones, cold. In the female, cubebs and copaiba are of little comparative use, for they scarcely act on the vagina. Their action only extends to the urethra, by which canal they are carried out of the system. Where the urethra is affected in the female, they should be given.

The best injections, as has been mentioned before, are solutions of alum, acetate of lead, sulphate of zinc, tannin, decoction of oak bark, &c. Their strength should be gradually increased, as the acute stage is further past, till an ounce to the pound of water is used; for it should be observed that much stronger treatment, whether abortive or otherwise, can be used in the female than in the male; where the narrowness of the canal renders strong applications hazardous. By means of these injections, and plugs of lint dipped in the same liquid, and kept in the vagina, M. Ricord says, that he succeeds in curing sixty cases in a hundred, and in a period of from twenty to sixty days.

But the chronic stage often resists all these modes of treatment, and is very tedious. In these cases, where the discharge seems to be kept up by the heat and moisture, high up in the vagina, an excellent plan is to fill that cavity with dry lint, renewed twice or thrice daily. If the surgeon himself apply this, which is much the best way, he should use the speculum. This is often successful, especially where the discharge is white and milky, and the cervical canal is not involved.

If there be any change of tissue keeping up the discharge, it must be first cured. Ulcerations and papular granulations should be cauterised with nitrate of silver, previously drying the parts with lint.

After the cure, injections of cold water should be used twice daily for some time, to give tone to the parts. They should be omitted four or five days before and after menstruation.

Although a radical cure can generally be effected by these means, and although M. Ricord's enegetic treatment is so often successful; still it is obvious that very great care and perseverance are necessary, on the part both of the patient and surgeon, to produce this result.   Unless the injections be properly given, which, as was formerly mentioned, is most effectually done by another person: unless due care be taken by examination with the speculum and other means, thoroughly to cure the changes of tissue, which are so frequent both in the vagina and the cervical canal ; a radical cure cannot be expected.   Now in this country these essentials of success are very rarely present.   Mr. Langston Parker in his able work on Venereal Diseases, says, "Many causes contribute to render the treatment of gonorrhœa in the female tedious and unsatisfactory ; and the disease more difficult to cure in this sex, than in the male."   Thus, he says, "I believe that gonorrhœal diseases in the female are very rarely completely cured.   This in most cases arises either from neglect on the part of the patient ; or the want of a proper knowledge of the disease, careful examination of the parts affected, and an appropriate topical medication on the part of the surgeon."

We see from this what fearful deficiencies there are in medical education and medical treatment, with respect to the sexual diseases of women ; deficiencies which are caused by the morbid delicacy on these subjects. The treatment of gonorrhœa in the female is, in the hands of very many medical men, a mere farce ; the prevailing morbid delicacy has prevented them from acquiring a due knowledge of these diseases, interferes with the necessary modes of diagnosis and treatment, and is a ready excuse for evading the troublesome and long continued means which are demanded for a cure.   In this way, not only are the unfortunate patients themselves left uncured, but the disease is suffered to spread to thousands, and cause incalculable misery.

Although gonorrhœa is so much more difficult to cure in woman than in man, (partly from the above reasons, and partly on account of the periodical return of menstruation, and also the large extent of surface affected) it is not of nearly so dangerous a nature ; because it is not liable to cause diseases which interfere with the passage of *urine*.   The urethra in the female is much wider than in the male, and stricture very rarely occurs.   Enlargement of the prostate, later in life, cannot in this sex be dreaded ; nor can seminal disease be excited.   The peculiar danger of gonorrhœa in man arises from the narrowness and vital importance of the canal where it occurs, and the connection of this canal with the generative functions.

However, the disease in the female may cause very great evils.   Its long continuance, like inveterate leucorrhœa, may greatly break down the strength, and favour the occurrence of other diseases.   Ulcers of the womb too, with all their miseries ; subacute ovaritis, and the various lesions of the ovaries and fallopian tubes, which are so often found in prostitutes, are frequently owing to this cause.

Syphilis in the female is in its main characters similar to that in the male.   There is one thing to be carefully remarked, that primary chancres almost always occur on the *external* parts ; namely, in the vulva, and not in the vagina or uterus.   They are very rarely seen on the womb,

the virus being apparently almost always deposited on the external parts, .
or at least not taking effect on the others ; probably because abrasions
are less frequent on them, and the mucous secretions wash away the
poison.

The treatment of the disease in its different stages, primary, secondary,
and tertiary, is the same as when it occurs in man.

For the *prevention* of venereal disease in the female, the parts should
be washed immediately after any mercenary intercourse, the lips of the
vulva being separated; urine should also be passed to cleanse the urethra.
These precautions are almost as effectual in woman as in man, for infectious matter, especially syphilitic, is so often deposited in the external
genital fissure.   The use of the sheath by the male of course protects
the female also, and is by far the most certain preventive.   The practice
of washing is very frequently neglected by women from heedlessness, or
from an unfounded dread of using cold water to these parts.   M. Ricord
says, " were women more cleanly, venereal diseases would be much less
prevalent."   He says moreover, that infection is very frequently given by
a woman, in whose organs the poisonous matter is retained, although
without affecting herself.   These cases would often be prevented by
washing.

But the great method of preventing venereal disease in the female, as
well as in the male, is to *prevent prostitution* or mercenary love; on
which subject I shall speak hereafter.

GENERAL REMARKS

ON THE

SEXUAL DISEASES.

THE above descriptions comprehend most of the functional and inflammatory diseases of the sexual organs in women, which form by far the greatest part of the diseases of these organs. I do not here speak of the organic malignant diseases, such as cancer, chiefly because the cause of these fearful affections is not yet known, and consequently a knowledge of them is not of such importance to society. Besides, however terrible these incurable diseases may be, and however dreadful the sufferings they frequently cause to their unfortunate victims, still they are comparatively so rare, that they are not of such social importance, as some of the much slighter diseases, nor do they cause on the whole nearly so much human suffering. The importance of a disease depends on the total amount of human suffering it causes; and I believe that by far the most important class of sexual diseases are those, which arise from sexual abstinence, or abuse; and which are characterised by genital enfeeblement, giving rise to general debility and mental irritation, discontent, and despondency. These are universally spread throughout our society in the present day, and spring naturally from the universal difficulties opposing the healthy exercise of the sexual organs. There are innumerable varieties and degrees of this enfeeblement; and very frequently, both in man and woman, the disease may be more of a mental than a physical nature, consisting in discontent, apathy, or irresolution, from the repression of the natural passions, without there being any tangible disease of the sexual organs.

The *prevention of disease* is one of the great leading ideas of this age. It is of very recent origin, and was not really and energetically urged on the attention of society, till the writings of Dr. Andrew Combe and some others within the last half-century. Before that time the prevention of disease was little thought of; as society, who were too much occupied with spiritual religion and national animosities to pay much attention to the bodily health, left the whole matter to the physicians, who attended solely to the cure and not to the prevention. But this is evidently of little comparative use; for society is little benefited, although disease be cured, if its cause be allowed to continue, and thus new diseases constantly permitted to succeed to the old ones. But in the prevention and eradication of disease, society is evidently even more directly interested than the phy-sicians ; and it is the former also, who by change of habits, and by their own intelligent exertions, can alone prevent it. Therefore, as soon as the idea of the prevention of disease was earnestly adopted, it was seen that the only possible mode of effecting this, was by getting the co-operation of all mankind. The great cause of disease was at once seen to be the general ignorance of the laws of health ; and hence arose the many admi-rable popular works on medicine, which have lately appeared, and which are among the most valuable parts of medical literature. It is not by the mere advance of science among medical men, that the health of man-kind can be elevated or diseases prevented ; but by the general knowledge of all.

Several excellent popular treatises have been written on the various bodily functions, and popular descriptions of many forms of disease given ; but with respect to the sexual organs, nothing of the kind has been done, except some meagre description of the venereal affections, and fancy por-traits of the traditional evils of excess. But of the real state of the sexual world, and of the natural laws which preside over these organs, no popular description has yet been given. And yet there is no subject on which knowledge is so much needed by all mankind. There is none upon which the general ignorance is so profound ; none on which depend questions of such vital importance in morals, health, and political economy. The sexual organs moreover are the citadel of the ignorance and degra-ding mystery, in which the whole body is shrouded from the eyes of the public ; and until they and their laws become generally understood by all educated men and women, mankind will never possess a due knowledge of the human frame. There is no part of our social fabric in so miserable a state as the sexual part ; and I do not think that even poverty causes so much misery as sexual disease and sexual difficulties, in which the de-gradation of secrecy and deceit is added to the other evils. However the two subjects are so closely connected together, as we shall see afterwards, that they cannot be separated.

There is no subject in which such difficulty is felt by a young man or woman, especially among the upper classes, from puberty till marriage, as the sexual one. They have no guide to a true knowledge of the new organs and passions developed in them ; and the promptings of nature are so completely at variance with conventional rules, that youth is quite bewildered. For a young man there are three ways open ; abstinence, abuse, or a mercenary love. Abstinence, besides the great moral evils of the discontent and unhappiness resulting from constantly repressed passions, exposes him to the most serious genital enfeeblement. Solitary indulgences are still more dangerous, and lead to the greatest disorders both of mind and body. Mercenary love, besides the fearful dangers of venereal disease, is exceedingly degrading ; and the amount of evil done to men, as well as to women, by this general degradation of their first sexual experiences, is little conceived. The young woman is in a much worse sexual position than even the young man ; for even mercenary love is far better than total sexual abstinence. The latter gradually destroys her balance of mind and body, making her hysterical and chlorotic ; and this, with the still greater evil of solitary indulgence, is all that is open to unmarried girls in the upper classes. In the poorer classes prostitution is another alternative, which thousands are driven into.

Thus we see that the present sexual condition of society is such, as necessarily to cause more or less disease and unhappiness to almost every individual of either sex. How are we ever to escape from these enormous evils, unless the subject become one of free and general discussion; and unless an intimate knowledge of the various facts, physical and moral, supply the materials of such discussion? Are we to hide our head in the sand, like the foolish bird, and hope that the destroyer will pass us by? In the present state of general sexual ignorance, there is no possible escape from these evils; their prevention and cure are equally impossible.

No man, who is not acquainted with the natural laws of the sexual organs, and with the diseased states arising from their disobedience, is capable of reasoning truly on sexual morality. And until within the last twenty years, before the researches of M. Lallemand had laid bare the sexual diseases in the male, and the introduction of the speculum had thrown a similar light on female disease, it did not lie in human power to erect a natural theory of sexual morality. The materials for *physical demonstration* were wanting; and without them, neither before nor since the time of these eminent men, could mere moral dialectics have any satisfactory result. Even yet our knowledge is excessively defective; we stand merely on the threshold of an acquaintance with the true sexual morality; but still I believe that with the materials afforded us by medical and moral research, together with the conclusions of political economy, it is possible to lay sure and natural foundations in this most important matter.

Before proceeding to the consideration of this great question, I shall give a short sketch of prostitution (of which, as of all other sexual subjects, so little is generally known,) in order to render somewhat more complete, the picture of the awful existing state of the sexual world. I shall then examine into the *great fundamental cause* of these evils, and the possibility of their prevention.

PROSTITUTION.

THE following description of this great social evil is in the main taken from the celebrated work of M. Parent Duchatelet. Several English works have been written on the same subject, but their authors have all drawn largely from him ; and their statements moreover, as far as I am acquainted with them, are not so trustworthy, from the want of that great caution and statistical accuracy, for which M. Duchatelet was so remarkable. He was a man, who devoted his whole life to the prosecution of sanitary researches, and was among the first and the chief of those eminent French physicians, whose statistical enquiries on medical subjects, have given quite a new aspect to the knowledge of disease. He spent the last eight years of his life in collecting and arranging the materials for his work on prostitution ; a work which for its accuracy, its benevolent spirit, and its interesting details, is of surpassing value. It is of prostitution in the city of Paris, that he treats : but as its character is essentially the same in all places, except as far as regards the peculiar surveillance of the Police in Paris, his description will give us a very true idea of the subject in our own large towns.

The question first arises "what is a prostitute?" To this the law answers, that it is one, who openly and with little or no distinction of persons, sells her favors for money: and who with this object endeavours to make herself publicly known as a prostitute. On the contrary, the woman, who does not court notoriety, but admits few lovers and in secret, although she receive money, cannot, and dare not, under penalty of damages for libel, be called a prostitute. This distinction is in Paris of great importance, for the police of that city exercise a surveillance over all the public prostitutes, who are obliged to enrol themselves in a registry, to receive sanitary visits &c., while they have no control over any other women. Hence the numbers, habits of life, and destiny of the prostitutes are much better known in Paris, than in any other city: and this gave M. Duchatelet facilities for gathering information, which he could have had nowhere else.

The number of prostitutes in Paris can thus be readily calculated, and is found to be much less, than the public opinion, ever prone to exaggeration on such matters, computes it. In 1831 there were about

3500 prostitutes in Paris. Very few of these, not more than 40 or 50, were foreigners; the rest were all Frenchwomen, of whom Paris alone furnished about half. The great majority are the daughters of working men, small tradesmen, and all the poorest classes of the community; very few indeed are from the upper classes. In Paris the proportion of illegitimate children and of foundlings among them, is estimated at about one-fourth. Their numbers in the towns of this country are not known; but probably they are much greater in proportion to the inhabitants than in France, where the moral code is not nearly so strictly observed by the rest of the sex as in this country, and where therefore they are not in such demand. The Bishop of Oxford estimated the prostitutes in London at 80,000; the magistrate Colquhoun at 50,000; but probably these numbers are exaggerated. However there is no doubt that in this respect as in almost all others, prostitution is a far graver evil in this country than on the continent.

Prostitutes may be divided into two classes, viz, those who live together in an establishment under the superintendence of a mistress; and those who live singly, whether in hired rooms of their own, or without any fixed abodes; lodging by the night, wherever fortune or misfortune may send them. Establishments of the former description are called in France, Maisons publiques, or Maisons tolerees, (public, or tolerated houses,) from the fact that the police administration grants them permission to be opened in certain localities. It does so, because it has found by long experience, that the presence of such houses is much more favourable to the public tranquility, than that each girl should live separately; as these houses have a character to support, and their mistresses are careful to avoid any disturbances which would damage their interests; and moreover they are much more easily brought under the inspection of the police. When any one wishes to set up a house of this kind in Paris, she has to apply for permission to the Prefect of the Police; who grants it or not, according as the applicant is considered a fit person, or the locality where she wishes to reside, a suitable one. These houses are not permitted in any quiet part of the town, where the inhabitants are all of the richer classes; nor close to a church, or school, as they would there present too striking a contrast; but in the populous streets they are confounded in the crowd. The police are always willing to tolerate them in the lowest parts of the town, as they purge, as it were, and collect into one focus, much of the vice and dissipation of the locality; and are a much better guarantee for the public tranquillity, than the private debauchery in the small taverns, &c., which leads to so much venereal disease and crime, and over which the police have much less control.

These houses are kept by *mistresses*, (dames de maison) who carry them on as a speculation, and sometimes make large fortunes by them. These women have in many cases been themselves prostitutes, and have, like many of that class, looked forward to this position as the height of their ambition; others have been kept mistresses; others again are married women, though the latter are found only in the poorest localities in Paris, where their husband probably keeps a neighbouring tavern, and they mutually share the profits. These house-mistresses, having obtained permission to open such a house, receive into it a certain number of girls, to whom they give board, lodging, and clothes, all of the most sumptuous kind. For this the girls give in return all the money they receive from visitors, none of which they are allowed to retain. This is the French agreement, but in this country I believe they generally keep a share of their gains, while they pay for their board, clothing, &c. In Paris the mistresses, who are for the most part, indeed it may be said almost without exception, of the most rapacious character, treating the girls worse than the most unfeeling labourer does his beasts of burden, sending them away without the least compunction the moment their charms have ceased to be productive, and hence cordially detested by all—vie with each other in making the living and clothing of their establishment, which is all the girls have to look for, as alluring as possible. They have no pity on the unfortunates, who are never permitted to refuse any suitor, however repugnant to them. All of them have this peculiar characteristic, that they think their occupation as justifiable as any other mode of industry, are very jealous of the dignity of their position, and enraged at any slight shown towards them. They exact from their girls the greatest deference, which is often very useful in maintaining their influence, and keeping order in the establishment. They live luxuriously, and thus often become exceedingly fat. They use every means which flattery and cajolery can suggest, to ingratiate themselves with those girls, who by their beauty and attractions are a source of gain to them; but this is generally solely for their own self-interest, and the deceit is rarely successful.

But they have other and more shameful means of binding these unfortunates to themselves. They are always anxious to get the girls some way into their debt, by lending them money to buy clothes, or other luxuries; and as these debts are generally held sacred, they in this manner hold them in their power. They frequently however sustain great losses by the girls deserting them, and carrying off their borrowed clothes, which are sometimes very valuable. There are constant complaints at the police board of such thefts. At first the complainants were advised to address themselves to the criminal tribunal, for the police board does not adjudicate in crimes; but the house-mistresses always shun anything which brings them before the public, as this injures their establishment. Therefore the police are wont to send for the culprits, and threaten them with prison, unless they restore the stolen clothes; and if this fail, which seldom happens, they wait till the girl is taken up for some public offence against decency, and then increase the severity of the penalty.

It may seem strange that girls should be willing to expose themselves to infection, and to all the disagreeables of such a life, without the prospect of any pecuniary gain; but this is owing to their, for the most part, extremely destitute state, many not having even a rag of their own to cover them. A large number of them are recruited from the hospitals in Paris, to which the girls from the surrounding country generally come, when suffering from venereal diseases; which, shameful to say, at the time when Duchatelet wrote, (viz., twenty years ago I know not how it may be now,) were in many provincial places not received into hospital. There are always several women in these large hospitals in league with the house-mistresses, who are on the look out for pretty country girls. They have also emissaries in many other quarters; some in the country, as travelling agents, &c.; others in town, such as the marchandes de toilettes, women who buy and sell old and new articles of female dress, and having been for the most part prostitutes themselves, tempt the servant girls, sempstresses, &c., to follow the same course. The mistresses also frequently exchange their girls with other establishments; although they generally bear towards such establishments much ill-will and rivalry; and nothing so provokes these feelings, as if another have succeeded in luring away from them a profitable inmate. To prevent the explosions of revenge, which frequently followed such abductions by rivals in the neighbourhood, the police thought it necessary to enact, that no girl should go to a neighbouring house, in less than fifteen days after leaving her former place.

Besides the gains which the girls earn by the ordinary exercise of their calling, the mistresses often make large sums, by allowing them to be taken out by the day or week, to pleasure parties in the country, or elsewhere. For this they receive from one to four or five pounds, according to the beauty, and still more the agreeability, of the girl. They also make much money, by letting their apartments as receiving rooms for an hour or two. In Paris they are obliged to take a whole house for their establishment; and therefore they let those rooms, which they do not require, to single prostitutes, who pay an exorbitant rent for them, and also for clothes, &c.; or else give a certain proportion or all their gains. These houses are in general very profitable to the proprietors, for they let at a high rent, and as soon as one tenant quits, another eagerly takes them; for when a house has once been used for this purpose, it continues to be so ever afterwards. Numberless petitions are sent in to the police by the residents in any locality, even the very lowest, where a house has been established, against this nuisance; but these are never listened to, and the police answer, that the same objections might be made in every quarter.

The house-mistresses, if they be orderly and provident, sometimes make large fortunes, with which they may withdraw to the country, and purchase a property. If however they be disorderly and spendthrift, and especially if they have several lovers, whom they entertain, and in whose society their attention to their establishment is distracted, they infallibly become bankrupt. Some grow old and die in the business, and bequeath it to their successors, perhaps an old servant or confidant; one or two of whom are always found in these houses, where they do the household work, help the mistress in her marketings, stand at the door to indicate the nature of the establishment to the passers by, &c.; having generally themselves grown old in a life of prostitution.

The other class of prostitutes are those who live *separately*, each providing for herself and being her own mistress. This life is much more to the taste of the girls, for a love of freedom and independence is one of the most marked characteristics of the class. In this mode of living, their gains belong to themselves; they can if they please make some choice among their suitors; and they can change their abode when they please, and exercise their calling, now in one quarter of the town now in another, and on holidays in the suburbs round Paris. Thus it was found by the police that the number of girls in the tolerated houses, was very small, until the enactment of several regulations, imposing restrictions on some of the practices of the separate girls; such as their inviting men on the public street, appearing in gaudy costumes, or stationing themselves in the Palais Royal and other public places; but since these regulations, the number of girls in the houses rose to one-third of the whole number of prostitutes.

Some of the independent prostitutes live in furnished rooms of their own, and in these a few of them receive their visitors; but more frequently they take them to a receiving house (maison de passe), where rooms are let by the hour or more, at a certain sum. These receiving houses are resorted to by all, who either have no home, where they can receive a lover, or wish to do so in secrecy, such as married women, maidservants, &c.; the latter of whom find time when going a message, to spend half-an-hour in these places, without losing their character. Some of them are especially frequented by the actresses, who are so numerous a class in Paris. Many endeavours have been made by the police to bring these receiving houses, which Duchatelet says are far more dangerous to morals and to health, than the tolerated houses, under their control; but no practicable method could be found; so they were contented with enforcing the residence of at least two registered prostitutes in the house, which acted as a check on the mistress, preventing her from aiding in the prostitution of children, and other offences; and also necessitating frequent sanitary visits to the house, which kept it under the eye of the police.

The isolated prostitutes frequent all the public places, the crowded streets, theatres, and other places of amusement, where they attract their visitors. They frequently become inmates of the tolerated houses for a time; and the girls in these houses, on the other hand, are as constantly changing to the separate mode of life: indeed nothing is more characteristic of the class than their necessity of locomotion, and restless change of place. At one time this was pushed to such an extreme in Paris, that they used to change their abodes once a week; and the police had to enact that they should stay at least twenty-five days in any tolerated house they might go to, in order to check the great confusion caused by this restlessness.

While one division of the isolated girls live in a room of their own, there is another very large class, who have no fixed lodgings; but live, as many thousands of the poorest workmen and vagrants in Paris prefer to do, from night to night in any place where chance may lead them. The lodging houses (garnis) to which they resort, are of the most miserable, squalid, tumble-down description, that imagination can conceive; the stairs covered with filth and ordure, the beds full of vermin. Here quarters are given at from one to three-pence a-night; and the poor prostitutes, here as elsewhere, are treated as those who have no friends, and made to pay more than others. These lodging houses have always been a thorn in the side of the police, for in them the prostitutes hide themselves, and carry on their calling without submitting to the sanitary visits : and as the police have no hold upon them, unless they be taken in the flagrant act of prostitution, they almost always escape free, and spread venereal infection on every side.

A peculiar class of girls are those, who are called the *soldiers' girls*, (filles a soldats.) These, who are always to be found in the neighbourhood of any place where soldiers are quartered, have in general followed their lovers from the country up to Paris ; and then have been obliged to take to prostitution, as a means of subsistence, separated as they are from all their friends. They sell their favours at the lowest price, one or twopence, and even, the unfortunate ones, for a morsel of bread, which they are too often in want of, their soldier lovers having nothing to give them ; for the French soldier receives only one penny a-day in Paris, and a half-penny in the country. The generous fellows have been known to half-starve themselves to give to their mistresses : so that a colonel of a regiment, having detected the cause of the emaciation of some of his men, gave orders that all should be searched on leaving the barracks ; but it was to no purpose, for the girls used to come under the windows, and receive the bread thrown out to them. They sleep at night in the lodging houses, and spend the day in the taverns and eating houses in the neighbourhood of the barracks ; where they dance and romp with the soldiers, and retire with them to dark closets, (cabinets noirs,) in which venereal contagion spreads like wild-fire. This mode of prostitution sets at defiance the police, who cannot succeed in obtaining control over these rebels ; for their escape is always favoured by the tavern-keepers, to whom the girls bring many customers, and cause a much greater amount of drinking and other expenditure. They try therefore to have as many girls as possible about their premises. Quantity is more regarded than quality, and indeed this class of girls are for the most part dreadfully ugly ; so much so, as Duchatelet says, that "it is only with drunken men and in the dark, that they could hope to find favour." In these low taverns, all sorts of criminals, thieves, pickpockets, &c., join in the amusement ; and the soldiers by mingling with them must necessarily lose in their order and discipline.

There are other prostitutes of a still lower class, who go by the name of *pierreuses* (girls of the stones) from the fact that, in consequence of their abject destitution, they often pass the night in unfinished buildings, in outhouses, or wherever they can find a place to lay their head. They have generally grown old in a life of prostitution, and are so hideously ugly, that they seek dark, sombre, and deserted places to hide their appearance. The name by which they call themselves, "masturbaters," (manuelles) indicates that their usual method of exciting and satisfying the sexual appetites, is anything but the normal one. In fact they are ready to lend themselves to all those artifices and degradations of licentiousness, which go under the name of unnatural vices. It is true that their natures are excessively degraded ; fear and hatred have, it can readily be believed, well-nigh extinguished in their breasts the natural feelings of love and kindness. Knowing the opinion of the world towards them, knowing the treatment they have received from it, hatred and secret outrages against the feelings of society have become their chief strength and support against despair. If society have cast them forth, they have their revenge in doing what they can to degrade and outrage the morality which scorns them.

I may take this opportunity of saying a few words on the subject of *unnatural vices*. These are said to be very common in Paris, in London. and other large cities; where every artifice that can whet a morbid and sated sexual appetite, is in the crowd of human beings, not only devised, but put in execution. A subject like this is generally held to be an unspeakable one, as if it would soil both him who talks of it and those who listen. But he who really loves truth, and his fellow creatures, has little sympathy with this rose-water morality; which cannot bear to scrutinise the deeds of our fellow-beings, nor even to hear of things which are daily done and suffered. Such scruples are as alien to the heart of the true moralist, as it would be for the true physician to shun the infectious disease, or to fly from the disagreeables of the dissecting room and dead-house. The very dread of approaching such subjects shows an inherent weakness and effeminacy in the mind, which all who desire really to aid their fellow creatures, should endeavour to divest themselves of. It is not the duty of the physician or moralist alone, to investigate the various phases of disease and crime; every one should be so much of a physician as at least to be willing to hear of, and seek to benefit all human ills, whatever be their nature. One of the chief reasons, why the mind of woman is so undeveloped, and her character so unreal and effeminate, is, that she is debarred from studying the phases of vice or crime in the moral world, as well as disease and decay in the physical; an error in her education, which destroys her powers of usefulness in vast numbers of the most serious evils of her fellow-beings. What can one do for others, if he or she do not know their real lives and their real actions? if they shrink back in dismay at every step, from the hideous forms of sin, which meet them, when they approach the realities of human suffering?

Sodomy, or the intercourse of two persons of the same sex, is common enough, especially in the prisons, where the most uneducated and degraded of the community, being shut up together, and left in idleness, take this mode of passing the listless hours. Instances now and then occur in venereal hospitals, of gonorrhœa or chancre of the anus, which the patients, when pressed hard, either confess, or tacitly admit to have been contracted by these unnatural practices; although at first, they always deny that the disease has such an origin, and ascribe it to an unclean water-closet, &c. The same diseases are much more frequently seen in the female venereal hospitals, especially in the one annexed to the prostitute prison; and Duchatelet remarks, that there are very few of the older prostitutes, who do not lend themselves to these practices, as well as many of the younger ones. However they always maintain an obstinate silence, when questioned on this point. Voltaire, Rabelais and other

writers (like Juvenal and Martial, under the Roman empire) make
several allusions to these practices: showing that even monarchs (for
instance Frederic the Great) were habitually guilty of them; and this
proves that they must exist to a considerable extent. Evils of such
gravity point to a serious want of reverence for nature; and demand a
much more earnest treatment, than either jesting allusions, or impotent
avoidance of the subject.

There is yet another unnatural sexual habit of much greater importance from its great frequency, on which M. Duchatelet gives some most
interesting details. It is the mutual loves between prostitutes themselves;
which are so common that, he says, about one fourth of their number
engage in them, including almost all the older ones; who are naturally
the most depraved. This class are called *tribades*, and the singular sexual
relation they bear to each other, much resembles the unnatural custom
of lovers among the Greek youth; who, like these prostitutes of the
present day, made it rather a boast to despise the other sex. In this
singular connection, two prostitutes enter into sexual relations with each
other, with all the ardour, impetuosity, and tenderness of passion,
that the most intense normal sexual love could inspire. They devote
themselves to each other, and practice together all devices of unnatural
voluptuousness. They feel for each other all the conflicting sexual passions, now burning with jealousy, now melting with tenderness; they
are distracted at separation, and follow each other every where. If the
one be committed to prison, the other gets herself also arrested, and they
seek to leave it together. They are much more jealous of desertion by
their female lover than by a male one; and if one has proved false, her
companion will seek revenge in every way. It is chiefly in the prostitute
prisons, where they are confined for breaches of the public decorum, that
such connections are formed. Here young girls are shut up together, often
for several months at a time; and thus it is not to be wondered at, that
they take to such practices, just as the male criminals do in the common
prisons. It is generally the older ones, who have been frequently in
prison, who cajole and entice the younger into such connections;
and the most ardent passion is generally found on the side of the younger.
"Thus," says Duchatelet, "they become in their old age more dangerous
for their own sex, than they have been in their youth for the other."
This class of unnatural lovers is generally recognised by the rest of the
prostitutes, who regard them with something of the general feeling of
disgust, and are not sparing in sarcasms, and sly allusions towards
them. They themselves veil all their practices in the greatest secrecy;
and, if ever questioned on the subject, answer indignantly, "We are
for men, and not for women," (nous sommes pour hommes, et non pas
pour femmes.) Many of the older prostitutes come at last to abhor all
men, and take pleasure only in these unnatural relations; a singular and
significant fact in these unfortunates, whose sexual experiences with the
other sex have been so painful and degrading.

In reviewing the whole subject of unnatural vices, I feel a deep and
earnest conviction, that it, like all others connected with the sexual
desires, requires to be regarded in a very different light, from that, which

is usual at present. One of the greatest causes of all irregularities in the sexual appetites is the destructive checks, obstacles, and degradations, to which they are exposed in their normal course. This has been shown to be the chief cause of masturbation, and so it is of these unnatural practices. The present harsh views of sexual morality give, at the outset, an underhand and degraded position to all unmarried intercourse, which is very favourable to the growth of the unnatural propensities. If even the normal sexual love be obliged to fly from the eyes of men, to hide itself in cabinets noirs, or other shameful retreats, what can we expect, that it will not degenerate into?

Again, all these vices have met with an opprobrium, far greater than they deserved; for the public mind loses all sense of justice, when it comes to consider a sexual fault, and is always far too harsh in its judgments. I should say, that of all acts none are viewed with such unjust severity, as these unnatural vices. A sentence which is too severe, is always, like Draco's laws, a very evil one; not based on natural justice, it rather provokes people into the commission of the acts it reprobates; which, like all those that are forbidden with a harshness and mystery unsuited to their gravity, have a kind of fascination for man. The moral guilt ascribed to such acts, which many people regard with as much horror and indignation as they do murder, incendiarism, or other crime of the first magnitude, is quite out of proportion to the physical evil they really cause; and this unsound physical basis shakes, as it will do in every case, the moral superstructure.

The true mode of eradicating these unnatural vices, is not to regard with horror and merciless disgust those who indulge in them; but with a loving and reverential spirit to examine into their nature, and remove their causes by the light of a true physical religion. Vice and crime are not to be bullied, nor suppressed, by any amount of so-called virtuous indignation; they depend on fixed and definite causes in our social circumstances, and till these can be changed, all our indignation and disgust are thrown to the winds. As long as the present obstacles continue to the gratification of the normal desires; as long as all unmarried love is regarded in a harsh and degrading light; so long will prostitution and unnatural vices flourish, and it will be out of human power to suppress them.

These observations lead me to an allied subject, namely, *clandestine* prostitution. By this is meant the prostitution of young girls before the age of puberty; an offence which is in France a criminal one, cognisable, and severely punishable, by the legal tribunals. Notwithstanding these laws, it is practised to a great extent in Paris, but in the most secret way. All kinds of devices are taken to hide it from the police. Thus the young girls or children of from ten to fourteen years of age, having been enticed into this life by some procuress, are either kept by a woman, who passes for their mother; or they merely go to play in her rooms during the day, by which artifice they can be said not to be kept on the premises; or perhaps a woman leads them about asking charity, or with other pretexts, to the hotels or houses where they may be required. All kinds of stratagems are resorted to, to escape the police, and thus they are very rarely detected. When they are so, it is generally from information given either by a house-mistress, jealous of her illicit rivals, or by some one who has received venereal infection from the children ; for diseases rage among these poor children with the greatest virulence, and they are a focus of infection. The cause of this severity of the diseases among them, is the dread of exposure, which prevents their mistresses from applying for medical aid for them. The little girls of course acquire the most dissipated habits ; and often, at the age of ten or twelve, are well-versed in every kind of debauchery. Even when the police do get information, they can scarcely ever succeed in convicting the offenders. In the first place it is necessary to have a search warrant to enter the house, and then the girls must be caught in the flagrant act of prostitution ; so that the parties almost always escape, as their character is generally supported by their neighbours, so ingeniously is this prostitution concealed.

There is yet another class of prostitutes, who should be mentioned. These are the *thievish* ones, a very numerous class. They are generally in league with pickpockets and other thieves, among whom they have their lovers and their bullies. Some of these girls are in the habit of accosting old men, and those who are least likely to follow them. When repulsed, they still persist ; and when shaken off, they raise a tumult, or else pick the pockets of their victims. Others will follow a raw and inexperienced youth, and surround him in a band ; and while he is defending himself from their pressing invitations, they treat him in the same way. Others watch and dodge drunken people. Many of the comparatively honest class of prostitutes do not hesitate to take any stray article from the pockets of their visitors ; but this they scarcely call stealing, it is only " minding their business." Those of the higher classes however, are generally above such actions, and the only thefts, which they are often guilty of, consist in the clothes lent them by the house-mistresses. Few of the above thefts meet with punishment ; for in general those who are robbed, do not like to prosecute, fearing the laughter or ridicule of society, and are contented to take their losses as an experience.

Besides the above-mentioned varieties of professed prostitutes, there are other classes, who either follow similar courses in a private way, or who in different modes aid prostitution. Those who go under the name of *femmes galantes* (courtezans), are for the most part kept-mistresses, who admit other lovers in order to increase their means of expenditure. Their great solicitude is to conceal their amours from those who keep them ; and thus they do not openly expose themselves, but allow themselves to be followed to their houses or to a convenient place, by those who are on the look-out for women of this class. They put a higher price on their favours, than the others ; and are often very attractive from the more select society they keep. The actresses also form a class, who have their peculiar manners and attractions. In Paris, where all modes of life abound, there are some women, who receive their lovers only during certain hours in the day ; after which they shut their door, and spend the evenings with their own favourite lovers at the balls and theatres. One of them, (to give an idea of the various methods they adopt,) guaranteed the health of all her visitors ; to secure which, she admitted only a select company of some fifty married men, who were allowed to join the society only with the consent of the rest, and were excluded if they became widowers.

The class of *procuresses* (proxenetes) is a large one, and plays an important part. They are for the most part women, who have been themselves prostitutes; and when age or other causes have made them abandon this mode of life, they make it their business to bring into it as many young girls as possible. They are in league with the house-mistresses, who pay them according to their success. Very many of them are marchandes de toilettes, and buy and sell articles of dress and of the toilette to servants and ladies-maids, whom they do all they can to seduce to prostitution.

Another set of women, called *marcheuses* (duennas) are the domestics in tolerated houses, and are generally old prostitutes, who have acquired great skill and tact in the exercise of that calling. Their business is to stand at the door of the house to show its nature, and also to walk about with the girls, and offer them adroitly to the passengers. These women are always in greater demand, when the police regulations are more strict.

Having thus given a sketch of the various classes of prostitutes, let us now inquire into their mode of life. Nine-tenths of them, says Duchatelet, spend their leisure time in complete idleness; lounging on a sofa or in bed, with scarcely the energy to go through the fatigue of dressing. Those of the lower class spend the day in taverns, where they eat and drink to excess, and talk with the idle characters who frequent these places. These excessive indulgences of the appetites are common to almost all prostitutes; and the latter, namely drinking, forms the greatest and most dangerous vice of the life they lead. Many of them eat as much as would serve three or four ordinary women; and to this and to their indolent life is to be ascribed the excessive fatness, to which they frequently attain. The grand vice of *drinking* however, is their bane; almost all of them drink to a greater or less degree. In the lower classes, drunkenness is almost habitual, and often plunges them into a slough of despond, physically and morally hopeless. The unfortunates are led to this ruinous habit at first, from the wish to banish care, and escape from thought and the stings of conscience; and it grows rapidly upon them. There is another reason which operates with this class, that the soldiers and workmen with whom they consort, think that if a girl does not drink, it is because she is diseased; knowing as they do the evil effects of drink upon venereal disease in themselves. Thus the unhappy girls are often forced to drink even against their inclination; and after several such orgies with different parties, they may be seen reeling along the streets, lying down in door-ways, or, if more sober, begging an asylum at the police-stations. Another cause which leads to their drinking, especially in this country, is to get over the feelings of shyness and bashfulness, felt by the girls themselves on first taking to this mode of life; and frequently by those also who are unused to the society of such girls.

The prostitutes of a higher class, rarely get drunk, as they know this would alienate all their suitors; but they drink large quantities of punch and wine, and this in time often leads to the same calamitous results. Few of them engage in sewing or other work in leisure hours, and still fewer in reading, though of course there are exceptions; and among their numbers there are some of considerable musical accomplishments. From

the habit they have, of always trying to drown serious reflection, they
come generally to have a peculiarly unstable fickle character of mind. It
is very difficult to fix their attention for any time upon a subject, or to
make them follow a train of reasoning. They have an extraordinary
love of locomotion, change of scene, and of action ; tumult is a favourite
element, for tempests drown the still small voice within.

Children of impulse, there are yet many impulses to which they are
rarely false ; among others to a strong esprit du corps, which induces the
friendless sisterhood, never to desert each other in adversity. If one of
them be unwell, or in destitution, they haste to offer her aid, even if they
have to strip themselves in so doing. In leaving the prison or hospital, if
one have no clothes, the others will lend her parts of their own apparel, even
though they may have had previous experience of her ingratitude. Some
have been known to aid in the support of poor old men, or other helpless
beings ; and not a few enter on this mode of life, to support infirm parents
or starving orphans. They make common cause against the police,
whom they all regard as their sworn enemies ; and rarely inculpate each
other.

Besides the peculiar instability of character, the class is distinguished
for its lying habits. Viewing all men as their enemies, trying at first to
deceive their parents and afterwards the police, being obliged constantly
to feign unreal feelings in their unnatural mode of life, their singleness
of nature becomes at last completely perverted, and it is as difficult to fix
them as the wind. The young ones are not well versed in this deceit,
and frequently contradict themselves, but the older ones are great adepts
in it : and hence those who busy themselves with the reformation of
prostitutes, such as the sisters of charity and other well-meaning persons,
have great distrust of the latter ; and no girl above 25, or under 18 years
of age is admitted into the Magdalen asylums in Paris.

With regard to the feelings, which they entertain towards their visitors, it may be said as a general rule, that when once the fresh appetite
for sexual gratification is over, they remain very indifferent to them ;
although there are certainly many, in whom the sense of sexual enjoyment remains keen for a long time, and who may continue this mode of life
with no other purpose than to gratify their insatiable desires. This general apathy to the venereal pleasures is probably the reason why prostitutes
suffer so little from their sexual excesses. The evils of excess are, I
believe rarely seen in them ; but rather in young married women, in whom
sexual intercourse is attended by the normal sensations.

If the heart of the prostitutes remains in general icy cold towards the
common crowd of those, with whom they consort, it is always warm
towards some favourite lover, who is really dear to them, and on whom
they lavish all their fondness. These, their real lovers, are not only admitted in general to their favours free of expense, but many receive
presents from their mistresses ; and not a few young men in Paris are
maintained entirely by the gains of their prostitute mistresses. When a
girl enters a tolerated house in Paris, she always stipulates for her lover's
admission, it may be three or four times a-week, free of expense ; and
these and other privileges are granted, for without them the girls would

not remain. These *lovers* are the bane of the house-mistresses. They are taken from all classes of society. The girls of a higher class generally choose some of the better ranks, preferring generally the students of law, medicine, or other branches. Those of the middle classes, take their lovers from among the tradespeople and shopmen, such as the journeymen tailors, jewellers &c. The lowest class choose theirs among the soldiers or workmen, and often from among the thieves and vagabonds of all descriptions, who are so rife in large capitals. The lowest class of sweethearts go by the name of *bullies* or supporters (souteneurs.) Their part is, to screen as much as possible, their mistresses from the police; if the girls wish to do anything against the regulations, their friends keep guard, and give warning, if any police inspector be seen approaching. If the girls be apprehended, their lovers try to raise a tumult, and by crowding the inspector, to rescue them. Sometimes they even come to blows. Again if any one has brought to punishment a girl, by whom he has been robbed, or who has given him a disease, the bullies, if they get hold of him, will not fail to take revenge, by serving him some ill turn. Hence this class of sweethearts is a thorn in the side of the police, who have often sought to put them down, but without success. They often act most tyrannically towards the girls. over whom they have gained an ascendancy; they learn whenever the latter have gained any money, and force them to spend it with them in drinking; so that the bond, by which their unfortunate mistresses are attached to them, is often one of fear rather than of love.

Indeed, it is rare that a prostitute meets with a return of affection from her favourite: on the contrary, this very tie, which the friendless one clings to, to fill the void in her breast, often proves the crown of her afflictions. The girls of the higher class are very often forsaken by their lovers, and suffer all the pangs of jealousy; a passion, of which all prostitutes are more susceptible than perhaps any other connected with love; while the lower classes often receive the most barbarous treatment from their tyrants, which their love frequently induces them to endure to a most incredible degree.

We can however conceive how this may be, when we reflect how much greater charms has reality, however painful, than the most splendid delusions; and what is nine-tenths of the life of a prostitute, but a tissue of delusions and counterfeits—feigned love, feigned pleasures everything feigned, but grief and embitterment; from which unrealities, they turn with double eagerness to their own true loves, the oases of their desert, however many disappointments or real anguish they may bring. With their lovers it is their delight to visit places of amusement, especially the dancing parties and public balls, which in Paris are so numerous, and afford so much happiness to youth; to exchange letters, burning with protestations of the most fervent passion, in which no obscene expressions are to be found; to share in fine " the hope, the fear, the jealous care " of love, even though its pain should so often predominate over its pleasures. If they ever become pregnant, they almost always ascribe this state to their lovers; for they have the very general belief, which prevails among women, that it is only when they love a man, and have an active share in the enjoyment of the venereal act, that they can be impregnated: a belief not warranted by science, for besides the numberless instances of women having children by those, whom they disliked or resisted, it has been shown, that even the introduction of semen into the vagina without coition, has in the lower animals been followed by fecundation. Still, very probably, there is some truth in the belief; and the subject certainly requires more elucidation, like all others connected with the intricate question of reproduction.

It is well known that pregnancies are comparatively very rare among prostitutes; a fact which is admitted by Duchatelet, though he shows that they are considerably more frequent, than is generally supposed. The reasons why they are so rare, are chiefly, the very intemperate and unnatural life which prostitutes lead, venereal diseases which often obstruct the entrance of the semen into the womb, subacute ovaritis, or adhesions between the fallopian tubes and peritoneum, brought on by venereal excesses; especially, it may be supposed, when these are indulged in during menstruation. Even during menstruation the work of prostitution suffers no interruption; for they make use of some means, by which they prevent the discharge from being apparent. Duchatelet, who mentions this, does not tell explicitly what these means are, from scruples which are very unsatisfactory to the investigator of truth; but we may suppose, that it is by some delicate membrane of similar materials with the sheath, with which they cover the vagina so as to retain the discharge. This means was also used to conceal disease from the sanitary examiners; but this deceit is now too well known to the medical men to be available.

Such abnormal excesses interfere greatly with menstruation, which in prostitutes is very often irregular, and absent for long periods. Several of these cases of amenorrhœa are owing to pregnancy, and are terminated by abortion; which is very common among prostitutes, and partly explains the rarity of childbirth. These abortions frequently occur at an early period of pregnancy, and are caused by their intemperate mode of life, rarely by criminal practises. Cases however do sometimes occur, in which death has been inflicted on the young fœtus by abortions, intentionally produced by instrumental means; and others where girls have been nearly killed by drugs taken by them for the same purpose. But these attempts are rare, for in general pregnancy is not at all dreaded by prostitutes; nay, it is often the object of their desires. Instead of diminishing, it increases their gains in a town like Paris, where everything at all out of the common renders a girl much sought after; such as, to give other examples, very tall or extremely diminutive stature, or even deformities, such as a humpbacked or crippled person, &c. Besides, child-birth, which to the modest unmarried girl is an object of the greatest dread, bringing with it, as it does, degradation in the eyes of the world, is rather ennobling to the prostitute, who takes a pride in fulfilling the maternal duties in the most tender manner; feeling that nothing raises her more in the opinion of others, and of herself, than having something really to love. Hence they are very fond mothers, and are tended in child-bed with the greatest attention and care by the other girls. The infant when born, becomes the object of the general care; and each vies with the other in performing towards it all the necessary acts of kindness.

As for the ultimate fate of these poor infants, everything proves that, almost without exception, they soon die, much to the grief of their mothers. Their premature deaths are to be ascribed to the intemperate lives of their parents, amid whose frequent intoxication and exposure to the inclemen-cies of the weather, they cannot long survive. The prostitutes rarely send their children to the foundling hospital, at which so many children are reared in Paris.

Having given this short sketch of the manners and morals of this class, let us now direct our attention to their *physical* life ; without a knowledge of which, our materials for judging of any human being are always of necessity most incomplete. Is prostitution injurious to the health ? is a question which few moralists have taken the trouble of asking, in their stormy denunciations of the subject ; and yet it is one so vitally impor-tant, that it may be called, like all other physical facts, the keystone of the whole. Duchatelet, after enumerating the diseases to which prosti-tutes are liable, for all of which he has statistical data, comes to the con-clusion, which he says is a very striking and sad one, that their mode of life with all its intemperance, and exposure to infection and inclemencies of the weather, is a much healthier one on the whole, than that of the needlewomen, sempstresses, and other females, whose occupations are of a sedentary and unrelaxing nature. Thus then, in one respect, the phy-sico-moralist will acknowledge that the life of the latter classes is a more sinful one than that of the prostitutes ; and for him who reverences the physical equally with the moral laws of health and virtue, this is readily intelligible ; for certainly the life of motion, sexual exercise, leisure, plenty of food, and variety of circumstance is much more healthy, and therefore more physically religious, than the constraint, hard work, and animal torpor, to which our unfortunate sempstresses are confined ; a state of sin against the natural laws, no less than of misery, which the physico-moralist must blame, if blame is ever to find its way between the loving heart and the sorrows of humanity. It is true that the unhappy ones cannot help their own sedentary and ruinous pursuits, that thy are fixed into them by the iron hand of necessity ; butthat does not make them less unnatural, and opposed to all the laws of moral and physical health.

The two greatest physical dangers to the prostitute are *syphilis* and *drinking*. Of the former I shall speak hereafter, in inquiring into the social question of its prevention. If it were not for the latter, namely drinking, a great part of the destruction moral and physical, attendant on their mode of life, would be taken away. It is true that the evil effects of it are not so prominent, as on those who work hard, especially at sedentary occupations, these banes of civilization, and drink at the same time ; a combination of exhausting causes, which no constitution can long withstand, and which gives rise to the ghastly lives and early deaths of our most wretched weavers, sweated tailors, and other unhappy classes, for whose bloody sweat, and miserable lives-in-death the heart of England is groaning. The impulse and excitement moreover caused by the sexual gratifications, give a buoyancy to the constitution, which enable it to bear much more deleterious liquors, than it otherwise could; which reasons account for the robust health, which prostitutes so often enjoy, and which makes some physicians ascribe to them "frames of iron" (santes de fer.) Mr. Acton says, "I shall be borne out by the concurrent testimony of all observers in the statement, that no class of females is so free from general diseases as the prostitutes." Still, drinking causes the ultimate ruin of very many of them.

Besides the evils it produces, which tell on the constitution later in life, causing diseases of the liver, kidneys, and blood-vessels, and making them very subject to inflammatory diseases; the affections to which prostitutes are most subject are sexual ones, such as amenorrhœa, menorrhagia, &c., and also wounds caused by violence. The uterine bleedings are caused by the excesses of their life, which over-stimulate the ovaries, and doubtless are frequently consequent on the abortions, which are with them so numerous.

Insanity is not uncommon among them; a fact which might have been expected, from the very violent and unbridled passions, to which they are subject; from the degraded, unhappy, and therefore mentally unhealthy condition in which they live; and from their extraordinary moral position, so apt to cause perturbed and maddening reflections in these despised pariahs of society. Duchatelet was struck by the frequency of weakness and imbecility of intellect, which he observed to be often urged, as a reason for mitigating their punishment, by the police. This imbecility was found, not among the young girls, but the old prostitutes, (among whom are several from 40 to 50 nay even to 60 years of age,) who had sunk to the lowest degree of misery and degradation. The unfortunate creatures! Let one but think of all their sufferings, the semi-consciousness of utter degradation and the merciless contempt of their fellow-beings; the feelings of revenge, hatred, and helplessness, ever growing feebler and feebler within their labouring breasts, too weak to bear such inhuman burdens; till at length reason, as if in pity, gives way! Can we conceive how much misery the growing sense of intellectual and moral decay in such wretched circumstances brings with it?

Every year many of these forlorn beings are sent, out of pity, to pass the winter in prison, where at that season several idiotical, mad, and imbecile ones are always to be seen. M. Esquirol, the admirable physician of the great female lunatic asylum in Paris, shows by statistical report that an average of twenty-one prostitutes annually, are received into that establishment, which is a very large proportion. Their disease is chiefly due to excess in wine, or misery; the latter arising from various causes, but principally from desertion by their sweethearts. Erotomania (madness, whose distinguishing feature is, to dwell on ideas of love and desire,) is almost unknown among these patients; their thoughts are rather occupied by dreams of wealth, power, and honours.

I now come to speak of the disease to which prostitutes are most of all exposed, namely, syphilis, and of the social means which have been taken in Paris to check its ravages. This disease, whose nature I have described before, is, as Duchatelet justly remarks, perhaps the most dreadful pestilence to which mankind is liable. Its effec.. are not, like those of epidemic pestilences, limited to certain countries and periods of time; but its extension is now universal over the surface of the globe, and in all seasons it rages unabated. "If then," says Du-chatelet, "mankind have instituted quarantines and other methods of preventing plague and cholera, should they not still more earnestly endeavour to prevent a disease, so much more terribly and widely des-tructive; of which the chief victims are among the vigorous youth, the most useful members of the state?"

Such praiseworthy motives have induced the Parisian authorities to take sanitary measures for securing the health of prostitutes, who are the centre point, whence syphilis is spread; and their efforts have been attended with signal success. These measures were first adopted with-in the present century, and consist in the compulsory enregistration of every prostitute in Paris, whose mode of life can be discovered by the police; and periodical examinations of her state of health by medical men appointed for the purpose. To secure these ends a great number of regulations had to be made and methods adopted; all of which show the consummate tact and management of the French police.

The city of Paris is divided into ten districts, for each of which there is an inspector of police, whose duties are to attend solely to the sub-ject of prostitution. These men have three duties entrusted to them. 1st. the care of the public way; 2nd. the care of the houses of prosti-tution; 3rd. the search after those girls, who will not submit to the enregistration, and also those who fail to appear at the sanitary visits. In the first of these duties, they have to watch that no breach of public decorum is made by a prostitute in the public street. If any such occur, they go up to the girl, make themselves known to her, and then seek to prevail on her by persuasion, never by violence, to go with them before the Police Board, or to follow them thither within a short time. If this gentle intimation be not obeyed, they are instructed never to use force, but to give information to the Board, who obtain constables from the executive force, and send to apprehend the culprit. But it is rarely necessary to have recourse to these means, as persuasion almost always succeeds; the girls being aware that any resistance will aggra-vate their punishment, while ready compliance and politeness to the inspector will mitigate it. Again if an inspector see a girl, who is not registered, either engaging in prostitution in a tolerated house, or in-viting people in the public street, or committing any offence against public decorum, their duty is to apprehend her, and draw up a minute account of all the circumstances under which she was taken, for the police board, to which they bring her immediately. The girl will gen-erally stoutly deny that she is engaged in prostitution; and in such a case the police, who must act with the utmost delicacy and caution, dismiss her, and do not insist on registering her, till she has been brought back three, or sometimes four times, for similar offences, which almost invariably happens. The inspectors have also to visit at short intervals the tolerated houses, and see that all the police regula-tions are there observed. Besides these duties, they have to seek out

s

the prostitutes, who fail to present themselves for sanitary examination; a duty which is often very difficult. To be able to discharge these various functions, they require much intelligence and tact, together with an intimate knowledge of the appearance of all the prostitutes in Paris; which they acquire from their presence at the registration, and frequent opportunities of seeing them.

The registration of prostitutes takes place in the three following ways; the girls present themselves of their own accord to be enrolled; or they are brought by the house-mistresses; or by the police inspectors. In the first case, the girls, knowing the necessity of complying with the police regulations, if they wish to follow such a calling, apply spontaneously for registration ; which is accorded to them, if, after a minute examination into their past and present history, no sufficient obstacle be found to their admission. In order to be certain of their personal identity, they are obliged to produce their certificate of baptism; and, as very few have it in their possession, the police send a letter to the magistrate of the parish, of which the girl says she is a native, asking for the certificate. If the girl have reached her majority, and thus be the mistress of her actions, the greatest delicacy is observed in the wording of the letter, which does not mention for what purpose the certificate is required. But if she be a minor, this purpose is expressly mentioned, and the magistrate is requested to communicate with her parents on the subject, so that they may, if they be willing, take steps for her reformation; a thing which however rarely happens, as her family, in general, cast off the unfortunate one. After receiving this certificate, assuring them of the real name of the applicant; and having previously put a number of questions to her, whether she be married or single, what are her reasons for adopting such a life, and many other queries, meant to throw a light on her history and character; the police give her a card, containing a declaration, to be signed by the girl, of her willingness to submit to the police regulations, and especially to the sanitary visits. The information received, and observations subsequently made on the girl's history, are preserved in a special memorandum at the office. The tact which the officers acquire, in judging of the character of the girls who come before them, is rendered wonderfully acute by long experience : and it is very difficult for a girl to deceive them. If they find, after sending for the certificate, that a false name has been given, they try to induce the girl by threats and various arguments to confess the truth ; and if she will not, they dismiss her, and keep her under observation, taking the opportunity of adding to her punishment for any fault she may commit; and by such means rarely fail to learn the truth. But it is seldom that false names are given, for the girls know how much more for their interest it is to comply willingly with the police regulations. The age of sixteen is fixed upon as the lowest for registration, which, in the case of minors, is conducted with great caution and delicacy ; so that it is only when the parents are unwilling to receive them, or are sunk in poverty or of bad character, that they are enrolled, though they may have been often detected in the practice of prostitution.

The next method of inscription is when they are brought to the office by the house-mistresses, who are directed under a penalty, to bring every girl, who is received into their house, to the office, within twenty-four hours after her arrival. Each house-mistress has a card with the names of all her girls upon it, and the dates and results of each sanitary visit. Duchatelet calculates that about one-third of the whole number of prostitutes are thus enrolled, while one-sixteenth are brought by the inspectors, and nearly two-thirds come of their own accord.

After receiving their cards they are examined by a medical man, who gives them a certificate of health or disease, according to which they are either dismissed or sent to the hospital for treatment. They are thenceforth subjected to the police regulations, and obliged to submit to periodical examinations by medical men. The isolated girls attend for this purpose once a fortnight at a dispensary, where they are examined with the speculum, and dismissed or kept under treatment accordingly, the day of their visit being marked on their card. The girls in the houses are examined twice as frequently, namely once a week, and if any one be found diseased, the house-mistress is bound to send her at once to the office, whence she is transferred to the venereal hospital; and if this be not attended to, and the girl be allowed to have connection with any one in the meanwhile, a very severe penalty is imposed on the house-mistress. If in any case the medical man be not satisfied of the contagious nature of a disease, (which is sometimes a most difficult question,) he consults with his colleagues; and if they be undecided, the girl is forbidden to exercise her calling for a certain time, when another examination is made. All these examinations are conducted with the utmost delicacy and propriety, so that the prostitutes may be taught in all matters apart from their own calling to behave with decorum; and by such means, together with the attention of the police, the character of the prostitutes in Paris is surprisingly improved in regard to propriety of behaviour.

Notwithstanding the more numerous examinations of the house-girls than of the separate ones, the number of the former found diseased is considerably greater than of the latter. Among the house-girls in 1832 the average of disease was 1 in 26; while among the separate ones it was only 1 in 60. This may appear strange, but on reflection the reasons for it will be evident. The single girls have it in their power to choose their suitors, to examine them, and if they please to make them adopt precautionary measures; while at the same time they are not forced to receive nearly so many visitors as the unfortunate girls in the kept-houses, who are never permitted by their inexorable mistresses to refuse any one, "even," says Duchatelet, "were he covered with ulcers."

These preventive measures, as M. Duchatelet shows by statistical tables, have been very effective in repressing disease. Among the lower orders of prostitutes, who will not submit to be enregistered, or to receive sanitary visits, and who sell their favours to crowds of the poorer classes for very small sums, it is found on the contrary, that when they are apprehended by the police, and examined, they are discovered to be diseased in the immense proportion of 1 in 4. Their diseases are also of a much more severe character than those to which the registered girls are subject, as the latter receive a timely treatment. All physicians remark moreover, how very much milder in form is the syphilis of the present day, than that with which they were acquainted several years ago. This is probably to be ascribed, not to any decrease of virulence in the syphilitic poison, (for, as Mr. Acton says, " the germ of the disease still lurks among us and in as concentrated a form as ever "), but partly to the more rational medical treatment, particularly as regards the more sparing use of mercury ; partly also to the care that is taken in Paris to attend in time to the diseases of the prostitutes ; and also in great measure, to the very different provision that is now made in the hospitals and dispensaries, for the treatment of this disease.

Although the form of the disease may be on the whole milder than formerly, it is still probably as frequent as ever ; at least in this country, where so little has been done to prevent it. Mr. Acton, who gives in his admirable work—probably the most complete we possess on Venereal and Genital Diseases—many valuable statistics on this subject, says, " I doubt if venereal complaints were ever more common than at present." Of the awful extent to which they have been permitted to gain ground among us, the following facts will give us an idea. Mr. Acton shows, that in the Army 1 man in every 5 is annually attacked by venereal disease ; in the Navy 1 in 7 ; and 2 of every 7 sailors (in the merchant service) admitted into the Dreadnought. In St. Bartholomew's Hospital 1 in every 2 of the out-patients are similarly affected, and in many other general hospitals and dispensaries the case is nearly the same ; while the Lock Hospitals are devoted entirely to the treatment of these diseases.

Syphilis is not to be regarded as a directly fatal disease ; although its effects are often so deplorable, especially in bad constitutions. In London during the three years 1846—7and—8, there were only 127 deaths (73 women and 54 men) caused by it. Infants and very young children are those in whom it most frequently proves directly fatal. It is *indirectly* that this disease, like gonorrhœa, is so very destructive to life ; syphilis, by poisoning and debilitating the frame, and thus exposing it to innumerable forms of disease ; gonorrhœa, by inducing affections of the genito-urinary organs, which are so very common and dangerous. Indirectly there are probably few diseases, which cause a greater amount of death, as well as of all forms of misery and destruction. In questioning patients in hospitals and dispensaries as to their previous history, how often is it found, that venereal disease has been the first link of the chain, which is dragging them to the grave.

Syphilis was first recognised in Paris in 1497 ; and in the subsequent history of its treatment, we have one of the most fearful instances of human barbarity to be found in the annals of history. For a long time no hospital would receive syphilitic patients, and the poorer classes of them were driven into the woods and fields, and left to die without comfort and assistance even by medical men. When at last parliament passed a law, that they should be admitted into one of the hospitals, every patient was *well flogged* before admission, which barbarism was rigorously carried into effect as late as 1700. But even this inhuman treatment was only for the male sex; unhappy woman. as usual, was still more shamefully treated. For this sex no provision at all was made, as if they were unworthy of any feeling but contempt; and we may picture to ourselves their miserable state as they rotted gradually from the surface of the earth, unpitied and abandoned, their hearts sickening with the bitterness of degradation, and racked by that agony of indignation, with which even the dim sense of wrong and injustice fills every human bosom. It was not till 1683 that a small ward in an hospital was devoted to their treatment; and what a ward! Imagination cannot call up a more hideous picture of filth and neglect, than is presented by Duchatelet in his description of this place; where the unhappy patients died in great numbers, or if they came out alive, were reduced to walking skeletons. To obtain even this miserable treatment, it was necessary to wait for a period, not exceeding a year, till it came to the patient's turn to succeed to a vacant bed: for there was provision for only one hundred patients, men and women huddled together. This horrible state of things was still existing in 1787; soon after which time, through the noble exertions of a benevolent physician, who was appointed to the hospital, better arrangements were made.

Does not our flesh creep on reading of such cruelties, as great proofs of barbarism as the rack and the wheel? and do we not feel what a long score of ill-usage we have to efface by our future treatment of such patients? And yet what is our treatment of them in the present day of so-called enlightenment? At the time when Duchatelet wrote, in 1835, there were few hospitals throughout the provinces of France, where venereal patients were received, and therefore the unhappy outcasts were forced to drag their sores to Paris for treatment, which even then they had often great difficulty in obtaining; as any one will conceive, who knows the imperfect provision made in respect of hospital accommodation for the sick poor, and especially for those, against whose complaints a narrow-minded physician may please to take a prejudice. A few years ago syphilitic patients were not admitted into the Middlesex hospital except by paying two pounds; and many people refuse to subscribe to the Lock hospitals from conscientious scruples. Hospital accommodation is much increased in Paris at the present time, but in this country it is still a mere island in the ocean of misery. How many hundreds are, of necessity, daily sent away from our crowded hospitals, suffering from these and other diseases, whose tottering frames have scarcely strength to bear them from the place!

But besides these deficiencies in hospital accommodation, which are often perhaps unavoidable, are not the contemptuous and abhorrent feelings, which so many still entertain towards the venereal diseases and their victims, but the remains of this miserable barbarism? Whoever at the present day is guilty of such feelings, would in a past generation have joined in the physical cruelties, which the better sense of those physicians, the true apostles of physical religion, have laboured to overcome. It is the very essence of all religion, to do in every case what is best and kindest to every human being.

Since Duchatelet's time good hospital accommodation has been provided in Paris for venereal patients. The Hopital du Midi under the care of M. Ricord, the Hopital du St. Lazare for prostitutes, of L'Oursine for married women, &c. are all excellent institutions.

In speaking of this subject, I would say a few words on the Lock Hospitals in this country—for so the venereal hospitals for prostitutes are repulsively termed. Of these I know nothing from personal experience, as medical students are not allowed to enter them; a privilege confined to the physicians of the establishments. This exclusion I earnestly protest against, as a part of the numerous exceptional methods, in which venereal diseases are regarded in this country. On the continent the venereal diseases of women are discussed, examined, and explained to the students in the most open and satisfactory manner; while here the mistaken feelings of a morbid delicacy are allowed to stand in the way of the scientific progress of young physicians, and to prevent us from acquiring knowledge on a subject, which is one of the most vitally important in our profession. Do not those who wantonly deprive us of such valuable opportunities, expect, that, when in future years our ignorance may cause to others the greatest misery and to ourselves the keenest regret, we may exclaim, " the blood be upon their heads, who caused our ignorance."

With regard also to the use of the speculum, which is now-a-days so much talked of, the depreciating way in which it is often mentioned, is most painful to him who has physical religion at heart. The men who have been most energetic in promoting the use of this instrument, (whose value, like that of the stethoscope, cannot be too highly estimated,) are spoken of with distrust and suspicion by many, whose morbid notions of sexual delicacy are offended by this necessary means of diagnosis. " It were better," I have heard it said, "even that many young girls should suffer for a time from genital diseases, than that they should be virtually deflowered by such a means. Since its introduction a morbid taste for such examinations has been spread abroad among women, many of whom even feign disease in order to be subjected to them; which prurient feelings there are always plenty of quacks ready to gratify." I cannot refrain from expressing the greatest reprobation of such sentiments. The idea that any morbid feeling of sexual delicacy should be allowed to interfere, one jot or one tittle, with the adoption of every means in the least likely to remedy a disease, is diametrically opposed to all real virtue and duty. There is nothing which more emasculates and denaturalises our society, than the mystery and secrecy on these subjects; than the morbid delicacy, which forbids all open discussion of sexual matters, and thus gives an unsound and superficial character to our various opinions, and to our social intercourse; which proscribes all allusions to the sexual organs, being careful even in our statues to cover them with the mystic fig-leaf—the visible symbol of the want of nature, and of what may be called the *spiritual castration* of our times.

What wonder, that women have such distorted views on these subjects, when men—and even excellent men, utter such opinions as the above: and as the following observation of Duchatelet, which I take to be the ne plus ultra of physical immorality. Speaking of some prostitutes, who have adopted that mode of life, on account of blindness preventing them from earning a livelihood in any other way, he says, "one could only reproach these unfortunates with not having preferred to die!" Here an unhealthy spiritualism is thrown into strong contrast with physical religion; and the greatest of physical sins, namely death, is thought preferable to a mode of life which is by no means devoid of virtue, and of value to mankind.

When a prostitute wishes to relinquish her calling, and to return again to society, as the vast majority do, (for Duchatelet takes great pains to impress on us the fact, that prostitution is in most cases, only a temporary interlude in life, lasting for from one to three years) her name is erased from the register; and in order to effect this, she must apply to the office, stating her reasons for withdrawing, and the mode of life she intends to adopt. The authorities decide, after hearing her account, whether she shall at once be struck off the list, or undergo a term of probation; during which she is kept under the eye of the police, who observe how she conducts herself in the new mode of life she has adopted; using the greatest delicacy and caution, so as not to make known her past history. This measure has been found necessary in most cases; for otherwise girls would have made any specious excuse, merely in order to be exempt from the police control and sanitary visits, and have secretly carried on their vocation. If it be found that they conduct themselves well, their names are struck off the list. Many never apply for their erasure, but leave Paris without giving any notice; and in these cases the police wait for three months, and if no tidings of them be heard, their names are then expunged.

I shall now speak of the prisons exclusively set apart for prostitutes, when they commit any offence against public decorum. The prison of St. Lazare s devoted to this purpose, and its inmates average from 450 to 550. It is excellently appointed, the lower part of the building containing the working rooms, and the upper the bed-rooms; and a spacious hall for promenading, in the midst of which is a water-basin, with materials for washing clothes, is thrown open to the prisoners during several hours in the day. The prisoners are all employed in occupations of various kinds, adapted to their capacity and previous habits; and this employment, which has only recently been introduced, has been found to have admirable effect in promoting quiet and order in the prison, which, prior to that, was the scene of the greatest turbulence and indecency. They have wholesome food, and are paid small sums for their work, with which they buy provisions at a canteen in the prison. They cook their own meals at stoves in the hall, and dine in pairs. It is often seen that a girl of a better class,

who receives money from her friends outside, as many do, shares her
dinner with a poorer girl.   They are also fond of buying flowers, for
which the whole class have a great love; and distribute them among
their companions with much generosity.   Sometimes one reads aloud
a novel or history, never an indecent work, and the others listen with
interest.   They are frequently visited here, as well as in hospital, by
the benevolent sisters of charity, and always treat them with great respect, nor are they ever known to ridicule them behind their backs.
These well-meaning ladies talk with them and exhort them to choose
a better mode of life; but in general, says Duchatelet, the prostitutes
are not much influenced by their exhortations, as they think the ladies
are only discharging their duty, and they feel that the simple sisterhood do not understand the circumstances of their lives.   He who
knows the duty that man and woman owe to their sexual organs, will
pereceive that the life of voluntary celibacy led by these ladies, as by
the priests, is, in a sexual point of view, quite as sinful a one, as that
of the prostitutes they endeavour to convert.

Notwithstanding the improvements in prison discipline, consequent
on the introduction of work, there are still frequent disturbances and
quarrels; besides other moral corruptions, which generally render a
girl more degraded at her dismissal, than at her incarceration.   Such
are the unnatural sexual relations, which girls enter into with each
other, when so suddenly deprived of their accustomed sexual gratifications, and which are often cemented with their partner at meals.   As
for their physique, it is observed that they are usually fatter on quitting
prison than on entering it.

The offences for which they are incarcerated are all of a *moral*
nature, consisting of breaches of public decorum, and of the police
regulations regarding prostitution; while for all *legal* crimes and
misdemeanours such as theft, they are tried, ike ordinary culprits,
before the criminal court.   Among the offences which are considered
of a less serious nature are, appearing in places where they are forbidden to go, as the Palais Royal, and some other parts of Paris; becoming intoxicated, and lying down in this state in the streets or arch-
ways; walking slowly through the streets in the day time, and
regarding fixedly the men whom they meet; tapping at their window
frames; asking charity; going out of doors with the head and neck
bare, &c.   These and several other minor offences are punished by
imprisonment for not less than a fortnight, and generally a month.
Among the more serious delinquencies are reckoned the following—
insulting in an outrageous manner the physicians appointed by the
authorities; failing to appear at the sanitary visits, and continuing to
pursue their vocation, knowing themselves to be diseased; uttering
obscene language in public; presenting themselves at the window in
a state of nakedness; attacking men with importunity, and insisting
on leading them away in spite of their resistance.   For such offences
the term of imprisonment is never less than three months, and sometimes five or six, according to the circumstances of the case, and the
previous habit and repute of the offender, which influence greatly the

sentence. There are many other offences for which they are punished, and of which Duchatelet gives instances; such as causing disturbances in families by seducing the affections of a married man from his wife, insulting the mother who wishes to detach from them her son, who is squandering on them his affections and substance; receiving the embraces of young boys, &c.

In these and in many other cases, where the men, with whom they commit any public breach of decorum, are equally or more to blame than they, still they alone are punished, as the administration has no authority over the others. This fact, which is worthy of all attention, brings me to the important question, as to the *legality* of this widely extended system of control exercised by the Paris authorities over the prostitutes. This question is fully discussed by Duchatelet, who admits that it is quite illegal, and endeavors by numerous arguments to show the necessity of its being legalised. "Individual liberty," says he, "is a right to which prostitutes cannot pretend; they have abdicated their perogative to it, and may be ruled by a different code of justice, from that to which any other member of society, however mean his station, is subjected."

This opinion, which forms the basis of all the arbitrary laws, to which prostitution, everywhere persecuted, is subject in Paris, and in many other parts of the continent, I look upon as utterly subversive of all justice, and a profanation of the sacred rights of the individual. Are then the unfortunate women alone to be punished and blamed for prostitution, when the men, who must share with them in it, commit the very same deeds? No wonder that to cloak such an enormous injustice, the police administration was obliged to do everything in secret; while the legislature dared not openly entrust to them powers, to justify which it would require that a new code of the different rights of man and woman should be devised. The French ministers have never ventured to speak openly in Parliament, of the necessity for adopting such measures to repress prostitution, but have merely connived at the efforts of the police board; efforts, well-meant it is true, but still most unjust, without any legal authority either for the registration of prostitutes, or their punishment for offences against public decorum. "But," says Duchatelet, "society is so generally convinced of the advantage of these coercive measures, that but few advocates, and those of the meanest class, have ever ventured to make any appeal against the arbitrary conduct of the authorities." Yes, there have been, alas! too few in all ages, who have taken up the cause of the weak and oppressed against the banded powers of society. It tells, I think, badly against the sense of justice of the French, that such arbitrary and illegal measures were allowed to be taken against any class of the community. If prostitutes are to be declared beyond the pale of social rights, let it be done publicly, and before the eyes of the world, by a legal constitutional act; and not in the dark, by illegal measures. Let us have so important a question discussed in the light of day, and see then whether men will dare to sanction such injustices.

It is considerations like these, which make me even on the threshold, object most strongly to the French system of arbitrary control, and to any coercive measures of a similar kind directed against women only, and not against the men, who are equally involved in the practice of mercenary love. Such measures, which appear to me both unjust and unmanly are frequently resorted to in the towns in this country, against the persecuted class of prostitutes, while those who go with them are not interfered with. We have not, it is true, the same systematic surveillance as in Paris; but neither have we that heartfelt desire to suppress, and if possible to eradicate venereal disease, which cannot be too much admired in the French, and which in part sanctifies the unjustifiable means they have taken to attain their object. It is the knowledge of the great benefits in the prevention of disease, which are so important to the prostitutes themselves, that has hitherto induced men to connive at the injustice of these measures.

No wonder the persecuted girls look on the police as their sworn foes, and do everything in their power to thwart and evade them. It is very right, that the authorities should be empowered to repress breaches of public decorum, and to punish in a legal manner such offences; but both men and women should be equally subject to these penalties. If unmarried love is to be controlled and repressed, let all of us, men and women, from the throne to the hovel, who take part in it, bear our share of the punishment; if any of us commit an offence against public decorum, let a punishment be impartially applied; if social preventive means are to be taken against the venereal diseases, let them apply to both sexes, and to all ranks alike; but let us be ashamed to see all the restrictions and all the punishments laid upon a poor, friendless, helpless class of girls, whose destitution, whose miseries, and whose wrongs are an ample excuse for any offence they may be guilty of. The illegality and flagrant injustice of the Parisian system, and of any analogous measures in this country; together with the degradation which a subjection to the police authorities necessarily entails, and the ill feeling it gives rise to; far more than counterbalance the benefit in the prevention of disease. Far other than this is the mode in which, I hope, mankind will ultimately contend with, and exterminate the destroyer; an infinitely important subject of which I shall speak hereafter.

What is the ultimate fate of these unfortunate girls? This is a question on which very vague ideas are generally entertained; and while those who know most of prostitutes, confess their ignorance, and are anxious to have more information on the subject, others make the most exaggerated statements regarding it, asserting that the life of a prostitute does not average more than three or four years; all of which statements, made at random, without statistical knowledge, and intended to inspire horror and dread of such a life, are, like all untruths, most pernicious. Duchatelet took great pains to investigate this matter, and the results of his valuable inquiries are the following. In the first place, prostitution in most cases is merely a period of transition, or as he calls it, " a temporary disease," from which girls recover in from one to three years, and then enter again into social life as wives, domestics, needlewomen, &c.; and this fact, as he justly observes, is an additional reason why every means should be taken to prevent their degradation, physical or moral whilst they follow such courses. Of those who continue for longer periods to practice the vocation, a limited number amass small fortunes, sometimes amounting to £40 or £60 per annum. This success is owing to naturally provident and economical habits, which here as elsewhere will make their way. Several of them make considerable sums by lending money to their companions at usurious interest; which debts, like those of honor, are almost always promptly paid. It is especially in the prisons that this system is carried on, and among the prisoners there are almost always several first-rate bankers. The savings-bank furnishes the means, by which some few are enabled to extricate themselves from a life of prostitution. Many who have been compelled by want to have recourse to such a life, look eagerly forward to the time, when they shall be able to escape from it.

It is rarely found that prostitutes leave that particular grade where they have made their first *debut*; and this is often a reason for their quitting the calling altogether. The girls, whose elegance and cultivation have gained them a place in the higher ranks of prostitution, seldom descend to a lower, unless they be either very stupid, or degraded by intemperate and careless habits; and on the other hand those of the lower class seldom rise, for they acquire a coarseness of manner by associating with rude and unpolished companions. There is a great rivalry and jealousy between the different orders; the more elegant ones looking down on the others with contempt, and feeling greatly insulted at being confounded with them.

Some prostitutes change their mode of life by marriage; and Duchatelet tell us, that the dispensary physicians sometimes recognise, in the wealthy and fashionable circles, ladies whose character would be destroyed, were their past history made known. Several become for a time kept-mistresses, and live with some one as man and wife; and it is very common for those of the humbler class thus to attach themselves to some old labourer or mechanic, whether widower or bachelor, whom they live with and tend, and at whose death they are sometimes forced again to betake themselves to their old calling. Others enter on a business of their own, and become washerwomen, marchandes de toilettes, &c.; in the practice of which they still continue to have intimacy with one or two favourite lovers, and also aid prostitution by trying to win over to it as many recruits as they can, for which they receive rewards from the house-mistresses. Others become domestics and duenuas in the tolerated houses; while a few are enabled by the portion they have amassed, to become mistresses in these establishments.

Duchatelet, besides the above details, endeavoured to obtain statistical information, as to the proportion cut off by death, and at what periods of life; but he could not get satisfactory information on this point. However he learned that several die in hospital from premature decay, brought on by excessive intemperance, and inveterate syphilitic diseases. We have seen above that a considerable number, averaging 21 per annum, are brought to the Salpetriere as insane. We may readily believe that where the causes of disease are so numerous, as in the life of the prostitutes, intemperate, reckless, passionate, improvident, and exposed to contagion as they are many evils must result; but even taken at their worst, they are not nearly so bad, as prejudiced writers would have us believe: nay, when we compare the life of the prostitute with that of almost any other *class* of women among us, it will be found, as Mr. Acton says, probably quite as healthy.

The foregoing facts must be taken as drawn from Duchatelet's description, and therefore applying chiefly to Paris. I am afraid that the lot of prostitutes, or their chance of escaping from their mode of life, is not nearly so good in this country, where they are viewed with so much more harshness and contempt; and where the poverty and difficulty of getting an honest livelihood, which of all secondary causes operates most to drive women into, and to keep them in, prostitution, are so much greater than in France. In our smaller towns especially, where prostitution is persecuted as much as possible; where its haunts are illegal; and where a hard and puritanical morality holds itself aloof from all sympathy with these unfortunate girls, as if their very sight were a pollution, there are far fewer avenues of hope for the friendless ones; and they, feeling their bitter degradation, drink to excess to drown their misery; and so draw ruin on themselves, and on the rest of society, by spreading throughout the land a taste for drunken pleasures, which is the disgrace of our country, and especially of Scotland, the stronghold or puritanism.

In London, however, from the size of the town and the minor austerity of the sexual code compared with the provinces, the ultimate fate of these girls seems very similar to what it is in Paris; and is for the most part far more favourable than is generally supposed. Mr. Acton says " I have every reason to suppose that by far the majority of them soon cease to have promiscuous intercourse, and return to a more or less regular course of life." He says again " One thing is certain, that before a prostitute has carried on her trade four years, she becomes thoroughly disgusted with it. She then abandons it, settles, and is amalgamated with the poorer classes of society; or becomes a married woman, after living in a state of concubinage with her husband. The better class of prostitutes become the wives of the mechanic, the clerk, and the petty tradesman; and as they are frequently barren, or have only few children, there is reason to believe they live in a comparative state of affluence, unknown to many virtuous women burdened with families."

What then are the views to be entertained, and the remedies to be adopted for prostitution,—that mighty fact, which occupies so large and important a place in the history of human society, spreading over all the world, and flourishing from the remotest antiquity? Is this a question, from which either man or woman, who would be thought a moralist, or a lover of their race, can submit to be held aloof by any effeminate scruples, which divide the conventional heart from sympathy with its fellow-beings? No; it is one, which claims the most earnest consideration from us all; and as it includes one of the modes, in which the workings of the mighty instinct of sexual love are manifested, it is full of the deepest interest to those, who desire to attain to a satisfactory solution of the great sexual problems · which, at the present day, are by far the most important of all.

Prostitution is a singular phenomenon. The fact that women should make it a trade to sell their persons, and those delightful intimacies of sex, which in our poetical ideals have been hallowed by so lofty an enthusiasm, for a price other than love, and mutual happiness; this fact is a very extraordinary one, and points to some fundamental difference in the position of the sexes. Why should women be less willing than men to taste of the joys of love, even although forbidden? The answer is to be found chiefly in the different sexual conditions of the two. Sexual intercourse entails on man no momentous physical consequences; a moderate indulgence gives him pleasures unmixed with pains, gratifying his passions, and giving new vigour to his frame. But woman has a widely different lot assigned to her; sexual intercourse has in her eyes a much more serious import, seeing that thereby she becomes subject to bear a tedious burden, and to undergo physical trials and sufferings, which the sustaining feelings of love, and the prospect of a happy and honored motherhood, can alone enable her to bear with peaceful mind. But when these consolations are denied her, when the anxious period of pregnancy has to be passed in fears and regrets, solaced only by stolen interviews with her lover, to whom she clings as to her only support, and when the infant, whose arrival should have been the end of her sufferings, seems but the beginning of her greatest degradation; then it is no wonder that women should shrink from pleasures, which may entail on them so much misery; while man, as long as he can himself escape scatheless, thinks little of his companions future lot, and is content to leave all the shame and disgrace on her shoulders. He therefore pays her well for the risk she runs; and as he has engrossed all the occupations by which a livelihood can be made, while she has only her person wherewith to purchase escape from want, the bargain is readily struck.

Then come the days of hollowness and deceit, of feigned delights and counterfeited passions, of momentary transports, succeeded by the loathing of satiety, or the gnawings of self-reproach, for love cannot be thus insulted with impunity; the destructive vice of intoxication to drown care and conscience, and the degradation in the eyes of the world, the crown of their sorrows. This is a melancholy, but in many respects a true picture of the life of the prostitute, a most unnatural and wretched one. What then has made it so necessary a part of our society? What are the great causes, which lead to it? For it is only by discovering and removing these, not by wrathful denunciations, or impotent avoidance of the subject, that we will be able to bring about a more natural state of things. Duchatelet and other writers take pains to show us the different ways, in which girls are led to adopt such a mode of life; as for example, the vices, ignorance, and harshness of their parents, want of education, wilfulness, and unbridled passions; the corruptions of large towns with their bands of seducers, procuresses, &c; and above all others, poverty; but they do not advert to that great cause, which is at the root of all the rest, and which will continue, throughout all ages, to bring men and women ever closer together, namely, *the necessity of sexual intercourse*, on which I have laid so much stress before. The sexual passions must always cause an immense amount of unmarried intercourse, and where the moral code is harsh, especially towards woman, and it is difficult for a woman to support herself by honorable means, such intercourse will assume the degraded character of prostitution. Thus the necessity of sexual gratifications, and the difficulties opposing marriage, (which difficulties, as will be shown presently, spring from the law of population) aided by female poverty, and harsh moral views towards woman, are the great cause of this evil. The natural passions, which irresistibly urge the youth of both sexes to the pleasures of love, cannot be so restrained; and every moral and social obstacle, which has been opposed to this primary want of our being, must eventually yield, however much misery they may still cause by blindly impeding the tide, which cannot be suppressed.

In what light then is prostitution to be regarded, when we take into consideration the great primary necessity of sexual intercourse? It should be regarded as a valuable temporary substitute for a better state of things. It is greatly preferable to no sexual intercourse at all, without which, as has been shown, every man and woman must lead a most unnatural life. Therefore the deep gratitude of mankind, instead of their scorn, is due, and will be given in future times, to those unfortunate females, who have suffered in the cause of our sexual nature. It is true that by doing so they have become degraded, have in many cases lost all love of mankind, by whom they were treated worse than dogs, have ruined their constitutions by intemperance, have been consumed by evil and unnatural passions; all of this, and more, have they done, but whose is the blame? Not theirs, the unhappy victims of our natural sexual difficulties, and of a hollow and inconsiderate moral code; but rather of us, their fellow-beings, whose unjust harshness and neglect have allowed them to sink so low. Surely, surely, we too have suffered, and still shall suffer bitterly for their degradation.

The mode of *preventing* prostitution, is to use every endeavour by the different training of the female sex, and by the precautions against over-population, to enable women to gain a livelihood readily for themselves, and not be dependent on man for their support, or obliged to make a barter of their love—the only marketable commodity, on which the poorest women among us have to rely; and also, and above all, to supply the inevitable want of sexual intercourse, on which prostitution essentially depends, in another and better manner. Unless this latter object can be achieved, the prevention of prostitution is a mere delusion and impracticable dream, of those who know so little of nature, as to imagine that her laws and her instincts can be forcibly suppressed. Sexual pleasures must be had at any price; and if they be not obtainable honorably and for love, they will be bought with money and degradation.

By these means (the fuller consideration of which, along with other questions, I reserve to a subsequent page), I earnestly believe and hope, prostitution with all its evils will ultimately be eradicated from our society; though long will be the struggle, and patient and enduring must those be, who seek to see such a reformation effected. But in the mean time as long as it continues among us, another great part of our duty should be, to raise as much as possible the unfortunate girls, who have suffered so deeply, as martyrs to the sexual passions. For this, *reverence* is the most essential means; reverence for them, as for all other human beings; any of whom, in their wonder and mystery, as much transcend any conception of the scorner, as his own real being does his self-consciousness. Reverence should be paid to themselves, to their actions, to their feelings; instead of neglecting, or reviling them, as the world has hitherto done, they should be made an object of the greatest solicitude, as well to their own sex as to ours. The legal restrictions, those flagrant injustices towards women, should be removed ; and man and woman should share alike in any verdict, moral or legal, passed upon unmarried love. What this verdict should be, I will examine more fully hereafter.

We shall find that if we love and reverence these girls, (at the same time that we endeavour totally to remove from our society the fearful evil of prostitution,) they will love and reverence us, and on no other consideration. If society enfold them in her bosom, they will soon learn gratefully to repay her love; but if she continue to spurn them, her punishment and sufferings will be no less than theirs. Her unnatural treatment has made them so degraded; and from that degradation only her repentant love and reverence will uplift them.

[Since the passing of the Contagious Diseases Act in 1866, a system essentially similar to the French, and consisting in the registration and periodical examination of prostitutes, and their compulsory detention in hospital if diseased, has been introduced in several towns of this country. These measures are so unjust in applying to women only, are such an interference with the rights and liberties of the sex, and have so many degrading influences attending them, that they have roused the most intense hostility. Their efficacy too in preventing disease has been disputed, and does not seem on the whole to be so very satisfactory, especially in large towns, in which, besides the registered women, there are always a much greater number of others who practise prostitution in a secret or clandestine manner; thus in Paris, where the system has been in operation nearly from the beginning of the century, M. Mauriac, surgeon to the Midi Hospital, estimates that about 5,000 new cases of syphilis occur annually. But though strongly opposed to these Acts, I think it is of the utmost importance that Government should take measures to eradicate syphilis, and to prevent individuals from spreading it. It seems to me that this might be done by other means, without injustice and without departing from the ordinary principles of legislation. If, as has been proposed by several writers, and among others by Mr. Berkeley Hill in his excellent work on Venereal Diseases, the communication of syphilis were made a punishable offence in either sex; and if, as has also been proposed, every case of syphilis and of other contagious diseases, such as small-pox, scarlet fever, etc., were reported by the medical attendant to the District Officer of Health, so that means might be taken to inquire into its origin and prevent its spreading, I believe that this would be found in the long run a more effectual preventive. It is far easier to trace the origin of syphilis than of other contagious disorders, such as small-pox, scarlet fever, or typhus. A man generally knows perfectly well from what woman he got the disease, and a woman often knows the man who infected her, though not, of course, where much promiscuous intercourse is indulged in. Surely this eminent *traceability* of syphilis should be the key to its prevention by the State. Moreover, every patient with syphilis who wishes to enter hospital, should be at once admitted and encouraged by kind treatment to remain till cured; and especially women of the town, who by the numbers they consort with, and by having thus to make their living, are far the most dangerous agents in spreading the disease. One great difficulty in preventing syphilis arises from the length of time its contagiousness lasts, which is now known to be about eighteen months or two years, owing to the infectious nature of the secondary symptoms. But still these difficulties might be overcome by persevering efforts. Syphilis never arises but from contagion ; no one need give it to another unless he or she chooses to do so ; and the knowledge of this, rightly used and deeply felt throughout society, should lead in time to the total and final extirpation of this terrible disease. 1876.]

THE LAW OF POPULATION.

Having thus given a short description of the existing evils of the sexual world, and endeavoured to convey some slight idea of the awful and widely spread miseries arising from sexual abstinence and abuse, and from venereal disease, in both sexes; I now proceed to the second great division of this subject, namely, the great *natural difficulty*, that opposes the normal and sufficient exercise of the genital organs, which we have seen to be so indispensable to the health and virtue of mankind. This arises from the *Principle (or law) of population*, so wonderfully explained by Mr. Malthus; and after him by many of the first political economists, among others by Mr. Stuart Mill. This is a subject whose extreme importance cannot be over estimated. It may be called *the* question of the age, for upon it, as Mr. Malthus and Mr. Mill have shown, depend the grand problems which are at present convulsing society; the wages of labour, poverty and wealth, &c. Upon it depends moreover, the greatest proportion of the *sexual* diseases and miseries, of which I have spoken, and which can neither be understood nor remedied except by reference to their grand cause. The usual mode of treating of these evils, whether in medical or moral works, where they are not traced to this cause, can have no satisfactory result.

Notwithstanding the paramount importance of the law of population, it is scarcely at all generally understood. In spite of the unanswerable reasonings of Mr. Malthus (and they are as conclusive as a problem of Euclid), in spite of the exertions of Mr. Mill and others, to show that attention to this law can alone enable mankind to solve the social problems, or to emerge from the miserable abyss of poverty, in which the greater part of our race is at present sunk, the subject is practically ignored, and there is not one man in thousands among those who reason on these questions, who pays any heed to it. We have still organizations of industry, socialism christian or unchristian, change in the government, national education, charitable institutions, &c., vaunted as the great remedies for poverty, low wages, and social embarrasments; but there is not one of these which has any real or direct power in the matter, or that when tried by the principle of population, can bear a moment's scrutiny as a proposed cure for social evils.

Mr. Malthus's great work was written fifty years ago, and his reasonings still stand impregnable, for truth cannot be overthrown. What
then is the reason that these vital truths have made so little impression,
that a knowledge of them is confined to a few of the most enlightened
minds, and that they have had little practical effect on individual conduct?

There are two great reasons for this. The first is, that the subject is a
sexual one, and like all similar subjects, has been prevented from being
openly discussed by the feelings of morbid delicacy, to the inevitable ruin
of mankind.

The second is, that the remedies which Mr. Malthus suggested were,
I believe, as erroneous and unhealthy as his principle of population was
undeniable; and the impracticability of the former led to the neglect of the
latter. Most people know nothing of Mr. Malthus's views, except from
some casual allusion to them by those, who probably have not read them,
and certainly have not understood their paramount importance. But
without a knowledge of these views, and in fact without their being taken
as an axiom in all our reasonings, it is utterly in vain to approach the
great social problems.

I do not know any work so important to the happiness of mankind at
present as that of Mr. Malthus. It alone explains the *real cause* of the
fearful evils both in the economical and sexual world: of poverty, hard
work, and early death, on the one hand, and of sexual abstinence, self-
abuse, and prostitution on the other; of the multiform miseries, which are
breaking the hearts and paralysing the arms of so many myriads among
us, and making the philanthropist despair. What can be done by any
effort to benefit mankind: how can disease be prevented or happiness
promoted, while poverty exists? Poverty is the fountain-head of evils
innumerable. Crime, disease, prostitution, ignorance, drunkenness, and
all imaginable miseries spring from it in endless exuberance: and while
poverty continues, every one must feel, that all efforts at social improvement will be of little avail.

Now what Laennec did for chest disease, what M. Lallemand did for
the diseases of the male generative organs, what Newton did for the law of
gravitation—that has Mr. Malthus done for poverty. He has shown its
nature and its only important cause; and in so doing, has conferred a boon
upon mankind, which cannot be sufficiently valued. To know the cause
of any evil is for man, but the preparatory step to devising a remedy: and
although, till Mr. Malthus showed the cause of poverty, it was not possible for society to escape from this, its greatest evil; I firmly believe
that, by the knowledge he has given us, the evil is no longer irremediable,
and that we will, by persevering and combined social efforts, ultimately be
freed from it.

As Mr. Malthus's celebrated essay is not very easily procurable by
every one, and as there are no truths, which deserve to be more universally known and deeply felt by all of us, than those which he explains, I
shall give here a short sketch of his work, using in most places the
author's own words.

I entreat the reader to study it carefully, and to make himself thoroughly master of the great law which it explains. By doing so, he will obtain a deeper insight into the complex problems of human society, the real difficulties with which our race has to contend, and the true cause of the evils existing among us, than if he studied every other branch whatsoever, of moral and political science, and omitted this; as is so frequently done. He will learn the profound errors on poverty and its remedies, which are still so prevalent; will be enabled to see through the fallacies on these subjects, which he will hear every day in conversation, from the pulpit, or the platform, or read in the pages of our newspapers, and other publications,—the very same fallacies, which Mr. Malthus so unanswerably exposed, but which are still widely, nay, almost universally spread, not only in this country, but on the continent; and will perceive the utter uselessness and superficiality of the usual discussions on poverty and low wages, and of the common routine practice of statesmanship, which tacitly ignore the real law of population and wages, " not, " as Mr. Mill says, "as if it could be refuted. but as if it did not exist."

ESSAY

ON THE

PRINCIPLE OF POPULATION.

BY THE

REVEREND Mr. MALTHUS.

" In an inquiry concerning the improvement of society, the mode of conducting the subject which naturally presents itself is

1st.—To investigate the causes, that have hitherto impeded the progress of mankind towards happiness ;

2nd.—To examine the probability of the total or partial removal of these causes in future.

To enter fully into this question, and to enumerate all the causes, that have hitherto influenced human improvement, would be much beyond the power of an individual. The principal object of the present essay is to examine the effects of one great cause, intimately united with the very nature of man ; which, though it has been constantly and powerfully operating since the commencement of society, has been little noticed by the writers, who have treated this subject. The facts, which establish the existence of this cause, have indeed been repeatedly stated and acknowledged ; but its natural and necessary effects have been almost wholly overlooked ; though probably among its effects may be reckoned a very considerable portion of that vice and misery, and of that unequal distribution of the bounties of nature, which it has been the unceasing object of the enlightened philanthropist in all ages to correct.

The cause to which I allude, is the constant tendency in all animated life, to increase beyond the nourishment prepared for it.

It is observed by Dr. Franklin, that there is no bound to the prolific nature of plants or animals, but what is made by their crowding and interfering with each other's means of subsistence. Were the face of the earth, he says, vacant of other plants, it might be gradually sowed and overspread with one kind only, as for instance, with fennel ; and were it empty of other inhabitants, it might, in a few ages, be replenished from one nation only, as for instance, with Englishmen.

This is incontrovertibly true. Through the animal and vegetable king-doms, nature has scattered the seeds of life abroad, with the most profuse and liberal hand; but has been comparatively sparing in the room and nourishment necessary to rear them. The germs of existence contained in this earth, if they could freely develope themselves, would fill millions of worlds in the course of a few thousand years. Necessity, that imperious all-pervading law of nature, restrains them within the prescribed bounds. The races of plants and of animals shrink under this great restrictive law; and man cannot by any efforts of reason escape from it.

In plants and irrational animals the view of the subject is simple. They are all impelled by a powerful instinct to the increase of their species; and this instinct is interrupted by no doubts about providing for their offspring. Wherever therefore there is liberty, the power of increase is exerted; and the superabundant effects are repressed after-wards, by want of room and nourishment.

The effects of this check upon man are more complicated. Impelled to the increase of his species by an equally powerful instinct, reason inter-rupts his career, and asks him, whether he may not bring beings into the world, for whom he cannot provide the means of support. If he attend to this natural suggestion, the restriction too frequently produces vice. If he hear it not, the human race will be constantly endeavouring to increase beyond the means of subsistence. But as, by the law of our nature, which makes food necessary to the life of man, population can never actually increase beyond the lowest nourishment capable of sup-porting it, a strong check on population, from the difficulty of acquiring food, must be constantly in operation. This difficulty must fall some-where, and must necessarily be felt severely in some or other of the various forms of misery, or the fear of misery, by a large portion of mankind.

That population has this constant tendency to increase beyond the means of subsistence, and that it is kept to its necessary level by these causes, will sufficiently appear from a review of the different states of society, in which man has existed. But let us first endeavour to ascer-tain, what would be the natural increase of population, if left to exert itself with perfect freedom: and what might be expected to be the rate of increase in the productions of the earth, under the most favourable cir-cumtances of human industry.

It will be allowed, that no country has hitherto been known, where the manners were so pure and simple, and the means of subsistence so abundant, that no checks whatever have existed to early marriages, from the difficulty of providing for a family, and that no waste of the human species has been occasioned by vicious customs, by towns, by unhealthy occupations, or too severe labour. Consequently, in no state that we have yet known, has the power of population been left to exert itself with perfect freedom.

In the northern States of America, where the means of subsistence have been more ample, the manners of the people more pure, and the checks to early marriages fewer, than in any of the modern States of Europe, the population has been found to double itself, for above a century and a half successively, in less than in each period of twenty-five years. Yet even during these periods, in some of the towns, the deaths exceeded the births; a circumstance that clearly proves that in those parts of the country which supplied this deficiency, the increase must have been much more rapid than the general average.

In the back settlements, where the sole employment is agriculture, and vicious customs and unwholesome occupations are little known, the population has been found to double itself in fifteen years. Even this extraordinary rate of increase is probably short of the utmost power of population. Sir William Petty supposes a doubling possible in so short a time as ten years.

But to be perfectly sure, that we are far within the truth, we will take the slowest of these rates of increase—a rate, in which all concurring testimonies agree, and which has been repeatedly ascertained to be from procreation only.

It may safely be pronounced therefore, that population, when unchecked, goes on doubling itself every twenty-five years, or increases in a geometrical ratio. *

---

* That population has the power, under favourable circumstances, of doubling itself in twenty-five years by procreation alone, is so extremely important a proposition—being the very foundation of the Malthusian arguments—that it seems advisable to show here more fully the statistical facts on which it rests. These are furnished especially by the Census Returns of the United States, which have been published every ten years since 1790, and are therefore of a later date than the first publication of the Essay on Population (in 1798). The results are given in the following extract from an article on "Population" in the *Encyclopædia Britannica*, which was written some years later by Mr. Malthus:—

"In the country to which we should naturally turn our eyes for an exemplification of the most rapid rate of increase, there have been four enumerations of the people, each at the period of ten years; and though the estimates of the increase of population in the North American colonies at earlier periods were of sufficient authority, in the absence of more certain documents, to warrant most important inferences, yet as we now possess such documents, and as the period they involve is of sufficient length to establish the point in question, it is no longer necessary to refer to earlier times. According to a regular census, made by order of Congress in 1790, which there is every reason to think is essentially correct, the white population of the United States was found to be 3,164,148. By a similar census in 1800, it was found to have increased to 4,312,841. It had increased then during the ten years from 1790 to 1800 at a rate equal to 36.3 per cent., a rate which, if continued, would double the population in 22 years 4½ months. According to a third census in 1810, the white population was found to be 5,862,092, which, compared with the population of 1800, gives an increase in the second ten years at the rate of nearly 36 per cent., which, if continued, would double the population in 22½ years. According to the fourth census in 1820, the white population was found to be 7,861,710, which, compared with the population of 1810, gives a

The rate according to which the productions of the earth may be supposed to increase, it will not be so easy to determine. Of this, however,

---

increase in the third ten years at a rate per cent. of 34.1, which, if continued,
would double the population in 23 years 7 months. If we compare the period of
doubling according to the rate of increase in the most unfavorable ten years of
this series, with 25 years, we shall find the difference such as fully to cover all
the increase of population which would have taken place from immigration.

"It appears from a reference to the most authentic documents which can be
collected on both sides of the Atlantic, that the emigration to the United States
during the last twenty-five years, falls decidedly short of an average of 10,000 a
year. Dr. Seybert, the best authority on the other side of the water, states that,
from 1790 to 1810, it could not have been so much as 6,000 a year. Our official
accounts of the number of emigrants to the United States from England, Ireland,
and Scotland, during the ten years from 1812 to 1821 inclusive, give an average of
less than 7,000, although the period includes the extraordinary years 1817 and
1818, in which the emigrations to the United States were much greater than they
were ever known to be before or since. The official American accounts, as far as
they go, which are only for two years from the 30th September 1819, tend to
confirm this average; and allowing fully for the emigrants from other European
countries, the general average will still be under the 10,000.

"Altogether then, we can hardly err in defect, if we allow 10,000 a year for the
average increase from emigration during the 25 years from 1795 to 1820; and
applying this number to the slowest period of increase, when the rate was such as
to double the population in 23 years 7 months, it may be easily calculated that in
the additional year and five months, a population of 5,862,000 would have increased
to an amount much more than sufficient to cover an annual emigration of 10,000
persons, with the increase from them at the same rate. Such an increase from
them, however, would not take place. It appears from an account in the *National
Calendar* of the United States for the year 1821, that of the 7,001 persons arrived
in America from the 30th September 1819 to the 30th September 1820, 1,959 only
were females, and the rest, 5,042, were males; a proportion which, if it approaches
towards representing the average, must very greatly reduce the number from which
any increase ought to be calculated. If, however, we omit these considerations, if
we suppose a yearly emigration from Europe to America of 10,000 persons for the
25 years from 1795 to 1820, the greatest part of which time Europe was involved in
a most extensive scene of warfare, requiring all its population; and further, if we
allow for an increase of all the emigrants during the whole period, at the fullest
rate, the remaining number will still be sufficient to show a doubling of the
population in less than 25 years. The white population of 1790 was 3,164,148.
This population, according to the rate at which it was increasing, would have
amounted to about 3,694,100 in 1795; and supposing it to have just doubled itself
in the 25 years from 1795 to 1820, the population in 1820 would have been 7,388,200.
But the actual white population of 1820 appears, by the census then taken, to be
7,861,710, showing an excess of 473,510; whereas an emigration of 10,000 persons

we may be perfectly certain, that the ratio of their increase must be totally of a different nature, from the ratio of the increase of population. Man is necessarily confined in room. When all the fertile land has been occupied, the yearly increase of food must depend upon the melioration of the land already in possession. This is a stream, which from the nature of all soils, instead of increasing, must be gradually diminishing. But population, could it be supplied with food, would go on with unexhausted vigour; and the increase of one period would furnish the power of a greater increase the next, and this without any limit.

From the accounts we have of China and Japan, it may be fairly doubted, whether the best directed efforts of human industry could double the produce of these countries, even once, in any number of years. There are many parts of the globe, indeed, hitherto uncultivated, and almost unoccupied; but the right of exterminating, or driving into a corner, where they must starve, even the inhabitants of these thinly peopled regions, will be questioned in a moral view. The process of improving their minds, and directing their industry, would necessarily be slow; and during this time, as population would regularly keep pace with the increasing produce, it would rarely happen that a great degree of knowledge and industry would have to operate at once upon rich and unappropriated soil. Even when this might take place, as it does sometimes in new colonies, a geometrical ratio increases with such extraordinary rapidity, that the advantage could not last long. If America continue increasing, which she certainly will do, though not with the same rapidity as formerly, the Indians will be driven further and further back into the country, till the whole race is ultimately exterminated.

Europe is by no means so fully peopled as it might be. In Europe there is the fairest chance, that human industry may receive its best direction. The science of agriculture has been much studied in England

---

annually with an increase from them at 3 per cent., a rate which would double a population in less than 24 years, would only amount to 364,592.

"If to these proofs of the rapid increase of population, which has actually taken place, we add the consideration that this rate of increase is an average applying to a most extensive territory, some parts of which are known to be unhealthy; that some of the towns in the United States are now large; that many of the inhabitants must be engaged in unwholesome occupations and exposed to many of those checks to increase which prevail in other countries; and further, that in the western territories, where these checks do not occur, the rate of increase is beyond comparison greater than the general average, after making the fullest allowance for immigration; it must appear certain that the rate at which the population of the whole of the United States has actually increased for the last 30 years, must fall very decidedly short of the actual capacity of mankind to increase under the most favourable circumstances."

From these and other facts Mr. Malthus draws the conclusion: "It may be safely asserted, therefore, that population, when unchecked, increases in a geometrical progression of such a nature as to double itself every twenty-five years."

and Scotland; and there is still a great portion of uncultivated land in these countries. Let us consider at what rate the produce of this island might be supposed to increase, under circumstances the most favourable to improvement.

If it be allowed, that by the best possible policy, and great encouragements to agriculture, the average produce of the island could be doubled in the first twenty-five years, it will be allowing probably a greater increase than could with reason be expected.

In the next twenty-five years it is impossible to suppose, that the produce could be quadrupled. It would be contrary to all our knowledge of the properties of land. That we may be the better able to compare the increase of population and food, let us make a supposition, which is clearly more favourable to the power of production in the earth, than any experience we have had of its qualities will warrant.

Let us suppose that the yearly additions which might be made to the former average produce, instead of decreasing, which they certainly would do, were to remain the same; and that the produce of this island might be increased every twenty-five years, by a quantity equal to what it at present produces. The most enthusiastic speculator cannot suppose a greater increase than this. In a few centuries, it would make every acre of land in the island like a garden.

It may be fairly pronounced therefore, that considering the present average state of the earth, the means of subsistence, under circumstances the most favourable to human industry, could not possibly be made to increase faster than in an arithmetical ratio.

The necessary effects of these two different rates of increase, when brought together, will be very striking. Taking the whole earth, emigration would of course be excluded; and while the human race would increase as the numbers 1, 2, 4, 8, 16, 32, 64, 128, 256, subsistence would only increase at the rate of 1, 2, 3, 4, 5, 6, 7, 8, 9.

In this supposition, no limits whatever are placed to the produce of the earth. It may increase for ever, and be greater than any assignable quantity; yet still the power of population, being in every period so much superior, the increase of the human species can only be kept down to the level of the means of subsistence, by the constant operation of the strong law of necessity, acting as a check upon the greater power.

I shall now speak of the general checks to population, and the mode of their operation.

The ultimate check to population, from the above considerations, appears to be a want of food, arising necessarily from the different ratios according to which population and food increase. But this ultimate check is never the immediate check, except in cases of actual famine.

The immediate check may be stated to consist in all those customs, and all those diseases, which seem to be generated by a scarcity of the means of subsistence; and all those causes, independent of this scarcity, whether of a moral or physical nature, which tend prematurely to weaken and destroy the human frame.

These checks to population, which are constantly operating with more or less force in every society, and keep down the number to the level of the means of subsistence, may be classed under two general heads, the preventive and the positive checks.

The *preventive* check, as far as it is voluntary, is peculiar to man, and arises from that distinctive superiority in his reasoning faculties which enables him to calculate distant consequences. The checks to the indefinite increase of plants and irrational animals, are all either positive, or, if preventive, involuntary. But man cannot look around him and see the distress, which frequently presses on them, who have large families; he cannot contemplate his present possessions or earnings, which he now nearly consumes himself, and calculate the amount of each share, when with very little addition, they must be divided, perhaps among seven or eight, without feeling a doubt whether, if he follow the bent of his inclinations, he may be able to support the offspring, which he will probably bring into the world.

In a state of equality, if such can exist, this would be the simple ques tion. In the present state of society other considerations occur. Will he not lower his rank in life, and be obliged to give up in great measure his former habits? Does any mode of employment present itself by which he may reasonably hope to maintain a family? Will he not at any rate subject himself to greater difficulties, and more severe labour, than in his single state? Will he not be unable to transmit to his children the same advantages of education, that he himself possessed? Does he even feel secure that, should he have a large family, his utmost exertions can save them from rags and squalid poverty; and may he not be reduced to the grating necessity of forfeiting his independence, and of being obliged to the sparing hand of charity for support?

These considerations are calculated to prevent, and certainly do prevent a great number of persons in all civilized nations, from pursuing the dictates of nature in an early attachment to one woman.

If this restraint do not produce vice, it is undoubtedly the least evil, that can arise from the principle of population. Considered as a restraint on a strong natural inclination, it must be allowed to produce a certain degree of temporary unhappiness; but evidently slight, compared with the evils, which result from any of the other checks to population; and merely of the same nature, as many other sacrifices of temporary to permanent gratification, which it is the business of a moral agent continually to make.

When this restraint produces vice, the evils which follow, are but too conspicuous. A promiscuous intercourse to such a degree as to prevent the birth of children, seems to lower in a most marked manner the dignity of the human character. It cannot be without its effect on men, and nothing can be more obvious than its tendency to degrade the female character. Add to which, that among those unfortunate females, with which all great towns abound, more real distress and aggravated misery are perhaps to be found, than in any other department of human life.

The *positive* checks to population are extremely various, and include every cause, whether arising from vice or misery, which in any degree contributes to shorten the natural duration of human life. Under this head therefore may be enumerated all unwholesome occupations, severe labour, and exposure to the seasons, extreme poverty, bad nursing of children, great towns, excesses of all kinds, the whole train of diseases and epidemics, wars, plagues, and famines.

On examining these obstacles to the increase of population, which I have classed under the heads of preventive and positive checks, it will appear that they are all resolvable into *moral restraint, vice, and misery.*

Of the preventive checks, the restraint from marriage, which is not followed by irregular gratifications, may properly be termed moral restraint.

Promiscuous intercourse, unnatural passions, adultery, and improper arts to conceal the consequences of irregular connections, are preventive checks, that clearly come under the head of vice.

Of the positive checks, those which appear to arise unavoidably from the laws of nature, may be called exclusively misery, and those which we obviously bring upon ourselves, such as wars, excesses, and many others, which it would be in our power to avoid, are of a mixed nature. They are brought upon us by vice, and their consequence is misery.

The sum of all these preventive and positive checks taken together, forms the immediate check to population; and it is evident that in every country, where the whole of the procreative power cannot be called into action, the preventive and the positive checks must vary inversely as each other; that is, in countries naturally unhealthy, or subject to a great mortality, from whatever cause it may arise, the preventive check will prevail very little. In those countries on the contrary, which are naturally healthy, and where the preventive check is found to prevail with considerable force, the positive check will prevail very little, or the mortality be very small.

In every country some of these checks are, with more or less force, in constant operation; yet notwithstanding their general prevalence, there are few states in which there is not a constant effort of the population to increase beyond the means of subsistence. This constant effort as constantly tends to subject the lower classes of society to distress; and to prevent any great permanent melioration of their condition.

These efforts, in the present state of society, seem to be produced in the following manner. We will suppose the means of subsistence in any country just equal to the easy support of its inhabitants. The constant effort towards population, which is found to act even in the most vicious societies, increases the number of people, before the means of subsistence are increased. The food therefore, which before supported · eleven millions, must now be divided among eleven millions and a-half. The poor consequently must live much worse, and many of them be reduced to severe distress. The number of labourers also being above the proportion of work in the market, the price of labour must tend to fall, while the price of provisions would at the same time tend to rise. The labourer therefore must do more work to earn the same as he did before. During this season the discouragements to marriage, and the difficulties of rearing a family are so great, that population is nearly at a stand. In the meantime the cheapness of labour, the plenty of labourers, and the necessity of an increased industry among them, encourage cultivators to employ more labour upon their land, to turn up fresh soil, and to manure and to improve more completely, what is already in tillage ; till ultimately the means of subsistence may become in the same proportion to the population, as at the period from which we set out. The situation of the labourer being then again tolerably comfortable, the restraints to population are in some degree loosened ; and after a short period, the same retrograde and progressive movements with respect to happiness, are repeated.

This sort of oscillation will not probably be obvious to common view : and it may be difficult even for the most attentive observer to calculate its periods. Yet that in the generality of old States some such vibration does exist, though in a much less marked, and more irregular manner, than I have described it, no reflecting man who considers the subject deeply, can well doubt.

One principal reason why this oscillation has been less remarked than might naturally have been expected, is, that the histories of mankind, which we possess, are in general only histories of the higher classes. The science of the history of the poorer orders may be said to be still in its infancy, and many of the objects, on which it would be desirable to have information, have been either omitted or not stated with sufficient accuracy. Among these may be reckoned the proportion of the number of adults to the number of marriages ; the extent to which vicious customs have prevailed in consequence of the restraints upon matrimony ; the comparative mortality among the children of the most distressed part of the community, and of those who live rather more at their ease ; the variations in the real price of labour ; the observable differences in the state of the lower classes of society, with respect to ease and happiness, at different times during a certain period ; and very accurate registers of births, deaths, and marriages, which are of the utmost importance in this subject.

A faithful history, including such particulars, would tend greatly to elucidate the manner, in which the constant check upon population acts ; and would probably prove the existence of the oscillations that have been mentioned ; although their periods would necessarily be rendered irregular from the operation of many interrupting causes ; such as, the introduction or failure of certain manufactures, a greater or less prevalent spirit of agricultural enterprise ; years of plenty, or scarcity ; wars, sickly seasons, poor laws, emigration, and other causes of a similar nature.

A circumstance which has perhaps more than any other, contributed to conceal this oscillation from common view, is the difference between the *nominal* and *real* price of labour. It very rarely happens that the mominal price of labour universally falls, but we well know that it frequently remains the same, while the price of provisions has been gradually rising. This is in effect a real fall in the price of labour, and during this period, the condition of the lower classes must be gradually growing worse, while the farmers and capitalists are growing rich, from the real cheapness of labour.

In savage life, where there is no regular price of labour, it is little to be doubted, that similar oscillations take place. When population has increased nearly to the utmost limits of the food, all the preventive and positive checks will naturaly operate with increased force. Vicious habits with respect to the sex will be more general, the exposing of children more frequent, and both the probability and fatality of wars and epidemics considerably greater ; and these causes will probably continue their operation, till the population is sunk below the level of the food ; and then the return to comparative plenty will again produce an increase, and after a certain period, its futher progress will again be checked by the same causes.

But without attempting to establish these oscillations in different countries, which would evidently require more minute histories than we possess, and which the progress of civilisation naturally tends to counteract, the following propositions are intended to be proved ;

1st.—Population is necessarily limited by the means of subsistence.

2nd.—Population invariably increases, when the means of subsistence increase.

3rd.—The checks which repress the superior power of population, and keep its effects on a level with the means of subsistence, are all resolvable into moral restraint, vice, and misery.

The first of these propositions scarcely needs illustration. The second and third will be sufficiently established by a review of the immediate checks to population, in the past and present state of society.

This review will be the subject of the following chapters."

In this manner, after having explained the great Law of Increase, inherent in the human species, as in all organiseu beings ; having shown as well by general reasoning, as by known facts, that the natural ratio of the increase of population is immeasurably greater than the usual ratio of the produce of the earth—or, in other words, that the increase of all plants and animals, including man, is of necessity very greatly limited by the limited size of the earth ; having shown that it is only in the case of new colonies, such as America, where the agricultural skill of civilised man is brought to bear upon fertile uncultivated territory (a case, which is a mere accident in human history, of temporary duration, and necessitating moreover, the dispossession and extermination of the native inhabitants) that food can be increased at all quickly enough to keep up with the geometrical increase of which population is naturally capable ; having shown that population *does* increase with extraordinary rapidity in such a case, doubling itself every twenty-five years for instance in the United States, while in all old countries it increases very slowly—Mr. Malthus next examines the question, *in what way* is population thus restrained in the latter countries? what are the *checks* which make it advance so slowly? Population cannot be checked except in two ways, either there must be fewer children born, or some must die; and it must be therefore by either or both of these two checks, called by Mr. Malthus the *preventive* and the *positive*, that the slow increase of our race in all old countries is effected. The modes in which these two checks operate may, he says, all be included under the three heads of *moral restraint, vice*, or *misery*; and these checks have been operating upon human society ever since its origin, and have only been suspended for short intervals in the case of new colonies &c.

This law of population is, it appears to me, by far the most important of all subjects for the consideration of mankind, and therefore I entreat the reader's earnest attention to it. It is not like the vacillating institutions of man, but is one of the fixed and immutable laws of Nature, which acts upon our race exactly as upon the humblest plant; from which no effort of reason can enable the civilised man any more than the savage to escape, and whose recognition has been impeded by the spiritual theories of the supremacy of mind over matter. Except in the accidental case of new colonies, and other rare and temporary circumstances, where the usual ratio of the increase of food is enormously increased, the law is, that if the preventive check do not operate, the positive must: if fewer children be not born, the surplus *must* die prematurely: there must be a rapid succession of necessarily short-lived beings to keep up the numbers, one generation being pushed out of existence before its time to make room for the next. The less the reproductive powers are restrained, the
• shorter *must* the general average of life be in the successive generations. Their premature death is certain; it is only the mode of it which is uncertain. It may be by famine or by war, by extreme poverty and slow starvation, or by quick disease; but in some shape or other it must come. Thus it is an enormous error to suppose, as is commonly done, that the wars, famines, pestilences, &c., which we read of in history, were occasioned mainly by man's evil passions, or want of industrial skill; they were primarily the effect of the natural sexual instincts, and were *absolutely inevitable*, as long as these were not restrained by foresight. More children having been born than the slow increase of food could support, they had to be cut off prematurely in some way; and thus, had war not operated, pestilence, famine, disease, &c., *must* have done so. If three or four times the number of children were born that could be supported, (a thing which must very frequently have taken place among uncivilised nations), either three-fourths of them had necessarily to perish in infancy, or in some other way, the general average of life had to be reduced to one-fourth of the natural one. It is generally thought that abstaining from marriage, sexual vices which prevent child-birth, such as prostitution, and premature death are accidental and avoidable evils; but this is the most radical of all errors. In all old countries some one or more of these checks to population *must* always operate with immense force; and they have thus operated in all such countries ever since the birth of history. Man has only a

choice *between* them; not independent of them. The more complete
the positive check, in other words the younger the age at which death
takes place, the less need is there for the preventive check. On the
other hand, wherever the positive check operates little, the preventive
one *must* operate greatly; a long average of life and few deaths can
only be procured in any old country by having few births.

Mr. Malthus next proceeds to examine in what manner the three
checks, moral restraint, vice, and misery, have operated on mankind in
the various conditions of human society. To do this he enters into a
detailed review of nearly all the nations of past and present times,
from the rudest savages up to ourselves, and points out how far each
of these three checks has operated upon them. This review occupies a
great part of his work, and is full of interest, both from the insight it
gives us into the workings of this mighty but unknown law on human
destiny, and also from its explanation of the complex problems of
society in its various stages ; problems which the principle of population can alone render intelligible. I shall give a short sketch of this
part of Mr. Malthus's work, begging the reader to supplement it by
reading the work itself.

Mr. Malthus first examines the checks to population among savages,
or those nations which subsist chiefly on the unassisted produce of
nature, as, for instance, the natives of Australia, Patagonia, the
North American Indians, &c. In these the main checks are similar to
those in the inferior animals ; namely the *positive* ones. The preventive check, or moral restraint, acts little upon them; they follow
blindly the promptings of the natural sexual instincts like the inferior
animals, and therefore the surplus population is cut off by starvation, ·
periodical famines, bloody warfares, &c. The condition of the women
among savages, moreover, is most miserable, and adverse to the bearing and nurture of offspring. They are used almost like beasts of burden ; and mothers among the American Indians, have been known to
destroy their female children to preserve them from such a life.

With regard to the checks to population in the Islands of the South
Sea, Mr. Malthus says, "M. Raynal, speaking of the ancient state of
the British Isles, and of islanders in general, says, ' It is among these
people that we trace that multitude of singular institutions which
retard the progress of population. Anthropophagy, the castration of
males, the infibulation of females, late marriages, the consecration of
virginity, the approbation of celibacy, &c. These customs, caused by
a superabundance of population in islands, have been carried to the
continents, where philosophers of our days are still employed in investigating the reason of them.' M. Raynal does not seem to be aware,
that a savage tribe in America surrounded by its enemies, or a civilized
and populous nation, hemmed in by others in the same state, is in
many respects circumstanced like the islander. Though the barriers
to a further increase of population be not so well defined, and so open
to common observation on continents, as on islands, yet they still present obstacles which are nearly as insurmountable. There is probably
no island yet known, the produce of which could not be further in-

creased. This is all that can be said of the whole earth. But as the bounds on population or small islands are so narrow, that every person must see and acknowledge them, an inquiry into the checks to population in them may tend considerably to illustrate the present subject.

If we turn our eyes to the crowded shores of Otaheite and the Society Islands, all apprehension of dearth seem at first sight to be banished from a country, that is described to be fruitful as the garden of the Hesperides. But this first impression would be immediately corrected by a moment's reflection. Happiness and plenty have always been considered as the most powerful causes of increase. In a delightful climate where few diseases are known, and the women are condemned to no severe fatigues, why should these causes not operate with a force unparalleled in less favourable regions? Yet, if they did, where could the population find room and food in such narrow limits? Effectual emigration or effectual importation would be utterly excluded, from the situation of the islands and the state of navigation among the inhabitants.

The difficulty here is reduced to so narrow a compass, is so clear, precise, and definite, that we cannot escape from it. It cannot be answered in the usual vague and inconsiderate manner, by talking of emigration and further cultivation. In the present instance we cannot but acknowledge that the one is impossible and the other glaringly inadequate. The fullest conviction must stare us in the face, that the people on this group of islands could not continue to double their numbers every twenty-five years; and before we proceed to inquire into the state of society among them, we must be perfectly certain, that unless a perpetual miracle render the women barren, we shall be able to trace some very powerful checks to population in the habits of the people."

These checks were promiscuous intercourse and infanticide, which were exceedingly common in Otaheite, when first discovered; and were universally practised by the members of the Arreoy societies, which included most of the youth of the upper classes. The same vices were very common among the lower classes also; and it was by these means —the positive check—that population was mainly kept down to the level of the food; although their action was not sufficient to prevent a very considerable degree of poverty.

Mr. Malthus next proceeds to the checks to population among pastoral and semi-civilized peoples. The nations of the north of Europe, who overthrew the Roman Empire, were of this description. It has puzzled historians to account for the numerous and successive armies which they poured down upon Italy and France, and which were so often annihilated, before the final triumph; but this can be readily accounted for by the great natural powers of multiplication. They must have increased very rapidly, for their morals, as described by Tacitus, were pure, and their life healthy; and thus their population was constantly increasing beyond the means of subsistence, and numbers of their youth were sent forth to gain new regions by the sword. The loss of life in these wars was prodigious; and it was in this way that their population was chiefly restrained.

The checks among the modern pastoral nations, as the Tartars and Bedouins, are chiefly of a similar nature, except that there is more poverty and famine, and less war. In many of the tribes the grinding poverty always borders on starvation. (Poverty, famine, and frequently pestilence, are the inevitable alternatives to war in all nations, where the preventive check to population does not operate. Therefore as this check operates very little among uncivilized nations, war, poverty, famine, or pestilence are constantly observed among them; and are indeed perfectly unavoidable from the laws of nature.) Moral restraint acts little among the Arabs, for 'a Mahometan is in some respects obliged to polygamy, from a principle of obedience to his prophet, who makes one of the great duties of man to consist in procreating children to glorify his Creator. Nothing can place in a more striking point of view the futility and absurdity of such encouragements to marriage, than the present state of these countries. It is universally agreed, that if their population be not less than formerly, it is indubitably not greater; and it follows as a direct consequence, that the great increase of some families has actually pushed the rest out of existence. While the Arabs retain their present manners, and the country remains in its present state of cultivation, the promise of paradise to every man who had ten children, would but little increase their numbers, though it might greatly increase their misery. Direct encouragements to marriage have no tendency whatever to change their manners, and promote cultivation."

The wives are bought of their parents, and therefore the poorer classes are sometimes unable to obtain them; so that the preventive check, by compulsion, operates in some degree.

In the various countries of Africa, the checks are also mostly of a positive nature; constant warfare, so that in some of the tribes Bruce says, that an old man is never to be seen, as they all die by the lance young; also famine and pestilence, the exportation of slaves, &c. The poorest classes are sunk in the most abject poverty.

In Hindostan, marriage is greatly encouraged by the religious code, which makes the procreation of male children one of the greatest merits. In the ordinances of Menu, it is said, ' By a son a man obtains victory over all people; by a son's son he enjoys immortality; and afterwards by the son of that grandson he reaches the solar abode.'' Thus marriage in India is considered a religious duty; and therefore, the preventive check operating little, the positive one must of necessity supply its place. The people are so crowded that the most excessive poverty prevails, and periodical famines have been always very frequent. Wars and pestilences have also at times carried off large numbers.

In Thibet on the other hand, the preventive check operates very strongly. "In almost every country in the globe, individuals are compelled by considerations of private interest, to habits, which tend to repress the natural increase of population; but Thibet is perhaps the only country where these habits are universally encouraged by government, and where to repress rather than encourage population, seems to be a public object."

In Thibet celibacy is deemed honourable, while marriage is almost a certain bar to a man's rising in the State; and the higher orders, who are occupied as priests or statesmen, leave to the husbandmen and labourers the business of populating the country. Even among the latter, moreover, it is the common practice for all the brothers of a family to have but one wife among them; so that here polygamy consists in a plurality of *husbands*; which of course is a great check to population.

In China the population is enormous, being upwards of 300,000,000, or about one-third of the human race. These vast numbers are owing to the goodness of the soil and climate, the very great attention that has always been paid to agriculture, and also the extraordinary encouragements to marriage, which here as in India is considered a religious duty; to be childless being held a dishonour. The preventive check therefore having operated but little, the positive has been the chief one. The most grinding and abject poverty prevails among the lower classes, together with an indefatigable industry and hard work; (a combination which finds a parallel perhaps in England alone). Periodical famines are very frequent, which sweep off vast numbers; and infanticide is very general. It is in these modes rather than by wars, (which, till lately, have not been so destructive in China), that the positive check operates.

"The check to population from a vicious sexual intercourse does not appear to be very considerable in China. The women are said to be modest and reserved, and adultery is rare.

The very great consumption of grain in making spirits has been dwelt upon by several writers as one of the great causes of the frequent famines among the Chinese; but this is a gross error." (The very same error is frequently committed at present with regard to the poverty in England). "In reality the whole tendency of this cause is in a contrary direction. The consumption of corn in any other way than necessary food, checks the population before it arrives at the utmost limits of subsistence; and as the grain may be withdrawn from this particular use in the time of a scarcity, a public granary is thus opened, richer probably than could have been formed by any other means. When such a consumption has been once established, and has become permanent, its effect is exactly as if a piece of land, with all the people upon it, were removed from the country. The rest of the people would certainly be in precisely the same state as they were in before, in years of plenty; but in time of dearth the produce of this land would be returned to them, without the mouths to help them to eat it. China, without her distilleries, would certainly be more populous; but on a failure of the seasons, would have still less resource than she has at present; and as far as the magnitude of the cause would operate, would in consequence be more subject to famines, and these famines would be more severe."

In ancient Greece "the philosophers and statesmen perceived the tendency of population to increase beyond the means of subsistence ; and did not, like those of modern times, overlook the consideration of a question, which so deeply affects the happiness and tranquillity of society. We must give them credit for seeing the difficulty, however we execrate the barbarous expedients they adopted to remove it." (In this case, exactly as in that of the speculum and female disease, which were in some degree known to the Greeks, attention to the all-important subject of population was afterwards prevented by the morbid sexual delicacy of the Hebrew-christian religion.)

Solon permitted infanticide by law ; Plato in his Republic says, that the magistrates should regulate the increase of citizens, and prevent undue multiplication ; also that men and women should be allowed to procreate only when at their greatest vigour, and that all weakly children should be destroyed. Aristotle proposed that the men should not be allowed to marry till thirty-seven, and the women till eighteen ; and also that each woman should be allowed to produce only a certain number, and if she afterwards became pregnant, an abortion should be induced. He said that if, as in most States, every one were allowed to have as many children as they pleased, poverty, the mother of crime and sedition, must result.

The preventive check therefore probably operated to a considerable extent among the Greeks ; and its deficiencies were supplied by the positive one in the shape of constant and bloody wars.

Among the Romans the positive check, namely the ceaseless wars, was the chief one. Under the Empire the preventive check also prevailed greatly, in the shape of all sorts of vicious sexual habits. Juvenal complains of the arts used to produce abortion, saying that scarcely any natural birth was permitted to take place. "In most countries, it is the frequency of marriage that causes promiscuous intercourse ; but in Rome during the later periods of its history, morals were so depraved, as to cause people to hate marriage and avoid it."

"All the checks to population, which have been hitherto considered in the course of this review of human society, are clearly resolvable into moral restraint, vice, and misery.

Of these, moral restraint, among the nations considered, has been seen to have operated but very feebly compared with the others. Vice also, though its effects seem to have been very considerable in the later periods of Roman history, and in some other countries, yet upon the whole, seems to have had much less influence on population, than the positive checks. A large portion of the procreative power appears to have been called into action, and the redundant population cut off by violent causes. Among these, war is the most prominent feature, and after this may be ranked famines, and violent diseases. In most of the countries considered, the population seems to have been seldom measured accurately, according to the average and permanent means of subsistence, but generally to have vibrated between the two extremes ; and consequently the oscillations between want and plenty are strongly marked, as we should naturally expect among less civilized nations."

Mr. Malthus next examines, how these checks operate on the nations of modern Europe, our own included. "In reviewing the states of modern Europe," he says, "we are assisted in our inquiries by the registers of births, deaths, and marriages; which, when they are complete and correct, point out to us with some degree of precision, whether the prevailing checks to population be of the positive or preventive kind; and give us, in many important points, more information respecting these states, than we could receive from the most observing traveller.

One of the most curious and instructive points of view in which we can consider these registers, is the dependence of the *marriages* upon the *deaths.* It has been justly observed by Montesquieu, that wherever there is a place for two persons to live comfortably, a marriage will certainly ensue; but in most of the countries of Europe, in the present state of their population, experience will not allow us to expect any sudden and great increase in the means of supporting a family. The place therefore for the new marriage must in general be made by the dissolution of an old one; and we find in consequence that, except after some great mortality, or some sudden change of policy, peculiarly favourable to cultivation and trade, the number of marriages is principally regulated by the number of deaths. They reciprocally influence each other. There are few countries, where the common people have so much foresight as to defer marriage, till they have a fair prospect of being able to support all their children. Some of the mortality therefore, in almost every country, is forced by the too great frequency of marriage: and in every country a great mortality, whether arising chiefly from this cause or from the number of great towns and factories, and the natural unhealthiness of the situation, will necessarily produce a great frequency of marriage.

The mean proportion of annual marriages in most countries is as 1 to 108. Wherever the average is much higher, it must arise from the greater average of death; as for instance, we find that in some Dutch villages, very unhealthily situated, the marriages were as 1 in 64 and the deaths as 1 in 22, while the births and deaths were nearly equal; or in other words the population nearly stationary. Compare this with Norway where the deaths are as 1 to 48, and the marriages as 1 to 130. The difference in both deaths and marriages is nearly double." (These statistics are to be understood as applicable to the time when Mr. Malthus wrote, but they illustrate the principle he is explaining).

"Unless when some sudden start in the agriculture, or other means of obtaining food, takes place, more marriages will only cause more deaths."

"The proportion of yearly *births* to the whole population must evidently depend, principally on the number of people marrying annually; and therefore in countries which will not admit of a great increase of population, must, like the marriages, depend chiefly on the *deaths.* Where an actual decrease of population is not taking place, the births will always supply the vacancies made by death, and exactly so much more as the increasing agriculture and trade of the country will admit. In almost every part of Europe, during the intervals of the great plagues, epidemics, or destructive wars, with which it is occasionally visited, the births exceed the deaths.

U

In thirty-nine villages of Holland, where the yearly deaths are as 1 in 23, the births are also as 1 in 23. In Sweden, where the mortality is about 1 in 35, the births are 1 in 28. In Norway, where the mortality is 1 in 48, the births are 1 in 34. In all these instances the births are evidently measured by the deaths, after making a proper allowance for the excess of births, which the state of each country will admit . In Russia this allowance must be great, as, although the mortality may be taken as only 1 in 48 or 50, the births are as high as 1 in 26, owing to the present rapid increase of population, which arises from the rapid expansion of the resources of the country."

Mr. Malthus then examines in detail, the checks which operate in these countries.

"Norway has been long free from war, has a very healthy climate, and in common years the mortality is less than in any other country in Europe. The proportion of annual deaths to the whole population is only as 1 to 48. Yet the population of Norway never seems to have increased with great rapidity.

Before we enter upon an examination of its internal economy, we must feel assured that, as the positive checks to its population have been so small, the preventive checks must have been proportionally great; and we accordingly find from the registers, that the proportion of yearly marriages to the whole population is as 1 to 130, which is a smaller proportion of marriages than appears in the registers of any other country except Switzerland. The proportion of yearly marriages is one of the most obvious criterions of the operation of the preventive check."

The chief cause of the fewness of marriages is the peculiar state of the country. There are few manufactures or means of emigration; and it is the custom among the farmers to have under them several labourers, to whom they give a house and some land, and a vacancy among these is the only prospect of maintaining a family. Therefore the great part of the agricultural population remain single till a late period of life. "Under such circumstances the lower classes cannot increase much, till the increase of mercantile stock or the division and improvement of farms furnishes a greater quantity of employment to married labourers. In countries more fully peopled, this subject is always involved in great obscurity. Each man naturally thinks that he has as good a chance of finding employment as his neighbour; and that if he fail in one place, he shall succeed in some other. He marries therefore, and trusts to fortune; and the effect too frequently is, that the redundant population, occasioned in this manner, is repressed by the positive checks of poverty and disease.

Norway is perhaps the only country in Europe, where the traveller will hear fears expressed of a redundant population; and where the danger to the happiness of the lower classes from this cause is in some degree seen and understood. This obviously arises from the smallness of the population altogether, and the consequent narrowness of the subject. If our attention were confined to one parish, and there were no powers of emigrating from it, the most careless observer could not fail to remark, that if all married at twenty, it would be perfectly impossible for the farmers, however carefully they might improve their land, to find employment and food for those that would grow up; but when a great number of these parishes are added together in a populous kingdom, the largeness of the subject, and the power of moving from place to place, obscure and confuse our view. We lose sight of a truth which before appeared completely obvious: and in a most unaccountable manner, attribute to the aggregate quantity of land, a power of supporting people, beyond comparison greater than the sum of all its parts."

"In Sweden the preventive check has not operated so largely, and therefore the mortality has been greater. The average proportion of deaths in Sweden is as 1 to 34½, which is a very large one considering the number of people employed in agriculture. The inhabitants of the towns are only as 1 to 13 to those of the country; while in well-peopled countries, they are nearly as 1 to 3. In Prussia and Pomerania, where there are many large towns, and the proportion of townsmen to countrymen is as 1 to 4, the average of death is as 1 to 37."

Seasons of severe scarcity have frequently occurred in Sweden, in which great numbers of the people were swept off. Much of the misery and mortality was doubtless caused by the mistaken efforts of the Swedish Government to increase population; to effect which they erected numerous lying-in and foundling hospitals. "But these have no tendency to increase population, but only to increase poverty and misery; the only true mode of increasing their population would have been to improve the state of agriculture."

"Positive laws to encourage marriage, not combined with religious feeling, as, in China, seldom produce the effect, and generally show ignorance in the legislator; but the apparent need of them shows a great degree of moral and political depravity in a State; as it is either institutions unfavourable to industry, and therefore to population, or else the prevalence of vicious customs, which seem to call for them."

"A good illustration of the law of population is afforded by the fact, certainly ascertained by the returns of the population made in France, since the great Revolution, that the population rather increased than diminished during that long and bloody struggle, in which it is calculated that France lost two and a half million of lives." The reason was that the increase of deaths led, as it always does, to a great increase of marriages, by which the vacancies were easily supplied. The enormous powers of multiplication, which had been repressed, were permitted to expand for awhile; and thus "France has not lost a single birth by the revolution. She has just cause to mourn the two and a half millions of individuals which she may have lost, but not their posterity; because if these individuals had remained in the country, a proportionate number of children, born of other parents, would not have come into existence.

Mr. Malthus thus examines in succession the checks to population in the other European countries; but we may pass on to his description of those which operate among ourselves in England. He says "The most cursory view of society in this country must convince us, that, throughout all ranks, the preventive check to population prevails in a considerable degree. Those among the higher classes, who live principally in towns, often want the inclination to marry, from the facility with which they can indulge themselves in an illicit intercourse with the sex. And others are deterred from marrying, by the ideas of the expenses they must retrench, and the pleasures of which they must deprive themselves, on the supposition of having a family. When a fortune is large, these considerations are certainly trivial; but a preventive foresight of this kind has objects of much greater weight for its contemplation, as we go lower.

A man of liberal education, with an income only just sufficient to enable him to associate in the rank of gentlemen, must feel absolutely certain, that if he marry and have a family, he will be obliged to give up all his former connections. The woman that a man of education would naturally make the object of his choice, is one brought up in the same habits and sentiments with himself, and used to the familiar intercourse of a society totally different from that, to which she must be reduced by marriage. Can a man easily consent to place the object of his affections in a situation, so discordant probably to her habits and inclination? Two or three steps of descent in society, particularly at this round of the ladder, where education ends, and ignorance begins, will not be considered by the generality of people, as a chimerical evil. If society be desirable, it surely must be free, equal, and reciprocal society, where benefits are conferred as well as received; and not such as the dependent finds with his patron, or the poor with the rich.

These considerations certainly prevent many in this rank of life from following the bent of their inclinations in an early attachment. Others, influenced either by a stronger passion or a weaker judgment, disregard these considerations; and it would be hard indeed, if the gratification of so delightful a passion as virtuous love, did not sometimes more than counterbalance all its attendant evils. But I fear it must be acknowledged, that the more general consequences of such marriages are rather calculated to justify, than to disappoint, the forebodings of the prudent.

The sons of tradesmen and farmers, are exhorted not to marry, and generally find it necessary to comply with this advice, till they are settled in some business or farm, which may enable them to support a family. These events may not perhaps occur till they are advanced in life. The scarcity of farms is a very general complaint; and the competition in every kind of business is so great, that it is not possible, that all should be successful. Among the clerks in counting-houses, and the competitors for all kinds of mercantile and professional employment, it is probable that the preventive check to population prevails more, than in any other department of society.

The labourer who earns eighteen-pence, or two shillings a day, and lives at his ease as a single man, will hesitate a little before he divides that pittance among four or five, which seems to be not more than sufficient for one. Harder fare and harder labour he would perhaps be willing to submit to, for the sake of living with the woman that he loves; but he must feel conscious, that should he have a large family, and any ill-fortune whatever, no degree of frugality—no possible exertion of his strength, would preserve him from the heart-rending sensation of seeing his children starve, or of being obliged to the parish for their support.

The servants, who live in the families of the rich, have restraints yet stronger to break through in venturing upon marriage. They possess the necessaries and even the comforts of life, almost in as great plenty as their masters. Their work is easy and their food luxurious, compared with the work and food of the class of labourers. Thus comfortably situated at present, what are their prospects if they marry? Without knowledge or capital, either for business or farming, and unused and therefore unable to earn a subsistence by daily labour, their only refuge seems to be a miserable ale-house, which certainly offers no very enchanting prospect of a happy evening to their lives. The greater number of them therefore, deterred by this uninviting view of their future situation, content themselves with remaining single where they are.

If this sketch of the state of society in England be near the truth, it will be allowed, that the preventive check to population operates with considerable force throughout all classes. And this observation is further confirmed by abstracts from the registers, returned in consequence of the late Population Act. These show that the annual marriages in England and Wales, are to the whole population as 1 to 123¼; a smaller proportion of marriages than obtains in any of the countries examined, except Norway and Switzerland.

In the earlier part of the last century, Dr. Short estimated this proportion as about 1 to 115. It is probable that this calculation was then correct, and the present diminution in the proportion of marriages, notwithstanding an increase of population more rapidly than formerly, owing to the more rapid progress of commerce and agriculture, is partly a cause and partly a consequence, of the diminished mortality, that has been observed of late years.

Those who live singly, or marry late, do not by such conduct contribute in any degree to lessen the actual population, but merely to lessen the proportion of premature mortality, that would otherwise be excessive. "

The annual deaths, like the marriages, bear a smaller proportion to the population in England, than in any other European country, except Norway and Switzerland. "This is owing to the superior cleanliness and healthiness of the people, and also in great degree to the prevalence of the preventive check."

The annual proportion of births moreover, is, like the deaths and marriages, the smallest next to these two countries; which marry latest, produce fewest children, and therefore have longest lives of the European States. "It has been hitherto usual with political calculators, to consider a great proportion of births, as the surest sign of a vigorous and flourishing state. It is to be hoped however, that this prejudice will not last long. In countries circumstanced like America, or in other countries after any great mortality, a large proportion of births may b a favourable symptom; but in the average state of a well-peopled territory, there cannot well be a worse sign than a large proportion of births, nor can there well be a better sign than a small proportion. In despotic, miserable, or naturally unhealthy countries, the proportion of births will generally be found very great. The desire of immediate gratification of the sexual passions, and the removal of the restraint to it from prudence, will in such countries prompt universally to early marriages; but when these habits have once reduced the people to the lowest possible state of poverty, they can evidently have no further effect upon the population. Their only effect must be on the degree of mortality; and there is no doubt, that if we could obtain accurate bills of mortality, in those countries where very few women remain unmarried, and all marry young, the proportion of the annual deaths would be 1 in 17, 18, or 20.; instead of 1 in 34, 36, or 40 as in European States, where the preventive check operates.'

"It has been calculated that the half of the surplus of births in Scotland is drawn off in emigration; and it cannot be doubted that this tends greatly to improve the condition of those who remain. Scotland is certainly still over-peopled, but not so much as it was half a century ago, when it contained fewer inhabitants.

"With regard to the population of Ireland, I shall only observe that the extended use of the potato has allowed of a very rapid increase of it during the last century. But the cheapness of this nourishing root, and the small piece of ground, which under this cultivation will produce the food for a family, joined to the ignorance and imprudence of the people, which have prompted them to follow their inclinations with no other prospect than an immediate bare subsistence, have encouraged marriage to such a degree that the population is pushed much beyond the industry and present resources of the country; and the consequence naturally is, that the lower classes are in a most depressed and miserable state."

Mr. Malthus, having thus examined in what proportion the two alternative checks to population, the positive and preventive, have acted, and do act, on the different nations of ancient and modern times, proceeds to some general deductions from this review. "That the checks which have been mentioned," he says, "are the immediate causes of the slow increase of population, and that these checks result principally from an insufficiency of subsistence, will be evident from the comparatively rapid increase, which has invariably taken place, whenever, by some sudden enlargement in the means of subsistence, these checks have been in any considerable degree removed.

It has been universally remarked, that all new colonies settled in healthy countries, where room and food were abundant, have constantly made a rapid progress in population." He instances the Greek, Portuguese, and Spanish colonies, and above all others the United States.

"From the late census made in America it appears, that taking all the States together, they have still continued to double their numbers every twenty-five years ; and as the whole population is now so great as not to be materially affected by the emigrations from Europe, and as it is well known that in some of the towns and districts near the sea-coast, the progress of population is comparatively slow; it is evident that in the interior of the country in general, the period of doubling, from pro-creation only, must have been considerably less than twenty-five years.

We have no reason to believe that Great Britain is less populous at present, for the emigration of the small parent stock, (which settled in America in 1643, being in number 21,200), which produced the present population. Whatever was the original number of British emigrants which increased so fast in North America, let us ask, why does not an equal number produce an equal increase in the same time in Great Britain ? The obvious reason to be assigned is the want of food ; and that this want is the most efficient cause of the three immediate checks to population, which have been observed to prevail in all societies, is evident from the rapidity with which even old states recover the desolations of war, pestilence, and famine. They are then for a short time placed a little in the position of new colonies, and the effect is always what might be expected. If the industry of the inhabitants be not destroyed, subsis-tence will soon increase beyond the wants of the reduced numbers ; and the invariable consequence will be, that population, which before perhaps was nearly stationary, will begin immediately to increase, and will con-tinue its progress till the former population is recovered.

The undiminished population of France after the revolution is a striking instance of this. The traces of the most destructive famines in China, Indostan, Egypt, and other countries, are by all accounts very soon obliterated ; and the most tremendous convulsions of nature, such as volcanic eruptions and earthquakes, if they do not happen so fre-quently as to drive away the inhabitants or destroy their spirit of industry, have been found to produce but a trifling effect on the average population of any state. *

Tables which have been made of the number of great and wasting pestilences and famines recorded in history, show how very frequent these have been. It appears from them that four hundred and thirty-one epidemics are known to have occurred, of which thirty-one were before the Christian era. "Thus then the periodical returns of such epidemics to some country that we are acquainted with, have been on an average at the interval of only four and a-half years."

"Of the two hundred and fifty-four great famines enumerated in these tables, fifteen were before the Christian era. Hence it appears that the average interval between the visits of this dreadful scourge, in some part of the world with whose history we are acquainted, has been only about seven and a half years.

How far these terrible correctives to the redundance of mankind have been occasioned by the too rapid increase of population, is a point which it would be very difficult to determine with any degree of precision. The causes of most of our diseases appear so mysterious, and probably are so various, that it would be rashness to lay too much stress on any single one; but it will not perhaps be too much to say, that among these causes we ought certainly to rank crowded houses, and insufficient or unwholesome food, which are the natural consequences of an increase of population, faster than the accomodations of a country with respect to habitations and food, will allow.

Almost all the histories of epidemics confirm this supposition, by describing them in general as making their principal ravages among the lower classes of people. Moreover a very considerable number of the epidemic years either follow or are preceded by, seasons of dearth and bad food.

Of the other great scourge of mankind—famine, it may be observed, that it is not in the nature of things, that the increase of population should absolutely produce one. This increase, though rapid, is necessarily gradual: and as the human frame cannot be supported even for a very short time, without food, it is evident, that no more human beings can grow up than there is provision to maintain. But though the principle of population cannot absolutely produce a famine, it prepares the way for it in the most complete manner; and by obliging all the lower classes to subsist nearly on the smallest quantity of food that will support life, turns even a slight deficiency from the failure of the seasons into severe dearth; and may be fairly said, therefore, to be one of the principal causes of famines."

"The highest average proportion of births to deaths in England may be considered as about 12 to 10; in France 11½ to 10. We have reason to believe that these proportions have not varied in any considerable degree, during the last century; and it will appear therefore, that the population of France and England has accommodated itself more nearly to the average produce of each country, than many other states. The operation of the preventive check, wars, the silent, though certain destruction of life in large towns and manufactories, and the close habitations and insufficient food of many of the poor, prevent population from outrunning the means of subsistence; and, if I may use the expression, which certainly at first appears strange, supersede the necessity of great and ravaging epidemics to destroy what is redundant.

In one of the States of North America, the proportion of births to deaths on an average of seven years, ending 1743, was 30 to 10 or 3 to 1. In France and England, the highest average proportion cannot be reckoned at more than 12 to 10. Great and astonishing as this difference is, we ought not to be so wonder-struck at it, as to attribute it to the miraculous interposition of heaven. The causes of it are not remote, latent, and mysterious, but near us, round about us, and open to the investigation of every inquiring mind. Since the world began, the causes of population and depopulation have been probably as constant, as any of the laws of nature, with which we are acquainted.

The passion between the sexes has appeared in every age to be so nearly the same, that it may always be considered, in algebraic language, as a given quantity. The great law of necessity, which prevents population from increasing in any country, beyond the food which it can either produce or acquire, is a law so open to our view so obvious to our understandings, that we cannot for a moment doubt it. The different modes, which nature takes to repress a redundant population, do not appear indeed to us so certain and regular; but though we cannot always predict the mode, we may with certainty predict the fact. If the proportion of the births to the deaths for a few years, indicates an increase of numbers much beyond the proportional increased or acquired food of the country, we may be perfectly certain, that unless an emigration take place, the deaths will shortly exceed the births. If there were no other depopulating causes, and if the preventive check did not operate very strongly, every country would without doubt be subject to periodical plagues and famines.

The only true criterion of a real and permanent increase in the population of every country is the increase of the means of subsistence. But even this criterion is subject to some slight variations, which however are completely open to our observation. In some countries, population seems to have been forced; that is, the people have been habituated by degrees to live almost upon the smallest possible quantity of food. There must have been periods in such countries, where population increased permanently without an increase in the means of subsistence. China, India, and the countries possessed by the Bedouin Arabs, appear to answer to this description. The average produce of these countries seems to be but barely sufficient to support the lives of the inhabitants, and of course any deficiency from the badness of the seasons, must be fatal. Nations in this state must necessarily be subject to famines.

In America, where the reward of labour is at present so liberal, the lower classes might retrench very considerably in a year of scarcity, without materially distressing themselves. A famine therefore, seems to be almost impossible. It may be expected, that in the progress of the population of America, the labourers will in time be much less liberally rewarded. The numbers will in this case permanently increase, without a proportional increase in the food.

Other circumstances being the same, it may be affirmed, that countries are populous according to the quantity of human food, which they produce, or can acquire; and happy, according to the liberality with which this food is divided, or the quantity which a day's labour will purchase. Corn countries are more populous than pasture countries, and rice countries than corn countries. But their happiness does not depend either upon their being thinly or fully inhabited, upon their poverty or their riches, their youth or their age; but on the proportion which the population and the food bear to each other. This proportion is generally the most favourable in new colonies, where the knowledge and industry of an old State operate on the fertile unappropriated land of a new one. In other cases the youth or the age of a State is not, in this respect, of great importance. It is probable that the food of Great Britain is divided in more liberal shares to her inhabitants at the present period, than it was two thousand, three thousand, or four thousand years ago. And it has appeared, that the poor and thinly-inhabited tracts of the Scotch Highlands are more distressed by a redundant population, than the most populous parts of Europe.

If a country were never to be overrun by a people more advanced in arts, but left to its own natural progress in civilization ; from the time that its progress might be considered as a unit, to the time that it might be considered as a million, during the lapse of many thousand years, there would not be a single period, when the mass of people could be said to be free from distress, either directly or indirectly, for want of food. In every state of Europe, since we first have accounts of it, millions and millions of human existences have been repressed from this simple cause, though perhaps in some of these States an absolute famine may never have been known.

Must it not then be acknowledged by an attentive examiner of the histories of mankind, that in every age, and in every state, in which man has existed or does now exist,

The increase of population is necessarily limited by the means of subsistence ;

Population invariably increases when the means of subsistence increase, unless prevented by powerful and obvious checks ;

These checks, and the checks which keep the population down to the level of the means of subsistence, are moral restraint, vice, and misery?

In regarding the state of society, which has been last considered, I think it appears, that in modern Europe, the positive checks to population prevail less, and the preventive checks more, than in past times, and in the more uncivilized parts of the world.

War, the predominant check to the population of savage nations, has certainly abated, even including the late unhappy revolutionary contests ; and since the prevalence of a greater degree of personal cleanliness, of better modes of building and draining towns, and of a more equable distribution of the products of the soil from improving knowledge of political economy, plagues, violent diseases, and famines have been certainly mitigated, and have become less frequent.

With regard to the preventive check to population, though it must be acknowledged, that that branch of it, which comes under the head of moral restraint, does not at present prevail much among the male part of society ; yet I am strongly disposed to believe, that it prevails more than in those States which were first considered ; and it can scarcely be doubted that in modern Europe a much larger proportion of women pass a considerable part of their lives in the exercise of this virtue, than in past times, and among uncivilized nations. But however this may be, if we consider only the general term, which implies principally an infrequency of the marriage union from the fear of a family, without reference to consequences, it may be considered in this light, as the most powerful of the checks, which in modern Europe keep down the population to the level of the means of subsistence."

Mr. Malthus then proceeds to consider many of the prevalent fallacies on the subject of human progress, and the law of population; to which I beg the reader's particular attention, as they are the very same, that are still constantly repeated.   The law of population is so novel and startling, so paradoxical, and so thoroughly opposed to the ordinary modes of reasoning on human affairs : and moreover by its unparalleled importance so completely throws other subjects into the shade, besides presenting such a gloomy picture of human destiny ; that it is scarcely to be wondered at, that men have refused to give it the attentive consideration which is needed for its clear comprehension, and have clung with a desperate tenacity to the old errors, however unanswerably they have been exposed.   But there is not within the whole range of human thought a single subject, on which ignorance or misconception is so inevitably ruinous ; and therefore none on which fallacies are so dangerous, and where more strenuous endeavours are required to extirpate them from every mind.   The law of population is as certainly true, and as clearly shown as that of gravitation ; and if it had been openly discussed, instead of suppressed by the morbid sexual delicacy, its truth would already have been universally recognised. Let any man only really examine it, and not take it on hearsay from those who have never examined it ; let him openly state any doubt or objection he may have, and he may be certain that they will be easily answered, and that his conviction of the truth of the law, notwithstanding its paradoxical appearance, will become absolute.   How can a man expect to understand any truth if he do not disclose his doubts, and seek more information on the subject ; in a word give it " fair play ?"

All that the law of population needs, is *open discussion*, and its recognition in a few years would be as universal as that of the circulation of the blood.   It is because people misconceive the very meaning of the law, and recklessly adopt any surface fallacy on the subject, that it is so little attended to.

In the first place with regard to the *systems of perfectibility*, and the idea that the evils of over-population are *at a distance*, and belong rather to futurity than to the present and the past, (a mistake still very commonly prevalent,) Mr. Malthus says " To a person who views the past and present states of mankind in the light in which they have appeared in the preceding pages, it cannot but be a matter of astonishment, that all the writers on the perfectibility of man and of society, who have noticed the argument of the principle of population, treat it always very slightly, and invariably represent the difficulties arising from it, as at a great and almost immeasurable distance.   They think that no difficulty from over-population or the tendency to it would arise, till the whole earth had been cultivated like a garden.   But the truth is, that the difficulty, so far from being remote, is imminent and immediate.   At every period during the progress of cultivation, from the present moment till the earth was become like a garden, the difficulty from want of food would constantly be pressing on mankind.   Though the produce of the earth would be increasing every year, population would be tending to increase much faster, and the redundancy must necessarily be checked by the periodical or constant action of moral restraint, vice, or misery."

Mr. Malthus applies the law of population to the schemes of human perfectibility brought forward by Mr. Godwin, M. Condorcet, and other writers; and shows how this great natural difficulty, which had not been taken into consideration, completely destroys all their bright anticipations of the future destiny of mankind. "Mr. Godwin in one place, speaking of population, says, 'There is a principle in human society, by which population is perpetually kept down to the level of the means of subsistence.' This principle, which Mr. Godwin thus mentions as some mysterious and occult cause, and which he does not attempt to investigate, has appeared to be the grinding law of necessity—misery, and the fear of misery."

"The great error under which Mr. Godwin labours throughout his whole work, is the attributing of almost all the vices and misery that prevail in civil society to human institutions. Political regulations, and the established administration of property, are with him the fruitful sources of all evil, the hot-beds of all the crimes, that degrade mankind. But the truth is, that though human institutions appear to be, and indeed often are, the obvious and obtrusive causes of much mischief to mankind, they are in reality light and superficial, in comparison with those deeper-seated causes of evil which result from the laws of nature and the passions of mankind." (This error is the prevailing one among the political and social reformers at the present day).

"How little Mr. Godwin has turned his attention to the real state of human society, will sufficiently appear from the manner, in which he endeavours to remove the difficulty of an over-charged population. He says, 'The obvious answer to this objection is, that to reason thus is to foresee difficulties at a great distance. Three-fourths of the habitable globe are now uncultivated. The parts already cultivated are capable of immeasurable improvement. Myriads of centuries of still increasing population may pass away, and the earth be still found sufficient for the subsistence of its inhabitants.'

"To suppose," says Mr. Malthus "that, in speaking of these effects of the principle of population, I look to certain periods in future, when population will exceed the means of subsistence in a much greater degree than at present, and that the evils arising from this principle are rather in contemplation than in existence, is, I must again repeat, a total misconception of the argument. *Poverty*, and not absolute famine, is the specific effect of the principle of population, as I have endeavoured to show. Many countries are *now* suffering all the evils which can ever be expected to flow from this principle; and even if we were arrived at the absolute limit to all further increase of produce, a point which we shall certainly never reach, I should by no means expect that these evils would be in any marked manner aggravated. The increase of produce in most European countries is so very slow, compared with what would be required to support an unrestricted increase of people, that the checks which are constantly in action to repress the population to the level of a produce, increasing so slowly, would have very little more to do in wearing it down to a produce absolutely stationary." •

Next of *emigration*, as a remedy for the effects of the law of population, (the most prevalent of all fallacies on the subject, and also the one which most naturally presents itself).

" It may be said that in the case of a redundant population, the natural and obvious remedy that presents itself is, *emigration* to those parts that are uncultivated. As these parts are of great extent, and very thinly peopled, this resource might appear on a first view of the subject an adequate remedy, or at least of a nature to ·remove the evil to a distant period ; but when we advert to experience, and the actual state of the uncivilized parts of the globe, instead of anything like an adequate remedy, it will appear but a slight palliative."

The obstacles which oppose the establishment of new colonies among the uncivilized nations of Asia and Africa are great; possession of these countries could not be obtained without a large armed force and frequent warfare with the natives, who must moreover be eventually exterminated with an immensity of misery. In Australia and America, these preliminary steps have been taken, and a secure possession gained ; and "for many years before the American war and since, the facilities for emigration to this new world, were unusually great ; and it must be considered undoubtedly as a very happy circumstance for any country, to have so comfortable an asylum for its redundant population. But I would ask whether, even during these periods, the distress among the common people in this country was little ; and whether every man felt secure before he ventured on marriage, that however large his family might be, he should find no difficulty in supporting it without parish assistance ? "

The ties of family, and love to one's native soil ; the doubts and uncertainties which ever attend distant emigrations, particularly in the apprehensions of the uneducated classes ; the expense and difficulty of so critical a step, and many other powerful obstacles, oppose emigration, and prevent it from ever being used to such an extent, as even to palliate materially for a short time the evils of poverty, far less to supersede wholly the usual preventive and positive checks, namely—moral restraint, prostitution, or premature death.

" Every resource, however, from emigration, if used effectually, must be of short duration. There is scarcely a State in Europe, except perhaps Russia, whose inhabitants do not often endeavour to better their condition by removing to other countries. Let us suppose for a moment, that in this more enlightened part of the globe, the internal economy of each state were to be so admirably regulated, that no checks existed to population, and that the different governments provided every facility for emigration. Taking the population of Europe, excluding Russia, at one hundred millions, and allowing a greater increase of produce than is probable, or even possible in the mother countries, the redundancy of parent stock in a single century would be eleven hundred millions, which, added to the natural increase of the colonies during the same time, would more than double what has been supposed to be the present population of the whole globe.

It is evident therefore, that the reason why the resource of emigration has so long continued to be held out as a remedy for redundant population, is, because from the natural unwillingness of people to desert their native country, and the difficulty and hardships of clearing and cultivating fresh soil, it never is or can be, adequately adopted. If this remedy were indeed really effectual, and had power so far to relieve the disorders of vice and misery in old states, as to place them in the condition of the most prosperous new colonies, we should soon see the phial exhausted; and when the disorders returned with increased virulence, every hope from this quarter would be for ever closed.

It is clear therefore, that with any view of making room for an unrestricted population, or superseding the necessity of powerful checks to it, emigration is perfectly inadequate."

Next of the *Poor Laws*, or any *artificial interference* in the *wages* of labour, as a remedy.

"To remedy the frequent distresses of the poor, laws to enforce their relief have been instituted, and in the establishment of a general system of this kind, England has particularly distinguished herself. But it is to be feared that though it may have alleviated a little the intensity of individual misfortune, it has spread the evil over a much larger surface."

"No possible sacrifices of the rich, particularly in money, could for any time prevent the occurrence of distress among the lower members of society whoever they were. Great changes might indeed be made. The rich might become poor, and some of the poor rich; but while the present proportion between the population and food continues, a part of the society must necessarily find it difficult to support a family, and this difficulty will naturally fall on the least fortunate members."

"The price of labour, when left to find its natural level, is a most important political barometer, expressing the relation between the supply of provisions, and the demand for them: between the quantity to be consumed and the number of consumers; and taken on the average, independently of accidental circumstances, it further expresses clearly the wants of society respecting population; that is, whatever may be the number of children to a marriage, necessary to maintain exactly the present population, the price of labour will be just sufficient to support this number, or be above it, or below it, according to the real fund for the maintenance of labour, whether stationary, progressive, or retrograde. Instead however, of considering it in this light, we consider it as something which we may raise or depress at pleasure, something which depends principally upon His Majesty's justices of the peace. When an advance in the price of provisions already expresses, that the demand is too great for the supply, in order to put the labourer in the same condition as before, we raise the price of labour, that is, we increase the demand, and are then much surprised that the price of provisions continues rising. In this we act much in the same manner as if, when the quicksilver in the weatherglass stood at *stormy*, we were to raise it by some mechanical pressure to *set fair* and then be greatly astonished that it continued raining. And yet many men who would shrink at the proposal of a maximum in the price of provisions, would propose themselves, that the price of labour should be proportioned to the price of provisions, and do not seem to be aware that the two proposals are almost the same, and that both tend directly to famine.''

" The poor laws tend to depress the condition of the poor in two ways. Their first obvious tendency is to increase population without increasing the food for its support. A poor man may marry, with little or no prospect of being able to support a family without parish assistance. They may be said therefore to create the poor which they maintain.

Secondly, the quantity of food consumed in workhouses, diminishes the share which would otherwise belong to the other members of society, raises the price of provisions, and thus in the same manner forces more to become dependent.

If men be induced to marry from the mere prospect of parish assistance they are not only unjustly tempted to bring unhappiness and dependence upon themselves and their children, but also, without knowing it, to injure all in the same class with themselves."

" If we examine some of our statutes strictly with reference to the principle of population, we shall find that they attempt an absolute impossibility. The famous 43rd of Elizabeth, which has been so often referred to and admired, enacts, that the overseers of the poor shall provide work for all the children, whose parents are not able to support them: and shall raise by taxation, from the inhabitants of the parish, materials to set all the poor to work.

What is this but saying, that the funds for the maintenance of labour may be increased at will and without limit, by a fiat of goverment? Strictly speaking, this clause is as arrogant and absurd, as if it had enacted, that two ears of wheat should in future grow, where one only had grown before. The execution of this famous clause is a physical impossibility ; and it is only owing to its incomplete execution that it still remains on our statute book."

" The attempts to employ the poor on any great scale in manufactures, have almost invariably failed, and the stock and materials have been wasted. Wherever they have been partially successful, their effect has been to throw out of employment many independent workmen engaged in the same manufactures ; for these cannot contend with competitors, supported by so great a bounty. It should be observed, in general, that when a fund for the maintenance of labour is raised by assessment, the greatest part of it is not a new capital brought into trade, but an old one, which before was much more profitably employed, turned into a new channel ; and this aggravates the absurdity of supposing, that it is in the power of a government to find employment for all its subjects, however fast they may increase."

" The poor laws, as a general system, are founded on a gross error ; and the common declamations on the subject of the poor, which we see so often in print, and hear continually in conversation, namely, that the market price of labour ought always to be sufficient decently to support a family, and that employment ought to be found for all those that are willing to work, is in effect to say—that the funds for the maintenance of labour in this country are not only infinite, but might be made to increase with such rapidity, that, supposing us at present to have six millions of labourers, including their families, we might have ninety-six millions in another century," &c.

Next of the fallacies of *waste among the rich,* and *uncultivated lands,* (which, with emigration and government employment, are the most prevalent fallacies still existing on the subject of poverty and its remedies).

"Among the other prejudices which have prevailed on the subject of population, it has been generally thought, that while there is either waste among the rich, or land remaining uncultivated, in any country, the complaints for want of food cannot be justly founded ; or at least that the pressure of distress among the poor is to be attributed to the ill conduct of the higher classes of society and the bad management of the land. The real effect however, of these two circumstances is merely to narrow the limit of the actual population ; but they have little or no influence on what may be called the average pressure of distress on the poorer members of society. If our ancestors had been so frugal and industrious, and had transmitted such habits to their posterity, that nothing superfluous was now consumed by the higher classes, no horses were used for pleasure, and no land was left uncultivated, a striking difference would appear, in the state of the actual population ; but probably none whatever in the state of the lower classes, with respect to the price of labour and the difficulty of supporting a family. The waste among the rich, and the horses kept for pleasure, have indeed a little of the effect of the consumption of grain in distilleries, noticed before with regard to China. On the supposition that the food consumed in this manner, may be withdrawn on the occasion of a scarcity, and be applied to the relief of the poor, they operate certainly, as far as they go, like granaries that are only opened at the time they are most needed ; and must tend therefore rather to benefit than to injure the lower classes of society.

With regard to the *uncultivated land,* it is evident that its effect on the poor is neither to injure nor to benefit them. The sudden cultivation of it will indeed tend to improve their condition for a time, and the neglect of lands before cultivated will certainly make their situation worse for a certain period ; but when no changes of this kind are going forward, the effect of uncultivated land on the lower classes operates merely like the possession of a smaller territory.

We should not be too ready to make inferences against the internal economy of a country from the appearance of uncultivated land, without other evidence. The fact is, that as no country has ever reached, or probably ever will reach, its highest possible acme of produce, it appears always as if the want of industry, or the ill-direction of that industry, was the actual limit to the increase of produce and population, and not the absolute refusal of nature to yield any more ; but it is never the question with regard to the principle of population, whether a country will produce *any more,* but whether it may be made to produce a deficiency to keep pace with an unchecked increase of people.

The allowing of the produce of the earth to be absolutely unlimited, scarcely removes the weight of a hair from the argument, which depends entirely on the differently increasing ratios of population and food ; and all that the most enlightened government, and the most persevering and best guided efforts of industry can do, is to make the necessary checks to population operate more equally, and in a direction to produce the least evil; but to remove them is a task absolutely hopeless."

Mr. Malthus next treats "of our future prospects regarding the removal or mitigation of the evils, arising from the principle of population ; and first, of *moral restraint*, and our duty to practice this virtue."

Moral restraint—that is, *sexual abstinence*—is in the eyes of Mr. Malthus *the only remedy* for poverty and other evil effects of the principle of population ; the preventive check being the only possible alternative to the positive one.

He says, " As it appears that in every state of society we have considered, the natural progress of population has been constantly and powerfully checked ; and as it seems evident, that no improved form of government ; no plans of emigration ; no benevolent institutions ; and no degree or direction of industry can prevent the operation of some great check to population ; it follows, that we must submit to it as an inevitable law of nature : and the only inquiry that remains is, how it may take place with the least possible prejudice to the virtue and happiness of human society. All the immediate checks to population, which have been observed to prevail in the same and different countries, seem to be resolvable into moral restraint, vice, and misery ; and if our choice be confined to these, it is easy to decide which it would be most eligible to encourage. It is better that the check should arise from foreseeing the difficulties attending a family, than from the actual presence of these difficulties.

The imprudent indulgence of all our appetites is followed by similar bad effects. If we eat or drink inmoderately, we suffer ; if we give way to anger we injure ourselves or our neighbours ; if we multiply too fast, we die miserably of poverty and contagious diseases. The evils attendant on increasing too fast, are not so immediately or obviously dependent on the conduct which leads to them, as in the other instances ; and this in great measure accounts for the inattention of mankind to the subject."

" The fecundity of the human species is a law, exactly similar in its great features, to all the other laws of nature. It is strong and general, and the evils arising from it are incidental to these necessary qualities of strength and generality, and are capable of being greatly mitigated and rendered comparatively light, by human energy and virtue. We have under our guidance a great power, capable of peopling a desert region in a small number of years ; and yet under other circumstances capable of being confined to any limits, however narrow, by human energy and virtue, at the expense of a small comparative quantity of evil."

" As moral restraint is the only virtuous mode of avoiding the incidental evils, arising from the principle of population, our obligation to practise it evidently rests on the same foundation as all the other virtues—the foundation of utility.

Whatever indulgence we may be disposed to allow to occasional failures in the discharge of a duty of acknowledged difficulty, yet of the strict line of duty we cannot doubt. Our obligation not to marry, till we have a fair prospect of being able to support our children, will appear to deserve the attention of moralists, if it can be proved that an attention to this obligation is of most powerful effect in the prevention of misery ; and that, if it were the general custom to follow the first impulse of nature, and marry at the age of puberty, the universal prevalence of every known virtue in the greatest conceivable degree, would fail to rescue society from the most wretched and desperate state of want, with all the diseases and famines, which usually accompany it.

One of the principal reasons, which have prevented an assent to the doctrine of population, is a great unwillingness to believe that the Deity would, by the laws of nature, bring beings into existence, which by the laws of nature could not be supported. But if, in addition to the general activity and direction of our industry, put in motion by these laws, we find that by moral restraint, which both reason and revelation urge upon us, we can avoid these evils, then will this apparent imputation on the goodness of the Deity be done away with."

Mr. Malthus then draws a picture of what he conceives the state of society would be, if all were to refrain from marrying till they could support a family. He says that if by this means, fewer children were born, the wages of labour would be raised, and " all squalid poverty would be removed from society.

The interval between puberty and marriage must, according to this supposition, be passed in strict chastity, because the law of chastity cannot be broken without producing evil. Promiscuous intercourse evidently weakens the best feelings of the heart, and degrades in a marked manner the female character ; and any other intercourse would, without improper arts, bring as many children into society as marriage, with a much greater probability of their becoming a burden on it.

These considerations show that the virtue of *chastity* is not, as some have supposed, a forced produce of artificial society, but that it has a real and solid foundation in nature and reason ; being apparently the only virtuous means of avoiding the misery and vice, which so often result from the principle of population."

" There are perhaps few actions, which tend so directly to diminish the general happiness, as to marry without the means of supporting children.

If we feel convinced of the misery, arising from a redundant population on the one hand, and of the evils and unhappiness, particularly to the female sex, arising from promiscuous intercourse on the other, I do not see how it is possible for any person, who acknowledges utility as the great foundation of morals, to escape the conclusion, that moral restraint is the strict line of duty; and this is strengthened and confirmed by the dictates of religion. At the same time, I believe that few of my readers can be less sanguine in their expectation of any great change in the conduct of men than I am."

"The duty is intelligible to the meanest capacity. It is merely not to bring beings into the world, for whom one cannot find means of support. From conversations I have had with some of their number, I should by no means say, that it would be a difficult task to make the common people comprehend the principle of population, and its effect in producing low wages and poverty."

"It does not seem visionary to suppose that if the *true and permanent cause of poverty* were clearly explained, and forcibly brought home to each man's bosom, it would have some, and perhaps no slight influence on his conduct; at least the experiment has never yet been fairly tried. Almost everything that has hitherto been done for the poor, has tended as if with solicitous care, to throw a veil of obscurity over this subject, and to hide from them the true cause of their poverty. When the wages of labour are hardly enough to maintain two children, a man marries, and has five or six. He of course finds himself miserably distressed. He accuses the low rate of wages; he accuses the parish for their tardy and scanty assistance; he accuses the avarice of the rich; he accuses the partial and unjust institutions of society; and perhaps, he accuses the dispensations of Providence. But he never adverts to the real quarter whence his distress arises. The last person he would think of accusing is himself, on whom in fact, the principal blame rests, except in so far as he has been deceived by the higher classes of society; who are however, generally as ignorant of the matter as himself. He may perhaps wish that he had not married, but it never enters into his head that he has done anything wrong. He has always been told, that to raise up subjects for his king and country, is a highly meritorious act. He naturally thinks that he is suffering for righteousness' sake, and is indignant at the cruelty and injustice of others, for allowing him so to suffer.

Till these errors and prejudices have been corrected, it cannot be said that any fair experiment has been made with the understandings of the poor; and we cannot justly accuse them of imprudence, till they act, as they now do, after it has been fully shown to them, that they themselves are the cause of their own poverty; that the means of improving their condition are in their own hands, and in the hands of no other persons whatever; that society and the government are without any direct power in this matter, and cannot assist them, however they might desire to do so; that when the wages of labour will not support a family, it is a certain sign that the country cannot support more inhabitants: that if they marry in this case, they are throwing a useless burden on society, plunging themselves into distress, and bringing upon themselves various miseries and diseases, which might all have been avoided, had they attended to the dictates of reason and the laws of nature.

The object of those who really wish to better the condition of the lower classes, must be, to raise the relative proportion between the price of labour, and the price of food. We have hitherto principally endeavoured to attain this end by encouraging the married poor, and consequently increasing the number of labourers, and overstocking the market with that commodity, (labour), which we still say we wish to be dear.   This has been tried in many different countries, and for many hundred years, and its success is just what might have been expected.   It is really time now to try something else.

In all old and fully peopled States it is *by checking the supply of labourers* and by this means alone, that we can rationally expect any essential or permanent amelioration in the condition of the poor.   Finding that however fast we increase the quantity of food, the quantity of consumers more than keeps pace with it, and that with all our efforts we are still as far as ever behind, we should be convinced, that our efforts, directed in this way only, will never succeed.   We should then try to proportion the population to the food, since it is impossible to proportion the food to unrestricted population.   Both objects indeed must be strenuously pursued ; and thus we might obtain the two grand desiderata, a great actual population, and a state of society, in which all squalid poverty and dependence would be comparatively little known.

A market overstocked with labourers and an ample remuneration to each labourer are matters perfectly incompatible.   In the annals of the world they never existed together ; and to couple them even in imagination betrays a gross ignorance of the simplest principles of political economy."

" But let those, who are unconvinced by these arguments, attend to the consequence of pursuing the opposite mode.

If we should wish all to marry young, and still hope to be able to surmount the evils, diseases, and misery, that this will cause, be assured all our efforts will be in vain.   Nature will not, cannot be defeated in her purposes.   The necessary mortality must come in some form or other ; and the extirpation of one disease by human skill, will only be the signal for the birth of another, perhaps more fatal.

In a country which keeps its population at a certain standard, if the average number of marriages and births be given, it is evident that the average of deaths will also be given ; and the diseases or channels of death will always convey away a certain quantity.   Now if we stop up one of these channels, or in other words extirpate one form of disease, others must become more fatal, so long as the same number of marriages and births takes place.   Thus it has often been remarked by physicians, that diseases change their forms at different periods, from causes they cannot account for.   Thus, while some diseases, as the plague, dysentery, ague, &c., have become less frequent in England, others, as consumption, gout, lunacy, &c., have become more frequent.   Sanguine hopes have been formed of the benefit which would accrue to the race, from the extinction of different forms of diseases ; but these hopes are demonstrably vain, as long as the same proportion of births takes place.

It cannot be said that we leave individuals free to follow their own choice on the matter; for at present the Poor Laws give a direct and systematic encouragement to marriage, and our private benevolence has often the same tendency, namely to facilitate the rearing of families, and to equalize as much as possible the circumstances of married and single men. Throughout all the ranks of society, moreover, the prevailing feelings respecting the duty and obligation of marriage, cannot but have a very powerful influence. A man who thinks that he will have failed in an important duty to society by going out of the world without leaving children, will be disposed rather to force than to restrain his inclination.

As to the effects of the knowledge of the principal cause of poverty on *civil liberty*, I believe that nothing would so powerfully contribute to a rational freedom, as a thorough knowledge of this subject; while ignorance of it, forms at present one of its chief obstacles. The pressure of distress on the poor, with the habit of attributing this distress to their *rulers*, appears to me to be the rock of defence, the guardian spirit of despotism. It affords to the tyrant the unanswerable plea of necessity. It is the reason that all free goverments tend constantly to their own destruction; that so many noble efforts in the cause of freedom have failed; and that almost every revolution, after a long and bloody struggle, has ended in a military despotism. When an established government has been destroyed, the poor, finding their evils not removed, turn their resentment against the successors in power; and so on without end, till the majority of the well-disposed people, sick of anarchy, are ready to throw themselves into the arms of the first sufficient power. A mob, which is generally the growth of a redundant population, goaded on by real sufferings, but ignorant whence they proceed, is of all monsters the most fatal to freedom.''

" There is one right, which man has generally been thought to possess, which I am confident he neither does nor can possess, a right to subsistence, when his labour will not fairly purchase it. Our laws indeed say that he has this right; but in so doing they attempt to reverse the laws of nature. A man has just the same right to live a thousand years, *if he can;* it is a matter of power not of right.

If men were only convinced of this truth, that they can have no *right* of subsistence, all the mischievous declamations against the unjust institutions of society, would fall powerless to the ground. If the real causes of their distress were clearly pointed out to the poor, and they were shown how small a part of their distress is attributable to government, a great part of that discontent and irritation, which exist at present among them, would cease, and when they did show themselves, would not be so much to be dreaded. ''

Mr. Malthus having thus shown that it is only by having fewer children, that it is possible for the poor to escape from poverty, and having urged upon them sexual abstinence as the only virtuous mode of effecting this, proceeds to some *auxiliary* and *secondary means* of promoting this preventive check. In the first place he proposes the gradual abolition of the Poor Laws, which had done so much harm to the poor, by tempting them to beget a family, without a prospect of being able to support it by their own exertions. However, it has been shown since, that if

parish assistance is coupled with very irksome conditions, it does not
tend powerfully to weaken the feeling of prudential restraint: and thus
the *right of subsistence* is still acknowledged by the State as belonging to
every citizen, though, as Mr. Mill says, this cannot, without ruinous
consequences, be coupled with the right of begetting children to be supported by charity.

"It is not enough," says Mr. Malthus, "to abolish all the positive
institutions that encourage population, we must endeavour to correct by
writing and conversation, the prevailing errors on the subject; to show
that it is not the duty of man simply to propagate his species, but to propagate virtue and happiness; and that if he cannot do the one, he is by
no means called upon to do the other.

Among the higher classes we need not apprehend the too great frequency of marriages. A proper pride and spirit of independence, in most
cases, prevent imprudent marriages among these classes; although even
among them, juster ideas might prevent many unhappy marriages. All
that a society can demand of its members is, that they do not have
families without being able to support them. This may be fairly enjoined as a positive duty; all beyond it is a matter of choice; but from
what we know of the habits of the higher classes, we have reason to
think that all that is necessary to obtain the object required, is to give a
greater degree of respect and liberty to single women, and place them
more on a level with married ones: a change which indeed the plainest
principles of justice demand.

Among the lower classes, the way to effect our purpose is evidently to
infuse into their minds a part of that prudence and foresight, which operates in the higher classes. The best way of doing this, would be by an
extended system of education; and in addition to the general subjects of
instruction, it would be well to explain the principle of population, and
its effect on the condition of the poor. The desirableness of marriage
should not be underrated; but it should be shown, that, like property, and
other blessings, marriage should be the reward of industry and other
good qualities.

It would be moreover of very great benefit to society, if the simplest
principles of political economy were also taught; for the common ignorance on these matters is very great, and exceedingly dangerous to a
State.

We have lavished immense sums on the poor, which we have every
reason to believe have only tended to increase their misery. But in their
education, and in the circulation of these important political truths,
which most nearly concern them, which are perhaps the only means in
our power of really raising their condition, and making them happier
men and more peaceful subjects, we have been miserably deficient.

It would add greatly to the advantages of a national system of education, if the schools were made the means of instructing the people in the
real nature of their situation; if they were taught, what is really true,
that without an increase of their own prudential restraint, no change of
government could essentially benefit their condition; that, though they
might by such a change get rid of some particular grievances, yet in the

great point of supporting their families, they would be but little, or not at all benefitted; that a revolution would not alter in their favour the proportion of the supply of labour to the demand, or the quantity of food to the number of consumers; and that, if the supply of labour were greater than the demand, and the demand for food greater than the supply, they might suffer the most extreme want, under the freeest and most perfect government, that the human imagination could conceive.

In most countries, among the lower classes, there seems to be something like a *standard of wretchedness*; a point below which they will not marry and propagate their species. This standard is different in different countries, and is formed by various concurring circumstances of soil, climate, government, degree of knowledge and civilization &c. The principal circumstances that contribute to raise it, are liberty, security of property the spread of knowledge, and a taste for the conveniences and comforts of life. Those which contribute chiefly to lower it are despotism and ignorance.

In our attempts to better the lower classes, our endeavours should be to raise the standard as high as possible, by cultivating a spirit of independence, a decent pride, and a taste for cleanliness and comfort. One of the most powerful means of so doing, is a wide-spread national education, and certainly no government does its duty towards its subjects, which neglects this."

He then speaks of *charity* as a mode of palliating the evils of poverty, and shows how often it tends, like the Poor Laws, when exercised in a thoughtless manner, to tempt people to become dependent, and to bring children into the world only to beggary. Hence he says, "We lie under a strong obligation to practise charity in a discriminating manner, for it has invariably been found, that poverty and misery, have increased in proportion to the quantity of indiscriminate charity.

Nothing can be clearer, than that it is in the power of money and the exertions of the rich, to relieve a particular family, a particular parish, or even a particular district. But it will be equally clear, that it is totally out of their power to relieve a whole country in the same way.

Even *industry* in this way is not very different from money. A man who possesses more of it than his neighbours, is indeed almost sure of getting a livelihood; but if his neighbours were equally industrious, his industry would be no security against want. Hume fell into a very great error, when he said that 'Almost all the moral, as well as natural, evils of human life arise from idleness.' It is evident that if the whole species possessed the greatest imaginable industry, if not combined with another virtue of which he takes no notice, it would wholly fail of rescuing society from want and misery, and would scarcely remove a single moral or physical evil of all those to which he alludes."

" We cannot in the nature of things, assist the poor in any way, without enabling them to rear to manhood a greater number of their children. But this is of all things the most desirable, both with regard to individuals and the public. Every loss of a child from the effects of poverty, must evidently be preceded and accompanied by great misery to individuals; and in a public view, every child that dies under ten years of age, is a loss to the nation of all that had been expended in its subsistence up to that period. Consequently, in every point of view, a decrease of mortality at all ages is what we ought to aim at.

It is impossible to do this : *it is not in the nature of things, that any permanent and general improvement in the condition of the poor can be effected without an increase in the preventive check to population ;* and unless this take place, either with or without our efforts, everything that is done for the poor must be temporary and partial ; a diminution of mortality at present will be balanced by an increased mortality in future : and improvements of their condition in one place will proportionally depress it in another. This is a truth so important and so little understood, that it can scarcely be too often insisted on.''

" In taking a general and concluding view of our rational expectations respecting the future improvement of society, and the mitigation of the evils arising from the principle of population, it may be observed, that though the increase of population in a geometrical ratio be incontrovertible, yet there are some natural results of the progress of society and civilization, which necessarily repress its full effects. These are especially great towns and manufactures, in which we can scarcely hope, and cer tainly not expect, to see any material change. These will probably always continue much more unhealthy than country employments and situations, and consequently, operating as positive checks, diminish the neccessity for the preventive one.

In every old State, it is observed that a considerable number of adults remain for a time unmarried. The duty of practising the common and acknowledged rules of morality during this period, has never been controverted in theory, however it may have been opposed in practice. Knowing how incompletely this duty has hitherto been fulfilled, it would be visionary to expect any·material change for the better in future.

But it is by no means visionary to expect, that some favourable change may take place in the extension of this period of celibacy, till we have the prospect of being able to maintain our children ; for it is found by experience, that the prevalence of this restraint is very different at different times and in different countries. It cannot be doubted, that in Europe generally, and more especially among the Northern nations, a decided change has taken place in the operation of this prudential restraint since the prevalence of those warlike habits, which destroyed so many people. In this country it is not to be doubted, that the proportion of marriages has become smaller, since the improvement of our towns, the less frequent epidemics, and the adoption of more cleanly habits.

Universally the practice of men in this respect has been better than their theories ; and however frequent may have been the declamations on the duty of entering into the married state, and the advantage of early marriage to prevent vice, each individual has practically found it necessary to consider of the means of supporting a family, before he ventured to take so important a step. That great *vis medicatrix reipublicæ*, the desire of bettering our condition, and the fear of making it worse, has been constantly in action ; and owing to this the prudential check to marriage has increased in Europe, and will probably make still further advances. If it do so without any marked increase of a vicious sexual intercourse, the happiness of society will evidently be promoted by it ; and it is to be observed, that those European countries, where marriages are least frequent, as Norway, Switzerland, England, and Scotland, are by no means the most noted for their profligacy of manners, but rather the reverse.

It is less the object of the present work to propose new plans for improving society, than to inculcate the necessity of resting contented with that mode of improvement, which is dictated by the course of nature, and of not obstructing the advances which would otherwise be made in this way. The limited good, which it is sometimes in our power to effect, is often lost by attempting too much, and by making the adoption of a particular system, essentially necessary even to a partial degree of success. I hope I have avoided this error. I wish the reader to remember, that though I may have given some new views of old facts, and indulged in the contemplation of a considerable degree of *possible* improvement, that I might not absolutely shut out that prime cheerer—hope ; yet in my expectations of probable improvement, and the means of accomplishing it, I have been very cautious. The gradual abolition of the Poor Laws, and the extension of education, are the only means I have proposed, and these would certainly benefit in some degree the condition of the poor ; but even though they be not adopted, I do not absolutely despair of some partial good effect from the general tenor of the reasoning.

If the principles I have endeavoured to establish be false, I most sincerely hope to see them completely refuted ; but if they be true, the subject is so important to human happiness, that it is impossible that they should not in time be more fully known and generally circulated, whether any particular efforts be made for the purpose or not.

Among the higher and middle classes the effect of this knowledge would, I hope, be to direct, without relaxing, their efforts for bettering the condition of the poor ; to show them what they can, and what they cannot do and that, though much may be done by instructing the poor, and in other modes elevating their character, so as to produce a greater amount of the preventive check, yet without the latter all the former efforts will be futile ; and that in any old and well-peopled State, so to assist the poor, as to enable them to marry as soon as they like, and rear up large families, is a physical impossibility.

Among the lower classes the effect of such knowledge would be, to make them more peaceable and orderly, less inclined to tumultuous proceedings in seasons of scarcity, and less influenced by inflammatory and seditious publications, from knowing how little the price of labour, and the means of supporting a family, depend upon a revolution. This would give to society the power of gradually improving their government, without the fear of those revolutionary excesses, which are the greatest foes to the progress of liberty.

From a review of the state of society in early times, compared with the present, I should certainly say that the evils attendant on population have rather diminished than increased, notwithstanding an almost total ignorance of their real cause. If we can indulge the hope that this ignorance will in time be dispelled, it may be rationally expected, that it will be even further diminished. The increase of absolute population which will of course take place, will not weaken this expectation, as everything depends upon the relative proportion between population and food, and not on the absolute population. In the former part of this work it appeared, that the countries with fewest inhabitants often suffered most from want of food; whereas in modern Europe, fewer famines and diseases from want have prevailed in the last century, than in those which preceded it.

On the whole therefore, though our future prospects respecting the mitigation of the evils arising from the principle of population, may not be so bright as we could wish, yet they are far from being entirely disheartening, and by no means preclude that gradual and progressive improvement in human society, which, before the late wild speculations on the subject, was the object of rational expectation. A strict inquiry into the principle of population obliges us to conclude, that we shall never be able to throw down the ladder, by which we have risen to our present height of civilization; but it by no means proves that we shall not rise higher through the same means.

It would indeed be a melancholy reflection, that while the views of physical science are daily enlarging, so as scarcely to be bounded by the most distant horizon, the science of moral and political economy should be confined within such narrow limits, or at least be so feeble in its influence, as to be unable to counteract the obstacles to human happiness arising from a single cause. But however formidable these obstacles may be, it is hoped that the general result of this enquiry is such, as not to make us give up the improvement of human society in despair. The partial good which seems attainable is worthy of all our exertions; and though we cannot expect that the virtue and happiness of mankind will keep pace with the brilliant career of physical discovery; yet if we are not wanting to ourselves, we may confidently indulge the hope, that to no unimportant extent, they will be influenced by its progress, and will partake in its success."

Thus finishes this wonderful Essay; the most important contribution to human knowledge, it appears to me, that ever was made. On rising from it, with a mind overpowered by the vastness of the subject, and the incomparable way in which it has been treated, I cannot but consider its author to have been the greatest benefactor of mankind, *without any exception*, that ever existed on this earth. I do not say that Mr. Malthus possessed the greatest genius, or most exalted moral character, that has appeared in history; but that the discovery of the law of population, which he made, and the service he thus rendered to his race, was of a higher nature than any other ever conferred upon mankind. It is a discovery, which, in fact, stands quite alone and unapproachable among discoveries, in its relation to human happiness. Compared with it, the labours of poets, of a Shakspeare, a Voltaire, a Goethe, or a Byron; of the physical inquirers—as Newton, Laennec, Humboldt, or Bacon, are utterly insignificant in their power over human happiness. The law of population is beyond all comparison the most important law ever discovered, and the most indispensable contribution to moral, medical, and political science. It explains to us the natural relation of the two very first essentials of human life and happiness, namely, Food and Love; without a knowledge of which, all other knowledge can avail us little. And yet the man, who imparted to his race this priceless knowledge, is little known, and mentioned, if at all, generally rather in terms of ridicule and contempt; while the conventional heroes of the world, poets, moralists, or religious innovators, are worshipped and idolised by all. We will yet learn better, to whom our chief thanks are due; and the incomparable boon, given to us by Mr. Malthus, will yet be estimated at its true value.

As it is of the utmost consequence that all of us should have a thorough comprehension of the great law of population, and a conviction of its paramount importance, I entreat the reader's attention to the description of it, given by Mr. John Stuart Mill, before I proceed to consider further its bearings on the sexual and social problems of the day. Mr. Mill is acknowledged to be the first existing writer on political economy; and his inimitable work on that subject, " the Principles of Political Economy," which, for its depth and closeness of reasoning; its iron logic, and brilliant eloquence of style; its wide and comprehensive grasp of social questions; and also its manly, liberal, and deeply sympathising spirit, ever taking the side of the weak against the strong, with a real philanthropy, equalled only by its profound enlightenment; for these and other matchless qualities, stands unrivalled among the works of the age, and far above my humble praise—this great work is built upon the principle of population as its keystone.   Mr. Mill shows, what every one, who deeply considers the question, must see, that this principle lies at the very first foundation of political economy, and also of moral science.   Mr. Mill's work should be carefully studied by all, who wish to obtain a true insight into the great social and economical questions of our times.

I should much prefer to give his views on the subject in his own words; but as I cannot take the liberty of making so large an extract from his work, I shall merely give the substance of his opinions, and refer the reader for further satisfaction to the work itself.

Mr. Mill first explains the power of increase inherent in the human species, as in all other living beings; showing, as Mr. Malthus did, that it is immense, if unchecked; and that it is a very moderate calculation to assume that each generation, in a good sanitary condition of the people, might be double that which preceded it, were the power of multiplication not restrained by different causes.

" Twenty or thirty years ago," says Mr. Mill, " these propositions might still have required considerable enforcement and illustration, but the evidence of them is so ample and incontestable, that they have made their way against all kinds of opposition, and may now be regarded as axiomatic; although the extreme reluctance felt to admitting them, every now and then gives birth to some ephemeral theory, speedily forgotten, of a different law of increase in different circumstances, through a providential adaptation of the fecundity of the human species to the exigences of society.   The obstacle to a just understanding of the subject does not arise from these theories; but from too confused a notion of the causes, which, at most times and places, keep the actual increase of mankind so far behind the capacity."

He then proceeds, like Mr. Malthus, to examine into these causes; which, he says, are not at all difficult to discern.   The increase of the lower animals is checked by the death of the superabundant progeny, whether from not having sufficient food, or from being killed by their enemies.   Such is the case also in the savage and uncultivated races of mankind.   But the foresight which forms the distinguishing feature of civilized man, prevents him from bringing beings into the world, which he sees cannot be provided for.   Therefore population is checked rather by the dread of want, than by want itself; by the preventive rather than the positive check; in proportion as man rises in civilization.   The fear of losing their social position, and of forfeiting their accustomed comforts and luxuries, is the form, which this prudential feeling takes in the upper parts of society.

In a very uncivilized state of society, the population is kept under by positive starvation, generally in the shape of periodical famines.

In a higher state it is not by more deaths, but by fewer births, that population is repressed. In different countries this, the preventive check, operates in different ways. In some, especially Norway, and parts of Switzerland, it arises from a prudent self-restraint. The labouring classes see that by having large families, they will sink below the condition of comfort to which they are accustomed; and therefore refrain from rash marriages and begetting too numerous off-spring. In these countries the average of life is the longest in Europe; both the births and the deaths bear the smallest proportion to the population; and there are fewer children, and a greater number of adults, than in any other part of the world.

In those countries of the continent which have Poor-laws, marriage is everywhere forbidden among those who are in the receipt of relief; and there are few countries which permit marriage, unless the man can show that he can support a family. Such is the case in Bavaria and Norway, in Lubeck, Frankfurt, and many other places. In other countries, as Prussia, Saxony, &c., every man is forced to serve for a time in the army, during which he is not allowed to marry. In some parts of Italy, it is the practice in all classes of society, for only one of the sons to marry, while the rest remain single.

But the enormous amount of reproductive power, which is repressed by these or other preventive checks, is always ready to expand, whenever their pressure is removed. Hence any amelioration in the state of the working classes, in general merely gives room for its expansion for a little; and the increased multiplication, which takes place, does away with all the benefit, and brings back the same state of things as before. Unless the habitual standard of comfort mentioned by Mr. Malthus—by which is meant that down to which they will multiply, but not lower—can be raised, the best endeavours for the elevation of the labouring people end in our having a population, increased in numbers truly, but not in happiness.

There are three elements of production, land, labour, and capital. The first differs from the others in not being capable of indefinite increase. It is limited in quantity, and also in productiveness; and it is this fact which forms the real limit to the increase of production.

But, since there is much land still uncultivated, and as that, which is already cultivated, could produce much more than it does; since in short we have not yet exhausted the resources of the earth; it is com-

monly thought, that this limit to population and production is at a
great distance.

" I apprehend this," says Mr. Mill, " to be not only an error, but
the most serious one to be found in the whole field of political economy.   The question is more important and fundamental than any
other ; it involves the whole subject of the causes of poverty in a rich
and industrious community ; and unless this one matter be thoroughly
understood, it is to no purpose proceeding any further in our enquiry."

He compares the resistance to production (and therefore to population) from this cause, not to an immovable wall, which stands at a
distance from us; but to an elastic band, which is never so tightly
stretched, that it could not be more stretched, but which always confines us, and the more tightly the more we approach its limits.

It is the law in agricultural industry that after an early stage in its
progress, every increase of produce is obtained upon harder and harder
terms.

" This general law of agricultural industry," says Mr. Mill, " is the
most important proposition in political economy.   Were the law different, nearly all the phenomena of production and distribution of wealth
would be other than they are.   The most fundamental errors, which
still prevail on our subject, result from not perceiving this law at
work underneath the more superficial agencies on which attention fixes
itself."

This law is shown by the fact that inferior lands are cultivated ; for
the very meaning of inferior land is that, which with equal labour
returns less produce.   The elaborate cultivation, moreover, of the well
farmed districts in England and Scotland is a sign of this law ; for
such high farming costs far more in proportion than the low.   In
America, where plenty of good land is to be had, and where labour is
dear, such careful farming is not to be seen, as there it would not be
profitable.

It is this law, according to which the returns of labour tend always
to become less and less, that causes the increase of production to be
accompanied by a deterioration in the state of the producers.

Therefore the preventive check to population would have not only
to be maintained, but gradually to be *increased* to enable a society
merely to hold its ground, and to retain its comforts ; were it not for
the progress of improvements, which facilitate production.   The ratio
of the increase of population would need to be progressively diminished, small though it already might be, were it not for these improvements ; which may perhaps at times be sufficient to counteract the law
of diminishing increase, and allow population to advance at its former
slow ratio ; or even at times in a somewhat faster ratio, though never
assuredly in any old country at a ratio at all approaching to that, of
which the reproductive powers are capable.   At other times, when the
improvements to production are not sufficient to counteract the law,
the check upon population must be increased, either in the preventive
or the positive mode.

The necessity for checking population is not peculiar, as is often thought, to a state of society, where there is an unequal distribution of property. This does not even increase the evil; which depends upon the fact that a larger body of men cannot in any case be provided for so well as a smaller; at most it can only make it sooner felt.

Whether the state of a people at any given time is improving or deteriorating, depends upon whether improvement is advancing faster than population, or population than improvement.

———

The rate of increase of the French is the smallest in Europe. In the ten years from 1817 to 1827 the annual increase of that nation was $\frac{43}{100}$, while that of the English was $1\frac{4}{10}$, and the Americans 3. It has been calculated from the population returns of France, that during the last fifty years, the annual increase has been only 1 in 200; and even this small increase has been owing to the decrease of deaths, for the number of births has remained nearly stationary. Now at no period in her history has the produce of France increased faster than in these fifty years; and hence there is a noticeable improvent in the condition of the working classes.

———

Wages are regulated in general by competition; and therefore depend upon the demand and supply of labour; in other words the proportion between the labourers and the capital. *They cannot be affected by anything else.* If they rise, it can only be because there is more capital or fewer labourers; if they fall, it can only be, because there is less capital or more labourers.

There are several common opinions in apparent contradiction to this fact, such as that wages are high when trade is good, that high prices make high wages, that wages vary with the price of food, &c.; but these are only complications in the concrete phenomena, which obscure and disguise the operation of the law of wages, and can be readily shown to be perfectly consistent with this law.

———

The various plans, of which there are always some before the public for making the working people a very little better off—such as the repeal of the corn laws, &c.—are of very little importance to the welfare of the labourers. Any slight temporary alleviation of the evils of their condition by such means, is very soon obliterated by the increase of population, which it generally gives rise to; and the state of matters becomes as bad as before. It is only from some very great and sudden improvement in their condition, which raises their habitual standard of comfort in a striking and marked degree, so as to induce them *to check their procreative powers* for fear of losing the advantages they have got, that a permanent benefit is to be hoped. The best instance of this is the case of France after the Revolution.

The condition of the labouring classes cannot be improved, but by altering in their favour the proportion between the number of labourers and the capital; and " every scheme for their benefit, which does not proceed on this as its foundation, is, for all permanent purposes, a delusion."

The rural population in many of the southern counties of England have lately attracted much compassion from their extreme poverty. In these districts they marry as early, and have as many children to a family, as if they were in America.

But unfortunately it is sentimentality and not common sense, which is applied to these evils; and while there is an increasing sympathy towards the poor, there is an almost universal unwillingness to recognise the *real cause* of their sufferings; and a tacit agreement to ignore completely the law of wages, or to dismiss it as " hard-hearted Malthusianism." Is not the hard-heartedness on the side of those, who misguide the poor as to the real cause of their poverty? Were it not for the increasing enlightenment and self-restraint of the manufacturing population, there is no reason, as far as regards the conduct of the rural districts, why we should not in time sink into as squalid poverty as Ireland; especially if our manufactures should cease to increase at the extraordinary rate of the last fifty years.

It is not reason, however, but a strong dislike to the population doctrines, which prevents their admission.

Many endeavours have been made, over and over again, to find out a mode of increasing wages, without the necessity of an increased check upon population, but they are all radically fallacious. It has been proposed, for instance, that there should be local boards of trade, consisting of delegates from the men and the masters, to fix a reasonable rate of wages; the state being bound to provide work, for those who cannot get it. Many believe that it is the duty of the rich or of the state to provide work for all. &c.

. In order to do this, the capital for the payment of increased wages must be raised by taxation. But to ensure work to all the members of the community would suspend all checks to population; and thus the taxation would need to be increased every year, so as to be able to support not only the first generation, but all whom they might call into existence; thus the whole wealth of the country would gradually be absorbed; and when that was done, the positive check to population could no longer be postponed.

These consequences of artificial interference in the labour question, have been so often pointed out by celebrated authors, that ignorance of them is no longer pardonable in any educated man.

If a man cannot support himself without assistance, those who assist him have a right to demand, that he shall not bring beings into the world to be maintained by the charity of others. If the State were to pledge itself to provide employment for all that are born, it must, if it is not to be ruined, prevent any one from being born without its consent; for if it remove the natural checks to population, namely, want and the dread of want, it must substitute others. If it take the feeding of the people into its hands, it must also take the control of their increase; or, on the other hand, if it leave their increase free, it cannot undertake to feed them.

If the natural checks to their increase be removed, neither charity nor promised employment can do them any real good, but on the contrary much evil; but if on the other hand they be put in such circumstances, as encourage their habits of foresight and independence, and teach them to avoid undue multiplication, they will be really benefited. No remedies for low wages have the least chance of success, which do not act on the minds and habits of the people.

"By what means then," says Mr. Mill, in an eloquent passage, which I cannot refrain from quoting, as it shows how utterly delusive are all the common views on the subject of poverty, (every remedy in fact except that of restraining the reproductive powers,) in the eyes of the profoundest social philosopher, the truest friend of the working classes, of our day, "By what means is poverty to be contended against? How is the evil of low wages to be remedied? If the expedients usually recommended for the purpose are not adapted for it, can no others be thought of? Is the problem incapable of solution? Can political economy do nothing but only object to everything, and demonstrate that nothing can be done?

If this were so, political economy might have a needful, but would have a melancholy and a thankless task. If the bulk of the human race are always to remain as at present, slaves to toil in which they *have* no interest, and therefore *feel* no interest—drudging from early morning till late at night for bare necessaries, and with all the intellectual and moral deficiencies which that implies—without resources either in mind or feelings—untaught, for they cannot be better taught than fed; selfish, for all their thoughts are required for themselves · without interests or sentiments as citizens or members of society, and with a sense of injustice rankling in their breasts, equally for what

they have not, and for what others have; I know not what there is
which should make a person with any capacity for reason, concern
himself about the destinies of the human race. There would be no
wisdom for any one but in extracting from life with epicurean indifference, as much personal satisfaction for himself and others with whom
he sympathises, as it can yield without injury to any one, and letting
the unmeaning bustle of so-called civilized existence roll by unheeded.
But there is no ground for such a view of human affairs."

Mr. Mill then states that *the only possible mode* of raising wages and
benefiting the poor, is by inducing them to exercise a greater control
over their reproductive powers. He says that this has never yet been
seriously tried; but on the contrary, that almost all public men,
whether statesmen, moralists, or clergymen, have rather encouraged
marriage and multiplication, (provided it were sanctioned by the marriage bond,) than otherwise; many having still a religious prejudice
against the true doctrines, and believing that it is opposed to the goodness of the Deity, or the usual bounty of nature, that the indulgence
in a natural passion should cause such miseries. The confusion of
ideas upon this subject, is, he says, in great measure owing to the spurious delicacy, which prohibits the open discussion of sexual matters;
but "the diseases of society can, no more than corporeal maladies, be
prevented or cured, without being spoken about in plain language."

The great object of statesmanship should be to raise the habitual
standard of comfort among the working classes, and to bring them into
such a position as shows them most clearly, that their welfare depends
upon themselves, upon their control over their reproductive powers.
For this purpose he advises that there should be, first, an extended
scheme of national emigration, so as to produce a striking and sudden
improvement in the condition of the labourers left at home, and raise
their standard of comfort; also that the population truths should be
disseminated as widely as possible, so that a powerful public feeling
should be awakened among the working classes, against undue procreation on the part of any individual among them—a feeling which
could not fail greatly to influence individual conduct; and also that
we should use every endeavour to get rid of the present system of
labour, namely, that of employers and employed, and adopt to a
great extent that of independent or associated industry. His reason
for this is, that a hired labourer, who has no personal interest in the
work he is engaged in, is generally reckless and without foresight,
living from hand to mouth, and exerting little control over his powers
of procreation; whereas the labourer who has a personal stake in his
work, and the feeling of independence and self-reliance which the possession of property gives, as, for instance, the peasant proprietor, or
member of a co-partnership, has far stronger motives for self-restraint,
and can see much more clearly the evil effects of having a large
family.

But such measures, to be availing, must be powerful and decided, for
"when the object is to raise the permanent condition of a people, small
means do not merely produce small effects, they produce no effect at

all. Unless comfort can be made as habitual to a whole generation as indigence is now, nothing is accomplished, and feeble half-measures do but fritter away resources, far better reserved till the improvement of public opinion, and of education, shall raise up politicians, who will not think that because a scheme promises much, the part of statesmanship is to have nothing to do with it."

Such then, are the views of Mr. Mill and Mr. Malthus on the Labour question ; and, as far as I know, they are held by most of the scientific writers on political economy, including Dr. Whateley, Mr. McCulloch, and others. . They show as this grand fundamental truth, that it is only *by checking still further the reproductive powers of our species,* that it is possible to remedy poverty and to raise wages ; and that all other means of effecting these objects, such as social or political reform, the removal of taxation, the spread of education, the change of religious beliefs, emigration, the advance of the various sciences and arts, in short every other conceivable form of progress is utterly impotent, and can have no direct influence in the matter.

These truths are absolutely incontrovertible ; and would long since have been universally admitted, not only by scientific men, but by the general intelligence, had it not been for the hopelessness they inspired. They have earned for Political Economy the name of the " dismal science," along with a general feeling of hostility and aversion ; as if the fault lay in the science, whose very highest merit is, that it is a faithful interpreter of natural truth. It is not by shutting our eyes to these mighty evils, nor childishly venting our anger on the science which explains them. and which thus gives to our race by far the most important *Revelation* which was ever given to it, that we may hope they will be overcome ; nature is never to be propitiated by such means, but, on the contrary, by an earnest consideration of her laws, and a patient and persevering endeavour to reconcile them with the interests of man, whatever difficulties this may cause us.

Before proceeding to examine more fully this question, I would wish to say a few words on two subjects ; viz. first, on a theory of population which has lately been opposed to the Malthusian by Mr. Doubleday and Mr. Herbert Spencer, (similar in substance to others that had been already brought forward by Mr. Godwin, Mr. Sadler, and other writers) ; and, secondly, on Socialism. I mention the first theory, not from its intrinsic importance, but because I wish the reader to see to what hopeless shifts men, and even talented men, are driven, to escape from the great population difficulty ; and also because I am desirous, that every one of us should have the most absolute and assured conviction, that there is no possible escape from this difficulty, except by manfully accepting, and patiently endeavouring to overcome it.

Mr. Doubleday asserts that the checks to population do not consist, as Mr. Malthus showed, in sexual abstinence, vice, and misery: but that the principal check arises from a change produced in the human constitution, by a luxurious mode of living; in fact, that the fertility of mankind depends chiefly upon what they eat. The poor, he says, are much more prolific than the rich, because they live upon vegetables and fish; while those who live upon animal food, and are in good circumstances, have comparatively feeble reproductive powers. Fertility is, he says, increased by the *deplethoric* condition, but diminished by the *plethoric*. As proofs of this, he instances the Islands of Scotland, whose over-population he ascribes to their fish-diet; and also Ireland, where it arises from the use of potatoes. In India and China the cause of the great population is the living on rice. On the other hand, the small population of Asiatic Russia and other pastoral countries, arises, he says, from their living so much on animal food. In the large families and swarms of children, which are seen in the poors' districts of our towns and country villages; and in the decay of our noble families, few of which last for many centuries, without the necessity of perpetual new creations, we have further signs of this, which Mr. Doubleday calls the true law of population. As illustrations of these propositions, he mentions the fact, that plants, when too highly manured, tend to develope leaves instead of flowers; and that the latter are often double and infertile.

Thus then, he says, population always increases rapidly among the poor, remains pretty stationary in the middle, and decreases in the upper classes of society, in an exact ratio with the kind and quantity of food and other comforts of life enjoyed by each.

This view may be characterised as a mere baseless hypothesis, in which the real meaning of the facts adduced is not understood, and the cause mistaken for the effect. Mr. Malthus showed that people were poor because they had too many children; Mr. Doubleday asserts that they have so many children because they are poor.

The fact that pastoral countries are poor in population, and grain countries the reverse, is, as Mr. Malthus showed, easily accounted for by the knowledge that the former do not produce nearly so much human food as the latter. The belief that a fish or a vegetable diet is peculiarly favourable, and animal food unfavourable, to reproduction, is an old popular error, founded partly on the same mistake of cause for effect. Mr. Doubleday has in these matters merely taken Mr. Malthus's facts, and read them the wrong way.

As for the dying-out of the noble families, and of any other community or body of men, it is, as far as it is a fact, owing to the agency of very many other forms of disease and destruction besides the deficiencies of the reproductive powers, arising from unhealthy modes of life; and, in general, sterility forms but an insignificant part of these destructive influences.

It is true that too great manuring and too high feeding, produce a

plethoric state in both plants and animals, which is adverse to the pro.
per performance of many of their healthy functions ; but this state of
plethora is a *disease*, and whenever it operates as a check to the reproductive powers, it comes under the head of Mr. Malthus's positive check
which includes all forms of death and disease. Mr. Doubleday admits
this himself; he says, " In the human animal luxuriousness and over-
feeding are generally admitted by physiologists and physicians to be the
root of most organic diseases." Believing this, it is not easy to see how
he remains satisfied with his theory ; seeing that the very check, which
he designates as a proof of the benevolence and goodness of the Deity,
could only be, even in the cases where it might operate, one of the forms
of disease and misery mentioned by Mr. Malthus.

Mr. Herbert Spencer's exposition of the same theory of population,
has a more scientific appearance, but is as completely fallacious.   He
begins with stating that in all living beings, the powers of reproduction
are in an inverse ratio to those of individual preservation. Thus in the
humblest plants and animals, there are an enormous number of seeds
and eggs ; while in the higher there are but few. In the elephant, and
man, the reproductive powers are smallest ; because they have the
greatest power of self-preservation.

From this proposition, which may perhaps be granted, he proceeds to
the totally unwarrantable inference, that, as the reproductive powers
decrease in the *different* species in ascending the scale of being, so do
they decrease in the *same* species, namely in man, during his advance in
civilization. The evident want of analogy between these propositions
scarcely needs to be pointed out ; and, as the author has not given any
illustrative proofs of this decrease of fertility in man, (probably thinking
the loose statistics of Mr. Doubleday sufficient on that point,) his argument is rendered valueless at the very beginning. To admit the astound-
ing proposition, that the progress of civilization tends so totally to alter
the nature of the human frame, as to diminish its reproductive powers
to the extent required to keep mankind at a just level with the increase
of food, would demand a very different kind of evidence from this ; which
is in fact, no evidence at all, but merely the vaguest and most illogical
analogy.

" Every generative product " says Mr. Spencer, " is a deduction from
the parental life, and, as already pointed out, to diminish life is to
diminish the ability to preserve life. The portion thrown off is organised matter ; vital force has been expended in the organization of it;
which vital force, had no such portion been made and thrown off, would
have been available for the preservation of the parent. Neither of these
forces, therefore, can increase, except at the expense of the other; in
other words, individuation and reproduction are antagonistic."

These assertions are perhaps as good examples as could be cited, of the
fatal errors into which men, whatever be their abilities in other matters,
constantly fall from want of physiological and medical knowledge. Had
Mr. Spencer been aware of the phenomena and causes of genital disease,
of the laws of the generative organs, or in fact of the most general principles of health, he could scarcely have adopted such opinions.   The

fact is, that instead of the powers of reproduction being in antagonism with those of individual preservation, they are, like all other powers in the body, in the closest harmony with them; that instead of it being injurious to the vital powers of either man or woman to reproduce their species, there is scarcely anything which is more indispensable to their health. The seminal fluid and the menstrual discharge are secretions, and are intended, like all other secretions in the body, *to be cast off*; in fact, they are more or less poisonous to the system if they be retained, just as all other secretions are; and to suppose that the vital force which was expended on their production is a loss to the powers of the economy, or could have been applied elsewhere more profitably to the parent, betrays a great ignorance of physiology. It would be just as reasonable to say, that the vital force used in producing any other secretion, as, for instance, the bile or the saliva, would have been better preserved to the individual. The retention of the secretion of the germ-cells and menstrual discharge in woman, which is always liable to take place unless the secreting organs receive their due stimulus, has a most withering effect upon the health; and probably many of the evil effects, which abstinence has on the male system, and which are not so openly manifested as they are in women, by the arrest or disorder of the reproductive secretion, depend really on its non-elimination from the want of the natural stimulus, and the consequent deterioration of the blood, and enfeeblement of the nerves. Want of energy of body and mind, despondency, weakness, and a benumbed and torpid state of the bodily and mental functions, are perhaps the most characteristic effects of sexual abstinence in man; and correspond to the hysterical and chlorotic affections of woman.

The truth is, that in this case as in others, the interests of all our different organs and functions are inseparably bound up together; and the same influences which promote the true and healthy development of any one of them, will promote that of the others also. The powers of reproduction cannot, any more than those of digestion, respiration, or absorption, languish or decay without the whole organism suffering; in other words, disease or imperfection in these parts must be either the cause or effect of the disease of the whole frame.

Therefore, wherever the reproductive powers have been checked by luxurious living, or by modes of life in which too much attention is paid to the cultivation of the intellect and too little to that of the senses, it is a certain sign of a diseased and morbid state; which, so far from meriting the name of progressive civilization, is merely one of the forms of disease and misery included under Mr. Malthus' positive check. The disproportionate size of the brain, which is found in highly intellectualised nations, and which is generally mentioned with much satisfaction, is in fact the physical expression of that diseased spiritualism, of which I have formerly spoken, and is a prolific cause of the wide-spread nervous maladies, which characterise our times. A luxurious mode of life and sedentary and studious pursuits have evil effects on many other organs, besides those of reproduction, and the brain; indeed they interfere with every function of the body, and produce constipation, indigestion, &c. It would be just as reasonable to say, therefore, that the alvine or digestive secretions would decrease, or the power of these organs decay in the progress of civilization, as that those of the organs of generation should do so.

The fact is, that there are few, if any, bodily functions, over which these injurious influences have *less* power than over those of reproduction. It might have been expected, that when such sweeping assertions as to the decrease of the fertility of the species were made, and visionary theories of human perfectibility founded thereon, their authors would have resorted to the only possible mode of satisfactorily ascertaining their truth ; namely, an investigation into the real nature and causes of sterility, as shown by medical writers, who are the only men that have the means of furnishing a knowledge on this subject. Now when we do examine medical works, we find that the vague term *plethora*, or a luxurious or studious mode of life, is very rarely used to account for sterility. The tendency of medicine, especially of late years, has been to assign some more definite form of *local* disease as its cause, and to do away with these vague and popular expressions, which were in general merely a cover for ignorance ; and the real demonstrable causes of this disease, (for sterility is always a disease,) have been in many cases made out, and shown to be curable. Dr. Whitehead, in his able work on this subject, says, "the cause of sterility is usually attributed, and correctly so, to the faulty condition of the female organs ; the non-existence of the procreative power in the other sex being, in reality, *extremely rare*." Now, if either plethora or intellectual developement were a frequent cause of sterility, why should it not operate still more on men than women ? and yet sterility is a rare disease in the male, and, occurs chiefly from the worst forms of spermatorrhœa, or from malformation of the sexual organs. The causes of barrenness on the female side, Dr. Whitehead says, are rarely congenital malformations, for nature is so abundantly liberal in her gifts, and so wonderfully correct in all she does ; " the more frequent causes consist in diseased states of the uterus and its organic products ; and are, generally speaking, susceptible both of demonstration and cure." Many of these causes of sterility have been already mentioned in the description of female diseases, and consist in the various inflammations and painful affections, which interfere with the powers of conception. Another cause, mentioned by Dr. Whitehead as frequently occurring, is an acid, instead of the natural alkaline state, of the mucus secreted from the womb, which kills the spermatozooids. When sterility exists, it may generally be traced to some such tangible cause operating in the individual ; and in fact, the vague idea of a gradual and progressive failure of the reproductive powers of our species, is wholly without countenance from any thing observed in nature. Sterility, except as far as it arises from prostitution, is one of the most insignificant of all the checks to population ; for one child that remains unborn from this cause, there are hundreds which are so from sexual abstinence ; and of the various causes of this insignificant check, *plethora* is one of the least important, or rather, strictly speaking, scarcely deserves the name of a direct cause at all.

As for the analogy between the effects of high cultivation on the human species and on plants, (that unlucky idea, which probably first suggested, this train of false reasoning), it is very unscientific. A most important law of physiology is, that the humbler the organism, the more is its form and original type susceptible of being modified by external circumstances, and the higher it is, the less ; and thus, to make a comparison in this matter between man and the lower organisms, is a fruitful source of error. The human constitution has a wonderful power of adhering to its natural type, and of defending itself from external impressions ; without which man would not be fitted for his many-sided and 9ninivorous life.

But, in reality the very *reverse* of these theories is the truth. The powers of reproduction, instead of being lessened by a true progress of civilization, must necessarily, as well as the other vital powers, be greatly *increased;* for no civilization is a true one, which does not include the advancement of every faculty of the human constitution. Their increase will take place in two ways; first, by the longer average of life, which will give greater time for their exercise; secondly, by the adoption of more healthy modes of life, and the better prevention and cure of sterility. Therefore, the difficulty from this cause, instead of diminishing, will assuredly greatly increase, in the progress of civilization.

It may perhaps give us a clearer idea of the reproductive powers of our species, than any statistics, to examine them by what we know of the female constitution. The sexual life of woman lasts from its maturity at fifteen, to its decline at about forty-five years of age ; that is, during a period of about thirty years. Thus if we allow two years for the production and nurture of each child, which is amply sufficient if the woman live a healthy life, she could produce in all about fifteen children.   This is a moderate average of the reproductive powers of woman, when these powers have their full scope, and are not checked by different circumstances. The possible rate of increase of mankind, is therefore much greater, than any actual rate which was ever known, even in America ; and we must remember, that it is this possible rate which is to be considered, in any inquiry into the possible progress of mankind : for progress, by increasing the average of life and health in the female sex, must always tend to increase their reproductive powers. But these powers at present in our country do not produce one-fourth part of the children, of which they are actually capable, nor one-sixth of those of which they are potentially capable. On looking round us in society the causes are easily perceived.   The great majority of women do not marrytill several years after they are capable of reproduction, and very many do not marry at all ; while vast numbers die before their sexual life is over, and the reproductive powers of others are quenched in the mire of prostitution. We do not see one woman in thousands, who has fully exercised her reproductive powers.   And yet with all this restraint, these powers are still so enormously over-exercised, that the most grinding poverty prevails, and a large proportion of the poorest classes are pushed out of existence, before the third of their natural term of life is past.

On analysing the various checks to the fertility of woman, with regard to the proportional effect of each, it may perhaps be said, that sexual abstinence, with its so frequent attendant—self-abuse, is by far the most important of all; that perhaps next comes premature death, before the reproductive age is over; next, prostitution; next abortion; and perhaps lastly, sterility, as far as it is not dependent on prostitution. These checks to the fertility of woman, together with the corresponding checks to that of man, and death at more advanced periods of life, form the sum of the positive and preventive checks to population.

The fallacious theory of a change in the human constitution is an admirable instance of· that short-sighted Optimism, in which so many thinkers have indulged in the world's history. By optimism is meant the belief, that there is some self-adjusting power in Nature, or some merciful guiding Providence, by which human ills all work for good, and are ultimately to be overcome. In this case we are to console ourselves with the encouraging prospect, that the human constitution will gradually undergo a change in our favour; to wait helplessly till the stream of misery has flowed past us, and then we shall enter the promised land of indefinite perfectibility. But we may sooner expect that the river will return to its source, or the seas cover the mountain tops, than that the fundamental character of the human frame will alter; for it is much less changeable than they. These and similar delusive hopes, springing from the want of perception of the mighty difficulty opposed by nature, are extremely dangerous, and have led to an immensity of evil.· By the discovery of the law of population, Mr. Malthus gave the death-blow to all such views, and to every theory of human progress, which had been erected in ignorance of it. He showed to demonstration the *real cause* which opposed the satisfactory advance of mankind; and also that the indispensable condition of such advance was a great increase in the preventive check to population. He first, like M. Lallemand in spermatorrhœa, traced the surface evils of society, which had till his time been mistaken for the radical ones, to their hidden source; he was the true physician, who alone saw the real meaning of the appalling disease, under which the human race has been labouring ever since it appeared on this earth; *the only true friend* the poor ever had, the friend who had not only the heart, but the head, to help them: and whose profound revelation, gloomy and apparently almost hopeless as it showed their lot to be, was yet infinitely more valuable to the poor, than the most splendid dreams of visionary perfectibility ever conceived.

Socialism is one of these short-sighted schemes, and is built upon the same false foundation as the rest; namely, that it is possible that man should make satisfactory progress, without a great increase in the preventive check to population. Socialism, like other schemes, leaves this matter out of the question, and confines its attention to various methods of increasing the produce of human industry, and equalising its distribution; which, whatever be their merits, are, without the other, not worth a moment's scrutiny. Put all the various human advantages, to the acquisition of which Socialism and all the usual efforts of society are directed, on one side, and diminished reproduction on the other; and we may be certain that every struggle for the former will be utterly vain and futile, so far as the great part of society is concerned, without the latter. The one cannot be got without the other.

"The poor ye have always with you," was said two thousand years ago, and would have been as appalling a truth at any time before or since. Let us mount to the remotest antiquity; let us regard the countless myriads of China and Hindostan, of our own, or any other country of the old world at the present day; and we shall find poverty, and her sister Hard Work--the want of Food, and of Leisure, everywhere plunging the great mass of our race in an abyss of misery and degradation. It is this universal prevalence and constant continuance of poverty, which have in a great measure accustomed men to its evils, and prevented them from either sufficiently feeling, or conceiving any hope of ever escaping from them. The ignorance of the great cause of poverty moreover, which is even yet so prevalent, notwithstanding the writings of Mr. Malthus and others, has made many people view it rather as a disgrace, and as brought on by individual laziness, drunkenness, or misconduct; a belief which interfered with their pity for it, and rendered totally abortive any effort they might make to alleviate it. Unacquainted with its cause, men think it an absolutely inevitable evil : and thus try to reconcile themselves to it, and to avoid a subject, whose consideration would almost lead them to despair of human society.

"It is easy to bear the ills of others with christian fortitude." Yes; although we, who look on, may reconcile ourselves to this horrible condition of the majority of our fellows; although we may seek to disguise it, by vain boasts of the advance of civilization, the progress of society, and the splendour of individual virtue, talent, and the other bright spots in human life, which dazzle the superficial gaze, and prevent it from seeing the dark shades of vice and suffering which hang around; alas! the poor themselves can never be reconciled to poverty, their human flesh and blood cannot stand its insufferable miseries, and to them all big talk of the progress of mankind is a delusion and a lie.

The life of our working classes is worse than that of most of the beasts of burden. They toil unremittingly for ten or twelve hours a-day at a laborious, monotonous, and in many cases a deadly occupation; without hope of advancement, or personal interest in the success of the work they are engaged in. At night their jaded frames are too tired to permit their enjoyment of the few leisure hours; and the morn wakens them to the same dreary day of ceaseless toil. Even the seventh day, their only holiday, brings them in this country little gaiety, little recreation; a solemn sermon, and two hours of sedentary constraint is all that is provided for them. The clergy and others, who are indignant that a poor working man does not go to church on his only holiday, should themselves try his life for six months, and see then what appetite they will have for church; when their limbs are wasting with incessant toil, their nerves beginning to give way, and their hearts embittered by a life of constant drudgery and care.

Thus have the poor to toil on, as long as their strength permits. At last some organ gives way, the stomach, the eyes, or the brain; and the unfortunate sufferer is thrown out of work, and sent to the hospital, while his wife and family are reduced to the brink of starvation. Often the man, rendered desperate by his hopeless position, plunges into drink and gives himself over to ruin. At other times, the working classes in a frenzy of rage at their infernal circumstances, determine that they will have higher wages or perish. Hence result the disastrous strikes, and the terrible social revolutions, that have in recent times so often convulsed society. But they are vain ; they are but the blind effort of men to do something or die, the fruitless heavings of a man in a nightmare. The mountain of misery invariably falls back again upon their breasts, with only increased pressure ; and forces them, worn out by impotent struggles, to bear it quietly for another little season.

Till within the last half century, it may be said that the evils of poverty were very little either understood or sympathised in by the richer and better educated part of mankind. The richer classes took little more interest in, and had little more communion with the poorest class, than if they had been an inferior order of beings. Was it not the lot of the poor to slave and toil for the pleasures of the rich, and were they not paid for so doing? The unhappy class-feelings also, which totally prevented and still prevent, the richer among us from mingling freely with the poorer, and treating them with that equal mutual respect and politeness, which should exist between all men, fostered the ignorance on the subject of poverty. But of late years this subject has become one of the most engrossing and wide-spread interest ; and there are few among us now-a-days, who are not tolerably well aware of the inconceivable wretchedness of the poorest classes among us, and of the fearful evils of hard work, unhealthy occupations, and low wages, under which this country groans. · Writers on political economy, and on medical and moral subjects, have almost all come to the conclusion, that the evils of poverty, and the wretched destitution and ignorance of our poorer classes, are the most pressing subject for the consideration of all men. Several admirable works of fiction, pre-eminent among which stands Alton Locke, have made the life and struggles of the poor the theme by which they awakened the deepest sympathy in the minds of all ; and now there are few novels or poems of much merit, in which the sufferings of poverty do not throw a shade over the brighter scenes, and cloud the heart of the writer and the reader. We do not care now for the artificial glitter of court etiquette, nor the hollow ceremonies of fashionable life ; we have comparatively little sympathy with the caprices of high-born lords and ladies, who have engrossed so unfair a share of man's attention : we wish to know the inner life of man, and most of all the thoughts and sufferings of those, who have been the most neglected by their fellow creatures.

There is perhaps no work of the day, which gives so mournfully interesting an insight into the lives of the poorest classes, as Mr. Mayhew's inimitable "London Labour, and London Poor;" and the truths which he lays bare to us in that work, are such as to freeze our blood with horror and anguish. It is the account of the manner, in which hundreds of thousands of our fellow beings are gradually ground and pressed to death and multiform destruction by hard work, and want of food. It tells us of starvation, disease, prostitution, crime, and every conceivable moral and physical degradation, to which these unhappy ones who are born at the foot of our social scale, are inexorably doomed. No hope, no chance of rising in the mire they were born, and in the mire they must, sooner or later, with greater or less misery, be engulphed.   Education, religion, political or social interests, are to them unknown ; the ceremonials of worship, the solemnity of debate, the pomps and glorifications of science, and all the vaunted results of human enlightenment, are in their eyes a mummery got up for the edification of the rich.   What avails anything to a man if he cannot, though he sweat to death for it, get enough to eat?   To attempt to cheat his misery by anything else than *food*, is a vain and heartless delusion.   All other human blessings are to him a mere dream, have for him no existence, if he cannot get food, the first essential of life ; or if he have to toil beyond human endurance to obtain it.

The fearful miseries of want of food, and of leisure, which the poor among us have to endure, are gradually pressing themselves more and more on the attention of all men.   We cannot walk through our streets, though we avoid the poorest districts, and station policemen to keep the poor within their purlieus, without witnessing enough of wretchedness to wither our hearts within us ; if we really took it earnestly to heart. The miseries of the poor are gradually darkening our society ; they are throwing a gloom over every heart, and intruding like a spectre upon the brightest scenes of gaiety.   Who can enjoy his life, can eat, drink, and be merry, when he sees the ghastly faces, heart-broken despair, or envious scowls of his unfortunate fellow-men, to whom fate has denied all those blessings ?   We cannot if we would ; and the cares and anxieties of the poor, joined to our own insufferable evils, have so overshadowed our society, that when we look around us among our friends and acquaintances, we can scarcely find a single individual, whose life we could call a happy one.   For my part, I do not think that I know in this country a single such case, and I have heard the same opinion from others.   All of us are worn by anxiety, and depressed by the atmosphere of misery, that overspreads our society.   So true is this, that the saying is constantly on our lips, "man is born to trouble," and the world is commonly termed the "vale of tears."   Let it not be for a moment supposed, that such sorrow is man's natural state ; it is only a sign of the fearful evils, with which our society has to contend, and of the gloom which the wide-spread want of food, love, and leisure, has poured round the common heart of man.   It is an absolute impossibility that any class can long enjoy happiness, if another is miserable ; sooner or later sympathy must unite them in a common lot of weal and woe.

Do not let us suppose either, that *we* escape from evils of an analogous nature to those, by which the poor are ground to death.   The cares and anxieties of the business and professional men among us are proverbial ; it is so difficult to make a livelihood in the press of competition, that we are driven into disease or insanity by the sweat and anxiety of the mind, just as the working man is by that of the body.   The great principle of population moreover presses upon us in a different, but scarcely a less fearful manner, than upon the poor.   It produces among us the want of *love*, just as it does the want of food among the poor ; and the former is almost as blighting and withering an evil among the richer classes, especially the young ladies, as the want of food and leisure among the poor. It slowly undermines health and happiness, and has made our society, our parties, balls, promenades, a hollow and artificial masquerade, where the joyless gaiety ill-disguises the aching hearts beneath. The immense number of unmarried men and women, whose sexual hopes have been blighted by the want of love, or by genital or venereal diseases, cast a gloom and constraint over all the sexual relations, like the spectre of poverty at a banquet. Married people and fortunate lovers do not like to reveal their happiness, when there is so much sexual misery and disappointment around; and were it not for the utterly selfish views of love which prevail among us, this feeling would be more common. Do we think that those who are suffering from the want of love, are not as real objects of our sympathy, as those who suffer from want of food?

But it is as vain for those who engross the love, as for those who engross the food, to expect to be happy, while others are miserable from the want of it. The sexual disappointments and anxieties darken the whole sexual atmosphere, and have fostered the puritanism, which has of late years increased among us, and has given a sombre and painful character to all love. No one likes to make allusions to sexual matters, a subject fraught with anguish to so many. Discontent is as infectious as happiness, and the number of minds soured by a life of forced abstinence embitter all social joys. Envy and jealousy pervade the general mind on sexual subjects, and hence the harsh judgments passed on those, who have dared to taste, except in the ordinary mode of marriage, which has been made as unenviable and rigorous as possible, the pleasures for which so many sigh in vain. It is from this terrible *want of love*, and not from the direct want of food, that the richer classes among us suffer; but the two wants represent each other, being the only two alternatives, as Mr. Malthus has shown, which the law of population leaves us. It is just a choice between two modes of death; by poverty, or by sexual misery; by want of food and leisure, or by want of love. This terrible choice may be called the *Malthusian dilemma.* Poverty, taken in its widest sense, means the want of *love* as well as of food; and the ignorance or disregard of this truth is the greatest of all errors in reasoning upon social matters.

The want of love is indeed fearfully felt in every grade of our society, but by no class so much as by young ladies. The young men among the richer classes, palliate this insufferable evil, by having recourse to a mercenary intercourse; from which arises all the misery and degradation of prostitution. The poor in general, rather than want love, will want food and leisure, and live only a small fraction of their natural term of life; and marriages take place at an earlier age, and are proportionally more numerous among them than the rich. In the last census the mean average of life in England is stated as forty years; which is not, the Report says, one-half of the possible average, which it estimates at one hundred years. In Manchester and Liverpool, the average is only twenty-five years.

To convey a slight idea of the state of poverty to which our working classes are reduced, I shall give one or two facts, which are enough to paralyse with dismay any heart that feels for its fellows; and to show us the great truth, that unless this state of things can be altered, we cannot expect that our society will long hang together as it is. It was lately found by the Government Commissioners of Inquiry, that the average amount of food procured by country labourers for their families, is 122 ounces per week. Hence the working man's share may be calculated as 140 ounces,—134 bread and 6 meat. Now the gaol dietaries (which Sir James Graham says were made from the advice of the most eminent medical men,) allow 254 ounces of food per week to the prisoners on hard labour, which the medical men declared was the very smallest amount which could safely be given. Hence the labourer gets only about half as much food as the criminal, whose allowance is the smallest neid compatible with health and vigour. I quote this awful fact from Mr. Mayhew's work.

Thus the rural population of many parts of England are, as a general rule, half-starved. They have to toil like bond-slaves, with no leisure for amusement, education, or any other blessing, which elevates or sweetens human life; and after all, they have only half enough of the very first essential of life. Better would it have been for the wretched ones, if they had never been born.

The working classes in the towns, are also miserably paid, often half-starved; and are sweated to death in unhealthy sedentary drudgery, such as tailoring, cotton-spinning, weaving, &c. Mr. Mayhew moreover informs us by the concurrent testimony of all the poor street-sellers in London whom he consulted, that poverty has greatly *increased* of late years : that the working classes have now no pennies to spend on superfluities; and hence that the gains of the street-folk have been diminished nearly to a third of what they were some twenty years ago. This is partly owing to the too rapid increase of our own people, and partly to the immense immigration of the Irish; that most unfortunate nation, whose abyss of poverty is deeper than our imagination can conceive, and who have flooded all the poorest occupations in this country, and reduced the wages to the starvation point. "We don't live," said many of the street-folk to Mr. Mayhew, "we starve."

Low as are the wages of the men, they are still far above those of the women. What are the pittances, on which our poor women manage to bear starvation for a few years, before they are ground to death? The mantle-maker earns about 4s. 8d. a-week, when in work, the "slacks" occurring twice in the year, each of three months duration. The embroideress, and upholsteress can make from 10s. to 12s. a-week, but on an average they do not earn half that sum. The garter-maker works from eight in the morning till nine at night, to earn about four shillings a-week clear. The shirt-maker makes shirts for 2s. a dozen : her usual time of work is from five in the morning till nine at night, winter and summer ; and for all this she earns on an average 2s. 10½d. per week, or 2s. clear, after deducting cotton and candle. The waistcoat-maker's earnings average from 3s. to 4s. a-week, out of which, all deductions made, she has about 1s. 10½d. to live upon. Of the workers for the Army Clothiers, the one working for the soldiers earns 2s. a week, and finds her own thread : the other, working for the convicts earns 3s. s week when in full work, but has to deduct thread and candles, " which is quite half." The shoe-binder works about eighteen hours a-day, earning 1s. 6d. per week, out of which she has to pay 6d. for candles. The brace-maker earns from 1s. to 1s. 3½d. a week, working six days of twelve hours, and finding cotton and candles ; she has three months slack in the year, during which she gets about 4½d. a-week, paying a halfpenny for cotton.

These are but specimens which might be multiplied indefinitely ; they are selected from the report of the Morning Chronicle Commissioners made in 1849. These awful miseries, at which our imagination reels and our hearts sicken with horror, arise from the fact, that the supply of " hands" is so great, that the workers are totally in the power of the employers : and dare not refuse, from fear of dismissal, the very lowest wages.

Such are the means, on which these miserable women sustain their life-in-death ; such the penury which drives them so frequently to prostitution,—the only refuge, which our horrible social state has left them ; and for having recourse to which they are despised and abhorred by the well-fed and well-married moralists, who do not enter into the necessities of their life. What is virtue or any other consideration to those who cannot get food ? Words, heartless words, which only serve to increase the misery and embitterment of the sufferer. Well may the noble-minded Mr. Maurice, lately expelled from King's College for his rejection of the withering doctrine of everlasting damnation, write thus, " I think the inference of those wt walk the streets of Christian London, from their observation of what is passing there, might naturally be, that it would be good for ninety-nine hundreds of its people, and of all the people in the world, if they had never been born. This natural opinion is immensely strengthened by the current doctrine among religious men, respecting the fixed doom, which is awaiting those hereafter, who are sunk so low here."

Alas ! I do not know, how we can have the heart to blame any human being, for any action he or she may commit in our present social state. Life is far too difficult for all of us ; we cannot, if we would, be good and happy ; and it is rather surprising now man can nave any virtues at all, amid our withering social evils. Let those who will, blame this man and that woman for actions to which they have been inevitably driven by the iron hand of our destiny: the earnest, loving heart, has other things to do. Instead of blaming, it eagerly seeks to save, and asks the question of questions " Can nothing be done to alter this horrible state of matters, and to prevent these unspeakable evils ? "

Before proceeding to consider this momentous question, 1 shall first entreat the reader's attention to the two following corollaries, which flow from the principle of population ; and which appear to me to be the most awful subject for the consideration of mankind, of any that could be mentioned. I believe moreover, that the more deeply the matter be reflected on, the more will their truth be perceived.

The first is, *that hitherto there has been no real progress among mankind in old countries, and that every good has had its necessary counterbalancin*

z

evil. This arises from the fact, as shown by Mr. Malthus, that the positive check to population is only to be avoided by using the preventive check; in other words, that it is only by sacrificing a proportional amount of love, that men can have an increased supply of food or of leisure. It is only by an increasing preventive check upon population—in other words by an increase of sexual abstinence, that the positive one can be diminished, and that the comforts of the poor can be increased. But it is not food alone, but every other advantage whatsoever, which must inexorably be paid for by the same price. Is the average of life longer now-a-days than formerly? are wars less frequent, are efforts being made to shorten the working hours, to improve the dwellings, to render more healthy the lives of the poor? These blessings also have *inevitably* to be bought by a diminished amount of love; or else the longer lives would only create greater misery, by still further crowding the population. In like manner every virtue, moral and physical, (which all naturally tend to the preservation of life and health, and therefore, by prolonging life, necessitate a diminished number of births,) has to be bought with the same fearful price.

But this price, namely, sexual abstinence, is itself an evil, and one of the very greatest of evils. It leads, as has been abundantly shewn above, to the most miserable physical diseases, to unhappiness and discontent; in so much, that it may be said, that a life without love is not worth having, though there should be every other blessing. The two great primary necessaries of life and happiness, namely, Food and Love, have hitherto been *antagonistic* to each other; and under these circumstances it was not in the nature of things, that man should be other than wretched. The checks by which population has been hitherto kept down to the level of the food—the most vitally important of all the influences which have acted on human destiny—have been *all* of an evil nature, the preventive as well as the positive. Thus for every virtue, for every blessing that we see among us, we may be certain that there is *an inevitable compensating evil*. All human efforts have led to increased *sexual* difficulties, to an increase of sexual abstinence sexual disease, and prostitution; and this not incidentally, but by an absolute and inexorable certainty.

We have partially escaped from the horrors of the *positive* check, namely, wars, infant mortality, famine, &c.; but it has only been, and could only be, to land in the equal horrors of the *preventive* check, namely, the diseases of abstinence and abuse, prostitution, and the most heart-rending poverty and hard work. Quick famine and destruction have given place to *slow starvation* from want of food and of love. Hence we see that there has been hitherto no such thing as real progress in human society. This has been, and is a delusion; and will ever remain so while food and love are antagonistic.

The second great corollary, that may be deduced from the principle of population, and which is enough to turn our hearts to stone, and to confound us with horror and bewilderment, is this; *that hitherto all happiness has been built on the misery of others*. No man at present can be happy himself, without inevitably causing his neighbour's misery. He cannot, where all are struggling for food love, and other advantages, enjoy any of these, without depriving others of them.   Mankind are like a forest of trees too thickly planted.   All indeed suffer more or less, but the more robust struggle upward, and in so doing destroy their weaker neighbours. So do we ; any of us who have greater talents or virtues, more robust bodies or minds, and who are born in more favourable circumstances, struggle onwards to the possession of the hardly-contested blessings of life ; and in so doing we destroy those who are weaker.   This age, and all past ages in old countries, have been ages of *mutual destruction*.   We eat the food of our fellow-beings, we breathe their air, we enjoy their loves, we suck their life's blood.   Hence talents or virtues, instead of being a blessing to those around, are rather a curse to them ; and thus talent and virtue are unworthy of their name.   Among the poor, this death-struggle is seen for the first necessary of life, namely *food* ; among the rich it is seen rather for other blessings of life, and especially for *love*. Those whose talents enable them to succeed in life, marry and mono-polise the blessings of love and offspring, and thus deprive others of them.   At present, when, on account of the large average of children to each marriage, but a limited number of the community can marry, every one who marries may know that he is preventing the marriage of some one else, and thus plunging his neighbour into the misery and disease of a life of celibacy.

Thus, the more deeply we consider this great subject, the more we shall perceive, that virtue, talent, happiness, have hitherto been mere delusions ; mere names, which their possessor had no right to.   It mat-ters not what the virtues have been ; christian or unchristian all are alike ; hitherto every quality which tended to advance a man in life, and to make him happy, has been *inevitably* exerted to the destruction of some of his fellow-beings ; and in this way may almost as well be called an evil as a good quality.   This confounds all commonly-received ideas on the difference of good and evil ; shows us that a deeply-rooted scepticism on human affairs, for which so many thinkers have been blamed, is in reality the only view warranted by the real state of matters ; and that morality has been hitherto a radically false and unsound science.   Do you wish to lead a good life ? you may recognise, that in the present state of human society, it is an absolute impossibility, and that perhaps the best thing you can do on the whole for your fellow-creatures, would be, to cease to live, and so leave them more room to enjoy their life.   No man has ever yet in any old country, where the checks to population are sexual ab-stinence, prostitution, and poverty, lived a good or a virtuous life.   What avail the efforts of the wise, the struggles of the philanthropist, the yearnings of the loving heart to benefit its fellows, while these things are so ?   They are all shattered to pieces on the principle of population and its corollaries, as these have hitherto worked in human affairs. Morality, medicine, religion, law, politics, are solemn farces played before the eyes of men ; whose imposing pomps and dazzling ceremonies serve but to divert the attention from the awful tragedies behind the scenes.   We may be absolutely certain of this, that unless we can attain to some other solution of the social difficulties, our society must for ever continue, as it ever has been, a chaos of confusion, of wrongs, and misery.

These reflections would not appear to us so strange, if we were not accustomed to regard the world from the more favourable point of view, occupied by the better educated and more fortunate classes. Had we been born amid rags and wretchedness, and forced by the pressure of circumstances into crime or prostitution to avoid starvation; had we been ground to death by toil, and found no friend to help us, but been driven from door to door by police and parish officers; we would have had a very different idea of the state of the world; and the increase of wealth and civilization among our neighbours would only have added to our bitterness. We would then have felt in our agony the awful truth, that to the poor the progress of mankind is a hollow lie; that the very prosperity of others is built upon their toil, their sufferings, and their ruin. The self-congratulations of the more fortunate part of mankind on the vast progress of civilization, are a constant insult to the poor and the suffering, and are as foundationless as they are unfeeling. The least we can do to those suffering from the want of food, love, and leisure, is not to insult their misery by vain boasts of the advance of human happiness.

I have dwelt on these considerations, because I wish to impress the deep conviction, that our present state of society is one *so horrible*, when we look beneath the surface, that it cannot possibly long continue as it is; that human affairs, when tested by the population principles, are found to be a hideous phantasmagoria, as if got up by some mocking fiend; and that if a radical change cannot be effected in our society, by which the destructive agency of the principle of population can be counteracted, man's destiny is hopeless. All other questions are insignificant compared to this; religion natural or supernatural, education, medicine, politics, all are alike trivial beside it, and are indeed incapable of solution, without the prior solution of this. The question is not, " are we to have improved morality, religion, or medicine; " but, " are we to have any at all?" Hitherto we have had none; all efforts at improvement in these matters have been totally neutralised by the principle of population, which " dragged at each remove a lengthening chain" of evils behind it. We have lived *just like the inferior animals*, in a state of *mutual destruction;* the only difference being that the *manner* of the destruction has been different, and that it has been to a great degree unconscious and unintentional.

I come now to the great question, "can anything be done to prevent these evils." There is but one possible mode of preventing any evil, namely, to seek for and remove its cause. The cause of low wages, or in other words, of Poverty, as has been so wonderfully explained to us by Mr. Malthus, and following him, by Mr. Mill and others, is over-population; that is, the existence of too many people in proportion to the food, of too many labourers in proportion to the capital; a state of things, produced and constantly kept up by the over-exercise of the reproductive powers. It is of the very first importance, that the attention of all who seek to remove poverty, should never be diverted from this great truth. The disproportion between the numbers and the food is the *only real cause* of social poverty. Individual cases of poverty may be produced by individual misconduct, such as drunkenness, ignorance, laziness, or disease;

but these and all other accidental influences must be wholly thrown out of the question in considering the permanent cause, and aiming at the prevention of poverty. Drunkenness and ignorance moreover, are far more frequently the *effect* than the cause of poverty; and it is a most serious error to overlook this. It is worse, it is an enormous injustice to the poor; and has led many to talk and think harshly of poverty, as being the result of such misconduct.

Hitherto all endeavours to alleviate poverty have been a mere vanity and delusion, from the want of knowledge of, and unremitting attention to, its only true cause. People have sought to remove it, by giving charity, by trying to elevate the moral condition of the poor, by crusades against drunkenness and other of its fearful effects, by the spread of Christianity; or, it may be, by a scheme of national education, socialism, or other means. But in all these the real root of the evil is quite overlooked, and it is not remembered, that none of them can have any permanent *direct* effect upon low wages; the only way it can possibly affect them, is by instructing people to prevent excessive population. If the proportion of the people to the food can be made a smaller one, poverty will be benefited; but by no other conceivable means. The only possible way to remove poverty is to have fewer children.

The common error which prevents the recognition of the population truths, and which we hear repeated over and over again whenever the subject is brought forward, is one which betrays a total ignorance of the Malthusian law, and which men should by this time feel ashamed of uttering, as it is has been so often exposed. I beg the reader to remark it, when next he hears the subject spoken of. Men say, "the idea of over population is absurd; is not the earth wide, and many parts of it uncultivated; and is not an immense quantity of the produce wasted by idlers, who have more than they know what to do with?" Can those who utter such opinions, suppose that the ablest political economists who have existed among us, have devoted their chief energies to the explanation of a palpable absurdity—one which any child would laugh at? Mr. Malthus did *not* say that the earth was *absolutely* over-peopled, or could not support far more inhabitants than now exist; he said that it is *relatively* over-peopled, and has been so to a greater or less degree ever since the birth of history; and this arises from the fact, that the ratio of increase of population is incomparably higher than that of the increase of food; so that population not only easily keeps up with *any* increase of food, that can possibly take place in an old country, but is always pushed beyond it by the force of the great sexual instincts, so that very many of the people (and those naturally who are in the poorest circumstances) are fearfully straightened and over-worked to gain subsistence; nay, are crushed out of existence by the others. Population and food, like two runners of unequal swiftness chained together, advance side by side; but the ratio of increase of the former is so immensely superior to that of the latter, that it is necessarily greatly *checked;* and the checks are of course either more deaths or fewer births, that is, either positive or preventive. The preventive check, or sexual abstinence, is so great an evil, that it is never adequately used, and far more people are brought into the world than can live in comfort on the existing produce; and hence come poverty and early death. It is only in new colonies like America and Australia, that food can be increased at all in the same ratio as population, and hence that the latter can advance with its natural rapidity. But in old countries, so many unavoidable difficulties attend emigration, increased cultivation, or any other conceivable modes of rapidly increasing the food, that they are quite inadequate to enable it to keep up with unchecked population. If these resources were readily available, they would very soon be exhausted, and would long ere this *have been* exhausted. Any one by reflecting on the subject will easily see, that they never can be made so available, as very materially to lighten poverty, even for a few short years, as their effects are speedily obliterated by increased procreation; and practically we know that they never have had this effect, nor have they ever permitted population in an old country to expand at anything approaching its natural ratio. Mr. Malthus showed all these things incontrovertibly, and hence made it apparent that population must be, and is, most powerfully checked in old countries either by more deaths or fewer births; and therefore that the only way of preventing poverty and early death is not by any conceivable means of increasing the produce in this country or emigrating to another, but by having fewer children. As for the rich, it is evident that although there were no rich, poverty would be quite as bad or worse; and would only differ in being universal, and in the absence of the glaring inequalities in human conditions.

Among the lower animals we can easily observe the enormous destruction caused by the law of population. In fishes we see what countless myriads of the young are destroyed; in the domestic animals, as dogs and cats, we have ourselves to be the instruments of this destruction. Poverty, or habitual difficulty of procuring food, together with incessant toil, is a state peculiar to man; and it is by it, as well as sexual abstinence and prostitution, that a similar destruction is effected, just as certainly as in the case of the lower animals, though in a more complicated manner. The average of life in man would be, proportionally, as short as it is in all the inferior animals, were it not, firstly, for the existence of the preventive check, both branches of which, moral restraint and vice, are peculiar to him; and secondly, his greater power of acquiring increased food, which always obviates a part of the necessary destruction.

Those who talk slightingly of the "supply and demand theory," or exercise their wit upon "that bug-bear of over-population," do not know that they are laughing at the most awful and overwhelming laws, that were ever apprehended by mankind; laws which are, and have been ever since our race appeared on this earth, crushing and grinding us to pieces; and which will continue throughout all time as silently, and as inexorably to destroy us, unless we can find a mode of escaping from them. The law of population forsooth is a paradoxical abstraction, and does not act at present, if it ever did act, on human affairs! Alas! do we think that it acts the less, because we refuse to look at its action? Its action is seen at present, exactly as in all past times in old countries, by the necessary existence of the preventive and positive check to population; of poverty and early death on the one hand, and of sexual abstinence or abuse, and prostitution, on the other. Our choice at this hour is exactly the same, as was that of our forefathers; namely, *between* moral restraint, vice, and misery, not independent of them; and whichever of them we seek to mitigate, we must necessarily by so doing *aggravate the others*. Thus if we wish to avoid premature death, and to raise the average of life, it cannot *possibly* be done (while food is increasing at its usual ratio) except by increasing sexual abstinence, or a sexual intercourse which hinders, like prostitution, the birth of children. A decrease in any one of the three immediate checks, moral restraint, vice, or misery, is *necessarily* attended with an increase in the others. In this way we see that premature death in former times obviated the necessity of sexual abstinence or prostitution; while the longer average of life at present has *necessitated* a great increase of these two evils.

The preventive check, in the shape of sexual abstinence, is operating among us at this day with so tremendous a power as was probably never before known in the world. In England and Wales the average age of first marriages among the men is twenty-five years and eight months; among the women twenty-four years and six months. Do we know what these numbers imply? We have become so accustomed to the unnatural sexual lives of our women, that twenty-four years and a-half seem a tolerable average age for the first gratification of the powerful passions, which have awakened ten years previously. These numbers show that the reproductive powers in women are restrained for nearly one-third of their sexual life, even in that proportion of the sex who do marry. But immense numbers never marry, nor exercise at all their reproductive powers. In some parts of England and in many counties in Scotland the proportion of spinsters is as high as forty-one per cent of the women, from the age of twenty upwards. There are 1,407,225 women between the ages of twenty and forty, who have never married; and 359,969 old maids of the age of forty and upwards. Those who are at all aware of the misery and disease of sexual abstinence, will be able to form a slight idea of the suffering arising from this form of the preventive check. The ten years of abstinence before the average age of marriage, of themselves amply account for the universal prevalence of hysteria, menstrual diseases, and the other evils before mentioned.

Prostitution is the mode, which has been adopted in all old countries to palliate in some measure the evils of want of love; and to treat of it, without the knowledge of this, as is generally done, is totally useless. Had it not been for the extraordinary, and still imperfectly explained, fact that a promiscuous intercourse tends powerfully to hinder, if not wholly to destroy, the reproductive powers in woman, mankind would long ere this have been driven to utter desperation from the want of love, as well as of food. It is not understood by those who treat of prostitution, that its increase hitherto has lightened the other necessary checks to population, moral restraint and misery; and therefore has been one great cause of the longer average of life, and the comparative rarity of famine, &c., in modern times. On the other hand, those who seek to do away with prostitution, are unaware of the immense natural difficulties opposing them; namely, that thereby, if other things remain the same, sexual abstinence or premature death *must* be increased.

Unless the *necessity* of the preventive or positive checks to population be perceived; unless it be clearly seen, that they must operate in one form, if not in another; and that *though individuals may escape them, the race cannot;* human society is a hopeless and insoluble riddle.

The difficulty of comprehending the principle of population arises from the extraordinary *peculiarity* of the principle itself. It differs from all truths hitherto discovered in this awful feature: that two great natural laws of our constitution *cross each other,* and are in antagonism; or in the words of Mr. Malthus, that "human beings are brought into the world by one law of nature, who by another law of nature cannot be supported." Between these two crushing laws our race has been, and is, inexorably devoted to misery and grinding destruction; and will ever continue to be so, unless we can reconcile this antagonism. In all other matters it is by obedience to the laws of nature that our safety is secured, but in the case of the reproductive powers, to obey *their* natural laws is certain destruction; while on the other hand, to *disobey* them is no less certain destruction. It was an unguarded, and incorrect comparison which Mr. Malthus made, between the misery resulting from multiplying too fast, and the effects of intemperance in drink; in the former case it is the *normal use,* not the overuse or abuse of the appetites, which is destructive. Were it otherwise, and did the fault lie in human error, the difficulty would be comparatively trivial; but the question is infinitely more awful than this, indeed is totally different from any other which, as far as I am aware, man has ever had to solve; it is, "can we escape from the antagonism of two laws of *Nature?*" Had this antagonism not existed, the whole past and present history of our race would have been radically different.

"Millions and millions of existences" says Mr. Malthus "have been destroyed by this simple cause." This antagonism *necessitates* the continued existence of moral restraint, vice, and misery—in other words of the diseases of abstinence, self-abuse and prostitution, poverty and premature death—in all old countries: in short, of the great social, moral, and physical evils, which exist among us. The ignorance of this antagonism has rendered abortive all human efforts at improvement: in seeking, with Sisyphean labour, to obey more fully one set of laws, men have been *forced* into greater disobedience of another, no less important.

Those who vainly try to remedy poverty by the usual routine means of education, emigration, charity, or political changes, do not reflect, that the problem is not to remove the existing poverty only, but also the sexual abstinence and prostitution; for unless this is done, and not for one generation only, but for all time, the same over-crowded state is constantly kept up by the expansion of the reproductive powers. Such efforts are exactly as delusive, as to seek to empty a cistern, while the stream which supplies it, is suffered to run on unheeded. *Poverty is a sexual question,* not a political or a charity one: and cannot possibly be remedied by any other than *sexual* means. It is one of the great sexual problems, just as truly as abstinence or prostitution; and depends like them upon the restrictive sexual law, discovered by Mr. Malthus.

Poverty and the present social difficulties' are a *compromise* made by mankind in this and all preceeding ages, between the two fearful wants, —the want of food and of love. Rather than resign love, rather than practise increased sexual abstinence, and so check population, they have been willing to submit to the smallest proportion of food and leisure which the human frame could for a season endure. The want of love is so miserable a state of constraint, and moreover so destructive to the health of body and mind, that people who have a choice in the matter will rather put up with any evils than endure it. This it is, which roused the intense disgust against the inexorable population doctrines ; and has made men steadily refuse to look at them, but rather madly cling to any fallacious hope, that might present itself elsewhere, in socialism, emigration, education, &c. What, resign more love? when even at present our life is a constant drudgery and monotony, when there is already not the sixth-part of these sexual pleasures among us, which would be needed to make our society a healthy or a happy one ; resign the dearest solace of our life, the poor man's only enjoyment, and the poet's brightest dream? there is madness in the thought. Instead of less love, we need infinitely more love, to make this world other than a dreary desert, as it is at present to the sexual sufferers, whose name is legion.

Hence we see, that the remedy which Mr. Malthus proposed for the evils of over-population, was of itself such a frightful evil, that all men recoiled from it ; and loaded with invectives the man, *the only man*, who had shewn them the true difficulties of their life. Rather than adopt his remedy, rather than renounce, as he advised, all sexual intercourse till a comparatively late age, they were content to remain sunk in the mire of poverty and hard work ; and to palliate their miseries by the old routine of prostitution, masturbation, and other morbid sexual outlets. The great error in Mr. Malthus's reasoning was, that he, like most of the moralists of his and our own age, was unaware of the frightful evils, and fearful natural sin of sexual abstinence. *The ignorance of the necessity of sexual intercourse to the health and virtue of both man and woman, is the most fundamental error in medical and moral philosophy.* However clearly Mr. Malthus saw the law of population he by no means fully saw its awful nature ; for he did not see the evil of one of his three necessary checks, namely, sexual abstinence. The want of medical knowledge, added to the erroneous austerity on sexual matters, prevented him from recognising them ; made him unhesitatingly advocate the increase of sexual abstinence, one of the most terrible causes of disease and suffering in modern times ; and thus threw him into strong antagonism with all those, who had deeply seen and felt this. He did not recognise the fact, that these evils are so enormous as to render his proposed remedies totally impracticable and visionary. They are impracticable, because they are worse, I firmly believe, than the evils they propose to cure. A society in which all men and women should restrain their sexual desires till the age of thirty or upwards, would be a scene of such horrible restraint, such absence of manliness and nature, such wide-spread genital disease, spermatorrhœa, chlorosis, hysteria, and all the allied signs of sexual

enfeeblement and morbidity, that it would be next to impossible to
find a single healthy or natural individual. If we are to dream of
Utopias, they should at least be of a somewhat more desirable character.   The difference between such a state of society and the present
one, would be, that the miseries would be more equally distributed, so
that no one would have a life worth the possessing.

No ; if there be no other means of increasing the proportion of food
and leisure among mankind, than that of sacrificing the love, human
affairs are hopeless.   It will not, it cannot be done ; and all human
effort will be a mere oscillation, a mere higgling between these two
necessaries of life, as it has been hitherto in all old countries.   To
resign either food or love is despair and death ; and that is the only
choice which mankind has yet had.   If we cannot have *both*, there is
no happiness or virtue for man ; and human society must ever continue, as it ever has been, a scene of confusion, where the strong
strangle the weak, and where the only progress, if progress it is to be
called, has been in the changed form, and more equal distribution of
the miseries.

The real problem for solution is ; to remove *both* the alternative
evils, preventive and positive, of the law of population ; to save our
society from the necessary existence of moral restraint, vice, or misery
—sexual abstinence, prostitution, and poverty—which are ingrained
into all old countries.   The usual attempts at solution—emigration,
socialism, change in the government, pulling down the church, the
aristocracy, and the rich, the spread of religion or education—still
repeated in persistent ignorance or contempt of the law of population,
in the face of the unanswered and unanswerable demonstrations of Mr.
Malthus and the experience of the whole past history of our race, are
futile.   The solution proposed by Mr. Malthus, although guided by
a profound knowledge of the true cause of the evils, (and therefore the
only one which had the slightest chance of being right), was in fact no
solution at all ; it merely recommends, as a remedy for the difficulties, the very thing, namely, sexual abstinence, which itself constitutes
the difficulty.

The hopes of man lie in a nutshell ; they are all comprehended in
this question of questions—Is IT POSSIBLE TO HAVE BOTH FOOD AND
LOVE ? Is it possible that each individual among us can have a due
share of food, love, and leisure ? in other words, is it possible to reconcile the antagonism of the two laws of nature, and to escape from the
horrors of mutual destruction ?

I firmly believe that it is perfectly possible, and that this greatest of
human difficulties has only to be clearly perceived and determinedly
approached, to be ultimately overcome.   But it is evident on the outset, that the means by which this is to be effected, must be very different from any that have been hitherto tried, since all these have
been so utterly inadequate.   It is evident, that it can be by no slight
palliative measures, such as have been hitherto resorted to, and which
have been all rendered abortive by the principle of population, that
any real improvement can be effected ; but that we must go to the
true root of the matter which is a *sexual* one, and that some great

radical change in the sexual life and opinions of mankind is required before it is even possible to escape from these evils.

I earnestly entreat the reader not to prejudge this greatest of questions, nor to allow commonly received opinions to divert him from its steadfast consideration. If he be deeply penetrated by the conviction of the horrible state of human affairs at present existing in old countries; of the utter hollowness and worthlessness of our social fabric; and of the delusive nature of all our schemes of morality, religion, medicine, &c., neutralised as they are by the principle of population; he will perceive that a change is to be sought at all hazards, and if it cannot be got, that human society cannot be expected long to hang together. When once the population truths and the mutual destruction of mankind become generally known, (and they must be before long), all will perceive, that a thorough reconsideration of the first principles of human society, and of sexual morality, is absolutely necessary; for the present state of things is incapable of continuance.

There is a way, and but one possible way, of surmounting these evils, and of securing for each individual among us a fair share of food, love, and leisure; without which human society is a chaotic scene of selfishness, injustice, and misery. I believe too, that this means, however strange it may be to the common ideas upon sexual matters, contains within itself little real evil, or at least the smallest possible amount of evil, which the laws of population leave us the choice of. I am absolutely certain that in time, however much opposition it may at first meet with, it will be universally adopted; for I will defy human ingenuity to imagine the bare possibility of any other escape from the economical and sexual evils of old States, when the magnitude of the difficulties from the want of food on the one hand, and of love on the other, is duly recognised.

The means I speak of, the only means by which the virtue and the progress of mankind are rendered possible, is PREVENTIVE SEXUAL INTERCOURSE. By this is meant sexual intercourse, where precautions are used to prevent impregnation. In this way love would be obtained, without entailing upon us the want of food and leisure, by overcrowding the population.

Two questions arise here, first—Is this possible, and in what way? second—Can it be done without causing moral and physical evil?

In answering the first question, I will give an account, as far as I am acquainted with them, of the different modes in which preventive sexual intercourse has been tried or proposed; for it must not be thought that these means of checking population are new or unusual; they are on the contrary I believe, very common, both in this country and still more in some parts of the continent. People have been driven to devise and adopt them in numberless instances, to prevent an increase in their families, or to avoid having offspring in an unmarried intimacy. I shall first give the great method of preventive intercourse, proposed by M. Raciborski, of whose important contributions to the physiology of the female sexual organs I have spoken above. His views are peculiarly interesting, as being expressly intended to counteract the population evils.

He says, "In marrying girls in our climates at from twenty to twenty-four years of age, we leave them from twenty-four to twenty-six years for reproduction. Let not the length of this period terrify the disciples of Malthus. Science has now the means of reassuring them. She can offer them means capable of arresting in time a rapid increase of the population, in each family which is menaced by it. These means are but the consequence of the progress of the physiology of the species. It is no longer with the destruction of living beings, nor the forced abortions of beings ready to live, that we have to do. Remedies of this kind are destined to remain for ever in the hands of barbarous nations, inaccessible to the lights of the Christian religion and of philosophy." The means he recommends is, "to adopt a certain order in sexual intercourse. It results from my investigations, that, though there may not be periods, as M. Pouchet has lately asserted, when conception is physically impossible, there are nevertheless periods, when it is infinitely less likely to happen than at others. Thus I have found, that in one hundred women we cannot reckon more than six or seven at the outside, who become pregnant at periods considerably distant from the menstrual epoch. In most women, conception dates from intercourse either during menstruation, or a few days before or after it. Hence it results, that in abstaining from intercourse from the second or third day before the menstrual epoch till the eighth day after it, one may be certain to diminish considerably the chances of reproduction."

M. Bischoff, the celebrated German physiologist, is nearly of the same opinion. He says that the egg escapes from the ovary in woman when menstruation is just about to cease, and that, to be impregnated, it must meet the semen in the oviduct; hence, he says, sexual intercourse, to be fruitful, must take place within from eight or twelve days after the menstrual period. Professor Naegele, who is acknowledged to be perhaps the first living authority on midwifery, is accustomed to reckon the duration of pregnancy at nine months and eight days since the last menstrual period; and he says that in normal cases he has never been wrong by this calculation. Very many other physiologists and physicians have the same views, which indeed may be said to have much the greatest weight of evidence on their side.

If these views be true, (and they have every appearance of truth,) they almost of themselves surmount the population difficulty; and are of an importance to mankind, which cannot be over-estimated. But I do not know how far they are true. On account of the rigid and ruinous secrecy, that is kept up on all sexual subjects, no individual gives the result of his or her experience on these matters; and it is almost impossible to ascertain, whether such means have been tried, and whether they have been found efficacious or not. Unless this secrecy and mystery be got rid of, and sexual subjects be discussed freely among us, the greatest of all human difficulties must remain buried in obscurity. Probably the chief reason that has opposed the discussion of the question of preventive intercourse, has been the feeling, that if such intercourse were shown to be of easy accomplishment, it would lead to an immense amount of unmarried love. Women, if they had not the fear of becoming pregnant before their eyes, would indulge their sexual desires, just as men do.   Hence the vehement prejudices in favour of our present code of sexual morality, and of the institution of marriage, together with the determined hostility to anything in the shape of unmarried intercourse, at least on the part of women, are the chief obstacles to the consideration *of the most important of all subjects*, preventive sexual intercourse.

In accordance with the views of these distinguished men, it is only necessary for woman to abstain from sexual intercourse during a certain part of the month; and this would leave them about the half of each month for the free indulgence of their sexual appetites, without the danger of adding to an over-crowded population.   This, if true, would be a boon of incomparable value; and if even this amount of sexual intercourse were available to all women, it would probably prevent in great measure the evils of sexual morbidity, repressed sexual desires, and un-exercised sexual organs, as they are seen in the numberless cases of chlorosis, hysteria, and diseases of menstruation.   Nothing could be of greater value to mankind, than to know how far these views are true; and this can only be brought about, by an ample experience of them, freely laid before the public.

But besides these preventive means, which may be called the *natural* ones, and which are as yet scarcely at all known to the mass of mankind, there are others, which are much more widely known, and much more generally adopted.   Dr. Ashwell alludes to these, as we have seen above, when he says that incomplete sexual intercourse is, he fears, not unfrequently practised, to avoid adding to the cases of an already numerous family.   The means to which he refers, are the *unnatural* or mechanical ones, which are of different kinds; but have all the same object, namely, to avoid impregnation, by preventing the seminal fluid from entering the womb, and thus preventing the meeting of the sperm and germ cell, which is the essential part of impregnation.   In this way the accessory and sensational part of the venereal act is obtained, while the essential and unconscious part is avoided.   This is done either by the withdrawal of the penis immediately before ejaculation takes place, (which is very frequently practised both by married and unmarried men); by the use of the sheath. (which is also very frequent, but more so on the continent than in this country); by the introduction of a piece of sponge into the vagina, so as to guard the mouth of the womb, which lies high up in the vagina; or by the injection of tepid water into the vagina immediately after coitus.

The first of these modes is physically injurious, and is apt to produce nervous disorder and sexual enfeeblement and congestion, from the sudden interruption it gives to the venereal act, whose pleasure moreover it interferes with   The second, namely the sheath, dulls the enjoyment, and frequently produces impotence in the man and disgust in both parties; so that it also s injurious.

These objections however do not, I believe, apply to the third, namely, the introduction of a sponge or some other substance, to guard the mouth of the womb. This could be easily done by the woman, and would scarcely, it appears to me, interfere at all in the sexual pleasures, nor have any prejudicial effect on the health of either party. (Any preventive means, to be satisfactory, must be used by the *woman*, as it spoils the passion and impulsiveness of the venereal act, if the man have to think of them.) I do not know how far this preventive means has been tried, or with what success, but I earnestly hope and believe, that either it, or some analogous simple means, will prove to be satisfactorily available for the grand object, the *practical solution* of the greatest human difficulties,—a preventive sexual intercourse, of easy adoption, and not of a physically injurious nature. The injection of tepid water into the vagina, immediately after intercourse, would also be a very effectual means of preventing impregnation; as it would wash away the seminal fluid, and also, as Wagner asserts, destroy the fecundating properties of the spermatozooids, whose movements speedily cease in pure water.

By far the best of these mechanical means I should take to be the sponge, and it might be used during that part of the month, in which fecundation can take place; or, if M. Raciborski's views prove erroneous, might still, of itself, surmount the population difficulties. The sexual desires in women are generally strongest just after menstruation, (a sign that that is the time, when they are most liable to impregnation;) and it would be an enormous evil to the female sex, which would render their life much more irksome than man's, if their strongest desires were to be systematically denied, and they were only to have one half, and that the least enjoyable half, of their sexual gratification. The law of population has always pressed more heavily on woman than on man (except in respect of the want of *leisure*) on account of the different sexual conditions of the two; and it is most difficult to enable her to escape from its evils.

I believe that by the natural means proposed by M. Raciborski, and the mechanical ones mentioned above, or others which may be discovered to be more satisfactory, it is perfectly possible to have a preventive sexual intercourse, which would enable mankind to surmount the greatest of all their difficulties, and to obtain a sufficiency of food, without the sacrifice of love. No greater boon could be conferred on mankind, than to increase and disseminate the knowledge of these preventive means; and every effort should be made to obtain this knowledge, by a wide induction of individual experience. It is very possible that some means superior to any of the above might be devised; and there is not in the whole range of human thought a single subject, on which ingenuity could be so valuably exercised.

The second question was, can these means be used without causing physical and moral evils? I firmly believe that they can; or at least that the evils they may cause, would be totally insignificant when compared with the present ones, arising from the principle of population. If by these means, together with other changes in our sexual code of which I shall speak hereafter, each woman in our society could have a due share of the pleasures of love, and also of the blessings of motherhood, it appears to me that this could be done, with little, if any, necessary injury to the health. The question is just this, could woman live a healthy life, if she permitted impregnation to take place only twice or thrice in her lifetime, and prevented it in the modes mentioned above at all other times? I believe not only that the average of female health would be immeasurably improved, if this were generally done throughout our society, but that the life of woman could be *perfectly* healthy in these circumstances; that two or three children are sufficient to maintain the health of her sexual organs; and that a due amount of preventive intercourse during the rest of life, would have a purely beneficial effect upon her health, physically and morally. Impregnation and child-birth are certainly of the very greatest importance to the health and happiness of woman, and hence every woman should produce her fair share of offspring; but it is probable that two or three children during life would be quite sufficient to secure these advantages. If such be not the case, alas for woman! for otherwise it is *absolutely impossible* to make the life of the sex a healthy one.

As regards the moral side of the question of preventive sexual intercourse, many people have an objection to it, because, they say, it is *unnatural*. But sexual abstinence is infinitely more unnatural; in fact it is so unnatural, and therefore sinful, that it is totally incompatible with health and happiness, and produces the most wide-spread and desolating diseases. It is granted that preventive intercourse is unnatural, but the circumstances of our life leave us no alternative. If we were to obey all the natural impulses, and follow our sexual desires like the inferior animals, which live a natural life, we would be forced to prey upon and check the growth of each other, just as they do. We must of an absolute necessity act unnaturally; and the only choice left us is to take the course from which the smallest amount of physical and moral evil will result. It is not with nature that preventive intercourse is to be compared, but with the other necessary checks to population, sexual abstinence, prostitution, and poverty. We have to choose *between* these checks, not independent of them.

Some people object to preventive intercourse, that it is a sort of murder, and that by it a life is lost to the world. This is akin to the superstitious dread of the Hindoos, lest any child should remain unborn, which makes them marry every girl immediately after her first menstruation; the consequence being, that the miserable people are sunk in the most hopeless mire of poverty, and are decimated by the positive check to population, in the shape of periodical famines, which are certain to be of frequent occurrence, where the preventive check is not attended to. Potential children are lost to the world every-day; every time that a woman menstruates, or a man's seminal fluid is re-absorbed or discharged without reproduction, a child is lost; in short exactly as many children are lost to the world in this way, as form the difference between the number born in a country doubling its population, as the United States do, in twenty-five years, and an old country whose population is nearly stationary.

But it is a total confusion of ideas to connect preventive intercourse with infanticide. The moment a human embryo is produced by union of the spermatozooid with the egg, its life is as sacred as that of the adult, and to take it away is murder; but to prevent impregnation is a totally different matter. We do prevent impregnation every day, when we refrain from sexual intercourse; and we do waste seminal fluid and eggs every day, and the only alternative left us is not whether or not they shall be wasted, but whether or not we ourselves shall be wasted and destroyed along with them. "We must do no harm to any one," is the golden rule of morality, and therefore the young embryo, when formed, is inviolable; but *before* it is formed, its elements are just like the other secretions of the body, utterly destitute of an independent vitality.

Those who make baseless accusations against preventive intercourse, should rather look to their own actions; which must before long rise up in fearful judgment against many, whose sexual conduct has been thought blameless. Instead of being murder, *preventive intercourse is the only possible mode of preventing murder*, which, as has been already shown in speaking of the mutual destruction of mankind, is taking place around us in society every moment, in its most insidious and painful forms. Instead of being immoral, *preventive intercouse is the only possible way of introducing real morality into human society*, where it has hitherto been a mere name; and although I cannot tell what evils may be found to be inseparable from it, yet I earnestly hope that they are few and slight, and feel deeply convinced that, compared with the present evils, they will be found to be totally insignificant.

Preventive sexual intercourse then, is the mode, and the only possible mode, of reconciling the opposing difficulties of the population problem; and is *the only possible solution* for the great social evils of this and other old countries. I stake my life, I would stake a thousand lives, on the truth of this. There is no subject on which I have thought so long, and felt so deeply, as the sexual one. It has been ever present to me for many years; and long before I read the works of Mr. Malthus and Mr. Mill, my mind was absorbed in the evils I saw and read of, from sexual abstinence, and other sexual difficulties and diseases. At that time I had little idea of the iron-hand of necessity, which was causing all this deprivation and misery, and blamed for it, as many have done, the tyranny of our moral codes, and the monopoly of our sexual institutions; but Mr. Malthus's great work revealed to me the real source of the evil. I then saw that the marriage monopoly was not the real cause of the sexual abstinence, any more than the unequal distribution of wealth was the cause of poverty; but that it arose from the inexorable necessity of checking population, and keeping it down to the level of the food. Marriage was a mere outpost, which screened from view the foe, which was destroying us. The two great opposing difficulties then stood out in the clearest light; those from want of love on the one hand, which I had so long lamented, and those from want of food, which, as I learned from Mr. Malthus, were inseparably connected with the former. I saw then, that the sexual evils and the evils of poverty were in fact merely two different forms of the same grand evil, caused by the law of population: that both sprang from the same source, and could be cured, if curable at all, only by the same remedy. Was this possible? did their cure lie in the nature of things? could these difficulties be reconciled? for, if they could not, the more deeply I considered the question, the more hopeless appeared human affairs. By preventive sexual intercourse, and by this alone, they can, I believe, be perfectly reconciled. It is not without a long and anxious scrutiny from all the points of view within my reach, that I have been led to this conclusion; and I feel earnestly convinced, that it will prove a true means of escape from the social evils. If it should not, alas for our race! In that case this work, and every other work which has ever been written on any subject, have been written in vain; and are impotent to produce any real improvement in human destiny.

But even although preventive intercourse were universally adopted, and found to be sufficient for its object, it would by no means thoroughly remedy the sexual evils, although it would greatly mitigate them: and although it might wholly remove poverty. Many of the sexual evils most widely spread among us, depend directly upon the errors of our code of sexual morality. According to this code, all love except married love, is considered sinful. Marriage, it is held moreover, should bind people together for life, without leaving them the power of indulging in any other sexual intimacy, or of divorce from each other, unless either the husband or wife commits adultery. If this, which is the view of marriage generally entertained in this country, were to continue, there are very many fearful sexual evils which could not be removed.

In the first place, what is, or should be, the grand object of any social institution for uniting the sexes? It is, that *each individual in society, every man and woman, should have a fair share of the blessings of love and of off-spring, and that the children should be duly provided for.* But if marriage be the only honorable way of obtaining sexual and parental pleasures, very many must be excluded from them; for, even supposing that there were room for the exercise of all the reproductive powers, as in America, or that by preventive intercourse the proportion of children in each family were to be small, so as to allow of a great many marriages, still there would be a large number of women, and even of men, who from plainness and other unattractive qualities, would find no one, who would be willing to be rigidly bound to them for life. Even in America there are, I believe, not a few old maids. Were these inevitable cases still fewer, they would be enough of themselves to show the insufficiency of marriage. In this country, from the great preponderance of the female sex, very many would necessarily remain single, though every man were to marry. In Scotland, where the disproportion of the sexes is highest, the census of 1851 shows that there are 110 women to 100 men; a fact which of itself, under our present sexual code, reveals an immensity of suffering.

But these are but drops in the ocean of miseries, which the rigorous institution of marriage inevitably causes. Marriage is based upon the idea, that constant and unvarying love is the only one, which is pure and honourable, and which should be recognised as morally good. But there could not be a greater error than this. Love is, like all other human passions and appetites, subject to change, deriving a great part of its force and continuance from variety in its objects; and to attempt to fix it to an invariable channel is to try to alter the laws of its nature. Youth, when the passion is strongest, is especially prone to change, according to the beautiful command of Nature, who intends that our experiences should be varied, and our different faculties and emotions called forth. To deplore this inconstancy in youth, or to call it an instance of perversity, or original sin, is to think to set ourselves above the wisdom of Nature. A young man and woman at puberty, when their new senses are awakened, fall in love with the first tolerably fair face they meet. It is ten chances to one that were they to marry this first object, in a few years they would bitterly repent. How can they tell, without experience of love, how many objects of greater attraction and congeniality they may yet encounter; they, who know as yet scarcely anything of character, even of their own?

Marriage thus tempts young people, blinded by the promptings of their novel passion, and by their inexperience, to rush into a state which will be the source of future years of grief. It denies all sufficient experience in the choice of a sexual companion; one of the most important essentials of our happiness. Though the man and woman may know a little of each other's exterior, and of some of their surface qualities, yet they have no idea how they shall *sexually* suit each other, before they enter into this irrevocable contract; so that the greatest miseries have frequently arisen from the existence of some sexual malformation on either side, from impotence in the husband, or even from total ignorance of all sexual matters on both sides—an ignorance worthy of the childhood of our race, but an extraordinary anomaly in the nineteenth century.

Many individuals in our society have a strong conscientious objection to the marriage vow, which is in fact a satire upon all vows, promising love till death; a promise, which is evidently in many cases utterly beyond the power of him or her who makes it, to fulfil. Again, the promise of the wife to *obey* is a standing shame to the whole formulary, and has tended to give a handle to those acts of domestic tyranny, which are, it may I believe be said, the rule, and not the exception, in married life.

Marriage cannot, in general, be used in those innumerable cases, where sexual intercourse is indispensable to the cure of genital diseases, such as many forms of spermatorrhœa, chlorosis, hysteria, and the diseases of menstruation. When a young man or woman has one of these diseases, sexual intercourse cannot be obtained promptly through the cumbrous machinery of marriage, (even were it morally advisable for an invalid, whether man or woman, to link his uncertain fortunes indissolubly with another;) and the deeper the unhappy sufferer sinks into the abyss of misery, the more hopeless does the prospect of marriage become; for, if a young man, he has neither the will nor the power to look about for a partner for life at such a time; and, if a girl, the more sickly she becomes, the less chance is there of her finding a husband. Therefore *marriage deserts us at our greatest need*; and if it should continue to be the only attainable sexual intercourse, the cure of vast numbers of genital diseases would be, as at present, impossible, and might be given up in despair. But not only the cure, the *prevention of* these diseases in any satisfactory degree would be impossible; for unless all young people were to marry about puberty, which would create the most fearful subsequent repentances, an immense amount of genital disease would be certain to arise, were no other honourable provision made for the gratification of the first and most impetuous passions. It is very generally about and shortly after the age of puberty, that masturbation begins to be practised among both sexes; chlorosis is most frequent in girls still in their teens; in short, it is an *absolute impossibility* to prevent the developement of an immense amount of genital disease and morbidity, if marriage be the only sexual provision for youth.

The irrevocable nature of the marriage contract, and the impossibility of procuring divorce, lead to the most fearful evils. Mr. Hill shows this in his work on Crime, telling us that the great majority of murders and brutal assaults now-a-days, are committed by husbands upon their wives; and showing that it is in the nature of all long and indissoluble contracts to cause similar evils. All contracts, binding two human beings together in an indissoluble manner for long periods, are the fruitful source of crimes and miseries. So it was with the cumbrous machinery of apprenticeships, formerly prevalent in the trades, which is now being gradually abandoned. It is certainly a fearful and miserable anomaly that two persons who have ceased to care for—nay, who have come to hate each other, should be bound together with iron rigour, in what should be the bonds of love. Surely it is a bitter satire upon love, and on the dignity and freedom of man and woman. It is said, with the austerity that characterises all the sexual opinions in this country, that the happiness of the parents in such a case should be sacrificed to the interests of the children, and that therefore a divorce should not be permitted; but could anything be more adverse to the happiness or welfare of the *children themselves*, than to dwell with a father and mother whose temper is soured by mutual hatred? For all parties it is infinitely desirable that a divorce should take place. It is from such rational considerations that in many parts of the continent, as for instance in Germany, the unnatural indissolubility of marriage has been abandoned, and divorce is permitted, if the parties find that they are unsuited to each other. Many are already in favour of a similar alteration in the marriage laws of this country.

Marriage is one of the chief instruments in the degradation of women. It perpetuates the old inveterate error, that it is the province of the female sex to depend upon man for support, and to attend merely to household cares, and the rearing of children—a belief which is utterly incompatible with the freedom or dignified developement of women on the one hand, and with the economical interests of society on the other. It is the emblem too of all those harsh and unjust views, which have given to woman so much fewer privileges in love than man, and have punished so much more severely a breach of the moral code in her case. For a man to indulge his sexual appetites illegitimately, either before or after the marriage vow, is thought venial; but for a woman to do so, is the most heinous crime. The wife has been held, in the true spirit of the oriental harem, to be in a manner the sexual *property* of the husband, whom no one had a right to touch, and who had no right to have a thought for any one but her own lord and master.

It is easy to compare monogamy, as it exists among us, with polygamy, and to boast of its superior justice; just as we hear Protestants every day easily triumphing over the effete Roman Catholicism. It is not with Roman Catholicism but with Natural Religion, that Protestantism is to be compared; and it is not with polygamy, but with nature, that marriage is to be compared: and it will be found infinitely further behind the truly natural sexual justice, than it is superior to ploygamy. It has been made the engine by which woman has been terrified into, and imprisoned in, the most rigid rules of sexual discipline, while man has taken to himself all the sexual privileges. The husband, who himself would not scruple in the slightest to break his marriage vow, thinks his *honour* implicated in his wife's rigid observance of it; and would be ready on the shortest notice to shoot a man through the body, who should dare to approach his wedded property, to whom he is perhaps totally indifferent. Are not things like these a mockery? do they not make fools and puppets of us. and pour scorn upon our vaunted institutions? Marriage delivers woman bound into the hands of man; it gives her moral and legal disadvantages, compared with him; tempts her to become entirely dependent on him for support, and do nothing but breed and rear children to overstock the world: by its hopeless indissolubility, it takes away her spirit, and makes her submit to hardships and indignities, which otherwise she would never for a moment endure; it puts her in the power of man, and tempts him to abuse his gift of superior strength; it is in short the instrument, in numberless cases, of making the man a tyrant and the wife a slave.

Marriage is a step so irrevocable and hazardous, that few would take it, were they not driven to it, by the want of any other honourable outlet for their sexual desires. Many men feel that it would be to them a great loss of freedom in various respects: and the number of those who remain bachelors, not from want of means, but from dislike to the married state, is very large; and is continually increasing, as the advance in intelligence makes men less willing to take problematical and irrevocable steps, in matters so closely connected with their happiness in life. Marriage is like the gambler's stake, all or nothing; and is fitted for the early stages of human developement, but not for an advanced state of society. There is nothing more degrading to the dignity of man and woman, than such irrevocable contracts; they make children of us, confining our affections and actions by rule and measure, as if we were unfit to have any freedom, and to guide our own sexual conduct throughout life.

The icy formality of the marriage ideas is a constant damper to the enjoyments of youth; it spoils the social pleasures between the young of both sexes, and casts a chill upon that intimacy and close sympathy, which they should have for each other. No warm feelings are countenanced between the sexes, unless marriage is in prospect; a young man must not address a young woman except with a certain constraint.

for fear of exciting in her hopes of marriage, which he does not mean to realise ; neither a man nor woman must *flirt* (that miserable word) with any of the opposite sex, for fear of entangling their hearts, and causing their misery ; in short, the only sexual conduct which is considered quite conventionally honourable, is to look about for one suitable partner, and keep at a due distance from all the rest of man or womankind, both before and after marriage. This it is, which has frozen our society, given an effeminate and unhealthy character to all love, as if young people could not take care of their own feelings, and deadened the frank gaiety and impulsiveness of our youth ; converting the dignified intercourse of men and women, into a scene of stiff and artificial marriage-hunting, where the girls and their mothers are bent on looking out for good matches ; where the unmarried women are tormented by the miserable apprehension of being left old maids, feelings destructive to the dignity of the female character; and where the men are frequently hooked into marriage by arts and stratagems, or bullied into it by the fear of having " gone too far " in attentions to the lady. This has had the effect of banishing true and natural love as much as possible from our society, and substituting for it interested calculations.

The romance and impetuosity of love are well-nigh extinguished among us, and are to be met with chiefly in works of fiction; where people indulge in a day-dream of what should be the feelings between the sexes. A great proportion of the marriages we see around us, did not take place from love at all, but from some interested motive, such as wealth, social position, or other advantages; and in fact it is *rare* to see a mariage in which true love has been the predominating feeling on both sides. This is especially the case as regards *woman*. It is comparatively rare, that a woman marries the man whom she most loves; we see matches every day in which a young girl marries an old man, or where the fear of remaining an old maid, or the wish to obtain the social advantages and protection of marriage, is the real motive which influences the woman. Such marriages are in reality cases of *legalised prostitution*, and are utterly alien to the true spirit of love. It is not woman herself but her unfortunate social position, that is to be blamed for them. From the dependent state of woman, which makes her think rather of a protector and maintainer than a lover ; from want of the power or active selection on her side ; and from the great population difficulties, which surround our society, and which have made marriage hitherto attainable but to a limited number and at an advanced age ; the influence of true love among us has been curtailed to an immense degree, and all other feelings have as far as possible been substituted for it. But by this, there is an incalculable loss to the happiness and virtue of mankind, and especially of youth, for on no age does the rigour of the marriage code press so suffocatingly as on youth; on youth, the season of ardent passion, of impulse, of change ; of generous spirit, as yet untamed by the griading difficulties of life, and beaming with that sexual halo, then only to be seen, which displays the freshness and power of the newly developed passions.

The complete *exclusiveness* of marriage, gives rise to very great evils

Both men and women, but especially the latter, often fall desperately in love with one object; and if they cannot have the full and sole possession of this, they resign themselves to despair. From hopeless love, especially in woman, what fearful evils arise daily! The sufferer loses all relish for the rest of life, pines away, and probably falls ultimately into the hands of our great national destroyer, Consumption. The most intense jealousy too is fostered among us, by the exclusiveness of marriage. Lovers paying their addresses to the same girl, or girls who are rivals for the affections of a man, are consumed with jealousies and anxieties; for they know that it is a question of all or nothing, and their whole happiness in life seems bound up in the issue. The exclusiveness of marriage is thus one great cause of *that intense anxiety of mind*, which is so conspicuous in our national character, and wears men down as much as hard work.

The custom moreover of selecting one sole object of love, and steeling one's heart, as far as sexual desires are concerned, against all the rest of man or womankind, has a very narrowing effect on our capacity for affection, and appreciation of what is good and amiable in the different characters we see around us. Hence, in great measure, has arisen that *fastidiousness* in love, which is so marked among us, and is the sign of a narrow and effeminate culture. There is perhaps no society, so full of little trifling dislikes and repugnances as ours; even the young, who should be averse to see any faults in the opposite sex, are full of the most captious criticisms against them; instead of admiring each of their neighbours for those good qualities which they possess, they must have them suit exactly their narrow ideal, or, if not, they despise them. These petty dislikes arise inevitably from a rigourous institution like marriage; and are the modes in which the heart of man or woman *instinctively* steels itself against others, and devotes itself to one sole object. Where a rigid puritanism sternly forbids even the very feeling of sexual desire towards any person save one's married companion, or any sexual intercourse except in a rigourous marriage, the heart is necessarily driven, if it is not to become the prey of conflicting emotions, to harden itself against the rest of the sex; and these are some of the ways in which this is done.

Another very common way is by the feelings becoming callous to the passion of love altogether; the husband turning his attention wholly to the pursuit of wealth, fame, or other objects, and the wife to rearing children, or, if she have none, to pietism. Thus constancy is secured by the partial or total extinction of the passion of love; and this is the case not in solitary instances, but I believe almost in the majority of married lives. This is one of the most important secondary reasons of that intense thirst for money-getting, which is so prominent a feature in the English and American character. When love becomes extinguished, from the influence of habit, of cold puritanical feelings, or other causes in marriage, some other passion must step in to supply its place in an energetic mind; and that passion is generally in this country the love of wealth. The effect of habit in dulling our passions is little understood as yet; and I believe we are little aware of how much the sum of sexual enjoyments is diminished, by the rigid monotony of our sexual institutions.

Marriage and the strictness of the sexual code is the chief secondary cause of *prostitution*. It excludes any honourable provision for sexual connections of a temporary kind; but these are so absolutely essential that they must be obtained at any cost; and since they are stigmatised as immoral, they assume the degraded and clandestine shape of prostitution.

But all these evils of marriage, fearful though they be, are as nothing compared with the miserable part it has played in the grinding population-difficulties of our race. Marriage has been, and is, in fact, a *monopoly* of honourable love, and the blessings of offspring, by a limited class; who have shut out all the rest from these blessings, and plunged them into the awful gulph of sexual evils, prostitution, masturbation, diseases of sexual abstinence, and venereal disease. It has been the rock on which a certain number have saved themselves from the sea of sexual sufferings; and whence they have looked, not in awe and pity, but rather in scorn and hatred, on their unhappy fellow-beings, who were struggling with the waves. But this is not all. By the *large families* they have had on the average, they have permiettd as few as possible to escape from the evils of celibacy; and have overcrowded the population to such a degree, that the most awful poverty, and hard work, and the greatest difficulty of getting a livelihood have ensued.

It is difficult to conceive greater evils than have existed, and do exist, under the present sexual code. Poverty could scarcely be more widespread and grinding than it is; and I think it would be difficult to imagine a state, where, on the whole, less sexual pleasures and more sexual evils exist. than in our present one. It is customary to boast loudly of the happiness of the married state, and to give the institution of marriage credit for that sum of sexual happiness, which we witness around us, and which is sure to be seen chequering the darker shadows of human life, wherever the two sexes dwell together, and by whatever tie they are united; but such boasts also are a vanity. Even among the richer classes, I believe just as little sexual happiness exists, as could be at all expected from any kind of relations, by which man and woman are held together in a civilized society; there is about as little pleasure in begetting the swarms of legitimate children, as could well be extracted from venereal intercourse; and when we go beneath our little surface of society, and look at married life among the poor, we find it full to the brim with miseries; cares, ill-usage, drunkenness, children a burden to their parents, and especially to their hard-worked mother; the wife generally sick of all sexual pleasures, which have loaded her with such cares, and perhaps submitting to them only from fear of her husband. Alas! Dr. not let us mock such fearful evils with the name of "Holy and blessed institution." In what way does the institution of marriage, in which such miseries can exist, deserve the thanks or the admiration of mankind? What has it done for us, Oh we unhappy! that we should bow down and worship it so blindly?

Married people have made an awful use of the privileges entrusted to

them, namely, the monopoly of the loves, by which our race is continued
From ignorance or heedlessness, they have totally disregarded the great
sexual responsibility, which is incumbent upon every member of human
society, and should be regarded by all of us as the most sacred duty,
namely, *not to bring into the world more than our fair share of children.*
This great duty, which is one of such supreme importance, little though
it be yet recognised, that it is not only by far the most sacred of all in
regard to our *sexual* conduct, but probably is *the most important of all
possible duties*, was not understood to be a duty at all until Mr. Malthus
wrote. He however showed clearly, that without attention to it, all
other virtues are in vain ; that the exercise of all the Christian, or any
other conceivable virtues, without this, would be totally unable to remove
a single one of the great evils which oppress our race.

I believe however, that Mr. Malthus, and even Mr. Mill (although
the latter says, that the population question is one in which not only the
labourers, but all the richer classes, whose children are educated to any
profession, are concerned), have limited too much the incumbency of this
great duty. Mr. Malthus defined it thus, " That no man should bring
into the world children whom he could not support." This has had the
effect of laying the whole burden of the duty upon *the poor and working
classes ;* and has been one great reason, why its sacredness has been so little
recognised. These were exactly the classes, who, from their want of
education and developement, could least understand the question ; and
even if they had understood it, could least be expected to exercise such
prudence. The rich were too well content that the irksome duty should
not be laid upon their shoulders ; and as they did not clearly see how
their own interests were involved in it, they were content to avoid the
question.

While the duty is made incumbent only upon the poor, there is comparatively little hope of its incomparable importance being felt. But I
am firmly convinced, that it has an infinitely wider applicability ; that it
is not a class duty, but a *universal human duty.* It is not a question of
poverty or the want of food merely, but also of the want of *love.* The
question is not—Can we support any number of children that we are able
to bring into the world ? but—How many children is each individual in
an old country morally justified in bringing into the world, when he has
consideration for the health, happiness, and virtue of others? The case
is simply thus. There is room in old countries (and, in two or three centuries more, which in the history of our race, are but as a day, even
America and Australia, will be old, or in other words well-peopled
countries,) for but a very small number of children, compared with
that which the reproductive powers of our species would admit of ;
and the question is, how, and by whom, are these children to be produced? If the rule of morality is to be, that a man or woman may
produce as many of this limited number of children, as he or she can
support, it must result, that a limited class will, as at present, *mono-
polise all the reproductive functions ;* and the rest be compelled either to
bring no children into the world, or, if they do, to overcrowd the population, and thus produce poverty, hard work, and early deaths.

At present every man or woman who marries, prevents some one else from marrying; every man or woman who gets a child, prevents some one else from having one. In this way, to have a large family of children is *the worst of all sexual sins* a man or woman can be guilty of. There is scarcely anything which causes so much misery to others. Suppose the circumstances of a society to admit of only from two to three children on an average by each woman, (which is the case at present in our own country), every married couple who have more than this number, are inevitably plunging some of their fellow-creatures either into sexual abstinence, whose horrors it is vain to disguise, or into prostitution, masturbation, or sexual disease. Therefore *large families are the primary cause of the sexual evils, as well as of poverty;* and to bring a large family into the world is in reality much more morally guilty, than prostitution or other sexual faults. Among the *poor*, the large families operate by crowding the population, increasing poverty, and causing hard-work and early death, (the poor in large towns only live one-third of their natural term of life); among the *rich*, they prevent other marriages, producing abstinence or masturbation among the young women, with all the miseries of a blighted sexual life; and mercenary love, abstinence, and other sexual evils among the young men; besides crowding all the professions to a degree, which produces the most destructive *want of leisure* and mental anxiety, makes the weaker despair and the stronger work himself to death.

The whole blame for sexual misconduct is laid upon those, who are the *victims* to the imprudence of married people. The poor prostitutes, the masturbator, the unhappy sufferers from venereal disease, the hysterical, the hypochondriacal, are either savagely despised or treated with ridicule and disdain; but the *real cause* of their sufferings and degradations, namely, to bring large families into the world, is thought rather a virtue than a fault. Thus it can be seen that *our* interests are just as much bound up in the great population question, as are those of the poor; and that *the duty of limited procreation is as incumbent upon the rich as the poor.*

To have offspring is not to be regarded as a *luxury*, which the rich man alone has a title to, as Mr. Malthus's reasonings tend to show it to be, but as a great *primary necessary* of health and happiness, of which every man and woman should have a fair share; which no class should be allowed to appropriate to themselves, without incurring the reproaches of their neighbours; and which no individual should be so selfish, as to wish to engross, without consideration for others. Childbirth is one of the grand *physical necessaries* for the health of woman. Without it her reproductive powers remain unexercised, and her constitution is almost sure to suffer in consequence. It is not enough to have sexual intercourse; the pleasures of love alone are not sufficient in woman to satisfy the wants of her organization, and to fulfil her sexual life. The blessings of offspring moreover, are one of those great *moral necessaries* of happiness, which the heart of every man and woman naturally yearns for. Both man and woman must feel, that their life is incomplete without offspring. To be childless deprives an individual of many of the most elevating experiences that belong to humanity; leaves him solitary in old age, and excludes him from those softening and purifying influences, which this great moral tie naturally brings with it. Therefore, even although by the adoption of preventive sexual intercourse, every individual could have a due share of *love*, still it would be impossible to secure a healthy and a happy life to the mass of mankind, and still more of womankind, unless each woman should also have a fair share of *offspring*.

It is a matter of the very first importance for the welfare of society, that the *necessaries* of life should be distinguished from the *luxuries*; and that society should be so arranged, that every individual should have a due share of the necessaries. Society should regard as its very highest principle and aim, that no single individual should be forced to live an unhealthy life; and it is a sacred duty, binding upon every one of us, to act in such a manner, that we shall not render health and happiness impossible to some of our fellow-creatures. Children stand in a perfectly different category from the luxuries of life. These luxuries, such as costly dresses, wines, handsome furniture, or other ornaments of life, are not naturally indispensable to the health and happiness of mankind; and therefore it is not incumbent upon the different members of society to see that all their neighbours, as well as themselves, are provided with them; but sexual intercourse and offspring are absolutely indispensable, and therefore it is morally binding upon every member of society, to take only such a share of them, as to leave a sufficiency to his fellows.

Therefore, any man or woman, it matters not what be their station in life, whether their destiny be a palace or a hovel, who has more than the small proportion of children which the circumstances of an old country allow, as the fair average to each individual, *is an irreligious being;* and disregards one of the most sacred of all the moral duties, thus inevitably causing disease and misery to some of his fellow-creatures. This is the most important of all the obligations of sexual morality; and ignorance of it, which was so universal until Mr. Malthus wrote, although it may lead us to pardon, and view with sorrow instead of blame, the faults of married people, does not in the least alter the great natural sin of disregarding this duty. *Large families are the ruin of us all;* they are the fountain-heads of the hard work, low wages, starvation, and prostitution among the poor; and of the mercenary love, sexual abstinence, and all the train of sexual horrors, together with the toils and anxieties of over-wrought professional life, among the rich. By them has the great mass of the misery we witness around us been caused; and it is only by concentrating our attention upon this parent source of evils, and stemming it at its origin, that it is even conceivably possible to remedy the miseries arising from the want of food, love, and leisure.

It is the most awful of all reflections, and yet it is absolutely undeniable, that no class of human beings have been the cause to their fellows of ruin or destruction, in the slightest degree comparable with that which arises from the imprudent procreation of married people.

How is it to be expected that our race should make real progress, or human society should be other than a chaos, when from a morbid delicacy the most important of all actions, namely, the giving life to new beings, is left to the mercy of ignorance and recklessness?

All should view with a jealous eye those who have more than a small number of children, so long as there remain any among us, who are suffering from the want of food or of love. Every man or woman who has a regard for his fellow-creatures, and a sense of the sacredness of moral duties, should refrain from bringing into the world more than a very small number of offspring, until the evils of poverty, and sexual abstinence, are removed. By thus refraining, he will do more for his fellow-men, than if he lavished upon them his whole wealth, and toiled for them in every other manner; but on the contrary, if he bring into the world a large family, while our society is labouring with the awful population-difficulties, as at present, all other imaginable virtues and efforts cannot make him other than a *destroyer of his fellow-beings*.

These reflections show us, that the great burden of the sexual sins should be laid on the shoulders of the married people, who have large families; and not, as is done at present, on the poor friendless prostitutes, unmarried lovers, and other sexual sufferers, who are the victims, not the causes, of our sexual sins. None of their faults are so great or so destructive to the interests of society, as that of having a large family; and moreover they are, in reality, mainly the *effects* of this great primary fault.

It becomes manifest, moreover, from these reflections, that the views commonly entertained as to the sexual duties are exceedingly unnatural; and that it is absolutely necessary to remodel in many respects our sexual code; to form it upon the great natural foundation of equal justice between man and woman, and in accordance with the principles of morality, arising from the laws of the generative organs and of population; of which our forefathers, who framed the present code, had no knowledge. The great *natural sexual duties* of man and woman do not, as is commonly imagined, consist in being a constant husband or wife, or in avoiding unmarried intercourse; but are of a very different nature.

In the first place, as has already been said, the most sacred of all the sexual obligations should be, not to have more than one's fair share of children. This share, in the present circumstances of our society, is a very small one; for we are already so overcrowded, that the object of every one should be, to thin our numbers *by avoiding all unnecessary births*, until poverty is completely removed, and the population is brought to bear a due proportion to the food. In fact, the fewer children either a man or woman could have at present, the better for their fellow-creatures; and no possible conduct could be so meritorious in any individual, as to refrain from having children altogether, unless they are necessary for the health of the mother, until the weight of our social difficulties is somewhat lightened. *The duty of limited procreation* may well be deemed the very first and highest of all duties, for if it be well performed, it makes all others comparatively easy; but if it be neglected, it is absolutely impossible that any other duty can be of avail to mankind, or that our race can make any real progress in virtue or happiness.

The next sexual duty, is to educate well those children whom we bring into the world. It is a sacred obligation upon every man and woman, to provide for their offspring to the best of their powers, and to train them to become good members of Society. Children at present are exceedingly ill-provided for, from the squalid poverty in which their parents are often plunged; and from the frequency of large families, in which the children are a drag upon their parents, and are too numerous to be attended to. Another great reason of the imperfect nurture, which many children receive, is the dependent and degraded state of their *mother*. She cannot support herself, but trusts for support to her husband, and of course the children share in her helplessness. Were women as a general rule able to gain a livelihood for themselves, not only would the character of the sex be greatly raised, but the children would have a far surer guarantee for being well cared for. A mother who could earn a good livelihood, would rarely, if ever, desert her child, even although the father might do so. There is no secondary cause of poverty more important, than the dependent and helpless state of woman. To have to support his wife as well as his children, is a heavy additional tax on the energies of man. Therefore for all parties, for man, woman, and child, it is of the utmost consequence that woman should cause to be dependent upon man for support, as she has hitherto been; and that every woman in society, just as every man, should be able to earn an independent livelihood for herself. Nothing would have a greater effect in elevating the female character, and in advancing the best interests of society.

There are two things requisite to enable woman to become independent. In the first place, *the wages of female labour must be greatly higher* than at present; and this can only be effected, exactly as in the case of male wages, by diminishing the number of workers. This is to be done only by checking population by means of preventive intercourse. Thus the means, by which the wages of man are to be raised, will at the same time raise those of woman. With regard to the exceedingly small wages of woman, of which specimens have been given before, Mr. Mill says, " The explanation of the fact that the peculiar employments of women are so ill-remunerated, must be that they are over-stocked; that although so much smaller a number of women than of men support themselves by wages, the occupations which law and custom make accessible to them are comparatively so few, that the field of their employment is still more over-crowded." He says also that from our present domestic customs, competition may depress much lower the wages of women than of men; for a man's wage is calculated by what is necessary to support a wife and small family, since it is the general custom for the wife to depend on the husband; whereas a woman's wage is only for her own support.

From these remarks of Mr. Mill it is seen, that the great causes which depress the wages of women are that there are so few occupations left open to them by law or custom ; while those which are open to them, are immensely overstocked. This leads us to the second requisite for the independence of woman. It is that *the sphere of her activity should be enlarged*, and that all professions and occupations in which, by her natural powers, she is fitted to engage, should be thrown open to her. Nothing would more powerfully promote the welfare of our race, than the developement of woman. It is to woman that the reproduction of the species is peculiarly entrusted ; and it is she, on whom will specially devolve that most important of all duties, the regulation of the number of offspring. It is therefore indispensable to the interests of mankind, that the independence, and foresight of woman, should be increased as much as possible, and nothing would have a more powerful effect on this, than to enlarge her sphere of action ; so that her pursuits might be as important and varied as those of man, and that every woman might have the power of gaining an honourable independence. On this subject I shall again quote Mr. Mill's words.

"It appears to me impossible but that the increase of intelligence, of education, and of the love of independence among the working classes, must be attended with a corresponding growth of the good sense, which manifests itself in provident habits of conduct, and that population therefore will bear a constantly diminishing ratio to capital and employment. This most desirable result would be much accelerated, by another change, which lies in the direct line of the best tendencies of the time, the opening of industrial occupations freely to both sexes. The same reasons, which make it no longer necessary that the poor should depend on the rich, make it equally unnecessary that women should depend on men ; and the least which justice requires is, that law and custom should not enforce dependence, (where the correlative protection becomes superfluous), by ordaining, that a woman who does not happen to have a provision by inheritance shall have scarcely any means open to her of gaining a livelihood, except as a wife and a mother. Let women who prefer that occupation adopt it, but that there should be no option, no other *carriere* possible for the great majority of women except in the humbler departments of life, is one of those social injustices which call loudest for remedy. Among the salutary consequences of correcting it, one of the most probable would be, a great diminution of the evil of over-population. It is by devoting one-half of the human species to that exclusive function, by making it fill the entire life of one sex, and interweave itself with almost all the objects of the other, that the instinct in question is nursed into the disproportionate preponderance, which it has hitherto exercised in human life."

The life of young ladies is most vapid and unnatural. They have no substantial occupation, and their energies are frittered away upon trivial accomplishments, which should form only the ornaments of life. Very many of them feel this keenly, and desire nothing so eagerly as a suitable occupation, to engage their often highly cultivated minds, and give them an independent position ; but our social arrangements render this an impossibility. When they marry, the rearing of children seems the only kind of real occupation, which can save them from ennui and self-reproach for their uselessness; and thus they are tempted to have large families, to the destruction of their fellow creatures.

These two great sexual duties, namely not to have more than our fair share of children, and to provide carefully for them, are those which a society has a right to demand from all its members. If a man or a woman fulfil these great duties satisfactorily, they have fulfilled their chief sexual duties to society. Whether the children have been born in marriage or not, is a matter of comparatively very little importance; and if these duties have been neglected—if an individual have brought into the world a large family, or have not provided for them well—the empty title of constant husband does not prevent him from having been one of the destroyers of his race.

It is of the highest importance, that the attention of all of us should be steadfastly concentrated upon the real sexual duties, and not dazzled by mere names. *Marriage diverts our attention from the real sexual duties*, and this is one of its worst effects. It also conceals from the superficial view the law of population. Those, who are not acquainted with this law, believe that people remain unmarried either from their own choice, or from their unattractive qualities. They do no not see the great restrictive principle which is operating beneath. This common error is very similar to that of calling drunkenness or idleness the cause of poverty, and is in reality a mockery of the evils of celibacy. The peculiar defects of marriage itself, doubtless make many persons, especially men, unwilling to enter into it, if freer sexual connections are at all obtainable, and this helps still more to divert attention from the great natural obstacle; but in countries like Australia where the latter is removed, and mercenary intercourse comparatively little obtainable, almost all the women marry, and at a very early age.

Besides these natural duties there are others, which each individual owes to himself and his fellows. Every individual, man or woman, is bound to exercise duly his sexual organs, so that the integrity of his own health shall not be impaired on the one hand : and so that he shall not, on the other, interfere with the health and happiness of his neighbour. Every individual should make it his conscientious aim, that he or she should have a sufficiency of love to satisfy the sexual demands of his nature, and that others around him should have the same. It is impossible, as has been shown before, that each individual should have this in an old country, unless by the use of preventive means. The use of these means therefore comes to be *incumbent* upon all those, who seek to enjoy the natural pleasures of love themselves, without depriving their neighbours of them.

Hitherto love, of whose disinterestedness and unselfishness so much has been said by poets and others, has been, on the contrary, an utterly selfish passion. Men and women have all been eagerly intent on securing it for themselves; and provided they got it, they have thought little of the anguish and misery of those, who were forced to go without it. Nay more, as has been shown already, by the very act of taking it to themselves, they have deprived others of it, and thus been the cause of their misery and disease, often of their death, from sexual sufferings. Thus we see, that the vaunted unselfishness of love has hitherto been, like all other human virtues, a vanity. There never yet was a happy love, crowned with off-spring, however exalted, tender, and self-sacrificing it apparently was, which was not, by its very existence, grinding some other hearts to death. The world has sternly shut its eyes against sexual miseries; and happy lovers and married people have ridiculed old maids and others, of whose sexual sufferings they are themselves the cause. Love has been held to be a subject, on which every one must look out for himself, and allow his neighbours to find the road to ruin as best they can. Seldom has a thought been wasted by the more fortunate, on the despair of those whom they have deprived of some beloved object, or on the sorrows and loneli-ness of a blighted sexual life. It is only within a few years, that the hearts of the rich have been awakening to the miseries of the poor; but to the *sorrows of sexual sufferers* mankind are not yet awakened.

But a true sexual conscience does not admit of such fearful disregard of the interests of our fellow-beings, in love, any more than in other pro-vinces of morality. In love, it is our duty to consider our neighbours' happiness as well as our own, and to see that they are not deprived of sexual pleasures by our selfishness. It is in this way that unselfishness and true morality are to be shewn; by taking to ourselves only a fair share of love, and by endeavouring to promote the sexual happiness of all around us, as well as of ourselves.

Another great sexual duty is to be true and sincere in all our dealings with the opposite sex, and to do nothing if possible in a *clandestine* way. We should endeavour to act in an open and dignified manner towards those, with whom we have any sexual relations; and never to deceive them. It is the degradation of character by intrigues, trickery, and deception, which makes the English mind revolt from the French and Continental habits of sexual life. Neither man nor woman should ever pretend to be constant, when they are not so, nor feign a passion which they do not feel. Deceit or pretence in love, as in other actions of life, degrades all who indulge in it, and spoils the honour, sincerity, and trust-worthiness of the whole character. No man or woman should ever be contented to indulge in love in an underhand manner. If the sexual code forbid freedom and openness in unmarried love, as is at present the case over the whole world, we may find an excuse for those who are thus forced into sexual deceit, at present so universally prevalent in every nation of the earth; but their conduct is none the less undignified and degraded. *Sexual deceit* arises mainly from two things; first, the un-natural restrictions of the moral code, and secondly, the dependence of woman; and it is only by removing its causes, that we can hope to get rid of this inveterate evil. The great safeguard for the purity of love is, that it should be open and free from deceit; and whenever we see that it is not so, we may be certain that great miseries must result. We should make it our aim, that the loves of each individual should be of a sincere, an open, a dignified, and a disinterested kind.

It is *absolutely impossible* to have a free, sincere, and dignified sexual morality in our society, as long as marriage continues to be the only honourable provision for the union of the sexes, and as long as the marriage bond is so indissoluble as at present. We might be certain of this, even on the first view of the matter, from observing how very frequently the common moral code, which has the institution of marriage for its symbol, is disobeyed. It may be said as a general rule, that it is only by women, and but by a limited number of that sex, that it is at all strictly observed; and the great mass of mankind break it every day. The very fact of the code being so often disregarded, shows that there is something fundamentally unnatural in it. The greatest disgrace is theoretically attached to the breaking of these moral regulations, and yet they are broken and set at naught daily. The reason of this is, that *the sexual code is not based upon the laws of Nature*, and that it is totally incompatible with human welfare, that it should be obeyed. There is no natural law, moral or physical, which commands either man or woman to limit their sexual affections to one object throughout life, and the attempt to assert such a law must be an utter failure; even although people should be burned alive for breaking it, as was the custom among the Jews. On the contrary, Nature expressly enjoins upon the young, by her own unerring impulses, that change and variety in love to a certain extent, is the most natural, and therefore the best, sexual conduct in them. There is a great difference in this respect in different characters. Some are born, or are moulded by circumstances, into a character, which is fitted to draw its greatest happiness from constant and unvarying love: others on the contrary are born to be changeable; and to attempt to fix all down by the same rigid sexual bonds, is certain to render many of them miserable; and to frustrate the happiness, which Nature intended that each variety of character should spread around, if its natural developement be not interfered with.

The rigour of the marriage theory does not prevent an immense amount of unmarried intercourse in all countries, for that is impossible; but it renders it clandestine, degraded, and miserable. It does not prevent adultery, for that is impossible, (on the Continent, and even in the large towns in this country, adultery is very common;) but it renders it in like manner stealthy, degraded, and destructive to the morality of all parties.

It is absolutely necessary therefore, before we can attain to a higher state of sexual morality, that the unnatural rigour of the marriage ideas be altered, and that other modes of sexual intercourse be considered honourable and legitimate. If a man and woman conceive a passion for each other, they should be morally entitled to indulge it, without binding themselves together for life, upon these conditions—that they do not bring into the world too many offspring, and take due care to rear them. All parents should be legally forced to support their children, if they be not willing to do so; a thing which would very rarely happen, if wages were higher, and women independent; and if the disgrace attaching to illegitimate children were removed. It is often this disgrace which leads the father to disown a child, whom otherwise he would have welcomed with delight, and so terrifies the unhappy mother, that she destroys her own offspring.

The true guarantee for the due maintenance of the children is not the empty name of marriage, but *the independence of both parents*, and especially of the mother. Marriage rather leads to the neglect of the children, by tempting the wife to be dependent for support on her husband. If every woman, not incapacitated by ill-health, were independent, and if none had more than the small proportion of children, which the circumstances of an old country admit of, there would be no fear of the children being neglected. We would not see, as at present, the melancholy spectacle of a troop of ragged spectres hanging about a helpless mother; or the father, in a fit of desperation, deserting his offspring and his wife together, from inability to support them. Instead of being regarded as a burden, children would be viewed by both parents as the dearest blessing and solace of their lives; would be claimed as a privilege, instead of abandoned, neglected, or frantically destroyed.

To make an honourable provision for unmarried love, *is the only possible mode of preventing prostitution*. If young people could have a due amount of the sexual pleasures in an honourable and open way, without binding themselves down for life, mercenary and prostituted love would soon become extinct. This is a subject of enormous importance. There is no other possible way of getting quit of the unspeakable evils of prostitution, venereal disease, and all the social demoralisation, which springs from these causes. Prostitution would indeed be greatly checked, if poverty were removed, and if women could easily earn an independence; but even were that the case, there would still, as is seen in America, be a great deal of prostitution, if there were no honourable provision for love, except in marriage. If there were such a provision, prostitution would inevitably cease; for no one would pay for a degraded and counterfeit intercourse, if true and genuine love could be honourably obtained without money, and without an indissoluble tie: and if sexual connections without the risk of impregnation, could be had otherwise than by promiscuous intercourse. Therefore it is only by relaxing the rigour of the marriage bond, and allowing greater sexual freedom, that it is possible to eradicate prostitution, and with it venereal disease.

That love should be bought with money, is a standing shame to all of us, both men and women; and no society where such degrading compacts are prevalent, deserves the name of a sexually moral society. Indeed such a name, when applied to any existing state of human society, is a mockery. Youth, whose interests are especially concerned in this matter, should use every effort to get rid of the abomination and misery of mercenary love. This is not to be done by sexual abstinence, (which is even a greater natural sin than mercenary love); but first by removing poverty, and making woman independent; and then by endeavouring to promote a greater sexual freedom in society, and to obtain that necessary of human welfare, unmarried and unfettered love, in an honourable manner.

It should be made a *point of honour* in the youth of both sexes, as soon as women have been rendered capable of gaining their own livelihood by honest work, and the burden of poverty has been lightened, *never to buy or 'sell love for money*; but on the contrary, to make every effort to show the perfectly justifiable nature of their temporary sexual connections, provided the great sexual duties, already spoken of, be fulfilled; and thus be able to indulge in them in an open and dignified manner.

It is in this way, and in this alone, that it is possible to escape from the awful miseries of prostitution; miseries whose chief cause (of course excepting the law of population, the primary cause of all the great sexual evils, which, it must always be remembered, are only the *secondary modes* in which its destructive agency is carried out, and therefore, though seemingly accidental and avoidable, are *essentially necessary* in some form or other, unless they are obviated by preventive intercourse) is the austerity of our sexual code, and the absolute inapplicability of an indissoluble institution like marriage to the nature of man. In this way moreover, and in this only, would it be possible to extirpate venereal diseases; an object whose importance in increasing the virtue and happiness of our race cannot be over-estimated. It is the existence of mercenary love, with its callousness towards a society which scorns it, that keeps alive these accursed diseases; and if mercenary love were removed from among us, it might be certainly anticipated, that the venereal diseases would not long remain behind. This great end should be promoted by every effort, social and individual. Syphilis and gonorrhœa should be uprooted wherever they are found, not by harshness, but by kind and prompt attention to every case which occurs; and everything should be done to effect their radical extinction.

Such hopes may appear to us at present almost visionary, surrounded as we are by the all-engrossing miseries of poverty, hard work, mutual destruction, and every kind of social despair; but I feel convinced that if once poverty and prostitution were overcome, and mankind were more united in mutual confidence, such plans as the total and final extirpation of syphilis, would not seem so very difficult of accomplishment. Blessed will be the generation, and honoured by all posterity, which shall effect this great purpose. It is by such means, and not by partial and unjust police measures, that I earnestly hope our race will one day annihilate this dreadful disease. If unfettered love were obtainable in an honourable way and not for money, and if the great sin of communicating a disease to a fellow-being were once openly recognised, there would be few of either sex, who would be guilty of such a deed. It is not unmarried love, but mercenary love, and the communication of disease, which really disgrace an individual; and to confound all these different actions together in one sweeping condemnation, as is done at present, is to lose all moral power over any of them, and to confuse the sense of right and wrong.

I am aware of the difficulties which attend any alteration in our sexual code; difficulties so great, that they have in general deterred even the boldest thinkers from proposing any definite change in it, however deeply they felt, and ably exposed its evils. But these difficulties do not decrease by our avoidance of the subject: on the contrary, they constantly accumulate, as man becomes more civilized; and the miseries caused by the long continuance of this unnatural sexual institution, nearly in its primeval Hebraic austerity, in the midst of modern society, have become countless. On the Continent, they have sought to palliate these evils, by resorting to all modes of intrigue and clandestine intercourse. The rigour of the marriage contract is, as M. Balzac says, very largely tempered by adultery in French society; and the immense evils of this in corrupting and sowing dissension among families, he eloquently exposes. Divorce has, moreover, in Germany, and for ought I know, in other parts of the Continent, been rendered very easily obtainable; incompatibility of temper being considered a valid cause for it. Now, in reality, *facility of divorce does away with marriage;* it thoroughly alters the theory of the institution, and makes it in reality nothing more, than an agreement between two people to live together as man and wife, so long as they love each other. And such is the only true mode of sexual union; it is the one which Nature points out to us, and we may be certain, that any institution which defies the natural laws of love, as marriage does, will be found to be the cause of immense evils; ever accumulating as the world rolls on, and mankind become more free, and more enlightened in the physical and moral laws of their being.

The great difficulty that men have found in proposing any definite change in our sexual code, is, that it is almost impossible *to alter at all, without totally overthrowing,* the theory of marriage. Easily obtainable divorce does virtually overthrow the theory of marriage; and yet there is nothing more indispensable to the sexual welfare of married people, than this. To make unmarried intercourse honourable and legitimate, evidently overthrows the theory of marriage; and yet without this, it is absolutely impossible to escape from the most fearful evils,—from prostitution, masturbation, genital and venereal disease, and innumerable other miseries.

On the Continent, the theory and practice of love are very inconsistent. The nominal theory of sexual union is marriage, as with us; and yet this, by the facility of divorce, is *virtually annulled,* and put on a par with any other kind of temporary sexual intercourse; so that it may be said that *marriage has ceased to exist* in those countries, where divorce is easily obtainable for such causes as incompatibility of temper. If divorce be readily obtainable in marriage, what is the use of marriage at all? Why go through an empty and ostentatious ceremony, if the contract can be dissolved at pleasure any day? why make so much ado, and drag forward love, which shrinks from observation, before the public eye? why not deem a sexual union without this empty formulary equally honourable? On the Continent moreover, prostitution, masturbation, venereal disease, together with all the degradation of intrigue, and stealthy undignified intercourse, exist in abundance. Young people deride the austere rules of morality, and set them at naught; and yet nominally the marriage theory remains the same, however totally at variance with the general practice.

The existence of a rigourous sexual theory such as marriage, necessitates one of two things; either puritanism and sexual austerity with all their

blighting influences, or a regular system of intrigue, deception, and disobedience to the sexual code. The former of these, together with the
most wide-spread prostitution and self-abuse, is the effect of marriage in
England, the latter on the Continent : marriage, of course, acting as *a
subordinate instrument of necessary destruction* under the grinding law of
population.

There are three great reasons, why the institution of marriage has remained so long unchanged among us, notwithstanding its innumerable
evils and injustices, deeply though these have been felt by many moralists.
The first and chief is the pressure of the great population-difficulties. These
difficulties are the *parent source* of all the most important sexual evils ;
and beside them the influence of any human institution sinks into total
insignificance. As long as the principle of population continues to exert
its destructive agency, as it has ever hitherto done, it matters little what
the sexual institutions are ; with or without marriage, or any other form
of sexual union, the misery of mankind is *certain*, while food and love are
antagonistic. If we must perish, it may as well be by the hands of marriage, as any other sexual arrangement. This truth, although it may
not have been definitely perceived, has been dimly felt by most of the
thinkers, who have considered the imperfections of our sexual code.
They saw clearly its errors, but they felt, however dimly, that there was
some far more powerful principle behind, whose destructive action could
not be obviated by changing the marriage code ; and thus, as they saw no
escape from these evils, they were content to leave it uninterfered with.
It is in vain to propose a great reconstruction of our social institutions,
unless it can be clearly shown, that such a course will lead to real advantages ; and no sexual code which was not based upon the law of population, and the sexual necessities of man, could have afforded any rational
hope of remedying the evils, existing under the present one. In this way
then, marriage has remained, not from its own merits, but from the lack
of anything better ; and the grinding miseries of mankind, the want of
food, love, and leisure, have forced them to put up with all its evils, and
have been its main safeguard.

The second great cause of its long continuance is the profound ignorance
of moralists on sexual matters ; and the morbid delicacy which forbids
the discussion of sexual questions. Our moral code bears in every line
the marks of having been framed by those who were ignorant of the fundamental laws of our sexual nature ; who had neither a knowledge of
nor reverence for, the generative organs ; who were perfectly unacquainted
with the principle of population ; and full of that childish mystery and disgust
in sexual matters, which characterises most nations in their infancy, and
is in none so conspicuous as in the Jews, from whom we have inherited
our sexual code. The ignorance of the nature and laws of the genital
organs, which obtains among moralists even to the present day, has deprived them of the materials necessary for forming a more natural
system of morality, even though they felt keenly the evils of the existing
one. Moreover, *till Mr. Malthus wrote, it was not possible to have a true
sexual code*, for no man knew the principle of population, on which alone
it could be based ; and till M. Lallemand and M. Recamier led the way

to the better knowledge of the sexual organs and their laws, a true physiological foundation was wanting. When we add ` to this deeply rooted ignorance the morbid delicacy which has hitherto veiled all such subjects we have another very sufficient reason for the unmodified persistence of marriage.

The third reason is, that the present sexual code has been supported by the authority of supernatural religion. It has been inseparably interwoven with the Christian and Hebraic beliefs, and is in fact one of the grand Jewish institutions, which is considered to share in the perfection and inspiration of the Bible. There is scarcely anything on which so much stress is laid in the Old and New Testament, as the institution of marriage. Fidelity and constancy to the marriage vow are regarded as the very highest virtues ; and all unmarried connections, which are stigmatised as fornications, and carnal lusts, are classed among the deadly sins. Hence the institution of marriage has been made a religious ceremony, and is believed in by great numbers as firmly as Christianity itself, of which it is considered a part. To doubt or to deny it would be to deny the whole. It is this *divine right* of marriage which has rendered most people blind to the evils of the institution, and has raised a storm of indignation against any one, who ventured to point them out. The institution is guarded as jealously as Supernaturalism itself. In the same manner the divine right of kings was long and furiously contended for; but it has now become a name, which even despots themselves are almost afraid to utter. But not for much longer will a divine right avail ought to protect any earthly thing ; nor can any institution which is based upon Supernaturalism, and not upon Nature, long continue among us. Men will not much longer be content to take the laws of their actions from any other source than *Nature*, and all institutions will be tested by this, and this only.

The assertion of the theologians, that "marriage suits the nature of man," is exactly analogous to the famous decree " the sun moves round the earth." Both are taken from supernatural authority, and the one is as false in the living, as the other in the lifeless world. Those among us who are the most strenuous in the support of existing sexual institutions, and most authoritative in laying down the laws of sexual morality, are the very men, who, like the judges of Galileo, are most incompetent to give an opinion on the matter. Have they studied the sexual organs? Are they well acquainted with the law of population? Are they conversant with the passion of love, as it is seen in all its various phases in our society, with the true, the false, the mercenary, the morbid, the unnatural forms of it, and their manifold and complicated causes and history? Have they followed it through all its degradations and obscenities, with an earnest perseverance and reverential sympathy, which nothing can disgust or fatigue? The very reverse of this is the case. The loudest supporters of our present system are in general the most deeply ignorant on sexual matters, and on the nature and laws of the sexual organs ; and are the most filled with that morbid delicacy, which absolutely unfits any one from handling these questions with any profit. They trust blindly to authority for the rules they boldly lay down, perfectly unaware of the awful and

complicated nature of the subject they are dealing with so confidently,
and of the horrible evils their inconsiderate systems are attended with.
They themselves break through the most fundamentally important of all
the moral laws daily, in utter unconsciousness of the misery they are
causing to their fellows.   The clergy among us are noted for the large
size of their families; whereas the Roman Catholic clergy err as much on
the other side, by the great natural sin of celibacy.   Are these the men
who are to expound to us the natural laws of sexual morality?   It is not
from the want of will, for the zeal and devotion of many of their members
in the service of mankind is beyond all praise; but from want of knowledge.   They may wish with their whole hearts to serve their fellows,
but they cannot possibly do so unless they study Nature.   The immovable laws of Nature are not to be softened by tears, nor overcome by the
emotions of the heart, however it may yearn for the sufferings of mankind.

It is by these props that our sexual code has hitherto been principally
supported; but when they shall be removed, marriage will be tested by
its own real merits; and all of us will gradually learn to see its insufficiency, as the sole honourable provision for the union of the sexes.

In what way then are its defects to be remedied, and how should it be
modified, so as to prevent the innumerable sexual and economical evils,
which exist at present; and to secure for every human being at least
the possibility of having a happy and virtuous sexual life?

The only way to do so, is to attend to the various modes, in which *Nature*
points out to us the true path of sexual duty; and to endeavour to prevent all those evils arising from disobedience to her laws, several of which
have been spoken of above.   In order to obey the sexual laws, it is
first necessary to have a knowledge of them.   It is therefore of primary
importance that Anatomy and Physiology should become a leading
branch of general education; that all educated people should have a
knowledge of the nature and laws of their body, and, more especially in
reference to our subject, those of the sexual organs.   This knowledge
should be imparted to both sexes before the period of puberty, so that they
should not fall from ignorance into the lamentable practices of masturbation, or other sexual errors, and should know how to guard against venereal disease.   A knowledge of the great law of population should also be
extensively spread throughout society, so that every individual, man,
or woman, should understand it, and feel the sacred duty of limiting their
reproductive powers.   Unless these great truths become generally known
and acted upon, science and art may progress, but man must remain stationary.   It should be inculcated upon those who are about to enter on the
sexual period of life, that the true path of virtue lies in moderation, and
in a due and healthy exercise of their new powers; abstinence on the one
hand, and excess or lasciviousness on the other, being alike shunned.
Openness and sincerity should above all be enjoined; all mercenary and
underhand dealings discountenanced; and the enormity of the crime of
spreading venereal disease exposed.

With minds prepared in this way, and not filled with that chaos of childish ignorance and morbidity, with which our youths at present enter upon

the most critical period of life, they would be enabled to meet in a genuine and manly way the real sexual difficulties, which surround all of us ; to speak freely of those mighty sexual questions, without the open discussion of which we are impotent as children in the hands of Fate, and all our science and philosophy are an empty babble ; and to show themselves worthy of that greater sexual freedom, which we may hope that our posterity, more fortunate than we, shall enjoy. It would not be desirable, even were it possible, that this increase of freedom should come suddenly. On the contrary, it is by very gradual steps, that mankind may be expected to modify their present sexual ideas, and to attain to a higher moral state.

This will be brought about gradually by the course of things. When the great primary duty of limiting offspring has come to be generally acted upon, and preventive intercourse has been recognised as consistent, and *alone* consistent, with the highest dictates of morality, and as the only mode, by which the population-difficulty can be surmounted ; when in this way poverty shall have been removed, as I firmly believe that it will, and women and men are alike independent, then will indissoluble marriage gradually lose its hold upon mens' minds, and appear an unnecessary bond ; fraught with numerous evils, without compensating advantages. If a woman is to have only two, or at most, and in comparatively rare cases, three children ; can easily gain a livelihood for herself, and therefore requires no protection nor aid, beyond what the laws afford to each of us ; why should she tie herself indissolubly to one man for life ; or on the other hand, why should a man do so ? It is the *large families* and the *dependence of woman*, which appear to make marriage advisable. As woman advances in independence, as more occupations are thrown open to her, and her wages are such as befit a human being, she will become ever less willing to tie herself indissolubly down, and to put herself in the power of one man. Why should either she or man bow their heads to the old accustomed yoke, when even the apparent necessity for it has passed?

All of us must reflect, that even though we adhere rigidly to the institution of marriage, and discountenance any change in its indissolubility, the great duty of limited procreation is *equally incumbent* upon us. Whether we marry or not, this supreme duty is equally to be observed. If married people change their conduct in this way, as they are morally bound to do, they must either adopt preventive means, or they will feel how wretched and enfeebling for mind and body, is the state of sexual abstinence ; and thus be gradually weaned from their implicit faith in our present system. A personal experience of the evils of abstinence will gradually give them a sympathy with the unfortunate sexual sufferers, whom they have so little comprehended ; and a remorse for the part they have played, however unconsciously, in causing their miseries. In this way they will be prepared gradually to accept of changes in their long cherished institutions.

Another circumstance will greatly aid in this change. When once the modes of preventive intercourse become universally known, and their indispensability a matter of general discussion ; without which, as has already been shown, not a single step can be made in human progress, and our race must remain sunk in the population-horrors ; it will be found to be totally impossible to confine woman by the present narrow sexual restrictions. In fact, preventive intercourse, if it be found to be really efficient and satisfactory, will put the two sexes almost on a par in sexual freedom. A woman will be able to indulge her sexual desires, with the same exemption from after consequences as a man ; and it will rest entirely with herself, whether she shall have offspring or not. This cannot fail to make a signal alteration in the habits of woman ; for there is no natural reason except the fear of getting children, which makes her less willing than man to gratify her sexual desires. It is a rare exception, that a man passes through life without indulging in unmarried love, even under the strictness of our present sexual code; and it is certain that were the fear of getting a child removed, woman, who is the natural counterpart of man in her modes of feeling and action, would do the same ; more especially when the harshness of our sexual views becomes gradually relaxed, and the divine right of marriage comes to be questioned.

When the universal applicability of the great law of exercise to all our organs is understood, every one will perceive, that he is *morally bound* to exercise duly his sexual organs throughout the period of sexual life. Thus the young man on entering upon puberty, will feel that Nature commands him to indulge to a moderate extent his sexual desires ; and when once he is fully convinced of the natural rectitude of this, he cannot fail to perceive the insufficiency and unnatural character of our moral code. He will therefore assert, and gradually obtain, a greater liberty of indulging honourably in unmarried love, which is at that age most of all indispensable. When once the commands of Nature are felt as they should be, and the dictates of physical are equally attended to with those of spiritual religion, *conscience will give youth no peace* till they be obeyed, and all obstacles to an honourable and disinterested outlet for the sexual desires surmounted. The sacred duty of the normal exercise of her generative organs is equally incumbent upon *woman;* and, when once adequately felt, will impel her to assert in like manner her title to a greater sexual freedom in spite of all opposition. The cause of sexual liberty, advocated not merely as a right but as a *duty,* will thus become the most sacred in the eyes of the youth of both sexes. By advancing it, they will gradually get rid of those sexual miseries, which now oppress them like a nightmare. Sexual impotence, morbid bashfulness, hysteria, and the gloomy train of menstrual diseases ; spermatorrhœa and masturbation, prostitution and venereal disease, will all gradually be extirpated, if youth be only true to itself, and assert resolutely and perseveringly its natural laws and duties ; and if all mankind fulfil conscientiously the great duty of limited procreation.

Let those who will, marry ; but those who do not wish to enter upon so indissoluble a contract, either on account of their early age, or from a disapproval of the whole ceremony, should deem it perfectly honourable and justifiable to form a temporary connection. If they refrain from undue procreation, rear their children carefully, and act in an open, sincere, and loving manner to their partner, they are fulfilling the *real* sexual duties; and although the world may for a time frown upon them, they will have the approval of their own consciences, the best and noblest of rewards, and will be laying the foundation of a truer sexual morality, than the world has yet known. It is singular, that among a large part of the poorest and most abject members of society, the empty formulary of marriage is very frequently dispensed with. Mr. Mayhew says, that not more than one in twenty of the street folk in London, who live as man and wife, are married; as they deem it a needless and expensive ceremony. Among the working classes too, such partnerships are very common, and are on the increase, even in this country, and still more on the Continent. It is common for the rich to keep mistresses, with whom they often live almost as man and wife; and it is chiefly among ladies of the educated classes, that such connections are rarely, if ever, met with. But when educated women come to understand the real nature of the sexual laws, and the sacredness of the duty of healthy exercise, they will feel that if they have not the opportunity of marriage, or are averse to enter upon that indissoluble state, these temporary and unfettered connections are the only resource for them. To remain an old maid is a thing, which no woman, who attends to the voice of natural morality, can consent to. She must feel that by so doing she is not fulfilling the laws of her being.

I do not speak of divorce, for it is a *far more radical change than divorce*, however easily to be procured, that is requisite, before love can be rendered sufficiently attainable by all human beings, to prevent the miseries of prostitution, masturbation, and sexual debility. If love be made too difficult of attainment, especially for youth, which has so little experience, and knows so little how to guide itself amid the sexual shoals, masturbation and prostitution are *sure* to be practised. On the other hand it should not be made too easy of attainment, nor should a moderate and invigorating indulgence be allowed to degenerate into *licentiousness*, which is one of the most demoralising of all influences.

No trust is to be put in the common modes of guarding against licentiousness, viz. the rigourous puritanism, which throws as many difficulties as possible in the path of love, and the austere and unnatural sexual code, which forbids any indulgences except within the most irksome bonds. To enforce sexual abstinence except in marriage, is about the worst possible way to guard against licentiousness. By this austerity the intensity of the sexual desires is greatly and morbidly increased, and exerts an undue sway over the whole mind. The young people in our society think far too much of love, and in great measure because they are so harshly debarred from it. At the same time the existence of *prostitution* gives ample scope to the most unbridled licentiousness; over which the moralist, by his inconsiderate austerity, has lost all controul. Prostitution or *mercenary* love in any shape, is the true and certain sign of licentiousness, and is infinitely

more demoralising to a society, than almost any conceivable amount of
sexual freedom could be. The true mode of checking licentiousness is to
point out its great evils to youth ; to impress upon them, that the conduct which is alone really virtuous, and which moreover can alone lead
to real happiness, is to indulge only to a moderate degree in venereal
pleasures, and never permit themselves to become plunged in sensual
excesses, which ruin the health of body and mind ; to exercise rather a
manly self-denial, and to think of the sexual happiness of others, as well
as of themselves. The evils which arise from excess, and which are
rather to be seen on the Continent than in this country, proceed chiefly
from the want of a true standard of sexual morality. Young people deride
the existing code, but they have no other guide to sexual virtue ; and
thus they plunge into all sorts of excesses, and become heartless and
effeminate.

The true antagonist to licentiousness is the knowledge of the greatly
superior happiness and virtue, which lies in moderation ; and also an
active engagement in other pursuits. No man or woman need hope for
happiness, who seeks it in love and sexual gratification alone ; no one
who does not live a life of useful industry, need look for a contented
mind. It is not unnatural austere rules, but a due amount of healthy
employment in other matters, which can give either sex a well balanced
mind, and guard them from licentiousness. Do you wish to keep your
wife or your mistress constant ? Give up bolts and bars, and conventional
restrictions, and give her instead an interesting occupation. If the sphere
of woman's activity be enlarged, and every woman be educated to gain
for herself an independence, there will to an absolute certainty be much
less licentiousness in our society than there now is, however much the
sexual freedom be increased. Idleness, mercenary love, and a narrow
culture are the chief causes of licentiousness ; and the true way to guard
against the latter is to remove them. Youth should be taught to take an
equal pride and delight in the developement of *all* its faculties ; and
especially of those physical powers, which have been so miserably neglected.
Athletic exercises and manly sports are the safeguards against effeminacy and sexual debaucheries ; and if these be duly attended to, both man
and woman will gradually acquire a sense of what is truly noble and
lovable in character ; and will be unwilling to let their manhood degenerate into a sickly licentiousness.

It is a very false, as well as degrading opinion to entertain of man,
that he is naturally prone to licentiousness or other vices. Nature has
taken far better means to promote our virtue than any imperfect codes,
by making our *happiness* necessarily dependent on it ; and therefore
fore the timid moralist need not be under any apprehensions for the progress of virtue, *if the true obstacles to it can be removed*. The general
estimates of human character are taken from man, in a state of bewildered misery from the necessary destruction caused by the unseen law
of population, and a total confusion of ideas on sexual morality ; and
consequently are full of fallacies. It is this law, operating beneath
the surface, that has made *chastity*, or sexual abstinence, be regarded as
a virtue ; for men, even when ignorant of the law, still dimly felt, that

the reproductive powers could not be fully exercised, without destructive consequences, and hence they considered sexual abstinence a virtue.   The error lay in not perceiving, that no exigencies of human society could alter the laws of the generative organs, or make sexual abstinence, however indispensable it might be, other than a *natural sin.*

As a further safeguard against licentiousness, it is very desirable that a more intimate *friendship* between the sexes should be promoted; and youth should feel that love, if not conjoined with mutual esteem, loses half its charms.   The sexes should mingle more freely, and share in each others pursuits, so that there may be as many bonds of sympathy between them as possible; and that the sexual passion may not be, as at present it so often is, almost the only common feeling which draws them together.

The great aim of the moralist should be, not so much the intensification, as the *universal distribution of the pleasures of love* among the whole race.   Hitherto this has been very little thought of; and yet it is as important as the *more equal distribution of the food* and other advantages, which is now the chief aim of the political economist.   It is not of so much importance that some few individuals, poets or fortunate lovers, should have their transports still more exalted and refined; but that the great mass of mankind, that every man and woman of us, should be able to obtain a sufficient share of the pleasures of love, and to enjoy them in their own way.   Love, like power, wealth, and other blessings, has hitherto been chiefly cherished for the rich, the refined, and the intellectual; while the loves of the mass of mankind, the poor, the ignorant, and the uncultivated, have had little attention.   It has been too much the practise for the highly refined—the spiritual aristocracy, to look down with contempt on the loves of others, and stigmatise them as gross and sensual; but no one should ever permit himself to think in a degrading or unsympathising way, of the joys of any of his fellows.   It is true, all are not equally refined or lofty minded; just as all are not born equally rich or beautiful; but each of us has his own emotions, and his own sources of pleasure, which should be sacred in the eyes of others.   Let us seek by our sympathy, and self-denial, to procure the means of sexual happiness for even the humblest of our fellow-beings; and rather to elevate by kind advice than to crush by disdain.   Let us not rest contented, while a single individual in society is excluded by avoidable circumstances from the pleasures of love.

Before leaving the subject of marriage, I shall give a quotation from the work "On the Sphere of Government" by Baron Wilhelm von Humboldt (elder brother of the great traveller), which has recently been translated into English, and reviewed in an admirable periodical; and which conveys to us an idea of the mode in which many earnest thinkers, especially on the continent, are beginning to approach the important subject of the union of the sexes.   He says "the effects which marriage produces are as various as the characters of the persons concerned, and, as a union so closely allied with the very nature of the respective individuals, it must be attended with the most hurtful consequences, when the State attempts to regulate it by law, or, through the force of its institutions, to make it repose on anything save *simple inclination*. The radical error of such a policy seems to be, that the law commands, whereas such a relation cannot mould itself according to external circumstances, but depends wholly on inclination; and whenever coercion or guidance come into collision with inclination, they divert it still more from the proper path. Wherefore, it appears to me that the State should not only loosen the bonds in this instance, and leave ampler freedom to the citizen, but that *it should entirely withdraw its active solicitude from the institution of marriage*, and both generally and in its particular modifications, should rather leave it wholly to the free choice of the individuals, and the various contracts they may enter into with respect to it. I should not be deterred from the adoption of this principle, by the fear that all family relations should be disturbed, or their manifestations in general impeded; for although such an apprehension might be justified, by considerations of peculiar circumstances and localities, it could not fairly be entertained in an inquiry into the nature of men and States in general. For experience frequently convinces us, that just where law has imposed no fetters, morality most surely binds; the idea of external coercion is one entirely foreign to an institution, which, like marriage, reposes only an inclination and the inward sense of duty; and the results of such coercive institutions do not at all correspond to the designs in which they originate."

By curing the sexual evils, we at the same time cure *poverty*. Poverty exists because our sexual habits are erroneous; the want of food springs from the same source as the want of love; *they are inevitable alternative products of all modes of sexual intercourse, except the preventive one;* and the means, which can alone cure the one, can alone cure the other also. To remedy the want of love, and to enable every individual to have a due amount of sexual pleasures and offspring, the only possible means is the general practice of preventive intercourse, and limited procreation: and these are the only possible means, by which Poverty also can be cured. That it can be perfectly cured by these, and by no other conceivable means, I feel the profoundest conviction. It is with the want of love that the *richer* classes have most directly to do, and therefore it is the young and unmarried people among them, that should chiefly concern themselves in remedying this want; but the *poor* are most immediately interested in the want of food. It is to them therefore that the following observations are principally addressed, in the spirit of the deepest sympathy and reverence.

The working classes have their fate in their own hands. There is one method and one only, by which they may escape from the great evils which oppress them—the want of food and leisure; hard work and low wages. This is, by reducing their numbers by preventive intercourse, and so lessening the supply of labour in proportion to the demand. All other means, which have been held out for getting rid of Poverty, are a mere delusion; socialism, emigration, national education, organisation of industry, are all, if not purely visionary and incapable of realisation, at best but slight palliatives, which lead ultimately to the no less formidable evil of want of love. No remedy for poverty has been hitherto proposed, which was not to be purchased by the sacrifice of an equivalent amount of love, which in fact rendered it totally unavailing. While the reproductive powers are managed by mankind as they are at present, and checked only by abstinence, prostitution, or death, it is a mere dream to talk of remedying poverty. Therefore the attention of the working classes should be steadily concentrated upon *the only real remedy* for their evils; and they should refuse even to listen again to any schemes which are not based upon the laws of population. All others are but will-o'-the-wisps, over which time and effort are utterly wasted, and which can lead only to a deeper slough of despond. They should use every endeavour to test the efficiency of preventive sexual intercourse; and disseminate as widely as possible, the knowledge of this means, and of the indispensable duty of limited procreation. *They should help themselves, nor wait for the tardy help of others.* If this great duty were to become widely known and generally fulfilled, in a very short time the burden of poverty would begin to be lightened, and eventually it would be wholly removed.

It would be desirable, that there should be as few children born as possible, until poverty be removed. Were no unnecessary offspring produced, none that were not indispensable to the physical health of the mother, in six years the evils of poverty would, I believe, be strikingly diminished; and in twelve years the working classes might dictate their own terms, and have wages and other advantages, to which at present they do not aspire even in thought. The rate of wages, that important political barometer as Mr. Malthus called it, is the index by which their efforts should be guided. Their steadfast, indefatigable, and united aim should be, to prevent by the means already mentioned, all unnecessary births, until wages are so high, as to ensure the comfort and independence of every man or woman; to leave a broad margin for the casualties of sickness, or other adverse circumstances, which may oppress any individual; to make it easy to earn a livelihood, even for the weakest woman, or dullest and slowest workman, for these should be cared and provided for as well as the rest. For this purpose the customary wages, even those which are called good wages, are miserably too low; and a much higher standard of comfort should be aspired to. Another persevering aim should be, that there should not be a single *unhealthy occupation;* and that men should not be forced, as at present, by the pressure of want, to engage in employments, which are certain death in a few years. They should also secure to themselves a much greater share of *leisure*, than they now have; *less work with higher wages;* and not be ground down by constant toil, but have a sufficiency of time for enjoyment, and for educating and developing their various faculties of body and mind. No human being should work, I firmly believe, more than six or seven hours a-day, except it be for some temporary purpose; and at many occupations even this length of work is far too much. In fact, the hours of labour should be regulated according to the health and the real interests of man. All these aims and innumerable others can, I feel convinced, be accomplished by the general adoption of preventive intercourse, and by a steady and undeviating attention to the true cause and only cure of Poverty.

The working classes have it in their own power to attain all these advantages; in fact to make almost any terms with the capitalists, if they sufficiently reduce their own numbers. It is by these means, and not by hopeless strikes or bloody revolutions, that any amelioration in their state can be effected; and the knowledge that the richer classes have *their own* bitter difficulties to contend with; that they are suffering from the destructive action of the law of population, just as really, though not so patently, as the poor; that the hearts of many among them are full of anguish for the miseries of the poor, and eager to assist them by any efforts, if they only knew how; and moreover that the poor are themselves as much to blame for the existence of poverty as the rich, seeing that it depends chiefly on their own improvident procreation: all these considerations may serve to assuage the unhappy class animosities, and to draw us all nearer in mutual sympathy. Alas! we have all sinned, consciously or unconsciously, against the most sacred social laws; we have all enough of sorrows and evils to contend with, without warring with each other!

Although preventive intercourse may appear strange to many, as the means by which alone human progress is rendered possible, yet I feel convinced that it is already far more generally practised, than we have any idea of; nay more, that wherever there has been any real and permanent progress in the condition of man made by an old country, it has been by means of preventive intercourse. To take the example of France for instance, we have seen from Mr. Mill's statement, that the progress of that country since the first revolution has been extraordinary; that at no time in French history have its resources increased so immensely and yet that the population is almost stationary, not on account of the increase of deaths, but the diminution of births. In consequence of this, the comforts of the whole French people have been greatly augmented. Now, although I do not know it as a fact, I am perfectly certain that this stationary state of population in France *must be* owing to the general use of preventive sexual intercourse; for any one who is acquainted with the habits of the French must be aware, that sexual abstinence is far less practised among them than in this country. An old maid is as rare a sight in France as common among us: and on the whole it is certain that there is far more sexual intercourse in the former country. Prostitution, also, or promiscuous intercourse to such an extent as to prevent the birth of children, (which, with sexual abstinence and premature death, are the only possible alternatives to preventive intercourse) is, I believe, not nearly so common in France as in this country. Now it is not possible to reconcile this with the very small proportion of births, otherwise than by inferring it to be the effect of preventive intercourse; for the fecundity of woman is nearly the same in all countries. Preventive intercourse must therefore be very general in France, and probably in the other continental countries; in none of which, not excepting even Norway and Switzerland, is sexual abstinence nearly so prevalent, I believe, as in this country. However, although it has produced considerable real improvement, it has not been able to raise adequately the condition of the working classes, nor to remove the sexual evils, because it has not been recognised openly as a great social duty, but has merely been adopted by individuals, and rather as a means of retaining than increasing their comforts; it is only when the law of population is well understood, and preventive intercourse is not used furtively and by single individuals, but is made the means of *a great and open social effort*, that it will enable us not only to avoid the lowest depths of poverty, but to *elevate* our whole society to a condition befitting the dignity of man.

This effort, moreover, should be made by all old countries together, for if any do not share in it, the wretched condition of their poor will drag down the others more or less; unless they be too uncivilized to compete with them for the provisions. The continued, although diminished, misery of the French poor, notwithstanding their adoption of the only means of relief, depends partly, I believe, on the abject poverty in 'this country and in Ireland; for our wealthy capitalists and hungry population become competitors for the products of French agriculture. In this way it is seen how inseparably the economical interests of all countries are bound up together. Each nation is in itself a society, but all form part of the great society of mankind; and no nation can expect long to flourish without the rest.

One blessed effect, which would result from the introduction of truer views of sexual morality among us, would be, to draw us nearer in sympathy with the French and the other Continental nations; whom we would then see to be suffering, just like ourselves, from the great sexual difficulties, and from whom nothing has more estranged us than the difference of views on sexual matters. We will learn to feel, that all of us have been in the wrong, and that along with much that is good, there is, and in the existing state of our sexual knowledge could only be, more that is evil, in the various codes of morality, which are at present prevalent in the different countries of the world; and the recognition of our own errors and sufferings will make us more lenient than we have been, to the errors and sufferings of others.

It is a mistake, moreover, to suppose that it is only in the *old* world, that the law of population is causing misery, or preventive intercourse needed. I believe that the extreme hard work, for which the Americans are as remakable as the English, and which is assuredly incompatible with the best interests, either moral or physical of man, essentially depends, not, as is generally thought, on a love of money or spirit of rivalry, (although doubtless these operate too as secondary motives), but on the immense difficulty of increasing the food, even in America, in a geometrical ratio, so as to keep up with a population doubling itself every twenty-five years. If the working classes in America wish to have still higher wages, with less work, they too can only do so by preventive intercourse. It is not a feverish increase of wealth and cultivation, nor a boasted superiority over the old world, whose circumstances are so infinitely worse, that is desirable in America; it is that every one should have *leisure* as well as food and love; should have time for enjoyment and the cultivation of their various faculties; and should have only so much healthy work, as will ensure the comparatively slow progress of population

and food, which, even in America, is compatible with the satisfactory con
dition of mankind.

In an old country, food and population cannot increase with rapidity,
except by an extraordinary succession of industrial or agricultural improvements, coupled with the most indefatigable labour.   In Great Britain
during the last half-century, we have the most remarkable of all instances
of this.   The population of this country, as we learn from the census of
1851, has doubled itself in the last 53 years.   The chief cause of this has
been the unexampled progress of the physical sciences and arts during that
time;   the introduction of steam, railways, machinery, &c., which have
made this country the great workshop of the world, and have enabled her
to command a large share of the food of other countries ; and the application of chemistry and other sciences to agriculture, which has so much
increased our own produce.   Another essential cause, acting and re-
acting on the increase of wealth, has been, as the Census says, the increase of marriages and births, which, by constantly pressing the
population hard against the means of subsistence, has produced that
indefatigable and exhausting labour, for which the English are distinguished above all other old nations except the Chinese, and also the
heart-rending poverty which we witness among us.   A large number of
births in any old country *must* produce one of two things ; either a very
short average of life, as we see among the Chinese, Hindoos, and uncivilized
nations in general : or the most terrible and universal hard-work, along
with wide-spread poverty, as we see among ourselves.   In this country
the rapid multiplication, falling on a people of higher civilization and
more skilful energy, has given rise to such efforts and such sacrifices
to increase the food and stave off destruction, as are wholly without
parallel in history.   And yet, notwithstanding these efforts, which have
reduced the great majority of us to working machines, the mighty tide
of population so easily keeps up with any increase of food they can effect,
that the most awful poverty, bordering on chronic famine, prevails on the
one hand, and an amount of celibacy and sexual abstinence, probably
as unparalleled as our industrial efforts, on the other.

In every line of the Census, the action of the terrible Malthusian Law
is distinctly visible ; this law alone can explain the continuance of unabated
poverty and misery among us, notwithstanding all our toil and progress
in wealth ; it alone explains how our population so easily keeps pace
with, and passes beyond the immense increase of food, although the age of
marriage is so late, and celibacy and prostitution so prevalent ; it alone
explains the miserably short average of life, notwithstanding all our sanitary efforts ; it alone explains the vast tide of emigration, which we have
sent forth : every one of us, who is suffering from the want of food, love,
or leisure, (and how few in our society are not or have not been !) is a
living proof of its action ; without it, in short, human society, and the
Census, are a totally unintelligible riddle ; and yet the author of the
Census Report (namely, the Registrar-General aided by his coadjutors,)
openly denies the law, and attempts by the most surface fallacies, which
had already been clearly pointed out by Mr. Malthus, to refute it. I

would not alude to these fallacies, were it not for the incomparable importance of the subject, and the character of the Census Report, which by its
wide circulation, and valuable statistical facts, is so dangerous an organ
for spreading error.

Its author asserts that the unparalleled increase of production in this
country, has been mainly owing to the improvements in the marriage
laws, and to the great increase of births: although he grants that the
industrial inventions and agricultural discoveries have had a good deal to do
with it. He says that the law of population, though it may apply to savages
and the inferior animals, cannot apply to civilized man ; for the latter
has such superior powers of increasing the produce. Thus he concludes,
that the large proportion of births and rapid increase of population, have
been *the chief cause* of the great progress of this country, and as such are
a signal advantage; in short, that the great procreation of married people,
with their increased care of their children, has mainly produced our
national wealth, and that to them therefore our *thanks* are owing. In
support of this assertion, he appeals to a work published in 1767, by Sir
James Steuart. On this point I shall give a quotation from Mr. Malthus,
which I omitted in the review of his work; not having at that time read
the Census Report, and having therefore thought that the fallacy it
brings forward was obsolete.

Mr. Malthus says, " I should be the last to deny that an increase of
population, when it follows in its natural order, is both a great positive
good in itself, and absolutely necessary to a further increase in the annual produce of the land and the labour. The only question is, which is
the natural order of its progress ? On this point Sir James Steuart, who
has in general explained this subject so well, appears to me to have fallen
into an error. He determines that multiplication is the efficient cause
of agriculture, and not agriculture of multiplication. But though it may
be allowed that the increase of people beyond what could easily subsist on
the natural fruits of the earth, first prompted man to till the ground ;
and that the view of maintaining a family, still operates as the principal
stimulus to cultivation ; yet it is clear that these products in their
actual state, must be beyond the lowest wants of the existing population,
before any permanent increase can possibly be supported. We know that
a multiplication of births has in numberless instances taken place, which
has produced no effect on agriculture, and has merely been followed by an
increase of diseases ; but perhaps there is no instance where a permanent
increase of agriculture has not effected a permanent increase of population, somewhere or other. Consequently agriculture may more properly
be termed the efficient cause of population, than population of agriculture ;
though they certainly react upon each other, and are mutually necessary
to each other's support. This indeed seems to be the hinge on which the
subject turns, and all the prejudices respecting population have perhaps
arisen from a mistake about the *order of precedence.* From a want of
attention to this most important distinction, statesmen, in pursuit of the
desirable object of population, have been led to encourage early marriages,
to reward the fathers of families, and to disgrace celibacy ; but this is to

dress and water a piece of land without sowing it, and yet to expect a crop."

Mr. Malthus here acknowledges, what in fact does not need to be pointed out, that an increase of births tends most powerfully to increase national wealth and population, by pushing the people to the last extremities to gain subsistence, and therefore making them work like slaves; exactly as we know that the more powerful the stream which flows against a slowly yielding barrier, the more quickly will the barrier recede; but this is at the expense of greater pressure upon all the particles of the water itself. In this manner, a country which is bent upon attaining a hollow superiority over others in aggregate wealth and population, and is reckless of human life, toil, and suffering, cannot probably take a better course than by encouraging rapid multiplication; at least if its inhabitants be at all civilized, energetic, and patient of toil, for otherwise the increase of births would only cause increase of deaths. The folly and inhumanity of the effort would be less, if the barrier against which the hearts of the working classes were broken, were ultimately surmountable; but it is totally insurmountable, nay, as Mr. Mill has shown, its resistance even *increases*, in the progress of cultivation. We are, forsooth, according to the Census-Reporter, to pride ourselves on our feverish industrial achievements, our national wealth, our population of 28 millions of *half-lives*, (by no means equal to 14 millions of whole ones,) nay more, on the *sexual morality* of our married people, from the throne downwards; we are gratefully to regard their virtuous and overwhelming procreation, as the main source of our pre-eminence among the nations, and forget the poverty, the squalor, the toil, the bloody sweat, the crushed average of life, the celibacy, the masturbation, the prostitution, the venereal diseases, it has also occasioned. We are to thank, as the authors of our national greatness, the very people whose reckless procreation has been the parent cause of our miseries. Alas! we may *forgive* them, but thank them we cannot. The routine and short-sighted boasts of the industrial glory of England, cemented as it has been by the blood of millions; of its splendid institutions, and above all its superior *sexual virtue*, are most painful to any one, who feels for his fellow creatures, and recognises the law of population. To boast of our sexual institutions, and the rapid procreation of our married people, is, in reality, *the most thoughtless insult* which could possibly be paid to the miseries of this country. It is not an emulative increase of wealth and population, without happiness, and at the expense of the most wide-spread suffering, that is desirable in any country; but that both population and food should increase only so fast, as to allow of the satisfactory state of all mankind, and a natural term of life for each generation. This is the only true aim for any country: the other is a foolish chase, which leads only to misery.

The other arguments by which the author of the Report opposes the Malthusian Law, are such as disclose a great ignorance of political economy, and of the law itself. He says, "the products of industry increase in proportion to the number of civilized men." If this means that a larger body of men require, and can produce, more food than a smaller, it is a truism; if it means that the produce in this or any other old country can keep up with unchecked population, or that men can marry as early, and support a large family as easily in this country as in America or Australia, we all know practically that it is false, and Mr. Malthus and Mr. Mill have demonstrated the reason of this. Again he says, "future generations of Britons, if they have genius, science, skill, industry—and if they are more numerous—will necessarily produce more than the country now yields." Who ever denied this? And again, "the share of the produce of every kind, that falls to a family in the most populous state of America, is incomparably greater than the share of the Indian hunter's family, when there was not one person to every square mile of territory." Mr. Malthus not only never denied these oracular truisms, but himself specified them. He did not however make a statement like this, "the character of every race of men is the real limit to its numbers in the world, if allowance be made for its accidents of position and time." It was never doubted by anybody that national character is one limit to production and therefore to population; but the main limit, which no energy of character can remove, was shown by Mr. Malthus to be the laws of Nature.

Can either the Registrar-General, or any other man in his senses, believe that the population of this country can *continue* to increase at the insane rate of the last 50 years? which rate after all is not half as fast, as that of the United States, nor probably much more than a quarter as fast as the possible rate. Can he believe that in another fifty years we may have 50 millions of inhabitants; in a century, 100 millions; in two centuries, 400 millions: in four centuries, 6,400 millions? This is the question which should be put to those who deny the law of population; and all who see the absurdity of supposing that population and food can for any length of time be increased in such a ratio, thereby *acknowledge the truth of the law;* which indeed, no more admits of dispute, except on the fallacious hypothesis of a change in the physical constitution of man, than a problem of Euclid. The proofs of the law are so self-evident, that it is probable that the great majority of those who deny or ignore it, have in reality never paid any adequate attention to them, nor are at all conversant with the modern science of political economy; which has, in fact, undergone a complete revolution since the publication of Mr. Malthus's essay,—"the era," says Mr. Mill, "from which better views on this subject must be dated." The old school of political economists, for instance Adam Smith, virtually treated the increase of population as a constant quantity; and, like most of the current writers of our own day, paid little attention to this matter, in their inquiries into the elements of national welfare. Thus, of the three main parts of which industrial progress consists, namely, increase of capital, increase of population, and improvements in production, they omitted attention to the second, which is incomparably the most important of all; and hence their reasonings are fundamentally vitiated. It is evidently of little avail to increase capital or to improve the arts of production, if population be allowed to increase in an equal proportion; for in this case, although there is a greater aggregate produce, yet, as there are more people to share it, no one is better off than before. Capital or produce might be increasing with immense rapidity, and yet the condition of mankind getting worse, if population were allowed to advance still more rapidly, as it could so easily do, if not checked. On the contrary, even though capital were not increasing at all: in other words, although a country had reached what political economists call *the stationary state;* yet if due care were taken proportionally to repress population, the condition of every one might be improving. It is not the *absolute* amount of wealth which a nation possesses, but the *relative* amount in proportion to the number of its inhabitants, and the satisfactory distribution of that wealth, which constitutes it a truly prosperous nation. A rapid increase of capital, to which the old political economists attached such importance, is no proof of national prosperity.

In the ordinary course of industrial progress, namely where as we see among ourselves, the working classes remain pretty much as they were, Mr. Mill shows, that, of the three great classes into which our society may be divided—landlords, labourers, and capitalists—the landlords are *the only sharers* who are really benefited, while the capitalists are losers ; for population, by increasing, raises the demand for, and therefore the price of, food, more quickly than the improvements in production can lower it. Thus the landlords gain, and the profits of the capitalists, unless the labourers submit to a reduction of their standard of comfort, must fall. Hence the aim of the most eminent political economists of our day, is no longer the delusive one of an increase of capital and improvements in production merely, which tends only to benefit the landlord, to injure the capitalist, and to leave the labourer where he was, but that there should be a *better distribution* of the produce, which is only obtainable by checking the increase of population, so that there may be fewer people to share the increasing produce. Their aim thus is twofold; to *increase produce* on the one hand, and to *repress population* on the other ; and the latter aim is beyond all comparison the more important of the two, for it is so little generally understood, and is also so much more influential in human destiny. " It is only in the backward countries of the world," says Mr. Mill, " that increase of production is an important object; in those more advanced, what is economically needed, is a better distribution, of which one indispensable means is a stricter restraint on population." " Only when, in addition to just institutions," he says again, " *the increase of mankind shall be under the deliberate guidance of a judicious foresight,* can the conquests made from the powers of Nature by the intellect and energy of scientific discoverers, become the common property of the species, and the means of improving and elevating the universal lot."

The discovery of the principle of population has thus made a thorough revolution in the doctrines and aims of Political Economy: and it must before long make a similar revolution in Medical and Moral Science, whose efforts at present are exactly as delusive as were those of the economists before Mr. Malthus wrote, namely, to increase the virtue and health of mankind, without attending to the increase of the species. Political Economy is as yet the only science concerning man and society, which rests upon a sound basis, and whose aim is a true one ; the others are radically delusive, and attempt impossibilities.

How little the Census-Reporter has studied the science whose fundamental principles he so recklessly denies, is shown by the following comparison between the increase of capital and that of population. "Capital," ne says, "increases, it is always assumed, when terms of years are considered, in a geometrical progression, and, at compound interest, the increase is much more rapid than the increase of population in any European state. The interest of money, indicating the annual increase of value, is the produce of property, and bears a rather close analogy to the increase of the means of subsistence. At three per cent per annum, compound interest, the value of capital is doubled in twenty-four years ; and a population increasing at three per cent, which is near the natural rate, doubles in the same time ; while actually the British population has increased at the rate of 1.3 per cent. annually for the fifty years, 1801-51, and has doubled in fifty-three years. Thus—if we take this indication—the means of subsistence have increased faster than the numbers of the people ; for, while the population has doubled, the value of capital under investment, at three per cent. compound interest, has quadrupled." These statements are full of the greatest errors. In the first place, it is *not* assumed by political economists that capital increases in a geometrical progression : on the contrary, Mr. Mill shows in the most masterly manner, in the first chapters of his fourth book, that the Law which governs Profits is that they are constantly *tending to fall*, and to reach a minimum, in the progress of industry. The reason of this, as has just been stated, is, that when population increases, (if the labourer does not people down to a lower standard of comfort, and, as the standard is already so low, this could have but little effect,) more food is required, and this, according to the fundamental law of agricultural industry, is procurable only at a greater proportional cost : and therefore profits must fall. The tendency of profits to fall in the course of industrial progress was always noticed by political economists, for instance Adam Smith ; but it is only lately that the true *reason* of this has been seen, namely, the want of fertile land, which makes food be produced at a greater proportional cost. Thus then, the *Law of Profits*, depending on the *Law of Wages*, and the *Law of Agricultural Industry*, is that they tend to fall, in the progress of civilization. But when profits fall, the *increase of capital* is much interfered with, because people have less inducement to save from their annual income in the hope of growing richer ; and, were this fall of profits not counteracted by several circumstances, it would soon reach what Mr. Mill calls the *minimum of profit*, namely, the smallest profit which would tempt people to save from their incomes, and employ their savings productively, in order to grow richer ; and when this minimum (which varies in each country, according to the saving habits of the inhabitants and the security of industrial enterprizes) was reached, no further increase of capital could for the time take place. Therefore, instead of increasing naturally in a geometrical progression, *capital always tends to increase more and more slowly*, and would ultimately reach the point where it would not increase at all, (called by political economists the *stationary state*), were the fall of profits not retarded by several circumstances. "When a country," says Mr. Mill, "has

long possessed a large production, and a large net income to make savings
from, and when, therefore, the means have long existed of making a great
annual addition to capital ; (the country not having, like America, a
large reserve of fertile land still unused) ; it is one of the characteristics
of such a country, that the rate of profits is always close to the minimum,
and therefore the country on the verge of the stationary state." The
chief causes which check the fall of profits in such a case, and thus allow
of further increase of capital are, he says, first, the *waste of capital*, by
ov r-trading and rash speculations. These constitute the commercial
cr ises, that so frequently occur among us, and are in a great measure
caused by this tendency of profits to fall : for this makes men engage in
rash speculations, to gain a larger profit. In the stagnation which follows these crises, moreover, much capital is consumed unproductively.
But this is not the principal cause which arrests the fall of profits,
otherwise capital would not increase ; while it does increase, and very
rapidly. The second cause, is *the introduction of agricultural or industrial improvements*, which cheapen corn, or other articles consumed by
the labourers, and thus raise profits ; for the labourer soon loses the advantage of the cheapness and transfers it to the capitalist, by peopling
down to his old standard of comfort again —the only use, which our
labourers ever make of any advantage, being, as Mr. Mill says, "to convert it into food for so many more children." The third cause is increased facilities of getting food or other necessaries *from abroad*, which
comes to the same thing as the preceding. But, as additional food is not
obtainable in the countries from which we get it, except by increase of
agricultural skill, which is of slow growth and diffusion, or by increase
of capital, which, in the corn-exporting countries of Europe, increases
slowly, and in America not more rapidly than their own population
— English capital must be sent abroad to procure it for our increasing
population ; and this, namely, the *overflow* of English capital into other
countries, where profits are still high, is the fourth great cause, which
retards the fall of profits, and therefore permits a further increase of capital. It is one of the chief causes which keep up profits in a country,
whose capital increases faster than its neighbours', and therefore whose
profits are nearest the minimum. "This perpetual overflow of capital
into colonies and foreign countries to seek higher profits, than can be got
at home, I believe," says Mr. Mill, "to have been for many years one of
the chief causes, by which the fall of profits in England has been checked."
Thus then, the chief causes, which check the fall of profits in England,
are these four—waste of capital, improvements in production, facilities
of importation, and overflow of capital into foreign countries. But by
the first of these, a large amount of capital is destroyed, or transferred to
foreigners ; and by the last also, it is sent into other countries, so that it
supports their labourers, not ours, except in so far as their increased production cheapens our food. Therefore the increased capital in this
country is only *in part* shared among our own labourers, and it is a
great error to compare it with our own population. Were the capital
indeed to be employed in this country and among our own people alone, its
increase would very soon be arrested, because profits would fall so low ; or

at least it would slacken so much as no longer to outstrip the comparatively slow march of agricultural improvements in our own country. It is because a great part of the increasing capital is sent *abroad*, that the rate of profits in all old and well-peopled countries, is prevented from falling in a very few years, to the minimum point, at which all increase of capital must for the time cease.

To say that " the interest of money bears a rather close analogy to the increase of the means of subsistence, " is another great error. The rate of interest depends upon many other elements, besides the profits of capital or increase of the means of subsistence; which moreover, as we have just seen, is by no means divided among our own people alone. It depends on the proportion between those who are ready to lend, and those who are ready to borrow money, and thus is greatly influenced by the desire to save, and to use savings productively, in each country. If the rate of interest were a true index of the increase of capital, the latter would increase most rapidly, where the interest is highest ; and thus would be increasing much faster in the Oriental countries, where money brings 20 or 30 per cent, than in England. In many European countries the rate of interest is higher, I believe, than it is in England, and therefore a sum would double much more rapidly at compound interest in them ; but their capital is not increasing nearly so fast.

As for some other misapprehensions of Mr. Malthus's writings, such as that " he attempts to reconcile us to the loss of lives by shipwreck, small-pox, close habitations, or low sites ;" that he made the assertion that " the disappearance of small-pox, cholera, or of other epidemics, must be followed immediately by famine or other diseases ; " and some vain wit on " the absurdity of applying the law of population to civilized man though it may hold of rabbits," they are scarcely worthy of notice. Had the author of the Report been satisfied with arranging the statistical facts of the Census in the admirable manner in which he has done it, he would have discharged a most valuable duty ; but as he has gone out of his way to deny the terrible law, which alone explains our society or the Census itself, nay, has endeavoured to make it a subject of thoughtless ridicule, his work must be regarded as one of the most dangerous to the sexual morality and social welfare of this country. There is nothing which is so *inevitably destructive* to the working classes, to the sexual sufferers—nay to married people themselves, as to deny or ignore the law of population ; and the statesman, who in ignorance or contempt of this law, encourages rapid multiplication, deserves, as Mr. Malthus said, the title of the ' destroyer of his people.' Without its guidance, society is a chaos, and poverty, celibacy, hard work, prostitution, are totally unintelligible, and therefore *irremediable.*

The time will come yet, when the law of population will be viewed in a very different light : when it will be universally accepted as beyond all comparison the most important truth, which was ever revealed to our race ; as the solution, made for us by Mr. Malthus, of the sphynx-riddle or *paradox of Nature*, which mankind have had ever since the birth of history, to solve, or to die ; the truth, which will form the boundary-line between ancient and modern society ; which, so far from being ignored or laughed at, will be jealously guarded and steadily kept in mind by all, as the bulwark of their liberty and happiness, the sacred principle of action on which alone a true social fabric can be based.

While preventive intercourse is the only *direct* means which will avail in the least to remedy poverty, there are many *auxiliary* measures, which should be adopted, to enable the working classes to escape from it as soon as possible. These are most admirably explained by Mr. Mill. The two measures which he lays most stress upon are *emigration* and *national education.* He proposes that an extensive and liberal scheme of emigration should be undertaken by the government, so as to carry off at once a large number of the surplus population; and thus raise in a sudden and striking manner the wages of those left at home. By this means the working classes would become accustomed to a higher standard of comfort, as was the case in France after the Revolution, and would *refuse to people down* to a lower standard again. Even though this should not be done, individual emigration should be promoted as much as possible, so as to aid in reducing the numbers. It is to be remarked, that means of relieving poverty which are of little or no use without preventive intercourse, may be of great service in accelerating its extinction, when its fountain head is at the same time stopped up. Thus Charity, which does almost more harm than good at present, would, if preventive intercourse were once generally adopted, be *a most useful auxiliary* in raising as quickly as possible the condition of the poor; and might be freely given, without the sickening consciousness, that it was perhaps rather injuring than benefiting its unhappy objects, and could do the poor no possible permanent good. A broad scheme of national education would also be of great service, both for the general enlightenment, and as preparing the poor to understand the law of population, and the remedy for the evils that surround them.

Besides these, there is another admirable auxiliary in the cure of poverty and the elevation of the working classes, on which Mr. Mill lays great stress. It is the change from the present system of Employers and Employed to that of *Independent and Associated Industry*. Mr. Mill (from whose great work I cannot refrain from quoting a few more passages, in order to show more fully that the distinguished expounders of the law of population, instead of being, as they have been so often represented, inimical to the interests of the working classes, are in reality *their truest friends*) says, "I cannot think it possible, that the labouring classes will be permanently contented with the condition of labouring for *wages* as their ultimate state. To work at the bidding and for the profit of another, without any interest in the work—the price of their labour being adjusted by hostile competition, one side demanding as much, and the other paying as little, as possible—is not, even when wages are high, a satisfactory state to human beings of educated intelligence, who have ceased to think themselves naturally inferior to those whom they serve." He says moreover, "as the general status of the labouring people, the condition of a workman for hire is almost peculiar to Great Britain.' In other parts of Europe the number of day-labourers is very small. The chief part of the agri-cultural population in Norway, Switzerland, France, &c., are *peasant proprietors*, (namely, the possessors of small independent properties of from five to twenty acres or thereabouts, which they till themselves); of which class Mr. Mill says, (in the course of an analysis of the com-parative merits of the various systems of agricultural industry preva-lent in different countries,) "It is not to the intelligence alone, that the situation of a peasant proprietor is full of improving influences. It is no less propitious to the moral virtues of prudence, temperance, and self-control;" and again, "The French peasant is no simple countryman, perhaps he is, if anything, only too calculating. That is the stage which he has reached in the progressive developement, which the constitution of things has imposed on human intelligence and human emancipation. But some excess in this direction is a small and a passing evil, compared with recklessness and improvidence in the labouring classes, and a cheap price to pay for the inestimable worth of the virtue of self-dependence, as the general characteristic of a people; a virtue, which is one of the first conditions of excellence in a human character—the stock, on which if the other virtues are not grafted, they have seldom any firm root: a quality indispensable in the case of a labouring class, even to any tolerable degree of physical comfort; and by which the peasantry of France and of most European countries are distinguished beyond any other labouring population."

In summing up the comparative merits of the various systems of agricultural industry, Mr. Mill comes to the conclusion that the system of peasant proprietors is quite as favourable as any other to the most effective use of the powers of the soil; and that no system at present in use, has so good an effect on the morals of the peasantry, by promoting the virtues of frugality, independence, and, what is most of all indis-pensable to their happiness—prudence in begetting children.

Mr. Mill, although he states so clearly the many advantages of the system of peasant proprietors over our own system of day-labourers, under which the recklessness and improvidence of the rural population are notorious, does not however advocate the adoption, at least to a large extent, of such a system in any part of the British empire, ex-cept Ireland; for which country he recommends it in the strongest terms, as by far the most powerful means of raising the population from the abject state of misery, in which they are sunk, and training them to those virtues in which they are most deficient, namely, the spirit of independence, and prudence in begetting children; the want of which, fostered by the most miserable of all systems of agricultural industry, namely, the Cottier system, has been the true cause of the ruin of Ireland. He says, "A people who have once adopted the large system of production, either in manufactures or in agriculture, are not likely to recede from it; nor, when population is kept in due proportion to the means of support, is there any sufficient reason why they should. Labour is unquestionably more productive on the sys-tem of large industrial enterprises; the produce, if not greater abso-lutely, is greater in proportion to the labour employed; the same number of persons can be supported equally well with less toil and greater leisure, which will be wholly an advantage, as soon as civilization and improvement have so far advanced, that what is a benefit to the whole, shall be a benefit to each individual composing it.   The problem is, to obtain the efficiency and economy of production on a large scale, without dividing the producers into two parties with hostile interests, Employers and Employed; the many who do the work being mere servants under the command of those who supply the funds, and having no interest of their own in the enterprise, except to fulfil their contract and earn their wages.

A solution of this problem is afforded by the extension and developement of which the *co-operative, or joint-stock principle*, is susceptible. That principle supplies means, by which every one who contributes to the work, whether by labour or by pecuniary resources, may have a partner's interest in it, proportionally to the value of his contribution. It is already a common practice to remunerate those, in whom particular trust is reposed, by means of a percentage on the profits ; and cases exist, in which the principle is, with the most excellent success, carried down to the class of mere manual labourers."   And further, " Under this system the labourers are in reality taken into partnership with their employer.   Bringing nothing into the common concern but their labour, while he brings not only his labour of direction and superintendance, but his capital also, they have justly a small share of the profits ; this however is a matter of private arrangement in all partnerships ; one partner has a large, another a small share, according to their agreement, grounded on the equivalent which is given by each.   The essence however of a partnership is obtained, since each benefits by all things that are beneficial to the concern, and loses by all which are injurious.   It is in the fullest sense the common concern of all."

" The value of this organisation of industry," he says again, " for healing the widening and embittering feud between the class of labourers and the class of capitalists, must, I think, impress itself by degrees on all who habitually reflect on the condition and tendencies of modern society.   I cannot conceive how any such person can persuade himself, that the majority of the working-classes will for ever, or even for much longer, consent to hew wood and draw water all their lives, in the service and for the benefit of others ; or can doubt, that they will be less and less willing to co-operate as subordinate agents in any work, when they have no interest in the result; and that it will be more and more difficult to obtain the best work-people, or the best services of any work-people, except on conditions similar to those mentioned above.   Although therefore arrangements of this sort are now in their infancy, their multiplication and growth, when once they enter into the general domain of popular discussion, are among the things which may most confidently be expected."

This great organic change from the system of hired labour to that of independent or associated industry, is of immense importance to the welfare of the working classes.   They should make it therefore one of their steady and determined aims, to attain to this independence ; and gradually to get rid of our present system of hired labour, with its many degradations, and small prospect of rising to a higher position. The chief obstacle to these associations is the poverty and dependence of the working classes, together with the present state of the law, which makes each member of a partnership liable with his whole means, in the event of the failure of the enterprise ; and therefore renders one, who has much to lose, unwilling to link himself with those who have little or nothing. Were the law changed, so as to admit of *partnerships with limited liabilities*, of which change Mr. Mill is much in favour ; and were the working classes better off, and able to make desirable terms with the capitalists, there is no doubt that such associations would become very common, as they are in some parts of America. As the wages of labour rise by means of duly limiting procreation, the working class will have less difficulty in effecting this change ; and they should not rest satisfied till their condition has been recognised as equally independent, and equally entitled to the respect and deference of mankind, as that of any other members of society.

Let not the attention of the reader be diverted in the slightest by these secondary and auxiliary means, from the only real remedy for the social difficulties, namely, *preventive intercourse*. If it be so, they had better not have been mentioned ; for without that primary and radical means, all the rest are not worth talking about, and can have no real effect in advancing human happiness ; for they, like all other schemes, if tried alone, can lead only to the aggravation of the want of love, and therefore are delusive. Preventive intercourse is of itself sufficient to remove poverty, without any of these auxiliaries ; and if poverty were removed, the other parts of social progress would become comparatively easy, and the working classes would attain without an effort the advantages, which they at present toil after in vain ; while on the contrary all those auxiliary means, or any other imaginable ones, are, without preventive intercourse, utterly impotent, or could at most only relieve poverty a little, at the expense of increased sexual abstinence and consequent miseries.

Without preventive intercourse and limited procreation, let us not vainly imagine that we can cheat our doom ; or make any real impression upon the appalling evils, moral and physical, which exist among us, and two-thirds of which arise from the fatal antagonism of food and love. If we ignore this antagonism, and shut our eyes as we have hitherto done, to this and other sexual subjects, we may do what else we like ; we may bully, we may bluster, we may rage, we may foam at the mouth ; we may tear down heaven with our prayers, we may exhaust ourselves in weeping over the sorrows of the poor ; we may narcotise ourselves and others with the opiate of Christian resignation ; we may dissolve the realities of human woe in a delusive mirage of poetry and ideal philosophy ; we may lavish our substance in charity, and labour over possible or impossible Poor-laws ; we may form wild dreams of socialism, industrial regiments, universal brotherhood, red republics, or unexampled revolutions ; we may strangle and murder each other, we may persecute and despise those whose sexual necessities force them to break through our unnatural moral codes, we may burn alive if we please the prostitutes and the adulterers ; we may break our own and our neighbours' hearts against the adamantine laws that surround us, but not one step, not one shall we advance, till we acknowledge these laws, and adopt the only possible mode in which they can be obeyed.

But if we do this, it is my earnest hope and belief that we shall ultimately triumph over that mighty difficulty, that *sexual dead-lock*, which has hitherto laughed to scorn all the efforts of our race ; that a new era will dawn upon the world, the only real era of improvement in the whole of human history ; a blessed era, which shall usher in the golden age, when truth and virtue shall be no longer a mocking phantom, and progress not a dream ; when every advance in science and art shall bear its true fruit, unembittered by the necessary sacrifice of an equivalent amount of love ; when the poor friendless prostitute shall no more be seen in our streets, the able-bodied pauper in our workhouse, or the helpless beggar at our gate ; when all of us shall have a share in the blessings of independence and sexual love, befitting the exalted position of the human race ; when the poor-houses shall be shut up, and the gaols nearly emptied of their tenants, poverty, the chief cause of crime, having been removed ; when the various classes of our society, no longer separated from each other by impassable difference of circumstances, shall fuse into one great and united whole, and learn to look back, with mingled pity and amazement, on the dark ages of mutual destruction and delusive struggles, in which their less fortunate ancestors were plunged. A true Sexual Religion can alone save mankind from the mighty wants of Food, Love, and Leisure.

END OF PART II.

PART III.
NATURAL RELIGION.

PART III.

NATURAL RELIGION.

DIGNITY, LIBERTY, AND INDEPENDENCE

" Live and let live."

MAN stands at the head of the universe, and we can form but a very inadequate conception of the wonderful majesty and glory of his being. We admire the extraordinary energies and transcendant perfections of the simplest organised substances; we can watch a humble plant construct a huge complex fabric, by the magical powers inherent in a cell, almost inconceivably minute; but when we come to reflect on the natural powers inherent in man, which build up our wondrous being from a cell no less minute, to a perfection of developement, which no imagination can reach, our astonishment can know no bounds. Man is beyond all comparison the most powerful and elevated part of Nature, and the majesty of his position cannot be too highly estimated. If a thing is to be valued in proportion to the great time and care spent in its production, in proportion to the grandeur of its construction and its purpose, and the multiplicity of the energies it possesses, Man cannot be too highly valued. It needed myriads and myriads of ages, for the working powers of life to develope this their master-piece; and it is only by this patient and long continued elaboration, that we could have been produced.

Of the boundless energies of Man how shall we obtain a conception? In every little cell within us reside occult powers of life and death, whose study is worth a life-time. By their united agency an individual is formed, so perfect, and with such various endowments, as to deserve the name of the microcosm; for his manifold being is an epitome of the whole universe. *Man is nature become self-conscious;* the crowning effort of Nature to understand herself, to know, as well as to be. And

It would almost seem as if the scale of being, having been developed so far, need not go further; for man, unlike other animals, contains in himself the powers of indefinite progress. It is probable, that there is scarcely a secret in Nature, (who has, as it has been beautifully said, in various places told all her secrets,) which man may not gradually learn, and that to all legitimate questions he may obtain an answer. Another reason for supposing that developement will not proceed higher than Man, is that the inferior organisms, whether existing or extinct, seem to prefigure man, who has thus been called the fulfilment of the geological prophecies.

If we thus, forgetting that we belong to the human race, and viewing it in an objective, not a subjective, light, consider man's unapproachable elevation in the universe, we must regard him as the greatest and most glorious manifestation of nature; and if we look up to the heavens and around us on this beautiful earth with wonder, and almost with awe, we must still more look up to man, as a being far more incomprehensible, and immeasurably further above our conception in his natural sublimity. He who does not profoundly feel the unutterable grandeur of humanity, does not feel that of nature; for man is nature incarnate. We may give the reins to our imagination, and form the most extravagant ideal of perfection; nothing that we can conceive or express of power, virtue, or sublimity, will give the least idea of the perfection of a human being, who contains in himself the concentrated energies of the universe.

When we reflect on the elevation of man's position, and observe the wondrous products of his power; the sciences, the arts, the material and mental wealth he has accumulated; the way in which he has bent to his purpose the various agencies in nature, and in which he is looked up to by the other creatures as their lord and master; we would expect that the possessor of such powers would have a due sense of his own dignity, would be able easily to raise himself above the grosser wants of inferior beings, and enjoy a much freer and more independent life. But alas! when we look upon the present state of mankind, we find this by no means the case. We see the world's Lord reduced to contend on every side with the most degrading evils, which take away the sense of liberty and dignity, that so lofty a being should possess; and make him cringing and timid, the slave instead of the master of fortune.

Dignity, liberty, and independence, are among the most valuable of human possessions. *Independence*, or the capability of self-maintenance, is indeed the very foundation of all other advantages; and from it comes the delightful sense of dignity and liberty, which is so essential to happiness. The great aim in social economy should be, *that every adult should be independent*; that every one should be able to obtain for himself the necessaries of life; and that no one in this essential respect should be more in the power of his neighbour, than the latter is of him. Of course there must exist a mutual dependence, which indeed is the great bond and condition of society; but this should be reciprocal, and as equal as possible, else there can be no satisfactory liberty. Upon individual independence alone, possessed by every adult member of the community, can social freedom or secure political institutions be based; for a state of dependence on others is so opposed to the welfare of man, that discontent and disorder are sure to result, where it exists. No man, even if he had the wish, could provide for another, as well as the latter could for himself; and whenever one man has undue power over another, we know from too sad experience, it is certain to be abused. Hence it is, that all institutions and systems, which have for their objects to make one part of mankind dependent on another, are radically erroneous ; and that the patriarchal forms of government, and the feudal ideas of noble beneficence surrounded by grateful dependents, are rapidly giving way to the far truer and more ennobling principle of universal independence in the essentials of life, which is, it may be said, the great leading idea of the civilized nations of modern times. Even if charity and brotherly love could be secured on the side of the more fortunate among us towards the more destitute, charity is no proper support for man, and grateful dependence no fit sphere for him. It is well that each of us should give and receive *mutually* from each other, and where there is this feeling of equality, there will be true gratitude and love ; but where the favours are all on one side, the natural feelings of independence revolt from them, and gratitude or content, even under the best treatment, is not to be expected. But a dependent need never look for good treatment ; for the only true foundation of this between man and man, is a mutual reverence, arising from equal independence. The noble desire for independence is one of the finest points in the English character, the main cause of the country's unrivalled progress in the industrial arts; and it has enabled her to struggle onward under the most overwhelming social difficulties.

But notwithstanding all our struggles for these grand essentials of life— liberty and independence—society is still very, very far, from having attained such an aim. In fact, if we look around us on the various individuals of whom our society is composed, we will find very few, who can be said to enjoy an adequately free or independent life.

In the first place there is a mass of *paupers*, to the humiliation of our race, who are unable to find employment, and are utterly dependent for their bare life on the charity of others. Helpless and dejected, covered with shame and contumely, their lot is a constant wretchedness to themselves, and a misery and reproach to the rest of us, who cannot find the means to prevent such awful calamities.

If we now regard the condition of the *working classes*, we shall find that there are few, if any, among them, who can be said to enjoy much freedom or independence. In the hot-press of competition, at present existing among us, all their energies are enslaved to the gain of their daily bread, and they are dependent on the least smile or frown of fortune. The fear of destitution always hangs over them, and even their greatest efforts are often insufficient to prevent them from sinking into the gulph of pauperism or crime. Those cannot be said to be free men, who are forced to toil from morning to night at a work, from which their jaded limbs revolt ; and who, after all, are perhaps half-starved. It matters little whether it be fortune or a tyrant that sets the task; the state of slavery

2 D

is nearly the same. They can have little sense of man's dignity, who are subject to so many hardships, and put to so many sordid shifts; and who are besides exposed to the caprices of a master, on whose favour they are dependent. The working classes are as a body dependent on the richer classes, for the difficulty of procuring a livelihood is so great, that to offend an employer is ruinous. Hence the marked subservience of the poorer among us to the richer; a thing which should by no means exist, as there should be an equal mutual reverence among all men. All have an equal natural dignity and title to reverence, whatever be their occupations, whether a prime minister or a costermonger; and it is most pernicious that this reverence should be given to certain classes alone, or it is man himself, and not his accidental external condition, that claims our reverence. But as long as the poorer classes, from an over-crowded state of the population, are dependent for their livelihood on the favour of the richer, there never can be either adequate mutual respect, or a due feeling of independence and freedom in every bosom; and discontent and unhappiness must result.

Even among the *richer classes* we find by no means a sufficient independence. Even here, the struggle for a livelihood, or for the means of marrying and supporting a family, is still very great; too great often for the powers of the individual; and the man must toil like a slave, or if he relax at all his efforts, sink to a dependent condition.

But the position of man with regard to independence, degraded though it be, is still infinitely before that of *woman*. The latter is so generally dependent on man for her support, that this state is very frequently held to be the one natural and fitted for the sex. But this is an immense error, and the source of fallacies and miseries innumerable. If we regard all the inferior animals, we will find, that the female is never dependent on the male. The females are generally as powerful, and frequently much more so than the males, and in all cases live just as independent lives. There is no doubt that woman is perfectly fitted by nature to live independently, that is, to gain her livelihood by her own exertions; and there is as little doubt that she is intended to do so. She is formed with boundless powers and faculties of body and mind, just as man is, with, however, marked differences in some respects; and there are very few operations in which he may engage, which she is not also fitted to perform, though with a different degree of power. Now the natural aptitude for any thing, shows that it should be done; for all the inborn powers demand their due exercise. It is true that the developement of woman has of late made considerable progress, but it is still very far behind that of man: and as a general rule, her lot may be regarded as one of comparative slavery and dependence.

If we review the condition of the female sex, from the most neglected prostitute to the Queen of our land, we shall find but very few in any class, who have a due share of independence, or that feeling of liberty or dignity which befits the Queen of Nature. *Single women* of the poorer classes, are still more dependent on fortune than men. There are so few occupations in which women are employed, that the vast competition for them among the hosts of poor women, reduces the wages to a mere trifle, scarcely enough to keep breath in the living skeleton. If such wretched means fail, the dreary workhouse, with its joyless abasement; opens to them.

We cannot wonder that so many are driven by these fearful hardships into prostitution, that great house of refuge for destitute women.

Forlorn and degraded as in the state of the very poor among our women, that of the *prostitutes* is in some respects worse. There is no class of society which stands in so degraded a position in the eyes of the world, scarcely even the criminals: and although some of these ill-used girls may not have much difficulty in gaining a livelihood, yet it is very precarious, and gained in a way which is eventually destructive to their happiness, sense of dignity, and self-respect.

The women among the *richer classes* have a lot, which I would be tempted to call even more unhappy than that of the labouring poor; except indeed of those, who are sunk in the lowest mire of poverty or prostitution. There are still fewer employments open to them; in fact, with the exception of the unpleasant situation of a governess, there is scarcely any employment fit for an educated woman. Hence they are almost entirely dependent on man for their support, their noble powers are allowed to lie dormant, and a few trivial accomplishments brought into a forced existence in their stead; and thus they have to wait till the arbiter of their destiny deigns to smile on them, and relieve them from their unpleasant position by marriage, which has been truly called, woman's only profession. In this way, woman is made dependent on man's love for her main hopes in life; by which the sex is unutterably degraded. Unhappy truly is the lot of those, who depend on a thing so varying and so deceitful as sexual love, especially in the hollow existing state of the sexual world. Such dependence on the affections of man has spoiled woman's character; has made her unreal, trifling, and weak, seeking rather what is pleasing and graceful in his eyes, than what is true and noble in her own; and this unnatural dependence could not but result in the unhappiness of both. The anxiety about being married, and the fear of remaining an old maid—feelings inseparable from the existing sexual institutions and circumstances of our society—have broken her spirit, and cowed her into a state of timidity, most destructive to happiness and the sense of dignity.

There is perhaps no lot in life with less dignity, liberty, or independence than that of a *young unmarried lady* in the richer classes, especially after she has passed the first season of youth, and finds how completely her happiness and liberty in life depend on her chance of marrying. What is open to the unfortunate in such a case? She is sick of her frivolous accomplishments, which should form the ornaments, not the substance of life; she has no field for the exercise of those transcendant natural powers, which, like the unruly spirits of old, are constantly crying out for "work, work" within her; she has no liberty of locomotion or of action. and she is probably dependent for her subsistence on those around her; and dependent too for love, that great essential of human happiness, on an unpropitious fortune.

Marriage, although a great improvement upon such a state, has still mmense disadvantages. The *wife* is still wholly dependent on the husband; and he who knows human nature could foresee, that, from this, enormous evils must result. From this she is to a great degree in his power, and in the main must suit herself to his wishes. Her privileges are few in comparison with his; he takes the lion's share of liberty, and expects deference and obedience, (which indeed have even, to our shame, been made part of the religious formula of marriage). It is true that in many cases the inherent human nobility and devoted love will in part remove these inequalities; but it is not by exceptional cases that our judgment should be guided. It is a certainty, in the case of woman as of all others, that she who is dependent for the main essentials of her existence, for food and for love, upon others, cannot expect to have a free, a dignified, or a happy lot. She may chance to attain it, but she is always at the mercy of external circumstances. The charity which supports woman, may be gilded over by the name of love; but in the main it is *charity* still; and no class of beings who depend on this, can look for a happy lot. No true sense of dignity or liberty can exist without the feeling of independence.

But it is not woman alone, who is depressed by her state of dependence, on *man* also it presses very heavily. He must work to support two, which is a great additional tax on his energies. In this way the wife or the daughter is constantly put in the humiliating position, of being a drag upon him whom she loves. It is often said that the wife contributes her share to the business of the family in managing the house, and in nursing and rearing the children. But this is a great fallacy, especially with regard to the educated classes. It is by no means an adequate sphere for an energetic and well-educated woman, to spend all her thoughts on domestic economy, or to act chiefly as a head-nurse. Even at the present day, when the propagation of the species is monopolised by a limited number of women, and when the solecism of large families is the general rule in married life, such duties ought by no means to absorb her attention; and in future ages, when it is to be hoped, there will be a very different proportion of children in each household, much less attention will be needed.

It is a great mistake to suppose that a mother should devote herself so completely to the children, as is generally seen among us. By this the characters of both, instead of being improved, are injured. The great secret of bringing up children well and happy, is to let them be very much in the society of *other children* of their own age, with whom they can play, and from whom they learn infinitely more than by constant contact with an adult, who is not their natural companion. However devoted a mother may be to her child, she will generally seek in vain to make it either happy or good, by all the pains she can lavish on it, unless she provide it with play-mates of its own age, whose modes of feeling and thought are so much more suited to its comprehension. It is from this reason, that we generally see the children of the poor, who are in at all tolerable circumstances, much happier, and less spoiled and perverse, than those of the rich. They have plenty of play-mates of their own age; and their mother, who has, as all human beings should have, some work of her own to mind, is not always looking after them, and encumbering them with help, exhortation, and advice, as among the rich. But the mother, as well as the child, is spoiled by her over-attention to it. An adult woman is not intended to be always in the nursery, or to have children for her chief companions, any more than a man is; and the strength of her mind, as well as that of the child's, is impaired by it. Although all ages should intermingle, yet it is certain, that as a general rule, children are more suited to the society of children, and adults to that of adults. Woman seeks the nursery, because she has few pursuits in common with man, who often comes in this way to hold but a secondary place in her affections.

The married women in the *poorer classes* have in some respects a more dignified and independent life, than those of the richer. They sometimes assist their husband at his work, or have washing, cooking, and other employments, and are not so wholly absorbed in the children. But even here, woman has a dependent condition; for as a general rule it is the man only, who supports the family. The necessity of supporting these tells very heavily upon the strength of the husband. He has to compete with young unmarried men in the labour market, and by this his wages are lowered to a degree insufficient for the wants of a family. It is no wonder in this case, that brutal usage of the wife by the husband is so frequent among the poorer classes. The man does it, and the woman bears it, why? because he feels that she is a drag upon him, and in his power; and she, knowing her dependence on him, dares not resist. It is neither the inferiority of physical force, nor love, which makes her endure it; but simply because she would be reduced to destitution if she left him. Were woman independent of man, there would be an end of the ill-usage and tyranny of the husband towards the wife; but not till then. It is easy for those in less oppressive circumstances to blame husbands, to call them brutes and monsters for abusing their wives; but it is utterly useless to do so, as long as the present system lasts. We may be absolutely certain, that so long as woman continues dependent on man for the necessaries of her life, so long will she have the invariable usage of a dependent.

In this manner we see, that there are immense numbers of individuals in society, who are dependent upon others, or enslaved by Necessity, for the simple gain of the first essential of life, their *daily food*. In this respect, man, the paragon of nature, is worse off than the inferior animals, whose livelihood is in general obtained with much greater ease and certainty; at least by those which grow to the age of maturity, and escape the destruction caused by the principle of population. The want of food is the greatest of all wants, as food is the very first essential of life, and of all its powers and virtues. No man who has undue difficulties in obtaining a plentiful supply of food, can be said to possess a free, a dignified, or an independent life. And no one who is dependent for this supply on the good will of others, need hope to possess these advantages.

But there are many other great obstacles to a free and dignified existence, besides the want of food. By far the most important of these in the present state of our society, is the want of *sexual love*.

This might be almost said to be at present a greater want than that of food, but the two subjects are so intimately connected together that they cannot be separated. It is from the want of food, that the want of love arises; and from the improvident indulgence in love, that want of food results.

Sexual love is a requirement of our being so essential, that it should be included among the *necessaries of life*. By these is understood at present only those things, such as food, fresh air, &c., which are absolutely essential to the life of the individual; but it is a grand error, and one which has pervaded and rendered utterly fallacious all theories hitherto formed of human nature, and systems of human society, to suppose that the exercise of the reproductive faculties is not also essential. In the humblest organism, in the simple cells of the protophytes, reproduction as well as nutrition is always one of their essential vital characteristics; and in man too the exercise of this function is absolutely essential to the health, happiness, and integrity of his being. The appetites for food and love are the two grand conservative powers of life. The one provides for the maintenance of the individual, and the other for that of the species; and man is dependant on a due gratification of both, for a free, a healthy, or a happy life. The man who cannot satisfy his hunger, and who has to toil from morning to night to effect this, may be said to be enslaved to this appetite; and he who cannot satisfy his sexual desires, and who suffers therefore from the dissatisfaction of mind and debility of body, the penalty imposed by nature for the frustration of her great purpose, may in like manner be said to be enslaved to this passion. Neither of them have a free, a dignified, or an independent life. A due gratification of these appetites for food and love is the foundation of our health and content; and without this, our life must always be bound down to a state of dependence.

There is nothing in which the liberty and dignity of mankind are so much impaired, as in sexual love. There is no subject which is so full of humiliation for man; none in which there is so vast an amount of secrecy, deceit, shame, compulsion, and all methods and forms of indignities; so much so in fact, that it is generally avoided, no one liking to open up this pest-house, or to disclose this greatest opprobrium of our society. It is the great principle of population, as has been already shown, which is the parent source of these evils, and of what may be called the tyranny of Love as well as Food; but, as it is by secondary restrictions and impediments thrown in the path of love, (which indeed generally divert attention from the primary one,) that this limiting principle acts in our society, it is on these that I would wish to make some further remarks.

The exceedingly strict rules of sexual morality, forbidding all sexual intercourse except in marriage, which state is attainable by the majority only at a comparatively late age, have given rise to a regular system of secret and mercenary intercourse, ingrained into all civilised societies; in which human dignity and liberty are almost as much degraded, as even by pauperism. Secrecy and deceit are the deadly enemies of liberty and dignity.; and as long as the present sexual system lasts, there is no such thing as a dignified life for youth. Mercenary love 'in itself is an abomination, utterly abhorrent to nature, and full of degradation to all concerned in it.

Both sexes have the dignity of their lives greatly lessened by the sexual difficulties, but in a very different degree. In the first place let us take the *young man*. If he abstain from forbidden intimacies he has anything but a free and dignified life. If he have strong sexual passions, which is almost always the case in early youth, and is the sign of a healthy mind and body, he is the slave of them ; they torment him, fill his mind, and hinder the developement of his powers in other directions ; perhaps lead him to masturbation, than which there is scarcely anything more destructive to the sense of dignity. Even if he is not driven to this, the unfortunate youth is constantly uneasy : in the company of his comrades, who talk about their love affairs, he feels awkward, and has by no means that glowing consciousness of virtuous self-denial, which those who do not know human nature, would wish to make us believe attendant on sexual abstinence : he carries with him the "celled-up dishonour of boyhood," the natural consciousness of the imperfection of unexercised powers. The Christian moralist may tell him he has acted virtuously ; but almighty Nature, although he may not understand her unerring voice, speaks a very different language to his disquieted heart.

But this is not all—the sexual impulses are so strong in youth, that it has been found impossible to restrain them, except by *weakening their force*, and thus tampering with the main-springs of vital energy. Hence sexual shame, sexual shyness and bashfulness, have been fostered in our youth ; and wherever sexual morality is very strict, they are sure to be apparent. Such feelings are diametrically opposed to the sense of a free and dignified existence; indeed shyness or awkwardness is the outward expression of an undignified and fettered mind. But whenever the natural force of a passion is thus interfered with, the powers of life are necessarily impaired. To weaken the sexual passions by infusing shyness or sexual timidity into the mind, as is the almost universal effect of the sexual puritanism, which pervades our country, especially in Scotland, is just as if we were to try to appease healthy hunger by taking doses of a nauseating substance ; we obtain our object, but at the expense of the happiness and integrity of the frame. Thus it may be truly said, that it is not possible for a young man to have a natural, dignified, and manly character, if all sexual intercourse be denied him.

If the young man be not sexually abstinent, how many difficulties must he encounter in his intercourse with the opposite sex. If he rest contented with mercenary love, as the great majority do, he prostitutes and degrades his nature, and his ideal of love must become debased. Love is a passion which elevates in proportion to its intensity, moral and physical ; in proportion to the feeling of reciprocal attachment, esteem, and mutual reverence between the parties. But in mercenary connections, in general, there is not this mutual reverence : and a love which is given for money is either cold and apathetic, or purely lascivious. Alas for the heart of youth, brought up amid such degrading intimacies. Besides these degradations, and the secrecy too, which must accompany them, and which inevitably produces deceit in the young man's character, he is exposed to the venereal diseases, which have ruined so many thousands of our race—blasted their hopes, embittered their hearts—in a word *poisoned* them. There is nothing more degrading to the dignity of character, than a protracted suffering from one of these diseases. The secrecy they necessitate, the miserable way in which they prostrate the powers, and take away from the enjoyment of life, and the fear which ever afterwards pursues their victims, unspeakably degrade the human character. They hang like a Damocles' sword over the head of youth; and so long as they exist, sexual intercourse will never have a truly free and dignified character, for fear and suspicion are incompatible with this.

If the young man, unwilling to prostitute himself to mercenary love, seek rather an unmarried intimacy of a higher nature, indignities even more formidable oppose him. The secrecy that such an intimacy involves, and the fear of detection, are much greater, for, strange to say, society is far more embittered against such an alliance, than any amount of mercenary love; which is considered a very venial fault in a young man, indeed, by many people, rather a point in his favour. Stolen interviews, fear of discovery and of consequent loss of character, place the youth here too in a most undignified position. In fact in all sexual intercourse, except in marriage, the young man has to act and feel like a pickpocket; shunning the light, and being for ever on his guard against discovery; and it can readily be perceived, what an effect this must have in degrading his character. For daring to indulge in one of the fundamental passions of his nature, he is treated as if he were guilty of a great crime, such as robbery, or a pernicious vice, such as drunkenness; and in fact almost all of us, (for how many men are there in society, who have not had more or less sexual intercourse before marriage?) are placed for a great part of our lives in the position of malefactors. Is this to continue? How long will youth tolerate this shameful position? No ingenuous mind can bear, without the keenest suffering, the necessity of secrecy and stealthy action. We must be able to justify our deeds, or else renounce them; and it is a standing reproach to youth to rest contented with their present stealthy and undignified position. The great rule of dignified action is " Never to do anything we are afraid to own;" in fact, openness is the safeguard of probity. At present all sexual relations except that of marriage, and even this in very many cases, especially on the continent, are full of concealment, deceit, and indignities; and as long as such a state of things continues, it is in vain to hope for happiness from sexual intercourse.

The want of freedom and 'dignity in love overshadows all the rest of life, and degrades the whole character. A man or woman, who has in many of the most important relations in life, been put in the position of a pickpocket, has his sense of honour vitally wounded, and cannot be expected to have so ingenuous a character. Clandestine love fills the whole of society with deceit and suspicion; every one suspects his neighbour, and is in his turn the object of suspicion; and even were there no other obstacles to the elevation of the human character, this alone, as long as it continues to exist, must be fatal to the hopes of the moralist. .

But if man be placed in so humiliating a position in sexual matters, unfortunate *woman* is infinitely more so. In the first place we have the vast multitude of *prostitutes,* on whose awful degradation one cannot think but with dismay and anguish. That there should be among us a class of unfortunate women, who are treated worse than dogs; who are hunted about by the police, despised and abhorred by their own sex, and abused and neglected by man, to whose wants they minister, is a page of human shame too dark for tears. It is the greatest disgrace of civilized society; a disgrace deeper even than negro slavery. And for what are these poor girls hunted down in this merciless manner? In truth for acting exactly in the same way as all of us; as all young men, who go with them, enjoy ourselves with them, and then desert them, and leave them to their fate; for supplying a want in our society, which man, by the necessities of his nature, cannot do without, and which only they, who know little of human nature, imagine may be withheld without the most destructive consequences. Instead of contempt, these poor neglected girls deserve the warmest thanks of society, for the heroic mode in which they have borne the misery and the burden of our shame. Notwithstanding the enormous evils which they aid in causing, they have been in the main *exceedingly serviceable* to mankind, by palliating in some degree the other alternative evils of the law of population, namely sexual abstinence or premature death: and thus, as already mentioned, they should be regarded as sexual martyrs.

If youth is to be humiliated and disgraced for indulging in sexual intercourse, at least let all of us bear our share, and be ashamed to throw the whole-burden on poor helpless woman. While so glaring an injustice exists, how can we talk of the nobility or dignity of man? In truth no one member of the human family, no prostitute nor criminal, can be degraded, without dragging down all the rest. In the case of prostitution the whole of society is concerned in it. Men, it may be said, are as a general rule all prostitutes; for there are but an inconsiderable section of them, who do not indulge more or less at some period of life in mercenary loves, and it matters little in such a case whether the money be given or received. The general character of woman also is exceedingly debased, and their dignity and freedom lessened, by the existence of such a class among their sex. The coarse and irreverent way, in which men learn to speak and think of this part of womankind, is inevitably extended to all: and has a much more powerful influence than is generally believed, in their views and treatment of the sex at large. He who has learned to despise or speak harshly of a prostitute, or of any other human being, has taken the first lesson in general irreverence, and will not be slow to extend it to others.

It may also be observed, that the liberty of women of the richer classes is very much impeded by the existence of the class of prostitutes; they cannot walk about in the street in the evening, without the liability of being taken for one of that class ; and hence either stay at home, according to the inveterate sedentary habits of the sex, or require the encumbrance of a conventional protector. But it is in vain for any of us, to hope for a free and dignified life for ourselves, or for the social class to which we belong, as long as any of our fellow-beings are permitted to remain in such a state of degradation ; we must assurdly pay the penalty for our irreverence and neglect of them, nor can we rise to a more dignified life ourselves, till we elevate them along with us.

Of the exceedingly undignified and constrained position of a *young unmarried lady* with regard to love, I have already spoken. One great evil is, that she dare not express her feelings, and the want of freedom of expression is one which is most opposed to human happiness. Shame and concealment prey upon her in most of her loves, and eat into her strength like a canker-worm. Sexual shyness moreover has been even more fostered in girls than in young men, and with the same fatal effects : weakening or rather making morbid, the natural sexual desires, but at the same time vitally injuring the integrity of mind and body. Hence comes hysteria, and its train of miseries, which overthrow the sense of dignity.

If a young lady, on the other hand, dare to indulge in any forbidden sexual intimacy, the whole of society is roused against her, and she is in many respects ruined for life. Hence the greatest fear, difficulties, and anguish attend any such step, and a series of endless degradations. The injustice here committed by society, is as flagrant as in the case of the prostitutes. A young man has very considerable liberty granted him, and sexual indulgences are considered venial in him, but if a young woman do the same and be discovered, her character is gone. This injustice is a crying shame to our society, and confuses all ideas of morality. Man sets at naught the golden moral rule, "do to others as you would have them do to you." He indulges himself in sexual pleasures, but if a woman do the same, he at once joins in the cry against her. Is this manly, is this just or righteous? No. If man expects woman, either married or unmarried, to renounce all sexual indulgences except the one prescribed by the present moral code, let him himself renounce them ; but for a brother or a husband, who has, as it is called, sown his wild oats, to expect perfect abstinencé in his sister, or perfect constancy in his wife, is an evident injustice. Unless the female sex be placed exactly on a par with the male in sexual freedom and dignity, there cannot be either justice or happiness. Is man ready to renounce all sexual intercourse except that of marriage ? then let him ask of woman to do the same ; but if he be resolved to have a freer and more dignified state of sexual relations than at present exists, he can only do so by giving to woman exactly an equal share of feedom.

In married life the *wife* has far less freedom in love than the husband. The latter, in the large towns in England, not infrequently keeps a mistress, or goes with other women, and little is said about it : but if the wife should be inconstant, the greatest scandal is caused. Thus all illicit intercourse on her side is carried on at the expense of fears and indignities innumerable. On the continent where wives are very frequently inconstant to their husbands, many married women may be said to lead a life constantly suspected; and the restraint and disgrace of such a position are easily understood.

In this way we see what very great indignities are suffered by the different members of our society, from the want of greater liberty in *love*. There is perhaps not a man or a woman among us, whose sense of honour and dignity has not suffered deeply from this cause; not one whose character is not more or less defaced by it. There is scarcely a human breast, in which the love experiences are not the ones most sedulously concealed from view, as being those which could least bear scrutiny. There is no subject, in which the freedom and dignity of man and woman are so vitally attainted.

Besides these two supreme tyrannies of food and love, which have their primary origin in the laws of nature, there is another, of inferior influence and depending on human institutions, by which the freedom and dignity of mankind are greatly diminished. This is the tyranny of *religious belief*. There are few countries in the world, in which this is not a most powerful engine in the degradation of man. We all know to what an extent the people of less civilized countries, such as Hindostan, China, &c., whose vast population numbers the half of our race, and in whose welfare and advancement we should feel a profound interest, are enslaved to idol worship. But even among ourselves, notwithstanding our comparatively advanced grade of enlightenment, when we consider the way in which man's dignity and liberty are interfered with by this cause, we shall find that we have little reason for self-congratulation. Although insignificant when compared with the two causes already mentioned, for these are constantly operating, being connected with the most fundamental wants of our nature; still the religious tyranny has a very powerful effect in lessening the liberty and dignity of each of us.

In the first place, there is a large and constantly increasing class in this country, who have no belief on the commonly received religious views. The dignity and liberty of this class are very seriously affected by the restrictions placed on the free expression of their opinions, by the intolerance of their neighbours. Instead of the opinions which they have conscientiously adopted, being received with that reverence, which is due in every case by one man to his fellow; instead of being met by free discussion and by an open and respectful dissent, such beliefs are too often treated with the bitterest animosity or contempt, and those known to entertain them are regarded in the most irreverent manner. Hence they are forced in most cases to conceal their opinions, and to adopt manners and habits quite at variance with those which their conscience approves. Their life is a constant succession of deceptions and false positions, most destructive to the sense of freedom and dignity. Instead of openly expressing their beliefs on the great and elevating subjects of the destiny and duties of man, they are afraid to disclose them, and must therefore have a frequent sense of self-reproach and humiliation; save where this is replaced by the still more unfortunate feeling of secret contempt for the neighbour, whose intolerance is the cause of the concealment. There is scarcely a more fruitful cause of mutual contempt among us than this:

the Christian despises the Atheist and the Infidel, and the latter returns the contempt, with the additional virulence of a forced secrecy. What is to be said of religious beliefs on either side, that admit of such uncharitable and irreverent feelings towards one's fellow beings?

The man who openly declares his disbelief in Christianity, is subject to a host of inconveniences and indignities He is looked upon with horror dislike, or contempt, by a great mass of his fellows; and besides the deep, wound which this gives to one who truly loves his kind, it is constantly humiliating to his sense of honour and dignity. He is put in the category of the worst malefactors, his actions misconstrued, and his noblest aspirations for the service of mankind treated with suspicion and ignominy. The free expression of the opinions, which he believes so essential to human happiness and virtue, is very much restricted. His nearest friends and relations look coldly on him, and lose no opportunity of degrading his cherished beliefs. Truly the man who resolves nobly to express his independent religious convictions, has much to encounter; and the service of truth is still a martyrdom.

But while those who dissent from the usual form of religious belief have so undignified and fettered a position, those who adopt it have one quite às much so. All the current religions, which assert the dominion of the supernatural over man and nature, strike at the very foundation of human dignity and liberty. They proclaim that man is under the irresponsible rule of a sovereign master. over whom he has no power whatsoever; whom he cannot comprehend, to whose will his own must be subservient, whom he must endeavour to propitiate by humbling himself in the dust before him, whose words and injunctions he must not even discuss the justice of; in short to whose service he must consecrate his life, under penalty of the most unheard-of vengeance. If this be so, the dignity and liberty of man are but names, and have no existence. The idea of an irresponsible sovereign is one so totally subversive of all liberty and moral dignity, that, where it exists, there can be no true conception of these virtues. An exact equality of mutual responsibility between all thinking beings, is the bulwark, the grand aim of freedom and virtue; and wherever the idea of unequal responsibility intrudes, it is fatal to both. To be in the power of any one, over whom you have not an equal power, is prostrating to the self-reverence. What are we, where is the dignity of our lives, if we are subject constantly to the fiat of another, who can do with us whatever he will, while he has to give us no account of his actions?

But in truth the idea of *irresponsiblity* is radically false, and one of the monstrous and impossible conceptions, of which the whole idea of the supernatural is composed. It is utterly impossible for any being to be irresponsible; all are indissolubly linked together, and all must render an account for every action. Man need not suppose from his exalted position, that the inferior animals and the rest of Nature are in his power; we are just as much in their's, and for every injustice or error we commit in our relations to them, we will surely have to pay the exact penalty, the happiness of all being mutually interdependent. If they suffer, surely we shall suffer too, for no one being or class of beings can remain happy, if others suffer. It is a philosophical error, as well as a great moral oversight, to believe in irresponsibility. To imagine a being whose happiness is not inseparably bound up with that of all others, or a scheme of salvation, which permanently excludes any living beings, is an immense error, and leads to endless immoralities. The only true scheme of salvation, the only one which could satisfy the ideal of moral perfection, is that which includes every living being; and which has for its first principle, that the permanent happiness of one is absolutely unattainable without that of all. It is owing to the neglect of this great principle, that so many attempts have been made to secure happiness for a limited class; that despots have sought happiness at the expense of their slaves: that the rich have thought to be happy without the poor; that men have dreamed of attaining to paradise, while their fellows were doomed to eternal perdition; that supernatural existences have been imagined, some of them infinitely happy, and others infinitely miserable: but all such endeavours, all such conceptions, are alike futile and impossible. The moral sense revolts from them, and our calm judgment tells us their irrationality.

In reverencing God, man has forgotten to reverence Man. There is perhaps nothing which has so frequently caused one man to despise or to ill-use another as religious zeal; as the preference, namely, of God to Man. Since the days of Tamerlane, of Mahomet, of the Inquisition, down to our own time, what hecatombs of victims have been sacrificed to this! Reverence to God was thought by all these men to be the grand essential of virtue; reverence to man formed no part of their creed. These monstrous ideas are it is true fading away before our enlightenment, but they still form the spirit of our religious beliefs. The chief end of Man it is said, is to glorify God. It is from this cause that the various religious sects, while bending down in humiliation before deity, regard each other often with the greatest irreverence; that they look down on their fellow-man with contempt and hatred for daring to disbelieve in the object of their reverence; in short that they prefer God to Man. They dare not think of God but with awe and adoration, they prostrate themselves before him; but on turning to their fellow-beings, they fill their hearts with scorn and irreverence. They turn with abhorrence from those who deny their religious beliefs, and with contemptuous loathing from the prostitute; and upon the most trifling provocation are ready to take irreverent, degrading, and angry views of their fellow-mortals. John Knox, whose religious character is much admired by many among us, was at one time very desirous, indeed I believe petitioned the ruling powers, that all the Roman Catholics in Scotland might be put to death. In what respect do the religious feelings of such a man radically differ from those of a Mahomet or a Tamerlane?

But this is a certain truth, that any human being, any one of us, no matter how fallen or degraded, is an infinitely more glorious and adorable being, than any God that ever was or will be conceived. *Man* is the true object of man's reverence and love, and it is to him that our service and homage are due, however unhappy, however degraded he may have become. Man, the consummation of Nature, is infinitely above any supernatural conception.

What is the meaning of reverence? why is it a virtue and a duty Because by it we can elevate and support; because by it we can *benefit* the object of our reverence. To bestow reverence on any being, who cannot be benefited thereby, is merely to waste it; and even on the supposition that there is a supernatural being, we could have no possible duty to reverence him, as we could do him no good thereby. But the idea of a deity is one which is passing from the world, and is so totally at variance with what we now know of life and nature, that it cannot long continue in any form. But man exists; man, our own real natural brother, bone of our bone and flesh of our flesh; man, bent down so often with suffering, quivering with anguish, and steeped in degradation, on whom our reverence and our love are never spent in vain. Oh! let not the heart which truly loves its fellows, ever be beguiled from their real weal and woe, by the imposing pomp of a visionary worship.

If we look back on the history of the world, we will find the vast difference in the result of lives spent in the service of God, and of those spent in the service of Man. All acknowledge the comparative uselessness of the lives of monks, nuns, and others, who have devoted themselves to the service of God; and had it not been for the human element in the Christian religion, which essentially consisted in love and reverence to *Man*, it would never have stood a day. Had reverence and humanity to one's fellow-beings formed the religious creed of mankind, how infinitely better would it have been for the world! The sword and the stake, the anathema and the religious intolerance, would not then have been disguised in the mask of holiness, but would have stood forth in all their natural hideousness. We would not now see men trusting to gain eternal happiness by going to church and adoring Deity, while they hold irreverent views of many of their fellow-creatures; and while the criminals, the paupers, and the prostitutes, are permitted to wander in shame and ignominy in the midst of us. Ah! the only true religion is that which makes us reverence and love all our fellow-creatures; which leads us to seek for and believe in no happiness for ourselves alone, while our companions are suffering, but makes us resolve to die with, rather than desert them; it is not the following of a cold idea, or allowing one's heart to be steeled against one's fellows, by a set of icy formulas, which pretend to give us reasons for hardening ourselves against any human being.

Another great cause which degrades the sense of liberty and dignity in each individual, is the adoption of *one standard* of moral excellence for all men. The character of Christ is taken as the perfection of all virtue, and men are exhorted to imitate this, no matter what their peculiar moral constitution may be. By this every other kind of character is degraded, and its liberty of self-developement interfered with. All of us, in comparison with the Christian character, are thrown into the shade, and urged, instead of freely developing ourselves according to our natural tendencies, to imitate Christ, and to prefer his character to our own. But this is an enormous error. The true rule of dignified morality is,

" *Be thyself,* imitate no one whomsoever ; thou cans't not possibly be anything so great as thy own true self." Every individual differs naturally
from all others, and therefore every one has naturally a different standard
of excellence, to which he is fitted to attain. Comparisons between man
and man are always very liable to fallacy ; it is with his own nature and
his own circumstances that each one should be compared. It is destructive to morality, to the sense of dignity and content, that all should be
struggling after the same standard. Hence arise jealousy and envy of
our neighbours, who are more fortunately constituted than ourselves ;
endless mortifications and disappointments by striving for virtues and
powers beyond our reach ; and a discontent with those natural powers
which every man has in his own peculiar degree, and which in every
human being are transcendant beyond all power of conception. Men
strive after a moral shadow, and neglect the infinitely more glorious substance within themselves. They judge themselves and their neighbours
by the Christian standard, and adapt their scale of reverence according
to this ; and from this reason all those characters whose natural virtues
are of a different, although of an equally high order with the Christian
ones, are degraded, while the latter receive an undue share of reverence.
The *physical* virtues especially (whose omission is the most radical
defect in the Christian standard) have been degraded in comparison with
the moral ones ; and their consequent neglect has been the source of the
most deplorable evils, which it will need all the efforts of physical religion
for generations to remove.

The fundamental idea too in the doctrine of *Redemption,* is utterly degrading to human dignity. It is indeed acknowledged to be so, and
constantly used as an instrument of abasement, by those who delight to
humble themselves or their neighbours in the dust before the Deity.
This idea is, that the moral nature of man is essentially vicious and perverted, that he is born full of *Original Sin.* There could not be a
doctrine more fatal to human dignity and liberty than this. What are
we, how should we have any self-reverence or self-confidence, if we knew
that we were corrupt at the core, that our moral nature was radically
erroneous, and sought evil rather than good ? But such a conception is
a total error, as entirely unphilosopical, as it is dangerous to morality. Any one who has studied the nature of life, and of the various organs
and faculties which the human frame possesses, knows that one of the
laws, which must never be lost sight of in inquiries into the vital
phenomena, is this ; that *every organ or faculty in the body works
invariably, in all cases and at all times, for the good of the whole.*
In health and disease this is alike true ; every process in health and every
process in disease is intended by nature for the preservation of the
individual ; that is, every act of every organ is essentially *good.* This
law applies exactly in the same way to all the intellectual and moral
operations; every thought and feeling of the mind must by the necessity of our being, tend to the preservation and not to the destruction of the organism, and therefore must be in like manner essentially
good. In this manner all those moral affections, which are generally
called the *bad* passions, and cited as instances of the natural human

depravity, are found, when carefully studied, to have invariably for their object the good of the being, so far as their powers go; exactly as the processes of disease have been all shown to aim at the preservation of life.   This is a great philosophical truth, which has not yet been sufficiently apprehended, from the want hitherto of any natural mental science; and indeed it is only lately, that the real nature of the processes of bodily disease has been perceived.   The want of perception of this truth is a fundamental error pervading our moral and religious philosophy and leads to the most lamentable mistakes as to the nature and proper treatment of the human mind in health and disease; mistakes exactly analogous to those of the ancient physicians, who had no trust or belief in the workings of nature, but were always trying to thwart and counteract her mighty plan.   It is now acknowledged by the profoundest physicians, that the object of medicine should be to study carefully the efforts of nature, and aid them by every means in our power, not to go blindly against them, calling them morbid, evil, or perverted, as the moralists do at present, in the case of mental phenomena.   As long as moralists work as at present, looking down upon the transcendantly beautiful moral constitution of man, and stigmatising as wholly vile, those wondrous passions, by which our all-perfect nature shows its intolerance of circumstances, injurious to its happiness or developement, we can have little hope of a satisfactory advance of moral science; or of the practical benefits, which it should have, in elevating and giving strength and self-reverence to mankind.

This may be assumed as an axiom, that the *mind* of man is as glorious, as wondrous, and as perfect in all its manifestations, as is his body; that however little we as yet comprehend either of them, we know enough to be assured, that in all their actions they are alike replete with that infinite perfection, which every part of Nature possesses; and that it is only by reverently studying them in all their phases of health and disease, that we can gain a true idea of moral or physical virtue; not by forming to ourselves, out of our own imagination, any vain and distorted image of these things.   The ways of nature are not as our ways, her real virtues are not like our shadowy preconceptions; and any one who knows the infinite depth of her phenomena, must feel, that any theories we can yet have of virtue or vice must be as far short of her infinity, as the few shells which Newton gathered on the shore of her ocean.   But we may be assured, that, whatever we do, whatever we become—if we die of cancer or syphilis, or fall into madness, idiocy, or crime, or any other abyss of misery in which so many of our race are at all times sunk—the wondrous natural powers of good continue equally at work within us to the last, and we cannot, if we would, help being full of an ineffable virtue. To him who despises any human action, the nature of man is a sealed book; but to the reverent eye, which strives to recognise the one grand principle of action in all its varied forms, every human condition teems with unspeakable interest.

The mind of man, as his body, is set to virtue like the needle to the pole, and cannot by any possibility swerve from it.   In the body, this is now recognised, and the chief reason that it is not so in the mind is, firstly,

the spell-bound state of morality from the influence of supernaturalism; and, secondly, the mode in which moral phenomena are obscured,
by the conflicting duties towards one's self and others. All the powers
in one individual tend to self-preservation, and in like manner all individuals tend towards the general preservation; but these tendencies
often cross each other, while all are constantly hindered and obscured
by external circumstances. However, there is no doubt that the same
Principle of Good, without which indeed life could not exist, prevails in
all; and that by attentive study we shall be able in time to gain a
fuller and fuller knowledge of its workings. The radically unsound
doctrine of Original Sin has had a most pernicious effect on our general
habits of thought and feeling. It has degraded the general estimate of
human nature, and thus acted powerfully to make men despise their
fellow-beings. We all judge far too harshly of each other on all subjects; and this is most inimical to human dignity and self-reliance.
These harsh judgments and degrading criticisms are especially remarkable, wherever, as in Scotland, the doctrine of Original Sin is most
prominently brought forward. Such views, together with the allied
sexual puritanism, are the causes of the marked national shyness, and
fear of the opinions of others, among the Scotch, which are so blighting
to the happiness, especially of young people. We cannot wonder that
where Nature, the all-perfect, is treated with so little reverence in the
person of Man, her living representative, the greatest evils should
result.

Another class of the community, in whom the liberty and dignity of
man receive a vital wound, are the *criminals*. The position of these
unfortunates is full of shame and humiliation. They are viewed with
aversion and contempt, if not with horror, by their fellow-men; their
liberty is taken from them, and they are forced in many cases to perform the most degrading labour, and to observe the most galling rules
of prison discipline. When at liberty, they lead a life of constant fear
and degradation, skulking from the presence of their fellows, hunted
about by the police, the object of general suspicion and dislike. There
cannot be a life more fatal to all sense of dignity and freedom, and
therefore more repugnant to human nature. Few, if any, would adopt
such a life, unless forced into it by the most adverse circumstances.
But in this case, as in that of prostitution, and all other instances of
the degradation of a class, the whole of society must share in it. It
has been truly said, that the liberty of the thief is the bondage of the
honest man; and the more crime there exists in society the more is
the liberty and dignity of each individual curtailed. All of us have to
live a life more or less of fear and watchfulness, as long as crime
exists among us; and every crime which is committed, causes
suffering in the honest part of the community. Moreover where
crime is rife, as it is in all our large towns, every one is more or
less the object of suspicion to his neighbours, and has himself
to entertain the most harassing and degrading suspicions of others.
Besides this, the ignominious and too often barbarous punishments,
and the awful state of degradation of the unhappy criminals, throw a

have little to do? Nursed in poverty, with its endless indignities and temptations; brought up perhaps by criminal parents, who enforce crime as a duty on their child; beaten and abused, what wonder if the unfortunate child of man becomes a wanderer and an outcast, his hand against every man, for everyone's hand is against him? Even amid all this, it is hard to extirpate the inherent human nobility; and in the dreary walls of a prison, beautiful are the gleams of gratitude and attachment, which kindness to these unfortunates so often awakens. "The governor of the prison," says Mr. Hill, "is often the first friend that the prisoners have known in life; the first who has treated them with kindness, given them good advice, and shown an interest in their welfare; and the affection and gratitude, which a benevolent governor excites among them, are most striking." "The first essential," he says, moreover, "in a good governor, and in good subordinate officers, is that they take a warm interest in the prisoners and their amendment, and treat them with kindness; this is more important than even the best devised prison discipline, and without it nothing can be done." These truths have a more general application, for in fact all members of society are the keepers of the criminals; and unless we bear towards them a spirit of brotherly love and reverence, and show a heartfelt desire for their reformation, little can be done with crime. But on the other hand, by carefully tracing all its causes, and making use of every means for its prevention and the reformation of offenders, in the ways which Mr. Hill has so admirably pointed out, we have, as he says, a right to expect, that "in time, crime will become so very rare, as not materially to affect the happiness of society."

I need not here dilate on the indignities and restrictions which man suffers under a system of *political oppression*. These are too well known by all; and in this country, human liberty and dignity are fortunately not so much compromised by this cause. Still, even among us, there is by no means a satisfactory political freedom, and the number of political malcontents is very large. In the first place we have the glaring indignity of a restricted suffrage. The great mass of our people are not even allowed a voice in political matters, and where this is the case, one of the first essentials of political freedom and dignity is wanting. It is impossible to satisfy the sense of justice without *universal suffrage*. Every adult member of the community, who has not broken the laws, should have a voice in framing them. This is the broad natural axiom of political justice, and until this be obtained the sense of political wrong must exist. It is a matter of humiliation for a society, if a large portion of its members be in so degraded and uneducated a state, that they are deemed unworthy of having a voice in the affairs which interest all. The consciousness of the possession of such a voice, like that of property, is a great instrument of moral elevation, and tends to give a man a dignified position in his own and his neighbour's eyes; while the want of such advantages allows him to fall into the lowest depths of degradation. Had there been universal suffrage in this country and in Ireland, the poor

could scarcely have fallen into such an abject state of misery and ꭢring--
ing abasement, as they have done; especially in the latter country
where human dignity is reduced to its lowest stage. The rich would then
have found, that they were dependent in some measure on the voice of
the poor, and would have been forced to pay them more respect, and not
look down on them as utterly beneath their notice, as has so often been
done. All such inequalities loosen the bond, which should unite the
different classes, and operate to the ultimate ruin of both; for the degradation of the poor must sooner or later drag down the rich.

In like manner the existence of an *aristocracy* tends very muc
to lessen the equal and mutual reverence, which each member of the
community should possess. The privileged few who are born to a
title, are constantly prone to regard the rest of society as beneath them,
and to lose sight of the equal dignity which invests all men, as men.
Among the other classes, the aristocracy are either fawned upon and
toadied, in a manner most repugnant to the sense of dignity; or are
envied and hated for the possession of such extraordinary privileges. If
we look moreover to the foundations, on which a permanent aristocracy
is based, we shall see that they consist for the most part in rights
and privileges most destructive to the interests of society. Thus our
aristocracy derive their main support from the laws of *primogeniture
and entail*; without which it would probably be impossible for them to
retain their power, or continue for any length of time in their present
elevated position. If it were not for these laws, their fortunes would
very soon be broken down, and their immense power at the same time
destroyed: so that it may be said, that a hereditary nobility necessitates
for its continued existence in a free country, the laws of primogeniture
and entail. But these laws are most destructive to the interests of society,
and are opposed to all natural feelings of justice. The law of entail has,
together with the Cottier system of land tenure, been one of the chief
causes of the ruin of Ireland; keeping the land constantly in a burdened
state, and preventing its transfer from the social drones, who would do
nothing for it, to the industrious agriculturists, who could have done so
much.

All titles tend to lead astray both their possessors, and the rest of
society; to make men bow down before the shadow and neglect the
substance; to make us forget, that it is man, and the real human
virtues, that should claim our reverence, and not high-sounding names
or accidental distinctions. He who has a greater reverence for a
Queen on the throne, than for the forlorn and ragged sempstress
in a garret, has no true conception of natural human dignity. *Reverence for reverence* should be the principle of each of us: treat me with
respect, and I will so treat you, but do not expect that you, my
friend, are to have all the respect, and I all the contempt. Each man has
an exactly equal natural dignity and title to our reverence. Were t e
poorer classes independent of the rich; were each man able to gain for
himself his livelihood, without thinking of the favour or the custom of
this gentleman or that lord, we should not see that one-sided subservience
and obsequiousness, that flunkeyism, as it has been termed, so degrading

to all human dignity. The working classes at present are bitterly exasperated at this servile position. In London very many among them regard the aristocracy and the richer classes with concealed hatred and embitterment, but, knowing that they are in their power, they dare not disclose those feelings. How long is this miserable state of things to last? It must last till the possession of *general independence* gives all classes the power of asserting their equal title to the reverence of their fellow-creatures. Till then, we shall not see these pernicious class-barriers removed, and the class prejudices put an end to, which are so dangerous to the happiness of all, and to the security of society. Till we have an equal mutual reverence among all classes, it is in vain to hope that the offended sense of justice and dignity will be satisfied. Our nature is not made to exist in such circumstances without disordered and diseased action.

I have thus given a short sketch of the four main influences which impair the dignity, the liberty, and the independence of mankind: and which therefore we should seek to remove by steady and persevering efforts in order to obtain these blessings. These *four great tyrannies* operate in different degrees in different countries. Thus, among ourselves, there is much less political tyranny than upon the Continent; but on the other hand the tyranny of food, love, and religion is in many respects much greater than in many parts of Europe. In neither France nor Germany do we see the abject and squalid poverty, that exists among us, nor are the working classes so enslaved to their toil. In none is the difficulty of gaining a livelihood so great, and the hot-press of competition so exhausting. In neither of these countries again, is the tyranny of love or religion nearly so oppressive as with us; and from these causes there is perhaps a larger sum of happiness and real freedom in them than in England, notwithstanding their unfortunate political subjection. It is a great mistake to suppose, that the latter comprises the whole question of liberty. As has been shown, there are many other matters, which affect just as vitally the freedom of each individual: and from which all the inherent nobility and independence of the British character have not been able to defend us. Foreigners, who know nothing of England but by hearsay, come to us with the most glowing ideal of British liberty, but by living among us they generally arrive at a totally different conclusion; and exclaim against the want of social and religious freedom, the stiffness and exclusiveness of our richer classes, and the fearful degradation of our poor.

It matters little in reality whether a man be enslaved by a tyrannical government, or by the necessities of his life. In fact the latter, as for instance the necessity of gaining a livelihood, and of procuring the sexual necessaries of health and happiness, are infinitely more important causes of bondage and degradation, than perhaps any possible form of government; much more than the government of this country, which in many respects is so admirable. The chief difference is, that men are more embittered by the evils which they obviously suffer at the hands of other men, than by those which appear to come from necessity. But this difference is more apparent than real, for, as has been shown in a former essay, the difficulties of obtaining food and love, which are by far the most important evils in society, arise from the monopoly of love and an undue procreation by a limited number, who thus inevitably subject their fellow-beings to these fearful wants; and are really, although unconsciously, the cause of their sufferings, as truly as the political oppressor. It is not necessity, but the imprudence of married people, which forces the rest of mankind to a life of toil and sexual privation.

It has been beautifully said, "Love thy neighbour as thyself," but the precept, "*Reverence thy neighbour as thyself*," is no less true, and is even more needed among us. We all reverence ourselves; a man never entirely loses his self-reverence. Upon his own actions he uniformly puts the best construction; and he does this from the beautiful natural instinct, which teaches him that he is innately noble and good. But in our judgment of our neighbours we act very differently; we are ready on the most trivial pretexts to adopt contemptuous views of them, to misconstrue their actions, to regard them with aversion or disgust. If we attended to this great principle of morality, "Reverence thy neighbour as thyself," should we judge them so very differently from ourselves?

Reverence is even more needed among us than love, for it has been far more neglected. The doctrines of universal love have been preached for ages by the Christian moralists, while those of reverence for *man* have been comparatively disregarded. Reverence implies belief that a man is essentially good; and therefore is not compatible with the doctrines of original sin or eternal punishment. Without reverence, love can do little, and indeed never can continue long. The love mingled with pity, with which it is the delight of the Christian moralist to regard mankind, the fallen race as he terms us, can do at present but very little for man, for it debases while it soothes. Pity is no natural sphere for so majestic a being as man, and his powerful nature instinctively recoils from it. It is not pity, however loving, that our paupers, our criminals, and, more than all our prostitutes, require; it is *reverence*, the reverence that elevates and infuses self-respect into the hearts of those neglected unfortunates, which alone can become the basis of a real reformation.

And reverence is the only true feeling, with which one can regard so wondrous a being as man, whatever state of accidental degradation he may have fallen into. Can we understand a man, that we despise him? In all cases the invariable principle of good still rules his life; and this all-perfect natural force demands our profoundest admiration. It is to these unfortunates too, that the earning heart of the philanthropist instinctively turns to pay its homage. Where should we rather bestow our reverence, than there where it is most needed? While others bow before the shrine of riches, rank, and virtue, Oh, let the heart which truly loves mankind, seek out the despised inmates of the workhouse, the gaol, and the brothel, where his brotherly love and reverence can do so much more for the elevation of his fellow-creatures! Let him prostrate himself before the eclipsed majesty of these ill-fated sons and daughters of man; and register an inward vow, never to join in the general contempt, nor to desert them, till they have been raised from their present abject condition, and till there is no member of human society in the awful position of an outcast from its bosom.

No man should ever allow himself to despise another. It is as foolish as unfeeling; for it assumes that we may have an elevation over a fellow-creature, which no man can possess. There is no part of nature, which is so unutterably above our comprehension as a human being; and therefore nothing, where all is perfection, which we can so little pretend to 'ook down upon. He who despises another, degrades himself thereby, for the irreverence inevitably recoils on our common humanity. It is our duty to reverence all, for by reverencing we elevate and benefit them; and it is our duty to do so, as far as lies in our power. A mutual reverence is the basis of politeness, dignity, and good-will throughout society, and is the bond of the social virtues. The reverence moreover should be paid to man as man, and not veer like the wind from every slight difference of fortune, talent, virtue, rank, or other accidental advantage. At present every little difference in these circumstances; in party feeling, in religious belief, in moral conduct, in tastes or pleasures, in class, in manners or education; is held sufficient to justify the profoundest contempt between man and man. The spiritualist looks down on the sensualist, and the latter returns the compliment; the noble despises the plebeian, and the intelligent radical despises the brainless patrician; the clever man sneers at the stupid one, and the saint draws back from the sinner; beauty looks down upon ugliness, which fortifies itself in a contempt for a fair exterior with a shallow mind. In this way there is scarcely one among us, who has not his pet objects of contempt among his fellow-men, thinking to elevate himself at the expense of his neighbour's degradation; and who is not himself the object of the contempt of some other. Alas! is human life made to be taken up by such unworthy feelings as these? Life is difficult enough for the most of us in any case, with all the evils, social, moral, and physical, which each has to contend with; and to many it becomes hopeless indeed, when we have also to struggle with the contempt and unkindness of our fellows. Besides, all such errors of feeling and judgment invariably recoil on our own head. No man is happy, as long as he consents to despise any human being. Nature will not permit such a monstrous injustice; and torments, by her own inimitable retributive evils, all who are guilty of such errors. For every irreverence shewn to any one of her children, the rest have invariably to pay the exact penalty; and the Nemesis, which slumbers not nor sleeps, pursues our race, till every indignity, every suffering inflicted on any individual, has been exactly avenged.

A reverence which depends on accidents, is unworthy of our attention. Which of us can tell to what lot in life he might have been born, or reduced by circumstances? Whether he should inherit a noble fortune, power, talents, virtues; or be born in a garret, amid rags and wretchedness, constitutionally prone to disease and crime, from being ill-suited to contend with surrounding circumstances? As long as reverence is to be given merely to fortune's favourites, to the rich, the powerful, the virtuous, the intellectual, what is it worth? who can tell that he will possess it? Alas! those who are born without these advantages, need our reverence, love, and assistance, most of all; so that we may in part make up to them for the niggardliness of fortune. And, after all, to him who looks beneath the surface, the merit of all men is, in one respect, equal; for all strive towards good in a measure exactly proportional to their natural powers, and to the suitability of their external circumstances. While this accidental reverence is the rule of our actions, no man is safe, no man can depend upon his fellows ; do what we may, we are constantly exposed during life to the contempt of others, which must always degrade us. As the true moral principle is not, "love this man and hate that one," so it is not, "reverence this one, and dispise the other," "but have an equal reverence for all," no matter what they are. While the philosophic mind should ever keep in view this great principle, so should we strive in every way to make it generally felt throughout society, by removing as far as possible those obstacles, which oppose the dignity, the freedom, and the independence of mankind ; for it is upon the universal possession of these great advantages alone, that a state of satisfactory mutual reverence can be based. By the want of them, by having to contend with a lot of dependence, slavery, and indignity, however imposed, a man's self-reverence is impaired, together with his reverence for others. Until the destructive action of the principle of population be obviated by the general adoption of preventive intercourse, it is a mere dream to talk of human liberty. It is not till every adult member of society shall possess an independent life: till every man and woman has a due share of sexual love; till all are able to assert openly their conscientious beliefs, without incurring the contempt or hatred of their neighbours; till secrecy and duplicity have become rare, and men are able to speak freely their inner thoughts, and make their outer life harmonise with the inner; it is not till then, that we shall see a true measure of dignity, liberty, and independence existing among us, and that Britain will truly deserve the name of a *free* country.

NATURAL RELIGION

In the present century there is being gradually accomplished the greatest revolution, which has ever taken place, or which perhaps ever will take place, in human Belief. This great change is, the progress from a Supernatural to a Natural Religion. From the beginning of human existence on this earth up to the present time, the idea of the supernatural has accompanied man in all countries and in all circumstances. He has chosen as the chief object of his reverence and worship, powers and virtues external to nature, and, as he imagined, superior. He has formed to himself conceptions of Beings, to whom those agencies which he saw at work in himself and in the world around him, were subservient; from whom they took their origin and the laws of their action, and from whom they were liable to constant interference.

This belief in the supernatural has existed in many different phases in different nations, and in the course of time, has been gradually changed from its original gross form to the more refined and exalted one, in which it at present exists among ourselves. At first man, being unable to account for any of the phenomena he saw around him, attributed everything to a supernatural cause. Thus he made a God the immediate cause of the storm and the calm, of the growth of the plant and animal, of human happiness and misery, and the current of human events. In short, whether he imagined a single supernatural being, or a plurality of them, he supposed this being to be constantly interfering with the course of things, and the mightiest and most active power in the universe.

But by little and little through the ages, science has shown us that all these phenomena, which we see around us, take place from *natural causes*; and that if we search narrowly there is never any other power than nature at work in all actions, no matter how mysterious they seem to us. In this way the doctrine of immediate supernatural interference has gradually yielded to the comparatively truer one of secondary causes, in which many enlightened minds now believe. In this form of belief, the idea of a supernatural being is still retained ; but instead of making him the active agent in all the phenomena of nature, he is believed to have only at first formed nature, and imposed upon her laws, according to which she could of herself do everything afterwards. This is very generally the belief of men, who, while, from their knowledge of physical science, they see that the natural laws are never departed from, that no event ever occurs except according to such laws, and that there is never the slightest sign of any interference with the course of nature, wish to reconcile this absence of all appearance of the supernatural, with the ordinary mode of religious belief.

But the ordinary form of belief admits very much more of supernatural agency than this. It asserts not only that all the universe, animate and inanimate, has been originally created by a supernatural being, but that this being constantly interferes in the affairs of man even in the present day. Thus it is currently believed by the Christians, that God gives to us health or disease, that he is the source of our happiness and misery. It is believed that his 'spirit operates upon our minds, so as either to convert us to what is termed a holy state of mind, or to harden us to unbelief. If we analyse carefully the Christian doctrines, we shall find that gradually, step by step, the idea of divine interference in the course of nature has been forced to yield to that of natural causation, throughout almost the whole domain of Physics. In Geology, Astronomy, Chemistry, Natural Philosophy; and in the natural sciences, Botany, Zoology, &c, no educated man ever thinks of introducing the idea of *supernatural interference* to account for any of the phenomena witnessed. Even to minds unversed in science, the idea that a chemical change, the diurnal revolution of the earth, or the rising of the sap in a tree, is produced immediately by supernatural interference, would scarcely for a moment occur. It has not been without a hard struggle, that supernaturalism has yielded its cherished empire over these sciences : inch by inch the ground was disputed, and many an astronomer or geologist has been laid under the ban of the supernaturalists, for what they conceived to be his impious theory of natural causation, before the truth was clearly established.

It is chiefly in the world of *mind*, that the immediate interference of deity is still insisted on. Men at present scarcely believe, that God acts on the material world to produce changes; that he turns aside the natural course of a stream for instance, or alters the natural operation of chemical affinities, for these things are too palpably untrue, and we see that this is never done; but they believe that he produces changes in the mind, that his spirit works upon mind, and produces joy or sorrow, belief or unbelief.

It cannot be said however, that the belief that even *material* phenomena are sometimes owing to immediate supernatural interference, is altogether extinct. It has been forced to yield in all the natural phenomena, which are now best understood, and whose invariable laws and definite chain of causation have been tolerably made out. But in those provinces of science where the chain of causation is not so well understood, the belief that supernatural agency sometimes operates, still exists. For instance, many people believe that the weather and the seasons are liable to supernatural interference. A mysterious occurrence also, such as the potato failure, whose natural cause has not been discovered, is ascribed to supernatural agency. The diseases to which our bodies are liable. especially such as are of a particularly terrible and mysterious nature, as the Cholera, are very frequently set down as due to supernatural interference. Accordingly prayers are offered to the Deity to send rainy or dry weather, to avert the potato disease, and to restore a sick man to health. Those who put up such prayers, do not consider, that it would be exactly as reasonable to implore Deity to build a city, or to solve for them a mathematical problem. Such prayers are founded on the radically false supposition, that any supernatural interference ever takes place in the course of Nature; that her laws are being constantly broken, and then patched-up again, by a supernatural hand. The laws that influence the weather and the seasons, that rule over the health of the potato and of the human body, are equally invariable and equally incapable of being interfered with, as those of mathematics, or of house-building. If we supplicate Deity to alter the course of nature in one thing, why should we not in another? Every man would feel the utter fruitlessness of asking for Divine interference to build a house for him, and would deem such a petition childish and irrational; but the exactly equal fruitlessness of a prayer for such interference in the natural operations of the frame and turns of the seasons, is not considered.

But the *laws of mind* are not one whit less definite and invariable than those of matter. The more attentively we examine mental phenomena in ourselves and others, the more clearly do we perceive, that they, just as material phenomena, are absolutely and entirely dependent on natural causation, invariably moving according to natural laws, and never in any case subject to the shadow of supernatural interference. Mental and moral science have been completely blighted by the neglect of this great truth; and hence, while the physical sciences have of late made such immense progress, the mental ones have remained spell-bound. Physiology, the science of the actions of the living body, was long retarded in a similar way by the dogmatic belief in a Vital Essence; some vague supernatural force, which was supposed to rule over the functions of the body, and to be totally beyond our comprehension. Hence every vital action was ascribed to this vital essence, and it was thought impious to search further for its cause. But we now know that all the vital actions take place according to definite laws, which are just as truly natural as the physical and just as comprehensible by us, although they are more complicated. In the same way moral and intellectual science are still retarded by the belief, that mind is an essence of a peculiar incomprehensible nature, subject to constant supernatural interference; and that it is not governed by laws just as fixed and definite, and just as truly fitted for our investigation and comprehension, as those of the rest of the universe. But it is a certain truth, that the workings of the mind are just as absolutely removed from all supernatural, from all spiritual interference, as those of matter. Its laws are never broken. There is not a thought, not an emotion within us, that does not depend entirely on natural causes, and may not be traced entirely to them. The laws of the emotions and of the thoughts, the conditions on which happiness or sorrow, virtue or vice, depend, are as certain and invariable as those of Chemistry; and are just as capable of being discovered and comprehended by us, although from the great complexity of mental phenomena, they are more difficult to determine. Still we have this advantage in investigating the laws of the mind, that they operate within ourselves, and thus are brought more thoroughly within the sphere of our consciousness.

The belief in the subjection of the mind to supernatural interference, and the connection of the soul with supernatural essences, has completely paralysed all true moral science, and has closed the door upon that path of investigation of mental processes, which could alone lead to any valuable result. Hence we have at present no natural moral science. The laws of the health of mind, on which its happiness and its virtue depend, exactly as those of the body upon its laws, have not been made out, or arranged in any scientific form. The effect of this is exactly as if the laws of the body had not been investigated. Wherever the laws of health, whether of body or mind, are not understood, or are disobeyed, misery is certain to result; and every error we make in endeavouring to comprehend the natural moral laws, which preside over our virtue and happiness, has to be atoned for by our sorrow and degradation.

The science of mental health may be said to be still quite rudimentary. Its very first fundamental axioms are not admitted, but all is involved in a paradoxical, mystic, supernatural obscurity. Thus, as has been shown in a former essay, the two great natural guides to the understanding of mental health and disease are disregarded, namely, Joy and Sorrow, which correspond to the feelings of Pain and Pleasure in the body: and hence there is the greatest confusion and misconception, as to what constitutes a really healthy or virtuous state of mind. Our common standards of moral excellence are not healthy, and therefore cannot be virtuous, or suitable objects for our aims. Many of the characters most admired by the christian moralist are in reality full of moral disease. From the want of a true natural standard by which to judge of mental health and disease, we fall into constant errors in the conduct of our own mind, and in the judgment we pass on others. We indulge excessively in modes of feeling and thought, which we imagine to be good but which in reality are very pernicious; and hence we become miserable, perhaps go mad, quite unconscious that the reason of our unhappiness lies in our infringement of the laws of mental health. Little as the laws of physical health are generally understood, those of mental health are almost less so.

It is a certain truth, that all unhappiness arising from mental causes, invariably results from our disobedience to the laws of moral health; that all insanity results in like manner from a greater degree of such disobedience; and that the opposite states of joy, health, and strength of mind can only arise from our obedience to these laws. All virtue arises from our observance of the natural conditions which lead to it, and all vice from their neglect. A virtuous state of mind comes invariably from natural causes: and to supplicate supernatural interference or assistance to make us virtuous, is just as unreasonable as to ask for bodily strength or health, or to entreat Deity to build a house for us. Yet prayers are constantly put up to the Deity to give us a contrite heart, or a loving and pious spirit, all of which are as fundamentally erroneous, and as full of danger to the suppliant, as the belief that supernatural interference will restore a sick man to health.

There is nothing more pernicious, than the belief that anything is to be obtained by supernatural means, either in the mind or in the body. It prevents us from seeing clearly the only means which can possibly be availing, namely, the natural ones; and paralyses our efforts, by leading us to depend on a succour which never possibly can reach us, and never has reached any human being, and thus to neglect the natural means, which we might by diligent search attain to. In the treatment of bodily disease also, it was common in former times to use prayers and religious rites, instead of the natural means; but fortunately for mankind these have now all but disappeared from among us, and prayers for the restoration of the sick by an interruption to the natural laws, are now only used as a form, which few men put any faith in. Who, when he sees a man dying of cancer or consumption, ever lets the idea of supernatural interference enter into his expectation of the inevitable issue?

But in the mind these supernatural agencies are still constantly resorted to. If a man become unhappy in mind, if his temper be spoiled, in other words if his mind become diseased in any way, instead of investigating narrowly, just as in the case of bodily disease, the natural causes which have led to this unhappiness, and removing them by substituting the natural conditions of mental health; the supernatural moralist, who knows but of one cause of moral disease, namely original sin, and but one cure, namely, spiritual conversion, prays over the sufferer, that a healthy state of mind be given him by supernatural interference, and that thus, he may be restored to happiness and to virtue. Our body, if diseased, is treated naturally; our mind supernaturally.

But nature knows of no such supernatural means; in her infinite variety, there is no such thing as one cause or one cure of disease. Every faculty of the mind has its own peculiar laws of health and happiness, just as every organ of the body; and this method of treating all mental diseases by one supernatural panacea, leads to nothing but accumulated error, confusion, and misery. It is partly owing to this unnatural moral treatment, (of course acting, like all other evils at present, merely as a subordinate to the law of population, which *necessitates* an immense amount of misery in some shape or other), that there is so much unhappiness in this country, and that insanity is so common, and is, indeed, even on the increase. In fact the spiritual panacea itself, that mental state which is considered to be the highest form of human virtue, is most assuredly, when analysed by the natural tests of moral health, quite the reverse of a healthy or a virtuous moral state; so much so, that the moral physician must regard the religious spiritualism, with its asceticism, and proneness to gloomy and serious views, which is so widely prevalent in our country, as one of the most fatal forms of moral disease now existing among us.

We cannot expect a state of satisfactory virtue or happiness among mankind, as long as the present supernatural views of mind exist; as long as all conditions of happiness and unhappiness, all virtues and vices, sanities and incipient insanities, are treated alike; while a moral panacea

taken from authority is applied to all, and the great book of Nature with
its infinite variety, and beautiful and unerring chain of natural causation,
is unstudied. Look at the fearful amount of misery and crime which
exists among us!   Our society in many of its grades is a moral pest-
house, which men are afraid even to look at.   An immense deal of this
misery is directly owing to our ignorance of the natural laws of happiness
and virtue, and to the constant substitution of the supernatural for the
natural efforts to remedy the evils.   What avail the prayers that God
will take pity on the poor, will remove poverty, or prevent drunkenness and
prostitution?   All the prayers under heaven will not remove one jot nor
one tittle of this misery or this vice; it is only by diligently studying the
natural causes which have led to it, and removing them, while we substitute the natural conditions of happiness, that so blessed a result is
conceivable.   How much time has been wasted, how much human agony
and degradation has been allowed to continue, through persistence in
these delusive means!

The idea of the supernatural has ever acted to paralyse the exertions of
men in the removal of miseries.   Poverty has been thought to be a sort
of necessary evil, sent upon mankind, possibly as a punishment for
human pride or sin.   Disease was for ages viewed in the same erroneous
light, till advancing medical science showed it to be entirely dependent on
infringement of the physical laws. "God has so willed it," or "the
finger of God is upon them," has been a constant phrase in the mouth
of those, whose thoughts ever run upon supernatural interference; and
in this way are the supernatural moralists wont to depreciate schemes
for greatly elevating and ameliorating the condition of mankind. "These
cannot succeed," they say, "for the main cause of poverty, and of all
other social evils is the natural inborn human depravity.'   Thus they
are contented to pray for supernatural interference to change men's minds,
and take comparatively little interest in the hopes or schemes of the
natural investigator.   But he, though full of sorrow at the present state
of human degradation, is no less full of hope, for he cannot forget the
great 'truth, that all these miseries arise from natural causes, from
natural laws which have been broken; that therefore there is no supernatural bar to their removal: and that by studying reverentially the
various causes of happiness and misery, vice and virtue, poverty and
crime, as we see them exemplified in the infinite variety of human lives
around us, we will in time be able to remove these evils, at least in a
great degree.   All of us will yet recognise the true comparative advantages
of these two different modes of religious belief, and religious effort.

Thus the more insight we obtain into the phenomena of the whole
universe, into those of mind as well as of matter, the more does it
become assured to us, that every effect is owing to natural causes; and
that fixed and invariable natural laws prevail everywhere, which are
never in any instance departed from.   There is never either in mind or
matter the shadow of a sign of supernatural interference. This great
fundamental truth lies at the bottom of all the sciences, and must before
long be universally conceded: in the mental and moral, as well as the
physical sciences.   When it is clearly understood, all of us will see the

utter fruitlessness of ever looking beyond nature for the causes of good or evil fortune, or of any event which takes place in the physical or moral world ; and the utter futility of any request for a supernatural interruption to these wondrous laws, in whose admirable precision and invariability their chief beauty, and our own safety, consist. Before long, in mind, as well as in physics, the doctrine of immediate interference must be totally abandoned ; and we must recognise that Deity, if existing, at least never in any one instance interferes in the natural course of events. In this way the supernatural moralist must inevitably soon be compelled to adopt at most the doctrine of *secondary causes*, in mind as well as in matter.

Let us now examine this doctrine of Secondary Causes. In it the idea of a supreme supernatural being is still preserved, and it is believed that this being at first originated the material universe, and impressed upon matter its laws, which should never afterwards be interrupted, except in the creation of the different species of animals and vegetables : which, it is held, nature unaided could not have produced. The recorded supernatural interferences of the Biblical narrative are by some included in the primary laws laid down for matter, special provision having been then made for these miraculous occurrences. Thus, according to the doctrine of secondary causes, supernatural agency has operated on the universe only at two epochs ; namely at its first origin, and again at the creation of the different races of living organisms. The laws once made, according to this doctrine, have never been interfered with, and the agency of the supernatural is never now apparent in the world ; and we are only to infer that it exists as a sustaining or supporting force.

This doctrine is certainly greatly preferable to that of direct supernatural interference. It removes to a much greater distance the disturbing idea of such interferences, veiling all direct operations of the first cause in the primeval origin of things ; and leaves it to mankind to investigate those laws, which have been primarily laid down, and to act according to them. It leaves them no hope of any supernatural aid ; nor does it countenance the idea, that it is the duty or the interest of man to seek such aid, instead of trusting entirely to natural means. The doctrine of secondary causes in physical phenomena is now the prevailing one among men of science, who adopt Christian beliefs , and it is compatible with a very considerable freedom of research into nature. Would that an equal degree of freedom, and an equally advanced mode of belief had prevailed in moral science ! But the doctrine of immediate spiritual interference is so ingrained in the moral world, the whole history of Christianity is so inseparably connected with this, that such a belief as that of secondary causes, could find no place in it.

But even the doctrine of secondary causes is very far from being a true or a satisfactory one. How are we warranted in saying that a supernatural power sustains the operations of Nature, or even exists at all, if we never in any case see the slightest sign of its presence or its action ? If there is never the slightest sign, in any of the operations of mind or matter, of a force different from the natural forces, how can we say that such a force exists ? The phrase that the universe is *sustained* by supernatural power, although such power never interferes in the minutest sensible degree with the natural phenomena, is quite destitute of meaning. To sustain anything requires the exercise of an active extraneous force, and this force, it is allowed, we never have the slightest sensible sign of. When we see Oxygen and Hydrogen unite to form water, or observe that certain mental emotions excite within us the feelings of joy, we say that such effects are produced by the natural properties in the chemical bodies or the mental states. These natural properties or forces are sufficient in themselves to produce the result: and it is a totally gratuitous assumption, that there is any other force, any supernatural agency, acting beneath, which enables them to produce the effect. It is against all true philosophy to imagine such an additional force, of which there is not the slightest sign in the phenomena before us.

But besides this negative sustaining force, the doctrine of Secondary Causes asserts that supernatural agency was actively employed in the *creation* of the vegetable and animal kingdom. Here it acted not merely as a sustaining force to laws already invariably fixed, but actively interfered, giving to matter new impulses, and new forms, which, unaided, it could never have assumed. Men saw that the doctrine of supernatural interference could not now be received, as it once was, in the phenomena going on around us at present. No one now imagines that the developement and growth even of the highest animal, that the evolution even of our most complex organs, takes place by immediate supernatural causation. However mysterious a process may be, and however little we may yet understand it, we know with absolute certainty, that all is done by the workings of the natural forces, never interfered with, never assisted; and no physiologist would ever now think for a moment, of accounting for any vital action, by any other than natural causes. The man who would attribute the developement of an organ, which we could not yet understand, to immediate supernatural agency, would be thought almost insane.

But what right have we to assert that such supernatural agency was used in the creation of living organisms, any more than in the developement and preservation of those at present existing? The only reason that this is done, is because it is not yet understood, how such wonderful organisms could first arise by natural forces. But they have little faith in Nature, who thus presume to set bounds to her powers. What can Nature not do? To him who has studied the developement and growth of a living organism; who has reflected on the phenomena, wondrous and transcendant beyond all conception, which are there witnessed; any reasoning based on an arbitrary limitation of the powers of Nature is utterly valueless. The human being originates in a single cell, so small that it cannot be seen by the naked eye. In this cell our infant powers of mind and body lie first cradled, and by these powers, of which no one attempts to deny the truly natural character, we develope ourselves ; we build up our body to its perfection of physical organisation, and we build up no less our mind, by which we obtain so boundless an insight into every part of the universe. In this way we in fact *create ourselves;* for it is a radically false conception that any external supernatural force aids one tittle in our developement. He who reflects on the concentration of powers in this little primary cell, and on this display of natural forces, including the evolution of mind equally with that of body—for the mind is just as certainly built up by natural forces as the body—will be too much lost in wonder at their infinity, to venture to imagine that he knows their limits. What can be more wonderful or more inscrutable than these phenomena? How could we ever have imagined that such powers resided in us; in us as a part of Nature? Why should we believe that nature who can do this unaided, could not also unaided give origin to the various forms of vegetable and animal life at the beginning? She, the only power that we ever see at work, our mother, our preserver, our own innermost essence; she, who has powers and infinite sublimity, which no tongue can utter, and no mind conceive; in what respect has she ever failed to satisfy our most boundless yearnings for the infinite, that we should dishonour her thus, and seek to substitute another power for her too feeble energies?

The more we reflect, the more we study the developement and succession of animated beings, the more assured will become our conviction, that all those transcendant phenomena, however incomprehensible by us at present, are owing entirely and absolutely to the natural forces; and that there has been as little supernatural interference in the *origin of Life*, as we now see in its *continuance*. Every thing leads us to this conclusion. We see in the history of the developement of living beings, plants and animals, the same wondrous marks of constant adherence to a fixed and definite plan, of the absolute obedience to invariable and definite laws, which we find everywhere else in nature. Several of these laws of organic structure have already been made out; such as that of the invariable developement of the more special from the more general, the unity of type and of function, &c.: and it is to such researches as these, and not to that mis-named piety, which contents itself with vague wonder over a first cause, that we are to look for a true and elevating conception of the wondrous origin of Life. And yet it is deemed almost a sacrilege, to attempt to divest the origin of life of its supernatural character, and reduce it, as has been done with Astronomy, Geology, Vital Force, &c., to a natural and conceivable form. Such an attempt on the contrary is most admirable; and the author of the "Vestiges of the Natural History of Creation" deserves our warm gratitude for his endeavour, however imperfect all such endeavours must yet be, to show how Life could possibly have originated, and gradually ascended through the scale of being, without supernatural interference. We may be perfectly certain that it *did* do so, although it may take centuries of the most patient research to tell us *how*. The idea of supernatural interference paralyses all science; unless we have natural phenomena to analyse, all our reasonings are a vanity and a delusion: and the preconceived belief in such interference has ever acted to satisfy the minds of men with an explanation which is no explanation, and to oppose the progress of earnest and devout enquiry.

How did we come here? What is the nature and purpose of our being? What is Life, what Death? Momentous questions, which it is as vain to attempt to satisfy by the routine answers of supernaturalism, as to arrest the course of the spheres. The general answer to the question of the Origin of Life, is, "we were created by supernatural interference. An arbitrary will, by an interruption to the Laws of Nature, caused us to come into existence, and to assume this form for certain purposes." The problem of Life were indeed a hopeless one, if such were the case. But the natural answer to these questions is very different. "We came into being according to fixed and definite laws, as truly natural and independent in their actions, as those which make the two elements unite to form water. We exist, because our existence was a necessary result of the progressive tendency of Nature; there is nothing arbitrary, nothing supernatural, in our life. We are not removed by any such impassable gulph from the rest of the inanimate universe; all beings and all things are bound together in one chain of invariable natural causation, of which we learn the links one by one with advancing knowledge. We do not indeed see all these links, nor can we yet conceive how it was possible for the natural forces to give origin to life; but everything we observe around us, all our progress in knowledge, clears up more and more of this mystery, and we live in the earnest hope and belief, that the clue will yet be found to the labyrinth; that some one will yet be able to unite together the broken links of the chain of life, and to show the natural connection which exists between all living beings." That there are numberless indications of such a connection, is undoubted; the unity of type between the organs of different animals; the resemblance of the embryos of the higher animals to permanent forms in the scale below them; the wonderful manner in which the different sub-kingdoms of animals and plants are connected together by their lowest forms, which are evidently of a transitional character, passing over from one group into another; all these wondrous and interesting indications are the keys given us by Nature, to solve the problem of Life; and we may feel certain that such keys will not be given in vain. The deeper insight a man has into these phenomena, the stronger grows his conviction, that a natural chain binds all together; and Cuvier asked "why should not organic life some day have its Newton?" This at least is absolutely certain, that he who attributes them to supernatural interference, does nothing on earth to help us in the matter. At what exact point was supernatural interference used? to what extent did it derange the natural forces? Unless he can also say this, he in fact says nothing. Men like Owen, Oken, Goethe, Cuvier, are the Galileos of the science of organic life; and the results of their discoveries will as irresistibly banish the idea of supernatural interference from that field of knowledge, as did those of Galileo in the case of the movements of the spheres. All of us will yet feel to whom our thanks are due, and what inquirers have pursued the true path to a nobler religious conception of the mystery of our Life.

Thus it must ultimately be conceded, although it may take centuries before we can conceive how it could take place, that the Origin and Evolution of Life are as absolutely independent of supernatural interference, as we now-a-days see its continuance to be. It is true that we have no parallel at present to any such phenomena as the Origin of Life; that all living beings spring from similar parents, and from such alone ; and this it is, that makes the problem so excessively difficult, and forms at present an absolute bar to our imagination. But still less have we any parallel to anything approaching to supernatural interference; of that we have not the shadow of a sign in the present day; and were it not for recorded examples of such interference, which are innumerable among all nations in their infancy, we would never even think of resorting to such an explanation. The question is just this; whether is it more probable that supernatural agency has been used, a thing which we have found in every other department of science to be an absolute error, full of the most pernicious consequences to human progress ; or that, in this case, as in myriads of others, too low and degrading an estimate has been taken of the powers of Nature, and we have arrogantly presumed to settle the limits of her actions ? We cannot forsooth understand how unaided Nature could give origin to life; and therefore we take it upon ourselves dogmatically to assert that she could not. What do we know of what she can, and what she cannot do? At the very least any impartial mind would confess his own ignorance on this, as yet inscrutable, subject; and reverentially enquire how much this almighty Nature is capable of effecting, before he comes to so rash a conclusion. Of what value on so difficult a question are the judgments of those, who know so little of truth, that they do not see the invariability of the law that operate around us at present? Who do not perceive that the laws of the seasons, of health and disease, of the body and the mind, are exactly as fixed as those of Chemistry? Who would desire a supernatural interposition to send fine weather, and yet see the folly of imploring such aid to build a house or to cleanse a city ? And yet these errors are looked upon as signs of a religious mind, and any one who would earnestly seek to show how mistaken and dangerous they are, is treated as a enemy to his race. Oh mother Nature, thou knowest a very different religion! thou who invitest all enquiry and stiflest none ; whose great book is ever open to all our race alike, in all countries and in all times ; in whose mighty bosom all thy children are impartially embraced, portions of thee, and sharing in thy infinite sublimity ; who workest ever onwards, evolving in thy course endless worlds and forms of being, all bound together in thy own perfect fashion, the subject for the research and adoration of all ages.

From the conviction that 'all the phenomena we see around us at present, are of an invariably natural character, to the conviction that the Origin of Life, however incomprehensible it still is to us, was also entirely natural, is but a step; and it is but one step further, to exclude entirely the idea of supernatural interference in the primeval *Origin of Matter*. It is indeed not so difficult to understand the infinity of matter as the natural origin of life. We see that matter exists at present perfectly independently ; it has its own invariable laws of action and of being, and when we seek further, we find that it is absolutely indestructible ; that, so far as we can see, it is infinite. And if we follow, here as elsewhere, the only true guiding principle of inquiry, namely, *to reason from what we see to what we do not see*, we must conclude that matter is infinite; that every particle we see around us has existed and will exist through all eternity. What conceivable reason, except blind authority, have we for any other conclusion? On the other hand, the idea that mind created matter is a totally baseless hypothesis, not founded on a shadow of reason. There is not the slightest analogy in its favour, and it was merely conceived, when human reason was in its infancy; when the connection between the brain and the mind was not known; and when every new form given by the hand of man to matter was vaguely termed a creation. We now know, that such a thing as creation never takes place at present; that no new element is ever introduced by extraneous power, nor do the laws of one part of the universe ever bend or alter one iota, in obedience to any other part.

Why do we say that mind is more infinite, more noble, or more powerful, than matter? that it can create matter, give it laws and bend it to its purpose? Alas! our race has paid, and still pays, but too dearly, for this enormous injustice to the one great part of our being. How is it one whit more conceivable that mind should be infinite, than that matter should be so? Nay, it is rather infinitely less conceivable; and while we can give no possible reason for matter not being infinite, but are forced to come to that conclusion if we attend to nature; we can on the other hand find no possible reason in nature why mind should be infinite, but are forced by the study of nature to the conclusion that it is not so. Mind is a living essence, and all life is, from the very first conditions of its existence, subject to change, and therefore to *death*. Mind is transient, being absolutely inseparable from transient forms of matter; and is not a force alien from the rest of Nature, but an entirely natural one, inseparably linked with the rest in mutual interdependence.

He who has studied the progress of Physiology, cannot but be struck by the numerous instances in which phenomena in the living body, which used to be considered as purely *vital*, and therefore of a kind totally removed from physical analogy, and from our comprehension, have of late years been successively shown to be purely *physical*. Thus the process of Digestion was long thought to be strictly vital, whereas now it is universally allowed to be entirely physical, taking place according to the physical laws of Chemistry, heat, &c.; insomuch that the food, when introduced into the stomach, must still be regarded as essentially *external* to the body, that is, not yet forming a part of the tissues. In like manner the essential part of Respiration, namely the taking in of Oxygen and the giving out of Carbonic acid, is regulated by the entirely physical laws of the diffusion of gases, &c. Nutrition, also, or the absorption of the food by the blood-vessels and lacteals, has been shown to depend chiefly on the physical laws of endosmosis and exosmosis. Animal Heat is produced by the chemical union of Oxygen and Carbon throughout the frame, and is as entirely a physical process, as the burning of the fire in the grate. Many more instances could be given, but these are sufficient to show the great and significant fact, that the progress of Physiology is tending in every direction to banish the old vague idea of an unintelligible vital force, from the bodily economy, and to substitute intelligible physical laws. In fact the very phrase " Vital force " is now acknowledged to be merely provisional, to mean nothing, except that we have not yet arrived at an explanation of the fact, regarding which it is used. Gradually it is becoming apparent in num- berless instances, that the so-called vital forces are merely *physical ones in disguise;* and this gives us another key to the great problem, the con- nection of the organic with the inorganic world, and origin of life. From what has been already done in this direction, and from what we may infer from reflection, it appears extremely probable, that all vital pheno- mena are really physical; that they are really produced by physical forces, acting in certain new conditions. He who feels convinced of the natural origin of life, would be led to this conclusion by *a priori* reasons. If life originated entirely by means of the natural physical forces, as it most indubitably did, all the vital forces must have sprung out of the physical ones; and must in fact be an evolution of properties and forces always existing in matter, but lying dormant, until called forth by suitable circumstances.

It is absolutely certain that there is not a movement of a muscle in our frame, not a thought or feeling in our mind, which is not accom- panied and inseparably connected with chemical, mechanical, and other physical changes. Now what is the connection between this chemical and mechanical change on the one hand, and thought and feeling on the other? It is easy to brand all investigations into the connection of mind and matter, such as those of Leibig and others, with the stigma of materialism, and to rest contented with an explanation which is none; but such a course leads just to nothing, like the old doctrine of vital essence. Do we consider it a degradation for mind, to link and compare it with matter? Do we think that there is anything one jot more ele- vated, more transcendantly wonderful, in a mental phenomenon, that in the extraordinary and infinitely subtilised chemical change that accom- panies it? Here, as in all other speculations, there has been a constant endeavour to vilify matter; but therein men have merely shown that the divine beauty of one fundamental part of their nature is hid from them. Their eyes are shut, their hearts are closed to the wonder and majesty of the material universe; they will not take Nature as she presents herself to us, with her perfect natural harmony of elements, but prefer forming to themselves a vain and distorted image. Forsooth, these transcendant and inconceivable chemical actions; that wondrous refine- ment and exaltation of physical forces which goes on in the brain, is a poor and contemptible set of phenomena, unworthy of our most lofty thoughts, and utterly unfit to be put on a par with the manifestations of mind. But he who is deeply imbued with physical religion, can make no such invidious and baseless comparisons; he must claim for matter exactly an equal share in our wonder; he recognises with devout admiration the certain truth, that there is an inseparable connection and unity between the physical and the mental phenomena; that instead of saying, for instance, that an intricate problem was solved, or a deep feeling of love or devotion manifested, through certain mental processes, it is exactly equally true, to say that they were done by certain transcendant chemical actions, of whose wondrous and subtle character we have as yet no conception. There is a deep fallacy contained in the common expression, that the animal and vegetable substance we feed on " *support* life ;" the fact is that they " *become* life," in other words are converted into ourselves, and their inherent vital and spiritual properties are called forth.

Everything leads us to the belief that the chemical, mechanical, and other physical forces at work, are of one nature and inseparable from the mental phenomena; and that the physical forces which we know to be manifested in the actions of the brain, are in some inexplicable manner endowed with self-consciousness. Matter, when in the form of a muscle, can contract; when in the form of living nervous substance *it can think*. Thought is in some mysterious manner connected with *Phosphorus*, and must in some way or other be an exaltation and refinement of properties, naturally inherent in that substance, and in the other elements of the brain; but in what way is yet totally unknown. On reflection we perceive that, as there is a chemical action attending every mental process, just as there is one attending every act of life, every change in the mind must be connected with an exactly corresponding change in these chemical actions. There is not a greater difference between joy and despair, than there is between the chemical changes which accompany them; and there is an exactly equal beauty in the chemical change and the mental emotion. The thought or the feeling expresses the *meaning* of the chemical changes. Are we joyful? the chemical change which is taking place in our brain, is of an easy nature, and favourable to the powers of life and health within us. Are we sorrowful? the chemical change is a difficult one, and opposed to these powers. The infinite variety of thoughts and feelings are the conscious expressions of the equal infinity of the processes of the organic chemistry within us. These considerations appear to me to be the simplest corollaries from what we now know of the physiology of nervous action; and they sound strange only from our mistaken preference for spiritual views of the nature of life.

When we examine into the history of the earth, we find every thing leading us to the conviction, that *matter existed long before mind*; or in other words, that the simpler chemical combinations existed long prior to the more complex ones, which are a comparatively recent birth of time. The evolution of mind is one of the latest triumphs of the natural forces; and if we follow the true path of induction, we are led to the conclusion, that so infinitely complex an essence could not possibly have existed, except as the result of myriads of ages of elaboration. Slowly, slowly, on looking back through the interminable vistas of Geology, we see Nature evolving this her most wondrous production; throughout the series of plants (whose lives are *constructive*) a foundation for the mental existence (which is one of *destruction*) is laid; and in the animal series, mind rises by the most gradual steps, each of which took probably millions of years to surmount to the platform of humanity. We may be certain that these wondrous and infinitely protracted efforts are not in vain; in fact, that without this extraordinary elaboration, mind could not by any possibility have come into being, and that nature must have remained without self-consciousness. The *principle of Progress* (the same with the principle of Good, of which mention has been made above, as being the invariable guide of all living action) seems to form an inherent part of nature ; and to make the most complex essence the origin of all things is completely to reverse the natural order. The progress of nature in the animated series, has been shown by Von Bær to be always from the more general to the more special ; and thus the most highly specialized and complex form of life, namely, that of man, came last into existence.

But the Supernatural in any shape or form is *absolutely inconceivable* by the human mind ; and every attempt to conceive it has resulted in inextricable confusion and inconsistencies. A mind without a brain ; spirit without a substance ; life without change, beginning or end ; personality without limitation of extent or of consciousness, uninfluenced by changes of joy and sorrow, and yet full of love, mercy, and tenderness ; in short, every possible natural attribute has been applied to the Supernatural, and yet every one has been, in the same breath, denied. It is absolutely and inexorably impossible for us to form the slightest shadow of an idea of a Supernatural being ; we cannot really conceive anything out of Nature ; all we possibly can do, is to form an aggregation of natural incongruities.

Thus then everything leads us to the profound and earnest conviction, that *Nature is all in all ;* that there is nothing above, beneath, or beside her ; and that to her should be transferred all the allegiance, which has been hitherto paid to the Supernatural. This grand truth is the foundation of modern thought, and is probably the most important conclusion (next to the knowledge of the law of population, compared with which every other is insignificant), to which our race has yet arrived. It is true that it is but partially and dimly seen as yet ; but gradually and gradually it is dawning upon the world, and every new revelation of the book of Nature tends to engrave it deeper in our hearts. It is the foundation of Natural Religion, that mighty faith, · which will sooner or later include the whole human family, and before which scepticism and differences of creeds shall all alike disappear. He who has once clearly seen the impassable gulph which divides the Natural from the Supernatural, and the infinitely greater reality and transcendant beauty of the former, possesses ever after a profound reverence and absolute reliance in Nature, that nothing can shake. She can do all, she can solve every mystery ; and he who has faith in her, shall never be deceived. We, her loftiest children, are indeed full of ignorance and weaknesses ; but there is not a thought, not a sorrow, not a perplexity among us, of which she does not hold the keys, and for which there is not consolation in her mighty bosom. The life of many of us may seem a hopeless riddle, may be fraught with sorrow, disappointment, poverty or disease, doubt, imbecility, or degradation, but she will clear up all at last ; she who has an equal and impartial love for all, and for whom nothing exists in vain.

Natural Religion is the one and only true religious belief, which has ever existed on this earth. It is separated by a far broader line of demarcation from all the various forms of supernaturalism, than any of these are from each other. The progress of religious belief has consisted in limiting more and more the influence of the Supernatural, and admitting more and more that of Nature; so that the religion, which contained least of the immediate agency of the Supernatural, and most natural truth, was the best. But the very slightest shadow of a conception of the supernatural spoils the harmony of Nature, mixes itself inevitably in all our views of life, and is absolutely inconsistent with Natural Religion. In the latter, the very first and fundamental belief is, that there is not, never was, and never can be, anything out of Nature; anything which is not itself a part of the mighty whole; subject like the others to the natural laws of existence, acting and being acted upon by all the rest of Nature; and that the chief end of our life is to study her laws and live according to them.

This is the great truth to which all modern thought has been tending; which is now becoming widely spread over a great part of the civilized world, and which has formed the leading idea of most of the profound thinkers of late times both in this country, and still more on the Continent; the truth which is embodied, under various shapes and designations, in the Rationalism of Germany, the Secularism of this country, and other sects, all of which are essentially the same, or at least differ only on trifling points, are all moving in the same direction and will ultimately fuse into one great and united whole; the truth, which is branded by the name of Atheism and Infidelity by the advocates of the supernatural beliefs, who forget that the question is no longer whether a man have or have not *a deep and settled religious belief*, but whether he believe in supernatural religion or in Nature. Those who believe in the supernatural, deny the adequacy of the powers of Nature, and dethrone her from her sovereign sway over the universe and our hearts; which Natural Religion, on the other hand, devoutly acknowledges. Let us not deceive ourselves; we cannot serve two masters. *Belief in God is disbelief in Nature.*

To no faith is the term "Infidelity" less applicable than to Natural Religion; and those who are convinced of its certain truth, should reject with a lofty indignation, the application of such a term to their faith—the noblest, the sublimest, that the world has ever known. It is a faith whose foundations are broad and deep as Nature herself, and which cannot be shaken. When once it becomes fairly established among mankind, religious scepticism will disappear.

It is a striking anomaly, and one that of itself is sufficient to show the unsoundness of supernaturalism, that its very first positions, even now when it has existed so long, should be capable of absolute denial. A great deal of misery is caused by the difference of religious opinions, and the want of unanimity on the very first principles of belief. These unhappy religious differences separate nation from nation, and stand like a spectral barrier in the midst even of our social and family circles; so that there is scarcely a single one of us, who has not suffered from this cause. This arises from the fact, that the Supernatural is taken for the standard of truth, instead of Nature. When Nature shall become the universal standard, no one will be able to object to it; for no one can regard Nature. even in the most superficial manner, without perceiving her infinite perfection. No man ever did, or ever will, find the slightest flaw in Nature; and even those who seek most to exalt the Supernatural, and to limit the powers of Nature, are lost in wonder and admiration when they consider any of her phenomena. No man can by any possibility utterly disbelieve in Nature; while on the other hand there is not a single form of the supernatural, which is not utterly disbelieved in by immense numbers of mankind; especially by those whose powers of perceiving truth have been more cultivated by the study of Nature, and who have been freed, in whatever manner, from the fascinating influence of the supernatural, so as to be able to form an impartial judgment.

It is of great importance that Natural Religion should be spread, as widely, as universally, as possible; not in this country alone, but over the whole globe. There is nothing which would have a more powerful effect in drawing all of us nearer to each other, and awakening our hearts to a common human sympathy, than having one universal form of religion. Nothing at present more divides nations than the different forms of supernatural faith; and there can never be a true reconciliation until these be laid aside, and we be united in one great Natural Religion, whose infallibility all men will allow, for Nature is one and the same over the whole globe.

This great consummation seems indeed far, very far, distant at present, when Natural Religion is still in its infancy; when various forms of Supernatural Belief are dominant in every country in the world. But their supremacy is more in name than in reality; for already their hold upon most of the civilized nations of the earth is very much shaken. In France and Germany, the Christian religion cannot be said to be generally prevalent; it is rare in these countries to see an educated man, at least among the laity, who believes in it. Over the whole continent it may be said, that Christian beliefs are, as a general rule, chiefly confined to the least educated class, in whom they have usually the form of a gross superstition. In our own country the number of those, who do not believe in Christianity, is very large, and constantly increasing. The great majority of the mechanics and artizans in our large towns are, I believe, of this number. A very large portion also of the educated classes, especially of the generation which is now springing up, either doubt or totally disbelieve in it. Many of our greatest living writers and thinkers are diametrically opposed to the Christian theory of life; and there are comparatively few of them, who can be called orthodox.

A large number of these various classes agree in rejecting the authority of the Scriptures, but differ in several points with regard to their limitation of the supernatural. Some admit the existence of a supernatural being, and of a supernatural life for man, after the completion of his natural one, while others deny this, and believe in nothing beyond Nature. I feel deeply convinced that all will ultimately come to the conclusion, that the idea of the supernatural must be wholly and entirely laid aside; and that it is impossible for man to rest contented in any other form of belief than a purely natural one.

We are parts of Nature, living in her and through her, and we cannot go beyond her in the slightest degree, without falling into the greatest inconsistencies, and forfeiting the happiness and virtue of our lives.

But although there are some differences in the opinions of those who dissent from the Christian beliefs, all are agreed as to this great fundamental truth, namely, that it is from ourselves and from progressive human enlightenment, that we are to derive our religious convictions, and not from any past authority. Every man must form for himself his own opinions on the great subjects of the meaning and end of life Whatever principles of moral conduct, or whatever views of life and death may be advanced, must address themselves to the moral sense and reason of each individual, and be tested by them : and not urged upon us as articles of blind faith, backed by the promises of infinite rewards and punishments. Such promises and such threats corrupt all impartiality of judgment, and are unworthy of the dignity of so lofty a being as man. Every one of us is a judge, a legislator, as to the truth or falsehood of the various theories of life, natural or supernatural, brought before us ; and should be addressed with befitting deference, and not as if we were criminals at the bar, or slaves who had to do nothing but listen and obey. The laws for our guidance are not ready made to our hands, but are to be discovered only by our own virtue and patient investigation. Each individual is responsible to the rest of Nature for his opinions and actions, but to no other power whatsoever ; and the punishments or rewards consequent on these are always purely natural, and exactly proportional to their deserts ; and moreover are open to our investigation and thorough comprehension.

Many who doubt or disbelieve in the supernatural views, are restrained from making known their opinions, on account of the intolerance with which these are regarded ; an intolerance which only twelve years ago, threw Mr. Holyoake and others whose noble exertions and self-devotion in the cause of Natural Religion will yet be gratefully recognised by all, into prison for openly expressing their disbelief in the current supernatural doctrines. So many of us are dependent on the goodwill of others for our subsistence, so many are afraid of public opinion, that the most deeply cherished convictions are often suppressed ; and thus it is difficult to estimate the number of those who have laid aside the Christian theory of life. Religious intolerance is the most vehement of all in this country, with the exception of sexual intolerance ; and both feelings cause a great deal of misery, and are opposed to that true sympathy and mutual reverence which should exist between all men. It is one of the very first principles of religion that we should honour and love our fellows, and listen with reverence to all their conscientious opinions, however imperfect they may appear in our eyes. All real convictions are sacred, and must be rooted profoundly in the life of the individual ; and therefore should be dealt with as carefully and as reverentially as possible. Any form of belief, which allows a man to regard with irreverence his fellow beings, or to think himself entitled to look down upon them, either morally or intellectually, cannot possibly be a true one.

Those who embrace the Religion of Nature should sedulously endeavour to avoid this intolerance and irreverence. Love and reverence
for *man* should form their first moral principle : and they should never
allow any difference of religious opinion to interefere with these feelings,
whatever others may do. Man is the most exalted manifestation of
Nature, and thus the highest object of reverence to him, who is imbued
with natural religion. He stands infinitely higher than any of our
beliefs, and should command our deepest reverence.

But they, who adopt the natural faith, should not only reverence others,
but resolutely assert their own title to a like reverence in return.
Believing that their's is the one and only true religion, and that the
most vital interests of us all are bound up in its universal diffusion, they
should claim for it a due reverence in the eyes of men. Every measure
should be taken to uplift Natural Religion and its adherents from their
still unacknowledged and degraded position ; and to enable every individual
who adopts these beliefs to avow them openly, and to defend and
endeavour to advance them, without being treated with intolerance by
his neighbours. The worshippers of Nature should demand, that their
faith be received by society in the same way as the various forms of
supernatural religion are at present—namely, as the conscientious
religious convictions of a large and powerful body of men, who have a
right to occupy an honourable place in the eyes of their fellows. There
is nothing that Natural Religion requires more in the present day than
to define its principles, and to *unite* its efforts ; and to gain for itself *a
recognised place*, and a name which shall be able to protect its followers
from oppression or religious intolerance. A Roman Catholic does not
hide his religious convictions, neither does a Jew, nor a Dissenter; and
their opinions, although disapproved of, are listened to and socially recognised ; and Natural Religion should not rest till its tenets be equally
recognised, and all its adherents be able to speak as openly and as proudly
of their cherished convictions. To effect this, they who have laid aside
the supernatural beliefs, should earnestly endeavour to combine as much
as possible their strength ; to make common cause for mutual protection
and support, in the same way as other religious bodies. They should
endeavour to get one general name, which shall include all the different
sects : and unite under that, so as to form a powerful and recognised body
in the state, which could command the respect of society, and protect
from religious intolerance its adherents.

I believe that if this were done, and that if all those, who have laid
aside Christianity, were to disclose their beliefs, and to come forward as
the supporters of a new and natural faith, (in the noble manner in which
Mr. Holyoake, Mr. Francis Newman, Mr. Owen, Mr. Thomas Carlyle,
Miss Martineau, and many others have acted,) they would form *the most
powerful of all existing religious bodies ;* including the great majority of the
educated classes on the Continent, and a large portion of those in this
country. Not until an earnest religious movement of a *public* kind has
been made, can we expect that society will treat with becoming reverence
the opinions of those, who do not believe in the established religions. If
we do not speak openly, earnestly, and devoutly, of our own convictions,

we can scarcely hope that our neighbours will view them with due reverence.

With regard to the name by which these views should be designated, I would humbly submit that the term "Natural Religion" should be adopted. There is something cold and uninviting in the words Rationalism and Secularism, which do not seem to me moreover to express so well the peculiar character of the belief. The term Natural Religion shows its real foundation, namely, on Nature, and Nature alone: and throws it into strong contrast with all the various forms of supernatural belief. Moreover the word "Religion" is inwardly dear to all of us; it is a name to which the noblest feelings of humanity have been consecrated; which has been hallowed by the virtues, the pious lives, and heroic deaths, of many of the most glorious characters in history; which has filled men's breasts with that heroic self-devotion that makes them undergo all trials and privations, to do that which their conscience tells them is right; which sends men to the wilderness to convert the heathen, and to the death-bed, and the haunts of crime and pestilence, to succour and console their suffering fellow-beings—oh may this name and all the devout, earnest, and loving feelings it breathes, sink into the minds of all of us, and may the followers of Natural Religion be animated by a no less exalted enthusiasm! The name of Natural Religion expresses, that the beliefs it represents, are but a continuation of the religious progress of the race; a progress which has been going on ever since the birth of history, and will advance till the end. It designates the continued aspirations of mankind to the True, and the Good, and the Beautiful; and their devout and enthusiastic sense of their duty to follow and defend them, at all risks, and with all sacrifices.

Whatever opinions we adopt, or whatever hopes we entertain of their effect on human life, let us not fall into that fatal error, which is ingrained into all the forms of supernatural belief; namely, that of attributing to human blindness or depravity, and not to their own imperfect systems, the continued existence of evils, which these systems are impotent to remedy. The proof of the truth of any system is its being found really to cure human ills—not its asserting that it can cure them; just as the only sign of the real efficiency of the physician is the restoration of his patient's health. Till the evils have been cured, in fact, nothing whatever has been done; no suffering has been relieved, and there has been nothing but an ostentatious talk, which to the physician, whose whole and sole object is the happiness of his patient, not his own vainglory, is absolutely valueless. If he has produced a cure, he is content, if not, he blames his own imperfect means, and want of skill; and is far, very far, from mocking his patient's miseries by laying the blame on him.

If we try by these tests the truth of any scheme for the satisfactory increase of human virtue and happiness, we must recognise that hitherto all such schemes have been a mere delusion; that hitherto there has been no such thing as a "saving faith," as a religious or moral system, which had the power adequately to contend with human evils; and that the persistence for so long a time in declaring the various religious systems to be panaceas, and in laying the blame not upon them, but upon mankind, has been perhaps the most miserable of all instances of the mockery of human wretchedness.

Mr. Malthus was a clergyman ; but by his discovery of the principle of population, he unconsciously gave the most fatal blow it had ever received, to the religion of which he was a minister. By showing the radical antagonism between food and love, he laid bare the real source of the great mass of human woes, and introduced a new element, namely, reproductive restraint, into the list of human duties ; an element which had been omitted in all previous systems, including the Christian but which is of such incomparable importance, that all the other virtues are, without it, utterly delusive. From ignorance of the law of population, and the great duty of limited procreation, the Christian scheme is as fundamentally vitiated, as every other theory of virtue or progress ; while its teachers, from want of attention to this subject, are rendered, like our statesmen, thoroughly impotent, as far as the main interests of mankind are concerned.

The great population difficulty has hitherto rather proved the safeguard of Christianity, as of marriage, by rendering abortive all schemes for remedying human ills ; and has thus forced men rather to cling to a religion of resignation than of hope and progress. But if, as I firmly believe, this great difficulty is to be overcome by the means of which I have spoken, nothing will then operate so powerfully in effecting a change in our religious beliefs; for it will be found that the only possible way of saving ourselves from these evils, is by thoroughly altering our sexual and religious opinions. Without this, indeed, progress is totally impossible.

On looking back upon the past history of our race, with reference to the action of the law of population, (without which, in fact, both past and present history are an insoluble riddle,) it may be divided into two tolerably well-marked epochs of *necessary destruction.* Ancient history is pre-eminently the epoch of the *positive* check, in the shape of wars, famines, and infant mortality. In it the average of life is very short, as it is in all the inferior animals ; but the average of health and strength among those who are fortunate enough to escape the necessary destruction, is very high, as it is in all undomesticated animals. Modern history is the epoch of the *preventive and positive* checks, in the shape of celibacy, prostitution, poverty, and over-work. Here the average of life is higher, chiefly on account of the prevalence of the preventive check, and the increased power of producing food; but the average of health and strength, irrespective of length of life, is much lower, chiefly from the same causes, namely, the unnatural celibacy, and the hard and unhealthy work. The Future, I earnestly hope and trust, will be the epoch of *preventive sexual intercourse,* by which alone the necessary destruction can possibly be obviated ; and will be characterised by universal independence in the essentials of life, and by an average both of life and of health and strength, gradually approaching nearer and nearer to the natural one.

No man ever did so much, however unconsciously, for Natural Religion as Mr. Malthus. Nothing ever threw into such strong contrast the power of Nature on the one hand, and the impotence of man and the supernatural, when opposed to her, on the other, as the discovery of the principle of population. What have availed all our efforts against the overwhelming and unseen laws of Nature? In what way have our great men, of whose achievements there has been so much vain-glorious talk, deserved the homage, the *hero-worship*, which has been paid to them; and which has tended so powerfully to divert attention from the supremacy of Nature, and the horrible condition of the masses of mankind? What have they done for us, the poets, fine writers, sculptors, statesmen, orators, moralists: in whose happiness and elevation forsooth, we are to find our own; with whose over-shadowing fame we are to console ourselves in our miseries; to worship whom is a sufficient privilege for the rest of us, the vulgar herd of mankind? We ask for bread, and they give us a stone: for love, and they give us a poetical or religious shadow of it. Poetry, painting, architecture, fine writing, oratory, religion, to a world plunged in the population horrors, are like music in the ears of a drowning man. They may dazzle our judgment; they may gild, but alas! they cannot cheat, our misery. It is the *necessaries* of life, it is food, love, and leisure that are at present chiefly needed among us; and till these be secured for every human being, man or woman, it is of little avail to talk of the *luxuries*.

It is alas! not difficult for any writer, as far as his *sexual* conduct is concerned, to win the short-sighted approbation of mankind. All that is needed is to avoid the sexual subjects, and tacitly at least, if not expressly, to acquiesce in the Reign of sexual Terror and Ignorance, that exists among us; but to do so is only to throw another stone upon the grave of human hopes. No real good can at present accrue to our race, except by meeting in a straightforward and manly way, the great sexual difficulties, and discussing them openly; and until this be done, although men may applaud our actions, let us not hope that we shall cheat Nature *Impotence and a radical delusiveness* characterise all the current views on man and society; and must characterise all views, which are not guided by the Law of Population, and based upon Preventive Sexual Intercourse.

END OF PART III.

.

PART IV.

SOCIAL SCIENCE.

THE MAIN ELEMENTS OF SOCIAL SCIENCE.

In the two first editions, this work ended with the preceding essay. However, as my main object is to demonstrate the truth of the Malthusian Law of Population; to show that this law is the real cause of the great social evils of old countries, and preventive sexual intercourse their only remedy; I am very desirous, before taking leave of the reader, to do everything in my power to promote the clear apprehension of these fundamental truths, by endeavouring to present them in a somewhat more systematic form. This appears to me advisable, not only from the incomparable importance of the subject, but also because it is still so little understood and so frequently misconceived. In parliament, and in other public discussions on social questions, the principle of population continues to be almost entirely ignored, and treated as non-existent; whereas a true art of legislation should be, in the main, based on this great principle, in the same manner as navigation on astronomy, or medicine on anatomy and physiology. In our newspapers and popular literature, whenever, at rare intervals, the Malthusian doctrines are mentioned, the very same fallacies and misconceptions are usually brought forward which were exposed by Mr. Malthus himself fifty years ago, and have been so often repeated since his time, that they may now be called traditional.

The great want of the age, as has been so admirably shown by Mr. Mill and M. Comte (although the latter, by his hasty and inconsiderate rejection of political economy and the principle of population, has signally failed in supplying it), is that there should be a Social Science. By this is meant, a body of ascertained laws relating to human society, which, like those that constitute the sciences of mathematics, astronomy, physics, chemistry, or physiology, should be definitely accepted and regarded by all men as beyond dispute. Until there be such a body of truths, universally acknowledged and

respected, society must remain in a state of profound disorder, whatever unanimity may exist upon matters of minor importance. In
order to obtain them, it is necessary that the subject should be treated
in the same careful and systematic manner, with the same attention
to the rules of induction and deduction, as the other sciences; and
not abandoned, as at present is so generally the case, merely to vague
and popular discussion. "If," says Mr. Mill, "on matters so much
the most important on which the human intellect can occupy itself, a
more general agreement is ever to exist among thinkers ; if what has
been pronounced ' the proper study of mankind' is not destined to
remain the only subject which Philosophy cannot succeed in rescuing
from Empiricism : the same processes through which the laws of many
simpler phenomena have by general acknowledgment been placed beyond dispute, must be consciously and deliberately applied to these
more difficult inquiries."

Although the science of society has hitherto received so little
general attention or recognition, that most people do not even know
of its existence, nay, deny its very possibility, it must by no means
be supposed that little has been done, or that the subject is still in its
infancy. On the contrary, I am convinced that by far the most important discoveries have already been made, and that the science is
already sufficiently advanced to meet the greatest practical wants of
mankind. It is true indeed, that it has not yet been exhibited as a
whole, and that many of its branches have been very imperfectly, if
at all, cultivated. But others, and especially political economy, the
science of wealth, are already in a highly advanced state; and above
all, the great principles have been ascertained, which give the true
scientific explanation of society in its principal features, in the same
manner as the law of gravitation explained the main phenomena of
the material universe. The law of population, together with the
more elementary laws of exercise, fecundity, and agricultural industry,
from which it is derived, may in fact be regarded as the groundwork
of the true theory of human society—as *the main elements of social
science.* These laws lie at the very root, not merely of political
economy, (of which, as we have already seen, Mr. Mill declares the
law of agricultural industry to be " the most important proposition "),
but also of sanitary and ethical science, and the other departments
of social philosophy. They are the principal causes of the deplorable
state of society in this and other old countries, and of the poverty,
prostitution, disease, and crime, by which in every age, so many millions of the human race have been oppressed. With a knowledge of
these laws, it is comparatively easy to understand the chief phenomena
of society, and to see the way to a true social regeneration ; without
them, this is not merely difficult, but impossible.

I would wish therefore to add to what has already been said, a
somewhat more methodical exposition of the above laws, in the hope
that it may assist the reader in thoroughly mastering the subject.
For this purpose, I shall first give a short statement and proof of the
law of population itself, and endeavour to show in what manner it

produces its three specific effects, poverty, prostitution, and celiba\`y; and then examine a little more fully the elementary laws of exercise, fecundity, and agricultural industry, and more especially the first of these, since it alone has not yet been generally and explicitly accepted by scientific men. I shall also give quotations from English and foreign writers on the law of population and its discoverer; for I am anxious that the reader should be aware of the general, nay, it might almost be said, universal acceptance of the Malthusian doctrines among those men of science who have paid due attention to the sunject. This is the more needed, because the opponents of these doctrines in our newspapers and elsewhere, are accustomed to represent them as bygone and refuted speculations, instead of being as they are, and as they have been for nearly half a century, definitely accepted principles of science; principles which are as well established as the rotation of the earth, or the circulation of the blood. It appears to me advisable also to add a short outline of the chief principles of political economy, including the laws of the production and distribution of wealth, and the three laws of value. No science is less generally understood, or more urgently needed, not only for the comprehension of economical questions in general, but more particularly in order to give a clear insight into the action of the population principle. It is only by a knowledge of the laws of political economy that we are enabled to understand accurately the influence of this great principle on wages, profits, rents, values, and prices.

Before proceeding to consider these subjects, a few remarks may be offered on the laws of nature in general.

It must be regarded as an ascertained truth, though as yet by no means generally admitted, that the Law of Universal Causation prevails everywhere throughout nature. This law, which forms the foundation of all the inductive sciences, is, that *every phenomenon in nature which begins to exist, arises from some cause or combination of causes, which it invariably and unconditionally follows.* The whole course of nature consists of uniformities of succession and of co-existence; every natural object, animate or inanimate, has its own laws or properties, according to which it invariably acts; and to discover these and trace them to their consequences, forms the sole problem of the various sciences.

This law of universal causation is the most important proposition of logic, the science of proof, and upon it, as Mr. Mill shows in his masterly work on that science, all the rules of induction depend for their validity. It is, to use Mr. Mill's words, " the foundation of every scientific theory of successive phenomena." No scientific conclusion would be justified, no general proposition could be sustained, unless we knew, from the uniform experience of ages, that the laws of nature are invariable, and that the same causes are always followed by the same effects.

Perhaps I should here allude to an ambiguity in the word *law* which causes a great deal of confusion and false reasoning. The word has two meanings quite distinct from one another. In the moral and political sense it means a *command*, as when it is enjoined that men shall abstain from a certain act, such as theft or falsehood, or perform a certain duty, such as paying a tax. In this sense a law may be obeyed or disobeyed, and rewards and punishments may be awarded accordingly. In the scientific sense, however, a law means an *invariable sequence or co-existence*, as, for example, the law that bodies, when once set in motion, tend to move in a straight line, and with uniform velocity, for ever; that the three angles of any triangle are equal to two right angles; or that health depends on the proper discharge of the bodily functions. It is with laws of this kind alone that science is concerned, while laws, in the sense of commands or rules, belong to the province of art. A science consists of a body of invariable sequences or co-existences; an art of a body of precepts or rules for practice. Science treats of what is, was, or will be, and the ultimate principle by which its laws or uniformities are justified is the law of universal causation; art treats of what shall be, or ought to be, and the ultimate principle which forms the justification of its laws or rules, is, as Mr. Jeremy Bentham so clearly and forcibly pointed out, the principle of utility, or of the greatest happiness of mankind. The scientific laws are not commands, but invariable truths, which are never defeated (though they may be counteracted by other laws), and therefore they cannot, strictly speaking, be said to be obeyed or disobeyed, or to be broken or violated. However, phrases of this kind are constantly used, as when, for example, it is said that disease or poverty results from a violation of the sanitary or economical laws; the latter being here regarded as commands, and not as uniformities of cause and effect, which they really are. Such phrases may be used without inconvenience, if it be understood that they are merely metaphorical, and if the real meaning of a scientific law be clearly perceived. Too often, however, the ambiguity in the word causes much false reasoning, especially on social questions, and leads people to confound the fundamental distinction between science and art, and to speak of social science or its branches, as if they were a collection of general maxims and precepts, instead of a body of invariable sequences or co-existences.

The laws or uniformities of nature, with which science is concerned, are either *ultimate* or *derivative*: that is, they are either properties of the elementary substances which compose the universe, or consequences arising from them. There are some bodies in nature, to which the name of Permanent Causes, or primeval natural agents, has been given, as they have existed and produced their proper effects, throughout the whole of human experience and for an indefinite time previously. Such are the sun, the earth and planets, the elementary chemical substances, and some of their combinations, as air, water, &c. Of the origin of these bodies we are utterly ignorant: nor can we perceive any regularity or law in their relative amount or position in space.

" All phenomena without exception which begin to exist," says Mr. Mill, " that is, all except the primeval causes, are effects either immediate or remote of those primitive facts, or of some combination of them. There is no Thing produced, no event happening in the known universe, which is not connected by an uniformity, or invariable sequence, with some one or more of the phenomena which preceded it: insomuch that it will happen again so often as those phenomena occur again, and as no other phenomenon having the character of a counteracting cause shall co-exist. These antecedent phenomena again, were connected in a similar manner with some that preceded them: and so on, until we reach, as the ultimate step attainable by us, either the properties of some one primeval cause, or the conjunction of several. The whole of the phenomena of nature were therefore the necessary, or in other words, the unconditional, consequences of some former collocation of the Permanent Causes."

The human body, and each of its different organs, digestive, locomotive, or reproductive, are governed by laws, just as definite and invariable as those of inanimate substances. To discover the laws of the body in a state of health is the province of physiology: while pathology investigates the laws of disease. The mind, also, forms no exception to the universal rule. Each of its three constituent states, namely, Thought, Feeling or Emotion, and Will, has its own fixed laws: the trains of ideas and sensations succeed each other according to definite principles of association, which are never departed from: and to ascertain these, forms the important aim of the science of psychology. Political economy, again, treats of the laws of the production and distribution of wealth; while social science, or, as it is often called, sociology (of which political economy is a branch), investigates the laws which determine the co-existence and succession of all the social phenomena. It examines the natural causes on which not only the wealth, but the political, moral, and sanitary condition of a people depend: the influences which determine the character, habits, social position, &c., of the various classes, and of the nation as a whole.

It is of the utmost consequence that all should have a clear idea of causation, and a due reverence for the laws of nature. There are three things which chiefly unsettle men's minds on these most important points. The first is, the belief in *supernatural interference:* the idea that the invariability of nature's sequences is liable to be interrupted by supernatural causes, of whose laws we can have no knowledge. The error and danger of this belief have been so fully pointed out by numerous writers, and so ably opposed, at the expense of social penalties and indignities, by many heroic and devoted men, that I need not further dwell upon them.

The second unsettling belief is, that there is one phenomenon in nature, namely, the *human will,* which is not subject to the law of causation, but has what is called a self-determining power. This idea, which generally accompanies the preceding, is most paralysing to the science of mind, and has greatly retarded its progress. But the will, like all other parts of nature, depends on definite causes which it invariably follows. All our actions are determined by *motives;* and this is practically recognised in our ordinary views of human conduct, however we may lose sight of it in theory. In judging of the actions of others, we always inquire what motives have led to them: what there is in the individual's character and circumstances that would naturally account for them: nor do we ever imagine that actions arise of themselves without any determining causes.

These two beliefs form the chief artificial obstacles to a recognition of the order of the universe. But the *real* obstacle is one which does not arise from our theories, but from the great complexity of the natural phenomena themselves. The difficulty in ascertaining the laws of nature mainly depends on the mode in which different causes counteract each other, and commingle their effects: thus making the line of causation very difficult to unravel. The same effect also is often producible by many different causes. It is by these circumstances, called respectively by Mr. Mill the *composition of causes*, the *intermixture of effects*, and the *plurality of causes*, that the progress of science is chiefly retarded: and it is from the mode in which different laws thus counteract each other, that the popular belief has arisen, that " there is no general rule without an exception." But the truth is, that there is *never* an exception to a law of nature. All apparent exceptions are merely cases where the effect is counteracted by some other law. Nay, in the ordinary case of the composition of causes, each cause, even although counteracted, still produces its full and characteristic effect. For instance, if a body be held in the hand, the law by which it tends to fall to the ground is counteracted: but it still produces its full effect, as we feel by the sensation of *weight.* The exception to the ordinary rule of the composition of causes—that causes produce their full and characteristic effect even when counteracted—is in the case of chemical combinations, where two bodies by uniting produce an effect of a thoroughly different nature; but even this is rather an apparent than a real exception.

In consequence of their liability to be counteracted, laws of causation are stated as *tendencies*, when scientific precision is aimed at. For instance, the law is, that bodies *tend* to fall to the ground, not that they always do so: for the tendency may be counteracted. Mistakes are constantly made, and a distrust in the principles of science often engendered by not attending to the fact that all laws of causation are subject to counteraction. This is especially the case in complex sciences, such as physiology or political economy, where so many conflicting causes are always at work. But the laws of these sciences are not one whit less invariable than those of astronomy. When once clearly ascertained by a sufficient induction, they too must be regarded as admitting of no exception, and definitely settled for ever.

With these preliminary remarks on the laws of nature in general, I proceed to consider the law which appears to me beyond all comparison the most important and terrible subject for the contemplation of mankind, namely, the law of population.

THE LAW OF POPULATION, OR MALTHUSIAN LAW.

The Law of Population—that is, the law which regulates the increase of mankind—may be arrived at from the following four propositions: the two first of which are undeniable, and must be granted by every one as soon as they are clearly understood; while the two last need proof.

PROPOSITION I.—Wherever in any country the actual increase of population is less than the possible increase, it is and can only be by some one or more of the six following causes or checks, viz., Celibacy, Prostitution, Sterility, Preventive Intercourse, Premature Death, and Emigration: whose collective amount varies inversely in proportion to the rapidity with which the population of the country is increasing, while the amount of each individually varies inversely in proportion to the others.

PROPOSITION II.—As a matter of fact, it is known that the population of different countries increases with very different degrees of rapidity. Thus the celebrated French statist, M. Moreau de Jonnès, has calculated, from the recent rate of their increase, the time which each of the undermentioned countries would take to double its population.

His calculation is as follows:—

Turkey	...	...	...	...	...	555 years.
Switzerland		...	...	...	...	227
France	...	...	...	...	...	138
Spain...	...	...	...	..	...	106
Holland	...	...	...	...	...	100
Germany	...	...	...	...	...	76
Russia	...	...	...	...	...	43
England	...	...	...	...	...	43
United States (deducting the contingents furnished by immigration)	...	...	25

From this we see that the rate of increase in the United States (a new colony) is very much greater than in any country of the old world; and that among the latter countries some, especially England and Russia, increase much more rapidly than others. Whatever, then, be the difference between the rates of increase in these countries, it is owing absolutely and entirely to some one or more of the six checks given above: whose collective amount varies inversely in proportion to the rapidity with which the population of each country is increasing or has increased, while the amount of each individually varies inversely in proportion to the others.

PROPOSITION III.—From a consideration of the Law of Agricultural Industry, and an estimate of the rate at which the means of subsistence could be increased in old countries, even under the most favourable circumstances, it may be inferred with certainty, that these means of subsistence could not possibly be increased so fast as to permit population to increase at its natural rate. Therefore the population of old countries must always continue to be, as it always has been, powerfully checked by some one or more of the six checks given above; whose collective amount will vary inversely in proportion to the rapidity with which the population of each country may increase, while the amount of each individually will vary inversely in proportion to the others.

Proposition IV.—Emigration is to be regarded, not as one of the permanent checks, to which man's choice is inexorably confined, but merely as a slight, temporary, and accidental palliative of the others. This is true even with regard to one old country alone, much more with regard to the whole world. The main causes which have retarded human increase, and some one or more of which have always acted, and will always continue to act, with enormous power in old countries, and in new colonies also as soon as their cultivation has increased to a certain extent, are the remaining five checks, namely, Celibacy, Prostitution, Sterility, Preventive Intercourse, and Premature Death; whose collective amount varies inversely in proportion to the rapidity with which the population of each country is increasing, and to the number of emigrants *minus* that of immigrants, while the amount of each individually varies inversely in proportion to the others.

I may here observe, that by the terms "possible" or "natural" increase in the above propositions, I mean the increase which would take place, if all the children were born which the reproductive powers admit of, and if every individual lived to the full term of life. By the term "celibacy" is meant sexual abstinence, whether practised by married or unmarried people; and by "sterility" is meant all cases of barrenness, not arising from prostitution. The population table in the second proposition, is quoted from the work of Mr. Rickards (late Professor of Political Economy at Oxford), on Population and Capital, and I would remark that although it may be found to differ more or less from other tables drawn up at different periods (since the population of a country often increases faster at one time than at another, owing to the progress of the industrial arts, and other causes), still the same main facts will be found in all correct tables, namely, that population always increases much more rapidly in new colonies than in old countries, and that, among the latter, it increases much faster in some than in others.

According to the last Census returns, the population of Great Britain, and still more that of France, is increasing more slowly than the rate given by M. de Jonnès; indeed the French population has of late years been almost entirely stationary.

The first of the four foregoing propositions is undeniable. It is merely an enumeration of all the modes in which the increase of the human race can be checked. These are obviously all reducible to the heads given above: or, in other words, to sexual abstinence, voluntary or involuntary unfruitful intercourse, premature death, and emigration: to there being fewer births or more deaths in a country than the powers of the human constitution would admit of, or a greater amount of emigration from it. If we can form an estimate of the possible rate of human increase, and are acquainted with the actual increase in any given country, it is evident that we can calculate the collective action of these checks upon that country. The slower the population of the country is increasing, the greater *must* be the collective action of these checks: that is, their action must be inversely proportional to the rate of increase. It is also evident that the share which each check has in the collective action must be greater in proportion as that of the others is less: in other words, that the individual amount of each must vary inversely in proportion to the others. The less the share of celibacy, for instance, the more must be that of the others: the greater the share of celibacy, the less that of the others, &c.

Before proceeding to the second proposition, it may be expedient to repeat the classification of the population-checks adopted by Mr. Malthus, which is exactly the same in reality as that given above, and presents merely a nominal difference. He divided the checks first into two great classes, the *preventive* and the *positive*. "These checks to population," he says, "may be classed under two general heads, the preventive and the positive checks." Under the first head he included all the modes in which the birth of children is prevented, namely, celibacy, prostitution, sterility, and preventive intercourse. Under the second head he included all the causes of premature death: such as, to use his own words, "all unwholesome occupations, severe labour, and exposure to the seasons, extreme poverty, bad nursing of children, great towns, excesses of all kinds, the whole train of diseases and epidemics, wars, plagues, and famines." But besides this primary division of the checks, he further subdivided them into three classes, namely, *moral restraint, vice,* and *misery:* in order to examine them more in detail, and to bring the subject more home to the mind of the reader. "On examining," he says, "the obstacles to the increase of population, which I have classified under the heads of preventive and positive checks, it will appear that they are all resolvable into moral restraint, vice, and misery." By the term moral restraint, as he further explains, he meant celibacy; by vice, he meant prostitution and preventive intercourse; and by misery, he meant premature death and the various forms of disease—thus including sterility, which is a form of disease or misery.

My reasons for nominally departing from this classification are, in the first place, that the terms moral restraint, vice, and misery, are in my opinion far too vague, and have tended greatly to confuse the subject in many minds, and to keep up the fatal obscurity which involves the sexual questions. In the second place, the terms moral restraint and vice are very misleading. Moral restraint seems to imply that celibacy is a voluntary state, which is by no means generally true, especially in the case of woman. To include, moreover, under the same head of vice two checks which differ so totally in their moral and physical character, as prostitution and preventive intercourse, is a great error: it is on every account of the utmost importance that they should be carefully distinguished.

The second proposition, to which I now return, is also undeniable, and scarcely requires additional illustration.   It is evident that as the six foregoing checks are the only ones which can retard increase, the different rates of increase known to exist in different countries must be owing absolutely and entirely to them.   If the French population increases much more slowly than the English, and the English than the American, it is because there is a much greater collective amount of these checks in France than in England, and in England than America.   The actual increase of each population, which is a known fact, is the exact measure of the collective amount of the checks; and thus though we may not be able to tell precisely their *absolute* amount, from want of exact knowledge of the possible rate of increase, we can tell at a glance their *relative* amount in one country as compared with others.   What share each separate check has had in the amount thus ascertained is not so easily determined; but we can calculate it with tolerable accuracy, by considering the average of life, the amount of emigration, and the sexual habits of each people; and we are at any rate certain, that it has varied inversely in proportion to the others.   Thus, whatever part of the difference between the total amount of the checks in France and England is not owing to celibacy, must be owing to the other five checks; whatever is not owing to premature death must be owing to the other five; &c.

Thus far of the two first propositions. From a consideration of them it may be laid down as a certain truth, that in every country of the old world there exist at present causes which retard human increase, and which, though less operative in some countries than in others, yet act with enormous power in all; and that these causes consist of celibacy, prostitution, sterility, preventive intercourse, premature death, and emigration, in varying proportions. Nay more; all statistical research into the past history of such countries shows that their population has always increased comparatively slowly; or, in other words, that some of these checks have *always* been powerfully active. Since, then, it is known that they have always acted, and do always act, the only question that remains is, *must* they always act? Can mankind escape from them, or do they arise from a necessity in nature? This leads us to the third and main proposition. Before entering on the proof of this proposition, it may be observed, that the very fact of the universal and constant action of these checks in every old country would of itself lead us to infer that they must always continue to act; that their cause must be some fixed and changeless law of nature, and no mere error of human character or institutions. Accòrdingly, on examining the matter, we can clearly ascertain that this is the case.

The third proposition affirms that the means of subsistence cannot possibly be increased so fast in old countries, as to allow their population to expand at its natural or possible rate; and that from this reason some one or more of the checks must for ever continue to act in such countries.

To prove this, it is necessary to form an estimate, firstly, of the possible increase of population; and, secondly, of the rate at which, under the most favourable circumstances, the supply of food could be increased in old countries; and to compare the two estimates. The first question, then, is, What is the possible increase of population? at what rate can the human race multiply when placed in the most favourable circumstances? There are two ways of estimating this: either by considering the most rapid increase which is actually known to take place in any country; or by calculating in the abstract the reproductive powers of the female sex, and observing by what means their action is checked in old countries.

First let us consider what is the highest rate known in any country. On this point all observers are agreed. "It has been established beyond all question," says Mr. M'Culloch, the eminent statistical authority, "that the population of some of the states of North America, after making due allowance for immigration, has continued to double for a century past in so short a period as twenty or at most five-and-twenty years." Even this falls very far short of the possible rate of increase, as is seen by the short average of life in America, and by the large amount of the reproductive power which, even in that country, is lost from celibacy and prostitution. However, for the demonstration of the Malthusian law, it is quite sufficient to take 25 years as the estimate of the possible rate of increase. It may be regarded, then, as an ascertained fact, that population, when the means of subsistence are sufficiently abundant, can easily double itself every 25 years. The capacity of increase in the human race, as in all other organised beings, is in fact boundless and immeasurable.

We arrive at a similar result by considering in the abstract the female reproductive powers. It is a moderate estimate to assume that each woman could produce ten or twelve children, were these powers not checked by various causes. Many individual women in our society do produce as many or more, and the causes which prevent others from doing so, are simple and obvious; they are, in fact, and can only be, the very same five checks already enumerated.

Having, therefore, ascertained that population under favourable circumstances can easily double itself every 25 years, the next question is, can the means of subsistence in old countries also do so? Can the supply of food be doubled every 25 years? We know both from reason and experience that this cannot possibly be done. In old and civilized countries all the most fertile land has long since been brought under cultivation, and land even of a very inferior quality has been resorted to; so that it is out of the question to suppose that the home produce could be doubled every 25 years. Importation of food, as Mr. Mill has shown, is also a limited resource, for the corn-exporting countries are either poor in capital, and therefore without the means of rapidly increasing their cultivation, or, like America, their own population is advancing so rapidly as to need the most of the food for their own support. All experience confirms these theoretical conclusions. Even in England, where, during the last half-century, the increase of the means of subsistence, by improvements in domestic agriculture and the importation of food, have been quite unparalleled in the history of an old country, it has not enabled population to advance with a rapidity at all approaching to that of America.

Thus we see that the true cause that checks the increase of food and population in old countries is the limited extent and productiveness of their land. The general law, which determines the productiveness of land, is called by political economists the "Law of Agricultural Industry" or the "Law of Diminishing Productiveness." It is, that the returns to agricultural industry tend to diminish; that after an early stage in the progress of cultivation, the produce of the soil does not increase in an equal proportion with the labour bestowed on it. The proof of this law is the fact, that inferior lands are cultivated; for the very meaning of inferior land, is that which with equal labour returns less produce. The elaborate cultivation seen in this and other old countries is another proof of this law; for such high farming costs much more in proportion than the low farming seen in America and other new colonies, where land is plentiful and labour dear.

"This general law of agricultural industry," says Mr. Mill, "is the most important proposition in political economy. Were it different, almost all the phenomena of the production and distribution of wealth would be other than they are." Were this law not counteracted by several tendencies of an opposite character, it would, by diminishing the proportional returns to agriculture, not only maintain but necessarily *increase* the population checks in each successive generation, until it had worn society down to what is called by political economists *the stationary state;* namely, where population and capital either do not increase at all, or very slowly. The circumstances which tend to counteract the law, are improvements in agriculture and the other arts of production; so that the question whether the condition of a people at any given time be improving or deteriorating, depends on the state of the balance between these two opposite tendencies; on the question whether improvement be increasing faster than population, or population than improvement.

The law of agricultural industry, therefore, or in other words, the impossibility of increasing the means of subsistence with sufficient rapidity, is the fundamental cause why population has always hitherto been checked in old countries, and must always continue to · be so. The law of population is a secondary or derivative law, arising from the laws of exercise, fecundity, and agricultural industry, in the same manner as the law of the earth's rotation arises from the opposing forces of gravitation, and of rectilinear motion. It is this natural antagonism between the laws of the human constitution, and those of the soil, which forms the true, though unseen barrier, on which the hopes of mankind have in every age been wrecked. The great social evils of old countries, when reduced to their simplest expression, are found to arise from the vast superiority of the powers of increase in man over the powers of increase in the land; from the antagonism between the laws of exercise and fecundity, which preside over the reproductive organs and passions, and the law of agricultural industry.

As a further illustration of the truth of the third proposition, and of the utter fallacy of all attempts to subvert it, let us apply the American rate of increase to the population of this country. Is it conceivably possible, that the population of England or any other old country should double itself every 25 years? In Great Britain there are now about 21 millions: is it conceivable that the means of subsistence could be so rapidly increased, as to allow these 21 millions to swell to 42 millions in the first 25 years; to 84 millions in the next; to 168 millions in the next, &c.? The supposition is evidently absurd. Even the rate of increase of the last 68 years (in which time the British population has doubled) cannot possibly be long continued. If it were, it would increase our population in three centuries to about 1300 millions; or in other words, to more than the total population of the globe, which is estimated at about 1000 millions. The rate of increase has already begun to slacken, as is shown by the last three Census Reports, which give a constantly diminishing proportional increase for each successive decenniad.

It may therefore be regarded as a settled truth, that the population of old countries must always remain under the powerful action of some one or more of the retarding causes; and that the only difference in this respect which can exist between such countries, is in the relative collective amount of the checks, and the proportional action of each individually. It is a mere question of *relative* amount; no old country, by any exertion, can escape from an immense *absolute* amount.

Let us now proceed to the fourth proposition. It is intended to expose the fallacy, which more than almost any other confuses the subject in many minds; namely, that *Emigration* is a mode of escape from the population-evils of old countries, and that it can supply the place of the other checks. But when we consider the power of human increase, as shown by the fact that population can easily double itself every 25 years, we can clearly perceive that no possible amount of emigration could suffice to neutralize it. All attainable means of emigration could not enable a single old country, much less all such countries together, to put forth its full powers of increase even for one generation. Emigration, moreover, is a mere accident in human history; and in the great majority of the countries of the old world its action as a population-check is quite insignificant. Even in this country, in which it has been carried of late years to an extent quite unparalleled, it has made but little perceptible difference in the grinding pressure of the other checks.

The full and complete statement of the law of population is contained in the concluding sentence of the fourth proposition, in which the main checks to population are reduced to five. But with a view to the popular discussion of the subject, which sooner or later must come, it is desirable to reduce the law to a shorter and more comprehensible form. In order to do this, one of the checks, namely, *Sterility*, may be struck off the list, for the following reasons. In the first place, its action, compared with that of the others, is insignificant. Secondly, it is not one of the true population-checks; namely, those which are caused *directly* by the law of population, and whose distinguishing characteristics will be given presently.

The term "Poverty," also, may be substituted for "Premature Death:" firstly, because poverty is far the most important cause of premature death in most civilized countries; and secondly, because it is more directly and obviously the effect of the law of population. Poverty, or a low rate of general wages, depends on there being too many labourers in a country, in proportion to its capital—a state of things produced and constantly kept up by the over-exercise of the reproductive powers. Poverty is also openly recognised as the chief social evil, while premature death has been little considered; so that it is better, for practical purposes, to take a part for the whole, and to use the term poverty, instead of premature death. For similar reasons, the terms "celibacy" and "prostitution" seem to me preferable to "sexual abstinence" and "sterility;" for although the latter are more comprehensive (celibacy being only one kind of sexual abstinence, and prostitution one kind of sterility), the others will be more readily understood and acknowledged as great social evils.

The list of the checks is thus reduced to four, namely, Celibacy, Prostitution, Preventive Intercourse, and Poverty, which should be called *the true population-checks.* The distinguishing characteristics of the true population-checks are,—

1st, That they depend directly on the law of population; that is, on the impossibility of obtaining a sufficiency of both food and natural love for all the inhabitants of an old country. And,

2nd, That their proportional amount is under human control; or, in other words, that any one of them can be increased, or diminished, though only by a counter-balancing diminution or increase of the others.

The law of population may therefore be shortly expressed in the following terms: "The natural increase of population has always been and must always continue to be, most powerfully checked in all old countries by Celibacy, Prostitution, Preventive Intercourse, or Poverty; whose collective amount varies inversely in proportion to the rapidity with which the population of each country is increasing, and to the number of emigrants as compared with that of immigrants, while the amount of each individually varies inversely in proportion to the others." To make this law scientifically correct, it is only necessary to use the terms premature death instead of poverty, and sexual abstinence and sterility instead of celibacy and prostitution. This is *the chief law of social science;* on which all effectual efforts to raise our society must be based. Previous to its discovery, the theory of society was an unintelligible chaos, which Mr. Malthus reduced to system and order. All views of human life which do not proceed from a full recognition of this terrible law of nature—however interesting they may be from the genius and benevolence of their authors—are radically fallacious, and are powerless to produce any real amelioration of the social evils. It is not a question of mental power merely, but of accurate knowledge; of that which in the social as well as the other sciences, constitutes the advantage possessed by the merest student of to day over the greatest minds of the past.

In order more fully to comprehend this law, let us examine it more narrowly. It affirms that some of these four population-checks exist at present to an enormous extent in all old countries; and that their existence does not depend on defects of national character, as is generally believed, but on a necessity in nature. Their collective amount in each country depends on the rapidity with which the population is increasing; which again depends partly on the industrial energies of the people, but mainly on their powers of obtaining the means of subsistence at home or abroad. These powers in all old countries are necessarily limited; and therefore, however the inhabitants may toil and save, they cannot possibly escape from an immense collective amount of the population checks. After this collective amount has been diminished to the utmost, none of the individual checks can be further diminished, except by a proportional increase of some of the others. Poverty, for instance, cannot decrease except by the increase of celibacy, or prostitution, or preventive intercourse; celibacy cannot decrease except on similar conditions, &c. Any one of them (excepting prostitution) may take the place of the other three; but solely on condition that it be increased in exact proportion as they are diminished. There is no other possible manner of getting rid of poverty, prostitution, and preventive intercourse, than by the increase of celibacy to an extent sufficient to supply their place; and poverty, prostitution, and celibacy, cannot possibly be got rid of, except by an exactly proportional increase of preventive intercourse.

The true social problem is thus seen to be, in which of these modes is the inevitable check to population to be effected? As it is universally admitted that poverty and prostitution are evils of so appalling a character that they must be removed at any cost, the choice is necessarily limited to celibacy and preventive intercourse; one or other of which two checks every thinker must choose, who would meet and not evade the real discussion of social questions. To seek to remove poverty or prostitution by any other means, is to bid defiance to nature, and to ignore her laws. From the inexorable necessity of his life, man's choice lies only *between* these checks, not independently of them; and thus we see that it is absolutely impossible for human society in old countries to live a *truly natural* life. Individuals may do so, but society cannot. These truths are as certain and indisputable as any with which we are acquainted.

But this is not all; the choice of mankind does not, really and practically, lie between celibacy or sexual abstinence, and preventive intercourse. The real choice is between preventive intercourse on the one side, and celibacy, prostitution, and poverty (that is, the present state of things), on the other; for population, I am convinced, never was and never will be in any country adequately checked by celibacy alone. Prolonged sexual abstinence is so intolerable an evil that it has never been borne alone, but has always been found associated with the alternative evils of prostitution and poverty. The difficulties of adequately practising sexual abstinence lead to poverty, and from poverty on the one hand and celibacy on the other arises prostitution; and it is vain to suppose that the same combination of evils would not continue to be found. Indeed, in order to remove poverty, and to admit all individuals to a just share in the sexual enjoyments, the state of sexual abstinence would need to be maintained by the whole of society till the age of from thirty to thirty-five or upwards; a state of things which it is not only quite visionary to expect, but which would probably be even more wretched than the present. Therefore, to choose celibacy as the desirable population-check, is in reality to choose along with it prostitution and poverty, or in other words, to accept as irremediable the present state of human misery and degradation. To choose *neither* celibacy nor preventive intercourse, and to suppose that no such choice is requisite, betrays, as already observed, an ignorance of the most fundamental difficulties of human life.

From the above considerations, it becomes apparent that *the sexual questions* are the true primary questions which demand the attention of mankind: and until they be earnestly investigated, instead of being suppressed, as at present, from a morbid delicacy, all treatment of social evils must be superficial and delusive. The three great social evils, Poverty, Prostitution, and Celibacy, are the immediate effects of the law of population, and are all of an essentially *sexual* nature. They should be called *the primary social evils*, for, like the deepest strata, they underlie all the others, and either directly or indirectly originate them. Crime, drunkenness, ignorance, disease, &c., although doubtless often arising from other sources, are in the main caused and kept up by poverty, prostitution, and celibacy—by the low rate of wages, the miserable condition of the labouring classes, and the fundamental sexual difficulties of mankind; and therefore they may properly be termed *the secondary social evils*. It is indeed often loosely said that crime, ignorance, or drunkenness, is the cause of poverty; but (unless by the term ignorance be meant an ignorance of the law of population, and of the means of limiting offspring) this is a very great error, and is completely to invert the real order of cause and effect. These secondary evils undoubtedly often produce *individual* cases of poverty; but they have no effect in causing *social* poverty, or, in other words, in lowering the general rate of wages, in a civilized and industrious country such as England; and this is the real question at issue. In such a country, it cannot be too often repeated, the only cause of social poverty is over-procreation. Since, therefore, the secondary evils are in the main caused by the primary ones, the former also must be regarded as having really, though more remotely, a *sexual* origin. According to this view of the order of causation, moreover, it is plain that the only effectual mode of removing the secondary evils is first to remove the poverty, prostitution, and celibacy, from which they mainly arise; and until this be earnestly attempted, the various efforts which are made for the prevention of crime, disease, ignorance, and other secondary evils, must be superficial, and can be attended with but a very limited success. Such is, in brief outline, the Malthusian or sexual theory of the causation of the social evils.

There is no part of the population-truths so difficult to convey to most minds as the *inexorable necessity* of the population-checks. Man is yet so little accustomed to consider himself as subject, like all other parts of nature, to fixed and invariable laws, and still less to a law so awful to contemplate as that of population—a law which renders it impossible for him in old countries to live a natural life—that it is very difficult fully to realize this truth. There are two things which chiefly tend to hide it from the inattentive eye. The one is, that single individuals may, and often do, escape from the population-checks—that they marry early, exercise fully their reproductive powers, produce and rear a large family, and yet live to an old age. But although individuals may thus escape, it is only at the expense of the rest of society. If they do not submit to their just share of the inevitable population-checks, they must aggravate the share that falls to others. Every one who in an old country has a large family, increases the amount of celibacy, prostitution, preventive intercourse, or poverty, in some other part of society. Thus, we see, that though individuals may escape, society cannot. If we regard society, and not individuals, we shall find everywhere throughout the old world, the population-checks existing in an amount inversely proportional to the rapidity with which their population is increasing.

The other circumstance which chiefly tends to hide the *necessity* of the checks, is the apparently indefinite degree to which they may be diminished by human energy. Thus, population in England has doubled in the last 53 years, while in Turkey at the recent rate of increase, it would need 555 years to do so. This is owing to the greater amount of industrial skill and energy in the former country; and it always seems to the uninstructed observer as if the energies which have done so much to diminish the *relative* amount of the checks, could remove them *absolutely*: but we have already seen the utter fallacy of this supposition. All that the utmost efforts of the best directed industry can effect in any old country is merely to stretch the iron girdle which confines human increase; to escape from it is impossible.

Nay more, as has been shown conclusively by Mr. John Stuart Mill, the most advanced social philosopher of this or any other age—the tendency of all industrial progress is not merely to maintain the population-check, but to increase it to the maximum in every nation of the world: in other words, all nations tend ultimately to *the stationary state*, in which capital and population either do not increase at all, or at most very slowly. The reason of this, as has already been mentioned, is the gradually diminishing productiveness of labour and consequent fall of profits, owing to the law of agricultural industry. Nor is the stationary state—the ultimate goal of all industrial progress —by any means so far distant from any old country, as not to be fully in view. Most of the Asiatic nations have been for ages almost stationary: and we have seen how very slow is the increase of population at least, in many European countries, such as Switzerland, Holland, and France: in which the slow progress assuredly does not arise from want of national energy, but from want of fertile land. The chief circumstance which in England postpones the stationary state, and prevents a rapid slackening in the increase both of population and capital, is that there are still some exceptional countries in the world, such as America and Australia, where labour is highly productive, and from which England can procure the means of subsistence at a cheap rate by international commerce—which tends to raise the productiveness of labour in the different parts of the globe. If all her labour and capital were confined to the comparatively unproductive field afforded by her own and the sister countries of the old world, no amount of energy could prevent a rapid slackening in the increase of both population and capital, and a consequent augmentation of some one or other of the population checks, in England.

Let us next proceed to *verify* the law of population, by comparing it, in a somewhat more detailed manner, with actual facts, and by observing whether its truth is attested by the state of society in this and other countries. Let us take any country of the old world—for instance, England—and examine whether the amount of the population-checks in it really corresponds to that which is indicated by the rate of increase of its population: whether their *absolute* amount is very great, as the law affirms to be the case in all old countries: and also whether their *relative* amount, on comparison with other countries, varies in proportion to the difference in the rate of increase.

The population of England has doubled in the last 53 years, that of the United States in 25 years. Is it then attested by known facts, that this great difference in the rate of increase is due to a greater amount of the population-checks in the former country? To ascertain this, it is necessary to examine the proportional amount of each check successively, as far as our knowledge may enable us.

In the first place, *sterility* need not be taken into consideration in comparing two countries together; for it may be reasonably assumed that the number of women who are barren from other causes than prostitution does not vary materially in different countries. Sterility is of importance rather with regard to the *absolute* than the *relative* amount of the checks; and even then its action is quite insignificant compared with that of others. Like almost all chronic diseases, it is probably less prevalent amongst uncivilized nations; but among those who stand nearly on the same grade of civilization, it may be taken, for practical purposes, as *a constant quantity.*

It is therefore in the remaining checks that the cause of the difference between the English and American rates of increase must be

sought. Let us therefore examine them methodically in succession.

1st. *Premature Death* is not the cause of the difference; for the average of life is not shorter in England than America, but on the contrary, rather longer. "The mean duration of life in the English race," says Mr. M'Culloch in his Geographical Dictionary, "has been inconsiderably affected by the climate of America. We have calculated the mortality of the cities of New York and Philadelphia, and it will be found to differ little from English cities of the same extent." Premature Death, therefore, though existing in a very great *absolute* degree in England (the average of life being only 40 years), does not account for the *relatively* slow rate of increase.

2nd. *Celibacy*, however, prevails in a very much greater degree in England than in America. This is clearly shown to be the case by the Census of 1851, which reveals the amount of celibacy in England by the following statement:

"The mean age at which marriages are first contracted in England and Wales is nearly 26 years for males, and 24½ years for females. There are in the kingdom 1,407,225 women between the age of 20 and 40, and 359,969 of the age of 40 and upwards, who have never married: while the number of men between the age of 20 and 40 who have never married, is 1,413,912, and of those aged 40 and upwards, 275,204. Of every 100 women in Great Britain of the age of 20 to 40, 42 are spinsters. If the whole of the population were married, the births in Great Britain would, instead of 700,000, be about 1,600,000 annually, if they bore the same proportio nto the wives at different ages as they do now." In the appendix to the fourth annual Report of the Registrar General in 1842, Dr. William Farr says, "The fact that one-fifth of the people of this country who attain the age of marriage never marry; and that the women, though capable of bearing children at 16, and certainly nubile at 17, do not marry until they attain a mean age of 24.3, the men until they are 25½, proves that prudence, or moral restraint, in Mr. Malthus's sense of the term, is in practical operation in England to an extent which had not been conceived, and will perhaps scarcely be credited, when stated in numbers."

In America, on the contrary, marriages are much more numerous, and also on the average much earlier. "Under the favourable circumstances presented by the States," says Mr. M'Culloch, "every man might enter into matrimonial engagements without being deterred, as in old-settled, and densely peopled countries, by the fear of not being able to provide for the children that might be expected to spring from them. In America, indeed, and in all similarly situated countries, a large family is a source of wealth: marriages in consequence are at once comparatively general and early." The number of children and young people in the United States, as might be expected from these facts, is remarkably great; for only one person in every six is 40 years of age and upwards.

3rd & 4th. With regard to *prostitution* and *preventive intercourse*, it is obviously difficult to form an accurate estimate of their amount in any country; but it is probable that both prevail to a considerably greater extent in England than in America, where a family is so much more easily provided for, and the number of unmarried people so much smaller. That prostitution does exist to a very great extent in all our large towns is well known. In London, Sir Richard Mayne, the Commissioner of Police, estimates the number of regular prostitutes, who live solely by the exercise of their trade, at from 8,000 to 10,000, exclusive of the city; while Mr. Talbot states, as the result of the most careful inquiries, that the number in Edinburgh is about 800; in Glasgow, 1,800; in Liverpool, 2,900; in Leeds, 700; in Bristol, 1,300; in Manchester, 700; and in Norwich, between 500 and 700. "If to these we add the number furnished by other towns," says Mr. Arthur Helps, in his essay on Prostitution, in the *Westminster Review* for July, 1850, "and the numbers who everywhere escape the knowledge of the police, the impression among the best informed is, that the number who live by prostitution, whose sole profession it may be said to be, cannot be under 50,000 in Great Britain."

5th. *Emigration* has also been an important cause of the difference in the rate of increase. For several years after the famine of 1847, the emigrants from the United Kingdom averaged above 300,000 annually; the greater part, however, being Irish. In the previous years the amount of emigration, though considerably less than this, was still very great. Thus there were 57,212 emigrants in 1843, and 93,501 in 1845.

It is evident, therefore, that in the case of England, the Law of Population is fully verified: that the *absolute* amount of the population-checks, which are known to exist in the country, are sufficient to explain the slow rate of increase: and also, that the *relative* amount of some of them, especially celibacy and emigration, is so much greater in England than in America, as to account for the different rates of increase in these two countries.

The immediate reason why there is so much more celibacy and emigration in England than in the States, is because there is so much more *poverty* in the former country. The difficulty of gaining a livelihood is so great, that immense numbers are induced to refrain from marriage or to emigrate in search of better fortunes. These efforts and sacrifices, however, although probably unparalleled in the history of any country, have been inadequate to prevent the existence of the most grinding poverty; as is shown by a consideration of the low rate of wages in many employments, and also of the number in receipt of parish assistance. The agricultural laborers in some of the southern counties of England receive when in full work only seven or eight shillings a week, with which they have to support their wives and families. The wages of the female workers in many occupations are still lower; the shirt-makers, shoe-binders, &c., being often unable to earn more than two or three shillings a week, even by working fourteen or fifteen hours daily. So indescribably appalling, indeed, is the degree of poverty and hard work in this country, that I quite agree in the opinion expressed by Mr. Ernest Jones in one of his noble addresses to the working classes in St. Martin's Hall:—"Though there are exceptions among the high-paid trades," he says, "yet speaking of the bulk of labor, manufacturing and agricultural, I fearlessly assert that the condition of the Hindoo Pariah, the Russian serf, and the Negro slave, is not so bad as that of the English working man." Mr. Mill observes that the wages of the English laborers "are, in proportion to their efficiency, quite as low as in Ireland."

The amount of pauperism is shown by the following statement from the Census of 1851. "According to the returns of the Poor Law Board, the number of paupers in receipt of relief, both in-door and out-door, in England and Wales, was 862,827 on 1st January, 1851; and 813,089 on 1st July, 1851. At the time of the Census, 126,488 paupers were inmates of workhouses in England and Wales."

The *secondary* social evils, such as crime, drunkenness, ignorance, and disease, are scarcely less fearful to contemplate; the number of habitual criminals being estimated at about 150,000. "Out of a total of sixteen millions souls in England and Wales," says Mr. Mayhew, in his London Labor and London Poor, "one-eighth, or 12 per cent. of the whole, continue their existence by pauperism, mendicancy, or crime."

In America, on the contrary, wages are comparatively so high, and employment so easily obtained, that there is little if any poverty for those who are able and willing to work; at least this has been the case until recently, but poverty seems to be gaining ground in the large towns in the eastern states, in consequence of their becoming gradually over-populated. We have seen, however, that notwithstanding this comparative absence of social poverty, the average of life is not higher than in England; and this fact shows not only the delusive character of the average of life, when taken alone, as a test of the social circumstances of a people, but shows also the propriety of substituting the term poverty, instead of premature death, in the popular discussion of the law of population. Poverty is a far better test of the action of the population law on civilized countries than the average of life; for this is lowered by many other causes than poverty and hard work, and therefore cannot be said to depend so directly on the law of population. Poverty, however, as will be shown more fully presently, is directly, and indeed almost entirely, caused by this law. "Poverty," says Mr. Malthus, "is the specific effect of the principle of population." Moreover, poverty is in all old and civilized countries by far the most important cause of premature death, and the chief obstacle to all sanitary improvements.

Let us next examine whether the Law of Population be verified by what we know of the state of society in France. In this country the rate of increase is very much slower than even in England. We have seen that the time needed for duplication has been calculated by M. Moreau de Jonnès at 138 years. Nay, it is stated by M. Legoyt, from an analysis of the official returns, that in the years between 1841 and 1846, the increase was not much more than one in 200; and at the two quinquennial Censuses which have taken place since that time, the increase has been so small that the population may be said to be stationary. M. Leonce de Lavergne, in his essay on Agriculture and Population, in the Revue des Deux Mondes, for April 1st, 1857, says, "The progress of the population has almost come to a stand. From 1841 to 1846, the population had increased in five years by 1,170,000 souls; from 1847 to 1851 there was only an increase of 383,000;" and from 1851 to 1856, an increase "of 256,000 souls." In 1790 the French population amounted to 26½ millions; in 1856, or 66 years later, it amounted to 36 millions. But the English population has doubled itself in the 53 years previous to 1851; and there must therefore be an immense difference in the relative amount of the population-checks in the two countries. To ascertain clearly what share each check has had in the difference, it is necessary, as before, to examine them in succession; sterility, for the reasons already given, being omitted.

1st. *Premature Death* is not the cause of the difference, especially of late years; for the average of life does not differ much in the two countries. In England, it is stated by the last census as about 40 years; in France, according to the census of 1846, it was 39 years. The average of life in both countries has risen greatly since the beginning of the century. The very slow rate of increase exhibited by M. Legoyt, is, he says, wholly the effect of a diminution of deaths, the number of births not increasing at all; while the proportion of births to the population is constantly diminishing. 2nd. Nor is *Emigration* the cause of the difference; for instead of being greater, it is very much less in France. In fact, the influence of emigration as a check to population in France may be said to be null. "The emigration to Algeria, California, and America," says M. de Lavergne, "does not carry off on an average more than 10,000 persons annually, and it is almost compensated for by the foreigners—Belgians, Germans, Swiss, &c.—who come to establish themselves in France, and especially at Paris. . . The influence of emigration is almost nothing." 3rd. Nor is *Celibacy* the cause; for not only are marriages more numerous, I believe, in France than in England, but it is a well-known fact that sexual abstinence is far less practised by unmarried people in the former country. 4th. Nor is it *Prostitution;* for the number of women in whom the reproductive powers are lost from this cause is, I believe, less in France than in England. M. Duchatelet states that in 1831 there were 3,500 prostitutes in Paris, which is a smaller proportional number than in London.

How then is the difference to be explained? What has become of the prodigious amount of reproductive power which has to be accounted for, when we consider not only the very slow rate of increase, but the comparatively small degree of the other population-checks, celibacy, prostitution, and emigration? Unless it be assumed, in the words of Mr. Malthus, that "a perpetual miracle renders the women barren," there is no other possible mode of accounting for the difference than by ascribing it to the only remaining check, namely, preventive intercourse. Accordingly, this is found, on inquiry, to be the true solution of the difficulty.

5th. *Preventive intercourse* is known to have become of late years very prevalent, indeed, I believe, almost universal in French society. In proof of this, I may quote the statement of Dr. Felix Roubaud, who in his admirable work on L'Impuissance et la Sterilité (the latest and most complete treatise on these diseases) speaks of "the habits of incomplete sexual intercourse, which the necessities of our social state have imposed on almost all the classes of society." Dr. A. Mayer, in his work on the Rapports Conjugaux (Conjugal Relations) alludes to preventive intercourse as being "so deeply rooted in our manners, that it may be affirmed that very few families are exempt from it." "I include in this affirmation," he says, "all the classes of society, except those who are sunk in the lowest depths of misery and hope-lessness." Mr. Robert Dale Owen says in his admirable work on Moral Physiology, "As every intelligent traveller in France must have remarked, there is scarcely to be found among the middle and upper classes (and seldom even among the working classes) a large family—seldom more than three or four children. A French lady of the utmost delicacy and respectability will, in common conversation, say as simply (ay, and as *innocently*, whatever the self-righteous prude may aver to the contrary) as she would proffer any common remark about the weather: 'I have three children; my husband and I think that it is as many as we can do justice to, and I do not intend to have any more.' I have stated notorious facts—facts which no traveller who has visited Paris, and been admitted to the domestic life of its inhabitants, will attempt to deny. However heterodox therefore my view of the subject may be in this country, I am supported in it by the opinion and practice of one of the most refined and socially cultivated nations in the world." M. de Lavergne says in the essay already referred to, "France is the country where the counsels of Malthus have been the most attacked; it is also that in which they have been the most instinctively followed;" (that is, as far as the limitation of offspring, though not the mode of effecting that limitation, is concerned). A medical friend told me that when conversing lately on the sexual questions with one of the most eminent surgeons in Paris, the latter said to him, "We are all Malthusians here." He informed him that the practice of preventive intercourse is very general among the French; the means usually employed being that of withdrawal previous to ejaculation. "Among the modes of preventing conception, which may have prevailed in various countries," says Mr R. D. Owen in his Moral Physiology, "that which has been adopted, and is now practised by the cultivated classes on the continent of Europe, by the French, by the Italians, and, I believe, by the Germans and Spaniards, consists of complete withdrawal on the part of the man, immediately previous to emission. . . In France, where men consider this (as it ought ever to be considered when the interests of the other sex require it) *a point of honor*, all young men learn to make the necessary effort; and custom renders it easy, and a matter of course."

This restraint on population has had a marked effect in lessening

poverty. "The slow growth of the numbers of the people," says
Mr. Mill, "while capital increases much more rapidly, has caused a
noticeable improvement in the condition of the laboring class." Sir
Francis Head bears a similar testimony with regard to the working-
classes in Paris. He visited the poorest quarters in that city along
with Lord Shaftesbury, and declares that they were unable to discover
anything at all approaching to the squalor and wretchedness of the
corresponding parts of our large towns. The French workmen, he
also remarked, did not labor so hard or so unremittingly as the English. M. Ambrose Clement, in his Recherches sur les Causes de
l' Indigence (Researches on the Causes of Indigence), published in
1846, says, "The classes of our population who have only their wages
to support them, and who are consequently the most exposed to indigence, are now-a-days much better provided with food, clothing,
and lodging, than they were in the beginning of the century. . . .
This fact is attested by all persons who can remember the former of
the compared epochs. . . . If any doubt should remain on the
point, it may readily be dissipated by consulting the old peasants and
artizans, as we have ourselves done in several localities, without meeting
with a single contradictory opinion. The facts collected on the subject
by an accurate observer, M. Villermé (Tableau de l'Etat Physique et
Moral des Ouvriers) may also be cited." M. de Lavergne, although
he deplores the arrest of the French population during the last 10
years, makes the following remarks with regard to the preceding
period: "According to Malthus, the virtual power of multiplication
in man is such, that if it were not checked by want of subsistence,
population could double itself every 25 years; on this calculation it
might have been more than 100 millions in France, in 1846. What
has checked it, is the deficiency of the means of subsistence. We
know in effect that from 1790 to 1846, the produce of agriculture has
only been doubled. On the other hand, if population had increased
exactly in the same proportion, it would in 1846 have amounted to
53 millions; it was however only 35½ millions. Whence comes this
new difference? From a progressive amelioration in the average
condition of the people. The division of the means of subsistence
among the inhabitants gave, I will suppose, 100 francs a head in
1790; the same division in 1846 gave 150 francs. If we add the produce of manufactures, and suppose for example that this amounted
in 1790 to 50 francs a head, and in 1846 to 150, the average of comfort
would have been doubled; and, in effect, this is what must have taken
place; and if we attend to the element indicated by Malthus, as the
true measure of the prosperity of a people, namely, the average of life,
we find that in this interval, it has increased from 28 to 39 years."
From these statements, it would appear that preventive intercourse has
already done more to lighten the burden of poverty in France, than
the vast amount of celibacy and emigration, aided by the most unrivalled industrial efforts, have been able to effect in England.

It may be mentioned that at the time when the stationary state of
the French population was made known by the census of 1856, it was

ascribed in a leading article of the *Times*, in *Reynolds'*, and in some of our other newspapers, to *sterility*, instead of to the use of preventive measures. This view is similar to that of Mr. Doubleday and Mr. Herbert Spencer, already considered ; the chief difference being that the latter writers regard sterility as an instance of the beneficent adaptations of nature, whereas the writers in the *Times* and in *Reynolds' Newspaper*, deplore it as an evil, and a sign of the physical degeneracy of the French people. As far as the existence of the check in question is concerned, both views are equally groundless, and proceed from a hasty and superficial consideration of the subject. Sterility, except in so far as it arises from prostitution, never was nor will be in any country other than a most insignificant check to population ; as any one will readily see who considers the prodigious powers of human fecundity, the comparative rarity of sterility, and the changeless nature of the physiological laws. The law of fecundity, like all the other bodily functions, is a law of adamant, which can never be expected to vary one iota as long as man exists on the earth ; whereas Mr. Doubleday, Mr. Spencer, and the writer in the *Times*, appear to regard it as a law of wax, liable to be profoundly affected by the varying circumstances of society. As well might it be supposed that the number of the heart's pulsations, or of the respiratory movements, would be altered by such causes. It may be asked also, Is sterility the cause of the slow increase of population in Norway and Switzerland ? or in Great Britain, as compared with the United States ? Is it the cause of the very different rates of increase which have taken place in our own and other countries at different periods of their history ? We learn from the Census of 1851 that "the people of Great Britain amounted to more than seven millions in 1751, and to more than twenty-one millions in 1851; they having increased more than fourteen millions in the hundred years ; while the increase of numbers in the preceding century, 1651—1751, was only one million." No one surely will venture to ascribe this great difference in the rate of increase to the sterility of our ancestors ; and yet it is just as groundless to ascribe to such a cause the slow increase of population in France. Far truer is the explanation given in a leading article in the *Daily News*, of April 18th, 1857. "The French," says the writer, "are a people who *will not* increase in numbers, without an increase in wealth, and this resolve does them infinite honor."

To obtain one further illustration of the truth of the law, let us take Switzerland. The rate of increase in this country is extremely slow, the time needed for duplication being, as we have seen, 227 years. That this is not owing to the *positive check*, is shown by the high average of life, and the comfortable circumstances of the people. In several of the Swiss Cantons, as has been attested by numerous observers, there is a total absence of pauperism, and (it might almost be said) of poverty. "In no country of Europe," says Mr. Inglis, "will be found so few poor as in the Engadine. In the village of Suss, which contains about six hundred inhabitants, there is not a single individual who has not wherewithal to live comfortably, not a

single individual who is indebted to others for one morsel he eats."
Emigration also is proportionally less from Switzerland than from
England. *Prostitution* is also rare, especially in the pastoral cantons,
where population increases least rapidly. The cause of the slow increase *must* therefore lie in one or other of the preventive checks,
celibacy, or *preventive intercourse:* and accordingly we find on inquiry,
that the age of marriage is very late, and the number of births extremely small. "Concerning both Norway and parts of Switzerland,"
says Mr. Mill, "there happens to be unusually authentic information:
many facts were carefully brought together by Mr. Malthus, and
much additional evidence has been obtained since his time. In both
these countries the increase of population is very slow: and what
checks it is not multitude of deaths, but fewness of births. Both the
births and the deaths are remarkably few in proportion to the population; the average duration of life is the longest in Europe: the
population contains fewer children, and a greater proportional number
of persons in the vigor of life, than is known to be the case in any
other part of the world. The paucity of births tends directly to
prolong life, by keeping the people in comfortable circumstances; and
the same prudence is doubtless exercised in avoiding causes of disease,
as in keeping clear of the principal cause of poverty." The only
question is, whether the small proportion of births be owing to
celibacy or preventive intercourse? From what is known of the
general character of manners on the Continent, it may be inferred,
that in all probability the latter cause is far the most influential.
Mr. Robert Dale Owen, as we have seen, speaks of preventive
intercourse as being "now practised by the cultivated classes on the
continent of Europe; by the French, the Italians, and I believe, by
the Germans and Spaniards." There is probably no country in the
world where, if the truth could be ascertained, sexual abstinence would
be found to exist in nearly so great a degree as in England; notwithstanding the comparatively rapid increase of population in the latter
country, and the enormous amount of poverty, prostitution, and
emigration

The above analysis (which has no pretension to statistical exactness,
but is rather intended as an instance of the manner in which such
inquiries may be conducted) is sufficient to show that the law of
population is fully verified by what we know of the state of society
in France and Switzerland: in both of which countries the births are
found to be so very few in proportion to the population, as to account
for the extremely slow rate of increase, and the comparatively minor
degree of poverty. If we were, in a similar manner, to pass in review
each nation of the old world, Germany, Turkey, China, or India, we
should obtain an equal verification of the law: we should find the
preventive and positive checks everywhere present in an enormous
degree, and varying inversely in proportion to each other: we should
find either the average of life very short, or the number of births very
small; and we should find, wherever we had means of gaining information, the collective amount of the checks exactly corresponding to

what was indicated by the rate of increase. All that is necessary in estimating the action of the population-law on any country, is to ascertain the rate of increase, and then to examine methodically in succession the share which each of the checks has had in retarding it. In this way, the law may be easily verified, in a rough and approximate manner, in every country of which we have any statistical knowledge at all : and no one, who has considered the impregnable character of the Malthusian arguments, can doubt, that if we had only adequate information, its truth could in every country be confirmed, even in the very minutest particular.

The law of population, therefore, however appalling to contemplate, must be accepted by every earnest and unprejudiced mind as the chief among those fixed and invariable laws of Nature which reign supreme over man's destiny on this earth : which he can as little hope to alter or evade, as to bind the planets in their course, or reverse the chemical affinities. More deaths or fewer births are inexorably necessitated by Nature in all old countries ; and celibacy, prostitution, preventive intercourse, or poverty, is the choice she offers to the human race. No nation of the old world ever has escaped from this choice, or ever will: poverty, prostitution, and celibacy, never have been, nor ever can be, removed in such a nation, except by an exactly corresponding increase of preventive intercourse. Nay more, when the tendency of industrial progress towards the stationary state is considered, it is clear that no human efforts can avail even to prevent a great *increase* of one or more of the population-checks: much less to remove them.

All therefore, that man can do, is clearly and openly to recognise the necessity of his life: to select from among the population-checks the one which involves least human suffering; and to see *that every member of society, whatever be his or her station in life, bear a just and equal share of the sexual difficulties common to all.* Until this be done, until the Law of Population be openly acknowledged, as the only true foundation of social morality, human society must continue, as it has hitherto been, a chaos of misery and injustice: a scene of confusion, where one man surfeits in a palace, while another starves in a hovel: where the toils of the poor never cease, and the cry of social distress is never silent: where one life is brightened by all the blessings of love and offspring, while another is shadowed in the gloom of celibacy or prostitution.

The method which has been pursued in the foregoing exposition of the law of population is similar to that adopted by its discoverer, Mr. Malthus. His work, it may be observed, is an admirable instance of the *concrete deductive method* of proof, which Mr. Mill, in his Logic, shows to be the only mode of arriving at the laws of complex phenomena, where many different causes are at work together. This method consists in reasoning from general laws of nature to their consequences, and then verifying the conclusions by an appeal to actual facts. It includes therefore, three processes, induction, deduction, and verification; the first of which consists in obtaining the general laws of nature by observation or experiment, the second in deducing theoretically the consequences of these laws, and the third in comparing the results arrived at with actual facts. Thus Mr. Malthus first establishes, by direct observation, the laws of fecundity and agricultural industry; then shows that these laws necessitate a powerful check to population, either preventive or positive, in all old countries; and lastly, verifies this conclusion by reviewing the past and present history of the different nations of the globe. It is in this way only, and not by specific observation or experiment, that the laws of complex phenomena can be ascertained. "To such cases," says Mr. Mill, "the Deductive Method, setting out from general laws and verifying their consequences by specific experience, is alone applicable."

Let us next proceed to consider somewhat more closely, the *manner* in which the law of population produces its three primary effects; and more particularly the manner in which it causes poverty through the economical *law of wages*. The mode of its action may be shortly described as follows.

The limited extent and productiveness of the land in all old countries prevents capital from increasing so fast as to allow population to expand at its natural rate. Population is therefore checked either by want, or the dread of want; by poverty or celibacy. But the powers of increase are so enormous, and their restraint so painful and irksome (in consequence of the Law of Exercise, which presides over the reproductive organs and emotions), that far more people are always brought into the world than can be supported in comfort; and the privations fall on the least fortunate part of society. That *too great numbers*, resulting from the enormous power of the principle of increase, are the immediate cause of poverty and low wages, appears in the clearest light from a consideration of the law of wages, as laid down in all scientific treatises on Political Economy.

The *Law of Wages*, which should be ineffaceably engraven on every mind, is, that *Wages depend on the demand and supply of Labor*: in other words, on the proportion between the laborers and the capital. Wages cannot rise except by there being more capital or fewer laborers; nor fall, except by there being less capital or more laborers. The proofs of this law are simple and obvious. It is evident that the share which each laborer will obtain of the fund destined for the payment of wages, depends on the amount of the fund, and the numbers among whom it is divided. The natural rate of Wages in any country is that which distributes the whole wages-fund, among the whole of the laborers. Wages cannot, in a state of free competition, be for any length of time kept *above* this natural rate; for if they were, some laborers would be thrown out of employment, and their competition would bring back the rate to its natural level. Nor can wages fall *below* this rate; for if they did, some of the capital would be left unemployed, and the competition of the capitalists would again raise wages to their natural level. Labor is a commodity brought to market and offered for sale like other commodities; and in a state of free competition, it cannot by any possibility be prevented from falling under the general laws of value. "The value of the commodity Labor," says Mr. Mill, "never depends upon anything but demand and supply."

The reason why wages are high in America is that capital is plentiful, and laborers scarce; while in this country, and still more in Ireland, they are low, because capital is relatively scarce, and laborers plentiful. In America, from the great extent of fertile land, profits are so high, and capital increases so rapidly, as to permit population to double itself every twenty-five years without a fall in the rate of wages; but this cannot possibly take place in any old country.

It is evident, therefore, that there are only two ways in which the natural rate of wages can be permanently raised: either by increasing the capital, or diminishing the number of laborers. But when we consider the circumstances of old countries, and especially of England, there cannot be a doubt, that it is mainly in the latter mode that any increase of wages could be obtained. The rate at which capital has increased in England during the last half-century has been so great, that we cannot even hope that it could be for any length of time *maintained*, far less accelerated. The extraordinary succession of inventions and improvements—the power-loom, the railway, and the rotation of crops—aided by the most indefatigable industry, has caused an increase of capital quite unexampled in the history of an old country; and has thus enabled population to double itself in 53 years. But the low rate of wages has been little, if at all raised; and the reason simply is, that the number of laborers has increased in an equal proportion with the capital. It is therefore only by diminishing the number of laborers—by an increase in the preventive check to population—that any general and permanent improvement in the condition of the working classes can be effected. "All schemes for their benefit," says Mr. Mill, "which do not proceed upon the principle of altering in their favour the proportion between labor and capital, are, for all permanent purposes, a delusion."

The mode therefore in which the vast superiority of the reproductive powers causes *poverty*, is by keeping the labor-market always overstocked; by bringing too many laborers into a country in proportion to its capital. *Celibacy*, again, is caused by the difficulties of providing for a family, and the fear of losing what is called one's position in society. The laborer sees that by having a family he would need to work harder, and probably fare worse; and the richer classes see that by marriage they would run the risk of sinking in the social scale, and involving themselves in pecuniary embarrassments. Both are thus induced to postpone marriage, or refrain from it entirely: but these prudential motives operate more powerfully among the latter class, partly because they have more advantages to lose, and partly from the resources offered by prostitution.

The mode in which the population-law causes *prostitution*, is not merely by the difficulties it creates in the way of marriage; this of itself could have little effect in causing prostitution. The circumstance by which prostitution, as a great social phenomenon, is

rendered possible, is the extraordinary fact, that a promiscuous intercourse tends to destroy the female reproductive powers. Were it not
for this fact, prostitution would present as insuperable difficulties as
marriage; and sexual abstinence, preventive intercourse, or premature
death, would alone be found, alternating with each other, in every
country of the old world. The fact however being as it is, the law of
population causes prostitution, by the insurmountable obstacles it
opposes to the normal exercise of the powerful reproductive passions
on the one hand, and by the low rate to which it reduces woman's
wages on the other; and thus prostitution has been resorted to by all
classes of society, but especially by those whose means better enabled
them to purchase a mercenary love, as a mode of escape from the
alternative miseries of poverty or celibacy.

It may be observed, that several treatises on Prostitution have
lately been published, and the subject has been discussed at the
meetings of the Social Science Association and elsewhere; but all the
treatises which I have seen (including those of Mr. Acton, Dr. Ryan,
Professor Miller, Mr. Arthur Helps, and the interesting investigations
of Mr. Mayhew) are, in my opinion, fundamentally mistaken with
regard to the *cause* and *cure* of this evil, in consequence of the writers'
ignorance, or (in the case of all the above-mentioned writers) their
rejection, of the law of population. Without a knowledge of this
great principle, indeed, it is quite in vain to attempt to deal with prostitution or any other of the great social evils, except in the most superficial manner. Unless it be clearly seen, that prostitution, like poverty,
is one of the population-checks, and that it cannot be diminished except
by a proportional increase of some of the others, its effectual treatment is hopeless. The question which should always be put to those
who aim at the removal of prostitution, as of poverty, is, What other
population-check do you propose to substitute in its place? As I
have already endeavoured to show, the true remedies for prostitution,
consist, firstly, in substituting for it preventive intercourse, so as to
remove its two primary causes, poverty and celibacy; and secondly,
in altering the strictness of the marriage code, the chief secondary
cause of prostitution.

In a country, such as England, where preventive intercourse is
comparatively little practised, the immediate checks to population
are poverty, prostitution, and celibacy; emigration acting at intervals
as a slight palliative, when the pressure of the others is felt to be too
insupportable, or some brilliant prospects of gain appear in another
part of the globe. The *collective* amount of the population-checks
depends, as we have seen, on the rate of increase which can be
attained by the industrial energies of the country, and on the amount
of emigration. The *individual* amount of each, as we have also seen,
depends upon that of the others; but the principal cause by which
this individual amount is determined deserves a closer examination.
This cause was called by Mr. Malthus, and by political economists
since his time, *the standard of comfort;* by which is meant, the point,
whatever it may be, down to which the people of any country will

multiply, but not lower. This standard varies in different countries: in Ireland it is extremely low, while in Switzerland it is comparatively high. The amount of poverty, and therefore of the other checks, is determined in all old countries by the standard of comfort, that is, by the degree in which the people will consent to restrain their reproductive powers; and by no other cause whatsoever.

"Wages," says Mr. Mill, "depend on the ratio between population and capital. As the ratio between population and capital, everywhere but in new colonies, depends on the strength of the checks by which the too rapid increase of population is restrained, it may be said, popularly speaking, that *wages depend on the checks to population;* that when the check is not death by starvation, or disease, wages depend on the prudence of the laboring people; and that wages, in any country, are habitually at the lowest rate, to which, in that country, the laborers will suffer them to be depressed rather than put a restraint upon multiplication." This shows still more clearly the indubitable truth of the conclusion to which we have already arrived by the abstract consideration of the Malthusian Law, and which is verified by all experience: namely, that no industrial efforts, or improvements of human institutions, can of themselves permanently lessen poverty; for the powers of human increase are so prodigious that they easily keep pace with any such improvements, and speedily obliterate their effects. This is illustrated by the fact, shown by the marriage registries, that in the seasons when trade is brisk, and the working classes comparatively prosperous, marriages are always more numerous; and thus the over-crowding of the labor market is constantly kept up. Indeed, an increase in the number of marriages is constantly cited by the Registrar-General, and by the *Economist* and *Times* Newspapers, as a sign of the prosperity of the working classes, and as a subject for national *congratulation;* whereas it is the very circumstance which (unless the procreative habits of the community be greatly changed, and preventive intercourse be practised) is *certain* in a few years to do away with any slight improvement which may have taken place in the condition of the people. An increase of sexual connections is indeed, in itself, one of the greatest blessings; but it is only a subject for true and unqualified congratulation, when it is not followed by a corresponding increase of offspring. It is on *the degree of reproductive restraint,* therefore, and on no other cause, moral, political, or economical, that the amount of poverty really depends. Celibacy, prostitution, preventive intercourse, or poverty forms the only choice of mankind; and the individual amount of each as stated in the Law of Population, varies inversely in proportion to the others. The exact point, at which, in a country where preventive intercourse is excluded, the other three population-checks tend to settle, is that, where the opposing evils of the want of food and of love most nearly balance each other in the estimation of the people.

The Law of Population is thus seen to be the true fundamental cause of poverty, prostitution, and celibacy: of the economical and sexual evils of old countries. There are two things which may be mentioned among many others, as at present greatly tending to disguise this grand truth, and to hide it from the general apprehension of mankind. The one is the institution of Marriage, the other Competition. The first conceals from many minds the true cause of the sexual evils: the second, that of the economical. Many have believed, and still believe, that the miseries of the sexual world depend primarily on the human institution of marriage; and it was on this error, that all the efforts of the sexual reformers of the last generation, Byron, Shelley, and Godwin, were shattered. The exquisite sense of social justice possessed by these men, revolted from the shocking inequalities in the distribution of love, which they saw around them in society; and thus they attributed the population-checks, celibacy and prostitution, to the monopoly of marriage. They were unaware that the true solution of the difficulty had already been given by Mr. Malthus; and that the primary cause of the evils they lamented, was a law of nature, and no institution of man. Marriage is merely a subordinate instrument of sexual restraint, acting under the law of population; and its removal would not make the slightest difference in the inexorable necessity of the population-checks. One of its chief evils at present is that it conceals the law of population, and prevents man from seeing clearly the true nature of his position. Those who are unacquainted with the law, think that people remain unmarried from choice, or pride, or their unattractive qualities, or from the great defects in the institution itself; but if so, there would be as little celibacy in England as in America or Australia. They do not see that the real obstacle to sexual union is opposed by Nature herself; and that indeed, the reproductive powers are already enormously over-exercised in every civilized country where poverty exists.

Competition has in like manner been made the scape-goat of the economical evils, by socialist and communist writers; and their views have largely infected the public mind. But the cause of poverty is evidently not competition, but *too many competitors*. Competition is merely the rule, according to which the produce is shared; and no other rule could possibly have increased the average amount of the shares, if the number of sharers had been proportionally great when compared with the capital. Competition exists among the employers as well as the employed; and is thus just as truly a cause of high as of low wages. In America the competition of capitalists raises wages: in Ireland, the competition of laborers preponderates over that of capitalists, and lowers wages. Wages, as we have seen, depend principally, nay, it might almost be said, *solely*, in any industrious and civilized nation, on the degree of reproductive restraint; and this determines their amount, whatever be the economical constitution of society; whether it consist of capitalists and hired laborers, of independent laborers, or of co-operative associations. In all states of society, the average share of the produce obtained by each individual, must depend on the aggregate amount, and the numbers among whom it is divided. If the institution of private property, and the rule of competition were abolished, and a community of goods substituted in their place, there would not be the slightest real change in the action of the law of population. Sexual abstinence, prostitution, preventive intercourse, or poverty, would still constitute the only choice of the human race.

Observations of a similar character may be applied to all other views on the causation of the great social evils, different from that which traces them to the law of population as their fountain-head. Thus, for example, drunkenness, idleness, want of education, or of Christianity, are the favorite explanations of the social evils among the aristocracy, the clergy, and the rich; artificial distinctions in rank or political power, and unjust laws of property, among the poor and the democratic party: but both of these views are radical and most dangerous errors. However shamefully unjust the present institutions regarding wealth, rank, and political power undoubtedly are, nothing could be more fatal to the hopes of the people than to mistake them for the cause of poverty.

By attending to the principle of population we can, in like manner, see the fallacy of the various popular schemes for permanently lessening poverty, and improving the condition of the working classes, when proposed as substitutes for limited procreation. The very fact that these schemes are still advocated, and still listened to, as constituting *in themselves* remedies for the social evils, shows the fatal ignorance of Political Economy which pervades the public mind. Among these schemes, some of which are always in vogue, tending to take off the attention of society from the true cause of its evils, may be mentioned the following: the organization of industry, parliamentary reform, socialism, communism, the cultivation of waste lands, emigration, universal suffrage and the other points of the Charter, artificial regulation of wages, tenant-right, industrial regiments, free trade, democratic and republican changes in the government, innovations in the currency, sanitary reform, the removal of supernatural beliefs and the substitution of positive philosophy in their place, Sunday recreation, the early closing movement, improved poor-laws, alimentary societies, equitable villages, the abolition of aristocracy primogeniture and entail, the temperance movement, national education, improvements in agriculture or machinery, the liquidation of the national debt, the removal of unjust laws and unequal taxation, &c.: in short every proposal which has been, or may be made, for improving the moral, political, or physical condition of society, irrespective of an increase in the preventive check to population.

I do not here speak of the general merits of any of these proposals, for with many of them I wholly agree, and with all I deeply sympathize, as proceeding from the noble desire to amend the deplorable state of society at present existing. I merely speak of them in their economical character, as far as they are declared, either virtually or expressly, to be remedies for the social evils, and substitutes for *the only true remedy*, namely, limited procreation. As such, we have already seen their utter futility. To believe that any or all of these

schemes can materially improve the economical state of society, shows
a profound ignorance of the true cause of poverty. Poverty, is a
sexual evil, depending on a sexual cause, and admitting only of a
sexual cure. This truth is so important, and so little generally
understood, that it cannot be too often insisted upon. The following
considerations may therefore be given as an additional aid to its clear
comprehension.

All of the above-mentioned proposals may be reduced to one or
other of two classes: 1st, plans for increasing the *production* of wealth
or of capital; 2nd, plans for equalising its *distribution*. Under the
first head come such schemes as the cultivation of waste lands, improvements in machinery or agriculture, the temperance movement,
free trade, &c.; under the second, the organization of industry,
socialism, the regulation of wages, tenant-right, &c. Many, perhaps
most of them, are indeed of a mixed character, being proposed both
as means of increasing production, and equalising distribution. But
with regard to the first class, it has already been shown, that no possible improvements could so increase the production of wealth in an
old country, as to enable population to expand at its natural rate.
However production might be increased, one or more of the four true
population-checks must still exist to an enormous degree in every old
society; and the average share of each individual in the aggregate
produce must still depend on the amount of reproductive restraint.
With regard to plans of the second class, it is equally evident that no
improvements in the *distribution* of wealth (irrespective of limited
procreation), could obviate the action of the principle of increase in
keeping down the remuneration of labor. All such improvements
merely tend, like improvements in production, to relax a little the
existing barriers which confine human increase, and to make some
slight additional room for its expansion. However quickly these
changes might be introduced: were we even to suppose that all injustices and inequalities in the distribution of wealth should be
immediately done away with, and that, by an equal division of the
property, every one should obtain a competent fortune; in a few
years, if the old standard of comfort were retained, and the reproductive powers as little curbed as before, the very same state of social
poverty would be induced, except that it would probably be more
universal. "The niggardliness of nature, not the injustice of society,"
says Mr. Mill, "is the cause of the penalty attached to over-population. An unjust distribution of wealth does not even aggravate the
evil, but, at most, causes it to be somewhat earlier felt." As however
all such improvements in distribution are generally of slow growth
and introduction, they rarely, if ever, produce even a temporary
alleviation of poverty, as their effects are at once obliterated by the
increase of population, to which they give rise. Their only perceptible
effect, at present, is to permit this increase of population: and thus
they have all hitherto ended in our having "a more numerous, but not
a happier, people." Emigration, in like manner, has merely had the
effect of making room for additional marriages, by which the vacancies
were speedily supplied, and the same state of poverty maintained.

It has already been seen, from a consideration of the **Law of Wages**, that the only two modes of permanently raising the rate of wages, are by increasing the amount of capital, or diminishing the number of laborers. All the above-mentioned plans leave the latter element out of sight: but we have seen that from it alone can any rise in wages be rationally expected. None of these plans could materially increase the rate at which capital during the last half-century has advanced in England. Nay, so far from *increasing* this rate, any plan for really improving the condition of the English laborers, must tend greatly to *diminish* it: for the extraordinary accumulation of the national wealth has been primarily owing to the exhausting toil of the working classes; and all true plans for their benefit must seek to lessen this toil, and thereby diminish the increase of capital. The only mode, therefore, of raising wages, and equalising the distribution of wealth, is by attending to that element, which is neglected in the popular schemes: namely, the regulation of the numbers of the community. This is the grand primary essential of social progress; to which all other measures of reform, or improvements in the production or distribution of wealth, however excellent, are subsidiary, and on which alone their success depends. "Only when, in addition to just institutions," says Mr. Mill, "the increase of mankind shall be under the deliberate guidance of a judicious foresight, can the conquests made from the powers of Nature by the intellect and energy of scientific discoverers become the common property of the species, and the means of improving and elevating the universal lot." It is apparent, therefore, that in whatever manner the law of population be viewed, whether its action be traced in the abstract or in the concrete, we arrive always at the same result: namely, that the positive check to population cannot possibly be avoided except through the preventive check—that poverty cannot possibly be permanently diminished in any other mode, than by a proportional diminution in the number of births.

THE LAWS OF EXERCISE, FECUNDITY, AND AGRICULTURAL INDUSTRY.

Let us next proceed to consider a little more fully the three laws of exercise, fecundity, and agricultural industry, from which the law of population is derived. The laws of exercise and fecundity are the most important laws of human nature (that is, the most powerful in their effects, and the most urgently demanding attention) with reference to social science, and an accurate knowledge of them is indispensable. They may with truth be termed the most important propositions of physiological and psychological science, as the law of agricultural industry is of political economy. Although properly

speaking belonging to physiology, the law of fecundity has been, as
Mr. Mill observes, interpolated into political economy, on account of
its very powerful influence on the production of wealth, and on
wages, profits, rents, and prices. To this law we may first direct our
attention. It has been repeatedly investigated by political economists
with reference to the law of population, and by physiologists as an
independent question of physiology; and is by no means difficult to
determine, at least in an approximate manner.

Every species of animal has its own peculiar law of fecundity, or
capacity of reproduction. This capacity varies greatly in the different
species, but is prodigious in all. "The capacity of increase," says
Mr. Mill, "is necessarily in a geometrical progression: the numerical
ratio alone is different." It is most remarkable in the lower animals,
and diminishes gradually on ascending the scale. Thus the common
cod is said to produce about four millions of eggs, the ling nine
millions. The reproductive powers of the lower mammalia are very
much less than this, and those of the higher orders, such as man and
the elephant, still less.

The law of fecundity in each species of animal is calculated from
three data: the length of the sexual period of life, the interval at
which births tend to occur, and the number of offspring produced
at each birth. In the human species these have long been familiarly
known; but it is only within the last few years that they have been
explained, by the discovery of the great leading fact in the sexual life
of woman; namely, the fact of spontaneous ovulation.

The Ovular or *Egg Theory of Menstruation* (with which, as with the
other important truths of anatomy and physiology, every one should
be well acquainted), was first arrived at through the researches of
M.M. Negrier, Coste, Raciborski, Pouchet, Bischoff, &c., and is now
generally received by physiologists. It is, that menstruation corresponds to the phenomenon of heat in the lower animals; and that
at each period of the menstrual flux, one minute egg, or in some
cases more than one, is ripened, and spontaneously discharged from
the ovaries.

"It may be concluded," say Mr. Kirkes and Mr. Paget, in their
Handbook of Physiology, "that the two states, heat and menstruation,
are analogous, and that the essential accompaniment of both is the
maturation and extrusion of ova." Ovulation and menstruation,
however, although generally concurrent phenomena, do not seem to
be always so; in other words, eggs seem in some cases to be discharged
at other times than at the menstrual epoch. "Perhaps the most
correct general statement on the subject," says Dr. Carpenter, "would
be that these two periods, though usually coincident, are not necessarily so: and that either change may occur without the concurrence
of the other."

The monthly discharge of eggs (and therefore, the reproductive
capacity), continues from puberty at fourteen or fifteen, till sexual
decline, at about forty-five—that is, during a period of about thirty
years: and in a healthy woman it suffers no interruption except

during the nine months of pregnancy, and from six to twelve of the first months of lactation. Allowing, therefore, from twenty to twenty-four months for the production and nurture of each child, and assuming that the reproductive power continues for thirty years, a woman could bear in all fifteen children or more. It is, however, believed by several physiologists that the child-bearing period is somewhat shortened in those women who bear many offspring in rapid succession; and that its average duration is not more than twenty-five years.

From this reason, as well as from the slight constitutional variations to which this function, like all others of the economy, is subject, there are some differences in the estimate of the reproductive powers made by various authors.

Thus Professor Allen Thompson, in the article on Generation in Todd's Cyclopædia of Anatomy and Physiology, says—"In the human female the number of children altogether produced is limited—first, by the number of Graafian vesicles in the ovaries; and secondly, by the length of time during which a woman bears children (the greatest extent of which is usually twenty-five years; that is, from the age of fifteen to forty, or twenty to forty-five), the length of this period again depending upon the rapidity with which the births succeed one another, and the number of children produced at each. Women most frequently bear every twenty months, but some have children at shorter intervals, as of fifteen or even twelve months. This often depends upon the circumstance that in some lactation prevents conception, in others it does not.

"A healthy woman bearing during the whole time, and with the common duration of interval, may have in all *from twelve to sixteen* children; but some have as many as *eighteen or twenty*: and when there are twins, &c., considerably more."

Mr. James Mill, the distinguished author of the History of British India, says, in his Elements of Political Economy, "That the rate of increase in the numbers of mankind depends upon the constitution of the female will not be disputed. The facts, which are fully ascertained with regard to the female of the human species, with the additions which the sciences of physiology and comparative anatomy enable that knowledge to derive from the analogy of other animals, the anatomy and physiology of which resemble those of the human species, afford the means of very satisfactory conclusions on this subject.

"Let us make such ample allowance for the female of the human species as shall include all interruptions, say one birth in two years. In Europe, to which we may at present confine our observations, the period of child-bearing extends from sixteen or seventeen to forty-five years of age. Let us make still more allowance, and say it extends only from twenty to forty years of age. In that period, at the great allowance of two years to one birth, there is time for *ten* births, which may be regarded as not more than the number natural to the female of the human species."

In his work on Sterility and Abortion, Dr. Whitehead estimates the number of births as *twelve;* and Professor Mohl, in the article on Population in the German Staats-Lexicon, as *at least* ten.

This estimate, and that of Mr. Mill, are made intentionally low, to avoid all risk of dispute; and the one given by Professor Thompson appears to me to be nearest the truth. In order to make allowance for differences of opinion, the Law of Fecundity may be stated as follows: *Each woman tends to produce from ten to fifteen children or thereabouts;* which statement may I believe be regarded as sufficiently accurate for practical purposes. The causes by which this law may be, and so generally is, *counteracted,* are the five population-checks.

The sexual period of life in man lasts considerably longer than in woman—namely, from puberty at about fifteen, till sixty or sixty-five, or even, when the health is vigorous, to extreme old age: during the whole of which period the reproductive or seminal fluid continues to be secreted. It must be observed, that in the human species, as in all other organized beings, the reproductive capacity is not a mere abstract endowment, but a most powerful natural *tendency;* in other words, the law of exercise invariably accompanies, and is inseparably connected with, the law of fecundity. It is from the combination of these two laws that the great human difficulties arise.

The sense in which the words *tend* and *tendency* are used in the above and other laws of causation should be well understood; for, as Mr. Senior and Dr. Whately have pointed out, there is an ambiguity in these words, which frequently leads to misconceptions and fallacious reasoning. The word tendency, like the word law, has two meanings. Sometimes it expresses a probability that, in the actual state of circumstances, a certain event will happen; as when it is said that the wealth of England tends, or has a tendency, to increase—meaning that it is likely to do so under existing circumstances. In another sense, it expresses the certainty that an event will happen, unless it be counteracted; as when it is said that "all bodies tend to approach each other with a force directly as their mass, and inversely as the squares of their distances;" not meaning thereby to give an opinion upon the probability of any particular bodies' approaching each other under actual circumstances, but merely stating the fact that all bodies will infallibly do so, unless this tendency be counteracted by some other law. It is in the latter sense that the words *tend* and *tendency* are used in the statement of the laws of fecundity, exercise, and agricultural industry, and of laws of causation in general. All that is meant by any law of causation is that the effect will certainly follow the cause *unless it be counteracted;* for all laws of causation are subject to be counteracted. The order of nature which we see around us, is produced by a multitude of causes, each of which, if uncounteracted, would invariably be followed by a certain effect, but whose operation is constantly impeded and modified by that of other causes. In seeking to explain the order of nature, science always tries to ascertain the effect which each cause would produce, if it operated *alone* and *uncounteracted;* after which the joint effect of various causes acting together can be computed.

Let us next proceed to the law of the increase of the produce of land. The increase of agricultural produce, as already mentioned, depends on two opposing forces—namely, on the law of agricultural industry, which tends to diminish the returns, and on improvements which tend to increase them. It is essential to have a perfectly clear idea of the Law of Agricultural Industry, which is, as Mr. Mill says, the most important proposition in political economy. It is, that *the proportional returns to agriculture tend to diminish;* in other words, that the produce of the soil tends to increase in a less proportion than the labour bestowed on it. A little attention will show this proposition to be undeniable. In the first place, it has never been questioned that there is an *ultimate* limit to the productive powers of the soil. It is indeed self-evident that the produce of a given tract of land could not possibly be increased so as always to yield undiminished proportional returns to whatever additional labour might be bestowed on it; but it is often thought that this limit is *at a distance,* and that the increase of produce is not yet retarded by it. "I apprehend this," says Mr. Mill, "to be not only an error, but the most serious one to be found in the whole field of political economy." He compares the resistance to production (and therefore to population) from this cause, not to an immovable wall which stands at a distance from us; but to an elastic band, which is never so tightly stretched that it could not be more stretched, but which always confines us, and the more tightly the more we approach its limits.

There are three things which show with certainty that the law of diminishing productiveness, instead of being at a distance, is operating at present, and has been operating from time immemorial, with enormous force on human society. These are, the cultivation of lands of inferior quality, the elaborate cultivation of the better lands, and the slow increase of population; which phenomena are observed in all old countries, but are absent, or at least exist in a very minor degree, in new colonies.

The cultivation of inferior lands is in itself a certain sign of the operation of the law; for the very meaning of inferior land is that, which with equal labour returns less produce. Had it not been for the fact that the proportional returns tend to diminish, none but the best lands would have been cultivated. The produce yielded by the best lands at present under cultivation in this country, is very much greater in proportion to the labour than that yielded by the worst. Now if it had been possible by increasing the labour on the better lands, to increase the produce in an equal degree, the inferior lands would not have been resorted to. The elaborate or high farming of the better lands is another sign of the law. It is much more costly than low farming; in other words, though the produce is increased by high cultivation, it is not increased in an equal proportion with the labour.

These two facts show with certainty that the agricultural law has long been in operation; and its disastrous action on human society is evidenced by the slow increase of population, and universal prevalence

of the population checks, in all old countries. No other cause than
this fundamental law of the earth's productiveness can possibly be
assigned for the fact that the increase of such civilized and industrious
communities as England, France, Switzerland, &c., is so very much
less than that of America. It is neither the want of industry and
skill, nor of the capacity and tendency to increase, that checks
the population and production of these countries; but the fact that
their land is limited in extent, and that its produce cannot be increased at more than a certain rapidity, without diminishing the proportional returns.

In the United States, fertile land is so plentiful that population is
enabled to double itself every twenty-five years; while in Switzerland, notwithstanding the energy of the people, the republican form
of the government, and the excellence of many of the social institutions, the population is almost stationary. Nothing but the limited
productiveness of the land can possibly account for this.

The causes which *counteract* the agricultural law, and enable an
additional quantity of labor to be applied to the soil without a diminution of the proportional returns, and rise in the price of food, consist
of all those improvements by which agricultural labor is made more
efficient, or the distribution of the produce facilitated. Thus an increase of agricultural skill, better means of conveyance by roads or
railways, mechanical inventions which cheapen the tools used in
husbandry, the application of machinery to the cultivation of the
soil, or to the preparation of its products for human use: as well as
the removal of burdens on the land, such as tithes and entails, or improvements in the tenure of land, whether by long leases, or by
granting to the cultivator a proprietary right in the soil: these and
many other causes tend to counteract the law, and enable the supply
of food to be increased without an increase in its cost. The counteracting agencies are in fact so various, Mr. Mill observes, that they
can scarcely be expressed by a less general term than *the progress of
civilization*. Thus then, the rate at which food, and consequently
population, can be increased, depends on the law of diminishing productiveness on the one hand, and the progress of civilization or improvement on the other. The progress of improvement varies greatly
in different countries, which accounts for the widely different increase of population in England, France, and Switzerland: but it is
never so rapid as to enable the population of any old country to
escape from the checks, or to increase at a rate at all approaching to
that of America or Australia.

It must be observed that it is by no means necessary, to show the
action of the agricultural law, that the proportional returns to agriculture should *actually* diminish, and the price of food rise. Whether
this takes place or not, depends on the comparative advance of population and improvement. If population outstrip improvement, labor
will become less productive, and the price of food will rise: if improvement outstrip population, the contrary effect will happen ; and
if both advance at a similar rate, as is frequently the case, the price

of food will remain pretty nearly the same. The operation of the agricultural law is shown not only by an actual diminution in the productiveness of labor, but by *the check on population;* not by misery alone, but also by the fear of misery.

Moreover, even when improvement and population are advancing at a nearly similar rate, so that there is no *absolute* diminution of the productiveness of labor, there is still a *relative* diminution. Improvements increase the productive powers of the land already under cultivation, at the same time that they permit additional labor to be applied to inferior land: so that, though the produce of the inferior land may not be less in proportion to the labor than that yielded by the better land, *before* the introduction of the improvement, it is less than what it *now* yields. The very fact that the proportional returns continue merely the same, and are not *increased*, by an improvement, shows the action of the agricultural law. The price of food would have been as much diminished by the late improvements in agriculture, as the price of manufactured goods has been by the mechanical inventions, had it not been for the advance of population, which by bringing into operation the law of diminishing productiveness, has obliterated the benefits of agricultural improvements, as speedily as they were introduced.

In the human species therefore and in the soil, the laws of increase are of a totally different nature. The former have an inherent power and tendency to increase indefinitely, and with extraordinary swiftness: while the increase of the latter has not only an ultimate limit, but is obtained on progressively harder terms long before that limit is reached. Agricultural improvements are a counteracting force to this law, but are never in old countries sufficient to enable production to keep up with unchecked population. When we compare the laws of fecundity and of agricultural industry, and reflect that they, like all other laws of nature, are fixed and immovable, we can clearly see that the former must always have been, and must always continue to be, most powerfully checked by the latter: and the only mode in which this can possibly take place, is by one or other of the five population checks.

That these checks *do* exist to an enormous extent in this and other old countries, is obvious to the most superficial view. Few individuals among us exert their reproductive powers in more than a very moderate degree, or, if they do, it is at the expense of the other members of society: and population on the whole advances at a comparatively slow rate. That the existence of the checks is owing to the agricultural law, is proved by the much greater rapidity with which population increases in America and Australia: in which countries wages are higher, and a family can be more easily provided for, in consequence of the abundance of fertile land. The presence of the checks in all old countries, and their comparative absence in new colonies, shows their real origin. Their existence, their cause, and their absolute unavoidableness under one or other of their five forms, are thus manifest; and it is not less manifest, on further considering the subject, that in their present shape they constitute the great social evils of old countries. Poverty, prostitution, and celibacy are, in fact, nothing else than these checks: the first arising from the destructive operation of the agricultural law, the others from the fear of its operation. The real disease under which this and all other old societies are laboring, is *reproductive plethora*, or excess of reproductive power: from this arises the permanently overstocked labor-market, the crowded ranks of prostitution, and the millions of both sexes living in a state of celibacy: and unless this great truth be clearly understood, and openly discussed, it is altogether vain to seek to escape from these evils.

Let us next direct our attention to the great physiological *law of exercise*, as it applies to the reproductive organs and emotions.

The Law of Exercise is that *the health of the reproductive organs and emotions depends on their having a sufficient amount of normal exercise;* and that a want of this tends powerfully to produce misery and disease in both man and woman.

The proofs of this law are gathered from three sources, physiology, pathology, and therapeutics; that is, from an observation of the facts of health, disease, and treatment.

First, of the proofs from *physiology*. It is laid down by physiologists as a universal law of the human body, that the nutrition and vigor of every organ is promoted by a due amount of appropriate exercise; while on the contrary mal-nutrition or atrophy, and enfeeblement, are attendant on a want of it. All parts of the frame are constantly undergoing a process of decay and disintegration, whether they be used or not. This is an essential characteristic of life. But if they are actively employed, each in performing its own special function, the waste is made up by the supply of new materials from the blood, and their vigor and development even tend to increase. The exercise of any part invariably draws towards it a current of blood, and it is from this fluid that every organ derives its nourishment. If, on the other hand, a part be not used, the natural process of decay is not counterbalanced, and a greater or less degree of enfeeblement results. Exercise, in short, feeds and strengthens an organ: want of exercise weakens and starves it.

The law of exercise therefore is a universal law applying to the whole body. It has been ascertained by conclusive observations and experiments, both in the case of man and the lower animals, and is verified by all experience. It forms indeed the most important and fundamental principle of physiology, and one upon which all scientific writers on that subject are agreed.

The following quotations from the Principles of Human Physiology by Dr. Carpenter may be given in proof of this.

"The demand for nutrition arises not merely from the exercise of the formative powers, which are concerned in the building up of the organism, but also from the *degeneration and decay*, which is continually taking place in almost every part of it, and the effects of which if not antagonized, would speedily show themselves in its complete disintegration." "The *muscular* and *nervous* tissues are doubtless subject, like all others that are distinguished by their vital activity, to the law of limited duration; for we find that when not called into use, they undergo a gradual disintegration or wasting, which is not adequately repaired by the nutritive processes. But the very manifestation of their peculiar vital endowments, determines an afflux of blood towards the parts thus called into special activity: and from this it comes to pass, that the nutrition of these tissues is promoted, instead of being impaired, by use: so that their constant exercise occasions an augmentation rather than a diminution of their substance—a due supply of the requisite material being always presupposed." "It is a general principle unquestioned by any physiologists, that when there is a local excitement to the processes of nutrition, secretion, &c., a determination of blood *towards* the part speedily takes place, and the motion of blood *through* it is increased in rapidity."

On the other hand, " The formative activity of muscles and nerves is so closely dependent upon the active exercise of their functional powers that *atrophy* is certain to supervene if this be interrupted." "Even the bones of a limb will suffer in consequence of atrophy of the muscles consequent upon disuse."

The *glands* or secreting organs, are subject to the very same law of healthy nutrition as the muscles and nerves. Their health and vigor depend on their having a sufficient supply of blood and nervous influence, which can be obtained only by an active discharge of their special functions. The chief difference is, that the vigor of the secreting organs and involuntary muscles is more directly dependent on the healthy play of the *emotions* (with which these organs are most intimately connected); and not, like that of the voluntary muscles and nerves, on the healthy play of the *will* Indeed nutrition and secretion are merely two forms of the same vital process, and in the main are subject to the same conditions of health. "There is no other fundamental difference between the two processes of nutrition and secretion," says Dr. Carpenter, "than such as arises out of the diverse destinations of the separated matters, and from the anatomical arrangements which respectively minister to these."

The same views are held by all physiologists, by Mr. Paget, Professor Alison, Professor Müller, and others; and are in accordance with the dictates of universal experience and common sense. Every one is aware that the vigor of the body is maintained and increased by exercise, and a due supply of nutriment Indeed the very meaning of a bodily organ is, a part which has a special function, and is intended by nature to perform it.

But the reproductive organs are mainly composed of muscles, nerves, and glands, and the very same law, which applies to these tissues in other parts of the body, applies equally to them. A due amount of appropriate exercise and nourishment is the first condition of their health and vigor: while enfeeblement and atrophy to a greater or less degree are sure to follow their disuse. In laying down the foregoin law of exercise for all the vital tissues, physiologists have already stated *by implication*, the law of the reproductive organs; nor can it be denied without an evident logical fallacy. The nutrition and health of muscles, nerves, glands, and other tissues, depends on their having a sufficient amount of appropriate exercise; the sexual organs are mainly composed of muscles, nerves, glands, &c.; therefore the nutrition and health of these organs depends on their having a sufficient amount of appropriate exercise—is a syllogism, which may be evaded, but from which, it appears to me, there is no escape. If the premises be admitted, as is done by all physiologists, the conclusion necessarily follows.

But the nutrition of each organ affects that of all the others. It is stated as a law by Mr. Paget, Dr. Carpenter, and other eminent authorities, that "each organ, by the very fact of nourishing itself, acts as an excretory organ to the rest of the body." That is, every organ selects from the blood the proper materials for its own nutrition, and in so doing, it renders the blood more fit to nourish the others. This is especially true of secreting organs, such as the ovaries and testicles, which produce fluids, that are intended *to be cast out* of the body, and are more or less noxious if retained. Hence, whenever any important organs are not duly engaged in their own special manner, not only is their own vigor impaired, but that of the others also. The ideal of health indeed cannot be stated otherwise than as consisting in the due performance of *all* the bodily functions.

The law of healthy exercise applies in like manner to the *Emotions* connected with the sexual system. These emotions form one of the great natural Appetites implanted in the human frame: on whose due regulation and satisfaction the health and happiness of mankind are so intimately dependent. The appetites have been divided into six principal classes, namely, Sleep, Exercise, Repose, Thirst, Hunger, and Sex. They are defined by Mr. Alexander Bain, in his great work on the Human Mind, (published in two parts, the first on the Senses and the Intellect, and the second on the Emotions and the Will), as *the cravings produced by the recurring wants and necessities of our bodily or organic life.* All of them have the same leading characteristics: they are powerful desires arising from deep-seated wants of the system; and if unduly repressed, they all tend, with greater or less force, to cause misery and disease. Their strength and universality are an exact measure of the importance attached by nature to their due gratification, and to the performance of the functions which they are intended to control and direct. In the case of all the appetites, *except those of sex*, the immense importance of attending to the true dictates of nature is insisted on by scientific physicians, and is generally admitted by the public.

It is stated by Mr. Bain as a general *Law of Emotions*, that they exercise a diffusive influence on the body; producing a flow of blood to various organs, along with movements, gestures, and expressions, by which the excitement is discharged or carried off. The influence of the feelings in stimulating, suspending, or perverting the functions of secretion: in disturbing the action of the heart, and the muscles of respiration, expression, &c.: and in modifying the nutritive processes, such as digestion or the elaboration of the blood, is pointed out by all physiologists. Different feelings affect different organs, and, as before stated, the glands and involuntary muscles are especially subject to their influence. "The glands liable to congestion," says Mr. R. B. Carter, in his very able work on Hysteria, "are those which by forming their products in larger quantity, subserve to the gratification of the excited feeling. Thus blood is directed to the mammæ by the maternal emotions: to the testes by the sexual; and to the salivary glands by the influence of appetizing odors."

The sexual emotions are primarily excited by the formation and accumulation of the reproductive secretions: and they react upon the organs which prepare these secretions, directing towards them a current of blood and nervous influence, from which their nourishment is derived, and their vigor supported. If the excitement be carried off by its natural channel, namely sexual union, the balance of health is maintained; if not, disorder of body and mind, varying in proportion to the strength of the arrested feelings and the susceptibility of the system, will result. According to the principle of the *composition of causes*, the emotion, though counteracted, still produces its full effect: but it operates now by deranging the other bodily and mental functions. Blushing, palpitation of the heart, hysterical convulsions, nervous irritability, and general disorder of the nutritive processes, are among the effects of repressed emotion, and consequently misdirected blood. The health of the mind suffers no less than that of the body. The will is rendered weak and irresolute by the conflict of the feelings: the thoughts are perturbed and the healthy links of association broken: restlessness, vehemence, anxiety, and hypochondria pervade the mind, and not unfrequently lead to confirmed insanity. Natural emotions, when unduly repressed, are as dangerous to the health of body and mind, as repressed secretions.

Let us next examine the proofs afforded by *pathology*, or the facts of disease. If the law of exercise be truly a law of nature, we should expect to find an immense amount of disease and misery, arising from the disregard of it: or in other words from the sexual abstinence which is so prevalent in old countries, and whose real origin, as already explained, is the law of population. This expectation is fully verified by facts. It is only after an examination of the history of disease, and an unprejudiced survey of the present state of the sexual world, that the havoc caused by the obstructed law of exercise can be duly estimated. The sexual evils are indeed productive of as large an amount of social wretchedness as even poverty They may be divided into three classes, namely, the *diseases of abstinence : self-abuse : and prostitution and venereal disease*. There are many other sexual diseases, such as inflammations, &c.: but the above classes comprehend those which result more directly from the law of population, or, in other words, from the obstacle which nature opposes to the normal exercise of the reproductive functions. It is of the diseases of *abstinence* that I shall chiefly speak at present, as they afford a clearer and more unmistakeable proof of the law of exercise: although the great frequency of prostitution and self-abuse is no less really a proof of its truth, and of the strength of the obstructed emotions. With regard to self-abuse, I may merely mention that Dr. Copland, in the article on Impotence and Sterility, in his Medical Dictionary, calls it "the modern Moloch of the species;" a phrase which will not appear exaggerated to those who are at all aware of the amount of mischief, moral and physical, caused by this habit in modern times. The habit itself arises in the main from the want of the natural sexual intercourse.

The *Diseases of Abstinence* consist principally of hysteria, chlorosis, and menstrual disorders, in woman: and of generative enfeeblement, spermatorrhœa, and hypochondria in man. These affections may doubtless, like many others, be brought on by other causes than abstinence, and this *plurality of causes* often gives rise to mistakes in reasoning upon them: but it is certain that they are all very frequently induced by abstinence. That this is true with regard to the female diseases is acknowledged by almost all medical men who have attended to the subject, both in this country and on the continent. With regard to the male diseases, the testimony of continental physicians, as far as I am acquainted with it, is equally unanimous, and is confirmed directly or indirectly by that of several English practitioners: although the peculiar prejudices upon sexual morality which are, unfortunately, so dominant in this country, have generally prevented the open acknowledgment of those natural laws, on which alone any true theory of sexual virtue, or health, can be founded.

The disease which in woman most frequently results from abstinence is *hysteria*. This is among the most prevalent of all chronic diseases in modern times. When arising, as it generally does, from abstinence, it consists mainly in disorder of the emotions, and of the sexual system: which give rise to a host of symptoms of greater or less severity. The physical evils, produced by or connected with hysteria, include convulsive fits sometimes so severe as to resemble epilepsy, nervous irritability and weakness, palpitation of the heart, spasmodic affections of the respiratory muscles, such as nervous cough and loss of voice, colic, intense headache, pain in the left side, indigestion, and many other disturbances of the various bodily functions. The mental evils are, deep-seated restlessness and discontent, vehement temper, caprice and instability of character, want of the power of concentrativeness, preoccupation of the mind by concealed feelings, corroding anxieties, violent bursts of passion or grief; which may, and by no means unfrequently do, proceed to insanity. The truth and ingenuousness of disposition are often thoroughly perverted by the restraint placed on the expression of the emotions; and hence various kinds of anomalous diseases, such as spinal complaints, pains in the joints, muscular rigidity or powerlessness, chronic vomiting, convulsions, and other affections are often *simulated* by hysterical patients, in order to excite compassion. These simulated diseases have given rise to many mistakes in medical practice, but are now well recognised. They are most graphically described in Mr. Carter's work.

The following quotations may be given in illustration of the frequency, cause, and nature of the disease. Sydenham in his essay on hysterical diseases, says that "they form one half of all chronic affections:" and Dr. Conolly and Dr. Ashwell coincide in this opinion. "We may almost admit, without qualification," says Dr. Conolly in the Cyclopædia of Practical Medicine, "the remark of Sydenham, that hysterical disorders constitute one half of all chronic distempers." With regard to the cause and the cure of the disease, Dr. Conolly says, "In a susceptible female temperament, and in the unmarried state, the system of reproduction, every change in which involves many other changes, acts strongly on the system at large, and in certain circumstances disorders all the functions of the body and the mind: the digestion of food, the circulation of the blood, the judgment, the affections, the temper: and in many of these cases all the mischief is removed by marriage, which by awakening the natural functions and normal sympathies, allays the whole series of irritations and morbid actions." In speaking of the unhealthy life of young ladies, he says again, "Then perhaps ensue the mortifications of celibacy, and the misery of growing old without an active and contented mind. As causes of disease, and especially of hysterical and other various disorders, none can deny the wide and powerful influence of these circumstances but those who have paid no reflection to the operation of human passions in society."

Similar views are expressed by Dr. Ashwell, Mr. Carter, M. Villermé, and indeed by all who are conversant with female disease. Mr Carter holds that hysteria is essentially a disease of repressed and concealed emotions, and especially those of sex. After giving a detailed account of the various modes in which emotion acts upon the system, he says, "It is reasonable to expect that an emotion, which is strongly felt by great masses of people, but whose natural manifestations are constantly repressed in compliance with the usages of society, will be the one whose morbid effects are most frequently witnessed. This anticipation is abundantly borne out by facts: the sexual passion in woman being that which most accurately fulfils the prescribed conditions, and whose injurious influence upon the organism is most common and familiar. Next after it in power may be placed those emotions which are usually concealed because disgraceful or un-amiable, as hatred or envy, &c." "The word 'hysteria,' the prevalent hypothesis that the disease depends on irritation of the ovaries and womb, and the universal consent of the medical profession," he says again, "may all be confidently appealed to, as bearing out by actual experience the theoretical conclusion, that the sexual passion is more concerned than any other single emotion, and perhaps as much as all others put together, in the production of the hysteric paroxysm."

"A disordered state of the emotional nature," says Dr. Carpenter, "seems to be the essential character of hysteria. There are certain forms of this disorder which graduate insensibly into moral insanity or monomania.'

"It is assuredly true," says M. Villermé, in the Dictionaire des

2 K

Sciences Medicales, "that absolute and involuntary continence is the most common source of this disorder. At the epoch of puberty, not only does the physical organization of woman undergo numerous changes, but her mental faculties become developed in a manner not less surprising: she experiences new wants: and the more pronounced these are, other things being equal, the more may we expect the explosion of this disease, if the purpose of nature be not fulfilled, if the imperious want of the organism be not satisfied." "Hysteria," he says again, "seems to have been known in all times, though less frequent formerly, from the minor restraint put upon the sexual passion: it is indeed an effect of *the law* common to all living beings, which impels the two sexes to an intimate union." "Nine out of ten cases of hysteria are owing to sexual abstinence."

Chlorosis, another very common disease in young women, and productive of manifold sufferings, is frequently owing to abstinence and disappointed desires. It consists essentially in a watery state of the blood, and is easily recognised by the deadly pallor, whence the name is derived. It proves not unfrequently fatal by leading to consumption. Dr. Ashwell after enumerating as predisposing causes the various debilitating and unwholesome habits in which girls are reared, mentions as the exciting causes "circumstances which depress the mind, and keep the feelings in a state of painful suspense or delay, unrequited affection, attachments opposed by relatives," &c. The same views are expressed by other authors.

Disorders of the menstrual secretion, such as absent and painful menstruation, to which Dr. Ashwell says single women are especially prone, are among the commonest forms of disease. They often cause intense and prolonged suffering, and may break down the health irretrievably. Sexual abstinence is a very frequent cause of these affections. It also acts powerfully as a predisposing cause of many of those inflammatory diseases of the ovaries and womb, which have in recent times been discovered to prevail so extensively. Dr. Tilt observes that the want of the natural stimulus to the ovaries which should promote their healthy action, is often the cause of their becoming the seat of morbid affections. The only natural stimulus to these organs is sexual intercourse and child-bearing.

The evil effects of prolonged abstinence on *man* are equally certain and indisputable. They are not indeed so often seen as in woman, nor do they manifest themselves so strikingly to the most careless observer. There are several reasons for this. Abstinence is by no means so generally practised by the male sex, and its effects are very frequently obscured and complicated by abuse or venereal diseases. By the peculiarity of his constitution, moreover, and the less unhealthy mode in which he is educated, man is not so subject to the dominion of the *emotions*, and can better repress their vehement manifestations. He has also a wider sphere of activity, and more facilities for mental distraction. But though the evils of abstinence are thus often obscured, and to some extent *counteracted*, they are equally undeniable. Indeed to admit them in the case of woman, as is done by all physicians who have attended to the subject, *is in fact to admit them in the case of man also:* for there is a thorough and universally recognised analogy between the laws of the two sexes.

Notwithstanding these complicating circumstances, however, the diseases of abstinence in man are most palpable to the attentive eye, and are universally acknowledged by all impartial observers. Though not perhaps so frequent as in woman, they are still extremely common, and cause an immensity of suffering. They consist chiefly in the baneful effects of *arrested emotion* on the bodily and mental functions ; including indigestion, nervous enfeeblement and irritability, constipation, numbness and torpor of the brain; together with mental anxiety, restlessness, hypochondria, shyness and embarrassment, a confused intellect and irresolute will, and a morbid persistency and undue prominence of those feelings whose natural expression has been denied. These effects are in part owing to the want of normal outlet for the reproductive or seminal *secretion:* and in many cases also to spermatorrhœa, or involuntary seminal losses, which grievous disease, as M. M. Lallemand, Ricord, Serrurier and others assert, is liable to be produced by sexual abstinence. Their experience is borne out by the fact that when once spermatorrhœa has been brought on by such causes as self-abuse, abstinence proves in many cases an insuperable barrier to its removal. Other evil effects on the reproductive organs produced by abstinence are such as arise from want of normal exercise, namely, wasting of the testicles, and more or less of generative debility or impotence.

The following quotations may be given in confirmation of these statements:—" It is well known," says Dr. Beatty, in the Cyclopædia of Practical Medicine, "that a state of inaction is often attended by atrophy of the testicles." " In this state of decay, impotence is the final result." " In some instances," says Dr. Copland in his Medical Dictionary, " prolonged disuse of this function is followed by wasting of the testes, and consequently permanent impotence is the result. These organs, like others of the economy, *are strengthened by moderate use,* are weakened by abuse: their functions being often entirely lost by protracted disuse." In the articles on Chastity, Continence, Celibacy, Seminal Losses, and Semen, contained in the Dictionaire des Sciences Medicales, and written respectively by M. M. Sedillot, De Montegre, Marc, Serrurier, and Devilliers, there is but one opinion expressed as to the pernicious effects of abstinence on both man and woman. " Nature," says M. Sedillot, " in commanding all beings to fulfil the great function of reproduction, is often opposed by the established usages of human society; and she punishes sometimes with extreme severity those who are rebellious to her laws." Among the consequent diseases he mentions nocturnal pollutions, insanity, hysteria, chlorosis, &c. " It is not always by severe diseases," he says again, " that the man, who is strictly chaste, is punished for his disobedience to the *immovable laws* of Nature: he lives alone on the earth, often sad and melancholy, and is neglected in his old age. Everything bears witness to the error he has committed against the physical and moral laws of the human constitution." "It is not with impunity," says M. De Montegre, "that the wants of nature are denied: there is an age when the physical gratifications of love become necessary to every well-organised being, and it is never without injury to the health, and to the tranquillity of the whole life, that a prolonged continence can be observed." If space permitted, many other passages might be given from English and Continental authors, in which the law of exercise in the case of man is either virtually implied, or openly acknowledged.

The proofs derived from *therapeutics* or treatment are not less conclusive. The natural and scientific treatment of a disease consists in reversing the process which led to it: in removing its cause and procuring an obedience to the natural laws which have been broken. The signal effects of sexual intercourse and child-bearing in removing hysteria, chlorosis, and menstrual diseases in woman, have been remarked by all observers. Dr. Conolly's opinion on this point has already been given. Dr. Ashwell remarks that marriage is frequently curative of chlorosis, absent and painful menstruation, and hysteria. M. Villermé, after reviewing the interminable list of medicines and other applications, which are still so constantly used, in the routine treatment of hysteria, says, "These external and internal applications can in general have merely an indirect and secondary action. The remedy which is most potent and whose influence is the most general and direct, is the pleasures of marriage. Hippocrates recommends marriage to young women subject to hysterics: Hoffmann, Reil, Pinel, Esquirol, Duvernoy, and all good observers in ancient and modern times, have adopted the same principle, which the most certain and authentic experience confirms every day."

The same is true of the diseases of abstinence in man. Spermatorrhœa, hypochondria, indigestion, and general debility, when proceeding from this cause, are in general readily curable by sexual intercourse, and by this alone. "The seminal losses, which depend upon absolute continence," says M. Sedillot, "must be treated by means conformable to the requirements of nature. Sexual intercourse is in certain cases the only remedy. In accordance, therefore, with all authors, we cannot but recommend marriage to those individuals, in whose case medical treatment can only imperfectly replace an act which belongs to all living beings, and from which but a very small number can refrain with impunity." "Whoever sees men as they are," says M. Ricord, "and without that disguise of morality which society imposes, must admit that there are circumstances in which sexual intercourse becomes indispensable, under pain of the most serious moral and social consequences in case of denial."

But the man who has done most of all by his arguments and treatment to demonstrate the law of exercise in the male, is M. Lallemand, whose great work on Involuntary Seminal Losses, is one of the landmarks of medical science. He habitually recommends a due amount of sexual intercourse in many cases of spermatorrhœa, proceeding from abstinence or abuse: and with the most successful results.

"The regular exercise of organs," says M. Lallemand, "will alone give all the energy of which they are susceptible, and those of generation are far from forming an exception to this general law. To complete the cure, it is necessary that sexual relations should be established." He treats these cases, in fact, on the same physiological principles as disease of other organs would be treated by a scientific physician: and the justice of these principles has been admitted by a large number of medical men on the Continent. "The more the function of an organ is used," says Dr. Felix Roubaud in his work on Impotence and Sterility, "the more it is nourished and increases in size. Unless this physiological law be a dream, it must be applied to the genital organs." In this country, too, these principles have made no inconsiderable impression, and have been approved of and acted upon more or less openly by many physicians.

These various proofs and quotations, which could be greatly multiplied, establish, I conceive, the truth of the law of exercise. It cannot indeed be denied, without ignoring the instincts of nature, and the plainest indications of science and common sense. It must be regarded, therefore, like the law of gravitation, or definite proportions, as one of the fixed and eternal laws of nature: a law which, according to the fundamental principles of physical religion, it is not merely the safety but the *duty* of man and woman to observe, and enable others to observe, as far as lies in their power; which neither bends nor moves to suit the exigencies of human society, but is the same yesterday, to-day, and for ever: which rewards the obedient, and punishes those who infringe it, with absolute invariability, regardless of the sexual institutions or theories of mankind. A clear and unvacillating perception of this law, as well as of the law of agricultural industry, and the law of fecundity, is necessary, in order to show in their full extent, the population-difficulties of our race: and can alone serve as a foundation for that on which the regeneration of society really depends, namely, a true theory and practice of Sexual Morality.

[As an example of the objections which have been made to the law of exercise and the natural duty founded on it, I may quote the following passage from the work on Prostitution by Mr. Miller, Professor of Surgery in the Edinburgh University. "We have good reason to know," he says, "that a popular delusion as to the physiological bearings of sexual indulgence, on the part of the male sex, widely prevails among high and low, young and old—fraught with the most pernicious consequences. It is supposed that occasional sexual indulgence, after the age of puberty, is essential to health, and not only may but ought to be transacted on purely physiological requirement. . . . . To show the folly of this physiological heresy, a short statement will suffice. God made man's body —perfect. The organs in their working, and with their appetites, are from his hand. Among others, he lodged those which minister to reproduction; their function and their appetite are from him. The latter, obviously, is meant to be indulged under certain restrictions, and these restrictions are specified; they are those of lawful wedlock. *You say* that it must be indulged, to maintain the health of the creature, in fulfilling the requirements of Nature, at all hazards—with or without wedlock, *per fas aut nefas.* Sexual indulgence, you say, irrespective of marriage, is needful, by the stern demand of a physiological law. But God, who makes and upholds all physiological laws, says that this is fornication, a flagrant violation of his moral law; that the soul who so sinneth shall die; and that fornicators by express command, are excluded from the kingdom of heaven. According to *you*, therefore, the matter would stand thus; the great and good God—all-merciful as all-wise and almighty—has made man with a certain bodily appetite and function, which in obedience to God's physical laws, which regulate its workings, requires occasional indulgence, even irrespective of that special limitation which God in his moral law has appointed; and yet, such infringement of his moral law, though necessarily arising out of his own physical law, God punishes with the highest penalty. Or, in brief, according to this popular and pernicious fallacy, God turns men into hell, for yielding to a physical necessity which he had himself ordained. This, we need not say, implies a moral impossibility."

In these remarks, Professor Miller speaks of the law of exercise and the duty founded on it, as a "popular delusion" and a "physiological heresy;" but, as the reader has seen, the necessity of sexual intercourse to the health and happiness of both man and woman is recognised, more or less clearly, not only by the common sense of mankind in general, but by a large number of the most eminent medical men in this and other countries.

With regard to Professor Miller's objections, it may be observed, in the first place, that they do not really apply to the law and duty of exercise, (against which he is ostensibly arguing), but merely to the indulgence in *unmarried* connections. These two questions are totally distinct from one another, and should never be confounded together. Whether sexual intercourse be necessary to the health is one question; how it should be indulged in is a totally different one. Indeed, properly speaking, there are *three* distinct questions involved; namely, first, Is the law of exercise true, or, in other words, is health dependent on the exercise of the sexual functions? Secondly, granting the law to be true, ought it to be observed? Thirdly, if it ought to be observed, in what manner is this to be effected—by early marriages, or in what other way? The first is a question of science or of a matter of fact: the two others are questions of art or of practical morality; and all three are quite distinct from each other. A man who rigidly adheres to the present marriage code, and condemns all unmarried connections, both may, and ought, if he attend to physiology, to admit that sexual intercourse is necessary to health; and he may hold the opinion that it ought to be indulged in, by means of early marriages, with or without the use of preventive measures. I am myself personally acquainted with one medical man who takes this view of the question, and doubtless there are many others who do so.

But in the second place, even if Professor Miller's objections did really apply to the law of exercise, objections of such a character are never admissible. Even among those who accept the Bible as their standard of morality, it is quite inadmissible to oppose its doctrines, or what a writer supposes to be its doctrines, to *the evidence of physical facts*. Physical facts can be met only by physical facts— that is to say, they can only be controverted by showing that they have been erroneously observed or interpreted; and not by assertions of what is, or is not, consistent with divine justice or benevolence, or with any statement contained in the Bible. This is the very same objection which was made to Galileo's theory of the earth's move- ment, and which has been so constantly repeated with regard to the principle of population, the geological theories, and so many other great scientific truths. In fact, at almost every step in its progress, science has had to struggle against similar theological objections. These objections are examples of the class of fallacies called by logicians *à priori* fallacies, or fallacies of simple inspection. "To this class" says Mr. Mill in his Logic, "belong Descartes' speculations, and those of so many others after him, tending to infer the order of the universe, not from observation, but by *à priori* reasonings from supposed qualities of the Godhead. . . . . Writers have not yet ceased to oppose the theory of divine benevolence to the evidence of physical facts, to the principle of population for instance. And people seem in general to think that they have used a very powerful argument when they have said, that to suppose some proposition true, would be a reflection on the wisdom or goodness of the Deity. Put into the simplest possible terms, their argument is, 'if it had depended on me, I would not have made the proposition true, therefore it is not true.' Put into other words it stands thus; 'God is perfect, therefore (what I think) perfection, must obtain in nature.' But since in reality every one feels that nature is very far from perfect, the doctrine is never applied consistently." Among those who, like myself, recognise no other standard either of scientific truth or of moral duties, than Nature, Professor Miller's objections can of course carry no weight.

I beg the reader to remark the above two fallacies—namely first, the fallacy of mixing up the question of the truth of the law of exercise with the question of prostitution, while ostensibly arguing against the former, and secondly, the theological objections—for they are the very ones which will probably be most frequently brought forward by the opponents of this great law of nature. The first is one of the prevailing errors in a series of articles on the sexual ques- tions by Professor Francis W. Newman, published in the *Reasoner* in 1855, and partly, though not expressly, directed against the present work. However widely I differ from Professor Newman and Professor Miller on the subject of Prostitution (both as regards their views on the cause and cure of this evil, and their general tone of feeling respecting it) as well as on the truth of the law of exercise, the two questions are quite distinct, and ought never to be confounded together.

"One other consideration," says Professor Miller, "before leaving

this part of the subject. In medical ethics, let it be clearly understood, that the practitioner who *prescribes* fornication to any patient,
under any circumstances whatever, commits a heinous offence, not
only against morals, but also against both the science and the
character of his profession. His advice is not more flagrantly immoral, than it is disgracefully unscientific and unsound." Fortunately
for medicine, and for the interests of suffering humanity, there are
already many eminent practitioners in this country and still more on
the continent, who take a very different view of medical duty on this
subject from Professor Miller. But here too it is necessary to make
a careful distinction; for Professor Miller has again confused the
question by mixing up the recommendation of sexual intercourse
with the recommendation of prostitution. It appears to me to be the
undeniable duty of a medical man, when he sees a patient, whether
man or woman, suffering from the effects of sexual abstinence, to tell
them candidly that this is, in his opinion, the cause of their disease,
and that sexual intercourse is necessary for their cure. However
frequently this duty may be evaded by medical men (especially when
the patient is a female), and however difficult and unpleasant it may
often be in the present state of society, yet surely it cannot be denied.
It is surely the duty of the physician *in all cases* to inform a patient
candidly of what he considers to be the true cause and cure of his
disease. If he does not, what is the real value of his advice? But,
in the case before us, to recommend sexual intercourse, is not to
recommend prostitution. All that the practitioner is, properly speaking, called upon to do, is to inform the patient that he considers
sexual intercourse necessary to his recovery; in what manner this intercourse is to be obtained, is a question mainly for the *patient* to
consider. It is for him to consider whether he will marry, or form
an unmarried connection with some one, or indulge in prostitution
(that is, intercourse with women of the town), or remain continent.
It is indeed true that in the present state of society, where sexual
intercourse is in very many cases attainable only by an indissoluble
marriage, or by prostitution—the first of which is so often impracticable, especially to an invalid, while the second is in many respects
degrading—the patient will frequently adopt the latter alternative;
but the practitioner is not responsible for this, nor is so miserable a
dilemma inherent in the nature of things. As I have already
endeavoured to show, the present system of prostitution and indissoluble marriage (which are closely connected together), might be,
and ought to be, superseded by preventive intercourse and by a
relaxation of the marriage code; when the diseases of abstinence and
abuse might not only be satisfactorily treated, but effectually prevented. As long however as prostitution continues to be in many
cases the only attainable intercourse, although I deeply deplore its
existence, it seems to me a far smaller evil that a man should indulge
in it, than that he should waste away under the miseries of spermatorrhœa or other evils of abstinence or abuse; and I admire from my
heart the eminent men, including M. M. Lallemand, Ricord, Roubaud,

and many others in this and other countries, who have both felt and acted upon this truth, whatever obloquy they incurred thereby. Had they cared more for their personal convenience, and less for the interests of their patients and of science, it would have been easy to have evaded the obnoxious question altogether.

With respect to Professor Newman's strictures, I shall only remark that in one place he makes the assertion that I have denied *chastity* to be a virtue. But this depends upon the definition given to the word. In the popular sense of the word, chastity is usually understood to mean "Complete sexual abstinence, for however prolonged a period, except during the married state." Benjamin Franklin however defined chastity to mean "the regulated and strictly temperate satisfaction, without injury to others, of those desires which are natural to all healthy adult beings." The late Mr. Robert Owen defined it in a similar manner, as "sexual intercourse with affection." If the word be understood according to the definition of Franklin and Mr. Owen, then I consider chastity to be a very great virtue; but chastity, in the sense of prolonged sexual abstinence, I cannot but regard as an infringement of the laws of health, and therefore *a natural sin* either in man or woman; though doubtless in the actual state of society there are certain cases in which it is unavoidable.

By the word *prostitution* I have meant here, and generally throughout this work, "indiscriminate and mercenary intercourse;" in other words, I have used it with special reference to the public women of the town. It is necessary to state this, for several writers have included under the word all kinds of *unmarried* intercourse, making little or no distinction between the moral character of any connections, which are not sanctioned by the marriage tie; or, at least, regarding all such connections as highly reprehensible. From this view, I need scarcely repeat that I entirely differ. On the contrary, the noblest sexual conduct, in the present state of society, appears to me to be that of those who, while endeavouring to fulfil the *real* sexual duties, enumerated in a former essay, live together openly and without disguise, but refuse to enter into an indissoluble contract of which they conscientiously disapprove.]

OPINIONS

OF

ENGLISH AND FOREIGN WRITERS ON THE LAW OF POPULATION.

———————

The four laws which have just been considered, namely, the laws of exercise, fecundity, and agricultural industry, with the derivative law of population, are, in my opinion, incomparably the most important truths with which man has to do. They form the true explanation of the chief phenomena of society, and hold the same relation to all other social theories, that the doctrine of gravitation does to the various theories of the planetary motions, which existed up to the time of Newton. I am unwilling to quit this great subject, without adding to what has already been said, the testimony of several distinguished writers, English and foreign, whose opinions are of far greater weight and value than my own. The following quotations will show the reader how general and complete is the acceptance of the Malthusian theory among those who have carefully studied, and rightly apprehended the question. In fact, the modern science of political economy is in the main based on this great theory, in the same manner as astronomy and mechanics are based on the laws of motion and gravitation. As Mr. Senior and Mr. Mill have shown, political economy as a science consists almost entirely of a series of deductions from the laws of fecundity and agricultural industry, and from the familiar law of human nature that "man tends to prefer a greater gain to a smaller." It is mainly by reasoning from these premises, that Malthus, Ricardo, and their successors have given to the science its present highly developed form. "Political Economy, properly so called," says Mr. Mill, "has grown up almost from infancy since the time of Adam Smith." To deny the Malthusian theory is therefore in reality equivalent to a rejection of the whole modern science of political economy, just in the same way as to deny the laws of motion and gravitation would be to reject the astronomical and mechanical sciences. It may be imagined with what extreme care principles of so fundamental a character have been examined by scientific men. Those who, in the present day, endeavour to refute the Malthusian theory, should know that they are arguing, not against an isolated proposition, or a single individual, but against a *science*, and a whole scientific body.

I may first quote the opinion of Mr. John Stuart Mill, the most eminent economist and sociologist of the age. After showing that the law of the Increase of Production depends on the laws of increase in the three agents of production—labor, capital, and land—Mr. Mill proceeds to consider the first of these agents. "The increase of labor," he says, "is the increase of mankind; of population. On this subject the discussions excited by the Essay of Mr. Malthus, have made the truth, though by no means universally admitted, yet so fully known, that a briefer examination of the question than would otherwise have been necessary, will probably on the present occasion suffice.

"The power of multiplication inherent in all organic life may be regarded as *infinite*. There is no one species of vegetable or animal, which, if the earth were entirely abandoned to it, and to the things on which it feeds, would not in a·small number of years overspread every region of the globe of which the climate was compatible with its existence. . . .

"To this property of organized beings the human species forms no exception. Its power of increase is indefinite, and the actual multiplication would be extraordinarily rapid, if the power were exercised to the utmost. It never is exercised to the utmost, and yet, in the most favorable circumstances known to exist, which are those of a fertile region colonized from an industrious and civilized community, population has continued for several generations, independently of fresh immigration, to double itself in not much more than twenty years. That the multiplication in the human species exceeds even this, is evident if we consider how great is the ordinary number of children to a family, where the climate is good and early marriages usual; and how small a proportion of them die before the age of maturity, in the present state of hygienic knowledge, where the locality is healthy, and the family adequately provided with the means of living. It is a very low estimate of the capacity of increase, if we only assume that in a good sanitary condition of the people, each generation may be double the number of the generation which preceded it.

"Twenty or thirty years ago, these propositions might still have required considerable enforcement and illustration; but the evidence of them is so ample and incontestible that they have made their way against all kinds of opposition, and may now be regarded as *axiomatic*." Mr. Mill then states the causes by which these boundless powers of increase are *checked* in old countries—namely, by want or the dread of want, by poverty or sexual restraint. "If the multiplication of mankind," he says, "proceeded only, like that of the other animals, from a blind instinct, it would be limited in the same manner with

theirs; the births would be as numerous as the physical constitution
of the species admitted of, and the population would be kept down
by deaths. But the conduct of human creatures is more or less influenced by foresight of consequences. . . . In proportion as
mankind rise above the condition of the beasts, population is restrained by the fear of want rather than by want itself."

Mr. James Mill, in his Elements of Political Economy, after stating
the law of fecundity, and adducing facts to show the powers of increase under favorable circumstances, says, "That population therefore has such a tendency to increase as would enable it to double
itself in a small number of years, is a proposition resting on the
strongest evidence, which nothing that deserves the name of evidence
has been brought on the other side to oppose." "We know well," he says
again, "that there are two causes by which it may be prevented from
increasing, how great soever its natural tendency to increase. The
one is poverty; under which, let the number born be what it may, all
but a certain number undergo a premature destruction. The other
cause is prudence; by which, either marriages are sparingly contracted, or care is taken that children, beyond a certain number, shall
not be the fruit." Again, in comparing the increase of population
with that of capital, he says, "If it were the natural tendency of
capital to increase faster than population, there would be no difficulty
in preserving a prosperous condition of the people. If on the other
hand, it were the natural tendency of population to increase faster
than capital, the difficulty would be very great. There would be a
perpetual tendency in wages to fall. . . . That population has a
tendency to increase faster than capital has, in most places, actually
increased, is proved, incontestibly, by the condition of the population
in almost all parts of the globe. In almost all countries the condition
of the great body of the people is poor and miserable. This is an impossibility if capital had increased faster than population. In that
case wages of necessity must have risen, and would have placed the
laborer in a state of affluence, far above the miseries of want."

In his article on Colonies in the Supplement to the Encyclopædia
Britannica, Mr. James Mill makes the following allusion to preventive intercourse. In speaking of the necessity of meeting the population difficulty in a straightforward and resolute manner, he says,
"This is indeed *the most important practical problem* to which the
wisdom of the politician or the moralist can be applied. It has till
this time been miserably evaded by all those who have meddled with
the subject, as well as by all those who were called upon by their situation to find a remedy for the evils to which it relates. And yet if
the superstitions of the nursery were discarded, and the principle of
utility kept steadily in view, *a solution might not be difficult to be found,*
and the means of drying up one of the most copious sources of evil—
a source which, if all other sources of evil were taken away, would
alone suffice to retain the great mass of human beings in misery—
would be seen to be neither doubtful nor difficult to be applied."

Mr. David Ricardo, in his Principles of Political Economy and

Taxation, says, "Of Mr. Malthus's Essay on Population, I am happy in the opportunity here afforded me of expressing my admiration. The assaults of the opponents of this great work have only served to prove its strength; and I am persuaded that its great reputation will spread with the cultivation of that science of which it is so eminent an ornament."

Mr. Senior, in his treatise on Political Economy in the Encyclopædia Metropolitana, bases the whole science on four elementary propositions, two of which are the law of fecundity with its checks, and the law of agricultural industry. "We have already stated," he says, "that the general facts on which the science of Political Economy rests, are comprised in a few general propositions, the result of observation or consciousness. The propositions to which we then alluded are these.

" 1. That every man desires to obtain additional wealth with as little sacrifice as possible.

" 2. That the Population of the world, or in other words the number of persons inhabiting it, is limited only by moral or physical evil, or by fear of a deficiency of those articles of wealth, which the habits of the individuals of each class of its inhabitants lead them to require.

" 3. That the powers of labor and of the other instruments which produce wealth, may be indefinitely increased by using their products as the means of further production.

" 4. That, agricultural skill remaining the same, additional labor employed on the land within a given district, produces in general a less proportionate return; or in other words, that though with every increase of the labor bestowed, the aggregate return is increased, the increase of the return is not in proportion to the increase of the labor.

" The first of these propositions is a matter of consciousness, the three others are matter of observation."

The first proposition mentioned by Mr. Senior, although not formally stated, is, he says, "assumed in almost every process of economical reasoning. It is the corner-stone of the doctrine of wages and profits, and, generally speaking, of exchange." The second proposition is the law of fecundity with its checks. The checks as enumerated by Mr. Senior are "moral or physical evil, or a fear of deficiency of wealth;" which correspond respectively to vice, misery, and moral restraint, in the language of Mr. Malthus. The third proposition relates to the employment of capital, as an instrument of production; while the fourth is the law of agricultural industry, or diminishing productiveness. Mr. Senior describes the two last propositions as being nearly self-evident. "No one who reflects on the difference between the unassisted force of man, and the more than gigantic powers of capital and machinery, can doubt the former proposition; and to convince ourselves of the other, it is necessary only to recollect that, if it were false, no land except the very best could ever be cultivated; since if the return from a single farm were to increase in full proportion to any amount of increased labor bestowed on it, the produce of that one farm might feed the whole population of England." Mr. Senior then proceeds to the further consideration and proof of each of these propositions, and to deduce from them the other doctrines of the science. Political Economy, it may here be remarked, though its first principles are of course obtained by induction, is in the main a *deductive* science; the laws of the distribution and exchange of wealth given in economical works, having been all ascertained by the *concrete deductive method* of proof, which has been already mentioned as the only means of arriving at the laws of complex phenomena.

In like manner, Mr. Cairnes, the present Whateley Professor of Political Economy in the University of Dublin, bases the science on the same elementary propositions, in his excellent treatise on the Character and Logical Method of Political Economy, published in 1857. After showing that the ultimate premises of political economy consist of certain facts of human nature and of the external world, he says with regard to these facts:—"Although so numerous as to defy distinct specification, there are yet some, the existence and character of which are easily ascertainable, of such *paramount importance* in relation to the production and distribution of wealth, as to afford a sound and stable basis for deducing the laws of these phenomena. The principal of these I stated to be, 1st, the desire for wealth, and aversion to labor, implanted in human beings: 2ndly, the principles of population derived from the physiological character of man, and his mental propensities; and 3rdly, the physical qualities of the natural agents, more especially land, on which human industry is exercised."

"There are no limits," says Mr. McCulloch in his Principles of Political Economy, "to the prolific power of plants and animals. They are endued with a principle which impels them to increase their numbers beyond the nourishment prepared for them. . . The progress of population in countries with different capacities for providing food and other accommodations, illustrates at once the operation of the law of increase, and the degree in which it is modified by a change of circumstances. In newly-settled countries, and especially in those which have a large extent of fertile and unoccupied land, population invariably increases with extraordinary rapidity. . . The population of some of the states of North America has, after making every reasonable allowance for immigrants, continued for upwards of a century to double in every twenty or at most, five-and-twenty years. .

But the principle whose operation under favourable circumstances has thus developed itself, is, in the language of geometers, a *constant* quantity. The same power that doubles the population of Kentucky, Illinois, and New South Wales every five-and-twenty years, *exists everywhere*, and is equally energetic in England, France, and Holland. Man however is not the mere unreasoning slave of instinct. . . In the United States every industrious individual who has attained a marriageable age may enter into the matrimonial contract without fear of the consequences: the largest family being there an advantage rather than otherwise. But such is not the case here; nor will it be the case in America after she has become comparatively populous. . . . Man cannot increase beyond the means of subsistence provided for his support; and it is obvious that if the tendency to multiplication, in countries advancing in the career of civilization, and where there is, in consequence, an increased difficulty of providing additional supplies of food, were not checked by the prevalence of moral restraint, or of prudence and forethought, it would be checked by the prevalence of vice, misery, and famine. There is no alternative."

In the article on Population in the Penny Cyclopædia, the writer says, "Mr. Malthus's theory is now generally accepted as the true exposition of the principle of population. Many of the objections that have been urged against it are hardly worthy of notice. Some are content to quote the Scripture command, 'Increase and multiply,' forgetful of the moral obligations which are imposed in connection with it." [Thus Professor Miller in the work on Prostitution already referred to, after recommending—like the *Times* newspaper, and the Roman Catholic priesthood—*earlier marriages* as one of the chief remedies for prostitution, says:—"But, say the political economists, perhaps—By such early marriages you will flood the labor market, and drown the population. Indeed, some wiseacres blame early marriage for prostitution, poverty, intemperance, and all the many evils with which the lower classes are so sore beset. Our answer is:— Let the marriage be 'early' under the limitations here specified, and we will answer for the consequences. 'Redundant population! Fudge! No fear of that. Man's mission is to 'multiply and replenish the earth.'" Now the very fact of the existence of social poverty in a country like England, is a certain sign that the procreative powers have *already* been enormously over-exercised by the community; therefore, to recommend earlier marriages, without at the same time recommending preventive measures, is just to recommend that poverty should be increased. With regard to Professor Miller's summary dismissal of the population principle, what would he, as a man of science, say to any one, who, without having ever really studied the subject, should reject in such a manner the most important principles of surgery?] "Others have imagined that they have discovered a supernatural law of fecundity which varies with the fluctuating circumstances of society. Dr. Price, Mr. Godwin, and Mr. Sadler entertained this notion. Mr. Senior is the only economist of any distinction who has objected to the theory of Mr. Malthus." This last remark refers to a discussion which took place between Mr. Senior and Mr. Malthus, and which arose from the ambiguous meaning of the word *tendency*, already alluded to; but it was soon perceived by both parties that there was no *real* difference of opinion between them. "Our controversy has ended," says Mr. Senior, "as I believe few controversies ever terminated before, in mutual agreement."

Again, in the article on Population in Rees' Cyclopædia, the writer says, "It hence appears that the checks to population may be divided into two general classes, viz.: those which operate in *preventing the birth* of a population which cannot be supported, and those which *destroy* it after it has been brought into existence; or, as they are denominated by Mr. Malthus, the preventive checks, and the positive checks. The necessary and constant effect of some checks being *fully established*, and these checks being divisible into the classes above mentioned, we cannot for a moment hesitate in determining which of these we should wish to see put in operation." In the Encyclopædia Britannica and Londinensis the articles on Population are by Mr. Malthus himself, so that they need not here be quoted.

"If the tendency of population be to increase in a geometrical ratio," says Mr. Francis Place in his reply to Mr. Godwin's attempted refutation of the Malthusian views, "and the period of doubling be a short one, it follows of course that the mass of the people in an old country must remain in a state of wretchedness, until they are convinced that their safety depends upon themselves, and that it can be maintained in no other way, than by their ceasing to propagate faster than the means of comfortable subsistence are produced."

In alluding to the subject of preventive intercourse, Mr. Place says, "If above all it were once clearly understood that it was not disreputable for married persons to avail themselves of such precautionary means, as would, without being injurious to health, or destructive of female delicacy, *prevent conception*, a sufficient check might at once be given to the increase of population beyond the means of subsistence; and vice and misery to a prodigious extent might be removed from society. The course recommended will, I am fully persuaded, at some period be pursued by the people, even if left to themselves . . . . If means were adopted to prevent the breeding of a larger number of children than married people might desire to have, and if the laboring part of the population could thus be kept below the demand for labor, wages would rise, so as to afford the means of comfortable subsistence for all, and all might marry." "It is time," he says again, "that those who really understand the cause of a redundant, unhappy, miserable, and considerably vicious population, and the means of preventing the redundancy, should clearly, freely, openly and fearlessly point out the means. It is childish to shrink from proposing or developing any means, however repugnant they may at first appear to be." So far from being "disreputable," preventive intercourse will, I am persuaded, in time be recognised as consistent, and alone consistent, with the highest dictates of morality; for it alone among the population checks (one or other of which, it must never be forgotten, is *inevitable*) fulfils the two great moral duties—the duty namely which one owes to others, and that which is due to oneself. Celibacy, or prolonged sexual abstinence, on the other hand, as already shown, is a violation of the laws of health, and therefore, like all other violations of these laws, must be regarded as *a natural sin*, either in man or woman.

I may here observe, that the use of preventive measures has been much more frequently recommended, as the true remedy for the population evils, than is at all generally known, or than I was myself aware of at the time when this work was first published. Besides such high authorities as Mr. James Mill and Mr. Francis Place, preventive intercourse has been zealously advocated by M. Joseph Garnier, Professor of Political Economy at Paris, and for many years the chief editor of the Journal des Economistes; by M. Raciborski; by Mr. Robert Dale Owen in his Moral Physiology; by the heroic Mr. Richard Carlile in his Every Woman's Book (the first work which openly described the preventive measures;) by Dr. Knowlton in his Fruits of Philosophy; by the author of Notes on the Population Question; and also in an excellent little treatise on Poverty, its Cause and Cure, just published by Mr. Truelove. In addition to these noble efforts, it was alluded to in some English newspapers in the year 1827, and about the same time a large number of handbills on the subject were distributed among the working classes in the northern counties of England. "It has been broached somewhat disguisedly in several newspapers," says Mr. Richard Carlile in his Every Woman's Book, "and preached in lectures to the people by a most benevolent gentleman at Leeds; it has been circulated by thousands of handbills through the populous districts of the north." Different writers have recommended different methods of prevention. Of the five methods which have been employed or proposed—namely, withdrawal, the sheath, the sponge, injections (chemical or simple), and attention to the monthly periods—Mr. Owen and the author of Notes on the Population Question give the preference to the first; Mr. Richard Carlile and the author of Poverty, its Cause and Cure, to the third; Dr. Knowlton to the fourth; while M. Raciborski, as we have already seen, has directed attention to the fifth. Without pretending to decide on a point on which so little experience has yet been made public, I may mention that although the two first measures are *the most certain*, yet the three others are in my opinion the best, and those which will be ultimately adopted; for they are the least injurious to health, and interfere little, if at all, with the pleasure of the venereal act. Dr. Knowlton speaks highly of the efficacy of injections containing a small quantity of sulphate of zinc, or alum, to be injected into the vagina by means of a female syringe, immediately after connection. "A lump of either of the above-mentioned salts," he says, "of the size of a chestnut, may be dissolved in a pint of water, making the solution weaker or stronger, as it may be borne without producing any irritation of the parts to which it is applied. These solutions would not lose their virtues by age." "I know," he says again, "the use of this check requires the woman to leave her bed for a few moments, but this is its only objection; and it would be unreasonable to suppose that any check can ever be devised entirely free of objections. In its favor it may be said, it costs nearly nothing; it is true; it requires no sacrifice of pleasure; it is in the hands of the female; it is to be used *after* instead of before connection, a weighty consideration in its favor, as a moment's reflection will convince any one; and last,

but not least, it is conducive to cleanliness, and preserves the parts
from relaxation and disease. . . . Those who have used this check
(and some have used it to my certain knowledge, with entire success,
for nine or ten years, and under such circumstances as leave no room
to doubt its efficacy) affirm they would be at the trouble of using injections merely for the purposes of health and cleanliness. . . .
I can only say I have not known it to fail. Such are my views of the
whole subject, that it would require many instances of its reputed
failure to satisfy me that such failures were not owing to an insufficient use of it. I even believe that quite cold water alone, if
thoroughly used, would be sufficient. . . . I hope that no failures
will be charged to inefficacy of this check, which ought to be attributed to negligence, or insufficient use of it. I will therefore recommend at least two applications of the syringe, the sooner the surer;
yet it is my opinion that five minutes' delay would not prove mischievous, perhaps not ten." Mr. Richard Carlile gives the following
description of the mode of employing the sponge, which he calls the
female's safe-guard:—"If before sexual intercourse the female intro-
duces into her vagina a piece of sponge, as large as can be pleasantly
introduced," (perhaps from the size of a walnut to that of an egg)
"having previously attached a bobbin or a piece of narrow ribband to
withdraw it," (or, without this, it may be withdrawn by the finger) "it
will be found a preventive to conception, while it neither lessens the
pleasure of the female, nor injures her health. When convenient, the
sponge should be dipped in cold water, or in warm water rather than
none. The practice is common with the females of the more refined
parts of the continent of Europe, and with those of the aristocracy
of England."

With regard to these preventive measures, the great desideratum
at the present day appears to me to be, not so much to know which
of them is best, (for this could be easily ascertained afterwards, and
at present all of them have their advantages), but that the subject
should be openly discussed, so that *every adult should be intimately acquainted with them;* and also that they should be recognised as not
only perfectly consistent with the highest morality, but as the most
fundamental requisite of human happiness and progress. They are
indeed, to use the words of Mr. James Mill, the solution of "the most
important practical problem to which the wisdom of the politician or
the moralist can be applied." Those who endeavour to vilify and degrade these means in the eyes of the public, and who speak of them
as "immoral" or "disgusting," are little aware of the moral responsibility they incur thereby. As already shown, to reject preventive
intercourse is in reality to choose the other three true population-
checks, poverty, prostitution, and celibacy. So far from meriting reprobation, the endeavour to spread the knowledge of the preventive
methods and of the great law of nature which renders them necessary,
is in my opinion the very greatest service which can at present be
done to mankind.

No one has more strenuously supported the population principle and the doctrine of moral restraint or celibacy than the eminent Scotch minister, Dr. Thomas Chalmers. He describes the main object of his work on Political Economy in the following terms:—"All the remedies which have been proposed against a state of general destitution in society," he says, "may be classified under two descriptions. By the first, it is sought to provide the adequate means for the increasing numbers of mankind. By the second, to keep down the numbers to the stationary, or comparatively speaking, to the slowly-increasing means. . . . It is our main design to demonstrate the insufficiency of one and all the remedies put together which belong to the first class—and to contrast, with their operation, the effect of the moral remedy, the prosperous economic state that will surely be realised through the medium of general intelligence or virtue, or by an action on the minds of the people themselves." After pointing out the error of Adam Smith (an error which is still so extremely common among writers of the "productionist" school) in attending chiefly to an *increase of production,* and augmentation of the physical resources, he says, "It was not otherwise to be expected; for his work, great and enlightened though it be, was long prior to the clear and convincing expositions of Malthus on the subject of population."

"In the more civilized state," says Mr. William Ellis in his Outlines of Social Economy, "capital is large, power developed, and if the country be but partially settled, as North America and the Australian colonies, large tracts of unoccupied land of great fertility and abundance of food await a rapidly increasing population; if the country be more fully settled, as England and France, the situation of the laborer is happy or miserable, according as the growing numbers are regulated by virtuous, sober, prudent forethought, or by—we must not say war, pestilence, and famine, for these would imply absence of civilization—but by insufficient and unwholesome food, inadequate clothing, scanty fuel, and confined and ill-ventilated dwellings."

"The grand principles are fully established," says Miss Harriet Martineau in her Illustrations of Political Economy, "which may serve as a key to all the mysteries relating to the distribution of wealth. Their application may require much time and patience; but we have them safe. Their final general adoption may be regarded as certain, and an incalculable amelioration of the condition of society must follow of course. These principles are two: that, owing to the inequality of soils, the natural tendency of capital is to yield a perpetually diminishing return, and that the consumers of capital [tend to] increase at a perpetually accelerated rate. The operation of these principles may be modified to any extent by the influence of others; but they exist; they are fully ascertained; and must henceforth serve as guides to all wise attempts to rectify an unjust distribution of the wealth of society. It is difficult to conceive how any sound mind can have withheld its assent to these grand principles, after they had once been clearly announced." The first of the principles, mentioned by Miss Martineau, is the law of agricultural industry, the second, the law of fecundity.

Mr. William Thompson (author of the noble "Appeal of Women") says in his work on the "Distribution of Wealth," in answer to the objections brought against his and Mr. Owen's communistic views by Malthusian writers, " It is admitted to these objectors that there is a physical capability of increasing the numbers of the human species, greater than any known physical capability of increasing the quantity of food necessary for human subsistence. It is also admitted that nothing could be more useful in the present state of human knowledge, than to bring forward this important question for *minute and uncompromising discussion*. . . . The remedy is absolutely indicated at the same time and by the same process, that the defect is discovered The defect is, the tendency to increase beyond the supply of food; this defect arising from the want of prudence in the regulation of a natural appetite, on the part of the great mass, the ignorant mass of mankind. If it be possible to impart prudence to the great mass of mankind, the evils said to arise from a want of prudence are plainly *not irremediable*." Mr. Thompson here expresses exactly the Malthusian views, and yet he speaks as if he were in some respects opposed to them. He seems to believe—as many have done—that Malthusian writers have asserted that the population evils *are* irremediable, and that the principle of increase must always give rise to poverty and wretchedness. But this, as the reader is well aware, forms no part of the population doctrines; according to which mankind have a *choice* between the four true population-checks, any one of which may be indefinitely diminished, though only by the substitution of some *other* check in its place.

Mr. George Combe, in the interesting sketch of the progress of his views in early life, prefixed to his latest work—" On the Relation between Science and Religion "—says, after describing his dissatisfaction with the chaotic state of opinion on moral and social subjects:—" In this condition of mind I continued for several years, and recollect meeting with only two works which approached to the solution of any portion of the enigma which puzzled my understanding. These were Smith's 'Wealth of Nations,' and Malthus 'On Population.' . . . I first read the work of Mr. Malthus in 1805, and he appeared to me to prove that God reigns, through the medium of fixed natural laws, in another department of human affairs—namely, in that of population. The facts adduced by him showed that the Creator has bestowed on men a power of increasing their numbers, much beyond the ratio of the diminution that, in favorable circumstances, will be caused by death; and consequently, that they must limit their increase by moral restraint, or augment, by ever-extending cultivation of the soil, their means of subsistence in proportion to their numbers, or expose themselves to the evil of being reduced by disease and famine to the number which the actual production of food will maintain. These propositions, like the doctrines of Adam Smith, met with general rejection; and their author, far from being honored as a successful expounder of God's method of governing the world, was assailed with unmitigated abuse, and his views were strenuously resisted in practice."

I may add, that Mr. Combe once told me himself that he never heard any one deny the Malthusian doctrines who understood them. I believe that every one who is well acquainted with these doctrines, and with the objections made to them, will confirm this assertion. In fact, with the exception of the *sterility* fallacy of Mr. Doubleday and others, I cannot remember a single argument against the population doctrines, which does not show an ignorance of their real nature, and a misconception of Mr. Malthus's meaning. Almost all these arguments are examples of the fallacy called by logicians *ignoratio elenchi*, or *irrelevant conclusion;* that is, the fallacy of arguing against what was never asserted, and therefore proving something which has nothing to do with the question. " The attempts to disprove the population doctrines of Malthus," says Mr. Mill in his Logic, "have been mostly cases of *ignoratio elenchi*. Malthus has been supposed to be refuted if it could be shown that in some countries or ages population has been nearly stationary: as if he had asserted that population always increases in a given ratio, or had not expressly declared that it increases only in so far as it is not restrained by prudence, or kept down by poverty and disease. Or, perhaps, a collection of facts is produced to prove that in some one country the people are better off with a dense population than they are in another country with a thin one; or that the people have become more numerous and better off at the same time. As if the assertion were that a dense population could not possibly be well off; as if it were not part of the very doctrine, and essential to it, that where there is a more abundant capital there may be a greater population without any increase of poverty, or even with a diminution of it." Besides these, there is another large class of objections to the Malthusian doctrines, which however can hardly be called arguments; for they consist in rejecting the doctrines at once, as opposed to what is called the bounty of nature or of providence, without even attempting to disprove the evidence on which they rest. "Writers have not yet ceased," says Mr. Mill, "to oppose the theory of divine benevolence to the evidence of physical facts, to the principle of population for example." Objections of this kind belong to the class of fallacies called by logicians *à priori* fallacies, or fallacies of simple inspection. A third class of objections do not apply to the law itself, but only to some of the practical inferences drawn from it; two perfectly distinct questions, but which have, unfortunately, been frequently confounded together. The truth of the law of population is one thing; how mankind should act in consequence of it, is another. The first is a question of science and theory, the latter of practice. Many however, overlooking this distinction, have rejected without examination the demonstrated law from not agreeing with the particular inferences drawn from it by this or the other writer. The law itself—namely, that the natural increase of population has always been, and must always be, most powerfully checked in all old countries by moral restraint, vice, or misery (that is, by celibacy, prostitution, sterility, preventive inter course, or premature death)—was as thoroughly and rigorously demonstrated by Mr. Malthus as the law of gravitation was by Newton.

Among the periodical publications, the only ones with which I am acquainted (though doubtless there may have been others) which have steadily and avowedly advocated the Malthusian doctrines, are the "Edinburgh Review," together with "The Republican," and "The Lion," edited by the brave and energetic Mr. Richard Carlile; whilst most of the other magazines, and almost all the newspaper press, have either ignored, or mentioned them only at rare intervals, sometimes with approval, but far more frequently with hostility and aversion.

The population principle is explained with admirable clearness in the Edinburgh Review for August, 1810, and is frequently alluded to in other numbers of the same periodical. But there is no work, in which these all-important questions have been more thoroughly and earnestly discussed, than in the very valuable journals edited by Mr. Richard Carlile. The population-principle and the subject of preventive intercourse are most ably treated in these journals by Mr. Francis Place, and by another writer signing himself R. H., the latter of whom especially enters very fully into these questions.

In addition to the foregoing authorities, the truth of the population principle has been acknowledged, (though usually in by no means a sufficiently straightforward and explicit manner), by many of the distinguished statesmen; and one legislative enactment, namely, the Poor-Law Amendment Act of 1834, was in reality based upon it. This measure was drawn up chiefly from the recommendations of the Poor-Law Commissioners of Inquiry, among whom was Mr. Senior; and was carried in both Houses of Parliament by large majorities, including members belonging to all the different political parties. The great object of the Act was *to raise the condition of the laboring classes*, who had sunk into the most deplorable state of pauperism and degradation under the former system of relief; to induce them not to rely for support on the delusive assistance of legal charity, but rather to control their increase, and thus to avoid the grand source of poverty. To effect these objects, the Bill provided that the condition of any one in receipt of relief should be *more irksome* than that of the independent laborer; a provision which the plainest dictates of common sense will show to be both just and necessary. It proposed that out-door relief should no longer be given to able-bodied persons except in cases of emergency, and above all that what was called "the allowance system" should cease. Under this system, which Mr. Mill describes as "worse than any other form of poor-law abuse yet invented," not only did the laborers, even while in employment, receive relief if their wages were held to be insufficient, but the relief given was in proportion to the size of their families; a system which placed the married laborers in a better position than the single, and operated in fact as a bounty upon children. The result of this most ruinous system (which was in operation for between thirty and forty years previous to 1834) had been not only to pauperize individuals, but to lower the wages of the working classes generally; so that in some parishes there was not a single laborer who did not receive assistance from the poor-rates, and the moral character as well as the material condition of the people had been most lamentably degraded. The allowance system had in short aggravated the wretchedness of the poor, by *weakening the prudential check* to population; and the main object of the Bill was to strengthen this check, by which means alone can the state of the poor be permanently raised.

Lord Brougham, at the time Lord Chancellor, in moving the second reading of the Bill in the House of Lords, entered more fully than any other speaker into the principle of population, and the dangerous tendencies of a bad system of Poor-Laws, and made the following allusions to Mr. Malthus:—" May I step aside for one moment to do justice to a most learned, a most able, a most virtuous individual, whose name has been mixed up with more unwitting deception, and also with more wilful misrepresentation, than any man of science in this Protestant country, and in these enlightened times. When I mention talent, learning, humanity, the strongest sense of public duty, the most amiable feelings in private life, the tenderest and most humane disposition which ever man was adorned with; when I speak of a man, the ornament of the society in which he moves, the delight of his own family, and not less the admiration of those men of letters and science amongst whom he shines the first and the brightest; when I speak of one of the most enlightened, learned, and pious ministers whom the church of England ever numbered amongst her sons, I am sure every one will apprehend that I cannot but refer to Mr. Malthus. The character of this estimable man has been foully slandered by some who had the excuse of ignorance, and by others, I fear, without any such palliative, and simply for having made *one of the greatest additions to political philosophy*, which has been effected since that branch of learning deserved the name of a science. . . . My Lords, those who framed the statute of Elizabeth [the statute which first introduced the system of legal relief for the poor] were not adepts in political science—they were not acquainted with the true principle of population—they could not foresee that a Malthus would arise to enlighten mankind upon that important, but as yet ill-understood branch of science—they knew not the true principle on which to frame a preventive check to the unlimited increase of the people."

On another occasion, Sir Robert Peel, in considering the advisability of introducing a system of Poor-Laws into Ireland, said, "Looking at the tendency of an increased population already in Ireland, I should rather think that the application of those laws to it would, by holding out a settlement to the poor, remove every check to population [that is, every prudential check], encourage early marriages, and a still greater subdivision of land."

With regard to the Act of 1834, I am aware of the odium which still exists against it among the working classes, and I merely adduce it as a proof that government has, although in a tacit and indirect manner, recognised the truth of the population principle. I believe too that this odium would never have arisen had it not been for two causes; namely, first, that the principle of population was not more clearly explained as the true foundation of the act, but was rather kept in the back ground by the government; and secondly, that the great social duty of limited procreation, which the Act was intended to promote, was not recognised as *equally incumbent upon all classes.* But the clearest principles of social equity demand that this duty should be impartially applied to every member of society alike, the rich as well as the poor. It is just that all mankind, whatever be their station in life, should bear an equal share of those sexual difficulties, which the laws of nature impose upon the human race. Hitherto the wealthy classes have set at naught this great duty, and have thrown the whole burden of it upon the poor. The aristocracy and clergy are commonly said to have on an average, the largest families in the community; and while such conduct is allowed to pass without disapproval in these classes, it is vain to look for any material improvement in social morality. "While the aristocracy and clergy," says Mr. Mill, "are foremost to set the example of incontinence, what can be expected from the poor?"

Had it not been for these two reasons, it appears to me that the fairness and necessity of the measure must have been generally acknowledged by society; whereas, from the manner in which government and its organs have all along evaded and mystified the population principle, the working classes are even at the present day, for the most part completely in the dark as to the intentions of the Act, and regard it rather as a scheme for defrauding them of their just rights to legal relief. It is often said that the aristocracy and the rich are favorable to the Malthusian doctrines; but this is a great error, as may be seen from the systematic manner in which parliament and the organs of the wealthy classes (such as the *Times* and *Economist* newspapers) have evaded these doctrines, and from the hostility which ever and anon they manifest towards them. The truth I believe to be, that there are no principles which the enemies of radical reform regard with so much fear and aversion; especially since the duty of limited procreation has been impartially applied by Mr. Mill and others to *all classes* of society alike.

Many other English writers might be quoted in support of the Malthusian principles, among whom may be mentioned Archbishop Whately in his Lectures on Political Economy, Mr. William Thornton in his Over-population and its Remedy, Mrs. Marcet in her Conversations on Political Economy, Mr. Edward Gibbon Wakefield in his Popular Politics, Mr. Travers Twiss, formerly Professor of Political Economy at Oxford, in his Progress of Political Economy, Dr. Traill, editor of the Encyclopædia Britannica, in his Medical Jurisprudence, Mr. Wade in his History of the Middle and Working Classes, Mr. Buckle in his History of Civilization in England, Mr. C. Morison in his Labor and Capital, Mr. W. Rathbone Greg in his Political and Social Essays, &c.

Among the professed English writers on Political Economy, though there is still considerable difference of opinion with regard to the *practical inferences* to be drawn from the Malthusian law, (by far the most important of which differences is in reference to the question, whether celibacy or preventive intercourse is the desirable population check), I scarcely remember a single one who has not acknowledged its scientific truth, except Mr. Rickards in his Lectures on Population and Capital, and Mr. Francis W. Newman in his Lectures on Political Economy. The objections of the former however do not really apply to the law itself (that is, to the necessary existence of the population-checks, which Mr. Rickards admits as fully as Mr. Malthus), but appear to me to have arisen from a misconception of Mr. Malthus's views as to the actual probability of social improvement—a misconception chiefly due to the ambiguity already noticed in the word *tendency*; while Mr. Newman, like most of the opponents of Mr. Malthus, has radically misunderstood his meaning, and the real nature of the question.

The following quotations from the works of several distinguished *foreign* writers, will show that the Malthusian doctrines are quite as widely diffused and as definitely accepted by scientific men in other countries as in our own.

I may first quote the opinion of Monsieur J. B. Say, the most celebrated French Economist of the last generation. In his Traité d' Economie Politique he says, " With regard to organised bodies, nature seems to despise the individual, and to bestow her protection only upon the race. Natural History presents us with many curious instances of the care which she takes for the preservation of species; but her most powerful means for effecting this purpose, consists in *multiplying the germs* with so vast a profusion, that, however numerous be the accidents which prevent them from coming into existence, or destroy them after their birth, there always remains a number more than sufficient for the perpetuation of the race. And if various forms of accident, destruction, and want of the power of development did not check the multiplication of organised beings, there is not a single animal, nor a single plant, which would not in a few years overspread the face of the globe.

"Man, like all the other animals, partakes in this faculty; and although his superior intelligence enables him greatly to multiply the means of existence, yet in his case also this power has its limits. . . . . Each individual family, and the nation itself (which is but a collection of families), subsists on the produce within its reach; and the total amount of the national produce necessarily limits the number of those who can be subsisted.

"Among those animals which are incapable of foresight in the gratification of their appetites, the progeny which result, when they do not become the prey of man or of other animals, perish as soon as they encounter an indispensable want, which they are unable to satisfy. But in the case of *man*, the difficulty of providing for future wants causes foresight to interfere more or less with the gratification of the natural desires; and it is this *foresight* alone, which averts from the human race a portion of those evils, which they would have to

endure, if their n mbers had to be perpetually kept down by violence
and destruction." In a note M. Say adds, "Consult especially on this
head the Essay on Population by Malthus, a work full of research
and of sound reasonings; a work which has withstood the numerous
criticisms directed against it, because it is founded on the experimental
method, and on the veritable nature of things." Again, in his Cours
Complet d' Economie Politique, M. Say, after observing that several authors previous to Mr. Malthus had incidentally alluded to the principle
of population (although without clearly seeing it) says, "Malthus has
confirmed, by philosophical investigations, the same principles, which
were never indeed disputed or vehemently attacked, until they were
placed beyond a doubt."

"There are few works," says M. Rossi, in his introduction to the
French translation of Mr. Malthus's Essay, "whose publication has
given rise to more discussion than the Essay on the Principle of
Population by Malthus. The illustrious author saw himself immediately surrounded by vehement opponents and zealous admirers. .
The question of Population affects everything—morals, politics, national and domestic economy. The state, the family, the individual,
are equally interested in this question. How diverse are the aspects
which such a subject presents! how many different points of view
does it open to the attentive observer! . . .

"That the human species can propagate itself with astonishing rapidity, is an ascertained truth, which no man of sense can deny. The
population of North America has doubled more than once in less than
25 years. Evidently what has taken place in America, could take
place everywhere. The physical organisation and the instincts of
man are not materially affected by degrees of latitude. . . .

"Let but prudence find its way into every household, and preside
over the birth of every family, and there would be no cause for
anxiety about the fate of the human race."

M. Joseph Garnier says, in his article on Population in the Dictionaire de l' Economie Politique, published in 1852:—"The man who
has most of all elucidated this subject, whose views form, so to speak,
the pivot of the discussions of economists, moralists, and writers of
every description, is unquestionably the celebrated Malthus. . . .
It is Malthus who has stated the question; it is he who has first demonstrated its supreme importance; it is he who has collected the
scientific materials of the argument in his celebrated Essay on the
Principle of Population; a work which was published in 1803, and
which had been preceded in 1798 by a first sketch of the subject, in
answer to the views of Godwin, who in his turn, twenty years later,
sought unsuccessfully to refute it. Some just ideas on the subject of
Population had indeed been thrown out by a few writers previous to
Malthus; for example, by James Stewart, Adam Smith, Wallace,
Hume, Gian Maria Ortes, &c.; but it is to the English philosopher
that the honor belongs of having made it the object of numerous
statistical and historical researches, and of having shed over the subject the clear light of science. . . . In his Essay on Population,

after having stated, by the aid of two well known propositions [the geometrical and arithmetical ratios] the law of the development of population, and that of the increase of the means of subsistence, the illustrious economist next proceeds to their verification, in a historical and statistical review of the nations of ancient and modern times, and shows by what *checks* the population has been retarded.

"Had the fact of duplication in 25 years, independently of immigration, been well attested in a single case only, it would have been sufficient to have induced science to accept *à posteriori*, the assertion of Malthus. But in the present day, the number of corroborative facts is so great, that to deny the law which we have announced, is, as it appears to us, *to repudiate evidence itself.*"

After showing that the choice of mankind is stringently limited either to the positive or the preventive form of the population-check, and that there can be no question as to which should be chosen, M. Garnier alludes to the subject of preventive intercourse in the following terms:—"I admit that the charge of inefficacy [one of the objections brought against Mr. Malthus's doctrine of *moral restraint*] would carry more weight with me. So much so that I am led to declare openly and positively, that by prudence is to be understood not only delayed marriages, not only celibacy for those who are capable of practising it, but prudence during the married state itself." He proceeds to defend the use of preventive means from the charge of *immorality*, which had been urged against them by various writers, and in particular by M. Proudhon in his Contradictions Economiques. "Can it be called immoral in the father of a family," says M. Garnier, "if he should wish to have only a limited number of children, proportioned to his means, and to the future which his affection fondly weaves for them, and if he should not, in carrying out this object, condemn himself to the most absolute and rigorous continence? But it is needless to enlarge on this point, and we content ourselves with leaving it to the decision of every enlightened conscience, and to that of M. Proudhon himself. . . Let any one ask himself, whether is it more moral, more conscientious, to give birth to children in the midst of privations, or prevent them being born—and let him then reply."

M. Michel Chevalier, Professor of Political Economy in the College de France, says, in his opening lecture in 1847, "What has been termed the theory of Malthus has given rise to controversies without end. . . The Essay on Population was saluted (by its admirers) as a blessing to the world, and it was said that this modest minister of the Gospel had discovered the law of the moral order of society, just as Newton had wrested from nature the secret of the mechanism of the physical universe. . . .

"The problem, how to effect a suitable provision for the destitute portion of the working classes, presents itself for our consideration at the present day, with no less urgency than it did in the time of Malthus . . . The amelioration of their condition would be certain, and would proceed with surprising celerity, if the increase of population were kept within due bounds, and if the éducation of the working man placed it within his power to produce an ever-increasing quantity of commodities in proportion to the labor expended in their production.

" Thus, gentlemen, behold us brought face to face with the precepts of Malthus in regard to the reproduction of the species. Let but population moderate its rate of increase, so as to *remain behind* the augmentation of the means of subsistence and employment; let mankind but exercise a sufficient self-control, a sufficient ascendancy over their passions, so as to adhere steadfastly to this guiding principle."

M. Villermé, one of the most distinguished medical men in Paris, whose views on Hysteria have been already alluded to, says, "Marriages generally become more numerous in proportion as the price of bread is lower, and *vice versa*. Such is found to be the case in all countries, and those words of Montesquieu, of which the celebrated work of Malthus on the Principle of Population might be regarded as the development, will be eternally true :—' Wherever there is room for two persons to live comfortably, a marriage is sure to take place; nature prompts mankind to this with sufficient energy, where her impulses are not checked by the difficulty of procuring subsistence.'"

M. Legoyt, who is at the head of the Statistical Office in France, in making a report to the Academy of the Moral and Political Sciences on Mr. Thomas Doubleday's work, entitled The Financial, Monetary, and Statistical History of England, says, " The author of this treatise made himself known for the first time in England, by a work published in 1845 under the title of The True Law of Population. This first publication already evinced in its author a love of paradox in the highest degree, and a sort of instinctive antipathy towards *the most generally received truths*. He there maintains that in every country the population increases in direct proportion to the deplethoric state of the species."

In another place, in considering the French census of 1846, and th general movement of population throughout Europe, M. Legoyt says, "According to these tables, France is the country of Europe where population advances the most slowly [the rate of increase being, as he showed, only about 1 in 200 annually]. Has France cause to complain of this inferiority in the increase of her population? We think not, and we believe that those will share in this opinion, who reflect that the states where population increases most rapidly, such as England, Ireland, Prussia, and Saxony, are precisely those where pauperism makes the most formidable progress.

" In France the population increases much more from the diminution of deaths than from the increase of births. A statistical document shows that *the number of children to a marriage* has sensibly diminished. Hence it is readily understood, that the working man, by not augmenting his family beyond a certain number, or by abstaining from marriage until either the rate of his wages, his savings, or perhaps the advantages of the union itself (for the workman now-a-days seeks a portion with his wife) enable him to marry—that he has thus increased the sum of his material comforts; which partly explains the diminution of deaths.

" In France the number of births to a marriage is *regularly diminish-ing*, while the number of *marriages* is increasing." These interesting facts are explained by the practice of preventive intercourse, which, as already mentioned, is almost universally spread throughout society in France.

M. Hippolyte Passy, author of " Aristocracy and Civilization," in reporting to the Academy of the Moral and Political Sciences, on a recent translation of the Principles of Political Economy by Mr. Malthus, says, " The Academy is well aware how eminent a position the works of Malthus occupy, and how great is the reputation of the ' Principles of Political Economy ' of this illustrious writer. . . . But the celebrity of Malthus is too high, and too well merited, to render it necessary for me to occupy the Academy with the characteristic qualities, and importance of his works."

M. de Molinari, Professor of Political Economy at Brussels, in commenting upon a new edition of Malthus's Essay recently published in Paris, says, " Since the publication of Malthus's Essay in the 'Collection complète des principaux économistes,' this great work has been the subject of renewed attacks. The socialist and protectionist writers, not to speak of a small number of self-styled defenders of religion, have combined to assail Malthus and his disciples with the most violent and unjust accusations. There has been a perfect concert of invective on the part of the ' Voix du Peuple,' the ' Constitutionnel,' the ' Nouveau Monde,' the ' Moniteur Industriel,' and the ' Univers Religieux.' How has this singular combination taken place? How comes it that writers who appear the most widely separated in opinion find themselves all at once united for the purpose of demolishing an economical doctrine? Simply because political economy is in their eyes *the common enemy*, and because the theory of Malthus, suitably disfigured and misrepresented, furnishes an inexhaustible theme for declamations and invectives against political economy."

[These remarks are not less applicable to our own country; where writers, who on other points differ most widely in opinion, unite in abusing political economy, and especially the Malthusian doctrines. Thus, for example, among the journals which have attacked these doctrines within the last two or three years, are included the *Times*, the *Daily Telegraph*, and *Reynolds's Newspaper*. The last-named journal especially has exceeded all bounds in the violence of its invectives against Mr. Malthus—the man who, by his discovery of the population principle, did more for mankind, and for the working classes in particular, than any other ever has done, or will do. These facts are an illustration of the following truth:—that, in the present day, by far the most important distinction between different social doctrines, is not the distinction between aristocracy and democracy, or between tory, whig, radical, republican, or socialist; it is the distinction between the Malthusian and scientific, and the non-Malthusian or unscientific theories of society.]

" Hence " continues M. de Molinari, " Malthus has had to run the gauntlet along the whole line. M.M. Proudhon, Burat, Pierre Leroux,

Denis, Louis Blanc, and Coquille, not to mention others, have vehemently attacked the 'Essay on Population.'

"But the work of the illustrious professor of Haileybury is entirely built on the solid basis of observation.

"We are aware, that our eminent and regretted friend Bastiat, after having commenced as a zealous Malthusian—that he too has pretended that Malthus was deceived, and that he sought to give a new solution of the population problem. But let any one read the works of Bastiat and what will he find? Conclusions expressed in other terms than those of Malthus, but whose sense is, in reality, absolutely the same.

"The theory of Malthus," continues M. de Molinari, "has withstood all the assaults of its opponents, whether old or new; and we do not hesitate to affirm, that every intelligent man, who will take the trouble to read, calmly and impartially, the Essay on the Principle of Population, with the striking introduction by Rossi, the biographical notice by Charles Comte, and the instructive and judicious notes by M. Joseph Garnier, will arise from its perusal deeply and irrevocably Malthusian."

M. Charles Comte, the friend of Bentham, and formerly secretary for life to the Academy of the Moral and Political Sciences, says, in his eulogium on Malthus, which was read to the Academy after the death of the latter in 1834, "There are few works so celebrated as the 'Essay on the Principle of Population.' There are few which have been more discussed, and upon which even educated people have entertained, and still entertain, more erroneous opinions. The misrepresentations of this work, which were published some thirty years ago, by writers interested in depreciating it, have spread abroad among society, and have become in the minds of a certain number of persons, inveterate prejudices. One often hears with surprise men, who, without ever having read his work, and without being acquainted with any of the attacks made on it at the time of its appearance, repeat with confidence, as universally received truths, the most groundless accusations which were then brought against it." M. Joseph Garnier remarks on the above passage:—"This opinion of Charles Comte was delivered 17 years ago; but it is equally true at the present day, as we may convince ourselves by considering all the abuse and opprobious epithets lately heaped upon Malthus, during the discussions which have arisen on the questions of socialism, &c."

In the course of the same memoir, M. Comte alludes to the great love of truth, for which Mr. Malthus was distinguished. "This never-failing love of truth," he says, "developed in him those private virtues of justice, prudence, temperance, and simplicity which marked his character. He had a sweet and amiable disposition. He had so much control over his passions, and was so indulgent towards others, that persons who had lived near him for fifty years, say that they scarcely ever saw him agitated, and never in a state of inordinate excitement or depression. No harsh word, no uncharitable expression, ever escaped his lips against any one; and though he was more the butt of injustice and calumny than any other writer of his own, or perhaps of any other time, he was rarely heard to complain of these attacks, and never attempted to retaliate.   He was one of the most zealous partisans of the Reform Bill, and desired to see the government enter on the path of progress.   Faithful to his political opinions at a time when they were far from leading to fortune, he never made them a claim to reward, when they had at last gained the ascendancy; he never condescended to make science the stepping-stone of ambition."

M. Quetelet, the president of the Central Board of Statistics, and Astronomer Royal at Brussels, says in his Système Social, "The animals and plants reproduce their species, according to an ascending progression, sometimes extremely rapid.

"These remarks are equally applicable to the human race.   Experience, as well as reasoning, proves that we have a natural tendency to reproduce our species, according to an ascending geometrical progression.   This principle, which has long been recognised, and has been substantiated in many works, and especially in those of Malthus, has never been seriously contested by any one."

After showing that there are limits which confine the increase of the animals and plants, M. Quetelet continues, "These limits exist in the case of man also.   There is therefore a cause which counteracts the effects of the principle previously laid down, and prevents our species from multiplying indefinitely.   This cause according to most of the economists and statists of modern times, is the difficulty of procuring the means of subsistence."

M. Charles Dunoyer, President of the Society of Economists at Paris, gave the following advice to the poor of his department, when he was Prefect of Amiens: "The classes of society whose lot is the most to be deplored, cannot escape from their miserable condition, except by the aid of industry, judgment, and prudence—and above all prudence in the conjugal union, and by taking extreme care not to render their marriage more fruitful than their industry."   M. Joseph Garnier, who quotes this advice in his article on Population, intimates that M. Dunoyer meant thereby to recommend the employment of preventive means.

Almost the only French economist of distinction who has not fully and unreservedly adopted the Malthusian theory, is M. Bastiat; but been in his case, the difference is apparent rather than real, as his views are in the main precisely those of Mr. Malthus.   M. Joseph Garnier, after quoting passages from the Harmonies Economiques, by M. Bastiat, which show that he fully grants the law of fecundity, and its necessary checks, and admits that reproductive restraint is the only safety for mankind, says, "This language of Bastiat is the language of Malthus, of the economists in general, of the moralists and philosophers who have reflected on this subject.   In delivering these opinions Bastiat has only fallen into one error; the error namely of supposing that he was saying anything new, whilst in reality he was only giving utterance once more, and in a very useful manner, to the truths which were explored and developed fifty years ago by Malthus, and which have been repeated by J. B. Say, Sismondi, Tracy, Dunoyer, and *almost all the economists*, and still more recently by the illustrious Rossi, and by Mr. J. S. Mill."

The foregoing extracts will suffice to show how thoroughly and unanimously the Malthusian theory has been accepted by the French economists. I am less acquainted with the economical writers in other countries of the Continent, but I believe they are equally agreed on this fundamental doctrine of the science. The following quotations may serve to illustrate their opinions on the subject.

Herr Rau, Professor of Political Economy at Heidelberg, says in his article on Population in the Allgemeine Encyclopädie, "The sole condition by which a due proportion between population and the means of subsistence can be maintained, consists in this, that only a certain number of new marriages be contracted. The apparent hardship of this sentence is necessarily involved in *the relation which man bears to the soil;* and it is generally recognised in the ordinary life of society, although with painful feelings. But where the foresight and the sense of duty which forbid the formation of a family without the probability of a suitable maintenance are wanting; where also manners, customs, and social arrangements do not effect this object: government can with difficulty and only indirectly, do much to promote it."

Professor Mohl, in his article on Population in the Staats-Lexicon, edited by MM. von Rotteck and Welcker, says, "As far as regards the simple laws of nature, it is an undeniable truth that man (with but few exceptions) is capable of begetting a large number of children, even in the state of monogamy. It is not less certain that the *inclination* to the increase and propagation of the species is deeply implanted in the moral and physical constitution of man, and is therefore common to the whole race." Professor Mohl estimates that " *at least ten* children would be the issue of a marriage, according to the simple organic laws of nature." He then shows that these great powers of fecundity are necessarily checked in old countries, " either by a deficiency of births, which is far the most desirable manner, or by the death of that part of the population which cannot find the means of support. Both of these causes operate constantly and powerfully, although indeed the chain of causation may escape the notice of the superficial observer, or of him who is not instructed on the subject, and who has no clear view of his own position and of the circumstances which rule his destiny.

"The Essay on Population," says Professor Hegewisch, the German translator of Malthus, "was a revelation of the laws of the moral world, comparable to the discovery of the laws of the physical world by Newton."

Thomas Cooper, M.D., formerly President of the South Carolina College, in the United States, and Professor of Chemistry and Political Economy, says in his Elements of Political Economy, "The next step in the advancement of this science [after Adam Smith's work] was the Essay on the Principle of Population of Mr. Malthus." After giving an abstract of Mr. Malthus's views, he continues, "Mr. Malthus has incurred much obloquy for these harsh doctrines; but their manifest truth and great importance have at length produced conviction in the minds of the greater number of those who have turned their attention to political economy; and they may now (1826) be considered as settled."

Don Florez Estrada, the most celebrated of the Spanish economists, says in his Course of Political Economy, " Malthus, for having established in the most luminous manner the doctrine of Population, on which theory depends the lot of the classes who live by their labor, is in my opinion the economist, who has given to the science the most important contribution since Adam Smith. This author, in his work published in 1798 under the title of 'Essay on the Principle of Population,' after examining with the greatest judgment and erudition the progress and the decline of population in different countries, shows that artificial encouragements, instead of augmenting population, have the effect rather of diminishing and demoralizing it. He shows that the only means of augmenting population without evil effects, is to augment the means of subsistence; that instead of falling short of these, population always tends to pass beyond them; and that if the propensity which prompts man to reproduce his species be not restrained by prudence, the population will be repressed by vice, misery, and the grinding law of necessity. The numerous assaults which have been directed against this work, have only served to prove more and more clearly its singular merit, and have given additional testimony to the fact, that there is no new truth which does not meet with resistance in direct proportion to its importance.

" Political Economy is indebted to Malthus not only for the doctrine of Population, but also for another very important discovery. In 1815 he published a small treatise entitled 'An enquiry into the nature and progress of Rent,' in which he demonstrates the origin and causes of the rent of land: without the knowledge of which it is not possible to levy a land-tax justly, nor to know upon whom such a tax would fall."

Signor Antonio Scialoja, formerly Professor of Political Economy in the University of Turin, says in his Principles of Political Economy, "The faculty of reproduction has in the human species an immense power. America doubles its population every 25 years, and the vacuum which wars and epidemics create in society, is soon filled up. . . . Where a man cannot find the means of subsistence, he is morally constrained to resist the impulses of his senses; and even if he does yield to them, his progeny is not numerous, for but a small proportion of these unhappy children, deprived of all the cares which are at that time so indispensable, survive the earliest stage of life."

The most distinguished among the Russian economists of the last generation is M. Storch, whose work, the Cours d' Economie Politique, was written in French, and was re-issued in Paris with notes by M. J. B. Say. " This work," says a reviewer in the Dictionaire de

2 M

l' Economie Politique, "is its author's principal title in the eyes of the science—that which places him in the rank of distinguished economists. A contemporary of J. B. Say, of Malthus, and of Ricardo, Storch treats with great clearness the same questions as these writers. Generally speaking, his principles and demonstrations are similar to those of Smith and of Say, from whom indeed he borrows many quotations. He seems to have been less acquainted with, or at least to have less deeply studied, the works of Ricardo."

The first original treatise on Political Economy in the Russian language, however, was published in 1847 by M. Bowtowski, a member of the Society of Economists at St. Petersburg. In a review of this work in the Journal des Economistes, a writer says, "M. Bowtowski adopts the theory of Ricardo on rent. He explains the rent of land, properly so called [that is, the sum which is paid for the use of the soil itself, and not for farm-buildings, &c., the latter of which is not, properly speaking, rent, but *profits*] by the difference between the price of agricultural produce and its cost of production. . . . We believe it is needless to add that M. Bowtowski fully adopts the theory of Malthus."

Among the other continental writers who have advocated the Malthusian principles may be mentioned M. Ambrose Clement, in his work entitled Recherches sur les causes de l' Indigence (Researches on the causes of Indigence); M. de Bruckère, burgomaster of Brussels, and President of the Congress of Economists which met at Brussels in 1847, in his Principles of Political Economy, written for the Popular Encyclopædia of Belgium; M. Wolowski, professor of Commercial law at Paris, in the Principles of Political Economy, published as one of the Cent Traités (Hundred Treatises)—a work which corresponds to our own Information for the People; M. Monjean, Principal of the College Chaptal, who has translated into French the Principles and Definitions by Mr. Malthus; Count Duchatel, formerly minister of the interior, in his work on Public Charity; Count Arrivabene, who has translated the Lectures of Mr. Senior, and the Elements of Mr. James Mill; M.M. Guillaumin and Coquelin, publishers of the Journal des Economistes, the Collection complète des principaux Economistes, &c.; M. Prevost, formerly Swiss Consul at London, the translator of the Wealth of Nations, and the Essay on Population; M.M. Fix, Daire, Leclerc, Horace Say, Cherbuliez, and others, members of the Society of Economists at Paris, &c. The Malthusian doctrines have indeed been for the last thirty or forty years, received as settled principles of the science of political economy; and this science, to use M. Garnier's words, is "one and the same from Naples to Moscow; its fundamental ideas, its general laws, its principles are everywhere the same." Wherever political economy is cultivated, the principle of population is taught, with greater or less clearness, as one of its leading doctrines; and the study of the science has now spread throughout every country of the civilized world, and is daily making further progress. Chairs of political economy have been established in almost all the Universities of Germany, Russia,

Belgium, Holland, &c., and in some of those in France and England. "There is scarcely a university either in Europe or America," says Mr. Senior, "which has not its chair of political economy." Instruction on the subject has also of late years been introduced into many of the primary schools in this country and in Ireland, owing, in great part, to the exertions of Archbishop Whately and Mr. Wm. Ellis; while in several continental countries, as for example in Russia and Belgium, it forms one of the regular branches of elementary education.

When the above facts and quotations are considered, it will not, I think, appear an exaggeration to say that the Malthusian theory, and the evidence on which it rests, must have been carefully scrutinised by hundreds of thousands of educated minds in this and other countries. It has withstood every test during the last half-century, with its rigorous methods of scientific proof, and vast accumulation of statisticalfacts, and has been embraced as the basis of their reasonings, by some of the greatest thinkers that have existed among mankind. However, therefore, these great principles may still be ignored or opposed by those whose judgment is swayed by prejudice, and not by evidence, or by those who have paid no adequate attention to the subject, they should be regarded, to use Mr. Mill's words, as *axiomatic* truths; as principles which are as well established as the rotation of the earth, the circulation of the blood, or any other of the best known laws of nature. Like the Newtonian theory of the solar system, the Malthusian theory of society is the only true explanation of the facts, and must in time be as universally accepted.

[The following particulars respecting the lives of the chief political economists above quoted, may be not uninteresting.

Thomas Robert Malthus, the discoverer of the chief law of social science, was born in 1766 at the Rookery, near Dorking, in Surrey. His education was at first carried on at home under the superintendence of his father Daniel Malthus, the friend and correspondent of Rousseau. He afterwards went to Jesus College, Cambridge, where he obtained a fellowship, and then became the clergyman of a small parish in Surrey. In 1798 appeared his first printed work, the Essay on the Principle of Population, which was subsequently much enlarged and improved, and ran through many editions. In 1799 he visited Norway, Sweden, and Russia, the only countries of the continent then open to the English traveller. During the peace of Amiens he visited France, everywhere collecting fresh facts illustrative of the law of population. In 1805 he married, and was soon after appointed to the professorship of political economy and modern history at Haileybury, where he continued till his death. He died suddenly in 1834, in his 70th year, leaving behind him his wife, and one son and daughter. He was one of the founders of the Political Economy Club, and of the Statistical Society; and was a member of many of the most eminent scientific bodies, in particular, the National Institute of France, and the Royal Academy of Berlin. His other principal works are the Principles of Political Economy, and Definitions in that science; and also an admirable treatise published 1815, in which he established the true theory of Rent.

Mr. James Mill, one of the profoundest thinkers of modern times, was of Scotch extraction, being born, I believe, at Montrose. Besides his Elements of Political Economy, which were composed as a school-book of the science, he was the author of an Analysis of the Human Mind, one of the ablest works on mental philosophy. He is best known however for his History of British India, of which his son Mr. J. S. Mill says, "This work has begun to spread the light of philosophy over the affairs of that country, and has placed its author in the first rank of political writers of the democratic school." Shortly after the publication of this work, Mr. James Mill obtained a high situation in the India House, which he occupied till his death. He was the intimate friend of Ricardo and Jeremy Bentham, and zealously advocated many of the latter writer's opinions on politics and moral philosophy.

Mr. John Stuart Mill, his son, was born in London in 1806. At an early age he entered the India House, where until lately he held one of the highest offices. His principal works are a System of Logic, published in 1843, Essays on some Unsettled Questions in Political Economy in 1844, the Principles of Political Economy in 1848, and an Essay on Liberty in 1859. His treatises on Logic and Political Economy were truly described in a late article in the *Saturday Review* as " the greatest works on these subjects in the English language."

Mr. David Ricardo is the writer to whom, together with Adam Smith and Malthus, the discovery of the chief laws of political economy is due. The researches of this great thinker into the distribution and exchange of wealth were much more accurate than those of Adam Smith. With regard to the laws of *distribution*, he threw additional light on the law of wages; gave the first clear statement of the law of profits; and although he was preceded in the discovery of the law of rent by Mr. Malthus and Sir Edward West, he explained the law and traced its consequences in so masterly a manner, that it is now generally known under the name of "The Ricardo theory of rent." He showed the tendency of the cost of labor to rise, and profits to fall, owing to the agricultural law, in the course of industrial progress. His contributions to the theory of *exchange* were not less important. He pointed out the fundamental principle which determines the value of commodities—namely, *the quantity of labor* employed in their production; and corrected several errors and inconsistencies into which Adam Smith, Mr. Malthus, M. Say, and others had fallen on the subject. He showed that agricultural rent is not an element of cost of production; and that a general rise or fall of wages does not cause a general rise or fall of values and prices. The subjects of Currency, Foreign Trade, Taxation, &c., were also greatly advanced by his researches. Ricardo was born in London in 1772. He entered into business on the Stock Exchange (of which his father also was a member) and made an immense fortune. Later in life he became Member of Parliament. He was intimately acquainted with Jeremy Bentham, Malthus, and other writers; and had a close friendship with Mr. James Mill. Mr. Ricardo was the author of several treatises on economical subjects, but his greatest work is the Principles of Political Economy and Taxation, published in 1817. He died in 1823, aged 51. Mr. James Mill says of him, alluding to his life on the Stock Exchange, " Amid this scene of active exertion and practical detail, he cultivated and he acquired habits of intense and patient and comprehensive thinking ; such as have been rarely equalled and never excelled."

Mr. Nassau William Senior was born in Berkshire in 1790, and was called to the bar in 1817. In 1826 he became professor of political economy at Oxford, and in 1836 Master in Chancery. Mr. Senior was appointed by the Government in 1832, as one of the Commissioners of Inquiry into the Poor-Laws; in 1838, as one of the Commissioners of Inquiry into the condition of the Weavers; and in 1847, again as professor of political economy at Oxford. His chief works are Lectures on Political Economy, which were first published in 1826; also an admirable treatise on Political Economy published in 1835 in the Encyclopædia Metropolitana. He likewise assisted in drawing up the Report on the Poor-laws, and the Report on the state of the Weavers, which were published by order of Parliament.

Mr. J. R. McCulloch was born in 1789 in Wigtonshire. He was for some time editor of the *Scotsman;* and afterwards became professor of political economy in University College, London, a situation which he retained for only three years. In 1838 he was appointed Controller of the Stationery Office. Mr. McCulloch is the author of numerous works on economical and statistical subjects; the chief of which are the Principles of Political Economy, the Commercial Dictionary, the Descriptive and Statistical Account of the British Empire, &c.

M. Jean Baptiste Say was born in 1767 at Lyons. In 1794 he became the editor of a Republican journal, the Decade Philosophique; and in 1799 he was appointed member of the tribunate under the French Republic. His principal work, the Traité d'Economie Politique, appeared in 1803, and has since passed through six editions; although the publication of the second edition was prevented for several years by Napoleon, who was pleased to object to its free-trade doctrines. In 1815 Say delivered the first course of lectures on political economy in France, at the Athenæum of Paris. It was not however till 1830 that a chair of political economy was founded in the Collège de France, of which Say became professor. He died in 1832. Among his other works are the Catechisme de l'Economie Politique, the Cours Complet de l'Economie Politique, and Six Letters to Malthus, with whom he had a discussion on the possibility of a general glut of commodities—a point on which Mr. Malthus entertained an erroneous opinion.

M. Rossi, one of the most eminent French writers on political economy and jurisprudence, was born in 1787, at Carrara, in Italy, and studied law at the universities of Pisa and Bologna. He afterwards settled at Geneva, as a political refugee, where he gave lectures on jurisprudence, and was elected to represent Geneva, at the Swiss Diet in 1832. He succeeded J. B. Say as professor of political economy in the Collège de France in 1833. In 1845 he was appointed by Louis Philippe and M. Guizot ambassador plenipotentiary to

Rome, to demand of the Pope the suppression of the society of Jesuits. He was assassinated in 1848 at Rome, by one of the extreme revolutionary party.

M. Joseph Garnier was born in 1813. In 1846, he was appointed to the chair of political economy which was then founded at the Ecole des Ponts et Chaussees (school of engineers), at Paris. He also holds the office of secretary to the Society of Economists, and is a member of the Statistical Society of London, and the Central Commission of Statistics in Belgium. In 1846, he became the chief editor of the Journal des Economistes, a journal which was established in 1841, and has ever since been the chief organ of the science in Europe. Among its sub-editors have been most of the economists and statists of distinction in France; for instance. M. M. Bastiat, Michel Chevalier, Dunoyer, Legoyt, Moreau de Jonnès, Leon Faucher, Rossi, Horace Say, H. Passy, Villermé, &c. M. Garnier is the author of several works on economical subjects, and among others the Elements de l' Economie Politique, which has been translated into Italian, Spanish, and Russian, and has been much used as a school-book of the science.

M. Michel Chevalier was born in 1806. In 1830, he became editor of the Globe, a journal which advocated the socialist doctrines of St. Simon. In 1840, he succeeded M. Rossi in the chair of political economy in the Collège de France. In 1845, he was elected member of the Chamber of Deputies, and in 1851, member of the Institute. His principal works are a Course of Political Economy in 1842. Letters on the Organization of Labour in 1848, &c.; also a recent treatise, which has been translated by Mr. Cobden, in which he shows the probability of a fall in the value of gold, in consequence of the Californian and Australian discoveries. "He belongs," says M. Blanqui in his History of Political Economy, " to that brilliant pleiad of Saint-Simonians, whose writings have thrown so much light on economical matters."

M. Frederic Bastiat was born in 1801 at Bayonne, and died of consumption at Rome in 1850. He is one of the best known and most popular of the French Economical writers, having taken an active part in the free-trade and other public movements. In 1846 he became the secretary of the various free-trade societies (associations du libre échange) throughout France, and edited the journal which represented the views of that party. In 1848 he was elected a member of the Constituent Assembly, and afterwards of the Legislative Assembly. He was the author of many treatises on economical subjects, the best known of which are the Sophismes Economiques, and the Harmonies Economiques, his principal work, which was left unfinished at his death.

M. Storch was born in 1766 at Riga, and died at St. Petersburg in 1835. He held the situation of Privy-Councillor and Vice-President of the Academy of the Sciences at St. Petersburg. In 1796 he published an important work, the Historical and Statistical Account of the Russian Empire. His Cours d' Economie Politique was published in 1815 at St. Petersburg, and a second edition in 1823 at Paris.]

THE CHIEF LAWS OF POLITICAL ECONOMY.

The name of Political Economy has been given to the science which treats of *wealth*, in the same careful and systematic manner as arithmetic and algebra treat of number, geometry of extension, chemistry of the elementary substances, or physiology of the functions of living bodies. Political Economy may be defined as *the science which treats of the laws of the production and distribution of wealth ;* in other words, it is the science which investigates the conditions according to which wealth is produced by human labor from surrounding objects, and is then shared among the classes in society who own the requisites of production. To this science belongs the consideration of the various questions relating to wealth. It is the province of political economy to consider the manifold influences which affect the wealth of nations, classes, or individuals; the causes of riches and poverty; the causes which promote or impede the production of wealth, and influence its distribution; which determine the value and price of commodities, making one commodity cheap and another dear, &c.

The laws of the *production* of wealth naturally consist of the laws or properties of human beings *by* whom it is produced, and those of material objects *from* which it is produced. The production and the increase of wealth depend on the efforts to attain it, and its attainability ; on the amount and efficiency of labor and capital on the one hand, and the powers of the soil, &c., on the other. The laws of the *distribution* of wealth, again, (in a country where, as in our own, the requisites of production are owned by three separate classes, namely, the laborers, the capitalists, and the landlords), consist of the laws of wages, of profits, and of rent: wages signifying the remuneration of labor, profits the remuneration of capital, and rent the remuneration of land. Besides these laws of the production and distribution of wealth, the science treats also the laws of its *exchange ;* that is, of the laws which determine how much of one article of wealth will be given for another, and which include the laws of value and price.

In order to understand the above definition of political economy, it is necessary to have a clear idea of what is meant by *wealth.*

Wealth is defined by political economists as consisting of all those objects *which possess an exchange value ;* that is, all objects which cannot be obtained gratuitously, and for which anything useful or agreeable would be given in exchange. The word "value" as used in political economy, means exchange value, or purchasing power, and not mere usefulness. The air we breathe has a high value in *use*, but it has no value in *exchange.* It is not therefore included among the objects of wealth, of which the science treats, and which consist solely of those articles (for instance, corn, clothes, money, diamonds, land, &c.) which have an exchange value or power of purchasing.

With these preliminary remarks on the nature and objects of political economy, I shall proceed to give, in the first place, a brief outline of the laws of production, as they are treated by Mr. Mill in the first book of his great work. I shall then examine the three laws of distribution, and consider in what way the condition of the laborers, capitalists, and landlords, is respectively affected by the population principle, through the medium of these laws. Lastly, I shall consider the three laws of value and price, and the effect produced by the population principle, through their instrumentality, on the value and price of the two great classes of commodities, namely, raw produce, whether agricultural or mineral, and manufactured articles. This, as shown by Mr. Mill, is the natural order in which the subjects of production, distribution, and exchange, should be considered; for it is evident that wealth must be produced before it is distributed among the producers, and distributed before it is exchanged.

PRODUCTION

The *requisites of production* are two; namely, labor, and the appropriate material objects.

Labor in the outward world is always employed in setting things in motion. The only mode in which man can act upon matter is by *moving* it; the properties of matter, or in other words, the powers of nature, perform the rest. The weaver, for example, moves his thread across the loom, and the cloth which is thus formed, is held together by the tenacity of its fibres; the sower moves the seed into the earth, but the development and growth of the plant are entirely the result of the natural forces. Human labor may be economised by using other motive powers, such as those of the steam-engine, or of the beasts of burden.

With regard to the *material objects* on which labor is exercised, it is to be remarked, as a distinction of primary importance, that some of them are *limited* in quantity, while others are, practically speaking, *unlimited.* The land, for example, in all old countries, is strictly limited in quantity; while the supply of water in some localities, and of atmospheric air over the whole globe, is practically unlimited. Now as long as any natural agent exists in unlimited abundance, it cannot, unless susceptible of an artificial monopoly, bear any value in the market; but as soon as the supply of it is less than would be used, if it could be had gratuitously, it acquires an exchange value, and a *rent* can be obtained for its use.

Labor is either employed *directly* upon the object intended to be produced, as for example, the labor of the baker or the tailor; or *in directly*, in previous operations destined to facilitate its production. With the exception of the labor of the hunter and fisher, there are few kinds of labor to which the returns are immediate.

One very important part of the past labor which is necessary to enable present labor to be carried on, is employed in preparing *food* for the laborers engaged in production. The remaining kinds of preparatory or indirect labor may be classified under the following five heads. Firstly, the labor of those workmen who produce *materials*, as for instance the miner and the flax-grower. Secondly, of those who make the *tools*, implements, and machinery. Thirdly, of those who *protect industry*, such as policemen, soldiers, shepherds, and also the workmen who erect buildings for industrial purposes. Fourthly, of those who help to render the produce *accessible*; to which class belong carriers, railway laborers, &c., and also the large and important body of tradesmen or dealers. The latter are often termed the *distributing* class, and are supplementary to the class of producers. They perform a valuable office in the economy of society, as there would be a great loss of time and convenience if the consumers had to deal directly with the producers. When production has increased beyond a certain point, a division of the distributing class into wholesale and retail dealers is found convenient; the former buying from the manufactories and supplying many retail shops.

The above are the modes in which labor, when employed on *external nature*, is indirectly subservient to production. All of them, with one exception, receive their remuneration from the commodity which is ultimately produced; although this remuneration is usually paid in advance by the capitalists. The single exception is in the case of that labor which is employed in producing *food* for the productive workmen; as this labor is remunerated from the food itself, or from the money which it brings.

Fifthly; the last kind of indirect or preparatory labor is that which is expended on *human beings*, in the technical or industrial training of the community. This labor also has to receive its remuneration from the future produce. Many other kinds of mental labor, as for instance that of the surgeon, the mechanical inventor, and even the speculative, thinker, are often indirectly of service to production.

There is much and very valuable labor, which has not for its object the production of wealth. Labor is therefore divided by economists into productive and unproductive—a distinction which does not imply any invidious comparisons between these two kinds of labor, as has often been erroneously supposed, but which has been adopted merely with a view to accurate classification.

Unproductive labor, in the language of political economy, is that which, however important and valuable it may be, does not aid in the production of *material wealth*, the special subject of the science; but which consists in a service rendered, or an immediate pleasure afforded. The labor, for example, of the judge, the poet, the actor, or the musician, is unproductive. *Productive* labor on the contrary is that which adds to the material resources of a country; including of course not only the labor of the workmen themselves, but also of those who direct their operations.

The *consumption* of wealth is in like manner divided into productive and unproductive. Although all the members of society are not laborers, yet all are consumers, and consume either productively or unproductively. The only productive consumers are the productive laborers; whilst all those who contribute nothing, either directly or indirectly, to production, are unproductive consumers. It should be observed, moreover, in order to have a full view of the subject, that a part of the consumption even of the laborers themselves, namely, what they consume on *luxuries*, is unproductive. From this it will be seen that there is a distinction even more important to the wealth of a community than that between productive and unproductive labor; the distinction, namely, between the labor which is destined for the supply of production, and that which is occupied in supplying the wants of unproductive consumers.

"It would be a great error," says Mr. Mill, "to regret the large proportion of the annual produce, which, in an opulent country, goes to supply unproductive consumption. It would be to lament that the country has so much to spare from its necessities, for its pleasures, and for all higher uses. The things to be regretted and to be remedied are—the prodigious *inequality* with which this surplus is distributed, the little worth of the objects to which the greater part of it is devoted, and the large share which falls to the lot of those who render no equivalent service in return."

Capital, which we next proceed to consider, is that part of the produce of industry which is engaged in carrying on *fresh production*. It is of great importance to understand thoroughly the function which capital performs in production, as there are many serious errors currently entertained on this point.

Capital must not be confounded with *money*. It is no more synonymous with money than wealth is. It consists of the tools, materials, industrial buildings, machinery, wages, &c., with which laborers are supplied to enable them to carry on fresh production. It is that portion of the produce of past labor which is employed in the support of present labor. The whole income of a capitalist is not capital, since a part of it is consumed unproductively by himself and his family; but that part alone is capital which he devotes to productive purposes. The sum of all the values so destined by their respective possessors forms the capital of a country.

All laborers are subsisted on capital, and without this essential pre-requisite no work could be carried on. The capital, however, need not be furnished by a capitalist, but the laborers may live upon their own funds, as in the case of the independent artizan, the peasant proprietor, or the members of a co-operative association. The following four fundamental propositions respecting capital, may help to convey a clear conception of its functions as an instrument of production:—

1st. *Industry is limited by capital.*—This proposition is so obviously true, that it must be admitted as soon as it is distinctly understood. There cannot possibly be more laborers in a country than are supplied with materials to work upon and food to eat. And yet opinions incompatible with this have been, and still are, very frequently advanced by political writers, especially on the continent. These writers believe that it is in the power of government, by protective laws, to create additional industry without creating capital. But though protective laws may create a new kind of industry, it is only by withdrawing capital from an old one.

Government, however, has the power, to a certain extent, of creating capital. This it can do by levying taxes, and using them either in production or in paying off debt. Taxes are generally paid, not out of what people would have saved and used as capital, but out of what they would have spent.

Every increase of capital can give increased employment to labor, and this without any assignable limits. If materials and food can be supplied, laborers may always be employed in producing something. This is in direct opposition to a belief which is very commonly prevalent, and which was entertained even by some celebrated writers, as, for instance, Mr. Malthus and M. de Sismondi; the belief, namely, that there may be a *general over-production* of wealth, and that the unproductive expenditure of the rich is necessary to the employment of the poor. This view, however, can readily be shown to be erroneous. Whatever part of their incomes the rich do not spend unproductively, they merely transfer in the shape of additional wages to the productive laborers. The latter may either increase their consumption, in which case the capital will be turned to the production of luxuries for them; or they may increase their numbers, in which case the capital will be employed in producing additional necessaries. It is never, therefore, from a want of *consumers* that production is limited, but solely from want of producers, or of capital to support them.

2nd. *All capital is the result of saving.*—It is the part of the produce which is not expended in immediate indulgence, but is set aside for the purposes of production. The immense capital of a country like England, has been gradually accumulated by successive generations of capitalists, constantly making larger and larger additions to their savings.

3rd. Although saved, and the result of saving, *all capital is nevertheless consumed.*—The word "saved" implies only that it is not consumed by the person who saves it. The capital which is saved by its owner, is consumed by the productive laborers. Money or goods which are not employed at all, but are laid by for future use, are said to be *hoarded.*

This is a point on which there is an inveterate popular error. A man who saves is often regarded in the same light as one who hoards; while the spendthrift, who lavishes his fortune in unproductive indulgences, is popularly viewed with favor, and is thought to give encouragement to trade. But the funds which are saved and invested are not less really consumed; the only difference is, that they are consumed by productive laborers, and therefore go to increase the resources of the country, whereas the income of the spendthrift is consumed by himself, and without yielding any return. Saving, in short, enriches, while spending impoverishes the community as well as the individual.

We see, therefore, that everything which is produced is consumed. There are many common expressions, such as "the ancient wealth of a country," "the accumulated wealth of ages," &c., which tend to disguise this truth. But, in reality, the greater part of the present wealth of England has been produced within the last year; and very little of it, with the exception of the land, the buildings, and other durable kinds of wealth, was in existence ten years ago. Capital, like population, is not kept up by preservation, but by constant reproduction.

This fact serves to explain the great rapidity with which countries in general recover from war expenses, or from devastation by hostile armies, earthquakes, &c. If the country be not depopulated, in the course of a year or two the amount of capital will probably be as large as before, although, during the interval, great privations may be experienced by the inhabitants.

4th. *A demand for commodities is not a demand for labor.*—The person who employs labor is the capitalist who advances the wages to the laborers, and not the consumer who buys the ready-made article. The latter does not in the slightest degree give employment to labor; he merely helps to direct labor into a certain channel, by demanding a particular commodity.

This proposition is perhaps less generally understood than any of the others. There is no belief more common than that a person who buys an article employs labor, and benefits the working classes, in the same way as the capitalist who pays them wages. This, however, is a radical and dangerous fallacy. The purchaser, who buys and consumes a commodity, does not, in the slightest degree, increase the demand for labor, or help to raise the wages of the working classes; it is solely by what he does *not* consume, but saves and employs productively, that he influences wages. A person does good to laborers, not by what he consumes on himself, but solely by what he does not consume.

Individual producers do indeed lose or gain by fluctuations in the demand for their commodities, but this merely shows whether or not they have produced the proper articles to suit the wants of others. When a thing is bought or sold, all that really happens is the *exchange* of one kind of wealth for another, for the sake of mutual convenience. The real remuneration of labor and capital consists in *the increased value* given to an article in preparing it for use, and not in the money obtained in exchange for it. This truth, namely, that production, not exchange, is the real remuneration of labor and capital, is fundamental, and demonstrates many common fallacies.

For instance, it has been often said that the income-tax does not fall upon the rich, but rather upon the poor; for the rich would have spent its amount on commodities, and would thus have given employment to labor. But in so far as the tax is paid out of what they would themselves have consumed, it falls upon them, and not at all upon the poor. Whosoever is compelled by a tax *to reduce his expenditure* is the person upon whom it really falls; for this is the unfailing test of the incidence of taxation. Taxes, moreover, unless when very heavy, are usually paid out of what would have been otherwise spent unproductively, and not out of capital; so that an income-tax probably benefits rather than injures the working classes, by being partly employed in the purchase of labor by the government.

Thus far of the fundamental propositions respecting capital. Let us next consider the distinction between what is termed circulating, and fixed capital.

Circulating capital is that which is consumed by a single use, and which needs to be perpetually replaced with a profit by each sale of the finished goods. The wages, materials, &c., are of this description. *Fixed* capital, again, is that which is sunk in machinery, tools, improvements in land, or other durable works, and whose renewal is spread over a corresponding space of time.

The effect which is exercised, on the gross or aggregate produce of a country, by circulating and by fixed capital, is very different. Circulating capital must be renewed with an increase or profit by a single use; whereas fixed capital is replaced with a profit only in the lapse of time, and after several uses of the more durable instrument.

It follows, therefore, that every increase of fixed capital, which takes place at the expense of circulating, must be, at least temporarily, prejudicial to the laborers. But in reality it rarely happens that fixed capital, upon the whole and taking all the departments of industry together, is increased at the expense of circulating. Costly machinery, permanent improvements in land, railways, &c., are generally made from the *annual increase* of capital, and not from funds which are already engaged in productive operations. Unless therefore they be introduced very suddenly, and to an unusual extent, they do not, even temporarily, diminish the wage-fund, or injure the working class in the aggregate; although in the particular departments in which the improvements are introduced, they undoubtedly often throw laborers out of work, and occasion much distress, which it should be the object of government to alleviate by every means in their power. "Since improvements which do not diminish employment on the whole," says Mr. Mill, "almost always throw some particular class of laborers out of it, there cannot be a more legitimate object of the legislator's care than the interests of those who are thus sacrificed to the gains of their fellow-citizens and of posterity."

There are two other considerations, which show that the ultimate tendency of machinery and other improvements is to *benefit the* laborers, as well as society at large. In the first place, these improvements generally increase the profits of capital and lower the price of commodities, and in both of these ways additional facilities for saving are afforded. Secondly, there are assignable *limits* to the increase of capital, owing to the fundamental laws of the soil; and all improvements in the arts of production tend to throw these limits further off, and to make room for further savings and for a larger gross produce than could otherwise have existed in the country.

We have now completed the inquiry into *the requisites of production;* which consist, as has been seen, of labor, capital, and material objects. Labor and material objects are the primary requisites; but capital, which is the produce of labor, requires also to be separately specified.

We next come to the *second great question* in the science of wealth, namely, On what does the productiveness of these three agents depend? What are the causes of the wide differences in the amount of wealth possessed by nations, whose population and extent of territory are nearly the same? Some of these causes are readily discernible, while others are not so obvious, but require a closer examination.

Amongst the more obvious causes of superior productiveness are, in the first place, what are called *natural advantages*, such as a fertile soil, a favorable climate, an abundant supply of minerals, and also the facilities of carriage afforded by a good sea-board or by navigable rivers. Secondly, the *energy of labor* among the inhabitants; meaning thereby not merely occasional efforts, but a steady and persevering application. Thirdly, the *skill and knowledge* possessed by the workmen themselves and by those who direct their operations. Under this head comes also the state of machinery, of agriculture, and the other arts of production. Fourthly, the *moral* qualities of the laborers, such as their honesty, sobriety, and trustworthiness. Great disadvantages in these respects are attendant on the present system of *hired labor* (a system which, Mr. Mill observes, is "almost peculiar to Great Britain," as the general condition of the laboring classes); and much loss is sustained, and time and trouble wasted, in watching that work is properly performed, where the workmen have no personal interest in the success of the business. Fifthly, *security* of person and property; which includes protection *against*, as well as protection *by*, the government, and is of first-rate importance to the productiveness of industry. In many Asiatic countries, the governments, which are little else than organised systems of robbery, have by their arbitrary exactions, paralysed the energies of the inhabitants, and prevented any marked industrial progress. Sixthly, just and enlightened *social institutions*. With regard to the general action of social institutions on the productiveness of labor, it may be observed, that they are beneficial in proportion as they hold the balance justly between man and man, and favor no one class at the expense of others; and in proportion as they give a free scope to industry, and secure to it as far as possible an equitable reward, giving most to those who have by their services done most to deserve it.

Another very important cause of superior productive power, consists in the *combination of labor*, or *co-operation:* and as this cause is not so obvious, nor so generally understood as the others, it deserves a fuller consideration.   One department of the subject, namely, the *division of labor*, has been much dwelt on by political economists, to the exclusion of others not less important.   A more fundamental principle, as Mr. Wakefield has ably pointed out, lies beneath that of the division of labor, and comprehends it.

Co-operation is divided by Mr. Wakefield into two kinds, namely simple and complex co-operation.   In the first, people work together in the *same* employment, as, for example, in reaping or sowing; in the other they co-operate in *different* employments; for those who are engaged in the various branches of industry do really, though in general unconsciously, act in co-operation with each other.

The importance to production of the *separation of employments*—one body of men producing food, another clothes, a third tools, &c.—is more fundamental than is usually supposed.   Many commodities would not merely be produced in smaller quantities, but would not be produced at all, were it not for the power of *exchanging* them for others.   Hence it is that a country will rarely have a productive agriculture, unless there be also a large town population, or a large export trade to supply a town population elsewhere.   On this principle is based the Wakefield system of Colonization, a great practical improvement which has been largely adopted.   According to this system, government sets a price upon the unoccupied lands, sufficient to prevent too many from betaking themselves to agriculture; and thus a town as well as a country population grows up, which is much more favorable to the progress of the colony.

But even after the primary separation of employments has become general in a country, there are reasons, equally real though less urgent, for a further division of labor; and thus many occupations, such as pin-making, card-making, &c., have been sub-divided into a large number of different processes, each of which is performed by a separate class of workmen.   The advantages of this *division of labor* are, in the first place, the increased dexterity of the workmen, and the smaller waste of materials in learning the business.   Secondly, the saving of time in passing from one occupation to another.   Too much stress was however laid on this point by Adam Smith; for one kind of labor acts rather as a rest and relief from another.   Thirdly, the greater probability of inventions being made, from the thorough knowledge of the business acquired by the workmen.   Fourthly, the more economical distribution of labor, by classifying the work-people according to their capacities.   This appears to be the most important advantage of the division of labor, next to the increased dexterity of the workmen.

The degree to which the division of labor may be carried is limited, in the first place, by the extent of the market; which may be narrowed either by too small, too scattered and distant, or too poor a population.   Hence railways, water-carriage, and other means of conveyance, by widening the market, exercise a powerful influence on the productiveness of labor. Another cause which limits the division of labor, is the kind of occupation. In agriculture, for example, it cannot be introduced to at all the same extent as in manufactures, since the same person cannot always be engaged in sowing or reaping.

Connected with the subject of co-operation, is the enquiry as to the comparative advantages of production on the *large*, and production on the *small* scale. Production on the large scale, by means of extensive manufactories, or shops, has several advantages in regard to the productiveness of labor : for in order to make labor most productive, it is often necessary that many workmen should combine. The division of labor, also, can be carried further in large establishments, and there is a saving in the business of superintendence. Moreover, when costly machinery is employed, the goods produced must be sufficient to come up to the full powers of the machine, in order to yield the maximum of profit; and this is another principal reason, which gives rise to large manufactories.

As a general rule, the expenses of a business do not increase at all in proportion to its extent. But there is one sure and simple means of ascertaining whether production on the large or small scale is most economical; namely, the power of *under-selling*. If the large producer or tradesman can sell his goods at a lower price than the small, it is a certain sign of superior productiveness of labor; and it is in consequence of this superiority, that large establishments are now being introduced into so many departments of industry, and driving their weaker rivals from the market. Although, in an economical point of view, this is manifestly a gain to society, yet it is in some degree counterbalanced by the loss of independence on the part of the small producer or dealer, who sinks from the position of a master, into that of a hired laborer.

Production on the large scale is greatly promoted by the formation of *joint-stock* companies, the members of which unite their capitals. It is in this way that railways, banks, insurance companies, &c., are carried on. The comparative advantages and disadvantages of joint-stock management, have been the subject of much debate. On the one hand, there is a want of that zealous interest in the success of the undertaking, which characterises the capitalist who manages his own affairs ; and there is also a disregard of small gains and savings. But on the other hand, it has to be considered, that the manager hired at a good salary by a company, has often a better knowledge of the business, and superior intelligence; and moreover, it is possible, by giving him a share in the profits, to awaken his personal interest in the success of the concern.

From these reasons, together with the great convenience attending a union of capitals, joint-stock companies have increased, and are likely to increase much further. Indeed it may be confidently expected, that associations of capital and of industry *among the laborers themselves*, are destined hereafter to supersede, to a very great degree, the present system of hired labor—a system which is in many respects so destructive to the interests of the working classes.

The possibility of substituting production on the large for production on the small scale, depends in the first place on the extent of the market. It is favored also by a rapidly progressive state of capital, by a high degree of industrial security and enterprise, and by the existence of large capitals in the hands of a few individuals; all of which circumstances are to be found especially in England, and hence the rapid increase of large establishments, which has of late years taken place in this country.

Although the superiority of the large system of production in the case of *manufactures* is undoubted, it is by no means so clearly made out in *agriculture*, in which, as we have seen, the benefits of co-operation and of the division of labor are far less available. Much difference of opinion exists on the question, whether the large farms, rented by capitalist farmers, and cultivated by hired laborers, which constitute the general agricultural system of this country; or the small independent properties, owned and cultivated by the peasants themselves, which prevail in many parts of the continent, are most favorable to the productiveness of agricultural labor. The majority of English writers have given the preference to the former system; but the testimony of continental writers, who have a better opportunity of gaining experience on the subject, is generally in favor of the peasant proprietors.

Mr. Mill, who enters very fully into this question both in his first and second book, and examines the influence of the peasant proprietary system not only on the *production* of wealth, but also on its *distribution*, and on the moral and intellectual character of the laboring classes, arrives at the following conclusions:—"As a result of this inquiry into the direct operation and indirect influences of peasant properties," he says, "I conceive it to be established, that there is no necessary connexion between this form of landed property and an imperfect state of the arts of production; that it is favorable in quite as many respects as it is unfavorable, to the most effective use of the powers of the soil; that no other existing state of agricultural economy has so beneficial an effect on the industry, the intelligence, the frugality, and prudence of the population, nor tends on the whole so much to discourage an improvident increase of their numbers; and that no existing state, therefore, is on the whole so favorable, both to their moral and their physical welfare. Compared with the English system of cultivation by hired labor, it must be regarded as highly beneficial to the laboring class." Mr. Mill accordingly recommends that the present system of the tenure and cultivation of land in England and Ireland, should be gradually superseded by that of peasant properties, and the joint ownership of the soil by associations of laborers.

Having examined the requisites of production, and the conditions on which their productiveness depends, we come now to the *third* great question in the theory of production, namely, What are its limits?

Production is not a fixed but an increasing thing. Two causes promote its increase; the desire to grow richer, and the growth of population. "Nothing in political economy," says Mr. Mill, "can be of more importance than to ascertain the law of this increase of production; the conditions to which it is subject; whether it has practically any limits, and what these are. There is also no subject in political economy, which is popularly less understood, or on which the errors committed are of a character to produce, and do produce, greater mischief."

The requisites of production, as already mentioned, are labor, capital, and material objects. With regard to the last of these, as we are now about to consider the *impediments* to production, we need only attend to those material objects, which are liable to be deficient in quantity and in productive power. These may all be represented by the term *land;* understanding by this term not only the soil itself, but also mines and fisheries.

We may say, therefore, that the requisites of production are labor, capital, and land. The increase of production must depend upon the properties of these three agents. It must depend upon the powers of increase either of the agents themselves, or of their productiveness; and the limit to production will be the limit set by the properties of one or more of them. The law of the increase of production must be a result of the law of the increase of labor, the law of the increase of capital, and the law of the increase of production from land. It is necessary therefore to examine these three laws in succession.

The Law of the Increase of Labor, is that the capacity of increase in the human species, as in all other organised beings, may be regarded as infinite. This law, together with the *checks* by which it is restrained in old countries, has been already so fully examined, that it need not be further dwelt upon in this place.

The Law of the Increase of Capital, is, that capital, like labor, has in itself the capacity of indefinite increase. In America, where plenty of fertile land is to be had, capital has increased so rapidly as to permit population to double itself every twenty-five years. In old countries, however, the actual increase of capital, like that of population, falls very far short of the capacity.

Since all capital is the result of saving, its increase must depend on two things, namely, on the amount of the fund from which savings can be made, and the strength of the desire to save.

The *fund* from which savings can be made, is that part of the produce which remains after deducting what is requisite to maintain the productive powers of the country; that is, after deducting the necessaries of the producers, replacing the materials, and keeping the fixed capital in repair. This surplus is the real *net produce* of a country, and forms the fund available either for further saving, or for the unproductive consumption of the producers themselves and of the rest of society The whole of this surplus might be, though it never is, saved; and more than this cannot be saved. Its amount is the index of the productiveness of labor, and the greater it is, the more inducements does it hold out for saving.

The *desire to save*, or, as it is often called, the effective desire of accumulation, varies greatly in different countries and individuals. The circumstances which tend to promote it are, a high rate of profits, industrial security, healthy and peaceful occupations, and the power of postponing present to future enjoyments; together with a wish to obtain the social advantages which wealth confers, or to make a provision for children. A deficiency in the desire to save, on the other hand, is produced by causes of an opposite character; for instance, by improvidence, by the want of intellectual and moral culture, by a strong taste for immediate enjoyments, or by the insecurity of property and of industrial enterprises, occasioned by tyrannical systems of government. In rude and semi-civilized countries, these causes have a most powerful influence in weakening the desire to save, and therefore in preventing the growth of capital and population.

When the increase of capital has come to a stand in any country from one or other of these two reasons, namely, either from the lowness of profits, or from the want of the effective desire to save, the country is then said to have reached *the stationary state.* In this state, though some individuals grow richer, and others poorer, the wealth of the community on the whole does not increase; nor consequently do the numbers of the population, for the growth of population depends upon the growth of capital.

In such countries as England, Holland, and many other parts of Europe, the increase of capital is not retarded by any deficiency in the desire to save, which, in the middle classes at least, rather exceeds than falls short of the limits prescribed by moderation. It is retarded by the other cause, namely, the low rate of profits, and the constant tendency to a diminution in the productiveness of labor. This tendency depends on the properties of *land,* to which we next proceed.

The Law of the Increase of Production from Land, or, in other words, the law of agricultural industry, is that the proportional returns to agriculture tend to diminish; in other words, that the produce of the soil does not increase in proportion as the labor bestowed on it is increased. "This general law of agricultural industry," says Mr. Mill, "is the most important proposition in political economy. Were the law different, nearly all the phenomena of the production and distribution of wealth would be other than they are." "The question," he says again, "is more important and fundamental than any other; it involves the whole subject of the causes of poverty in a rich and industrious community; and unless this one matter be thoroughly understood, it is to no purpose proceeding any further in our inquiry."

The reason why the rate of wages and of profits is low in this country, is simply, because the law of diminishing productiveness has been brought into too powerful operation by the pressure of the people on the land; or, in other words, because agriculture has been forced by the advance of population and the demand for food, *to descend to unproductive soils*, so that the returns yielded by the worst soils under cultivation are very small in proportion to the labor and capital expended on them. "It was stated by several of the witnesses examined by a committee of the House of Commons on the state of agriculture, in 1821," says Mr. McCulloch, in a note to the Wealth of Nations, " that the produce obtained from the lands under cultivation in England and Wales, estimated in wheat, varied from thirty-six and forty, to eight and nine bushels an acre. The required supplies of food could not be obtained without cultivating these inferior lands ; and it is this necessity of resorting to soils of a diminished degree of fertility that is the real cause of the comparatively high price of corn, and ther raw products, in highly populous countries." The only possible means of permanently raising wages, and lowering the price of food, is to restrain the increase of population, so as not to be compelled to cultivate land of so poor a quality. As will be shown in speaking of the laws of value and price, food cannot be cheap, nor labor dear, unless the *margin of cultivation* consist of highly productive soils ; for it is upon the fertility of the *worst* soils under cultivation, that the price of food, as well as the remuneration of agricultural labor and capital, really depend. The great practical doctrine of political economy therefore—the doctrine which is incomparably the most important precept derived from this, or indeed from any other science—is that *population should be restrained,* so as to remove the pressure on the productive powers of the soil. This is the most essential of all the conditions of human happiness, for it is the one and only cure of Poverty. If population were sufficiently restrained, poverty could be removed, with scientific certainty, in the space of a single generation ; and indeed, if a vigorous effort were made by the government to relieve the labor market and remove the pressure on the soil, by a sudden and very extensive measure of Colonization, as Mr. Mill strongly advises ; and if, at the same time, reproductive restraint were conscientiously practised by all classes, so as to prevent the over-crowded state from being re-induced, and the margin of cultivation again depressed ; in a few years every member of society would be easily able to earn a comfortable subsistence.

This is the settled doctrine of political economy, the science of wealth, upon the cause and cure of poverty. I would ask, whether a government which, like our own, continues year after year to ignore this great doctrine ; which refuses even to allude to the population principle, much less to adopt any adequate measure for the relief of the labor-market, as advised by the most eminent economists ; whether such a government can be considered as doing its duty to the people? If statesmen and other public men are not yet satisfied of the truth of the economical doctrine, why do they not attempt to disprove it, or make known their objections? Why do they not, at the very least, speak of the subject in a straightforward and genuine manner, so that the people may clearly understand what science declares to be the true cause and cure of low wages? Is it just to political economy, nay, is it just to the poor, and to mankind at large, to *ignore* principles of such unparalleled importance ; to pass them by, " not," as Mr. Mill says, " as if they could be refuted, but as if they did not exist? " Is not this a hollow trifling with the awful miseries of poverty? Surely, of all modes of dealing with scientific doctrines, the most unjustifiable, the most unworthy of any earnest and truth-seeking man, is to ignore them. To ignore the law of population is in reality to abandon the consideration of the chief social questions altogether

We see therefore that the Increase of Production is limited in old countries by one or other of two causes; either by a deficiency of fertile land, or of capital. The former is the true limit to production in the more advanced countries of the old world; whilst a deficiency of capital, arising from the want of the effective desire to save, is another cause which acts as a powerful check to production, among barbarous and semi-civilized nations.

DISTRIBUTION.

Having now briefly considered the Production of wealth, let us next direct our attention to its Distribution. The laws of distribution present in one respect an important and well-marked difference from those of production. While the latter, consisting as they do of the properties of human nature and of material objects, are of a fixed and immovable character, and cannot be changed by man, the former are essentially dependent on human institutions, and both may, and do, vary greatly in different countries, and at different times. "The laws and conditions of the production of wealth," says Mr. Mill, "partake of the character of physical truths. There is nothing optional or arbitrary in them. Whatever mankind produce, must be produced in the modes, and under the conditions, imposed by the constitution of external things, and by the inherent properties of their own bodily and mental structure. . . It is not so with the *distribution* of wealth. That is a matter of human institution solely. The things once there, mankind, collectively or individually, can do with them as they like. . The distribution of wealth therefore depends on the laws and customs of society. The rules by which it is determined are what the opinions and feelings of the ruling portion of the community make them, and are very different in different ages and countries; and might be still more different if mankind so chose." From these remarks we can see the error of those socialist writers who assert that the laws of political economy are applicable only to a society founded on private property and competition, and are consequently of a transitory nature. The laws of distribution are doubtless applicable only to such a state of society, but those of production, including the laws of fecundity and agricultural industry, are quite independent of the social institutions. Moreover, when once the laws which regulate distribution in a society constituted like our own are well understood, it is easy to see by what principles it will be regulated in any other form of society, actual or possible. "Whoever," says Mr. Mill, "is thoroughly master of the laws which, under free

competition, determine the rent, profits, and wages, received by landlords, capitalists, and laborers, in a state of society in which the three
classes are completely separate, will have no difficulty in determining
the very different laws which regulate the distribution of the produce
among the classes interested in it," under other industrial systems.

Where the institution of private property prevails (as it does in all
existing societies) the whole produce is divided, in the first instance,
among those classes who own the requisites for producing wealth, and
whose consent is therefore necessary to production. The requisites
for the production of wealth, as we have already seen, are three, labor,
capital, and material objects; the last of which may, for practical purposes, be represented by the term *land*, understanding by this term both
the soil and the minerals contained in it. It is among the classes who
own these three requisites—namely, *the productive laborers*, the
capitalists, and the *landlords*—that the whole produce is shared. "No
other person or class obtains anything," says Mr. Mill, "except by
concession from them. The remainder of the community is, in fact,
supported at their expense, giving, if any equivalent, one consisting of
unproductive services. These three classes, therefore, are considered
in political economy as making up the whole community."

In Great Britain, the laborers, capitalists, and landlords, form, as a
general rule, three *separate* classes, whose interests are in many respects opposed to one another. It must not be supposed, however,
that this system, which is attended with so many disadvantages to the
laboring class, is necessary, or even generally prevalent. "The fact
is so much otherwise," says Mr. Mill, "that there are only one or
two communities in which the complete separation of these classes is
the general rule. England and Scotland, with parts of Belgium and
Holland, are almost the only countries in the world, where the land,
capital, and labor employed in *agriculture*, are generally the property
of separate owners. The ordinary case is, that the same person owns
either two of these requisites, or all three." Thus, in the case of the
slave-owner or the peasant proprietor, all the three requisites of production are in the hands of the same individual; while in that of the
metayer, the Irish cottier, or the Hindoo ryot, they belong to two different persons. The peasant proprietor is himself the owner, and not
merely the tenant, of the land, which he cultivates with his own labor
and capital. The system of peasant proprietors prevails very widely
in the northern states of the American union, and on the continent
of Europe. It is the commonest kind of land tenure in the former
states, and one of the commonest in France, Switzerland, Norway,
Sweden, Denmark, and in parts of Germany, Italy, and Belgium. In
France, the number of landed proprietors is estimated at about five
millions, while in England (from the extravagant increase in the size
of estates, in consequence of the law of entail, the law and custom
of primogeniture, and the expenses attendant on the transfer of land,
owing to the difficulty of proving the title, &c.), it is only about
thirty thousand. Under the metayer system, which prevails in some
parts of Italy, Piedmont, &c., the landlord owns the land and the

capital, while the tenant furnishes the labor; and the produce is shared between these two parties, each usually receiving one-half. In the case of the Irish cottier, the Hindoo ryot, and in Asiatic countries generally, the land belongs to the landlord (whether he be a private individual or the government) and the labor and scanty capital are the property of the cultivator.

In *manufacturing* industry, there are never more than two classes who share the produce; namely, the laborers and the capitalists. These classes, although usually separate in this and other countries, at least in the larger kinds of industrial undertakings, are by no means necessarily so. Indeed Mr. Mill, as we have seen, confidently anticipates that the present system of employers and employed will ultimately be superseded to a very great extent by that of *associations* of labor and capital, either among the capitalists and the work-people, or among the work-people themselves. In his chapter on the Probable Future of the Laboring Classes he says:—"Unless the military despotism now triumphant on the Continent should succeed in its nefarious attempts to throw back the human mind, there can be little doubt that the *status* of hired laborers will gradually tend to confine itself to the description of work-people whose low moral qualities render them unfit for anything more independent; and that the relation of masters and work-people will be gradually superseded by *partnership* in one of two forms; temporarily and in some cases, association of the laborers with the capitalist; in other cases, and finally in all, association of laborers among themselves." After showing, both by general reasoning and by the experience of the numerous associations of working men formed in France after the Revolution of 1848, the manner in which the industrial system might be changed, not by any dishonest spoliation of the existing capitalists, but by fair competition with them, he says, "I agree then with the Socialist writers in their conception of the form which industrial operations tend to assume in the advance of improvement; and I entirely share their opinion that the time is ripe for commencing this transformation, and that it should by all just and effectual means be aided and encouraged." Similar views were expressed in a paper "On the Political Economy of Strikes" by Mr. Henry Fawcett, at the late meeting of the noble Association for the promotion of Social Science, at Bradford; in which paper Mr. Fawcett, after deprecating the remarks made by Lord Shaftesbury and Lord Brougham on the subject of strikes, showed in the most philosophical manner in what cases strikes are likely to succeed, and in what cases to fail; and expressed his opinion that their increasing prevalence arises from the growing intelligence and power of combination among the working classes, and from the defects of an industrial system, which places employers and employed in the relation of buyers and sellers, with opposite pecuniary interests; and that the true remedy for strikes is the admission of the laborers, by their employers, to a share in the profits of the business. In like manner Sir James Kay Shuttleworth, in an address delivered at the same meeting, says, with regard to strikes and interferences with the personal freedom of workmen;--"I have not only an unwavering confidence that these are transient forms of evil; they are even signs of an advancing civilisation. They are irregular and disturbing movements of a great social force, slowly, but with the certainty which marks the great operations of nature, adjusting the relations of labor and capital, so as to be consistent with that *partnership* between the free and intelligent workman and his employer, for which, step by step, our whole history has been a preparation."

Instances are not wanting in which this kind of partnership between employers and employed has already been tried with success; as, for example, in the case of the American ships trading to China, in which every sailor obtains a share of the profits of the voyage; in that of the crews of whaling vessels, (as stated by Mr. Babbage, who approves highly of this principle, and shows, in his Economy of Machinery and Manufactures, that it might be extended with advantage to all branches of manufacturing industry); in that of the Cornish miners, gangs of whom contract with the owners of the mines, or their representatives, to prepare the ore for market, at the price of so much in the pound of the sum for which it is sold, &c. The same principle of remuneration was adopted, some years ago, by M. Leclaire, a house-painter in Paris, who admitted his workmen to a share in the profits of his business, with the most beneficial results, moral and pecuniary, to both parties. This interesting experiment was described by M. Leclaire in a pamphlet published in 1842 (of which an abstract was given in Chambers' journal for September 27, 1845), and is alluded to by M. Michel Chevalier in his Letters on the Organization of Labor.

But, however valuable and important this kind of association may be in the present state of society, it is held by Mr. Mill that the ultimate form which the industrial system tends to assume, is that of partnerships between laborers themselves, and not between laborers and capitalists. "The form of association" he says, "which, if mankind continue to improve, must be expected in the end to predominate, is not that which can exist between a capitalist as chief, and work-people without a voice in the management, but *the association of the laborers themselves on terms of equality*, collectively owning the capital with which they carry on their operations, and working under managers elected and removable by themselves." That this great change in the industrial system, (the first conception and most zealous advocacy of which are due to Socialist writers), is perfectly practicable, was placed beyond a doubt by the events which followed the French Revolution of 1848. During that period of great excitement and generous aspirations, numerous associations of working men sprung up in France; of which there were upwards of a hundred in Paris alone, besides a considerable number in the provinces, which proved very successful. The history of these associations is given in a work on L' Association Ouvrière Industrielle et Agricole, by M. Fuegueray, published in 1851; and many details regarding them are to be found in the deeply interesting account of the Revolution of 1848, by M. Louis Blanc, who, in his capacity of member of the Provisional Government, was one of their chief promoters. Most of these associations were formed and carried on entirely by the working classes themselves; the tools, materials, and other capital being gradually accumulated by the heroic struggles and self-denial of the members, who in some cases lived for weeks together upon bread and water, and by the aid of small sums lent to them by other working men. Some associations received grants of money from the republican government, but these were in general by no means the most successful. The prosperity ultimately· achieved by many of these bodies, notwithstanding the painful privations they had at first to undergo, was surprising. "The associations founded within the last two years" says M. Fuegueray, "had many obstacles to overcome; the majority of them were almost entirely destitute of capital; all were following a path hitherto unexplored; they had to encounter those perils which always beset the pioneer and the novice. And yet, in many employments where they have been established, they have already become formidable rivals of the old-established places of business, so much so as even to excite numerous complaints among a portion of the trades-people; not merely among the proprietors of eating-houses, the sellers of lemonade, and the hairdressers—that is to say, in those employments whose peculiar nature permits the associations to reckon upon a democratic class of customers—but in others where they have not the same advantage. One has only to consult, for example, the makers of armchairs, of chairs, or of files, and one will learn from them that the most important establishments in their departments of industry, are those of the associations." An association of piano-forte makers, mentioned by M. Fuegueray, which started in 1848 with fourteen members and a capital of 2000 francs (£80,) had, in 1850, acquired funds to the amount of nearly 40,000 francs in tools, materials, finished goods, saved money, &c., and consisted of thirty-two members. It is a declared principle of these bodies, that they exist, not merely for the benefit of their own members, but for the promotion of the co-operative cause generally; and therefore additional members are admitted at once to all the benefits of the association, although they receive for a few years a smaller share of the profits. Several flourishing associations of a similar character have lately been set on foot in this country, one of which, the Rochdale Co-operative Provision Store, has been eminently successful; so much so that its members are now engaged in erecting a factory, to be conducted on the same principles.

It is painful to learn, as stated by Mr. Mill, that most of the provincial associations in France, and many of those in Paris, have, since M. Fuegueray wrote, been put down by the arbitrary power of Louis Napoleon; the man who, under the pretence of order, has stifled so much else of what was really great and noble in France, and fostered in their place the miserable passion for what is called military glory; and who has done more than any other for the last forty years, to revive the unhappy animosities between France and England, and to check those feelings of mutual appreciation, love, and esteem, which were growing up between the two countries, and which must be so dear to every true friend of human progress.

Where the whole produce belongs to one class, as in the case of the peasant proprietor, or where the division is regulated by custom or agreement, and not by competition, as in that of the metayer, or of the co-operative association; political economy has no general laws of distribution to investigate. It has only to consider the effect of each of these different systems on the production of wealth, and on the condition of the laboring classes. Where, however, as in our own country, the produce is shared between different classes under the rule of competition, the distribution can be shown to take place according to certain laws, namely, the laws of wages, of profits, and of rent, which determine the shares of the laborer, capitalist, and landlord respectively. A consideration of these laws will enable us to understand clearly the manner in which the principle of population influences the distribution of wealth. Its general action may be described as follows:—It *lowers wages, lowers profits,* and *raises rent.* I shall briefly consider each of these effects, together with the laws of wages, of profits, and of rent, through the medium of which they are produced; for it should be remarked that *all* causes which influence the distribution or exchange of wealth, must do so (whenever competition is the determining agency), through the medium of the laws of wages, profits, rent, value, or price.

Before entering on the consideration of the laws of distribution and exchange, given in economical works, it is necessary to state that they are all calculated on the supposition of *free competition.* There is however another agency by which wages, profits, rents, and prices, are sometimes more or less powerfully influenced, namely, *custom* or usage. "Under the rule of individual property," says Mr. Mill, "the division of the produce is the result of two determining agencies; Competition and Custom." In former times custom or usage was the principal rule by which the produce was shared; but the course of industrial development has tended more and more to bring transactions under the rule of competition. Custom however still frequently acts, especially on the continent, and still more in Asiatic countries; in which the spirit of competition is not nearly so active as in England or the United States. In some cases it alone determines the amount given or received, as in the case of the metayer cultivator, or in that of the fees of professional men. In this country however, although custom often acts, more especially in the retail market, it operates in general only as a minor counteracting agent, which prevents competition from producing its full effect. It should however be carefully kept in view; for many mistakes have been made in applying economical principles, and a groundless distrust of these principles has often arisen, from overlooking this counteracting force.

1st. The Law of Population *lowers wages.* We have already seen how it does so, namely, by bringing too many laborers into a country in proportion to its capital, and thus keeping the labor-market always over-stocked. The Law of Wages is that *wages depend on the demand and supply of labor;* in other words, on the proportion between the laborers and the capital. This law is merely a particular case of the general law of demand and supply, which, as will be shown presently in treating of the *exchange* of wealth, determines the market value, not only of labor, but of every other commodity whatsoever. The proofs of the law of wages have already been given, and need not be further dwelt upon.

There is often a slight verbal difference in the mode of expressing the law of wages in economical works. Wages are commonly said to depend on the ratio between *population* and capital. This is done for the sake of convenience, in making comparisons between the increase of capital and of population. It must be remembered, however, that by the term " population " is here meant only the productive laborers; and by the term "capital" only the part of capital which is devoted to the payment of wages. No other portion of capital, whether fixed or circulating, has any effect upon wages. The precise expression of the Wage-Law, therefore, is, that wages depend on the proportion between the productive laborers and the wage-fund. The condition of the working classes rises or falls according as this proportion is favorable or the reverse.

But it is not the productive laborers alone who live by wages, and whose condition is depressed by the population principle. Wages signify *the remuneration of labor*, the salaries paid for services rendered; and in this country the great majority of society are supported by this means. The judge, the barrister, the physician, the painter, the actor, live by wages, no less than the productive laborers. The only real difference is, that the wages or fees of the professional classes are fixed by *custom*, and are nearly invariable; whereas those of the productive laborers are for the most part regulated by *competition*, and fluctuate with the variations in the demand and supply of labor. Competition however acts most powerfully in the professions also, not by diminishing the fees, but by diminishing the chance of obtaining them. The anxieties of professional life—the struggles and sufferings of the many who fail, and the exhausting toil of those who succeed are proverbial, and are owing to the number of competitors being too great in proportion to the aggregate amount of fees to be distributed among them. The population principle, therefore, depresses the condition of the unproductive, in precisely the same manner as that of the productive laborers, namely, by keeping the ranks of the pro-fessions constantly overstocked.

The causes which we have hitherto considered as influencing wages, are chiefly those which determine the general or average rate of wages in a country; but it is necessary also to advert to the causes of the *differences* of wages in different employments—which differences are often so excessive, and so irreconcilable with any principle of natural justice. Wherever competition is the determining principle, the latter class of causes, as well as the former more general ones, produce their effect through the law of demand and supply in the particular trade or profession; and operate by adding to or diminishing the demand, or (what is the really important element in an industrious and saving country like England) the *supply* of the laborers engaged in it. Even where the wages are fixed by custom and not by competition, as in the professions, it is essentially by influencing the *number* of competitors, that causes produce an effect on the average rate of remuneration. According to Adam Smith, the different rates of remuneration in different employments are partly owing to the restrictions placed by governments or corporate bodies, on the perfect freedom of labor, and partly arise "from certain circumstances in the employments themselves, which either really, or at least in the estimation of men, make up for a small pecuniary gain in some, and counter-balance a great one in others." These circumstances he enumerates as follows:— " First, the agreeableness or disagreeableness of the employments themselves; secondly, the easiness and cheapness, or the difficulty and expense, of learning them; thirdly, the constancy or inconstancy of employment in them; fourthly, the small or great trust which must be reposed in those who exercise them; and fifthly, the probability or improbability of success in them;" each of which circumstances he has illustrated by numerous examples from the various trades and professions. But, as Mr. Mill shows in his profound chapter on this subject, the causes enumerated by Adam Smith, although they are the ones which *would* and *ought to* determine the relative wages of different employments, in a favorable condition of the labor market and a just state of society, and although they do operate at present to a considerable extent, are very far indeed from accounting for the actual differences of wages. So much is this the case, that the most disagreeable and laborious occupations, instead of being the *best* paid, as they would be according to these principles, are usually the *worst* paid; the reason being that, in the present over-crowded state of the labor market, they are filled by those who have no choice, and who are glad to accept any wages, however low, to save them from starvation or the workhouse. "Partly from this cause," says Mr. Mill, " and partly from the natural and artificial monopolies which will be spoken of presently, the inequalities of wages are generally in an opposite direction to the equitable principle of compensation erroneously represented by Adam Smith as the general law of the remuneration of labor. The hardships and the earnings, instead of being directly proportional, as in any just arrangements of society they would be, are generally in the inverse ratio to one another."

The *artificial* monopolies here mentioned by Mr. Mill, are those arising from direct restrictions on the liberty of following certain trades or professions, which have the effect of limiting competition in them, and thus keeping up wages; as, for example, legal enactments, the regulations or customs of corporate bodies, apprentice laws, the rules of trades' societies, &c. All such restrictions, however, with the exception of the last, have in modern times been greatly relaxed

In the more advanced countries, and will probably soon be altogether abandoned. A far more powerful cause of differences of wages in the present day, consists in what are called *natural* monopolies; that is, those which exist, not from any intentional restrictions, but from the circumstances of society, in favor of skilled labor, and especially of all kinds of labor which require any considerable degree of school education. Such an education has hitherto been beyond the reach of the great bulk of the people, and this circumstance has tended powerfully to limit the number of competitors in the professions, and to keep up their remuneration. Even those employments which require only the humble accomplishments of reading and writing, have been recruited from a limited class, and the wages in them are higher than in proportion to their comparative ease and agreeability. Indeed, this cause has hitherto acted so powerfully, as to be almost equivalent to the Hindoo distinction of *caste;* each profession and trade being usually recruited either from the children of its own members, or from other professions which stand on nearly the same . social grade; so that the average wages of each have hitherto depended rather on its own rate of increase and its own standard of comfort, than on those of the community at large. In the present day however, the barriers which have surrounded skilled labor are gradually giving way before the spread of education, and the effacement of social distinctions; so that each class is exposed to an ever-widening competition, from the other portions of society.

It is found, as a general rule, that in those employments where the wife and children work as well as the husband, as for example in hand-loom weaving, the wages are lower than in any other trades. The reason is, that the wages of any class depend in reality on their standard of comfort, or, in other words, on the sum which they consider necessary for their subsistence, and down to which they will multiply but not further; and it makes no difference, (or at least it has hitherto made none,) whether this sum is obtained by the labor of the husband alone, or by that of the whole family. It is even probable that the aggregate earnings of the family in such a case will be less than those of the man alone in other employments: for marriages are more readily contracted, when their immediate effect is to better the pecuniary circumstances of both parties. As a rule, then, in the actual procreative habits of society, the industrial employment of women and children does not ultimately tend to raise, but rather to lower, the income of a family. The increase of work is not attended, in the long run, by any increase of income; just as in the case of the working classes generally in modern times, who work much harder than their ancestors, although they do not, I believe, in most employments receive really higher wages. "No argument however" says Mr. Mill, "can be hence derived for the exclusion of women from the liberty of competing in the labor market. Even when no more is earned by the labor of a man and a woman than would have been earned by the man alone, the advantage to the woman of not depending on a master for subsistence is more than an equivalent. But in the case

of children, who are necessarily dependent, the infl ience of their competition in depressing the labor market, is an important element in
the question of limiting their labor, in order to provide better for
their education."

Where men and women work at the same employment, and where
their efficiency is equal, they sometimes receive equal wages; as, for
example, in hand-loom weaving, and also in some kinds of factory
labor. Where the wages are unequal, although the efficiency is
equal, the only explanation that can be given is, that this is the effect
of custom, which habitually remunerates the services of men at a
higher rate than those of women. This is well seen in the case of
domestic servants, where the wages are fixed by custom, and not by
competition, and where men receive a much higher salary than
women, although the efficiency of both may be equal.

In the employments *peculiar* to women, and in which the employers
take full advantage of competition, the rate of wages is usually
very much lower than in male employments of equal ease and agreeability. The reason of this, as already mentioned in a former essay,
is, in the first place, that the female occupations are still more over-
crowded; and secondly, that competition may, under existing circumstances, depress the wages of woman to a much lower point than
those of man; for, as it is the custom for the wife to depend on the
husband, a man's wage must be sufficient, as a general rule, to
support a wife and small family, whereas a woman's wage is calculated
only for her own support.

2nd. The Law of Population *lowers profits.* `This effect is owing to
the obstacle which the agricultural law opposes to the increase of
capital and population. The manner in which it is produced may be
stated as follows. The principle of increase augments the numbers of
the people, and consequently the demand for food, so rapidly, as to diminish the productiveness of agricultural labor, by the pressure on the
powers of the soil. The productiveness of labor decreases, in proportion as agriculture is forced by the advance of population, to descend
to less fertile soils, and adopt more expensive processes. This is
owing to the fundamental "law of diminishing productiveness,"
which, like other laws of nature, may be more or less completely
counteracted by agricultural or other improvements; and whose destructive operation need not be called into play if population be suffi
ciently restrained. When however population increases so rapidly as
to outstrip the antagonising agencies, the productiveness of agricultural labor is diminished and the price of food rises.

Now production constitutes the real remuneration of labor and
capital; and when the productiveness of labor decreases, the loss falls
on one or other of these two elements. When both capital and labor
are owned by the same individual, his aggregate earnings are lessened.
But when the capitalists and laborers are separate classes, as is
usually the case in this country, the mode in which they are respect-
tively affected by a diminishing productiveness of labor, is seen from
a consideration of the law of profits.

The *Law of Profits* is that *Profits depend upon Wages: rising as wages fall, and falling as wages rise.* This law was first clearly stated by Mr. Ricardo, to whom political economy is so much indebted. The following considerations show its truth. Under the existing social arrangements, the whole produce usually remains with the capitalist, who pays the other two sharers, for the use of their labor and land. In manufactures and trading establishments the capitalists and laborers are the sole sharers (with the exception of the sum paid for ground-rent): and it is evident that the share of each party depends on that of the other. All commodities are produced by labor and capital; and the advances made by a capitalist for purposes of production consist entirely of wages of labor. A great part of these advances consist in the *direct* payment of wages; and the rest (as for instance the sums spent on tools, materials, &c.) are an *indirect* repayment of the wages which were advanced by the capitalist from whom the tools or materials are bought. It is true that the latter capitalist receives a *profit* on his capital likewise, but this profit is *advanced* to him by the other capitalist before the completion of the undertaking, as a matter of convenience. "The fact remains," says Mr. Mill, "that in the whole process of production, beginning with the materials and tools and ending with the finished product, all the advances have consisted of nothing but wages; except that certain of the capitalists concerned have, for the sake of general convenience, had their share of profit paid to them before the operation was completed. Whatever of the ultimate product is not profit, is repayment of wages." In the case of agricultural industry the same is true. The capitalist farmer does indeed pay rent to the landlord as well as wages to the laborer, but rent, as will appear presently, does not enter into his expenses, nor detract from his profits. What really does so is the diminishing productiveness of labor, owing to the agricultural law. Rent is merely the sum paid for land of a better quality, and the farmer has for it a full equivalent.

The term "Profits" as used in the above law, means the *rate* of profit, or percentage on the capital, not the gross profits. The gross profits, or in other words the whole surplus that remains to the capitalists after repaying their advances, depend not only on wages, but also on the productiveness of labor. "The two elements," says Mr. Mill, "on which and on which alone, the gains of the capitalists depend, are, first, the magnitude of the produce, in other words, the productive power of labor; and secondly, the proportion of that produce obtained by the laborers themselves; the ratio, which the remuneration of the laborers bears to the amount they produce. These two things form the data for determining the gross amount divided as profit among all the capitalists of the country; but the *rate* of profit, the percentage on the capital, depends only on the second of the two elements, the laborer's proportional share, and not on the amount to be shared. If the produce of labor were doubled, and the laborers obtained the same proportional share as before, that is, if their remuneration was also doubled, the capitalists, it is true, would gain twice as much; but as they would have had to advance twice as much, the *rate* of their profit would be the same as before." For instance, suppose that the laborers produced 110 bushels of wheat, and received as wages 100 bushels. In this case the profit of the capitalist would be 10 per cent. on his outlay. But suppose that both the productiveness of labor, and its remuneration were doubled, so that the same laborers produced 220 bushels, and received 200. In this case, the *gross* profit of the capitalist would be 20 bushels, but the *rate* of profit would still be only 10 per cent.

It must be also remarked that the term "wages" as used in the law of profits, means the Cost of Labor to the capitalist, and not the real remuneration of the laborer: in other words, it means *money* wages and not *real* wages. There is a wide difference between the two. Real wages consist of the necessaries and comforts obtained by the laborer, and are the most important matter to him: while money wages are merely the pecuniary sums he receives, whose value depends on the price of food, &c. It is on the amount of the latter that the profits of the capitalists depend. In any given state of the productiveness of labor, where the capitalists and laborers are separate classes, the share of the one depends upon that of the other. Both profits and wages however may be high, as in America, or both may be low as in England, from the difference in the productiveness of labor in the two countries.

As therefore profits depend on wages, it is evident that if the productiveness of labor diminishes and wages do not fall, profits must. Now we have already seen that wages in old countries really depend on the *checks to population*, or in other words, on the standard of comfort among the laborers. In an old country therefore, where wages are already so low as not to admit of reduction, or where the laborers have a high standard of comfort and will not submit to a reduction, if labor becomes less productive from an increasing pressure of capital and population of the soil, the loss falls on profits not on wages Wages either cannot fall lower, or are not allowed by the laborers to do so. In the first case, when labor becomes less productive, and the price of corn rises, the numbers of the laborers are reduced by the positive check to population: in the second, by an increase of reproductive restraint. In either case the proportion of the laborers to the capital is diminished, and, though real wages remain the same, money wages rise: and thus the loss falls on profits. The same effect on profits is produced by a rise of the laborer's standard of comfort, even though the productiveness of labor do not diminish nor the price of food increase. If the laborers reduce their numbers in order to obtain a larger remuneration, real wages as well as money wages rise and profits fall. Or if, while the productiveness of labor and the price of food remain the same, capital increases faster than population: in this case also (which is virtually the same as the preceding) real wages as well as money wages rise, and profits fall In both of these cases the laborers have a real gain, while on the two former suppositions, their condition remained unaltered; and in all four cases, the loss falls on profits.

In the usual course of industrial progress therefore, as shown in

Mr. Mill's masterly exposition of the Dynamics of Political Economy, (that is, the part of the science which considers the economical phenomena as in a state of *motion*, or, in other words, as influenced by the progress of society, whereas the Statical part considers them as in a state of *rest*) profits have a different actual tendency from wages. They tend to *fall;* whereas real wages either remain the same as long as the standard of comfort does not vary, or may be greatly raised by an increase of reproductive restraint. Industrial progress consists mainly of three elements—*increase of population, increase of capital,* and *improvements in production;*—and the mode in which the three sharers in the produce are affected, depends essentially on the rapidity with which each of these three elements advances. Wages, profits, and rent rise and fall, in proportion as population, capital, and improvement outstrip or fall behind each other in the progress of society. An increase of population tends to diminish the productiveness of labor, and raise rent and the price of food, owing to the agricultural law: improvements in production, and especially in agriculture, have an opposite tendency. If population increases faster than improvement, the productiveness of labor is diminished, rent and the price of food rise, and the loss falls either upon wages, or, as is usually the case, upon profits: wages in old countries being habitually at what has been termed either the *physical* or the *moral* minimum, that is, being either incapable of falling, or not being permitted by the laborers to fall any lower. If on the other hand improvement advances faster than population, (which unfortunately has never been the case for any length of time in this country), the productiveness of labor is increased, and wages rise; or, if the laborers people down to their former standard of comfort again, profits rise. If the increase of population and improvement advance with equal rapidity, so that the productiveness of labor and the price of food remain nearly the same, the rise or fall of wages and profits depends on whether population or capital advances most rapidly. If population increases more rapidly than capital, wages fall and profits rise: if capital increases faster than population, wages rise and profits fall. Now as wages are habitually at, or close to, the positive or preventive minimum in all old countries, population can scarcely outstrip capital, though it may outstrip improvement: real wages cannot permanently fall to any very great extent, but money wages may rise: population may outstrip improvement, and thus diminish the productiveness of labor and raise the price of food, but if it do so, money wages will rise, and profits, not real wages, fall: whereas capital, on the other hand, may outstrip both population and improvement, and in a saving country like England, it constantly tends to do so. Population and capital, urged forward the one by the principle of increase, the other by the desire to grow richer, tread close upon the heels of improvement, and, (as has hitherto been the case), do not merely obliterate its effects, but even tend to diminish still further the productiveness of labor: and when this takes place, the loss falls on that element, namely, capital. which can alone bear it, and which under the existing circumstances has the power of increasing, and therefore the tendency to increase, most rapidly. Mr. Mill sums up the result of his investigation of the effects of industrial progress, in the following terms. "The economical progress of a society constituted of landlords, capitalists, and laborers, tends to the progressive enrichment of the landlord class: while the cost of the laborer's subsistence tends on the whole to increase, and profits to fall. Agricultural improvements are a counteracting force to these last effects: but the first, though a case is conceivable in which it would be temporarily checked, is ultimately in a high degree promoted by these improvements: and the increase of population tends to transfer all the benefit derived from agricultural improvement to the landlords alone."

Profits therefore are not only, like wages, already much lower in old countries such as England, Holland, or France, than they are in new colonies, as America, but they have a constant tendency to fall to the lowest point—or, in the words of Mr. Mill, "profits have a tendency to a minimum:" whereas wages are already habitually at or close to the physical or moral minimum in all old countries, and cannot or will not fall much lower. By the "minimum of profit" is meant the smallest profit which will tempt people to save from their incomes, and add to their capital; and when once this minimum (which varies in different countries according to the saving habits of the people, and the security of industrial enterprises) is reached, no further increase of capital, nor consequently of population, can for the time take place. The country has then attained *the stationary state*, to which state many of the countries of Europe and still more of Asia approach very closely, and to which every country in the globe eventually tends.

The tendency of profits to fall in the course of industrial progress was seen and pointed out by the early political economists, for instance, Adam Smith (and is indeed a matter of common observation): but the true cause of the phenomenon, namely, the increasing cost of labor owing to the agricultural law, was not understood. In a country like England, where the increasing capital and population press hard on the powers of the soil, the tendency of profits to fall is constant and powerful, and is productive of the most disastrous results. It is the true cause of those *commercial crises*, which have in recent times been of almost periodical occurrence. When capital and population have been quietly accumulating for a few years, profits fall, and there is a general complaint among business men that no money is to be made. Hence they are tempted to indulge in over-trading and rash speculations to gain a larger profit; and this leads to the simultaneous failure of many mercantile houses, the panic, the stagnation of trade, and the wide-spread ruin among the capitalist classes, which constitute what is called a "commercial crisis." The laborers suffer in a commercial crisis no less than the capitalists, for much capital is either wasted in the rash speculations which precede the panic, or consumed unproductively in the stagnation which follows it: and thus the wage-fund is diminished, and many laborers thrown out of employment.

Indeed in a country situated like England, with so small a reserve of fertile land, and so great a desire to increase its capital, profits have not merely a general tendency to fall: but, were it not for some *counteracting* influences, they would fall so rapidly as very soon to arrive at the minimum. "When a country," says Mr. Mill, "has long possessed a large production, and a large net income to make savings from, and when therefore the means have long existed of making a great annual addition to capital: (the country not having, like America, a large reserve of fertile land still unused): it is one of the characteristics of such a country that the rate of profits is always close to the minimum, and therefore the country on the verge of the stationary state." The counteracting influences which check the fall of profits, and permit a further increase of capital and population in England, are mainly of three kinds—namely, *improvements in the production*, or *facilities in the importation* of articles consumed by the laborers, together with the *overflow of capital* into foreign countries to seek higher profits than can be found at home. The first two tend to benefit the laborers in the first place, by cheapening food and thus raising real wages: but unless the standard of comfort be also raised, the laborers people down to their former standard again, and thus transfer the advantage to the capitalist, whose profits rise. It is for this reason that such improvements as the rotation of crops, or the abolition of the corn-laws, have had no permanent effect in raising the condition of the laboring classes: all have been converted, to use the words of Mr. Mill, "into food for so many more children." The third counteracting influence, namely the overflow of capital into foreign countries, operates powerfully in retarding the fall of profits. "The perpetual overflow of capital into colonies and foreign countries to seek higher profits than can be got at home, I believe," says Mr. Mill, "to have been for many years one of the chief causes by which the fall of profits in England has been checked." A fourth cause which keeps up profits, is the *waste of capital* in the commercial crises, and in ill-judged speculations: but this of course does not favor the increase of capital and population, nor avert the stationary state.

To resume then: the immediate manner in which the agricultural law checks population and capital, and produces that slow increase of both which we have seen to be invariably found in old countries compared with new colonies, is as follows. It checks population by *low wages* or *fear of low wages:* wages falling whenever population advances faster than capital and improvement. It checks capital by *low profits*, or *fear of low profits:* profits falling whenever capital advances faster than population and improvement. Slowly but surely the girdle which confines human increase tightens its iron clasp, and brings on the stationary state, by reducing both wages and profits to a minimum · and the only choice it leaves us, is whether that minimum shall be physical or moral, positive or preventive. The minimum of wages is the lowest wage which will tempt people to increase their numbers: the minimum of profit is the lowest profit which will tempt people to increase their capital. Wages are habitually at or close to the positive or preventive minimum in all old countries: profits tend towards it. The fall of profits may be produced in two ways: either by the gradually diminishing productiveness of agricultural labor, and consequent rise of money wages, while real wages remain the same: or by a rise of real wages as well as money wages, in consequence of the laborers' determination to restrain their increase and raise their position, which it is in their power to do to an indefinite extent. Nature sets no narrow bounds to the productiveness of labor, and the reward of industry in any country, *if the numbers of the people be sufficiently small:* but she opposes the most stringent and impassable barrier to the rapid *increase* of capital and population in all old countries. The closer they press against it, the lower do wages and profits fall, and the keener grow the anxieties of the capitalist and the miseries of the laborer.

In each country, it should be observed, the rate of profit on capital in all the different employments *tends to an equality:* unless there be peculiar circumstances attending any business, such as greater risks or unpleasantnesses, which require to be compensated for by a higher profit than usual. "After due allowance is made for these various causes of inequality," says Mr Mill, "namely, differences in the risk or agreeableness of different employments, and natural or artificial monopolies, the rate of profit on capital in all employments tends to an equality." The mode in which the *Equality of Profits* is brought about, is by capital being attracted towards the more flourishing employments, and withdrawn from those which are less prosperous. The rate of profits however, though either uniform, or at least constantly tending to uniformity, in the *same* country, at any given time, yet differs widely in *different* countries; so that each country has what is termed its own *ordinary rate of profits.*

Profits are *the remuneration of abstinence,* as wages are the remuneration of labor. They are the reward which an individual expects, and justly receives, for his self-denial in *saving* part of his income from unproductive indulgences, and using it productively, either in person, or by employing with it productive laborers. The mechanic whose savings are put into the bank and lent by the banker to producers or dealers, is a capitalist and employer of labor, in the same way as the extensive manufacturer: and the *interest* he receives is a just reward for his abstinence. Profits consist of three elements: interest, insurance, and wages of superintendence. In other words, a man who saves from his income, in order to increase his wealth, expects that he will obtain in the first place, a reward for his abstinence; secondly, a reward for the risk he incurs of losing his money; and thirdly, a reward for his labor if he superintend the employment of his capital in person. The owner of money may either invest in the funds, in mortgages, &c., in which case, as he runs little risk and takes no trouble, he receives only *interest,* or the reward of abstinence: or he may become a sleeping partner in a firm, in which case, besides interest, he receives *insurance,*

or a reward for the risk he incurs: or finally he may himself superintend the employment of his capital, in which case his profits must include all the three elements, interest, insurance, and wages of superintendence. We have already seen how the aggregate rate of profits
is depressed by the population principle, and the evils thus produced
in the commercial world. That part of profits which consists of
interest, is also depressed by the same cause. The rate of interest depends on the demand and supply of loans: in other words, on the proportion between the sums demanded by borrowers and those offered
by lenders. Now when the aggregate rate of profit falls, producers,
dealers, and other borrowers, cannot afford to pay so high an interest,
but either borrow less money, or give a smaller sum for it; and thus
the rate of interest is diminished, and the condition of all those who
live on the interest of their money deteriorated. The rate of interest,
like the aggregate rate of profit, is in ordinary times very much lower
in England than in America or Australia. In Holland it is lower
still: the interest given by the Dutch government being only about
two per cent.

3rd. The Law of Population *raises* rent. The manner in which it
produces this effect, will be understood by a consideration of the law
of rent.

The *Law of Rent* is, that the *worst land under cultivation pays no
Rent, but that Rent consists in the excess of produce yielded by all lands
of a better quality;* rising as this excess of produce rises, and falling
as it falls. "This is the theory of rent," says Mr. Mill, "first pro-
pounded at the end of the last century by Dr. Anderson, and which,
neglected at the time, was almost simultaneously rediscovered, twenty
years after, by Sir Edward West, Mr. Malthus, and Mr. Ricardo. It
is one of the cardinal doctrines of political economy: and until it
was understood, no consistent explanation could be given of many of
the more complicated industrial phenomena." The proofs of the law
of rent may be stated as follows.

Land in all countries is of different degrees of fertility: and it
depends on the price of corn and other agricultural produce, to what
extent its cultivation will yield a profit. In any given state of the
price of corn, some land is so barren as not to repay its cultivation at
all: some will yield the bare *minimum of produce,* in other words will
just support the laborers who till the soil and their *secondaries,* (by
which term is meant the laborers who make the tools, clothes, buildings, &c., of the husbandmen): some will give in addition to the
necessaries of the laborers, the ordinary, and no more than the ordinary, profits of the capitalist; others will yield more than this.
Now the worst land which can be cultivated at all is that which
barely yields the laborer's necessaries: this may be cultivated by the
laborer for subsistence, but not by the capitalist for profit. The worst
land which can be cultivated by the capitalist, is that which yields in
addition just the ordinary profits of capital, and no more. It is
evident that the latter description of land, and still more the former,
cannot afford to pay any rent. But it is also evident, that though it

can pay no rent, it will be cultivated; for there is nothing to prevent the farmer from cultivating as much of his land as he pleases, or from cultivating it as elaborately as he pleases; and he will naturally cultivate it just so far and no further, than it yields him the ordinary rate of profit. After he has once taken a lease of his farm, he may indeed be willing to lay out capital upon it for less than the ordinary profit; but before he takes it, he will naturally expect, like all other capitalists, to obtain the ordinary rate of profit on the whole of his capital.

In a country such as England therefore, where almost all the land is cultivated by capitalist farmers, it may be laid down as a general rule, that the worst land under cultivation at any given time, is that which just yields the ordinary profits of capital: and that this land pays no rent. Cultivation descends to, and takes in, this land, for the price of corn renders it remunerative to do so: but it cannot descend lower, until either the price of corn rises from an increase of population, or until the progress of agricultural improvement enables corn to be raised at the same price from inferior lands. This land then is the standard which determines the amount of rent. Rent consists in the excess of produce yielded by all lands of a better quality than the worst under cultivation: and the competition among farmers enables the landlords to appropriate to themselves this excess. —The lower cultivation descends, the wider grows the difference between the best and worst land, and the larger does the excess of produce which constitutes rent, become.

It is evident therefore that rent rises in proportion as cultivation descends. Cultivation is enabled to descend by two causes: either by a rise in the price of food, or by agricultural improvements. Food rises in price whenever the advance of population increases the demand relatively to the supply: and this rise of price makes it profitable to cultivate an inferior quality of land. Agricultural improvements tend to benefit the laborers in the first place, by increasing the productiveness of labor: and thus their first and abstract tendency, as Mr. Ricardo and Mr. Mill have shown, is to *diminish* rent, by enabling society to dispense with some of the worst kinds of cultivated land. However, in the usual course of things, these improvements, instead of diminishing rent, have the effect of greatly augmenting it, as they enable inferior lands to be taken in, and thus make room for a further increase of population. Hitherto their ordinary action has been, not to cheapen food, but merely to prevent its growing dearer: not to benefit either the laborer or capitalist, but only to permit a further increase of population and capital. "Agricultural improvement then," says Mr. Mill, "is always ultimately, and in the manner in which it generally takes place, also immediately beneficial to the landlord. We may add that when it takes place in that manner, it is beneficial to no one else. When the demand for produce fully keeps pace with the increased capacity of production, food is not cheapened: the laborers are not, even temporarily, benefited· the cost of labor is not diminished, nor profits raised. There is a greater aggregate production, a greater produce divided among the laborers, and a larger gross profit: but the wages being shared among a larger population, and the profits spread over a larger capital, no laborer is better off, nor does any capitalist derive from the same amount of capital a larger income."

Rent is the effect of what is called "a natural monopoly:" that is, it necessarily arises from inherent differences in the productive powers of the soil, and, as such, cannot be prevented from existing. The better qualities of land are like machines of superior power, and the excess of produce which they yield, must accrue to some one. The only question is, whether private individuals or society at large should profit by it? Hitherto every increase of rent has gone to the landlord class: but in so far as this increase has been due to the progress of population, and not to individual exertions on the part of the pro- • prietors, the latter have done nothing to deserve it. "They grow richer," says Mr. Mill, "as it were in their sleep, without working, risking, or economizing." It would therefore be no violation of the great principle on which private property is based, namely *the right of producers to what they have produced*, if the state were to appropriate this *spontaneous* increase of rent: and Mr. Mill proposes that it should in future do so by a *land-tax;* from which the present value of all land should be exempt, and which should be levied with due precaution, so as not to affect any rise in rent which may be owing to individual skill and expenditure on the part of the proprietor.

Mr. Porter, in his Progress of the Nation, makes the following statements, showing the vast extent of uncultivated land which has been brought under cultivation in this country within the last century, and the consequent increase of rent, "The whole number of acres brought into cultivation," says Mr. Porter, "from the beginning of the reign of George the Third (1760) to the end of the year 1844, has been 7,076,610." This statement moreover, as far as I understand it, refers only to the *common* lands, which have been enclosed by acts of parliament. "With scarcely any exception," he says again, "the revenue drawn in the form of *rent* from the ownership of the soil, has been *at least doubled* in every part of Great Britain since 1790. This is not a random assertion, but, as regards many counties of England, can be proved by the testimony of living witnesses, while in Scotland the fact is notorious to the whole population." "The increased rental of real property in England and Wales during the thirty-five years that we have now been at peace in Europe, exceeds forty millions."

From the foregoing description of the laws of wages, profits, and rent, it may be seen that a good test of the actual state of the distribution of wealth in any given country, is afforded by the productiveness of the land which forms the extreme *margin of cultivation.* "It is well said by Dr. Chalmers," says Mr. Mill, "that many of the most important lessons in political economy are to be learned at the extreme margin of cultivation, the last point which the culture of the soil has reached in its contest with the spontaneous agencies of nature. The degree of the productiveness of this extreme margin, is an index to the existing state of the distribution of the produce among the three classes of laborers, capitalists, and landlords." When the marginal soil is unproductive, as is at present the case in this country, it is a certain sign that both wages and profits are low and that rent is high. It shows, in the first place, that population is pressing too heavily on the soil and the capital, and therefore that *real* wages (that is, the necessaries and comforts obtained by the laborers) are low. Secondly, it shows, that *money* wages are comparatively high; for money wages have a close connection with the price of food, and the latter, as will be shown presently, must be high when the worst land is unproductive. If the standard of comfort among the laborers (which alone decides their *real* wages) do not vary, and they receive the same amount of commodities, it is obvious that their money wages must depend on the price of these commodities. Hence money wages will, generally speaking, be high in proportion to the price of food: a truth which is illustrated by the gradual rise in money wages, as well as in the price of food, which has taken place in the progress of society. Now whenever money wages rise, profits fall; for profits, as we have seen, vary inversely with money wages or the cost of labor. Therefore, whenever the worst land under cultivation is of a low quality, it is a sure sign that profits, as well as real wages, are low. It is a sign also, in the third place, that *rent* is high; for rent depends on the excess of produce yielded by all lands of a better quality than the worst land under cultivation, and rises in proportion as cultivation descends to lands of an inferior quality. Labor therefore cannot possibly be dear, nor food cheap, unless the margin of cultivation consist of a very productive soil; and all schemes for benefiting the working classes which do not keep this truth in view, are necessarily fallacious.

From the above considerations may be seen also the truth of the following proposition, to which I would particularly call attention, as it seems to me the most fundamental as well as the least generally understood of all the subjects relating to wages; namely, that low wages are essentially a question of *production* and not of distribution, that they arise from a *low productiveness of labour* and not from an unjust distribution of wealth. This is a point on which very erroneous views are usually entertained. It is evident that there are two ways in which low wages may be accounted for; it may be held either that the labourers do not produce enough to maintain them in comfort ; or that, although they produce enough, a large part of the produce is wrested from them by the exactions of landlords and employers. The latter opinion is exceedingly common, but it seems to me a radical and a most dangerous error. If we look closely into the matter, we shall find that the grand cause of low wages and long hours of work in this and other old countries, is not the mal-distribution of wealth, but the low productiveness of labour; in other words, the labourers receive little, not because a large part of the produce is taken from them, but mainly because they do not, under present circumstances, produce enough to support themselves in comfort even by working ten or twelve hours a day. The low productiveness of labour, again, arises from the fact that population is pressing too heavily on the land; that the excessive numbers of the people keep cultivation constantly depressed to poor soils, which yield but a scanty return even to the most skilful and long-continued efforts of industry. *Poverty and overwork are the effects of a low productiveness of labour, arising from the undue pressure of population on the productive powers of the soil.* To convince ourselves that the productiveness of labour is in reality very low in this country, we have but to consider attentively the great fact that the general rate both of wages and of profits is very low. Indeed, the remuneration of labour and capital is only about half what it is in the United States. Thus, M. Joseph Garnier, in his work on Political Economy, remarks that "in the present day, the average rate of wages in the United States is the double of that in Europe." Mr. Mill says also, that "the rate of profit is higher; as indicated by the rate of interest, which is six per cent. at New York, when it is three or three and a quarter per cent. in London." Now when the general rate both of wages and of profits is low in a country, it is a certain sign that the productiveness of labour is low. This will be clearly seen, if we attend to the mode in which the produce of industry is distributed. As already mentioned, the whole produce or wealth of the country is divided between the three classes who own the requisites of production, namely, the productive labourers, the capitalists, and the landlords. In manufactures and commerce, the whole of the produce (with the exception of the sum paid for the ground-rent of buildings) is divided between the labourers and the capitalists alone; and in agriculture also, these two classes divide between them the whole produce of the inferior soils—or, to speak more exactly, the whole of the returns to that part of the farmer's capital which yields no more than the ordinary rate of profit; while the excess of profit or of produce yielded by the better soils goes in the shape of rent to the landlords. If therefore, the general rate of wages and profits is low in England, it can only be, because the wealth produced by the workmen in manufactures and commerce, and on the inferior soils, is insufficient either in quantity or exchange value to give an adequate remuneration to labour and capital. The labour engaged in trade and manufactures is, no doubt, very efficient, if we look only to the *quantity* of the commodities produced by the workmen, and this is what blinds people to the real deficiency of productive power in the country; but we must remember that the *price* of manufactured articles is low, so that a man is unable, even by a long day's work, to produce enough of them to earn for himself and family a comfortable subsistence. On the other hand, the high price of food, the first necessary of life, shows in the clearest manner the low fertility of the inferior soils, and the real cause which depresses the general productiveness of labour; for the price of food (as will be shown presently) depends on its cost of production on the worst soils under cultivation, and therefore, whenever food is habitually dear, it is a sure sign that cultivation has been driven down to land of a poor quality, which yields but a scanty produce in proportion to the labour and capital expended on it. The only case in which labour is highly productive, both as regards the quantity and value of the articles produced, is that of the industry employed on the better soils; but this case is quite an exception to the general rule, and has no effect on wages and profits, since the whole excess of produce goes as rent to the landlords. These considerations seem to me sufficient to show that the fundamental cause of poverty and overwork in England does not lie in the distribution of wealth (however shamefully unjust this undoubtedly is), but in the low productiveness of labour, and that to remove the evil, what is above all needed, is a careful restraint on population so as to take off the pressure on the productive powers of the soil.

It may be seen too, from the above remarks, that the chief condition on which the well-being of a people depends, is not the distribution of wealth, however important that may be, but *the productiveness of labour*. Though comparatively little attended to in popular discussions, this seems to me by far the most important of all economical questions. It is the productiveness of labour which really and at bottom determines the rate of wages and profits and the hours of work in a country; where wages are high, as in America or Australia, it is because the productiveness of labour is high, and where they are low, as in England or France, it is because the productive powers are deficient. As Mr. Mill observes, in speaking of the law of diminishing productiveness in the soil, the question "involves the whole subject of the causes of poverty in a rich and industrious community." It is this law, called into play by the constant advance of population, which has counteracted the effects of the progress made in machinery and industrial skill, and which has lowered the productiveness of labour, and with it the rate of wages and profits, in all the civilised countries of the old world.

EXCHANGE.

We may next proceed to consider the laws of the *Exchange* of wealth, or in other words, the laws of Value and of Price. In a society like our own, exchanges are of such constant occurrence, that without a knowledge of the laws which govern them, it is impossible to have any clear or correct idea of the nature of economical transactions.

"In a state of society," says Mr. Mill, "in which the industrial system is entirely founded on purchase and sale, each individual, for the most part, living not on things in the production of which he himself bears a part, but on things obtained by a double exchange, a sale followed by a purchase—the question of Value is fundamental. Almost every speculation respecting the economical interests of a society thus constituted implies some theory of Value; the smallest error on that subject infects with corresponding error all our other conclusions; and anything vague or misty in our conception of it creates confusion and uncertainty in everything else. Happily there is nothing in the laws of Value which remains for the present or any future writer to clear up: the theory of the subject is complete."

First, with regard to the *definition* of the principal terms, we have already seen that the word "value" has two meanings: that people sometimes employ it to denote simply *usefulness*, and at other times *exchange value* or *power of purchasing;* and that it is in the latter sense that the term is used in political economy. This must be carefully remarked, for the ambiguity in the word has very often been the source of misconceptions and false reasoning. The distinction between value and price should also be noted. The *value* of a commodity means its general power of purchasing; whereas the *price* means the value in *money*, that is, the quantity of money for which it exchanges.

When we consider the meaning of the word "value," it is evident that it expresses no quality inherent in a commodity itself, but only a relation between it and other commodities. The value of a thing is the quantity of *other* things for which it exchanges. Value is therefore a *relative* term. When one thing rises in value, something else must necessarily fall. There cannot be a *general* rise or fall of values; the very idea of such an occurrence involves a contradiction. There may however be a general rise or fall of *prices*, from variations in the quantity of the circulating medium, whether of coins or notes. This distinction between values and prices, with regard to their *general* rise or fall, is obvious, and yet it is frequently overlooked. In fact, there is scarcely any topic in political economy, on which there has been so much false reasoning and baseless speculation, as on the advantages of a general rise of prices. Many writers (for example, the celebrated David Hume, Mr. John Gray, Mr. Attwood, Sir A. Alison, Mr. Thomas Doubleday, and others) have asserted that this is of vast importance to national welfare; and many schemes have been devised for effecting it, such as the adoption of an inconvertible currency, and large issue of paper money. There seems to be a vague idea, that when prices rise, values rise also, and every one grows richer. But such a thing as a general rise of *values* is impossible; and with regard to the rise of prices, instead of being an advantage, it is a great *evil.* Society in general are unaffected by a general rise of prices; for although people receive more money for their goods and services, they have also to pay more. The value of commodities in relation to each other remains as before, that of *money* alone being altered; and all the difference which this makes to society at large, is that they have more counters or pieces of paper to reckon by. It is therefore immaterial to the community at large, whether the amount of the currency be great or small. "The uses of money," says Mr. Mill, "are in no respect promoted by increasing the quantity which exists and circulates in a country: the service which it performs being as well rendered by a small as by a large aggregate amount. Two million quarters of corn will not feed so many persons as four millions; but two millions of pounds sterling will carry on as much traffic, will buy and sell as many commodities as four millions, though at lower nominal prices." The only persons who are really affected by a general rise or fall of prices (which is equivalent to a fall or rise in by no means the case. Suppose for example that the supply of corn in the market is one-third below the demand; in other words that there are purchasers willing to take one-third more corn at the market value than the quantity offered for sale. The value will rise; but it may rise in a very different proportion from one-third. When it has risen a third, the demand may still exceed the supply. The value may continue rising, until it has reached a point several times higher than the original deficiency in the supply: and its rise will only be checked, when from the increasing dearness, either the number of purchasers is diminished, or a larger quantity of corn is brought into the market, so that the demand and supply are equalized. "The price of corn in this country," says Mr. Tooke, the highest authority on the subject, in his History of Prices, "has risen from 100 to 200 per cent. and upwards, when the utmost computed deficiency of the crops has not been more than between one-sixth and one-third below an average, and when that deficiency has been relieved by foreign supplies. If there should be a deficiency of the crops amounting to one-third, without any surplus from a former year, and without any chance of relief by importation, the price might rise five, six, or even ten-fold." Again, suppose the converse case, that the supply of corn *exceeds* the demand. The value will fall, probably in a considerably greater ratio than the excess of the supply. It will settle at the point where the demand and supply are again made equal to each other; either by an increased consumption consequent on the cheapness, or by the farmers and corn dealers withdrawing part of the supply from the market, and storing it up for future sale. The rise or fall of value necessary to equalize demand and supply, is different in different commodities. It is generally greatest in the case of absolute necessaries, or of those luxuries the consumption of which is confined to a small class.

"Thus we see," says Mr. Mill, "that the idea of a *ratio* as between demand and supply, is out of place, and has no concern in the matter; the proper mathematical analogy is that of an *equation*. Demand and supply, the quantity demanded and the quantity supplied, will be made equal. If unequal at any moment, competition equalizes them, and the manner in which this is done is by an adjustment of the value. If the demand increases, the value rises; if the demand diminishes, the value falls: again, if the supply falls off, the value rises; and falls, if the supply is increased. The rise or the fall continues until the demand and supply are again equal to one another; and the value which a commodity will bring in any market is no other than the value which, in that market, gives a demand just sufficient to carry off the existing or expected supply."

It should be borne in mind that the reasonings upon values and prices contained in economical works are more particularly applicable to the prices in the *wholesale* market. Here competition is active on both sides; the buyers as well as the sellers are men of business, and are attentive to their own interests; so that in this case the economical axiom is generally true that "there cannot be two prices in the same

THE LAWS OF EXCHANGE.

such as ancient pictures or statues, or choice wines which can be grown only in peculiar situations. The second class comprehends the majority of marketable articles; such as shoes, hats, glass, &c. Agricultural and mineral products, and in general all the raw produce of the earth, belong to the third class. We will consider in succession the causes which determine the value of each of these three classes of commodities.

The value of those belonging to the first class depends on Demand and Supply. As the law of demand and supply is very important, and is often somewhat vaguely conceived, it deserves an attentive consideration.

The supply of a thing is the quantity offered for sale; but the *demand* for it needs some explanation. It is not a mere desire. "A beggar may desire a diamond," says Mr. Mill, "but his desire, however great, has no influence on its price." The demand, which *does* affect price, and with which we are alone here concerned, is defined by economists as *a desire combined with a power of purchasing*, and is termed *effectual* demand. But secondly, in order to obtain a clear idea of the relation between supply and demand, we should understand by the latter term *the quantity demanded;* for in this way only can an intelligible comparison be drawn between things of so different a nature as a quantity and a desire. Lastly, it should be remembered that the quantity demanded is not a *fixed* quantity, but varies with the price of the commodity. It generally increases when the price falls, and diminishes when it rises.

Understanding then by demand the quantity demanded, and by supply the quantity supplied, the law is, that the value of commodities always adjusts itself so that the demand is made *equal* to the supply. If the demand at any time exceed the supply; in other words, if a greater quantity of the article be required than can be supplied at a given value; the value will rise from competition among the buyers, until the demand be so reduced by the increasing dearness that the supply is again made equal to it. If on the other hand, the supply exceed the demand, the value will fall from competition on the side of the sellers, until additional purchasers are called forth by the cheapness, or until part of the supply is withdrawn from the market. In all cases, where competition is active on both sides, the value settles at that point, where the quantity demanded and the quantity supplied are exactly equal to each other.

The law therefore may properly be called the Equation of Demand and Supply. The value of commodities will be such that the demand and supply of them are made equal. Mr. Mill shows that this is a more correct expression of the law, than to say, that value depends on the *proportion* between the demand and the supply. The latter phrase is indeed frequently employed from its convenience (as for instance, in the law of wages, which is a case of the general law of demand and supply), but it is apt to suggest an erroneous impression. It might lead us to suppose that the value rises or falls, in the exact ratio in which the supply falls short of or exceeds the demand. But this is of indefinite increase, the value *always* depends on this law. The principal of these are Labor, and the Exports and Imports of International Trade. Why the value of exports and imports depends on demand and supply, and not on cost of production, is a question of International Exchange, into whose theory I shall not enter. The reason why this is the case with labor, is obvious. Human beings are not, like the other commodities which form the subjects of exchange, products of industry, nor is it with a view to gain that they are called into existence.

The value of labor is determined by the law of demand and supply exactly in the same way as that of other commodities. If the demand for labor exceed the supply, wages (which word expresses the *value* of labor) rise; if the supply exceed the demand, wages fall. In all cases, where competition is free and active, the value of labor will settle at the point where the demand and supply are made equal: that is to say, the rate of wages will be such as to distribute the whole wage-fund among the whole of the laborers. The greater the demand and the less the supply of labor, the higher will be the rate of wages. The same proposition—namely, that the greater the demand and the less the supply, the higher will be the market value—applies to all commodities whatsoever; and in the case of all *except labor*, it is universally admitted to be true. Every producer and dealer is familiar with the fact, and habitually acts upon it. If the supply of any article threatens to be deficient, tradesmen hasten to lay in a stock of it, knowing well that if their surmise be correct, a rise of price is certain to follow. On the same principle the monopolist limits the supply of his goods, in order to raise their value. If we ask any business man what it is that causes a rise in the market price of a commodity, he will at once answer, "a short supply and a large demand." In the case of *labor* alone is this great truth, with the most flagrant inconsistency, ignored or denied. Nay, we sometimes see apprehensions expressed, even in liberal journals, lest there should be a *scarcity* of labor; as if there were any possible or conceivable manner in which wages could be permanently raised *except* by labor being scarce, or in other words, by the laborers bearing a small proportion to the wage-fund. "A market overstocked with laborers, and an ample remuneration for each laborer," says Mr. Malthus, " are matters perfectly incompatible. In the annals of the world they never existed together; and to couple them even in imagination betrays an ignorance of the simplest principles of political economy."

Let us next examine the law of Cost of Production. This law determines the average value of all things, the supply of which can be *indefinitely increased*. These things, as already mentioned, are divisible into two great classes, between which there is a marked distinction; the first class being susceptible of indefinite increase at a *uniform* expense; the second (if the facilities of production remain the same) only at a *greater* expense. The value of the first is determined by their general cost of production, that of the second by their cost of production in the worst circumstances.

It is evident in the first place that the value of any article produced by laborers and capitalists cannot permanently be *below* the cost of production—understanding by this phrase not only the expense of producing the article, but also of bringing it to market. It must suffice to repay the outlay of the capitalist, and it must yield him, in addition, the ordinary rate of profit; for otherwise the commodity would not be produced. But it is also clear on further considering the matter, that the value cannot be permanently *above* the cost of production; that is to say, it cannot do more than repay the outlay with the ordinary rate of profit. If the value of any commodity were greater than this, the capitalist who produced it would obtain a higher rate of profit than his neighbours; and this cannot permanently be the case, where there is no monopoly, and where every one is free to employ his capital in the production of those articles which he thinks most advantageous. We have seen that in a state of free competition, the rate of profit in all employments of equal risk and agreeableness tends to an equality; and profits can only be equal, when things exchange for each other in the ratio of their cost of production.

The value, which corresponds to the cost of production of a commodity, is termed in economical works, the *natural* or the *necessary* value; whereas the *market* value is that which a commodity bears at any given time. The latter always depends on demand and supply, and is such that the quantity of the article demanded and the quantity supplied are made equal to each other. The market value may deviate more or less widely from the natural value, but has a constant tendency to return to it; and the manner in which the adjustment is effected, is by an increase or diminution in the *supply* of the commodity. If the supply be at any time deficient, so that the market value rises above the cost of production, more capital is attracted to the employment; the supply is increased; and the value again sinks to its natural level. If on the other hand, the supply be excessive, production is checked, until by a diminution of the supply, the value is raised to the natural level. The cost of production therefore forms as it were the centre point round which the market value oscillates; from which it may diverge during a certain period in consequence of changes in the demand or supply, but to which in the long run it always tends to conform. The market value may at one time be above, and at another below, the cost of production; but these deviations compensate for one another; so that, on an *average*, things sell at their cost value.

Cost of Production is made up of several elements, some of which are universally, and others only occasionally present. The *universal* elements, in the case of all things made by laborers and capitalists, are the wages of the labor and the profits of the capital; the former of which is much the more important. Most commodities require the successive labor of many different bodies of workmen to produce and bring them to market. For instance, among the laborers engaged in furnishing the market with cotton cloth, are included not only the weavers n spinners and planters, but also the sailors who import the raw

material, the bricklayers and carpenters who build the factories, the
mechanics who make the machinery, the wholesale and retail shopmen
who sell the finished goods; together with many others too numerous
to mention. The value of the cloth must suffice to remunerate the
labor of each of these classes of workmen. It must replace the
entire wages of those who are occupied solely with the commodity in
question, such as the cotton spinners and planters; and *part* of the
wages of those who are occupied not only with this commodity, but
with others also, as for example, the sailors, bricklayers, shopmen, &c

The comparative *quantity* of wages, or labor, expended in producing
a commodity is therefore the first circumstance which determines its
value. A second circumstance is the comparative *rate* of wages.
Some workmen, as for example jewellers, optical instrument makers,
and skilled laborers in general, are better paid than others; and the
value of the articles they produce, must be proportional to this higher
rate of remuneration.

It should be carefully remarked, however, that it is only the *comparative*, and not the *absolute* quantity and rate of wages which affects
the value of commodities. If the wages spent in producing any
single article were increased or diminished, the value would rise or
fall in proportion. But if the rate or quantity of wages were to vary
equally in *all* employments, values, generally, would be unaffected.
The relations which things bear to each other, are not changed by
causes which affect them all alike. A *general* rise or fall of wages
therefore cannot cause a general rise or fall of values. Indeed the
very idea of a general rise or fall of values, as already mentioned,
involves a contradiction. General *prices* however may rise; and it is
a widely spread popular opinion that "high wages make high prices."
But it is obvious that a *general* rise of wages cannot affect prices any
more than values. If the prices of commodities *were* raised by such
a cause, wages could not really rise at all; since the laborers would
have to pay dearer for every thing they purchased. It is *profits*, and
not values or prices, which are affected by alterations in the general
rate of wages. It has already been shown that profits depend on
wages; rising as wages fall, and falling as wages rise. Whenever
therefore there is a general rise in the rate of wages, the loss falls on
profits; and capitalists have no power of escaping from it by raising
the price of their goods. If the productiveness of labor remain the
same, and the laborers receive a larger share of the produce, the
capitalists must necessarily receive less.

The other universal element of cost of production is *profits*. The
abstinence of those who furnish the funds for an undertaking, has to
be remunerated from the finished product, no less than the *labor* of
the workmen. The value of the cotton cloth must be sufficient not
only to repay the wages of the laborers employed in producing it, but
also to yield a profit to the various capitalists by whom these wages
were advanced. Profits therefore form another component part of
value. The same observations however which applied to wages, are
equally applicable to profits. It is not the absolute, but only the com-

parative rate of profits, by which values are effected. High or low profits, when common to all employments, do not make high or low values and prices. It is only when the rate of profit is higher in one employment than in others, or when the capital has to be advanced for a longer time, that the value of commodities is affected.

For example, there are some occupations (such as those of the gunpowder manufacturer or of the butcher) in which the rate of profit is permanently higher than usual, to compensate for the peculiar risks or unpleasantnesses of the business. In these cases, the value of the commodities manufactured or sold, is proportionally raised. In other employments, again, although the *rate* of profit is not unusually high, yet the *time* during which the capital is advanced, is longer. A wine-merchant often keeps his wine several years before selling it: and the price he ultimately receives must be sufficient to repay him for so long a detention of his capital. In the case of all articles made by *machinery*, also, the capital is advanced for a longer time, than in those made wholly by immediate hand labor. Capital has first to be employed in making the machine, and afterwards in producing the goods with its assistance; and as the price of the goods must be sufficient to replace with a profit the whole capital expended in any stage of their production, it will evidently be higher in proportion to the length of the period, during which that capital, or any part of it, has been advanced. The greater the proportion of the capital which is spent in *previous operations* before the immediate work commences; in other words, the greater the amount, not only of machinery, but also of materials and buildings, which has to be provided; the more largely do profits enter into the cost of production, and therefore into the value, of the ultimate product. Greater *durability* in the fixed capital has the same effect as a greater *amount* of it. The more durable a machine is, the less necessity is there that its original cost of production should be speedily replaced, and the less does it stand in need of repairs. In those employments, therefore, where the machinery and buildings are of a very durable nature, a less proportionate amount of immediate hand labor is required, and the capital is advanced for a longer period; so that here also profits will enter more largely into the value of the ultimate product.

Hence it follows that even a *general* rise or fall of wages will, to a certain extent, affect values. It will not indeed raise or lower values generally (which is impossible); but, by its action on *profits*, it will raise the value of some things and lower that of others. Every rise of wages causes a fall of profits, and conversely. Now when profits fall, the relative value of those things into whose cost of production profits enter most largely, will be proportionally diminished. A fall of profits therefore will lower the value of things made by machinery, in comparison with those made by hand labor; and a rise of profits will have a contrary effect. This cause of variations in value is, however, but slight; since the alterations in the general rate of profit are confined within comparatively narrow limits.

The manner in which wages and profits affect the value of commodities, is shortly expressed by Mr. Mill in the following terms: "If two things are made by the same quantity of labor, and that labor paid at the same rate, and if the wages of the laborer have to be advanced for the same space of time, and the nature of the employment does not require that there be a permanent difference in their rate of profit: then, whether wages and profits be high or low, and whether the quantity of labor be much or little, these two things will, on an average, exchange for one another. If one of two things commands, on the average, a greater value than the other, the cause must be that it requires for its production either a greater quantity of labor, or a kind of labor permanently paid at a higher rate; or that the capital, or part of the capital, which supports that labor, must be advanced for a longer period; or, lastly, that the production is attended with some circumstance which requires to be compensated by a permanently higher rate of profit. . . . But every fall of profits lowers, in some degree, the cost value of things made with much or durable machinery, and raises that of things made by hand; and every rise of profits does the reverse."

Besides wages and profits, there are two other elements, which *occasionally* enter into cost of production. These are, *taxes*, and any extra cost caused by a *scarcity* value of any of the materials or instruments employed. As in the case of wages and profits, it is not absolute, but only *relative* taxation, which has an influence on values. If a tax be laid on a single commodity, or on several, their value would be proportionally raised; but if *all* things were to be taxed in the same degree, their values would remain unaltered.

The question, as to the manner in which cost of production is affected by a *scarcity* value of any of the requisites, has been the subject of much discussion. In some cases, it is easily seen that the expenses of production are increased by this cause. Suppose, for instance, that any of the commodities already alluded to, whose supply is limited either by nature or by a monopoly, were to be employed in the manufacture of other things, the expense of producing the latter would evidently be raised in a proportional degree.

But the case in which a scarcity value most frequently operates in increasing cost of production, is that of *natural agents*, or, in other words, the powers and forces of nature, among which are comprehended light, electricity, land, water, &c. Some of these, such as light, heat, and electricity, cannot be appropriated by individuals, but are free to all; and therefore a price cannot be charged for their services, nor can they form part of the expenses of production. Others, however, such as the land or rivers, may be, and in all old countries are appropriated. The sum which is paid for the use of an appropriated natural agent is termed *rent;* and the question is, Does rent enter into cost of production, and does it increase the value of commodities? In some cases there is no doubt that it does so. The rent paid by a manufacturer for the ground on which his factory is built, or that paid for the use of a fall of water by the miller, forms a part of their expenses, and must be replaced with a profit by the sale of the finished goods, or of the flour.   But the chief question is, whether *agricultural* rent enters into cost of production, and whether the price of corn is raised by it?   Adam Smith (who, it may here be mentioned, was born at Kirkaldy in 1723, and died in 1790, and whose great work on the Wealth of Nations, which laid the foundation of the modern science of political economy, was published in 1766) and most of the early political economists answered this in the affirmative.   They thought that agricultural produce is always at a monopoly price, because, they said, it not only yields the ordinary rate of profit to the farmer, but also yields something for rent.   But it was clearly shown by Mr. Ricardo, that this opinion is erroneous; for the price of corn is determined by the cost of its production on the worst land under cultivation, and this land pays no rent.   It is only the *better* lands which yield a rent, and it is not by them that the price of corn is regulated.   The existence of rent is therefore an *effect*, and not a cause, of the high price of corn; in other words, corn is not high because rent is paid, but rent is paid because corn is high.   Even if the landlords were to forego their rents, and give them over to the farmers or to the state, it would have no effect on the price of corn; for this price is a condition indispensable to the production of the required supply.   If the price were less, an equal quantity of corn could not, in the existing state of agricultural skill, be profitably grown, and the cultivation of some of the inferior lands would be abandoned.   "Rent therefore," says Mr. Mill, "unless artificially increased by restrictive laws, is no burthen on the consumer; it does not raise the price of corn, and is no otherwise a detriment to the public, than inasmuch as if the state had retained it, or imposed an equivalent in the shape of a land-tax, it would then have been a fund applicable to general, instead of private advantage."

A natural agent, even when appropriated, cannot, any more than other things, possess value, unless it be *difficult of attainment,* or in other words, unless the supply of it be limited.   Now it is only the *better* qualities of land whose supply is limited, and accordingly they alone can yield a rent.   The inferior lands are, practically speaking, unlimited; that is to say, the supply of them is far more than sufficient to satisfy the existing demand.   There are millions of acres, lying within the boundaries of farms, which are capable of cultivation, and yet are not cultivated.   The reason is, that they would not, at the existing price of agricultural produce, repay the expenses of the farmer and yield him the ordinary rate of profit.   The farmer might cultivate them if he chose, but he does not find it profitable to do so.   It is evident that *these* lands yield no rent; and it is not less certain, on further considering the matter, that the worst land which the farmer *does* find it profitable to cultivate, also yields no rent; for there is nothing to prevent him from cultivating his farm to as great an extent as will afford him the ordinary profit, and he will naturally do so.   The price of agricultural produce is the *cause* which determines the quantity of land which may be profitably cultivated, and also the amount of rent which the farmer can afford to pay to the landlord.

The comparative advance of population and improvement, is the
circumstance which fixes the price of agricultural produce; and this
in turn fixes the rent.

Rent therefore is determined *for* the landlord, not *by* him. At any
given price of corn, the worst land under cultivation will, as a general
rule, be such as barely to repay expenses with the ordinary profit,
and no more. The landlord cannot obtain a rent for this land. Even
if he should attempt to obtain it, and withhold the land from cultivation unless a rent were paid, the only effect would be, that the farmer
would apply his capital to the *more elaborate* culture of the better
lands; so that there would still be a portion of his capital which paid
no rent. As long therefore as there is any land which might be
cultivated, and yet is not, it may be laid down as a general rule that
the worst land under cultivation yields only the ordinary rate of
profit, and pays no rent. But as this land yields the ordinary profit,
all the *better* lands must yield more; and the competition among the
farmers transfers this *excess of produce* to the landlords.

The manner in which a rise in the price of food takes place (and in
which it *has* taken place by successive steps in the progress of society)
is as follows. Whenever population increases, more food is required.
Now we have seen that the general law of agriculture is, that the
produce of the soil does not increase in proportion as the labor
bestowed on it is increased; or, in other words, that an additional
supply of food is only obtainable at a greater proportional expense.
But we have also seen, that this law may be *counteracted* by the
progress of agricultural improvement. If improvement advance as
fast as population, an additional supply of food can be obtained
without any additional expense, and therefore without a rise in the
price. In order that the price should rise, it is necessary that population should *outstrip* improvement; that the numbers should increase
faster than the facilities of raising food at home, or importing it from
abroad. When this takes place, a greater expense is requisite in
order to obtain the supply from inferior lands; and the farmer will
not incur this expense, till the price has risen high enough to remunerate him. The price therefore will gradually rise to the
remunerative point, in consequence of the demand being in excess of
the supply. In the interval during which the price is rising to the
remunerative point, it partakes of the nature of a *scarcity* price, and
is governed by the law of demand and supply. As soon as it has
risen high enough, the farmer will take in additional land. This land
will thenceforth regulate the price of corn; for the corn grown on
the better lands obtains the same price as that grown on the worst.
"If the production of any, even the smallest, portion of the supply,"
says Mr. Mill, "requires as a necessary condition a certain price, that
price will be obtained for all the rest. We are not able to buy one
loaf cheaper than another, because the corn from which it was made,
being grown on a richer soil, has cost less to the grower. The value
therefore of an article (meaning its natural, which is the same with
its average value) is determined by the cost of that portion of the

supply, which is produced and brought to market at the greatest expense. This is the Law of Value of the third of the three classes into which all commodities are divided."

As the price of corn repays the expenses of growing it on the *worst* lands, it must *more* than repay the expenses on the *better* lands, and precisely in the ratio of their superior fertility. On the worst land the price is proportional to the cost of production, that is, it replaces the outlay with the ordinary profit; on the *better* lands it is *more* than proportional to the outlay, so that it yields more than the ordinary profit. If the farmer could keep this extra profit to himself, his gains would be higher than those of other capitalists; but competition forces him to pay it over to the landlord in the shape of rent. "Rent, in short," says Mr. Mill, "merely equalises the profits of different farming capitals, by enabling the landlord to appropriate all extra gains occasioned by superiority of natural advantages."

The value of the produce of *mines* and *river fisheries* is determined by the same law. The value of minerals depends on their cost of production at the worst mine; and the rent of the better mines is in proportion to the *excess of produce* which they yield. Even the worst mine itself may yield a rent, for mines are comparatively few in number, and their productive qualities do not graduate gently into each other, as those of land do; but the rent cannot be so high as to render it remunerative to work a still worse description of mine. The same observations apply to river fisheries.

Such then are the three Laws of Value. It deserves consideration, in what manner the two necessary conditions or elements of value, namely, Utility and Difficulty of Attainment, operate on each class of commodities. Utility in the object corresponds to *demand* in the pur chaser; while difficulty of attainment is represented by *supply* Wherever therefore (as in the case of the first class of commodities) the value depends on demand and supply, *both* elements of value have an effect in determining it. The greater the utility and the greater the difficulty of attainment; in other words, the greater the demand and the less the supply; the higher will be the value. But utility has nothing whatever to do with the natural or average value of commodities of the *second* class. This is determined solely by the difficulty of obtaining them, or in other words by their cost of production; while it is merely the *market* value that depends on demand and supply. In those cases, the demand decides only the *quantity* of the article which will be produced, and has no effect on its average value. Lastly, the commodities of the third class are of an intermediate kind, partaking of the qualities of both the others. At ordinary times, their natural value depends solely on difficulty of attainment, or in other words on cost of production; but in the interval during which the value is rising or falling from one cost of production to another, it is governed by demand and supply, and thus the element utility comes into play in deciding it. In this case therefore, demand decides not merely the *quantity* of the commodity, but also, to a certain extent, its natural value; the value rising whenever the demand increases so fast as to raise the cost of production, and falling in the opposite case.

We can now easily perceive the reason why "gold is more valuable than copper, and diamonds than corn." They are more valuable because their cost of production is greater; because a larger amount of labor and capital has been expended upon them; and their superior value is exactly proportional to their superior cost. We also see the reason why "the value of labor is so much lower in England than in America and Australia." It is so, because the supply of labor in this country bears a far less favorable proportion to the demand; in other words because the laborers are much more numerous when compared with the wage-fund. The two cases of value, which are paramount above all others in their importance, are those of *labor* and *food;* and the low value of the one depends on the same cause as the high value of the other—namely, on the undue pressure of population. The price of food is high, because population presses too heavily on the soil; the price of labor is low, because population presses too heavily on the capital. Arising from the same cause, they are curable only by the same remedy; namely, by a stricter restraint upon population. By this means the margin of cultivation would be enabled to recede, till a more productive soil regulated the price of corn; and the wage-fund would be distributed among a smaller number of laborers, so that each would receive a larger share. It is not the *knowledge* of these great truths which is now wanting; it is the inflexible determination on the part of society to recognize them openly, and act up to them. Science has performed her part towards us; she has shown us the *causes* of low wages and dear food with the same rigorous certainty with which she has demonstrated the laws of the planetary movements; and in so doing she has placed these evils entirely under our own control.

We can now also readily understand the action of the population law on the two great classes of commodities, raw produce and manufactured articles. Its action is *to raise the value and price of agricultural produce in relation to manufactured articles.* This effect has been strikingly illustrated in recent times, by the extraordinary fall in the price of cotton and woollen cloths, while the price of corn, meat, and other agricultural produce has varied but little. The reason is, that machinery and other improvements, by effecting a saving of labor, have lowered the cost of production of the former articles; whereas the improvements in agriculture, though almost equally extensive, have been neutralised by the constant advance of population. This has forced agriculture constantly to descend to poorer soils, so that the productiveness of the land at the margin of cultivation (on which alone the price of corn depends) has not materially varied. All the improvements, and all the saving of labor, have increased the productiveness of *better* lands only, and thus have all gone, in the shape of rent, to enrich the landlord class; while on the *worst* lands, from the constant advance of population, there has been no saving of labor,

—their productiveness, and therefore the price of food. have remained pretty nearly the same. The improvements in manufactures in short have been *uncounteracted*, while those in agriculture have been *counteracted* by the law of diminishing productiveness.

Before quitting the subject of Value, I may add the following short Summary of its theory, which is condensed from that given by Mr. Mill.

The Value of a thing means the quantity of some other thing, or of things in general, for which it exchanges. Value is therefore a *relative* term. When one thing rises in value, something else must fall. There cannot be a *general* rise or fall of values. The two necessary conditions of value are Utility and Difficulty of Attainment. The market value of all things, and the natural value of some, depends on Demand and Supply. The value always adjusts itself so that the demand is *equal* to the supply. The things whose natural value depends on demand and supply, are the *scarcity* articles; among which are included all things whose supply cannot be increased at all, or not sufficiently to satisfy the demand that would exist for them at their cost value. A monopoly value is a scarcity value. The natural value of all things which can be indefinitely increased by labor and capital, depends on their Cost of Production, if it be uniform; or, if it be manifold, on their Cost of Production in the worst circumstances. The universal elements of cost of production are the wages of the labor and the profits of the capital: the occasional elements are taxes, and any extra cost caused by a scarcity value of some of the requisites. Agricultural rent is not an element of cost of production. Value is not affected by the *absolute* but only by the *comparative* amount of wages and profits; except in this respect that every fall of profits lowers (though only in a slight degree) the value of things made by much or durable machinery, and raises that of things made by hand: and every rise of profits does the reverse. The comparative amount of wages depends partly on the comparative *quantity* of labor employed, and partly on the comparative *rate* of its remuneration. The comparative rate of profits depends partly on the comparative length of *time* for which profit is due, and partly on the comparative *rate* of profit in different employments.

Into the subject of *Price*, I shall not enter further than by stating that the laws which determine the price of commodities, that is, their value in relation to money, are just the same as the laws which determine their value in relation to other commodities. In other words the price of commodities depends either on Demand and Supply: the Cost of Production: or on Cost of Production in the worst circumstances. The ordinary laws of value are unaffected by the introduction of money, which itself, as an exchangeable commodity, necessarily comes under their operation. The exchange value or purchasing power of money, like that of other mineral products, depends temporarily on demand and supply, and, permanently and on the average, on cost of production in the worst circumstances. "The introduction of money," says Mr. Mill, "does not interfere with the operation of any of the Laws of Value laid down in the preceding chapters. The reasons which make the temporary or market value of things depend on demand and supply, and their average and permanent values upon their cost of production, are as applicable to a money system as to a system of barter. Things which would by barter exchange for one another, will, if sold for money, sell for an equal amount of it, and so will exchange for one another still, though the process of exchanging them will consist of two operations instead of only one. The relations of commodities to one another remain unaltered by money : the only new relation introduced is their relation to money itself; how much or how little money they will exchange for; in other words, how the Exchange Value of money itself is determined. And this is not a question of any difficulty, when the illusion is dispelled, which caused money to be looked upon as a peculiar something, not governed by the same laws as other things. Money is a commodity, and its value is determined like that of other commodities, temporarily by demand and supply, permanently and on the average by cost of production. . . Of the three classes into which commodities are divided—those absolutely limited in supply, those which may be had in unlimited quantity at a given cost of production, and those which may be had in unlimited quantity, but at an increasing cost of production—the precious metals, being the produce of mines, belong to the third class. Their natural value, therefore, is in the long run proportional to their cost of production in the most unfavorable existing circumstances, that is, at the worst mine which it is necessary to work in order to obtain the required supply."

The foregoing description, although brief, comprehends the main laws of the Science of Political Economy. The remaining portions of economical treatises are for the most part occupied with the applications of these laws, with the theory of currency, credit, and foreign trade, and with the discussion of practical questions of an economical character and relating to the functions of government—such as taxation, poor-laws, emigration, free trade, national debt, the laws of inheritance, entail, partnership, insolvency, usury, &c. Although these questions have engrossed so much of the attention of politicians and philanthropists, and are doubtless of great importance, they are in reality insignificant when compared with the population law and the duty of limiting offspring. Indeed, if the latter duty were conscientiously practised by society, the subjects of poor-laws, emigration, &c., would present but little difficulty. On the other hand, nothing that can be done by these or any other philanthropic schemes can have any substantial effect on the great social evils, while their true source continues to be ignored and neglected, and the duty of limited procreation set at naught.

I am unwilling to quit the subject of political economy, without making a few remarks on one circumstance, which more than almost any other hinders the diffusion of the science, and the inestimable practical benefits which would result. I allude to the unfortunate *prejudice against political economy and its followers*, which exists among the working classes, and among many other persons who are interested in the cause of human progress.   There is a prevalent belief that the economists are a heartless and unfeeling set of men, who care only for the increase of national wealth, and think little of the toils and sufferings of the poor.   Alas! that any such belief should prove the means of separating the working classes from their truest friends, and from the science in which alone their salvation is to be found.   No opinion could possibly be more erroneous.   Even if it were true; it the economists had done nothing more for the working classes than point out *the cause of poverty*, they would still have rendered them a greater service than any other men ever have done, or can do; for the first necessary step to the removal of an evil is to know its *cause*. What the working classes most of all need at present is to see clearly the cause of low wages.   A knowledge of this is of far more import-ance to them than any amount of commiseration for their sufferings. It is not charity and sympathy, but science and justice, that they most urgently require.   But, besides pointing out the cause of poverty, the economists, *as a class* (though doubtless there have been exceptions), have been remarkable for their democratic tendencies, and their de-votion to the interests of the working classes.   They have been unceasing in their efforts to raise wages, and procure a better dis-tribution of wealth.   If we regard the list of economical writers— Adam Smith, Malthus, Ricardo, Senior, Chalmers, James Mill, John S. Mill, Ellis, Place, H. Fawcett, Greg, Miss Martineau and others—I do not think that in any science we could find a greater number of writers distinguished for their liberality of opinions, their benevolence. and devotion to the cause of humanity.   With regard to their poli-tical views, several of the English, and still more of the French, economists, have, I believe, been in favor of the removal of monarchy and aristocracy, and the substitution, in their place, of a Republican form of government;—which appears to me also to be the most conducive to human dignity, independence, justice, and happiness, and therefore much the best, in any country where there is a due respect for the laws, and a sufficient degree of political intelligence and unselfishness.   Some economical writers have themselves be-longed to the working classes, as, for example, Mr. Francis Place in the earlier part of his life.   Mr. Place repeatedly urged on their attention the study of political economy, as the only science which could save them from their evils.   "Political economy" he says, "is *the science of the working classes;* nothing but a knowledge of its leading principles, aided by their own prudence, can ever rescue them from the degradation into which—they have not fallen—but from which they have never been able to emerge.   Political economists are neces-sarily friends of the working people; the very end and object of the science is to elevate them, to procure for them the greatest possible share of the produce of their labor."

I believe that much of the prejudice against political economy, has arisen from its being supposed that the thoughtless and unfeeling boasts of the "prosperity of England," and vast "progress of the nation," so frequently put forth by statistical and commercial writers, and by the *Times* and *Economist* newspapers (both of which are essentially aristocratic, and anti-Malthusian), afford a fair representation of the views of the economists; but nothing could be further from the truth. None know so well the really miserable state of this country, as those who have carefully studied the action of the population principle. None are so little apt to be dazzled by a surface glitter, or to be carried away by what Mr. Mill terms "the unmeaning bustle of so-called civilized existence," as those who are well acquainted with the *causes* of the present evils, and who are therefore in a position to form a comparison between society as it is, and society as it might be.

It may be observed moreover, that the earlier economists, although liberal in their own generation, were in some respects behind the most enlightened views of the present age. The great doctrines of *social equality* and the abolition of artificial distinctions of rank, were in their time but little known, and men had scarcely even begun to conceive the possibility of organic social changes. Better views on these points have been spread abroad chiefly by the Revolutions in France, and in other parts of the continent, and by the noble exertions of democratic and socialist writers. The earlier economists had so much to do in investigating the laws of their science, and have performed this task so admirably, that they may well be excused, if, in their general ideal of society, they fell short of the views of a later age. But whatever may be their deficiencies in this respect—and they are mostly deficiencies of omission not of commission—they have been amply atoned for by the work of Mr. John Stuart Mill, the most eminent living authority on the subject. The objects kept steadily in view throughout his whole work are first, that poverty should be removed, and wealth more equally distributed; and secondly, that (after making any necessary provision for the infirm, &c.) the income of each member of society should be as nearly as possible *in proportion to his exertions.* No writer could be more opposed to the present iniquitous distribution of wealth. Although differing widely (as all who recognize the population principle must do) from the general views of socialist and democratic writers on the cause and cure of poverty, Mr. Mill regards many of their moral conceptions as far in advance of existing social arrangements. "If," he says, in drawing a comparison between private property and a community of goods, "if the choice were to be made between communism with all its chances, and the present state of society with all its sufferings and injustices; if the institution of private property necessarily carried with it as a consequence that the produce of labor should be apportioned as we now see it, *almost in an inverse proportion to the labor*—the largest portions to those who have never worked at all, the next largest to those whose work is almost nominal, and so in a descending scale, the remuneration dwindling as the work grows harder and more disagreeable, until the most fatiguing and exhausting bodily labor cannot count with certainty on being able to earn even the necessaries of life: if this or communism were the alternative, all the difficulties, great or small, of communism, would be but as dust in the balance." In order to effect a better distribution of wealth, Mr. Mill recommends as the first and most indispensable means, (without which all others are futile), that the duty of limited procreation should be impartially applied to all classes alike; secondly, that the present system of hired labor should be gradually superseded by that of independent and associated industry; thirdly, that the laws of entail and primogeniture should be abolished, and the expenses attendant on the transfer of land removed; fourthly, that a tax should be laid on the spontaneous increase of rent; fifthly, that the right of inheritance should be limited, and that no one should be allowed to acquire by inheritance more than a certain sum, which should be fixed at a moderate competence; sixthly, that all the common lands, hereafter brought into cultivation, should be devoted to the purpose of raising up a class of peasant proprietors; seventhly, that there should be an extensive measure of colonization and of national education, so as to raise as rapidly as possible the condition of the poor, &c.

In his chapter on the Probable Future of the Laboring Classes, Mr. Mill makes the following remarks, in reference to those members of society who do nothing themselves, and regard as their inferiors all who are engaged in any useful occupation:—"When I speak either in this place or elsewhere of 'the laboring classes,' or of laborers as a 'class,' I use these phrases in compliance with custom, and as descriptive of an existing, but by no means a necessary or permanent, state of social relations. I do not recognise as either just or salutary, a state of society, in which there is any 'class' which is not laboring: any human beings, exempt from bearing their share of the necessary labors of human life, except those unable to labor, or who have fairly earned rest by previous toil. So long however as *the great social evil* exists *of a non-laboring class*, laborers also constitute a class, and may be spoken of, though only provisionally, in that character."

Fortunate would it be for the working classes, if they and all who really desire their elevation, would study the views of this great and benevolent thinker, and follow him as their true leader and guide. Sooner or later, I am convinced that they will do so. Notwithstanding the prejudices which now separate many of the working classes from political economy, I am persuaded that the time is not far distant when they will learn to know this science for what it really is; to know it as their best and truest friend—the friend which has never forsaken and never wittingly deceived them; and when they will regard with gratitude and admiration the noble-minded men—Adam Smith, Malthus, Ricardo, Mill and others—who have labored so long, so patiently, and with so sorry a requital in their service. Nothing could at present more powerfully advance the best interests of mankind, than a cordial and steadfast union between Political Economy and the People.

RECAPITULATION OF THE PRECEDING LAWS

In order to promote the clear apprehension of the laws of physiology, political economy, and social science, already considered, they may here be briefly recapitulated.

The *Law of Exercise.* The health of the reproductive organs and emotions depends on their having a sufficient amount of normal exercise; and the want of this tends powerfully to produce misery and disease in both man and woman.

The *Law of Fecundity* Each woman tends to produce from ten to fifteen children or thereabouts.

The *Law of Agricultural Industry, or Diminishing Productiveness.* The proportional returns to agriculture tend to diminish; in other words, the produce of the soil tends to increase in a less proportion than the labor bestowed on it.

From these three laws arises—

The *Law of Population, or Malthusian Law.* The natural increase of population has always been, and will always continue to be, most powerfully checked in all old countries, and in new colonies also as soon as their cultivation has reached a certain extent, by Celibacy, (that is, Sexual Abstinence), Prostitution, Sterility, Preventive Intercourse, or Premature Death; whose collective amount varies inversely in proportion to the rapidity with which the population of the country is increasing, and to the number of emigrants *minus* that of immigrants, while the amount of each individually varies inversely in proportion to the others.

These four laws may be called *the Main Elements of Social Science.* They are the laws which chiefly determine the distribution of *the necessaries of life*—which may, for practical purposes, be said to consist of three chief elements, Food, Love, and Leisure. The causes by which they may be *counteracted* are, in the case of the law of fecundity, the five population-checks; in that of the law of exercise, an unhealthy life in other respects, (for this will naturally tend to counteract the benefits of moderate sexual intercourse, while, on the other hand, a *healthy* life in other respects will tend to counteract the evil effects of prolonged sexual abstinence); and in that of the law of diminishing productiveness, agricultural or other improvements—

which however are never sufficient to enable old societies to escape from an immense amount of one or more of the population-checks.

As inferences from these laws arise the two following Duties; whose truth and paramount importance, together with the only method by which they can both be fulfilled, it has been the main practical object of this work to show.

The *Duty of Limited Procreation.* In an old country, it is the dnty of every individual, whatever be his or her station in life, to bring into the world only a very small number of children.

The *Duty of Sexual Intercourse.* It is the duty of every individual to exercise his or her sexual functions, during the period of sexual life; abstinence and excess being alike avoided.

The former of these duties is of a social, the latter of a self-regarding, character, (although each of them, doubtless, partakes of both characters). The first may be called the *primary social duty*, for it lies at the root of all the other virtues, and is most of all essential to the happiness of society. The removal of poverty and the mass of its attendant and consecutive evils, depends, in a country like England, on the conscientious practice of this duty and on nothing else whatsoever. Its impartial application to all members of society, whether rich or poor, is the real keystone of social justice. The second duty is, in my opinion, at present the most important of all duties of the self-regarding class; that is to say, it is the one which is most neglected, and whose neglect is attended with the greatest amount of misery; and which therefore most of all requires to be resolutely and perseveringly asserted. No one who deeply and earnestly reflects on this subject, should allow himself or herself to be prevented from fulfilling this great duty, and from obtaining a just share of the sexual privileges, by the imperfections of the existing moral code. Social regulations which (unless from the direst and most undeniable expediency) deprive human beings of *the necessaries of life*, ought not to be obeyed; for the allegiance which we owe to the laws of nature and the primary wants of our being, is far more sacred than that which is due to human institutions. On the proper observance of this duty depends the removal of the manifold diseases arising from sexual abstinence, self-abuse, and prostitution.

The duties of limited procreation and of sexual intercourse, like all the *real* duties, are founded on the laws of nature, or, what is equivalent, on the principle of utility; the former being an inference from the laws of fecundity and agricultural industry, the latter from the law of exercise. If it be granted that over-procreation is the cause of poverty; and if it be further granted that all members of society are bound to co-operate in the removal of this evil; the former duty must be admitted. Again, if it be granted that the law of exercise is one of the laws of health; and if it be further granted that every individual, male or female, is bound to observe these laws; the second duty is also undeniable. In order to fulfil *both* of these duties, the only method left by the law of population to the inhabitants of an old country, is Preventive Sexual Intercourse.

The economical laws of the Distribution and Exchange of wealt'
may also be recapitulated.

The *Laws of Distribution* are as follows:—

The *Law of Wages*. Wages depend on the Demand and Supply c
Labor; in other words, on the proportion between the Laborers an
the Capital.

The *Law of Profits*. Profits depend on wages (that is, on the Cos
of Labor); rising as wages fall, and falling as wages rise.

The *Law of Rent*. The worst land under cultivation pays no Ren(
but Rent consists in the excess of produce yielded by all lands of :
better quality; rising as this excess of produce rises, and falling as i
falls.

The Laws of Exchange are as follows:—

The Laws of Value. The Value of those commodities which canno
be indefinitely increased, depends on Demand and Supply; that o
those which can be indefinitely increased at a uniform expense, o(
Cost of Production: and that of those which can be indefinitely in
creased, but only at an increasing expense, on Cost of Production i(
the worst circumstances.

The Laws of Price are the same as the laws of Value; in othe
words, the Price of commodities depends either on Demand an(
Supply; on Cost of Production; or on the highest Cost of Prcductior

These laws of distribution and exchange are all deduced, cn th
supposition of free competition, from the simple law of huma(
nature that "man tends to prefer a greater gain to a smaller." Th
causes by which they may be *counteracted* are custom, ignorance. in
attention to one's own interest, or any other circumstance whicl
prevents competition from producing its full effect. It should alway
be remembered, that political economy, like other sciences whicl
treat of laws of causation, is a science of *tendencies,* which are subjec
to be more or less powerfully counteracted.

The Malthusian or Sexual Theory of the Social Evils may agai(
be briefly stated. It is that the laws of exercise and fecundity an
always powerfully checked in old countries by the law of diminishin(
• productiveness; and that the three primary social evils—povert(
prostitution, and celibacy, are different modes in which this inevitab(
check takes place. Poverty arises from an over-crowding of th
labor-market and an undue depression of the margin of cultivation–
a state of things produced and maintained from generation to gener(
·tion by the over-exercise of the prodigious powers of increas(
celibacy arises from the dread of poverty, and of the cares of a famil(
while prostitution springs from female poverty and the difficultie(
opposing marriage, together with the fact that the reproducti(
powers are thereby more or less completely destroyed. Povert(
Prostitution, and Celibacy, in short, are population or fecundit(
checks; the first arising from the *over-use,* the second from the *abus(*
and the third from the *non-use* of the reproductive powers; and on(
or more of these checks (or Preventive Intercourse) always ha(
existed, and always must exist to an enormous extent 'n all ol(

countries, in consequence of the different laws of increase in the human species and in the soil. The economical action of the population law, when more particularly considered, is, that it (or the law of diminishing productiveness from which it is derived) is the main limit to production; and, with regard to distribution and exchange, it lowers wages: lowers profits: raises rent: and raises the value and price of raw produce in relation to manufactured articles. Its sexual action when more particularly considered, is, that it produces the diseases of abstinence: self-abuse: and prostitution with its attendant venereal diseases. The *secondary* social evils, such as crime, drunkenness, disease, want of education, &c., are in the main caused and kept up by the primary evils of poverty, prostitution, and celibacy; and therefore they too are, in a very great degree, ultimately traceable to the law of population. It is indeed often said that the secondary evils are the causes of one another, as, for example, that drunkenness and want of education are the causes of crime; but (although these evils undoubtedly act and react upon each other) this is only to go back one step, and comparatively an unimportant one, in the line of causation.

The reader will now, I trust, admit the justice of the statement already made in an earlier part of this work. "The great social evils of old countries, when reduced to their simplest expression, are found to arise from the vast superiority of the powers of increase in man, over the powers of increase in the land; from the antagonism between the laws of exercise and fecundity, which preside over the reproductive organs and passions, and the law of agricultural industry." This truth, whose discovery we owe to Mr. Malthus, is beyond all comparison the most important ever apprehended by mankind. Until it was discovered, Man lay at the mercy of Nature, and was utterly ignorant of the primary source of the destruction which in all ages has involved his race. That source however, he can now, from a consideration of the Malthusian Law, clearly perceive to reside in his own limitless powers of reproduction, opposed as they are by the limited extent and productiveness of the planet he inhabits. It is from the reproductive laws of his own constitution—from his prodigious capacity, and powerful tendency, to increase—that his chief difficulties arise. It is with these laws that he has had, and will have throughout all time, principally to struggle; and it is on their due management and regulation that the regeneration of human society really depends.

In conclusion, I entreat the reader to take these views in the spirit in which they are intended, namely, in that of brotherly kindness and goodwill. If I have given offence by the manner in which they have been brought forward, I sincerely ask forgiveness; and hope that the fault may be imputed rather to awkwardness of expression, than want of humility. In speaking of the sexual and religious institutions, which exist among us, it has been my earnest desire to wound as little as possible, by the plain statement of my conscientious convictions, those feelings in which all of us have been brought up; and rather to carry my own and the reader's attention far beyond these surface institutions, into the presence of that mighty Sexual Difficulty, upon which the hopes of our race have been shattered, and in whose awful and solemnising contemplation, human systems and the contending strife of human passions seem but as the helpless waves, which break upon the iron rocks of Doom. It is against Nature, not against each other, that we should contend; it is she, who is as omnipotent in the weapons of death, as of life—who has been our grand destroyer; and from her crushing grasp the most persevering and united efforts can alone enable us to escape.

It is not for myself that I ask consideration; it is for the unfortunate sufferers to whom this work is devoted, and for whose benefit I would readily submit to any amount of obloquy—even from those I wish to serve. Alas! when I see around me the poor perishing in their squalid homes, the forsaken prostitutes wandering in our streets, the sexual victims pining in solitude and bitterness; when I look down into the fearful abyss of our social miseries and wrongs, and think moreover of the mutual destruction by which all this suffering is attended, the reflection overpowers me—that it matters little what becomes of myself. What am I better than they, that I should be happy when so many are miserable? If I can help my suffering fellow-men, it is the dearest wish of my heart—that for which I live—that for which I would willingly die; if not I am indifferent to my own fate. But I have a deep and abiding conviction that these evils are not insuperable; that the future of our race will be brighter than the past; and that what I have written, has not been written in vain.

THE END.

Lightning Source UK Ltd.
Milton Keynes UK
UKHW020643070922
408471UK00006B/688

9 780343 608866